*Wen xuan,* or SELECTIONS OF REFINED LITERATURE

# Wen xuan

## OR SELECTIONS OF REFINED LITERATURE

*VOLUME THREE: Rhapsodies on Natural Phenomena, Birds and Animals, Aspirations and Feelings, Sorrowful Laments, Literature, Music, and Passions*

## XIAO TONG (501–531)

*Translated, with Annotations by*

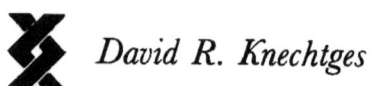 *David R. Knechtges*

PRINCETON UNIVERSITY PRESS

Copyright © 1996 by Princeton University Press
Published by Princeton University Press, 41 William Street,
Princeton, New Jersey 08540
In the United Kingdom: Princeton University Press, Chichester, West Sussex

ISBN: 0-691-02126-0

*Library of Congress Cataloging in Publication Data*
Wen hsüan. English.
Wen xuan, or, Selections of refined literature.
(Princeton library of Asian translations)
Translation of: Wen hsüan.
Contents: v. 1. Rhapsodies on metropolises and capitals.  v. 2. Rhapsodies
on sacrifices, hunting, travel, sightseeing, palaces and halls, rivers and seas.
v. 3. Rhapsodies on natural phenomena, birds and animals, aspirations and
feelings, sorrowful laments, literature, music, and passions.
    1. Chinese literature—Translations into English. 2. English literature—
Translations from Chinese. I. Hsiao, T'ung, 501–531. II. Knechtges,
David R. III. Title. IV. Title: Wen xuan. V. Series.
PL2658.E1W4   1982      895.1'08'002     81-47930
ISBN 0-691-05346-4 (set)              AACRS

Publication of this book has been aided by the Graduate School Fund and
China Program, University of Washington

This book has been composed in Baskerville by Asco Trade Typesetting Ltd ,
Hong Kong

Princeton University Press books are printed on acid-free paper and meet the
guidelines for permanence and durability of the Committee on Production
Guidelines for Book Longevity of the Council on Library Resources

Printed in the United States of America by Princeton Academic Press

10 9 8 7 6 5 4 3 2 1

# Contents

PREFACE                                                                    *vii*

INTRODUCTION                                                                  *1*


## Wen xuan

### 13. Rhapsody G, Natural Phenomena

RHAPSODY ON THE WIND    *Song Yu*                                             7

RHAPSODY ON AUTUMN INSPIRATIONS    *Pan Anren*                               13

RHAPSODY ON SNOW    *Xie Huilian*                                           21

RHAPSODY ON THE MOON    *Xie Xiyi*                                          31

### Birds and Animals, Part I

RHAPSODY ON THE HOULET    *Jia Yi*                                          41

RHAPSODY ON THE PARROT    *Mi Zhengping*                                    49

RHAPSODY ON THE WREN    *Zhang Maoxian*                                     57

### 14. Birds and Animals, Part II

RHAPSODY ON THE RUSSET AND WHITE HORSE    *Yan Yannian*                     65

RHAPSODY ON DANCING CRANES    *Bao Mingyuan*                                75

### Aspirations and Feelings, Part I

RHAPSODY ON COMMUNICATING WITH THE HIDDEN    *Ban Mengjian*                 83

### 15. Rhapsody H, Aspirations and Feelings, Part II

RHAPSODY ON CONTEMPLATING THE MYSTERY    *Zhang Pingzi*                    105

RHAPSODY ON RETURNING TO THE FIELDS    *Zhang Pingzi*                      139

### 16. Aspirations and Feelings, Part III

RHAPSODY ON LIVING IN IDLENESS    *Pan Anren*                              145

### Sorrowful Laments

RHAPSODY ON THE TALL GATE PALACE    *Sima Zhangqing*                       159

RHAPSODY ON RECALLING OLD FRIENDS    *Xiang Ziqi*                          167

RHAPSODY ON LAMENTING THE DEPARTED    *Lu Shiheng*                         171

RHAPSODY ON RECALLING OLD FRIENDS AND KIN    *Pan Anren*                   179

# CONTENTS

RHAPSODY ON A WIDOW    *Pan Anren*                                      *183*

RHAPSODY ON RESENTMENT    *Jiang Wentong*                               *193*

RHAPSODY ON SEPARATION    *Jiang Wentong*                               *201*

17. Rhapsody I, Literature

RHAPSODY ON LITERATURE    *Lu Shiheng*                                  *211*

Music, Part I

RHAPSODY ON THE PANPIPES    *Wang Ziyuan*                               *233*

RHAPSODY ON DANCE    *Fu Wuzhong*                                       *245*

18. Music, Part II

RHAPSODY ON THE LONG FLUTE    *Ma Jichang*                              *259*

RHAPSODY ON THE ZITHER    *Xi Shuye*                                    *279*

RHAPSODY ON THE MOUTH ORGAN    *Pan Anren*                              *303*

RHAPSODY ON WHISTLING    *Chenggong Zi'an*                              *315*

19. Rhapsody J, Passions

RHAPSODY ON THE GAOTANG SHRINE    *Song Yu*                             *325*

RHAPSODY ON THE GODDESS    *Song Yu*                                    *339*

RHAPSODY ON MASTER DENGTU THE LECHER    *Song Yu*                       *349*

RHAPSODY ON THE LUO RIVER GODDESS    *Cao Zijian*                       *355*

BIOGRAPHICAL SKETCHES                                                  *367*

NOTES                                                                  *401*

BIBLIOGRAPHY                                                           *413*

INDEX                                                                  *431*

# *Preface*

This volume completes the translation of the rhapsodies in the *Wen xuan*. Numerous other obligations, including a five-year term as a university administrator, have delayed my completing it. The format is generally the same as in volumes 1 and 2. The most important variations include the omission of complete publication data for the first citation of works in the notes, and of translated titles of Chinese and Japanese works in the Bibliography. This volume also contains more extensive information about textual variants. As in the previous volumes, line-numbering is based on the Chinese text. In determining the pronunciation of Chinese words, place names, and personal names I rely primarily on the *Ciyuan* (edited by Shanghai yinshuguan bianjibu) and *Hanyu dacidian* (edited by Luo Zhufeng). Old Chinese pronunciations are preceded by an asterisk. To comply with the request of readers, I have incorporated some material from volumes 1 and 2. Although notes are ample, some pieces did not require extensive annotation, or, as in the case of the rhapsodies on musical instruments, so little is known about matters of language or technical terminology that there is nothing I could add in the way of explication.

For the preparation of this volume, I am very much indebted to Stuart Aque. Mr. Aque set up the English-Chinese computer system that I used to produce the text. He patiently initiated me into the arcane world of Chinese word processing and Chinese character creation. Finally, he carefully read through the text numerous times, and corrected many egregious errors I had missed.

I must express gratitude to my wife, Chang Taiping, who, as in the past, helped me through difficult passages of classical Chinese. She also was a careful proofreader of the Chinese text. I want to thank Andrew Plaks for his careful reading of the manuscript and his many helpful suggestions for improving the infelicities in my translation. I wish to acknowledge the assistance I received from Princeton editors Deborah Malmud and Molan Chun Goldstein. Lorri Hagman is to be especially commended for her meticulous copyediting.

I owe special thanks to the Royalty Research Foundation of the University of Washington, which provided me with a grant to purchase a computer system for producing Chinese and English. The Graduate School and the China Program of the University of Washington have generously provided a subvention to cover part of the costs of publication. I wish to thank the acting dean of the Graduate School, Dale Johnson, and the chairman of the China Program, David Bachman, for their assistance and support.

# Introduction

This third volume in my translation of the *Wen xuan* consists of chapters 13 through 19, which comprise the last section of the *fu* 賦 (rhapsodies), excluding the beginning of the *shi* 詩 (lyric poetry) section. Unlike the first two volumes, which contained a small number of long rhapsodies, most of the *fu* in this volume are relatively short. There is one long *fu*, Zhang Heng's 張衡 (78–139) "Si xuan fu" 思玄賦 ("Rhapsody on Contemplating the Mystery"), that occupies almost an entire chapter. However, most of the pieces are examples of the so-called short *xiaofu* 小賦 form.

As in the previous volumes, the *fu* are grouped into categories established by the *Wen xuan* compilers. The first section, "Wuse" 物塞 (Natural Phenomena), includes "Feng fu" 風賦 ("Rhapsody on the Wind") by Song Yu 宋玉 (fl. 3rd cent. B.C.), which describes wind from two points of view, that of the ruler and that of the common people; Pan Yue's 潘岳 (247–300) "Qiu xing fu" 秋興賦 ("Rhapsody on Autumn Inspirations"), which enumerates the various emotions associated with autumn; "Xue fu" 雪賦 ("Rhapsody on Snow") by Xie Huilian 謝惠連 (ca. 407–433) and "Yue fu" 月賦 ("Rhapsody on the Moon") by Xie Zhuang 謝莊 (421–466), which use the personae of famous poets of the past to rhapsodize on the manifold qualities of snow and the moon.

The second section, "Niao shou" 鳥獸 (Birds and Animals), contains "Yingwu fu" 鸚鵡賦 ("Rhapsody on the Parrot"), in which the poet Mi Heng 禰衡 (ca. 173–198) expresses his own frustration using the persona of a captive parrot; "Jiaoliao fu" 鷦鷯賦 ("Rhapsody on the Wren") by Zhang Hua 張華 (232–300), in which the poet praises the virtues of "smallness" by telling of a wren who, because of its tiny size, is able to avoid capture and harm; "Zhe bai ma fu" 赭白馬賦 ("Rhapsody on the Russet and White Horse") by Yan Yanzhi 顏延之 (384–456), which is a panegyrical rhapsody on a dappled horse that was presented to the emperor; and Bao Zhao's 鮑照 (ca. 414–466) "Wu he fu" 舞鶴賦 ("Rhapsody on Dancing Cranes"), a poem describing a troupe of dancing cranes. The first piece in this section is Jia Yi's 賈誼 (ca. 200–168 B.C.) "Fu niao fu" 鵩鳥賦 ("Rhapsody on the Houlet"), which, in spite of its title, is not a poem about a bird, but actually is a Taoist philosophical essay in verse on the relationship between life and death.

The title of the third section, "Zhi" 志, is nearly impossible to render into English. Most of the pieces in this section are rhapsodies in which the poet uses the poem as a vehicle to resolve a dilemma faced at a critical juncture in his life. Service to the state, reclusion and escape from the world, and the role of fate and fortune figure prominently in these pieces. Since the poems explore questions that come directly from the poet's own experiences and express his personal aims and sentiments, I have rendered *zhi* as "Aspirations and Feelings." The first poem in this section is Ban Gu's 班固 (32–92) "You tong fu" 幽通賦 ("Rhapsody on Communicating with the Hidden"), a long philosophical poem in which the poet relates a dream journey to explore how the unseen world influences human life. Zhang Heng's "Rhapsody on Contemplating the Mystery" is a long spirit journey poem in which the poet relates his imaginary travels through the heavens in search of a solution to the question whether he should in the face of slander and hostility escape from the world, or instead remain in it and persist in the cultivation of his virtue. Two other poems in this section, Zhang Heng's "Gui tian fu" 歸田賦 ("Rhapsody on Returning to the Fields") and Pan Yue's "Xian ju fu" 閒居賦 ("Rhapsody on Living in Idleness") celebrate the delights of leaving the turmoil of the court and city and returning to the country to live.

The next category, a large section called "Ai shang" 哀傷 (Sorrowful Laments), is a miscellany of melancholic poems. "Changmen fu" 長門賦 ("Rhapsody on the Tall Gate Palace"), attributed to Sima Xiangru 司馬相如 (179–117 B.C.), is written in the persona of a palace lady who has been abandoned by her lord. "Si jiu fu" 思舊賦 ("Rhapsody on Recalling Old Friends") by Xiang Xiu 向秀 (ca. 221–ca. 300) is a lament for his two friends Xi Kang 嵇康 (223–ca. 262) and Lü An 呂安, both of whom were executed in 262. Lu Ji's 陸機 (261–303) "Tan shi fu" 歎逝賦 ("Rhapsody on Lamenting the Departed") is a general lamentation for kinsmen and friends who had passed away during the previous ten years, while Pan Yue's "Huai jiu fu" 懷舊賦 ("Rhapsody on Recalling Old Friends and Kin") is a mourning poem written upon visiting the graves of his father-in-law and brothers-in-law. This piece is followed by another rhapsody by Pan Yue, "Guafu fu" 寡婦賦 ("Rhapsody on a Widow"), written in 277 for the widow of Ren Hu 任護, who was married to the younger sister of Pan Yue's wife, née Yang 楊. The "Sorrowful Laments" section concludes with two rhapsodies by the late Southern Dynasties poet Jiang Yan 江淹 (444–505), "Hen fu" 恨賦 ("Rhapsody on Resentment") and "Bie fu" 別賦 ("Rhapsody on Separation"). In the first of these pieces Jiang Yan relates the manifold feelings of men who died filled with resentment and indignation at their unfulfilled aspirations, while in the second, he portrays different types of separation along with the various feelings associated with it.

The next category, "Wen" 文 (Literature), contains a single piece, the famous "Wen fu" 文賦 ("Rhapsody on Literature") by Lu Ji. In this piece Lu Ji writes about the process of writing, genre, style, and standards of literary excellence.

To complement the section on literature, the following section, designated "Yinyue" 音樂 (Music), includes four pieces on musical instruments: "Dongxiao fu" 洞簫賦 ("Rhapsody on the Panpipes") by Wang Bao 王褒 (ob. ca. 61 B.C.), "Chang di fu" 長笛賦 ("Rhapsody on the Long Flute") by Ma Rong 馬融 (79–166), "Qin fu" 琴賦 ("Rhapsody on the Zither") by Xi Kang, and "Sheng fu" 笙賦 ("Rhapsody on the Mouth Organ") by Pan Yue. This section also includes "Wu fu" 舞賦 ("Rhapsody on Dance") by Fu Yi 傅毅 (ca. 35–ca. 90), in which the poet describes in detail a special form of Han dance, and the "Xiao fu" 嘯賦 ("Rhapsody on Whistling") by Chenggong Sui 成公綏 (231–273), who poetically portrays the various aspects of the ancient Chinese practice of *xiao* (whistling), which in the Taoist tradition was a method by which a person reputedly could commune with the spirits and even achieve immortality.

The final category of *fu* is designated "Qing" 情 (Passions). It includes three rhapsodies attributed to Song Yu, a pre-Han poet who traditionally was regarded as one of the early creators of the *fu* form. The authenticity of these pieces is still controversial. Two of them, "Shen nü fu" 神女賦 ("Rhapsody on the Goddess") and "Gaotang fu" 高唐賦 ("Rhapsody on the Gaotang Shrine"), are variations on the same subject, the enchanting goddess of Wushan 巫山 in the state of Chu. The third, "Dengtu zi haose fu" 登徒子好色賦 ("Rhapsody on Master Dengtu the Lecher") is a humorous dialogue in which Song Yu defends himself against charges of being a lecher. The concluding piece is Cao Zhi's 曹植 (192–232) famous "Luo shen fu" 洛神賦 ("Rhapsody on the Luo River Goddess"), in which the poet recounts his encounter with the lovely Fu Fei 宓妃.

When I first began my translation project some fifteen years ago, except for some work that was being done in Japan, there was very little contemporary Chinese scholarship on the *Wen xuan*. That situation has changed dramatically in the past few years. First of all, there has been a revival of *Wen xuan* scholarship in the People's Republic of China. In 1986 the Shanghai guji chubanshe 上海古籍出版社 issued a carefully edited, punctuated edition, of the Hu Kejia 胡克家 Li Shan 李善 commentary. This is a valuable text that now makes the *Wen xuan* available in a form comparable to the Zhonghua shuju 中華書局 edition of the dynastic histories. Research also has been enhanced by two international conferences on the *Wen xuan* held in Changchun in 1988 and 1992.[1] A third conference was held in Zhengzhou, Henan, in 1995. Leading scholars in early and medieval Chinese literature have given important papers at these conferences.

A small Zhaoming *Wenxuan* 昭明文選 research group has been active in Changchun since 1987. They have prepared a comprehensive bibliography of *Wen xuan* scholarship,[2] and are working on an annotated *baihua* (modern colloquial) translation of the entire *Wen xuan*. Although the four volumes they have produced to date are far from perfect and could benefit from more careful attention to current scholarship,[3] they have been useful aids to me in preparing this volume.

An even more ambitious research project is now under way in Zhengzhou. Designated the Center for *Wenxuan* Research 文選研究中心, it is headed by Yu Shaochu 俞少初, who published a critical edition of the works of Wang Can 王粲 (177–217) in 1980.[4] His collaborators include some of the leading scholars in medieval Chinese literature: Cao Daoheng 曹道衡 and Shen Yucheng 沈玉成 from the Wenxue yanjiusuo 文學研究所 of the Beijing Academy of Social Sciences; Mu Kehong 穆克宏, a professor in the Guji yanjiusuo 古籍研究所 of Fujian shifan daxue 福建師範大學; and Xu Yimin 許逸民, ancient texts editor of the Zhonghua shuju. Among the works they plan to publish that should be of great use to anyone working in the field of medieval Chinese literature are *Wen xuan huibian* 文選匯編, which includes a collection of all *Wen xuan* commentaries, editorial notes, and critical remarks; *Wen xuan jinzhu jinyi* 文選今注今譯, a scholarly, annotated translation of the *Wen xuan* into modern Chinese; *Wen xuan xue yanjiu lunwen suoyin* 文選學研究論文索引, a bibliography of modern scholarship; and *Wen xuan xue yanjiu lunwenji* 文選學研究論文集, a collection of important scholarly articles.

In addition, in Taiwan there recently has appeared a translation of the *Wen xuan* into modern Chinese: *Zhaoming Wen xuan xinjie* 昭明文選新解 by Li Jingying 李景漾. To date, five volumes of that projected six-volume translation have been published.[5] Although designated as a "new interpretation," Li's work simply reproduces, often without acknowledgment, Li Shan's commentary. His *baihua* translation contains a surprising number of errors.

4

*Wen xuan,* or SELECTIONS OF REFINED LITERATURE

# 13

## NATURAL PHENOMENA

# Rhapsody on the Wind

## SONG YU

### I

King Xiang of Chu was amusing himself at the palace of Magnolia Terrace,[1] with Song Yu and Jing Cuo attending him.[2] A breeze suddenly blew in upon them, and the king opened his collar and faced the wind, saying, "How pleasant this wind! Do We not share it with the common people?"

Song Yu replied, "This is a wind for Your Majesty alone. How could the common people share it?" The king said, "The wind, being the breath of Heaven and Earth, blows vast and wide, and does not choose between noble or mean, high or low. But now you claim that this is Our wind alone. Can there be an explanation for this?"

Song Yu replied, "I have heard from my teacher that a gnarled and contorted tree attracts nesting birds,[3] and that holes and crevices attract the wind.[4] But the breath of the wind differs depending upon the nature of the places where things lodge."

THIS RHAPSODY is attributed to Song Yu, but most scholars now believe that it must have been written no earlier than the Han dynasty. The poem provides a description of the dual aspects of the wind. The male wind, which blows only upon the king and his palace, is comforting and cooling, while the female wind, which blows on the common people, is harmful and brings illness.

The piece has been previously translated by Erkes, "The Feng-Fu"; Waley, *170 Chinese Poems*, pp. 41–42, and *Translations from the Chinese*, pp. 5–6; Watson, *Chinese Rhyme-Prose*, pp. 21–24; and Idema, *Wie zich pas heeft gebaad*, pp. 9–11. For *baihua* translations, see Chen Hongtian et al., *Zhaoming Wen xuan yizhu* 2: 689–94; Li Jingying, *Zhaoming Wen xuan xinyi* 2: 80–83; and Chi et al., *Lidai fu cidian*, pp. 6–9. For a Japanese translation, see Obi and Hanabusa, *Monzen* 2: 160–65. For annotated texts, see Xiao Jizong, *Xian Qin wenxue xuanzhu*, pp. 262–64; Fu Lipu, *Fu xuan zhu*, pp. 11–13; Huang Ruiyun, *Lidai shuqing xiaofu xuan*, pp. 9–14; Li Hui and Yu Fei, *Lidai fu yishi*, pp. 1–11; Liu Zhenxiang and Li Fangchen, *Lidai cifu xuan*, pp. 78–83; and Bi Wanchen et al., *Zhongguo lidai fu xuan*, pp. 122–27.

L. 20: Cf. *Zhuangzi* 1.10b: "Great clods of earth expel breath—its name is 'wind.'"

L. 23: "Earthen sacks" (*tu nang* 土囊) are caves.

L. 24: It is not clear whether 泰山 should be understood as Mount Tai or "great mountains." Because the preceding lines do not indicate a specific place, I have opted for the latter.

L. 27: Li Shan (*Wen xuan* 13.2a) explains *biao nu* 熛怒 as "like the angry sound of flames." However, Hu Shaoying (*Wen xuan jianzheng* 15.2a) shows that *biao* actually means "swift."

L. 29: The alliterative binome *huixue* (\**gwəi-giwet*) 迴穴 has the meaning of "crooked," "bent," and, as in this context, "tortuously twisting." It is equivalent to *huijue* 迴沢 of *Mao shi* 195/1: "Plans and schemes are crooked and contorted." See Sun Zhizu, *Wen xuan buzheng* 1.35b; and Zhu Jian, *Wen xuan jishi* 13.12a.

L. 33: The rhyming binomes *pili* (\**phjai-lıai*) 被麗 and *pili* (\**phıaı ljai*) 披離 probably represent the same word, which means "scatter and spread." See Knechtges, *Wen xuan* 2: 22, L. 55n; and Wang Xianqian, *Han shu buzhu* 57A.12a.

L. 46: Li Shan (*Wen xuan* 13.2b) explains *qin heng* 秦衡 as the name of two different fragrant plants. He also cites the lost text *Fanzi jiran* 范子計然 attributed to Fan 范蠡, the famous minister of the state of Yue, which says that *qin heng* is a fragrant plant from the area of Tianshui 天水 in Longxi 隴西 (modern Gansu). Hu Shaoying (*Wen xuan jianzheng* 15.2b–3a) notes that *Taiping yulan* 994 cites the *Fanzi jiran* as referring to a plant native to Chu that was called *chu heng* 楚衡. He concludes that *qin heng* and *chu heng* are regional names for the same plant, commonly known as *duheng* 杜衡 (*Asarum Blumeı*, wild ginger).

The king said, "Where is the wind first born?"
Song Yu replied:

## II

20  "The wind is born from the earth,
Rises from the tips of green duckweed,
Gradually advances into glen and vale,
Rages at the mouths of earthen sacks,
Follows the bends of great mountains,
25  Dances beneath pine and cypress.
Swiftly soaring, blasting and blustering,
Fiercely it flies, swift and angry,
Rumbling and roaring with the sound of thunder.
Tortuously twisting, in chaotic confusion,
30  It overturns rocks, fells trees,
Strikes down forests and thickets.

## III

"Then, when its power is abating,
It scatters and spreads, spreads and scatters,
Charging into crevices, shaking door bolts.
35  All that it brushes is bright and shiny, dazzling fresh
As it disperses and turns away.

## IV

"Thus, this cool and refreshing male wind
Blows and swells upward and downward,
Scales and crosses high walls,
40  Enters the innermost palace.
Buffeting flowers and leaves, it scatters their fragrance.
Lingering amongst cinnamon and pepper trees,
Soaring above coursing waters,
It strikes the great blooms of the lotus.
45  It plunders basil herbs,
Disperses wild ginger,
Levels peonies,
Splits budding willows.

LL. 57–58: Similar lines occur in "Rhapsody on the Gaotang Shrine," also attributed to Song Yu (this volume, LL. 203–4). Wang Niansun, *Dushu zazhi* 讀書雜志 ("Zhi yu," B.32a–b) proposes that L. 57 should read 㵝慄憭㦬 in order to be parallel with the following line (the first binome describes the cold of the wind, and the second the emotional response to it), and also for purposes of rhyme between *qi* (\**tshiət*) 悽 and *xi* (\**hjət*) 欷.

L. 69: Li Shan (*Wen xuan* 13.3a) explains the rhyming binomes *boyu* (\**bhwət-jwət*) 勃鬱 and *fanyuan* (*bjwa-jwa*) 煩冤 as descriptive of the whirling movement of the wind. However, elsewhere (see *Chuci buzhu* 4.18b, 4.23a, 13.17b, 14.4b) *fanyuan* has the meaning of "sad and resentful." Thus, it is not clear how it could mean "whirling." I suspect that *boyu* has a similar sense. It perhaps is a variant of *fuyu* (\**pjət-jwət*) 怫鬱 (also written 茀鬱 or 沸鬱), which means "sad and dejected." Thus, rather than describing the wind's movement, these binomes refer to its "emotional" state.

L. 71: Li Shan (*Wen xuan* 13.3b) notes the variant *ou* 堰 (sand pile) for *ke* 堁 (dirt). Although Li Shan rejects the variant, Hu Shaoying (*Wen xuan jianzheng* 15.3b–4a) prefers it on the grounds of avoiding the redundancy with *ke* in L. 68 above.

L. 75: A house with windows made from jars with the bottoms broken out (*weng you* 甕牖) is a conventional figure for extreme poverty. See *Zhuangzi* 9.13a; and A. C. Graham, *Chuang Tzu*, p. 228.

L. 78: Hu Shaoying (*Wen xuan jianzheng* 15.4a) argues that *dui* 憝 is a miswriting for *bei* 愁 (confused); hence my rendering "dizzy and dazed" for *beihun* 愁涽.

It whirls into caves, assails hills,
50    Desolating the many fragrances.
Then, it rambles in the inner courtyard,
Northward ascends the jade hall,
Climbs gauzy curtains,
Passes into the inner chamber,
55    And at that time it becomes Your Majesty's wind.

## V

"Thus, when this wind strikes a man:
Its manner is simply so biting cold he shivers and shakes,
Yet it is so refreshingly cool he heaves a sigh of relief.
It is so clean and pure, fresh and cool,
60    It cures illness, dispels hangovers,
Soothes the body, comforts men.
This is what is called Your Majesty's male wind."

## VI

The king said, "Excellent indeed your exposition of the matter! Now may I hear about the wind of the common people?"

65    Song Yu replied:
"The wind of the common people
Gustily rises from a remote lane
Scooping out grime, raising dust.
Sullen and sad, fretting and fuming,
70    It dashes through holes, invades doors,
Stirring up sand piles,
Blowing dead embers,
Throwing up filth and muck,
Blowing rotten residue.
75    In oblique attack, it enters jar-windows,
Reaching into cottage rooms.

## VII

"Thus, when this wind strikes a man
Its manner makes him feel dizzy and dazed, downcast and dejected.

It drives heat upon him, inflicts him with dampness,
80  So that he becomes sad and sorrowful in his heart,
And he takes ill and develops fever.
Where it strikes his lips, sores break out,
Where it touches his eyes, they become red and swollen.
He gnashes his teeth, gasping and groaning,
85  Half-dead, half-alive.
This is what is called the female wind of the common people."


# Rhapsody on Autumn Inspirations

## PAN ANREN


In the fourteenth year of Jin,[1] when my years reached thirty-two, gray began to appear in my hair.[2] By virtue of my position as assistant to the Grand Commandant,[3] and concurrent post of Tiger-swift Commander of Palace Gentleman, I was assigned to the bureau of the detached cavalry.[4] The towering chambers reach so far into the clouds that sunlight rarely shines there. Officials wearing caps with cicada ornaments and

IN THIS RHAPSODY Pan Yue (zi [style name] Anren) uses the arrival of autumn to express his disillusionment with government service. He had served in low positions at the court since 266, and wrote "Rhapsody on Autumn Inspirations" in 278 while he was a member of the staff of Grand Marshal Jia Chong 賈充 (217–282). Autumn was a conventional theme of Chinese poetry. Poems such as "Nine Changes" attributed to Song Yu (Wen xuan, chap. 33), "Song of Yan" by Cao Pi (Wen xuan, chap. 27), and "Miscellaneous Poem" by Zuo Si (Wen xuan, chap. 29) portray autumn as the most sorrowful season. Pan Yue's piece includes most of the images of Chinese autumnal poetry, such as falling leaves and withered trees, cold wind and brisk air, southward-flying geese, and the chirping of cicadas and crickets. Although Pan Yue expresses the conventional feeling that autumn is the season associated with the approach of old age and death, he ends the piece on a distinctly Lao-Zhuang Taoist note and seems to indicate that he prefers a life of repose and retirement in the country to the constant danger and worry of official life.

The piece previously has been translated by von Zach in De Chinesiche Revue 3 (1929), rpt. in Die Chinesische Anthologie 1: 193–95; Obi and Hanabusa, Monzen 2: 166–71; Kōzen Hiroshi, Han Gaku Riku Ki, pp. 54–78; Chiu-mi Lai, "River and Ocean," pp. 184–95; and Idema, Wie zich pas heeft gebaad, pp. 29–31. See the baihua translations in Chen Hongtian et al., Zhaoming Wen xuan yizhu 2: 695; Li Jingying, Zhaoming Wen xuan xinjie 2: 84–89; and Chi et al., Lidai fu cidian, pp. 296–97.

L. 1: Cf. "Li sao," LL. 17–18 (*Chuci buzhu* 1.5b): "The sun and moon hasten on, never delaying; / Spring and autumn are in constant alternation."

L. 2: Cf. Jia Yi, "Rhapsody on the Houlet" (this volume) L. 49: "The myriad things are impelled around and around."

L. 3: See *Zhou yi zhushu* 3.21b (hexagram 25, "Commentary on the Image"): "The former kings, because things were flourishing, responded to the times to nourish the myriad things."

LL. 7–8: *Wen xuan* 13.5a reads *moshi* 末士 for the *Wuchen* (*Liuchen zhu Wen xuan* 13.6a) edition's 末事. A 末士 is a wretched, insignificant scholar, and presumably would be a self-deprecatory reference to Pan Yue himself. 末事 are "insignificant things or matters," and here refer to the process of growth and decay that Pan Yue mentions in the preceding lines. The You Mao text is highly ambiguous. It could mean "Even the glory and decline of a wretched scholar like me, / [Rouses] the human feelings of delight and disgust." Although the You Mao text represents the Li Shan version of the *Wen xuan*, Hu Shaoying (*Wen xuan jianzheng* 15.5a) shows that the original Li Shan reading was 末事. This reading makes good sense in the context, for the preceding lines pertain to the natural process of growth and decay. Following this reading, the lines say: "Even such minor things as splendor and decay / Rouse the human feelings of delight and disgust." What I have translated as "delight and disgust" is literally "good and bad" (*mei e* 美惡). The expression implies the different emotions that come with the change from splendor to decay.

LL. 10–13: These lines are cited from "Nine Changes" (LL. 1–4), attributed to Song Yu. See *Chuci buzhu* 8.1b–2a.

L. 16: Cf. *Lun yu* 9/17: "The Master stood on the bank of a stream and said, 'It passes away like this, never ceasing day or night!' "

L. 17: The *Yanzi chunqiu* (1.10b) has a story of Duke Jing 景 of Qi, who climbed Mount Niu 牛, from which he could view the entire state of Qi. He then sighed and said, "What can I do? Will I leave this great state and die? Suppose that in antiquity no one died— would that not be joyous?" Li Shan (*Wen xuan* 13.5b) cites this story as an example of "longing for the distant" (i.e., thoughts of the immensity of the world), and "grieving for the near" (worrying about impending death).

L. 18: Cf. *Mao shi* 203/2: "They go forth, they come back; / They cause my heart pain."

garbed in white and figured silks roam and rest here.[5] I am a man from the countryside, and when I take my rest, I have nothing more than a thatched hut and dense grove, and for conversation, my only guests are farmers and old peasants. I have been temporarily appointed by default and have been unduly assigned a court rank.[6] Rising early and going late to bed,[7] I have no time to get real rest.[8] I am like a fish in a pond or a caged bird, who long for rivers and lakes, mountains and meres. Thereupon, wetting a brush and with paper in hand, I heave a sigh and compose a rhapsody. The season is autumn, and thus I name the piece "Autumn Inspirations." The words of the rhapsody read:

## I

The four seasons hasten on in constant alternation;
The myriad things chaotically swirl and advance.
Observing the seasonal growth of flowers and plants,
I perceive that on which splendor and decay rest.
5    I am struck by the withering of winter and the display of spring;
I am moved by the luxuriance of summer and the wilting of autumn.
Although such splendor and decay are minor matters,
They, too, rouse the human feelings of delight and disgust.

## II

Excellent indeed are the words of Song Yu, who said:
10    "Mournful is the air that is autumn's!
In the soughing wind, leaves flutter and fall, turn and decay.
All is gloomy and sad, like traveling afar,
Climbing a hill, looking down on a stream, sending someone off on a
        homeward journey."

## III

When sending a person off, one harbors affection for his bosom friend;
15    When traveling afar, one feels a wayfarer's torment.
When looking down on a stream, moved by its flow, one laments its
        passing away;
When climbing a hill, one longs for the distant, grieves for the near.
These four sorrows pain the heart;

LL. 26–29: The light fan and grass-cloth clothing are used in summer. The rush mat and lined coat are used in autumn. What I have translated as "rush" actually are two plants —the *guan* 莞 (*Scirpus Tabernaemontani*, bulrush) and *ruo* 蒻 (*Typha latifolia*, common cattail). See Lu Wenyu, *Shi caomu jinshi*, pp. 45–46, no. 53; and p. 104, no. 115.

L. 32: Cf. *Mao shi* 197/4: "Lush are those willows, / The calling cicadas chirp softly."

L. 33: Cf. "Nine Changes" I, L. 13 (*Chuci buzhu* 8.2b): "Wild geese, honking loudly, travel south."

L. 34: The "high sky" is a common image in Chinese autumnal poetry. Cf. "Nine Changes" I, L. 4 (*Chuci buzhu* 8.2a): "Vast and open, the sky is high and cold."

L. 41: The cricket is commonly associated with autumn. See *Mao shi* 114 and "Nine Changes" III, L. 28 (*Chuci buzhu* 8.6a).

L. 43: The Fire Star is the lunar mansion known as the Heart (Xin 心). It corresponds to three stars in Scorpio. The Fire Star traditionally was thought to recede in the autumn. See *Mao shi* 154/10 and Schlegel, *Uranographie chinoise* 1: 140–41.

L. 44: The term *gengjie* 耿介 occurs in "Nine Changes" (VII, L. 4; *Chuci buzhu* 8.10a) in the sense of "staunch," "resolute," which is clearly inappropriate here. I suspect that Pan Yue is using it in the sense of *genggeng* 耿耿 of *Mao shi* 26/1: "I am restless and do not sleep." In fact, Hu Shaoying (*Wen xuan jianzheng* 15.6a–b) argues that *genggeng* is the original Li Shan text reading based on Li's citation of the *Mao shi* 26/1 line in his annotation to this line.

L. 45: Cf. *Mao shi* 1/2: "Tossing and turning, he turned from side to side."

L. 46: Cf. "Nine Changes," III, 23; and VIII, 5 (*Chuci buzhu* 8.5b. 8.11a): "The year hastens by and soon will end."

L. 51: Cloud-Han (Yun Han 雲漢) is one of many names for the Milky Way. Here it is a metaphor for high office.

Yet one alone is hard enough to bear.
20  Alas that autumn days are so sad!
Truly there is no grief they do not bring!
In the wilds there is a homing swallow;
Over the wetlands there is a hovering hawk.
Drifting miasmas rise at dawn;
25  Withered leaves fall at dusk.


## IV

Then do I discard my light fan,
Remove my fine grass-cloth garb,
Spread a rush mat,
Don a lined coat.
30  Courtyard trees are bare—the leaves have shed and scattered;
A strong wind blows fiercely against the curtains.
Cicadas chirp softly, coldly call;
Wild geese, gliding smoothly, fly south.
The sky, bright and clear, rises ever higher;
35  The sun, its brightness dimming, gradually fades away.


## V

In the fading brightness, how short the days!
One feels the chilly nights becoming longer.
The moon glimmers, holding back its light;
The dew, cold and pure, begins to freeze.
40  Fireflies glow by steps and doorways;
Crickets chirp by verandas and screens.
I hear the morning call of a stray swan,
Gaze at the lingering light of the receding Fire Star.
At night I am restless and do not sleep;
45  Alone, I toss and turn in my grand office chamber.
Aware that the year soon will end,
I sigh and bow my head in self-reflection.
White temple-hair, in long fringes, supports my cap;
White locks, thin and bare, fall loosely over my collar.
50  Admiringly I gaze on the traces of the great men:
They have ascended to Cloud-Han, where they roam and gallop.

L. 52: Cf. *Laozi* 20: "Everyone is merry and joyful, as though enjoying the Great Sacrifice, as though climbing the Spring Terrace." The Spring Terrace (Chun tai 春臺) here stands for palace pavilions and towers where officials strolled and relaxed.

L. 53: The hat described here is the military cap mentioned in the preface. The gold refers to the cicada ornaments. See n. 5 above.

L. 55: Cf. *Laozi* 26: "Heaviness is the root of lightness, and repose is the ruler of activity." Pan Yue portrays himself as a man of quietude and repose (*jing* 靜), and the high officials with whom he serves as restless and agitated (*zao* 躁).

L. 56: The Supreme Man (*zhiren* 至人), or Perfect Man, is the Taoist sage who has reached the stage at which he becomes oblivious of self, is unperturbed about the world around him, and sees all things as one. Cf. *Zhuangzi* 7.18a: Confucius asked Laozi what it meant to attain such a state. Laozi replied, "To attain it is supreme beauty, supreme joy. One who attains supreme beauty and roams in supreme joy is called the Supreme Man."

L. 57: The second chapter of the *Zhuangzi*, titled "Seeing Things as Equal," develops the idea that distinctions are fictions that prevent one from gaining a true understanding of the ultimate reality, which can be achieved only by viewing things as one. Cf. *Zhuangzi* 1.15b: "Rather than use the meaning to show that 'The meaning is not the meaning,' use what is not the meaning. Rather than use a horse to show that 'A horse is not a horse,' use what is not a horse. Heaven and earth are the one meaning, the myriad things are the one horse." Translation by A. C. Graham, *Chuang Tzu*, p. 53.

L. 58: Cf. *Zhou yi zhushu* 8.12a ("Grand Commentary," B/4): "Thus, when a gentleman is secure, he does not forget [the threat of] danger, and when living, he does not forget [the prospect of] death."

L. 59: This is one of several interpretations of the ambiguous line in *Laozi* 50: "One leaves life and enters death. Three of ten are companions of life, three of ten are companions of death."

LL. 60–63: These lines allude to a *Zhuangzi* (9.8b) parable in which Zhuangzi instructed Hui Shi in the "usefulness of the useless." Zhuangzi said to Hui Shi, "The earth is certainly vast and large, but a man uses only the portion that fits his feet. If, however, one were to dig by his feet down to the Yellow Springs, would the man still have use for it?" Hui Shi replied, "It would be useless." Zhuangzi said, "This being so, that the useless may be useful is clear after all." Pan Yue uses the parable to illustrate the dangers of restrictive, confining official life.

LL. 64–65: These lines also allude to a *Zhuangzi* (ibid., 6.14b–15a) parable. One day Zhuangzi was fishing on the Pu River when he was visited by two officials representing King Wei of Chu, who wished to offer him a government post. Zhuangzi continued his fishing, and without looking around, replied, " 'I have heard Chu has a sacred tortoise that has been dead for three thousand years. The king stores it wrapped and boxed in the ancestral temple. Would this tortoise rather be dead as an honored bone relic, or would he rather be alive dragging his tail through the mud?' The two officials said, 'He would rather be alive and drag his tail through the mud.' Zhuangzi said, 'Be gone! I shall drag my tail through the mud.' "

L. 67: Cf. "Distant Roaming," L. 124 (*Chuci buzhu* 5.8b): "Moving with easy, measured gait, I soar on high."

LL. 68–69: The "eastern paddy field" (*dong gao* 東皋) is conventionally associated with the life of a recluse. Cf. Ruan Ji's "Letter to Lord Jiang" (*Wen xuan* 40.1846): "I will plow the fields south of the eastern paddy field and contribute my taxes of millet."

L. 73: Cf. *Zhuangzi* 6.15a–b: "Zhuangzi and Huizi were strolling over the Hao breakwater when Zhuangzi said, 'The hemiculter have come out and are swimming so easily. This is the joy of fish.' Huizi said, 'You are not a fish. How do you know it is the joy of fish?' Zhuangzi replied, 'You are not I. How do you know I do not know the joy of fish?' "

Merry and joyful, they climb a spring terrace,
Their gold and sable caps resplendent and bright.
If pursuing and rejecting follow divergent roads,
55 How can one distinguish activity from repose?


## VI

I have heard of the refined manner of the Supreme Man,
Who equates Heaven and Earth to a single meaning.
Others know security, but forget danger;
Thus, they "leave life and enter death."
60 In walking, one plants his toes in a space no larger than his feet;
By hardly stepping at all, he obtains a secure foothold.
But if one digs around his feet down to the Yellow Springs,
Even a monkey or gibbon will not walk there.
The tortoise had his bones sacrificed in the ancestral shrine,
65 But wished instead to return to the green waters.


## VII

For now, I shall straighten my lapel and return home;
Soon will I discard official ribbons and soar on high.
I shall plow the rich soil of the eastern paddy field,
And contribute my levy of surplus millet.
70 Where a spring bubbles and burbles among the rocks,
And chrysanthemums waft their fragrance over the river bank,
I shall bathe in the rushing torrent of the autumn flood,
Play with the swimming hemiculter darting to and fro.
I roam at will by the banks of hills and streams;
75 Free and unfettered, I abide in the human world.
Relaxed and carefree
I shall end my days.

L. 5: The King of Liang 梁王 is Liu Wu 劉武, also known by his posthumous name of King Xiao 孝. During his reign, from 168 to 144 B.C., Liang was one of the most prosperous kingdoms of the Han empire, and Liu Wu invited many distinguished poets to become guest scholars at his court.

L. 6: Hare Garden (Tu yuan 兔園) was the pleasure park reputedly constructed by King Xiao of Liang. Also known as Liang Park (Liang Yuan 梁園), it was located east of the Liang capital. It is described in *Xijing zaji* 2.6a. It is not clear whether this is another name for the large preserve called Eastern Park (Dong yuan 東園). See *Han shu* 47.2208; *Shui jing zhu* 24.3b; and Zhu Jian, *Wen xuan jishi* 13.14a–b.

LL. 9–11: Scholar Zou is Zou Yang, a native of Qi, who began his career at the court of Liu Pi 劉濞, king of Wu (reg. 195–154 B.C.). After failing to convince Liu Pi to abandon his plans for revolt against the emperor, Zou Yang went to Liang, where he became a distinguished member of the entourage of Liu Wu. Elder Mei is Mei Sheng, the most venerated poet at the Liang court. Xiangru refers to Sima Xiangru.

# Rhapsody on Snow

## XIE HUILIAN

### I

The year was coming to an end,
The day was already dark,
Cold winds blew hard,
Sad clouds thickly gathered.
5    The king of Liang, cheerless,
Went roaming in Hare Garden.

He set out fine wine
And called over guests and friends.
He summoned Scholar Zou,
10    Invited Elder Mei.
Xiangru arrived last,
But sat to the right of the other guests.

Soon light sleet began to fall,
Followed by thick snow.

THIS RHAPSODY is a short prosopopoeia (literary impersonation) using the Former Han dynasty poets Sima Xiangru, Zou Yang 鄒陽 (ca. 206–129 B.C.), and Mei Sheng 枚乘 (ob. 141 B.C.) to portray various aspects of snow for the king of Liang (see L. 5, note). The rhapsody begins with a long virtuoso performance by Sima Xiangru, who affects the epideictic style of the Han rhapsody to provide a comprehensive account of snow. He begins by relating the pervasiveness of snow in space, history, and literature, then describes the effects of freezing air that comes with the arrival of winter, the actual falling of snow, its appearance and manifold transformations, and its whiteness and jadelike purity. He concludes by giving his personal reaction to snow. Next, Zou Yang presents two songs on the theme of two lovers who take advantage of the heavy snow to prolong their tryst. Finally, Mei Sheng presents an envoi, in which he philosophizes about snow, arguing that its basic essence is impermanence and changeability.

"Rhapsody on Snow" has been previously translated by von Zach, *Deutsche Wacht* 14 (1928), rpt. in *Die Chinesische Anthologie* 1: 195–98; Margouliès, *Anthologie raisonnée de la littérature chinoise*, pp. 359–61 (partial); Watson, *Chinese Rhyme-Prose*, pp. 86–91; Owen, "Hsieh Huilien's 'Snow Fu,'" pp. 14–22; and Idema, *Wie zich pas heeft gebaad*, pp. 34–38. For *baihua* translations, see Chen Hongtian et al., *Zhaoming Wen xuan yizhu* 2: 703–12; and Li Jingying, *Zhaoming Wen xuan xinjie* 2: 90–96; and Chi et al., *Lidai fu cidian*, pp. 391–92. There are notes in Huang Ruiyun, *Lidai shuqing xiaofu xuan*, pp. 111–19.

L. 15: "North Wind" (*Mao shi* 41) is a song in the "Bei Airs" ("Bei feng" 邶風) section of the *Classic of Songs*. The area of Bei, from which the Bei songs reputedly came, belonged to the Wei state. Thus, Xie Huilian designates "North Wind" as a "Wei Song."

L. 16: "South Mountain" refers to "Xin Nanshan" 信南山 (*Mao shi* 210), a poem in the "Lesser Elegantiae" section of the *Classic of Songs*. The opening lines of its second stanza read: "The sky above is a single mass of clouds; / It sends down snow thick and heavy."

L. 24: Snow Palace (Xue gong 雪宮) was a touring palace in the state of Qi (the "eastern state" of Xie Huilian's line). King Xuan of Qi received Mengzi there. See *Mengzi* 1B/4.

L. 25: The snowy mountains are the Tianshan 天山 of the Western Regions.

L. 26: Qi 歧 is the mountain area (located near modern Qishan 歧山, Shaanxi) that was the homeland of the Zhou founding house. Chang 昌 is the personal name of the Zhou founder, posthumously known as King Wen. He is attributed with *Mao shi* 167, the last stanza of which contains the following lines:

When we first went forth,
Willows were soft and tender.
Now, upon our return,
The snow falls thick and heavy.

L. 27: Man 滿 of the Ji 姬 is Duke Mu 穆 of Zhou. When people were crossing the Huangtai 黃臺 hills and heavy snow began to fall, Duke Mu composed a song in three stanzas to commiserate with the freezing people. The first line of each of the first two stanzas reads: "I have gone to Yellow Bamboo." See *Mu Tianzi zhuan* 5.4b. Yellow Bamboo (Huangzhu 黃竹) presumably is another name for Huangtai.

L. 28: *Mao shi* 150, a song in the "Airs of Cao" section of the *Classic of Songs*, has the line "Linen robes like snow" (stanza 3).

L. 29: The Chu song refers to "Rhapsody on Persuasion," attributed to Song Yu. Song Yu tells of coming to the home of a beautiful women who invites him inside. He is given a zither, on which he plays the songs "Hidden Boneset" ("You lan" 幽蘭) and "White Snow" ("Bai xue" 白雪). See *Guwen yuan* 1.8b.

L. 30: The Mao commentary to *Mao shi* 210, "Xin Nanshan," says that a bountiful harvest is always preceded by a heavy snow. See *Mao shi zhushu* 13.2.19a (1011).

L. 31: Li Shan (*Wen xuan* 13.9a–b) cites the apocryphon *Chunqu quantan ba* 春秋潛潭巴, which says: "When a great snow is very deep this means that later there is certain to be a female ruler. When it snows continuously for months, this means that the yin [female] force exercises authority."

L. 32: Xie Huilian here follows the phrasing of the "Commentary on the Judgment" to hexagram 33, "Retreat," of the *Classic of Changes*: "The significance of 'Retreat' with respect to time/season is great indeed!" See *Zhou yi zhushu* 4.7a–b.

L. 34: What I have translated as "time of darkness" literally is "dark pitchpipes" (*xuan lu* 玄律). In Chinese correlative thought each month corresponded to one of twelve pitches. Winter was the *xuan* (dark) season. Thus, Xie Huilian uses "dark pitchpipes" to designate the last month of winter.

L. 36: Scorching Creek (Jiao xi 焦溪) may refer to the stream mentioned in the *Shui jing zhu* (9.4a) as flowing south from Scorching Springs (Jiao quan 焦泉) in the vicinity of modern Hui 輝 xian, Henan. See Zhao Yongfu, *Shui jing zhu tongjian jinshi*, p. 19.

L. 37: Scalding Vale (Tang gu 湯谷) may refer to the stream of this name located in the Zi Mountains 紫山 north of Nanyang. See Sheng Hongzhi 盛弘之, *Jingzhou ji* 荊州記 (Notes on Jingzhou), cited by Li Shan (*Wen xuan* 13.9b).

L. 40: Although this is probably not a specific reference, Li Shan (*Wen xuan* 13.9b) refers

15 The king then sang "North Wind" from the "Wei Songs,"
And chanted "South Mountain" from the Zhou "Elegantiae."
He gave bamboo strips to grandee Sima and said:
"Draw forth your innermost thoughts,
Give free rein to lovely expressions,
20 Describe its features, portray it in fitting detail,
And rhapsodize on it for me."

## II

Thereupon, Xiangru left his mat, stood up, stepped back a bit, and bowed, saying:

"I have heard that Snow Palace was built in an eastern state;
25 And snowy mountains rise on high in the Western Regions.
Chang of Qi chanted of it in "Now, we return";
Man of the Ji sang of it in "Yellow Bamboo."
The "Airs of Cao" compared its color to linen robes;
In a Chu song it was paired with "Hidden Boneset."
30 If a full foot deep, it reveals a propitious omen for bountiful harvest;
But if more than ten feet, it manifests the calamity of the yin power.
The significance of snow with respect to the seasons is far-reaching
indeed!
Please allow me to speak of its beginnings:

## III

"Now, as the time of darkness reaches its peak,
35 And harsh air is ascendant,
Scorching Creek dries up,
Scalding Vale freezes,
Fire wells are extinguished,
Hot springs ice over,
40 Frothing pools no longer bubble,

to a bubbling well called Frothing Pool (Fei tan 沸潭) located near the Jizi Temple 季子廟 near Qu'e 曲阿 (modern Danyang 丹陽, Jiangsu).

L. 43: The "land of the naked" possibly refers to Luoguo 裸國 (Country of the Naked), which is variously located to the west or south of China. According to legend, the Great Yu entered this country naked (see *Huainanzi* 1.6b).

L. 65: King Mu 穆 (reg. 1023–983 B.C.) of Zhou built a terrace of layered jade for his concubine Sheng Ji 盛姬. See *Mu Tianzi zhuan* 6.1b.

Fiery winds do not rise.
On north-facing doors, panels are plastered;
In the land of the naked, men drape themselves in silks.


## IV

"And then, clouds rise on river and sea;
45  Sand flies on northern deserts.
Unbroken vapors, piled up haze,
Shroud the sun, veil the clouds.
First sleet comes pattering down;
Then snow, copiously clustered, falls harder and harder.


## V

50  "Such is its appearance:
Scattering and spreading, mingling and merging,
It swells up, then thins out,
Dark and dense, lightly drifting,
Thickly massed, high and heavy.
55  Unremitting, it flies and spatters;
Wavering, pausing, it forms piled drifts.
It begins by edging eaves, blanketing purlins,
Ends by opening blinds, entering cracks.
At first it whirls round stair and veranda;
60  Last it twists through curtain and mat.
Conforming to the square, it forms a jade tessera;
Meeting the round, it creates a jade disc.
Glance at the lowlands and see a million acres all like albescent silk;
Gaze at the mountains and behold a thousand cliffs all white.


## VI

65  "And then terraces rise like layered jade;
Roads stretch out like interlocking gems.
Courtyards are arrayed with chalcedony stairs;
In forests stand carnelian trees.
The albescent crane is deprived of its luster,
70  The silver pheasant loses its pristine whiteness,

LL. 75–76: The Candescent Dragon (Zhu long 燭龍), also known as Zhu yin 燭陰, was a spirit with a human face and reptile body. When he closed his eyes there was darkness, and when he opened them, daylight began. See Yuan Ke, *Shanhai jing jiaozhu*, 12.438. Mount Kun refers to the Kunlun Mountains.

L. 79: Pingyi 馮夷 is another name for Hebo 河伯, the god of the Yellow River. See *Zhuangzi* 3.6b, commentary.

L. 91: Xiang 湘 and Wu 吳 here refer to Xiangchuan 湘川 and Wuxing 吳興, famous wine-producing areas. Except as another name for the Xiang River, I cannot identify Xiangchuan as a specific place name. Wuxing was a commandery located in the modern area of Huzhou 湖州 City, Zhejiang. Li Shan (*Wen xuan* 13.11b) cites the *Wu lu* 吳錄 (Records of Wu) by Zhang Bo 張勃 (Western Jin), which says that Lingling 靈陵 Prefecture (modern Lingling, Hunan) of Xiangchuan produces fine wine, and Wucheng 烏程 Prefecture of Wuxing is renowned for its Ruoxia 若下 wine.

Silk-sleeved beauties are ashamed of their charms,
Alabaster faces conceal their fairness.

## VII

"When its piled whiteness has not yet melted,
And the morning sun shines bright:
75  It gleams like the Candescent Dragon,
Torch in mouth, illuminating Mount Kun.
Or when flowing droplets form hanging icicles,
Clinging to downspouts, clutching corners:
They are resplendent as if Pingyi
80  Had split open oysters and set out luminous pearls.
As for its aspect of plenteous profusion, chaotic confusion,
Its form of glistening brightness, glowing purity,
The manner of its whirling dispersal, twirling cumulation,
The wonder of its flying coalescence, gelid brilliance:
85  Truly it evolves and changes without end;
Alas, how can one understand it fully?

## VIII

"If one wishes to extend his pleasure and enjoyment without end,
At night, dark and still, many feelings are roused.
Wind strikes columns and echoes resound;
90  The moon shines on gauze windows, filling rooms with light.
I pour thick wine from Xiang and Wu,
Don a double cloak of fox and racoon dog,
Face a pair of jungle fowl dancing in the courtyard,
Gaze at a solitary goose flying among the clouds.
95  Treading the alternating drifts of frost and snow,
I pity the leaves parted from branches.
Letting my thoughts race a thousand leagues distant,
I yearn to take a dear one's hand and return together."

## IX

After hearing this, Zou Yang
100 Was shamed into submission,

27

LL. 124–27: Cf. *Mengzi* 6/13: Mencius asked Gaozi, "Is the whiteness of a white feather like the whiteness of white snow, and is the whiteness of white snow like the whiteness of white jade?" Gaozi said, "Yes." "If so," replied Mencius, "then the nature of a dog is like the nature of an ox, and the nature of an ox is like the nature of a human being." Mei Sheng follows Mencius in arguing for the different attributes of feathers, jade, and snow.

Yet wished to compose a lovely song,
And respectfully requested to follow with a humble tune.
Thereupon, he stood up and chanted "Song of Drifting Snow":
The song goes:
105 "Taking a fair one's hand, open a double drape;
Hugging a silken coverlet, sit on fragrant mats.
Kindle the incense burner, light a glowing candle;
Pour cinnamon wine, sing forth a clear refrain."

## X

He then followed with "Song of White Snow":
110 The song goes:
"The refrain has been sung, wine is set out;
Ruddy faces flush red, thoughts turn to dear ones.
I wish to lower the curtain and bring the pillows near;
I long to undo my girdle, loosen my sash.
115 I resent that the year so quickly comes to its close,
Lament that for future meetings there is no chance.
Have you seen the white snow on the stairs?
How can it remain dazzling bright in sunny spring?"

## XI

When the songs were done, the king then mulled them over, humming and savoring them, clapping and gripping his wrist as he watched. Turning to Mei Sheng, he had him rise and compose a finale. The finale goes:

"Although a white feather is white,
125 Its essence is lightness.
Although white jade is white,
Its basic nature is hardness.
They cannot compare with this snow,
Which appears and disappears with the seasons.
130 When dark yin forms, it does not conceal its purity;
When the sun warmly shines, it does not guard its firmness.
How is firmness my true name?
How is purity my true nature?

L. 1: The Prince of Chen 陳 is Cao Zhi. Ying and Liu are Ying Yang and Liu Zhen See Cao Pi, "Letter to Wu Zhi," *Wen xuan* 42.9a.

Resting on clouds, I ascend and descend;
135  Following the wind, I flutter and fall.
I am endowed form by the things I meet;
I am given shape by the places I land.
My immaculence comes from the things I encounter;
My soiling follows from external stains.
140  Unfettered, my heart is free and at ease;
Why worry, why fret?"

# Rhapsody on the Moon

## XIE XIYI

### I

The prince of Chen had just begun to mourn the death of Ying and
      Liu,
And he spent his days in grief and sorrow.
Green moss grew beneath galleries,
Fragrant dust formed on terraces.

THIS RHAPSODY by Xie Zhuang (*zi* Xiyi) is a short *yongwu* piece on the moon. Like
Xie Huilian's "Rhapsody on Snow," it is a prosopopoeia set in an earlier period, the Jian'an
era of Cao Zhi (196–220). The piece begins with Cao mourning the deaths of his friends
Ying Yang 應瑒 (ca. 170–217) and Liu Zhen 劉楨 (ca. 170–217), two of the Seven Jian'an
Masters, during the epidemic of 217. It is autumn, when constellations shift position and
white dew descends. As moonlight streams across the heavens, Cao recites lines from the
*Classic of Songs* that refer to the moon. He then hands a brush and tablet to Wang Can and
requests him to write a poem on the moon. Wang Can's rhapsody follows. He first presents
traditional lore associated with the moon: its *yin* essence; the light it obtains from the sun, in
the east when it is full, and in the west when it begins to wax; its two famous inhabitants,
the hare and the beauty Chang E; how its waxing and waning serve as warnings to humans
and their rulers; the illumination it provides to the palace of the Lord of Heaven; and the
good fortune it sent down on two great houses, the Han and Wu. Wang then follows with a
series of lines describing in typical *fu* fashion how the moon outshines all other celestial
luminaries to flood both earth and sky with its brilliant light. In the remaining sections he
tells of the human response to the moon: a prince leaves his candle-lit feast chamber to view
the moon while drinking wine and listening to zither music; on a cold, windy night a man
(or perhaps a woman?) is all alone in his chamber, and plays a zither and pours out his
sadness to the moon. As in "Rhapsody on Snow," at the end there are two short lyrical

31

LL. 13–14. The "slanting Han" is the Sky River, or Milky Way. According to Li Zhouhan (*Liuchen zhu Wen xuan* 13.16b), in autumn the Sky River inclined to the southwest. However, I can find no other textual authority to confirm this claim. Furthermore, left is east in traditional Chinese orientation, and thus it is not clear why Li Zhouhan would specify the direction as southwest. The Boreal Route (Bei lu 北陸), α of Equuleus and β of Aquarius, is another name for the Barrens (Xu 虛) constellation. See Schlegel, *Uranographie chinoise* 1: 225.

L. 15: The ascending of white dew (*bai lu* 白露) marked the beginning of autumn. "White dew" also was the name of the autumn solar period that begins around 8 September.

L. 17: The verses of Qi 齊 refer to *Mao shi* 99, which is in the "Airs of Qi" section. The second stanza begins with the line "The moon is in the east."

L. 18: The song of Chen 陳 is *Mao shi* 143, "The Moon Rises." Each stanza begins with the refrain "The moon rises bright." See ibid.

L. 20: Zhongxuan 仲宣 is the style name of Wang Can.

L. 22: The eastern border refers to Wang Can's native place, Gaoping 高平 in Shanyang 山陽 Commandery (southwest of modern Zou 鄒 xian, Shandong).

L. 25: The word *gu* 孤, which I have rendered "alone," may also be understood as *gu* 辜, "undeservedly."

LL. 26–27: Xie Zhuang borrows the phrases "sunken and submerged" and "high and brilliant" from the "Grand Norm" chapter of the *Shang shu*. The Kong Anguo commentary (*Shang shu zhushu* 12.15a, 404) says that "sunken and submerged" refers to Earth, and "high and brilliant" to Heaven.

5   Saddened by this he was sick at heart,
    And remained dispirited into the middle of the night.
    Then, thoroughwort paths were swept,
    Cinnamon park was cleared.
    As blaring pipes sounded from cold hills,
10  He halted his cart on an autumn slope.
    Looking down into a plunging chasm, he lamented the distantly
                departed;
    Climbing a lofty tor, he bemoaned the remoteness.
    And then, when the slanting Han was edging left,
    And the Boreal Route lodged in the south,
15  White dew dimmed the sky,
    Moonlight flooded the heavens:
    He softly intoned the verses of Qi,
    Heartily chanted the song of Chen.
    Taking out a brush, presenting a tablet,
20  He commanded Zhongxuan to write a poem.


## II

    Zhongxuan knelt and declaimed:
    "I am an obscure and humble scholar from the eastern border,
    And I was raised in hills and copses.
    Although ignorant in lore, deficient in learning,
25  I alone have received my wise lord's favor.
    I have heard that the sunken and submerged is the guiding norm,
    And the high and brilliant is the ruling constant,
    The virtue of the sun is yang,

---

songs: one about two separated lovers who, in spite of the great distance, can at least share the moon; the other about how the setting of the moon is a reminder to return home before it is too late. Xie Zhuang concludes the piece with the conventional words of praise: Cao Zhi commends Wang Can for his performance and rewards him with a toast and present of jade.

   "Rhapsody on the Moon" has been translated by von Zach, *Deutsche Wacht* (May 1928), rpt. in *Die Chinesische Anthologie* 1: 198–201; and Obi and Hanabusa, *Monzen* 2: 182–87. There are *baihua* translations in Chen Hongtian, *Zhaoming Wen xuan yizhu*, 2: 713–21; and Li Jingying, *Zhaoming Wen xuan xinjie* 2: 97–102. There are annotated texts in Qu Tuiyuan, *Han Wei Liuchao fuxuan*, pp. 183–89; Liu Zhenxiang and Li Fangchen, *Lidai cifu xuan*, pp. 285–91; Wang Chenguang, *Wei Jin Nanbeichao cifu xuancui*, pp. 90–101; Wei Fengjuan, *Wei Jin Nanbeichao zhujia sanwen xuan*, pp. 270–77; and Huang Ruiyun, *Lidai shuqing xiaofu xuan*, pp. 120–27.

LL. 30–31: Fu is Fusang 扶桑, a legendary mulberry tree located above the Dawn Valley (Yang gu 暘谷) at the extreme eastern limits of the world. According to legend, the ten suns bathed on the Fusang tree. Nine suns remained on the lower branches, while one rested on top. As soon as one arrived on a branch, another left. Each carried a three-legged crow. See Yuan Ke, *Shanhai jing jiaozhu* 9.260–61, 9.354–55. The eastern pool is another name for Dawn Valley. Ruo is the Ruo tree 若木, which was located in the extreme western limits of the world, where the sun set. Its scarlet blossoms cast light onto the earth (presumably explaining the red rays of sunset). See ibid. 12.437. The Western Gloom presumably is a name for Mei Gu 昧谷 (Dark Valley) or Meng Si 濛汜 (Murky Shore), the depression into which the sun sinks at the end of the day. See *Chuci buzhu* 3.3b; and *Shangshu zhushu* 2.10a, 251. Li Shan (*Wen xuan* 13.13b) explains that the moon reached its fullness in the east, thus the text says it "seizes" light from the Fusang tree; it begins to wax in the west, thus it "inherits" blossoms from the Ruo tree.

L. 32: Li Shan (*Wen xuan* 13.14a) cites a "Guan xiang fu" 觀象賦 ("Viewing the Celestial Phenomena") by Zhang Quan 張泉 (n.d.): "The Platform of Lapping Waters can be ascended." Zhang's note to this line reads: "The Platform of Lapping Waters is a name for the Lord of Heaven's Platform (Di tai 帝臺). Its four stars lie east of Weaver Girl." The Platform of Lapping Waters corresponds to four stars in Lyra. See Ho Peng-yoke, *The Astronomical Chapters of the Chin shu*, p. 83. The ancient Chinese believed that the moon was inhabited by a hare. One of the earliest explanations is in the *Ling xian* 靈憲 (Divine Pattern of the Heavens) of Zhang Heng (cited in *Hou Han shu*, "Zhi," 10.3216, commentary): "The moon is the ancestress of the yin. It gathers together to form an animal that resembles a hare." See Michael Loewe, *Ways to Paradise*, pp. 52–55.

L. 33: The Albescent Beauty (Su E 素娥) is more commonly known as Chang E 常娥 or Heng E 恆娥. According to the *Huainanzi* (6.10b), Heng E stole the herb of immortality from Yi 羿, who had obtained it from the Queen Mother of the West. She then fled to the moon. In his commentary to this passage in *Huainanzi*, Gao You adds that Heng E was Yi's wife. He obtained a drug of immortality from the Queen Mother of the West, but before he could ingest it, Heng E stole it. She ate it and transformed into an immortal. When she "entered the moon, she became the luminous essence of the moon." According to Zhang Heng's *Ling xian* 靈憲 (see *Hou Han shu*, "Zhi," 10.3216, commentary), Heng E was transformed into a toad that lived in the moon. Li Shan (*Wen xuan* 13.14a) cites Zhang Quan's "Guan xiang fu," which identifies the Heavenly Emperor's Court (Di Ting 帝庭) as the Taiwei Palace 太微宮, which corresponds to stars in Virgo, Leo, and Coma Berenices. See Ho Peng-yoke, *The Astronomical Chapters of the Chin shu*, p. 71.

L. 34: *Nü* 朒 is an abbreviated form of *suonü* 縮朒, which refers to the moon appearing in the east at the first of the month. See *Shuowen jiezi gulin* 7A.3000a–30001b. *Tiao* 朓 designates the moon seen in the west at the end of the month. See *Shuowen jiezi gulin* 7A.2999b–3000b. On the etymology of these words, see Boltz, "Evocations of the Moon, Excitations of the Sea," pp. 31–32. The idea conveyed by this line is that a moon not fully round was a sign of "deficiency." Thus, it was a warning to rulers to beware of complacency even in times of plenty and prosperity.

L. 35: *Fei* 胐 and *po* 魄 here probably are synonymous terms that designate the first days of the waxing moon (the second day after a "long" thirty-day month, and the third day after a "short" twenty-day month). There also was a tradition in which *po* was explained as the day after the full moon. However, that interpretation does not seem to apply to Xie Zhuang's usage in this line. For further discussion of the terms, see *Shuowen jiezi gulin* 7A.2995b–2999a; Wang Guowei, *Guantang jilin* 1.1a–4b; and Dubs, *HFHD* 3: 194–95, n. 19.9.

L. 36: There were twelve cyclical signs, one for each lunar month.

And the essence of the moon is yin.
30 The moon seizes the light of Fu from the eastern pool,
Inherits the Ruo tree blossoms in the Western Gloom,
Leads the dark hare to the Lord of Heaven's Platform,
Brings the Albescent Beauty to the Celestial Court.
The waxing and waning crescents warn of deficiency;
35 The new moon exemplifies modesty.
In accord with the horary signs, it circulates light;

L. 37: This line alludes to a passage in the "Grand Plan" chapter of the *Shang shu*: "As the moon follows the stars there results wind and rain." The Kong Anguo commentary explains that when the moon passes into the Winnow Star (Sagittarius) there is increased wind; when it meets the Net Star (Hyades) there is increased rain. See *Shang shu zhushu* 11.23b, 408.

LL. 38-39: The Chamber of Ministers (Tai Shi 台室) refers to the San Tai 三台 (Three Platforms), which represents the seats of the Three Ducal Ministers. They correspond to three stars in Ursa Major. See Schlegel, *Uranographie chinoise* 1: 529; Ho Peng-yoke, *The Astronomical Chapters of the Chin shu*, p. 80. The Carriage Palace (Xuan Gong 軒宮), also known as Xuanyuan 軒轅, included seventeen stars north of the Star (Xing 星) constellation (Hydra). It corresponded to stars in Leo and Lynx and governed the court of the empress and imperial concubines. See Ho Peng-yoke, *The Astronomical Chapters of the Chin shu*, p. 93.

L. 40: This line alludes to a story recorded in the *Soushen ji* 搜神記 of Gan Bao 干寶 (fl. A.D. 317) concerning Wu Polu 吳破虜, wife of Sun Jian 孫堅 (ob. 191). She was the mother of Sun Ce 孫策 (175-200), elder brother of the Wu founder Sun Quan 孫權 (182-252). While pregnant with Sun Ce she dreamed that the moon entered her breast. See Wang Shaoying, *Soushen ji* 10.122; and *Sanguo zhi* 50.1195.

L. 41: This line refers to a story concerning Wang Zhengjun 王政君, a wife of Emperor Yuan 元 of the Former Han (reg. 48-33 B.C.). Her mother was pregnant with Zhengjun when she dreamed that the moon entered her breast. Wang Zhengjun was the mother of Emperor Cheng 成 (reg. 32-7 B.C.) and, as Empress Dowager, was extremely influential at the end of the Former Han, especially when her nephew Wang Mang was in power. See *Han shu* 98.4015. Yang Xiong refers to this event in his "Dirge for Empress Yuan". See *Guwen yuan* 9.9b.

LL. 44-45: Cf. "Nine Songs," "Lady of the Xiang," L. 4 (*Chuci buzhu* 2.9a): "Lake Dongting ripples, leaves fall from trees."

L. 51: The long river is the Sky River.

LL. 52-53: In ancient Chinese thought the virtue of earth was described as soft or yielding. One of the attributes of heaven was roundness.

Following the stars, it brings moisture and wind.
It adds splendor to the Chamber of Ministers,
Casts luster upon the Carriage Palace.
40 It sent down its light, and the house of Wu flourished;
It let fall its shining essence and the course of Han was smooth.

## III

"Then, when the air clears over the ground,
And clouds withdraw to the sky's edge,
Dongting begins to ripple,
45 Trees gently shed their leaves,
Chrysanthemums spread fragrance over mountain peaks,
Geese mournfully call from river shoals:
Slow and steady rises a radiant form,
That casts down a soft and gentle light.
50 Constellations have their starry profusion dimmed;
The long river sheathes its light.
The yielding earth seems as if frozen by snow;
The rotund sky is like a pellucid pool.
One after another towers glisten white as frost;
55 All around stairs shine clear as ice.

## IV

"Then, when a prince tires of morning pleasures,
He enjoys himself with night feasting.
He cuts short the wondrous dancing,
Abandons his clear-toned bells.
60 Leaving his candle-lit chamber,
He enters a hall bathed in moonlight.
Fragrant wine is presented,
A melodious zither is played.

## V

"When on a cool night one feels lonely and sad,
65 And the wind blows a melody through bamboo groves:
With no kin or friend for company,

37

L. 68: The marsh bird is a crane. Cf. *Mao shi* 184/1: "A crane cries in the nine marshes, / Its voice is heard in the wilds."

L. 69: The northern pipe is the reed whistle, or Tibetan flute.

L. 70: The word for zither is literally "stringed paulownia" (*xuan tong* 絃桐), as it usually was made of paulownia wood.

L. 72: "Fang lu" 房露 presumably is equivalent to "Fang lu" 防露 ("Keeping off the Dew"), a song mentioned in Lu Ji's "Rhapsody on Literature" (L. 181). Xie Lingyun mentions a song of this name in his "Rhapsody on Dwelling in the Mountains": "A Chu guest was exiled and 'Keeping off the Dew' was composed." In his commentary to this line, Xie explains that this refers to Dongfang Shuo's "Seven Admonitions." See *Song shu* 67.1762. Zhu Jian (*Wen xuan jishi* 14.23a) suggests that it may be another name for the song known as "Yang'e xielu" 陽阿薤露 mentioned in "Responding to a Question by the King of Chu," attributed to Song Yu (*Wen xuan* 45.2a). However, this seems unlikely given that Xie Zhuang mentions the song "Yang'e" in the following line.

L. 73: "Sunny Bank" ("Yang'e" 陽阿, also written 揚荷 or 揚阿) is the name of an ancient Chu song. See *Chuci buzhu* 9.11a; and *Huainanzi* 18.17b.

And only wanderers constantly passing by,
He hears a marsh bird's night call,
Listens to a northern pipe's autumnal song.
70   And then, the notes of the zither mode are chosen,
And the manner of the tones is tender and gentle:
Slow and languid—'Keeping off the Dew';
Sad and mournful—'Sunny Bank.'
The murmuring grove stills its piping;
75   The wind-swept pond quiets its ripples.
Pent-up feelings, to whom can they be entrusted?
Sing a long plaint to the shining moon.


## VI

"A song goes:
'My fair one is far away, all news is cut off;
80   Although a thousand leagues apart, we share the same moon.
I sigh into the wind—how can I stop?
River and road are long and cannot be traversed.'


## VII

"Song and music have yet to end,
And the fading moon is about to set.
85   Everyone in the hall changes expression,
All are confused and confounded as if lost.
They then sing another song:
'The moon has set, the dew is nearly dry;
The year soon shall end, I have no one with whom to return.
90   This is a propitious time to go home,
For the frost may soon soak your clothes!' "


## VIII

The prince of Chen said, "Excellent!"
He then commanded attendants
To offer a toast, present jade discs.
95   "I admire your precious verses,
And I shall never weary of reciting them."

LL. 1–3: *Chan e* 單閼 is one of the astrological names used by the ancient Chinese to indicate one year of the twelve-year Jupiter cycle. *Chan e* designated a *mao* 卯 year. See Hao Yixing, *Erya yishu* B4.4a. Thus, Xu Guang 徐廣 (352–425) equates this year with the sixth year of Emperor Wen (174 B.C.), which was a *dingmao* 丁卯 year. See *Shi ji* 84.2497, n. 1. This also is the date given by *Mh* 3: 660. However, since Jupiter does not take exactly twelve years to revolve around the sun, the Jupiter-cycle chronology was behind the actual chronology, and thus adjustments must be made in converting the Jupiter-cycle date to the Western calendar. Qian Daxin corrects the date to the seventh year of Emperor Wen (173 B.C.). See *Nianer shi kaoyi* 5.10a. This date agrees with that established by Liu Tan, "*Lü lan* Tuntan yu 'Fu fu' Chan e *Huainan* bingzi zhi tongkao," 80–81. As Dubs has shown, month dates given in Han sources before the calendrical reform of 104 B.C. must be adjusted by adding three months. See Dubs, *HFHD* 1: 154–60. Thus, the fourth month actually corresponds to the seventh month. The *gengzi* day of the seventh month of the seventh year of Emperor Wen corresponds to 1 June 173 B.C.

# Rhapsody on the Houlet

## JIA YI

Jia Yi served as tutor in Changsha.[1] In his third year there a houlet flew into his house and perched on the corner of his mat.[2] The houlet resembles the owl, and is an unlucky bird. Jia Yi had been banished from the court and sent to live in Changsha. Changsha is low-lying and damp, and Jia Yi felt himself afflicted with sorrow and grief. He believed that his life span would not be long, and he thereupon composed a rhapsody to console himself. The words of the piece read:[3]

### I

In the year *Chan e*,
The fourth month, the first of summer,
At sunset on a *gengzi* day,
A houlet landed in my house,
5    Alighting on a corner of my mat,
Its manner very relaxed and tranquil.

IN THIS RHAPSODY Jia Yi tells of a bird called the *fu* 鵩 or 服, which landed in his house. *Fu* is a Chu dialect word for *xiao* 鴞, the standard Old Chinese name for owl. Early sources describe the bird as black, with a striped body. It reputedly received the name *fu* because of its shape. See *Shi ji* 史記 84.2497. However, it is not clear what shape this might designate (the most common meaning of *fu* is "garment"). In order to indicate its dialect origins, and also to distinguish it from *xiao*, I have rendered *fu* with the archaic English "houlet." In spite of its title, "The Houlet" is not a *yongwu* poem on a bird, but is a philosophical poem on life and death. Drawing upon lines from the *Laozi* and *Zhuangzi*, Jia Yi repeatedly makes the point that life and death are part of the natural process of change. Life is nothing to cling to, and death is nothing to fear. Much of the piece consists of a variation of statements on the inexorability of change, the vagaries of fate, and the resonating influence that exists among natural phenomena. Particularly artful is the third section, in

L. 7: *Shi ji* reads 集 for *Han shu*'s *zu* 崒. *Wen xuan* reads cui 萃. The latter two graphs are interchangeable, and all three have the same meaning of *zhi* 止 (to come to rest). Cf. *Mao shi* 141/2: "At the graveyard gate there is a plum tree; / An owl comes to rest on it." See Wang Niansun, *Dushu zazhi* 4/9.11b (297); Zhu Jian, *Wen xuan jishi* 13.17b–18a; and Hu Shaoying, *Wen xuan jianzheng* 16.1b–2a.

L. 10: *Wen xuan* and *Han shu* read *chen* 讖 (prognostication) for *Shi ji*'s *ce* 筴 (divining slips).

L. 12: The meaning of "depart" is not clear from the context. However, the traditional interpretation of this line is that it refers to death. Cf. *Xijing zaji* 5.7a: "When Jia Yi was in Changsha, a houlet landed on his dust curtain. According to Changsha custom, when a houlet enters a man's house, the master will die."

L. 17: The *Wen xuan* and *Han shu* read *su* (\*suk) 速 for *shuo* (\*sruk) 數 of the *Shi ji*. Both are variant graphs for the same word meaning "swift." See *Li ji zhushu* 19.18b (3029); and Wang Li, *Tongyuan zidian*, p. 299.

LL. 23–24: Cf. *Heguanzi* C.4a: "Things whirl and course, shift and move, / Verily without cease or rest."

A strange creature came to rest,
And I wondered the reason.
I opened a book and divined the question;
10   The oracle told me my fortune.
It said: "A wild bird enters a house;
The master will soon depart."

"May I ask Sir Houlet
Where should I go?
15   Is it auspicious? Then inform me!
Inauspicious? Tell me the misfortune.
Whether it shall occur late or soon,
Let me know the time."


## II

The houlet heaved a great sigh,
20   Raised its head and flapped its wings.
Since its beak cannot speak,
Let me reply what it thought.
The myriad things change and transform,
Verily without cease or rest.

---

which Jia Yi introduces two analogies for the process of creation: the fashioning of a pot on a wheel, and the casting of metal in a great forge. The constant turning of the wheel and the continuous transformation of substances in the forge represent the process of change. At the end of the piece, Jia Yi offers a portrait of the ideal Taoist sage, to whom life, self, riches, fame, and power do not matter. The man of broad vision is oblivious of all things except the Tao. Thus, he divests himself of all desires and attachment to self, and yields to whatever fate decrees for him.

There are many lines that are identical to passages in the *Heguanzi* 鶡冠子, a pre-Qin syncretic work heavily influenced by Lao- Zhuang thought. Although the authenticity of the *Heguanzi* has been questioned since the Tang dynasty, some recent scholarship has shown that at least part of it may be genuine. See Ogata Tōru, "Kakkanshi no seiritsu"; Wu Guang, *Huang-Lao zhi xue tonglun*, pp. 151-58; Neugebauer, *Hoh-kuan Tsi*; and A. C. Graham, "A neglected pre-Han philosophical text." Although I doubt that Jia Yi would have so shamelessly "plagiarized" another work, I have indicated the textual parallels in my notes.

Previous translations include Giles, "Poe's 'Raven'—in Chinese"; Richard Wilhelm, *Die chinesische Literatur*, pp. 111-12; Hightower, "Chia Yi's 'Owl Fu'"; Watson, *Records of the Grand Historian of China* 1: 512-15, rpt. in *Chinese Rhyme-Prose*, pp. 25-28; and Obi and Hanabusa, *Monzen* 2: 188-95. There are *baihua* translations by Chen Hongtian et al., *Zhaoming Wen xuan yizhu* 2: 722-29; Li Jingying, *Zhaoming Wen xuan xinjie* 2: 103-8; and Chi et al., *Lidai fu cidian*, pp. 26-27. Special studies include Schindler, "Some Notes on Chia Yi and his 'Owl Song'"; and Itō Tomio, "Ka Gi no Fukuchō no fu no tachiba."

L. 28: The *Wen xuan* reads *shan* 嬗 for *shan* 嬗 of the *Shi ji* and *Han shu*. Both forms of the graph mean "to transmute." See Zhu Jian, *Wen xuan jishi* 13.18a.

L. 30: Cf. *Heguanzi* C.3b: "Change and transformation go on without end; how can one express it in words?"

LL. 31–32: These lines are from *Laozi* 58. See also *Heguanzi* C.4a.

LL. 33–34: These lines are also found in *Heguanzi* C.4a.

LL. 35–38: King Fucha 夫差 (ob. 473 B.C.) of Wu led the army of Wu to victory over King Goujian 句踐 (ob. 465 B.C.) of Yue. Goujian then took refuge on the summit of Mount Guiji. Later, Goujian returned to rout Wu and become Hegemon of the States. See *Shi ji* 41.1739–47; and *Mh* 4: 420–33. Cf. *Heguanzi* C.4a: "Wu was great and its army was strong, yet Fu Cha was surrounded. Yue took refuge in Guiji, yet Goujian was acclaimed hegemon over the world."

LL. 39–40: Li Si 李斯 (ob. 208 B.C.), a native of Chu, traveled to Qin, where he became one of the First Qin Emperor's favored ministers. Later, when the Second Qin Emperor assumed the throne, Li Si was accused of disloyalty and executed. See *Shi ji* 87.2539–63; and Bodde, *China's First Unifier*. The five punishments in Qin times probably were tattooing, cutting off the nose, severing both feet, beating the person to death, and cutting the corpse into mincemeat in the market. See Chavannes, *Mh* 2: 210, n. 2.

LL. 41–42: Fu Yue 傅説 worked as a convict laborer at the Fu Cliffs until the Shang ruler Wuding discovered him and made him his minister. See *Shi ji* 3.102. *Xumi* 胥靡 literally means "bound together"; convict laborers were tied together. See *Han shu* 36.1924, Yan Shigu's commentary. For a reference to Fu Yue's service as a convict laborer, see *Lushi chunqiu* 22.7b.

LL. 43–44: Cf. *Heguanzi* C.4a: "Disaster and good fortune are like the strands of a rope."

L. 46: See *Laozi* 58: "Disaster is where good fortune rests, / Good fortune is where disaster lurks. / Who comprehends their limits?"; and *Heguanzi* C.4a: "The process ends only to begin again; who comprehends its limits?"

LL. 47–48: Variations of these lines appear in *Lüshi chunqiu* 16.16b and *Huainanzi* 15.11b. See also *Heguanzi* C.3b.

LL. 49–50: Cf. *Heguanzi* C.3b: "Soul and spirit are impelled round and round, pushing and propelling, turning one upon another."

L. 53. The *Shi ji* reads *zhuan* 專 for *jun* 鈞 of the *Han shu* and *Wen xuan*. These graphs are interchangeable in the sense of "potter's wheel." See Zhu Jian, *Wen xuan jishi* 13.18a–b. The *Shi ji* reads *pan* (*ba) 檠 for *bo* (*pa-) 播 of the *Han shu* and *Wen xuan*. I suspect that the word represented here is *pan* (*ba) 盤 (to form by revolving; to turn). Thus, I have translated it here as "shape."

LL. 55–56: Cf. *Heguanzi* C.4b: "Heaven cannot be preplanned; earth cannot be predicted."

L. 57: Cf. ibid. C.3b: "Late or soon, all is fate."

25 Swirling, coursing, shifting,
At times thrusting forward, then turning back.
Matter and spirit follow one upon another,
Changing, transforming, and transmuting.
The process is dark and deep, unending;
30 How can one express it in words?

Disaster is where good fortune rests;
Good fortune is where disaster lurks.
Grief and joy crowd the gate;
Good luck and bad share the realm.

35 Wu was powerful and strong,
But Fucha met with defeat.
Yue took refuge on Guiji,
Yet Goujian was acclaimed hegemon over the world.

Li Si traveled to Qin and attained success,
40 Yet in the end suffered the Five Punishments.
Fu Yue was a convict laborer,
But later served as minister to Wuding.

Disaster accompanies good fortune;
How are they different from strands of a rope?
45 Fate cannot be foretold;
Who comprehends its limits?

Water stirred begins to rage;
An arrow shot hard flies far.
The myriad things are impelled round and round,
50 Pushing and propelling, turning one upon another.

Like the rising of clouds, the falling of rain,
Things are complexly conjoined, intricately entwined.
The Great Wheel shapes all things,
Boundlessly, without limit.

55 Heaven cannot be predicted;
The Way cannot be preplanned.
Late or soon, all is fate;
Who can know the time?

ll. 59–60: Cf. *Zhuangzi* 3.9b: "Now I think of Heaven and Earth as a great kiln, and the fashioner of things as a great smith."

ll. 63–64: Cf. ibid. 7.23a: "Human life is a gathering of pneuma. When it gathers, there is life; when it dissolves, there is death." Cf. *Heguanzi* C.3b: "Things join and dissolve, wax and wane. Who knows their time?"

ll. 65–67: Cf. *Zhuangzi* 3.5b: "Happening to take on human form, one rejoices over it. A form such as man's undergoes a myriad mutations, and never is there an end."

l. 68: The *Han shu* reads *tuan* 揣 for *tuan* 搏 of the *Shi ji* and *Wen xuan*. The graphs are interchangeable. *Kongtuan* 控搏 literally means "to grasp and roll into a ball." Its extended meanings are "to grasp," "to hold," "to cling to." Cf. *Heguanzi* C.3b: "One's lot is received from Heaven, position is determined by Earth, and name is achieved by man, but the time of their arrival, how can it be turned back, how can it be held back?"

l. 72: Cf. *Zhuangzi* 6.9a: "Observed from the perspective of the Way, things have no value or meanness. Observed from the perspective of things, each values self and demeans others."

l. 74: Cf. ibid. 1.16a: "Things have that which makes them so, and things have that which makes them admissible. There is nothing that is not so, there is nothing that is inadmissible."

ll. 75–76: Cf. ibid. 4.4a: "The petty man will give his life for profit, the knight will give his life for fame, the grandee will give his life for family, and the sage will give his life for the world." Cf. *Heguanzi* C.4b: "The heroic man will give his life for fame, and the greedy man will give his life for profit."

l. 77: Cf. *Zhuangzi* 8.14b: "If his power and might do not increase, the ambitious man is sad." Cf. *Heguanzi* C.4b: "The ambitious man would die for power."

l. 78: The *Han shu* and *Wen xuan* read *mei* (\**mwəh*) 每 (to covet) for *Shi ji*'s *ping* 馮 (to cling to). *Mei* in the sense of "covet" also is written *mei* 拇; see Dai Zhen, *Fangyan shuzheng* 13.4a. It may be equivalent to *mao* (\**məkw*) 冒, which often means "to covet" in early texts. For a detailed discussion of this line see Zhu Jian, *Wen xuan jishi* 13.18b–19a.

l. 79: As Wang Niansun has suggested, the phrase *xu po* 忧迫 (enticement and repulsion) should be understood in the context of a *Guanzi* (13.2b) passage: "Thus, the gentleman is not enticed by his likes, and is not repulsed by his dislikes." See *Dushu zazhi* 4/9.11b–12a. Cf. *Heguanzi* C.4b: "The multitudes are muddled and confused and are enticed by their likes and desires."

l. 80: I follow Yang Shuda in reading *huo* 或 as *huo* 惑 (confused; madly). See *Han shu kuiguan*, p. 255.

l. 82: 亿 意 should be construed as *yi* 億 (million). See Wang Niansun, *Dushu zazhi* 4/9.12a.

ll. 85–86: Cf. *Heguanzi* C.3b: "The Perfect Man abandons things, consorting alone with the Way."

l. 87: Cf. ibid. C.4b: "The multitudes are muddled and confused."

l. 88: I follow Wang Niansun in reading *yi* 意 as *yi* 臆 (full). See *Dushu zazhi* 4/9.12b.

l. 91: Cf. *Zhuangzi* 3.14b: Yan Hui said to Confucius, "I let my limbs and body fall away, banish acuity and perception, leave form, dispense with knowledge, and become one with Grand Commonality. This is what is called sitting and forgetting."

l. 92: Cf. ibid. 1.10a: "Now I have lost self."

### III

Moreover, Heaven and Earth are the kiln,
60  The fashioner of things is the smith.
Yin and yang are the charcoal;
The myriad things are the copper.

Things join and dissolve, wax and wane—
Where is the constant rule?
65  A thousand changes, a myriad mutations,
Never is there an end.

If perchance one becomes a man,
How is this worth clinging to?
If one be transformed into something other,
70  How is this worthy of concern?

The man of small vision is egoistic,
Demeaning others, valuing self.
The perspicacious man takes a broad view,
And to him nothing is inadmissable.

75  The greedy man gives his life for riches;
The heroic man gives his life for fame.
The ambitious man would die for power;
The common man covets life.

Men driven by enticement or repulsion
80  Madly dash west or east.
The Great Man does not bend;
The million changes are all the same to him.

The foolish man is bound by the profane,
Constrained as if a prisoner bound.
85  The Perfect Man abandons things,
Consorting alone with the Tao.

The multitudes are muddled and confused;
Desire and hate fill their breasts.
The Realized Man is quiet and still,
90  Existing alone with the Tao.

Divesting himself of wisdom, abandoning physical form,
Dispassionate, he loses self.

L. 96: Or, following the *Shi ji*: "Meeting an isle."

LL. 99–100: Cf. *Zhuangzi* 6.2a: "His [the sage's] life is like a floating; his death is like a rest."

L. 102: Cf. ibid. 10.7b–8a: "He drifts like an unfastened boat, empty, roaming easily along." Cf. *Heguanzi* C.4b: "He drifts like an unfastened boat."

L. 105: "Cf. *Zhuangzi* 5.8b: "The Virtuous Man rests without thought, acts without plan"; 6.2a: "Thus [the sage] suffers no calamity from Heaven, and has no burdens from external things."

Feeling vast and empty, detached and distant,
He soars with the Tao.

95 Riding the current, away he goes;
Meeting an obstacle, he stops.
Yielding his body to fate,
He is not partial to self.

His life is like a floating;
100 His death is like a rest.
He is tranquil like the stillness of a deep pool;
He drifts like an unfastened boat.
He does not for sake of life value self,
But nurturing emptiness, floats about.
105 The Virtuous Man has no burdens;
Understanding fate, he does not grieve.
Minor matters, petty woes—
How are they worth concern?

# Rhapsody on the Parrot

## MI ZHENGPING

At that time[1] Huang Yi, heir designate to Huang Zu, hosted a large gathering. Someone presented him with a parrot. Raising his goblet to Heng, he said, "Retired scholar Mi,[2] today I have nothing with which to entertain our guests. However, I believe that this bird from afar, intelligent and bright, is a creature worth prizing among the feathered species. I hope that you would compose a rhapsody on it so that all our guests

THIS RHAPSODY by Mi Heng (zi Zhengping) is a yongwu poem written at a gathering hosted by Huang Yi 黃射, governor of Zhangling 章陵 (south of modern Zaoyang 棗陽, Hubei). Someone had presented Huang Yi with a parrot as a gift, and Huang Yi asked Mi Heng to compose a rhapsody to entertain the guests. This gathering probably occurred in 198, the last year of Mi Heng's life. "Rhapsody on the Parrot" is his only extant poem. Although it is a yongwu piece that describes the attributes of a parrot, it also expresses the poet's personal feelings and frustration. In the opening lines Mi Heng tells of the parrot's origins in the Western Regions (Central Asia), its cosmological association with both the

L. 1: The bird described here is the parrot (or perhaps more correctly, parakeet) of the Long Mountains 隴山 that stretch from Long *xian* in Shaanxi to Pingliang in Gansu. It probably is now extinct in China. See Schafer, "Parrots in Medieval China," pp. 272–74.

L. 3: In Chinese Five-Phases correlative thought, metal is the element of the west. The parrot was a native of the Western Regions, and its white plumage corresponded to the white color of the metal element.

L. 4: The original You Mao text reads *han* 含 (possess) for *he* 合 (accord with). I have followed the You Mao reading, which is generally regarded as correct. See Qu Shouyuan, *Zhaoming Wen xuan zashu ji xuanjiang*, pp. 54–55. Fire is the element of the south. Its color is red. According to Li Shan (*Wen xuan* 13.21a), this line refers to the parrot's red beak.

might share in this magnificent sight. Would this not be delightful?" Heng thereupon composed a rhapsody, without pausing his brush, and without making the slightest correction. The poem goes:[3]

*I*

A marvelous bird from the Western Regions,
Manifests a wondrous natural beauty.
It embodies the sublime substance of the metal essence,
Embodies the shining brilliance of fire's power.
5   Gifted with wit and acuity, it is able to speak;
Intelligent and bright, it can perceive the imperceptible.

Thus, it plays and sports on lofty peaks,
Nests and perches in secluded vales.
Whenever it flies, it does not land at random;
10   Wherever it soars, it is sure to choose a good grove.
It has reddish-black feet, a vermilion beak,
Green coat, azure mantle.
Bright and colorful, lovely in appearance,
It chitters and chatters in a lovely voice.
15   Although of the same genus as feather and down,
It is truly distinct in wisdom, different in mind.
It equals the beauty of simurgh and phoenix;
How can its attributes compare with common birds?

---

metal and fire phases, its intelligence and ability to speak, and its magnificent colors and uniqueness in the avian realm. He then relates how this marvelous bird is sought out by hunters, who capture it, clip its feathers, and put it into a cage. They carry the parrot across rivers and mountains and present it to a "kindly lord." At this point, it is clear that Mi Heng is no longer writing about a captive bird, but about himself. The parrot is very much like Mi Heng, who often offended his masters with his sharp tongue. Another theme of "Rhapsody on the Parrot" is homesickness. In the final section the parrot longs for its native place in the far west. Perhaps Mi Heng, like the parrot, yearned to return to his home in the north.

    Previous translations include William T. Graham, Jr., "Mi Heng's 'Rhapsody on a Parrot'"; and Obi and Hanabusa, *Monzen* 2: 196–203. There are *baihua* translations by Chen Hongtian et al., *Zhaoming Wen xuan yizhu* 2: 730–36; Li Jingying, *Zhaoming Wen xuan xinjie* 2: 109–13; Chi et al., *Lidai fu cidian*, pp. 242–44; and Kong Jingqing and Han Quanxin, *Liang Han zhujia sanwen xuan*, pp. 324–33. There is an excellent annotated version in Qu Shouyuan, *Zhaoming Wen xuan zashu ji xuanjiang*, pp. 45–64. Other annotated texts include Qu Tuiyuan, *Han Wei Liuchao fuxuan*, pp. 52–57; Pei Jinnan et al., *Han Wei Liuchao fu xuanzhu*, pp. 81–87; Huang Ruiyun, *Lidai shuqing xiaofu xuan*, pp. 43–48; and Liu Zhenxiang and Li Fangchen, *Lidai cifu xuan*, pp. 173–79.

L. 21: Longdi 隴坻 (lit., "slopes of Long") is another name for the Long Mountains on the Shaanxi-Gansu border. See Tan Qixiang, *Zhongguo lishi ditu ji* 2: 57–58, 5–8.

L. 22: Bo Yi 伯益 was the official in charge of mountains and rivers under Shun. He helped Shun tame the animals and birds. See *Shi ji* 1.43. The name later became a generic designation for hunter and animal tamer.

L. 26: Cf. *Wenzi* 16.36b: "When a bird is about to arrive, spread a net and wait for it. That which catches the bird is a single loop. However, if one were to make a net with a single loop, he would have no way to catch a bird."

L. 27: Cf. Jia Yi, "Rhapsody on the Houlet" (this volume), L. 6.

L. 41: The Min 岷 is the great mountain range that runs along the border between Sichuan and Gansu. The exact identity of Zhang 嶂 is not certain. Li Shan (*Wen xuan* 13.21b) says it is the name of a mountain. However, Zhu Jian (*Wen xuan jishi* 13.20a) argues that it is a river in Zhang Prefecture of Longxi 隴西 Commandery. See *Hou Han shu* 23.3517; and Li Jifu, *Yuanhe junxian tuzhi* 39.984. This prefecture is located in modern Zhang 漳 xian, Gansu. See Tan Qixiang, *Zhongguo lishi ditu ji* 2: 57–58, 5–6.

L. 46: Cf. *Mao shi* 138/1: "Beneath the cross-piece gate, / I can rest."

L. 51: This line literally reads: "The stench of its humble body."

## II

Thereupon, admiring its fair name that has spread afar,
20   Prizing its wondrous form in which all delight,
A lord orders his forester to Longdi,
Dispatches Bo Yi to Flowing Sands.
Crossing the Kunlun, they shoot corded-darts;
On top of the clouds and rainbows they spread their nets.
25   Although the fasteners and stays are fully deployed,
It is caught in the end by a single loop.

Moreover, it is relaxed and tranquil in demeanor;
Holding its composure, it rests unperturbed.
Press near, and it is unafraid;
30   Pet it, and it does not take fright.
It prefers docile compliance to avoid harm,
Rather than to stubbornly resist and thus lose its life.
Thus, he who presents an unblemished specimen receives reward,
While anyone who injures its flesh is punished.

## III

35   Then, submitting to its predicament, yielding to fate,
It leaves the flock, bereft of its mate,
To be shut in an ornately carved cage,
With its wing feathers clipped.
Drifting, wandering for ten thousand leagues,
40   Over rugged terrain, perilous defiles,
They traverse the Min, cross the Zhang,
Enduring winter's cold and summer's heat.
A girl leaves her family to be married;
A subject offers his life in service to his lord.
45   Even the wise and worthy, encountering hardship,
Must find a place to rest in travels abroad.
Let alone a petty creature like a bird—
Must it not submit to taming, content with its lot?
With constant longing it watches the westward road;
50   Gazing homeward, it waits with craned neck.
It knows that its vile and stinking flesh
Will be of no use in the cauldron and meat stand.

L. 53: Because they represent the imagined thoughts of the parrot, it would be possible to translate LL. 53–67 in the first person. In order to make it consistent with the voice of the preceding portion of the rhapsody, I have used the third person.

LL. 55–56: Cf. *Zhou yi zhushu* 7.19a–b (164). "Grand Commentary": "Wherever calamity arises, words are the stairway to it. If a ruler is not discreet, he will lose his minister. If the minister is not discreet, he will lose his life."

LL. 65–66: The Western Capital is Chang'an. The capital area was renowned for its rich soil. See Knechtges, *Wen xuan* 1: 185, "Western Metropolis Rhapsody," LL. 60–61. William Graham ("Mi Heng's 'Rhapsody on a Parrot,'" p. 48, n. 40) argues that in this line the Western Capital is a metaphor for Huang Zu's court, "and line 66 is a tactful statement that it is not to Mi Heng's taste, despite all its attractions." This is indeed a possible interpretation. However, it is not clear how the Western Han imperial capital can stand for the court of an Eastern Han local official. The Western Capital probably represents in this context any governmental center. Although it is a hub of excitement and pleasure, the parrot and Mi Heng take no delight in it. On the superficial level in this rhapsody, the Western Capital is literally the imperial capital. For example, in LL. 19–21 the poet implies that it is the emperor who sends out the forester and bird tamer to capture the parrot. (Note that the word *zhao* 詔 designates an imperial command.) Thus, on the literal level it is the capital to which the parrot is taken. Only in L. 62 is there a vague suggestion that the current owner of the bird is not the emperor, but a "majestic and stately lord." However, nowhere does Mi Heng indicate that the bird has been brought to the south. The route taken by the tribute bearers (see L. 41) in fact suggests a northern destination. I suspect that the reference to the Western Capital functions on several levels. First, it is the land of the fabled fertile soil and delightful pleasures. Second, it represents the court. On the surface level, it would be the imperial court to which the parrot was presented as tribute. As it applies to Mi Heng's personal situation, it stands for Huang Zu's court. The two lines can be paraphrased as follows: This place of rich soil and great pleasures is something the parrot should enjoy, but he "knows that misery and joy are relative things." Depending upon the situation, perceptions of misery and joy differ.

L. 67: Dai 代 is an old state of northern China (modern northern Shanxi); Yue is in the south (modern Guangdong and Guangxi). The Dai (northern) horse and Yue bird are stock images for the exile or wanderer who yearns for home. Cf. "Nineteen Old Poems," no. 1 (*Wen xuan* 29.2a): "The Hu horse leans into the north wind; / The Yue bird nests on a southern branch."

L. 68: Li Shan (*Wen xuan* 13.22b) says that "this" refers to Chang'an. However, as William Graham rightly observes, "this" refers to the bird's homesickness.

LL. 69–70: Shaohao 少昊 was the chief god of autumn; Rushou 蓐收 was its principal spirit. See *Li ji zhushu* 16.16b.

L. 82: Mi Heng here refers to *Mao shi* 199/7: "The elder of us played the ocarina; / The younger played the flute. / You and I were as if strung together." The ocarina (*xun* 壎) and flute (*chi* 篪) are conventional figures for the harmonious relationship between brothers.

L. 83: Wang Niansun (see *Dushu zazhi*, "Zhi yu," B.32b) proposes to emend *liang jue* 兩絕 (twain cut off/parted) to *yu jue* 雨絕 (rain ceases). He shows that Li Shan cites this line as *yu jue* in *Wen xuan* 23.25b and 31.15a and that *yu jue* is a common figure in Wei and Jin literature for separation (the rain-cleared sky represents the vast expanse that separates two people). Wang is followed by most other Qing dynasty commentators. See Zhang Yun'ao, *Xuanxue jiaoyan* 8.5b–6a; Liang Zhangju, *Wen xuan pangzheng* 15.10b; Hu Shaoying, *Wen xuan jianzheng* 16.5b–6a; and Zhu Jian, *Wen xuan jishi* 13.20a–b. Although there is much textual support for the *yu jue* reading, I have not followed it here. I agree with William Graham that *yu jue* is a much too dense a reading for this rhapsody and is difficult to link with the following line.

## *IV*

Alas, how meager the blessings fate has bestowed upon him!
Why has he met such vicious times?
55  Were words the stairway to calamity?
Or did indiscretion bring on his peril?
He is sad that mother and child are forever parted,
Sorrows that mates are separated in life.
It is not that he cares about his remaining years,
60  But he grieves for the innocent fledglings.
He has forsaken a lowly land of the Man and Yi,
To serve a majestic and stately lord.
Yet he fears that his reputation does not match reality,
And is ashamed that he lacks unusual talent.
65  Although he admires the rich soil of the Western Capital,
He knows that misery and joy are relative things.
Like the Dai horse and Yue bird, he longs for home;
Thus, whenever he speaks, he refers to this.

## *V*

Then, when Shaohao takes charge of the season,
70  And Rushou takes over the reins,
Severe frost begins to fall,
Cold winds howl:
Heaving long sighs, it longs for its distant home;
Its mournful cry stirs its fellow creatures.
75  Its voice is plaintive and shrill;
Its expression is haggard and sad.
Those hearing it are pained with grief;
Those seeing it shed tears.
The banished official repeatedly sighs;
80  The abandoned wife sobs and moans.

## *VI*

It recalls its lifelong companions;
They are as interdependent as ocarina and flute.
Why today should the twain be parted,

L. 84: Hu refers to the land of the Xiongnu in the north. Yue is the remote land of the south (see L. 67n). Cf. *Huainanzi* 2.6a: "If one looks at things from the perspective of their differences, they are like liver and gall [which represent closeness], Hu and Yue [which represent great distance]."

L. 88: When the giant Kuafu 夸父 raced with the sun, he died of thirst. His staff was transformed into the grove known as Denglin 鄧林 (Deng Grove. See Yuan Ke, *Shanhai jing jiaozhu* 8.238–39. It is not clear why the parrot longs for Deng Grove. Graham ("Mi Heng's 'Rhapsody on a Parrot,'" p. 49, n. 47) suggests that Mi Heng's home lay in its direction. However, the grove formed by Kuafu's staff is purely a product of legend. There is a place called Denglin near Xiangyang in Hubei (see *Shi ji* 23.1166, n. 15, but it probably has no connection with the legendary Denglin and certainly is far removed from Mi Heng's home in Shandong. I believe that Denglin does not refer to any specific geographical location, and simply designates the grove that is the parrot's home somewhere in the remote northwest.

In worlds different as Hu and Yue?
85 Following the bars of its cage, it looks up, then down;
Peering out the door, it paces back and forth,
And imagines the high peaks of Kunlun,
Longs for the spreading luxuriance of Deng Grove.
It turns its head and looks at the damage to its quills;
90 Yet, though he furiously flap his wings, where could he go?
His heart longs to return, yet he cannot do so;
He can only bear bitter resentment in his little corner.
If he is to serve his master with full devotion,
How can he turn his back on kindness and forget past favors?
95 Having entrusted his lord with his humble fate,
He offers his paltry body.
He hopes to abide until death to repay benevolence,
And is ready fully to express himself in order to offer humble advice.
Having relied on exalted favor in the past,
100 May it long endure and never change!

# *Rhapsody on the Wren*

## *ZHANG MAOXIAN*

The wren is a tiny bird. Born among the weeds, it grows up under hedges and fences, flies and lands within a span or double-span,[1] yet its means of sustaining life are sufficient.[2] Its plumage is drab, its body is small, and it is of no use to humankind. Diminutive in form, it lives in low-lying places, and nothing does it harm.[3] Multiplying and propagating its kind, it dwells in twos, travels in pairs.[4] Fluttering and flitting about, it provides its own enjoyment. Of the eagle, osprey, jungle fowl, swan, pea-

THIS RHAPSODY by Zhang Hua (*zi* Maoxian) is a *yongwu* poem on the *jiaoliao* 鷦鷯, which is the northern wren (*Troglodytes troglodytes*). The poet portrays the *jiaoliao* as a creature that is able to avoid harm because its small size makes it of no use to anyone. This idea is the old Lao-Zhuang notion of the "usefulness of the useless."
   According to Zhang Hua's biography in the *Jin shu* (36.1068–69), which also preserves a text of this piece, he wrote "Rhapsody on the Wren" when he was still young and

L. 6: This line literally says: "It has no black or yellow with which to make itself dear."

LL. 7–8: Cf. *Zuo zhuan*, Yin 5 (Legge, *The Chinese Classics* 5: 19): Zhang Boxi said, "When the flesh of birds and animals is not presented to the sacrificial stand, and their skins, hides, incisors, molars, bones, horns, hair, and feathers are not presented in the vessels, by not shooting them the duke conforms to ancient regulations."

L. 17: Cf. *Zhuangzi* 1.6a: "The wren nests deep in the woods on no more than a single branch."

cock, and kingfisher, some soar to the edge of the scarlet clouds,[5] others take refuge beyond the farther bounds of the world.[6] A sweep of their wings is enough to pierce the heavens, their beaks and talons are sufficient for self-protection. Yet they all are struck by the stringed-dart and tangled in the corded-arrow. Their feathers and plumes are presented as tribute. Why is this? It is because they are of use to man.

Some words are simple but convey a profound meaning. Some creatures are small, but they can illustrate a great truth.[7] Thus, I have written this rhapsody, which reads as follows:

## I

What manifold variety of Creation,
Which allots the multiple forms among the myriad beings!
Even a tiny bird, the wren,
Receives vital force to sustain its life.
5　Born with a tiny body that flits and flutters,
It lacks bright colors with which to make itself dear.
Its plumage has no use in adorning vessels,
And its flesh is not offered on the sacrificial stand.
If even the goshawk and merlin dip their wings and fly past,
10　Why should it fear nets and snares?
Where grass and trees are thick and lush,
This is where it plays and roosts.
It flies, but does not sail on high;
It takes wing, but its flight is not swift.
15　Its dwelling easily accommodates it;
Its needs are easily provided.
Nesting in a woods, it uses no more than a single branch;

---

unknown as a way of conveying his frustration. However, the *Jin shu* of Zang Rongxu (cited by Li Shan in *Wen xuan* 13.23b) says that Zhang composed the piece when he was serving as "gentleman of palace writers." Zang says that "although Zhang occupied a position at the imperial court, he felt frustrated and composed 'Rhapsody on the Wren.'" Lu Kanru dates the piece to 261, Zhang Hua's thirtieth year. See *Zhonggu wenxue xinian* 2:602.

　　There are previous translations by von Zach, *Deutsche Wacht* (June 1928), rpt. in *Die Chinesische Anthologie* 2: 201–3; and Obi and Hanabusa, *Monzen* 2: 204–10. There are *baihua* translations by Chen Hongtian et al., *Zhaoming Wen xuan yizhu* 2: 737–42; and Li Jingying, *Zhaoming Wen xuan xinjie* 2: 114–18. For annotations, see Huang Ruiyun, *Lidai shuqing xiaofu xuan* pp. 69–76. There is a study by Nakajima Chiaki, "Chō Ka no 'Shōryō no fu' ni tsuite."

L. 27: Cf. ibid. 3.16a: "A bird flies high to escape the danger of stringed arrows, and the field mouse burrows deep under a sacred mound to escape the calamity of being dug and smoked out. Do you have these two creatures' lack of sense?"

L. 29: Cf. *Zuo zhuan*, Huan 10 (Legge, *The Chinese Classics* 5: 55): Yu Shu possessed a fine jade. When his brother the Duke of Yu requested it of him Yu Shu refused, but later changed his mind, citing an old Zhou proverb: "A man has committed no crime—his crime lies in holding on to his jade." He then told his brother, "What use could I make of this jade? It would only court me harm."

L. 31: Cf. *Wenzi* 1.2b: "He is restrained in what he keeps, and he makes few the things that he seeks."

L. 32: Cf. *Huainanzi* 9.1a: "[The ruler], quiet and still, does not move; even when moving he is not agitated. Following the natural course of things, he entrusts tasks to those below him."

L. 43: Several ancient Chinese sources claim that wild geese carried reeds in their beaks to prevent stringed arrows and darts from striking their wings. See *Huainanzi* 19.8a; Ge Hong, *Baopuzi* 48.7b; and *Gujin zhu* B.3b–4a.

Whenever it eats, it takes no more than a few grains.

Wherever it roosts, it does not stay for long;
20  Wherever it roams, it does not linger.
It does not demean thorn or briar,
Nor honor angelica or thoroughwort.
It flaps its wings and is reposed;
Standing in place, it is at ease.
25  Yielding to fate, it accords with the natural order,
And is not at odds with the world.

## II

Oh, this bird so lacking in knowledge,
In deporting itself seems so wise!
It does not hold on to treasure, and thus courts no harm;
30  It does not adorn itself, and thus invites no trouble.
Resting, it is restrained and is never haughty;
Active, it follows the natural course of simplicity and ease.
Relying on spontaneous action for its basic substance,
It is not seduced by the hypocrisy of the world.

## III

35  Eagle and silver pheasant rely on beak and talons;
Swan and heron soar to the edge of the clouds.
The jungle fowl hides in secluded defiles;
Peacock and kingfisher are born in distant marches.
Those ducks flying at dawn and geese winging their way home
40  Beat their wings and rise aloft.
All have beautiful plumage and plump flesh;
And so, though blameless, they are put to death.
Vainly holding reeds in their mouths to avoid the stringed dart,
They end up slaughtered by the world.

## IV

45  The goshawk, for all of its ferocity, is tied to a leash;
The parrot, for all of its intelligence, is shut in a cage.

61

L. 51: Zhong 鍾 and Dai 岱 (variant 代) are mentioned together in the *Han shu* "Monograph on Geography" as places near the land of the "Hu [Xiongnu?] marauders." Commentator Ru Chun does not know the location of Zhong. See *Han shu* 28B.1656. The Qing dynasty expert on Han geography Qian Dian 錢坫 (1744–1806) identifies Zhong as an alternate name for the Yin Mountains 陰山 of Inner Mongolia. See Zhu Jian, *Wen xuan jishi* 13.21a–b. Dai was a Han prefecture northeast of modern Yu 蔚 *xian*, Hebei. See Tan Qixiang, *Zhongguo lishi ditu ji* 2: 17–18, 12–3. Presumably these areas were famous for their goshawks.

L. 52: Longdi was famous for its parrots. See Mi Heng, "Rhapsody on the Parrot" (this volume), L. 21n.

LL. 55–56: The *Guo yu* (4.5b–7b) records a story of a frigate bird that landed outside the east gate of the state of Lu. A Lu official explained that its arrival was a sign of a great storm at sea. I have followed Edward Schafer in translating *yuanju* 爰居 (variant 鶢鶋) as "frigate bird." See *The Vermilion Bird*, p. 38.

LL. 57–58: This bird is an ostrich. On Tiaozhi, see Knechtges, *Wen xuan* 1: 114, L. 135n.

L. 67: The *jiaoming* 焦螟 is the proverbial example of the smallest creature in the world. It was so small it reputedly built its nest on the eyelash of a mosquito. See *Yanzi chunqiu* 7.16a; and *Liezi* 5.6b.

One curbs his wild will and submits to taming;
The other is confined alone to the palace depths.
One changes its voice to comply with its master's wishes;
50  The other has its feathers clipped in order to be of use.
One longs for the woods and wilds of Zhong and Dai;
The other yearns for the tall pines of Longdi.
Although they now bask in great favor,
It cannot compare with the freedom of the past.

## V

55  The seagoing frigate bird
Arrived after fleeing a storm.
The giant bird of Tiaozhi
Came on its own across tall peaks.
One was carried and transported a myriad leagues;
60  The other, buffeted by the wind, was overawed by fright.
A body that is excessively large encounters obstructions;
Something rare in appearance is greatly prized.
The yin and yang mold and create:
A myriad things in a single realm;
65  Small and large are interspersed,
In numerous kinds, distinct types.
The *jiaoming* nests on a mosquito's eyelash;
The great peng fills a corner of the sky.
If one falls short in comparison with his betters,
70  He surpasses by far those below him.
Viewing the vast expanse of heaven and earth,
How can one know what is large or small?

# 14

BIRDS AND ANIMALS, PART II

# *Rhapsody on the Russet and White Horse*

## *YAN YANNIAN*

A good steed is praised not for his strength,[1] yet a magnificent horse is called a "dragon."[2] Is this only because the state exalts its mighty bearing, and the army wishes to harness its strength and speed?[3] In truth, in times past when light sprang from the river and a horse spat out a diagram, this was an auspicious token sent to a man of virtue.[4] Thus, men have extolled its wonders, and age after age has honored its arrival.

When our Exalted Ancestor founded the Song,[5] the peoples of the five directions declared allegiance,[6] and the four remote marches presented tribute. Rare treasures filled the storehouses, and teams of colored horses lined the grand stable. Then, there came a russet and white to draw the imperial chariot. Especially endowed with unusual traits, the splendid choice rested with His Majesty alone,[7] and he therefore granted it a place in the imperial stable. Harnessed and driven, it obeyed the coachman's will; racing and galloping, it conformed to the rules. Even in its declining years its skill and beauty did not change. Year after year cared for and

---

THIS RHAPSODY by Yan Yanzhi (*zi* Yannian) celebrates a marvelous piebald horse that had been presented to the founder of the Liu-Song dynasty Liu Yu 劉裕 (Emperor Wu, reg. 420–422). The horse, which was colored a reddish brown (*zhe* 赭) and white, apparently was very much favored by Liu Yu, as well as Emperor Wen 文 (reg. 424–453). When the horse died in 440, Yan Yanzhi was commissioned to write a rhapsody in praise of it. Yan Yanzhi draws on a vast array of horse lore to describe this magnificent steed. This piece is the source of many lines in later horse poems in the Chinese literary tradition.

Previous translations include von Zach, *Deutsche Wacht* (April 1929), rpt. in *Die Chinesische Anthologie* 1: 204–8; and Obi and Hanabusa, *Monzen* 2: 211–21. There are *baihua* translations in Chen Hongtian et al., *Zhaoming Wen xuan yizhu* 2: 744–58; and Li Jingying, *Zhaoming Wen xuan xinjie* 2: 119–28.

L. 1: Li Shan (*Wen xuan* 14.2b) says the twenty-second year of the Song was the seventeenth year of Emperor Wen (440), the second ruler of the Liu-Song. However, as Zhang Yun'ao (*Xuanxue jiaoyan* 8.6a–b) points out, the twenty-second year actually is the eighteenth year of Emperor Wen (441).

L. 5: The Grand Stairway (Tai jie 泰階) is another name for the Three Platforms, a six-star constellation corresponding to six stars in Ursa Major. The Grand Stairway was composed of three levels, each of which symbolized a rung in the social and political hierarchy. The upper level represented the emperor and empress; the middle level, the nobles and ministers; and the lower level, the scholars and common people. The harmonious working of the three levels signified peace and good order in the empire. See *Jin shu* 11.293; and Ho Peng-yoke, *The Astronomical Chapters of the Chin Shu*, pp. 80–81.

LL. 9–10: Dixuan 帝軒 is the Yellow Lord (Huangdi 黃帝). According to the *Huainanzi* (6.6b), when he ruled the empire, the horse Flying Yellow (Feihuang 飛黃) "submitted to being kept in a stall." In his commentary to this *Huainanzi* passage, Gao You describes Flying Yellow as resembling a fox, with horns on its back. Anyone who rode it enjoyed a longevity of three thousand years.

LL. 11–12: Lord Tang is Yao. Dapple Red (Chiwen 赤文) refers to the horse that appeared out of the Yellow River during the reign of Yao. The horse was the bearer of the shell on which was written the diagram that Yan Yanzhi refers to as the divine register, a sign that Heaven had granted Yao the mandate to rule. See Knechtges, *Wen xuan* 1: 244, "Eastern Metropolis Rhapsody," L. 50n. Note that in this line the red color seems to refer to the horse rather than the markings on the shell. See n. 4 to this rhapsody.

L. 13: The celestial steeds refer to the so-called blood-sweating horses of Ferghana that appeared during the reign of Emperor Wu of the Former Han (140–87 B.C.). See *Han shu* 6.202; Dubs, *HFHD* 2: 132–35; Waley, "The Heavenly Horses of Ferghana"; and Hulsewé, *China in Central Asia*, pp. 132–34, n. 322.

L. 14: The appearance of the horse from the marshes (ze ma 澤馬) was regarded as a sign of good government. Li Shan (*Wen xuan* 14.3a) cites the *Wei zhi* 魏志 (Chronicle of Wei), which says that one of these divine steeds appeared during the Huangchu period of Emperor Wen. For other mentions of it, see Knechtges, *Wen xuan* 1: 298, "Eastern Metropolis Rhapsody," L. 612n; and ibid., p. 461, "Wei Capital Rhapsody," L. 550.

L. 17: This line alludes to the horse that sprang from the Yellow River with the diagram of the eight trigrams in its mouth.

L. 18: This line refers to the songs composed to celebrate the presentation of the heavenly horses during the reign of Emperor Wu of the Former Han. The first song was composed to commemorate the birth of one of these horses at the Wowa 渥洼 River (near modern Anxi 安西, Gansu); the second was composed in honor of the steeds brought back from Central Asia by General Li Guangli 李廣利 in 104 B.C. These pieces were part of the repertoire of the sacrificial songs performed by imperial musicians in the Bureau of Music, here referred to as "master of pitchpipes." For texts of the songs, see *Shi ji* 24.1178 and *Han shu* 22.1060–61. They have been translated by Chavannes, *Mh* 3: 620–21; and Birrell, *Popular Songs and Ballads of Han China*, pp. 40–42.

LL. 21–22: The astral emanation refers to the Heavenly Quadriga (Tian si 天駟) constellation, which was composed of four stars in Scorpio. It also is another name for the lunar lodge named Fang 房 (Chamber). See Schlegel, *Uranographie chinoise* 1: 114–15, 329. Yan Yanzhi seems to be saying here that the divine horses were a response to this astral horse-team. Cf. Guo Pu 郭璞 (276–324), "Encomium for the Horse": "The horse comes from a luminous emanation, he is a scion of the Heavenly Quadriga." See *Yiwen leiju* 93.1622.

L. 23: The mandate is that of the Liu-Song.

L. 25: "Receiving the calendar" signified recognition of the legitimacy of a new regime

tended, it received generous imperial favor. At an old age its vitality was
spent, and it died in its palace stall. When young it expended all its
strength, and moved by extreme compassion, the emperor commanded his
attendants to set forth his feelings in a rhapsody. This lowly and humble
official dares to present a rhapsody along with them. The poem goes:

## I

It is the twentieth and second year of the Song,
And glorious achievement shines on into the second reign.
Our martial might is solemnly displayed;
Our civil teachings have liberally spread.
5   The Grand Stairway, with its order and peace, can be ascended;
The traces of the glorious kings can be followed.
We search for good deeds preserved in ancient histories,
Examine events of the regions transmitted in old documents.

Of old, when Dixuan ascended the throne,
10  Flying Yellow submitted to being kept in a stall;
When Lord Tang received the divine register,
Dapple Red awaited the setting sun.
The way of Han spread far and wide, and the celestial steeds showed
        their skills;
The virtue of Wei flourished, and a horse from the marshes displayed
        his fine traits.

15  Those peerless and wondrous steeds,
Which have continuously appeared since ages past,
Have been resplendently revealed in auspicious canons,
And their sacrificial song was presented by the master of pitchpipes.

Their purpose was to exalt and protect his divine majesty,
20  Guarding him and clearing his way.
The astral emanation harmoniously responded;
Divine creatures appeared all in proper order.

When the shining mandate was established,
All throughout the Nine Regions swiftly submitted.
25  Some, disregarding perils of travel, arrived to receive the calendar;
Others, traversing great distances, came to present tribute.
Hearing of the great splendor of the royal assemblies,

by rival and foreign states. See Knechtges, *Wen xuan* 1: 430, "Wei Capital Rhapsody," L. 40n.

LL. 29–30: The Six Dependencies are the six zones that radiate out from the royal domain. The Seven Rong is a Zhou dynasty designation for the Western Rong tribes, which in Yan Yanzhi's time probably simply referred to any of the peoples of Central Asia.

L. 34: The Angular Array is a group of six stars within the Purple Palace. It was the celestial counterpart to the Rear Palace (imperial harem) and had charge of the imperial guard. See ibid., p. 126, "Western Capital Rhapsody," L. 242n.

LL. 37–38: The sage founder refers to Emperor Wu of the Liu-Song, who gave the horse to his successor, Emperor Wen.

L. 39: Li Shan (*Wen xuan* 14.4a) cites the *Xiang ma jing* 相馬經 (Canon for Judging Horses), which says that a good horse can be judged by its muscles and bones.

L. 41: The *Xiang ma jing* (cited by Li Shan, *Wen xuan* 14.4a) refers to a high quality horse in whose eyes the full form of a man could be seen. "This means that the eyes are clear and bright like a mirror. Some say that the curly hair in the middle of the eyes forms a mirror."

L. 42: The *Xiang ma jing* (ibid.) says that cheeks of a horse should be round as jade discs. "They are round and full as the moon. This is the mark of an unusual feature."

LL. 45–46: Yan Yanzhi probably is alluding to a *Liezi* (8.8b) passage that tells of Duke Mu of Qin seeking advice from the great horse expert Bole on judging good horses. Bole replied, "A good horse can be judged by shape and form, muscle and bone. But the best steeds in the world will seem invisible, vanished, missing, or lost. Such horses raise no dust and leave no tracks."

L. 47: The Barrier Gate (Sai men 塞門) probably refers to the Great Wall. Li Shan (*Wen xuan* 14.4b) notes the variant reading *Han men* 寒門 (lit., "Cold Gate," referring to the extreme northern frontier), which he rejects. However, Zhang Yun'ao (*Xuanxue jiaoyan* 8.6b–7a) argues that the variant should not be ruled out, for the north was known as a horse-producing area.

L. 48: The Scarlet Watchtower refers to the imperial palace.

LL. 49–50: You 幽 and Yan 燕 are the ancient names for the territory corresponding to modern Liaoning and northern Hebei. Jing 荊 and Yue 越 refer to the area of modern Zhejiang and Hubei.

LL. 51–54: Yan Yanzhi alludes to a passage in the *Zuo zhuan* (Zhuang 23; Legge, *The Chinese Classics* 3: 105), which specifies the reasons that a ruler leaves his state: "The vassal lords have their obligations to the king, and the king has his tours of inspection, and they are performed in a grand manner. Except for such affairs, a ruler has no other movements. The ruler's movements must be recorded."

L. 57: The Five Commands (*wu ying* 五營), or, more literally, "Five Encampments," are the divisions in the Han dynasty military, each headed by a colonel. These commands were stationed near the capital, and thus designated the troops that guarded the emperor. See Bielenstein, *The Bureaucracy of Han Times*, pp. 114–18.

They knew of the plentiful abundance of the imperial realm.
From the Six Dependencies they collected the best stock;
30  From the Seven Rong they obtained prime strains:
Perhaps a fine descendant of a charger that rode the wind,
Or truly a great heir of a steed that outraced his own shadow.
Thus, the russet and white horse for two generations drew the
      imperial chariot,
For successive reigns was paired with the Angular Array.
35  As his years lengthened and increased,
The greater his worth and fame.
Truly this was a great gift from the sage founder;
Having gained imperial affection, he was always eager to run.

## II

Just look at his tight muscles, protruding bones,
40  Thickly sweeping tail, bristling mane,
Twin eyes fixed with mirrors,
Double cheekbones like full moons,
Uncommon frame rising like a mountain peak,
Unusual features so distinctly revealed!

45  Leaping, prancing, he leaves no dust or tracks;
Galloping, racing, he suddenly seems to vanish.
They chose this grand steed at Barrier Gate,
Presented him to the Scarlet Watchtower.
At daybreak he is curried at You and Yan;
50  By early morning he is fed in Jing and Yue.

To teach respect for the rules that never change,
And instruct the people in movements that must be recorded,
Like his ancestor before him, the emperor
Makes excursions, makes expeditions.
55  Light chariots, racing ahead, herald his arrival;
Mounted bowmen, encircling the cortege, clear the way.
The Five Commands are directed to order the march;
The harness bells sound to regulate the gait.
Accoutered with armor made of metal and cords,
60  And further adorned with vermeil and green,
He is ringed with jeweled studs that sparkle like stars,

L. 63. Li Shan (*Wen xuan* 14.5a) cites the *Tongsu wen* 通俗文 (Common Graphs) of Fu Qian 服虔, which says that *zhelie* 遮迣 was the name given to the Rapid-as-Tiger guard that protected the emperor when he went out of the palace.

L. 73: Li Shan (ibid., 14.5a) cites the *Dili shu* 地理書 (Book of Geography) by Lu Cheng 陸澄 (late fifth cent.), which explains Broadview (Guangwang 廣望) as the name of a tower in Luoyang.

LL. 85–86: Li Shan (ibid., 14.5b) explains that the speed of the horse's gallop causes the archers to shoot at a faster pace and the drummers to drum to a more rapid beat.

LL. 87–88: The black hoof (*xuan ti* 玄蹄) is a target made of a horse's hoof. The white target refers to the Yuezhi 月支, a target presumably depicting an effigy of the Yuezhi, a long-time foe of the Chinese in the Han period, when this type of target was used. Li Shan (ibid., 14.5b) cites the *Yi jing* 藝經 (Canon of Arts and Skills?) by Handan Chun 邯鄲淳 (130?–225?), which says that in shooting from horseback, there are three Yuezhi targets on the left, and two "horse hooves" on the right. Cao Zhi also mentions both of these targets in his poem "Song of White Horses". See ibid., 27.22a.

LL. 89–90: Yan Yanzhi lends this horse the attribute of the Heavenly Horses of Ferghana, which were famed for sweating blood. According to Ying Shao (*Han shu* 6.202), sweat exuded from their shoulder blades like blood. The bleeding probably was caused by a parasite. See Dubs, *HFHD* 2: 132–35. The sweat conduit (*han gou* 汗溝) was located where the foreleg and belly join. When the horse ran at a fast gallop, sweat poured from this spot. See Luo Zhufeng, *Hanyu da cidian* 5: 908b.

And figured designs are scattered like clouds.
Advancing at the fore, he joins the protective cordon;
Withdrawing to the rear, he follows the imperial chaise.
65   Suddenly, he rears up like a startled swan,
At times coiling and uncoiling like a soaring dragon.
He curbs his virile nature to draw the imperial chariot;
With docile and gentle heart he awaits the harness.

## III

Then, when dew is thick, the moon is pale,
70   Frost forms, and the autumn harvest is done:
The king issues a proclamation
To display his majesty and might to the world.
Looking down from Broadview Tower,
Seated a hundred stories high,
75   He judges riders' skills,
Grades chargers' speed.

Flowing finery drapes their bodies,
Melodious bells are set in rows.
Seeing their shadows, they loudly neigh;
80   About to dash ahead, they stop midway.
They severally gallop into a broad course,
To contest power and strength over a long track.
Distinct from his kind, superior to the herd,
The russet and white, with blazing speed, disappears in the distance
85   He quickens the nimble hands of brave bowmen,
Speeds the urgent beat of the ornate drum.
They split the "black hoof," and it scatters like hail;
They pierce the "white target," and it shatters like ice.
The horse's chest lathers red;
90   The "sweat conduit" runs with blood.
Curbing his stride, he returns to the palace roadway,
His pent-up fury not fully spent.
The emperor deigns to show some small delight;
Capital residents, awestruck, all express their joy.

95   Although his graceful, shifting movements now cease,
His frisky spirit has not abated.

LL. 101–4· Purple Swallow (Zi yan 紫燕), Green Kraken (Lü she 綠虵), Slender Black (Xian li 纖驪), and Splendid Blue (Xiu qi 秀騏) are names of famous horses.

LL. 105–6· The wastes of Kun refers to the Kunlun Mountains, the home of the Queen Mother of the West. The visit to her perhaps was in emulation of the voyage of King Mu of Zhou, who on his westward journey to her land obtained a number of fabulous horses. See *Shi ji* 43.1779. Ditai 帝臺 is a spirit who is renowned for hosting a feast for the gods. See Yuan Ke, *Shanhai jing jiaozhu* 5.142. Mount Xuan 宣, which is mentioned in the *Shanhai jing* (ibid., 5.170), is not otherwise known.

L. 115: Wu refers to Emperor Wu and his obsession with acquiring the heavenly horses of Ferghana. Mu is King Mu of Zhou, who traveled all over the empire in search of the eight fabulous steeds.

L. 116: Wen is Emperor Wen of the Former Han, who was presented with a great stallion that could gallop a thousand *li* in a day. The emperor refused the gift on the grounds that for felicitous occasions he traveled only thirty *li* a day, and on military campaigns, the most he traveled was fifty *li* a day. Thus, where could he possibly ride a horse that went a thousand *li* a day? See *Han shu* 64B.2832. Guang is Emperor Guangwu 光武 (reg. 25–57), the founder of the Later Han. In the twelfth year of Guangwu's reign (A.D. 36), a kingdom presented him with a famous horse, which he used to pull the drum cart. See Wu Shuping, *Dongguan Han ji jiaozhu* 1.10.

L. 119 Yan Yanzhi alludes to the story of Wangzi Wuqi 王子於期, who drove the chariot for Zhao Jianzi 趙簡子 (Viscount Jian of Zhao) over a thousand-*li* course. When they first set out, there was a boar hiding in a ditch. Wangzi Wuqi simply drove ahead at a steady pace. Suddenly, the boar dashed out, scaring the horses with the result that the chariot turned over. See *Han Feizi* 14.3b.

L. 120: When King Mu of Zhou went hunting, a black bird resembling a dove flew onto his chariot crossbar. The driver killed it with his whip. Startled by the sudden movement, the horse bolted and stumbled over the chariot. The king received an injury to his left thigh. See *Guwen Zhou shu* 古文周書 (Ancient Script Documents of Zhou), cited by Li Shan, *Wen xuan* 14.7a.

L. 126: Rusted millet is grain that has been kept so long it turns red. The horse was given so much grain he could not eat it all, and thus it had turned red. See *Han shu* 64B.2832.

LL. 129–30: According to Confucius, one should not discard a worn curtain, but rather use it for burying a horse. See *Li ji zhushu* 10.25a (2844).

Restrained by the control of bit and bridle,
Hampered by the narrow confines of the great city,
Longing for the Western Limits, he tosses his head,
100 Gazing toward the northern clouds, he stamps his feet.
The emperor will harness him together with Purple Swallow,
With Green Kraken flanking the wheel-hubs,
Slender Black following at the rear,
And Splendid Blue trotting beside.
105 He pays his respects to the Queen Mother on the wastes of Kun,
Meets with Ditai on the peak of Mount Xuan,
Traverses the tracks of the central realm,
Explores the route taken by spirits in their journeys.

A ruler may enjoy himself in excursions and hunts,
110 But finds a warning mirror in former kings.
As the head of the people he may indulge himself,
But he feels regret at departing from the proper way.
Then, the Son of Heaven halts his chariot to ponder his course;
He rests the retinue, and has the travel gear removed.
115 He takes warning from the examples of Wu and Mu,
Models himself on Wen and Guang,
Relieves the people's suffering,
Improves the state ordinances.
He takes precautions against a runaway boar upsetting his chariot,
120 Is on guard against a flying bird landing on his crossbar.
Therefore, he is careful about matters that are usually ignored,
And he prepares to protect himself against unforeseen events.

His carriage has the security of double wheel-hubs,
And his horses do not bolt and overturn his cart.
125 The russet and white is housed in the depths of the Sleek Dragon
                    stall,
And is fed with an allotment of rusted millet.
Such tending and feeding acquaints him with kindness,
And at an old age he dies a natural death.
Using a worn curtain,
130 They wrap his fallen hulk.
Imperial favor is all-embracing,
Royal grace is fully bestowed.
The Coda says:

73

L. 137: Li Shan (*Wen xuan* 14.7b) cites the *Chunqiu kaoyi ji* 春秋考異記 (Notes on Variants in the *Annals?*), which says that when earth came into being, the horse was created from the emanations of the moon. The Quadriga is the Heavenly Quadriga constellation. See LL. 21–22 above.

LL. 139–40: Cf. "The Song of the Heavenly Horses" (*Han shu* 22.1060): "Its mettle is beyond compare, / Its spirit is uncommon, unwonted." For the translation of *quanqi* 權奇 as "uncommon, unwonted," see Kroll, "The Dancing Horses of T'ang," p. 251.

L. 143: Li Shan (*Wen xuan* 14.8a) says the Yellow Gate refers to the post of *zhong Huangmen fuma* 中黃門駙馬 (attendant cavalry of the palace attendants of the Yellow Gate). However, Liu Liang (*Liuchen zhu Wen xuan* 14.9b) says it is the "central encampment."

L. 1: The mysterious canon (幽經), or perhaps the "canon of arcana," refers to the *Xiang he jing* 相鶴經 (Canon for Evaluating Cranes), an ancient manual of crane lore. The work does not survive intact, but is cited in such texts as *Yiwen leiju* (90.1563), *Chuxue ji* 30.726–27, and Li Shan's commentary to the *Wen xuan* (14.8a–b). According to tradition, the book was written by Fuqiu Gong 浮丘公, also known as Fuqiu Bo 浮丘伯. When Wang Zijin 王子晉 studied the art of immortality with Master Fuqiu he received the text, which he hid in a huge boulder on Mount Songgao 嵩高. During the Han dynasty, the Eight Lords of Huainan 淮南, who were retainers of Liu An 劉安, King of Huainan, acquired it while gathering herbs. Thus the text often is referred to as *Huainan bagong xiang he jing* 淮南八公相鶴經 (see *Sui shu* 34.1039). In spite of the reputed ancient pedigree for this text, it probably is no earlier than the third or fourth century A.D. See Upton, "The Medieval Animal Book in China and the West," p. 44; and Schafer, "The Cranes of Mao Shan," pp. 374–75, n. 12.

L. 2: In the Chinese tradition, the crane was thought not to be hatched from an egg, but "born of the womb" (*tai sheng* 胎生). According to the *Xiang he jing*, a crane must attain an age of 1,600 years before it can produce offspring from the womb. See *Bencao gangmu* 4: 2557.

L. 5: The Pot of Peng (Penghu) 蓬壺 is one of three pot-shaped islands of the Eastern Sea reputedly inhabited by immortals. According to the *Shiyi ji*, Penghu is another name for Penglai 蓬萊. See Qi Zhiping, *Shiyi ji*, p. 20.

Verily, when good virtue stirs Heaven,
A divine creature manifests itself.
135 At this time strong steeds
Fill the palace stairs and roads.
The russet and white received its spirit from the moon and
               Quadriga,
And is descended from the dragon in the clouds.
Its grand mettle is beyond compare,
140 And its spirit is uncommon, unwonted.
Both strong and good,
He submits to halter and bridle.
At the Yellow Gate he offers to run,
Giving his life in racing and galloping.
145 The emperor hoped always to show him kindness and care,
To "shade" him from root to branch.
But finally—faster than dew vanishes at dawn—
He has parted and gone forever.

# Rhapsody on Dancing Cranes

## BAO MINGYUAN

### I

I open the mysterious canon to investigate natural beings:
Grandest is the immortal avian born of the womb!
It concentrates in its elegant essence a carefree detachment,
And holds within its knowing heart a pure remoteness.
5 Heading toward the Pot of Peng, it flaps its wings;

THIS RHAPSODY by Bao Zhao (zi Minguan) is a poem on one of the most admired birds of the Chinese tradition, the crane. The crane described here probably is the *Grus japonensis*, variously known as the Japanese crane, Manchurian crane, or red-crowned crane. This is a beautiful white-bodied bird with a distinctive red crest and black cheek, neck, throat, and secondaries. See Johnsgard, *Cranes of the World*, pp. 197–98; and de Schauensee, *The Birds of China*, p. 201. The whiteness of the crane figures prominently in Chinese poetry. Edward Schafer has shown that the whiteness of the Manchurian crane is closely associated

L. 6: The Wastes of Kun Kun lang 崑閬) refer to Langfeng 閬風, the northern peak of the Kunlun mountains, on which immortals reputedly resided.

L. 10: In the Chinese tradition the crane is considered a bird of great longevity. According to the *Xiang he jing* cited by Li Shan, *Wen xuan* 14 8a), the crane undergoes a series of transformations every so many years. A lesser change takes place every sixteen years, and a greater change occurs every sixty years. When the crane reaches the age of 1,600 years, its body attains its final, fixed form, and its color is white.

L. 11: According to the *Xiang he jing* (ibid. 14.8b), the crane has protruding eyes containing a red essence *jing* 精 that enables it to see long distances.

L. 12: The color purple *zi* 紫 probably refers to the reddish color of the crest, which more commonly is described as *dan* 丹 cinnabar-red) or *zhu* 朱 vermilion).

L. 17: According to *Shiyi ji*, the ninth peak of the Kunlun Mountains had mushroom fields *zhi tian* 芝田 and basil gardens that were tended by immortals. See Qi Zhiping, *Shiyi ji* 10.221.

L. 18: Carnelian Pond Yao chi 瑤池) was a mythical pool located in the Kunlun Mountains. According to legend, it was the site of a banquet given by the Queen Mother of the West for King Mu of Zhou. See *Mu Tianzi zhuan* 3.1a.

L. 20: My "sky-net" literally is "cloud-net" *yun luo* 雲羅), a net that presumably caught birds as they flew in the sky.

Gazing toward the Wastes of Kun, it raises its screeching call.
Circling the Solar Realm, it whirls and soars;

Reaching the end of Heaven's concourse, it explores on high.
Far into the supernal precincts has it entered,
10  And now it has attained a holy old age.
Its eyes contain a red essence and sparkle like stars;
Its crest of purple is like a mottled mist.
Stretching its rounded neck so delicate and graceful,
It stands tall on long and stately legs.
15  Fluffing frosty plumage, it plays with its shadow;
Spreading wings of jade, it looks down from the clouds.

At dawn it plays in the mushroom fields;
At dusk drinks from Carnelian Pond.
Sated with river and sea, it travels to a marsh;
20  There it is caught in a sky-net and is held fast.

---

with the images of snow, frost, and ice. See "The Cranes of Mao Shan," pp. 391–93. The whiteness of the crane is central to the basic meaning of the word *he* 鶴 (Old Chinese *gak*), which is undoubtedly related to a number of words having something to do with "whiteness." See Wang Li, *Tongyuan zidian*. pp. 205–6. The peoples of all cultures have been fascinated by the movements of cranes. and the movement that has most entranced human observers is their dance. Especially during the breeding season, "cranes conduct an elaborate dance, walking around each other with half-open wings, leaping up from the ground, and bowing in front of each other" (see de Schauensee, *The Birds of China*, p. 200). The ritual crane dance has been amply studied and is the subject of a special monograph; see Lucas, *Der Tanz der Kraniche*. Bao Zhao's rhapsody is the most detailed account of dancing cranes in the Chinese literary tradition. The poem also is rich in crane lore, and many of its lines have become stock phrases in later poems about cranes, notably those by the Tang poet Bo Juyi 白居易 (772–846); see Spring, "The Celebrated Cranes of Po Chü-i."

    Bao Zhao begins his piece by describing a solitary crane that roams freely in the heavens and the realm of the immortals. He describes its beautiful white plumage and distinctive crest (here depicted as purple instead of red). On its travels it makes the mistake of flying over a marsh where it is caught in a net and taken away to become a member of a troupe of dancing cranes. Bao Zhao describes a performance of the cranes at the court, presumably of his prince Liu Yiqing. The description of the movements of the dancing cranes is difficult to translate, for one is never sure whether Bao Zhao is referring to the entire troupe or the single captive crane. Although there may be lines that refer to a solitary crane. for the sake of consistency in English, I have translated the section on the dance as if it refers to the entire troupe.

    This rhapsody also is contained in Qian Zhonglian. *Bao Canjun jizhu* 1.32–41 Previous translations include von Zach, *Deutsche Wacht* (July 1928), rpt. in *Die Chinesische Anthologie* 1. 208–10; and Obi and Hanabusa, *Monzen* 2: 222–26. See also three annotated translations into modern Chinese: Chen Hongtian et al., *Zhaoming Wen xuan yizhu* 2: 761–65, Li Jingying, *Zhaoming Wen xuan xinjie* 2: 129–33; and Chi et al., *Lidai fu cidian*, pp 396–97.

L. 23: The rhyming binome *zhengrong* (\**dẓhɛng ɣwɛng*) 崢嶸 (tall and lofty) most commonly describes tall buildings or mountains. Here Bao Zhao uses it to describe the "lofty" age of the crane.

L. 25: The "deadly season" is either autumn or winter, when the "deadly pneuma" (*sha qi* 殺氣), the destructive force of the cold and yin, is at its peak. See *Li ji zhushu* 16.24a (2972).

L. 28: The Winnow Star 箕星 (four stars in Sagittarius) is the asterism that was thought to control the wind. See *Shang shu zhushu* 12.23b (408); and Schlegel, *Uranographie chinoise* 1: 164–65.

L. 41: *Li* 唳 refers specifically to the cry of the crane. Schafer ("The Cranes of Mao Shan," p. 378) translates this word as "crunkle." The Western Jin poet Lu Ji is famous for exclaiming just before his execution in 303, "I wish I might hear the bugling of the cranes of Huating, but shall I ever do so?" See Yang Yong, *Shishuo xinyu jiaozhu* 33.672; and Mather, *Shih-shuo Hsin-yü*, p. 471.

It has left the lofty stillness of the Lord of Heaven,
And returns to the noisy baseness of the human world.
Its years are "high and lofty," and it grieves that its life has reached
        its eve;
Sad and sorrowful in heart, it laments separation from the flock.

25   And then, in the deadly season of fullest yin,
When quickened sunlight hastens the fading year,
Cold sand covers the plain,
And Winnow's wind shakes the sky.
Severe and harsh is the cruel fog,
30   Clear and cold are the sad springs.
Ice clogs long rivers;
Snow blankets massed mountains.

Then dark vapors recede at night,
Revealing a scene vast and bright.
35   Stars change position, the Sky River turns course,
And the morning moon is about to set.
Cranes are moved by cold roosters crowing the dawn,
And pity the frosted geese fleeing the northern desert.
Facing the whine of the fierce wind,
40   And gazing upon the glow of the streaming moonlight,
They bugle clear calls on the vermilion stairway,
And dance their fluttering forms in the golden pavilion.
To begin, they raise themselves, frolicking like phoenixes;
To end, they twirl and turn, prancing like dragons.
45   They pause, hesitant, reluctant to advance;
Then, with a sudden spread of their wings, they begin to soar and
        swoop.
Their swift bodies are like clumps of tumbleweed;
Their nimble wings fly like snow.
At times they part the line, to head in separate directions,
50   Then regroup the file to follow in close formation.
About to fly off, they stop midway;
Making as if to leave, suddenly they turn back.

Closely clustered, they intently stare,
Then withdraw, their pace slow and deliberate.
55   Their swift wings leave the dust behind;

79

LL. 57–58· These lines are ambiguous. It is not clear whether *hui* 會 (lit., "highway intersection") and *qi* 歧 (branch road) refer to the actual roadway on which the cranes perform or whether they metaphorically designate the merging and branching of the files of cranes. Similarily, it is not clear whether *gui* 規 and *ju* 矩 should be understood literally as "compass and square" (describing the circular and square formations of the troupe), or as "norm" and "rule" (the designated movements prescribed for the troupe). An alternate translation might be: "As their files merge, they fly in regular formation; / As they branch off, they stride in proper array."

L. 75: The Song edition of Bao Zhao's collected works and the *Liuchen zhu Wen xuan* read *luo* 羅 (spread out) for *ba* 罷 (end?).

L. 80: The lads of Ba are the performers of the famous Ba-Yu 巴渝 dances of the southwest. See Knechtges, *Wen xuan* I: 348, L. 110n.

L. 81: According to the "Monograph on Music" in the *Song shu* (19.551), the kerchief dance originated at the famous banquet given by Xiang Yu for Liu Bang at Hongmen. One of Xiang Yu's officers, Xiang Zhuang 項莊, rose to perform an intimidating sword dance before Liu Bang Xiang Bo 項伯 then stood up and danced, shielding Liu Bang from Xiang Zhuang's attack with his sleeve. Later versions of the dance were reputed to be representations of this event. According to the "Monograph on Music" (ibid.), the Whisk Dance originated in the lower Yangtze area. The *Jin shu* (23.713–15) preserves the lyrics of five Whisk Dance pieces.

LL. 83–84. Handan 邯鄲, the capital of the state of Zhao during the Warring States period, was renowned for its singers and dancers. During the Former Han, there was a troupe of Handan drummers at the Han court. See *Han shu* 22.1073. Yang'e 陽阿 was the name of a famous performer as well as a piece of dance music. See *Huainanzi* 16.13a, commentary. Cf. Xie Zhuang, "Rhapsody on the Moon" (this volume) L. 73n.

L. 85: Duke Yi 懿 of Wei 衛 (reg. 668–661 B.C.) was so fond of cranes, he allowed them to ride in his carriage. See *Zuo zhuan*, Min 2 (Legge, *The Chinese Classics* 5: 126).

L. 86: The daughter of King Helu 闔閭 of Wu committed suicide after her father requested that she eat a defiled fish Helu then built a large tomb for her outside the west gate of the Wu capital. As part of the mourning ceremony, he ordered a troupe of dancing cranes to perform in the market place. Ten thousand people came to view them. When the cranes marched out of the city, men and women accompanied them to the door of the tomb. They were then sealed inside "to escort the deceased." See *Wu Yue chunqiu* 4.7a.

Their soaring flight outdistances the road.
Heading to the intersection, they hover in a circle;
Nearing the branch road, they march in foursquare array.
Their carriage has a surfeit of grace,
60    And they give no semblance of stopping.

Advancing to a rhythm, stopping to a beat,
They cast contentious looks, each one holding himself apart from the
                    troupe.
With necks raised, they lightly race off;
Wing touching wing, in unison they sound forth.
65    Their slight traces intersect,
Their drifting shadows crisscross.

In manifold transformations, multiple postures,
Diversely disposed, tightly joined,
They blend into the mist, coalesce with the fog,
70    And seem to have lost their feathery essence.
Like a gust of wind they depart, like a sudden shower they return;
Their changes cannot be described in full.
They so distract the soul and blur the eyes,
One is bewildered and does not know where they have gone.
75    Suddenly they part like stars, pause like clouds,
Take on a solemn mien and compose themselves.
But upon gazing on the distant heights of the heavenly home,
More disheartened and downcast do they feel.

At this time, the beauty of Yan maidens pales beside them,
80    The lads of Ba feel shame in their hearts.
The kerchief and whisk dancers cease their stepping;
The ball and sword jugglers all halt their movements.
Even the Handan troupe would not dare to match them;
And how could Yang'e compete with them?

85    Cranes entered the state of Wei and rode the lord's chariot;
And upon departing the capital of Wu, they emptied the city.
Kept, trained, and tended for a thousand years,
They send forth a long lament into the myriad-mile vastness.

L. 1: Gao-Xu is a combination of Gaoyang 高陽 and Zhuanxu 顓頊, the clan name and reign name respectively of one of the Five Lords who reputedly ruled before the Xia dynasty. In Chinese correlative thought, Zhuanxu ruled by virtue of water, which was equated with north and the color black. He was considered the founder of the Chu house, to which the Ban family traced its ancestry. See *Han shu* 100A.4197. The opening line is similar to the first line of Qu Yuan's "Encountering Sorrow," in which the poet also declares his descent from Zhuanxu.

L. 2: The "blazing numen" refers to Ziwen 子文, the founder of the Ban clan of Chu. As an infant he was abandoned in a marsh, where he was then found and nursed by a tiger. Ziwen later served as minister in Chu. The Chu dialect word for tiger was *ban* 班 (the striped?), and his son was called Ban. When the family moved north after the Qin conquest of Chu, it took Ban as its name. See *Han shu* 100A.4197.

LL. 3–4: The *Han shu* reads *you* 繇 for *yao* 飖 of the *Wen xuan*. Yan Shigu (*Han shu* 100A.4214, n. 2) explains 繇 as equivalent to *you* 由 (follow). However, *yao* must have been the original reading, for Cao Dagu (*Wen xuan* 14.11a) explains *yao* as *piaoyao* 飄飖 (drift about). Thus, Hu Shaoying (*Wen xuan jianzheng* 17.1a) insists that Yan Shigu's explanation is mistaken. The "balmy breezes" refers to the land of the south (Chu). Toward the end of the Qin First Emperor's reign, Ban Yi 班壹 took refuge in Loufan 樓煩 (corresponding to modern Shenchi 神池 and Wutai 五泰, Shanxi) in the north, where he raised horses, cattle, and sheep. According to Ban Gu's "Autobiographical Postface" in the *Han shu*, in the early Han Ban Yi "by means of his wealth gained prominence in the border area" (*Han shu* 100A.4198).

LL. 5–6: In the tenth reign of the Han, the daughter of Ban Kuang 班況, Emperor Cheng (reg. 33–7 B.C.), was named Favorite Beauty. At that time Kuang and two of his sons held important positions in the capital. See *Han shu* 100A.4198. The terms "goose advanced" and "plumed ornament" are expressions from hexagram 53 of the *Classic of Changes* (9/6): "The wild goose advanced to the heights, / Its plumes can be used as an ornament." In Ban Gu's rhapsody, they refer to the success of the Ban family at court.

L. 7: Ju refers to Jujun 巨君, the style name of Wang Mang. See *Han shu* 99A.4039. Ban Gu also uses the expression *tao tian* 滔天 (defiant to Heaven) in his appraisal of Wang Mang contained in his "Autobiographical Preface": "Oh you rapacious vassal, / You usurped and defied Heaven" (*Han shu* 100B.4270). On the various meanings of the term, which first appeared in the *Classic of Documents* (*Shang shu zhushu* 2.19b), see Karlgren, "Glosses on the Book of Documents," pp. 65–66, no. 1236.

L. 8: After the fall of Wang Mang in A.D. 23, the Chang'an area was in turmoil. In A.D. 25 Ban Biao fled to join the satrap Wei Ao 隗囂 in eastern Gansu. It is not clear what Ban Gu means by "song" here. It could refer to the lines from *Mao shi* 241 that Ban Biao recited to Wei Ao in a speech advising him against trying to establish a regime to replace the Han. See *Han shu* 100A.4207. It also could refer to Ban Biao's "Northern Journey Rhapsody," which he composed during his journey from Chang'an to Wei Ao's court. In the piece, Ban Biao complains about the abuses of Wang Mang. See Knechtges, *Wen xuan* 2, chap. 9.

LL. 9–10: Cf. *Lun yu* 4/1: "A neighborhood's benevolence is what constitutes goodness. In selecting a residence, if one does not dwell in a place of benevolence, how can he attain wisdom?" Cao Dagu (*Wen xuan* 14.11b) comments: "This means: my father died young and left me a good example. What is the good example? He chose for me a place to dwell."

# Rhapsody on Communicating with the Hidden

## BAN MENGJIAN

*I*

Our lineage began with the "dark scions" of Gao-Xu,
Our clan descends from the "blazing numen" of the middle ages.
Drifting away, my forebears shed off the land of the balmy breezes,
And left for the northern wilds, where they gained prominence
        and fame.
5    In Han's tenth reign a goose advanced to the heights,
And we had a plumed ornament in the Supreme Capital.
Ju defied Heaven and destroyed the dynasty;
Encountering this troubled age, my late father sang a song.
In the end he preserved himself and bequeathed me a good
        principle:

THE TITLE OF this rhapsody could also be translated "Communicating with the Spirits." The title refers to Ban Gu's (*zi* Mengjian) attempt to examine how the unseen world, the realm of the "hidden men" (*youren* 幽人), influences human life. He wrote this piece just after the death of his father, Ban Biao 班彪, in A.D. 54. Ban Gu was only twenty-two at the time, and had not yet embarked on his career. Uncertain about his future, and concerned that he had no achievement to continue his family's legacy of fame and merit, he consults the "hidden men" to obtain advice on what course to follow.

    "Rhapsody on Communicating with the Hidden" also is found in Ban Gu's "Autobiographical Postface" to the *Han shu* (100A.4213–25). Li Shan cites extensively from an early commentary on the rhapsody by Ban Gu's younger sister Cao Dagu 曹大家 (Ban Zhao 班昭). For other translations, see von Zach, *Deutsche Wacht* (March 1929), rpt. in *Die Chinesische Anthologie* 1: 211–16; and Obi and Hanabusa, *Monzen* 2: 227–41. There are *baihua* translations in Chen Hongtian et al., *Zhaoming Wen xuan yizhu* 2: 766–85; and Li Jingying, *Zhaoming Wen xuan xinjie* 2: 134–45; and Chi et al., *Lidai fu cidian*, pp. 183–85.

L. 12: This is a variation of *Mengzi* 7A/9: "When in obscurity a man perfects his own person in solitude; when prominent, he perfects the entire empire as well."

L. 16: The *Han shu* reads *wei* 偉 for *wei* 違. Yan Shigu (see *Han shu* 100A.4214, n. 8) says that 偉 is equivalent to *wei* 韙, which he glosses as "this." Yan's explanation must be based on the *Shuowen*, which says that 偉 is the greater seal-script form of 韙. See *Shuowen jiezi gulin* 2B.728a-29a. However, Cao Dagu explains 違 as 恨 (regret). Liang Zhangju and Hu Shaoying follow Yan Shigu and construe 偉世業 to mean "the heritage of this [our] house." See *Wen xuan pangzheng* 15.17a-b; and *Wen xuan jianzheng* 17.1a-b, respectively. Zhu Jian (*Wen xuan jishi* 14.1a) notes that the *Guang ya* includes 偉 in a list of words all of which are glossed 恨. Wang Niansun argues for the equivalence between 偉 and 違 in the sense of 恨. See Wang Niansun, *Guang ya shuzheng* 4A.14b. Thus, Cao Dagu probably was following a current Han interpretation of 違 or its variant 偉 as 恨, and I follow her in my rendering of this line.

L. 18: The "past" here is the time of the ancestors.

L. 20: Cf. *Mao shi* 256/5:

A flaw in a white jade tessera,
Can be ground away.
But for a flaw in these words,
Nothing can be done."

Cao Dagu (*Wen xuan* 14.12a) paraphrases this line to mean: "I hope this unusual conduct will not defile the way of my forebears."

L. 22: Cao Dagu (*Wen xuan* 14.12a) comments: "What a person thinks about during the day comes forth at night in dreams. At that time one has contact with spirits."

L. 29: The Yellow Spirit is Huangdi (Yellow Lord), who is attributed with a dream-divination manual titled *Huangdi changliu zhan meng* 黃帝長柳占夢 'Yellow Lord's Tall Willow Dream Divinations'; see *Han shu* 30.1772.

L. 32: Cao Dagu (*Wen xuan* 14.12b) comments: "That the way shall be clear is a sign that one will not be confused."

LL. 33-34: Cf. *Mao shi* 4/1, which is one of the "Southern Airs" of the *Classic of Songs*: "In the south there is a tree with drooping branches; / Vines cling to it. / Joyful is our lord, / May good fortune soothe him." Cao Dagu (*Wen xuan* 14.12b) comments: "This is a sign of contentment and joy."

LL. 35-36: These lines allude to *Mao shi* 196/6 ("Be fearful and careful, / As if looking down on a ravine"), and *Mao shi* 195/6 ("Tremble, be cautious, / As if looking down on a deep abyss"), both of which are in the "Lesser Elegantiae." Although Ban Gu does not directly cite a line from the "Greater Elegantiae," Cao Daogu (*Wen xuan* 14.12b) quotes *Mao shi* 257/9: "People also have a saying: / 'Advancing or retreating, one has no recourse.' " It is not clear why she cites this line. She may have followed an interpretation of gu 谷 'dilemma' in its literal sense of "ravine"—advancing and retreating are a ravine" (about which one must be careful).

LL. 37-38: The auspicious sign is the dream of climbing the mountain, thus giving him the opportunity to meet with the spirits. The spirits perhaps are his deceased ancestors, who offer assistance and a "clear warning" about the dangers of the deep ravine, into which the incautious might fall.

10    Dwell in a neighborhood of the highest benevolence.
I admire the purity and goodness of my illustrious forebears;
Both in obscurity and prominence they helped the people.

Alas, this stupid and lowly orphan,
Will ruin their legacy, for I have not mounted the stairway to fame.
15    How am I worthy to carry it on?
I regret that the heritage of our house is such cause for concern.
Quietly I dwell in seclusion, constantly brooding;
Days and months elapse—the past becomes ever more remote.
I do not dare think I am better than my peers;
20    I only hope my words will not be defiling.

## II

My soul, solitary and alone, contacts the spirits;
True feelings come forth during night sleep.
I dreamed of climbing a mountain and gazing afar;
I glimpsed the semblance of a hidden man.
25    He grasped a vine and handed it to me;
Looking back at the deep ravine he told me, "Don't fall!"
At daybreak I awoke, and gazing upward began to reflect;
My mind, befuddled and confused, could not understand the dream's
        meaning.
The Yellow Spirit was far away, impossible to consult;
30    I used the oracles he left to conjecture a reply.
It said, "Climb high and meet the spirits.
Far, far ahead the way is clear—you will not lose your way.
The vines twist about the drooping tree:
Singing the 'Southern Airs' may soothe your soul.
35    Tremble upon gazing down on the depths—
On this the 'Two Elegantiae' cautioned.
Having given thee an auspicious sign,
We add to it a clear warning.
Why not strive to overtake the crowd?
40    The moment quickly passes, never to be repeated."

85

L. 44. Cao Dagu (*Wen xuan* 14.13a) comments: "This means that Heaven and Earth are infinite, but of the people who dwell within them, those who reach a longevity of 120 years are rare and few."

L. 45: This line draws phrases from the oracle texts of the *Classic of Changes*: hexagram 3, Zhun 屯, "Difficulty" (6/2: "Difficult and tortuous") and hexagram 39, Jian 蹇 "Obstruction" (6/4: "Going forth: obstruction; coming back: union"). Ban Gu seems to use the phrases all in the general sense of "difficulty."

L. 47: The *Wen xuan* reads *wu* 迕 (greet) for *wu* 寤 (awaken) of the *Han shu*. Cao Dagu's commentary contains 迕. I follow her reading.

LL. 49–50: These lines allude to the story of Viscount Shuwu 叔武, whose brother was Duke Cheng 成 (reg. 634–620 B.C.) of Wei 衛. In 632 B.C. Duke Cheng was driven from Wei and fled to Chu. During his absence, he left Shuwu in charge of the state. Shuwu represented the state of Wei at the Jiantu 踐土 Convention, at which a treaty was concluded with Jin that permitted Duke Cheng to return to his state. According to the *Zuo zhuan* (Xi 28; Legge, *The Chinese Classics* 5: 211), when Duke Cheng returned to Wei, some of his supporters shot Shuwu with an arrow as he was leaving his bath "to greet his brother." Duke Cheng felt his brother had been wrongly killed and ordered the execution of the assassin. The *Gongyang zhuan* (Xi 19), which has a different account, says that Shuwu was induced by Duke Wen of Jin to usurp the dukedom. When Duke Cheng returned to Wei, he himself ordered Shuwu's execution.

The expression *sang yu* 喪予 (lit., "destroyed me") is from *Lun yu* 11/18.

LL. 51–52: Guan Zhong 管仲 (ob. 645 B.C.) at one time served the enemies of Duke Huan of Qi. Before the duke assumed the throne, Guan Zhong's forces faced him in battle. An arrow shot by Guan Zhong glanced off his belt buckle. Later, Duke Huan appointed Guan Zhong prime minister. See *Zuo zhuan*, Xi 24 (Legge, *The Chinese Classics* 5: 191); and *Shi ji* 32.1485.

L. 55: Yong Chi 雍齒 had fought against Liu Bang before he was victorious over Xiang Yu. After Liu Bang became emperor, he enfeoffed Yong Chi as Marquis of Shifang. See *Shi ji* 55.2043; and Watson, *Records of the Grand Historian of China* 1: 144–55.

L. 56: Lord Ding 丁 was a Chu general who fought against Liu Bang. In one battle Liu and Ding were in close combat when Liu suggested that it was senseless for "two worthies" to fight. Ding then withdrew his troops. Later, after Liu Bang's victory over Xiang Yu, Lord Ding visited Liu. Liu seized him and ordered him beheaded, claiming he was a "disloyal vassal." See *Shi ji* 100.2733; and Watson, *Records of the Historian*, 103.

L. 57: Lady Li 栗 was the wife of Emperor Jing 景 (reg. 156–141 B.C.) of the Former Han. Her son Liu Rong 劉榮 (ob. 147 B.C.) was installed as heir-designate. However, she became increasingly jealous, and eventually so offended the emperor that he deposed Liu Rong. Lady Li was never again allowed to see the emperor, and she "died of grief." See *Shi ji* 49.1976; Watson, *Records of the Grand Historian of China* 1: 387–88; and *Han shu* 97A.3946.

L. 58: Empress Wang 王 was the wife of Emperor Xuan 宣 (73–48 B.C.) of the Former Han. She was first selected as a Favorite Beauty, but later was elevated to empress after the death by poisoning of Empress Xu. The emperor charged her with raising Empress Xu's son. Childless herself, Empress Wang became the foster mother of the future Emperor Yuan. See *Han shu* 97A.3969.

L. 60: The Old Man of the North, who lived on the northern frontier, had a horse that ran away to the Hu. When people tried to console him, he said, "Might this not suddenly turn into good fortune?" Several months later the horse returned, bringing with it a fine Hu charger. When people congratulated him on his "luck," the old man replied, "Might this not suddenly turn into misfortune?" Later his son broke his left leg riding the horse. This time friends came to express their sympathy, but the old man said, "Might this not suddenly turn

## *III*

I received divine instruction, but was doubtful;
Long I stood, hesitant, waiting.
I thought—Heaven and Earth are infinite,
But few men reach old age.
45   All is a mass of hardship and obstacles—
How much travail, how little wisdom!
The ancient sages, faced with hardship, extricated themselves;
How could they be impeded by the common crowd?
Of old, Shuwu of Wei greeted his brother;
50   His brother mistook him for a rebel and killed him.
Guan Zhong drew his bow intending to kill an enemy;
The foe became lord and made him minister.
With constant change there is constant reversal;
Who can predict the end or beginning?
55   Liu Bang detested Yong Chi, but rewarded him first;
He was kind to Lord Ding, but then put him to death.
Lady Li received grief in propitious circumstances;
Empress Wang obtained good fortune from something sad.
Things perversely turn and reverse like this;
60   The Old Man of the North knew well the vagaries of fortune.

into good fortune?" A year later the frontier was attacked by the Hu. His son was able to avoid military service because of his bad leg. The point of the story is that "Good fortune may turn to misfortune, and misfortune may turn to good fortune." See *Huainanzi* 18.6a–b.

LL. 61–62: Ban Gu alludes to a *Zhuangzi* (7.3b–4a) passage about Shan Bao 單豹 and Zhang Yi 張毅. Shan Bao was a hermit who lived on a cliff. He nurtured himself carefully, drinking only water and avoiding competition for gain. After seventy years he still had the complexion of an infant. One day he met a tiger, who devoured him. Zhang Yi, on the other hand, had lived a life of luxury for forty years when he died of "internal fever." Zhuangzi comments about them: "Bao nurtured himself inside, but a tiger ate his exterior; Yi nurtured his exterior, but disease attacked him from within." Cao Dagu (*Wen xuan* 14.14a) comments: "Treating the inside refers to controlling the breath."

L. 64: Yan Hui 顏回, Confucius's favorite disciple, died young at the age of twenty-nine. See *Lun yu* 6/2 and 11/7–8; and *Shi ji* 67.2188. Ran Geng 冉耕, also known as Boniu 伯牛, was another of Confucius's disciples. He suffered a terrible illness, about which Confucius exclaimed, "If it kills him, it is fate!" See *Lun yu* 6/8 and *Shi ji* 67.2189. The implication is that the harmony of the mean did not prevent these two good men from suffering early deaths.

LL. 65–66: Jie'ni 桀溺 was a farmer-recluse to whom Confucius sent Zilu to inquire about the ford of a river. Jie'ni tried to persuade Zilu to leave Confucius and join him in fleeing the world. See *Lun yu* 18/6.

LL. 67–68: Jie'ni used the expression *taotao* 滔滔 (chaotic) to characterize the conditions of his time. See ibid. 18/6.

L. 69: The "sage" is Confucius.

L. 70: When Zilu died defending the legitimate ruler of Wei, the ruler who usurped the throne ordered that Zilu's flesh be made into mincemeat. When Confucius heard about this, he had covers put on all of the mincemeat jars in his house. See *Li ji zhushu* 6.7b (2758).

L. 71: Cf. *Lun yu* 11/12: "When Minzi stood at his master's side, he was docile and quiet. Zilu was bold and warlike. . . . The Master was pleased and said, 'One like You [Zilu]—he will die a violent death.'"

L. 72: Cf. *Lun yu* 17/23: "Zilu said, 'Does the gentleman esteem courage?' The Master said, 'The gentleman most highly values what is right. If a gentleman has courage but not a sense of what is right, he will be a rebel. If an inferior man has courage but not a sense of what is right, he will be a bandit.'"

L. 73: Ban Gu uses the analogy of a tree to illustrate that one's fate depends to a certain extent on the "roots" (i.e., ancestors) from which it comes.

L. 74: The *Wen xuan* reads *ling* 零 (to fall) for *ling* 靈 of the *Han shu*, which Yan Zhigu (*Han shu* 100A.4218, n. 16) glosses as "good." Cao Dagu's commentary writes *ling* 零, which I follow. The word *hui* 彙 is problematic in this line. Ying Shao (*Wen xuan* 14.14b) glosses it as *lei* 類 (kind; class), which is the most common sense of the term. Yan Shigu (*Han shu* 100.4218, n. 16) explains it as *sheng* 盛 (to flourish). However, this interpretation seems redundant because of the occurrence of *mao* 茂 in the same line. I suspect that the literal sense of the line is: "The branches and leaves, depending upon type, fall or flourish."

LL. 75–76: These lines allude to the dialogue between Penumbra (wangliang 魍魉) and Shadow of the *Zhuangzi* (1.24b–25a): "Penumbra asked Shadow, 'Just now you were moving, and now you stop. Just now you were sitting, but now you stand. Why is it that you have no definite action?' Shadow replied, 'Do I rely on something that makes me act this way? Or does what I rely on also have something on which it relies to make it act this way? Do I rely on snake's scales and cicada's wings? How do I know what makes me act this way? How do I know what doesn't make me act this way?'" Ying Shao (cited in *Wen xuan* 14.14b–15a) explains that in trying to explain the tragic deaths of Yan Hui, Ran You, and Zilu, various

Shan Bao treated the inside, but withered from without;
Zhang Yi cultivated his exterior, but was attacked from within.
In the harmony of the mean one can nearly escape disaster;
But Yan and Ran did not attain long lives.
65 Jie'ni summoned Zilu to join him,
Claiming Confucius was not worth following.
Calm in the face of turmoil, Zilu did not flee,
And in the end lost his life in the travail of his time.
Being the disciple of a sage did not save him;
70 Although Confucius covered the mincemeat, to what avail was it?
Being so "bold and warlike," he was bound to meet disaster;
He avoided becoming a bandit or rebel by reliance on the Way.
Form and breath issue from the roots;
For they determine whether branch and leaf wither or flourish.
75 However, I fear that when Penumbra rebuked Shadow,
He did not fully understand the true essence of things.

people have either cast aspersions on their character or placed the blame on their teacher. They are as mistaken as was Penumbra, who tried to rebuke Shadow for his lack of independent action. Penumbra erred in not understanding that Shadow was dependent on other things. What happened to the three disciples of Confucius was determined by fate and nothing else. A simpler explanation of this line might be that just as Shadow cannot explain the causes of his action, it is impossible to determine the reason (blame?) for the tragic deaths of Yan Hui, Ran You, and Zilu.

LL. 77–78: Chong 重 and Li 黎 originally were the names of two persons, but by Han times they had coalesced into the name of a single person, Chongli. See Karlgren, "Legends and Cults," pp. 234–39. Chongli reputedly was the great-grandson of Zhuanxu. He served as director of fire under Lord Ku 嚳, Gaoxin 高辛. Because he was able "to illumine brightly the empire" he was given the title Zhurong 祝融, "Great Illuminator." Chongli was executed by Gaoxin for failing to quell the rebellion of Gonggong. His younger brother Wu Hui 吳回 succeeded him as Zhurong. Wu Hui's son Lu Zhong 陸終 sired six sons. His sixth son, Jilian 季連, took the clan name Mi 羋. His descendants were the founders of the ruling house of Chu. See Guo yu 16.2a–3a; Shi ji 40.1689–91; and Chavannes, Mh 4: 337–40. Si 汜 here is probably not the name of the Yangtze tributary mentioned in Mao shi 22 as suggested by Yan Shigu (Han shu 100A.4219), but means "shore" (see Cao Daogu, Wen xuan 14.15a and Ying Shao, Han shu 100A.4219).

L. 79: Ying 嬴 is the surname of the Qin ruling house. The Ying clan traced its ancestry back to Bo Yi (*prak *ʔje) 伯翳 or 柏翳, also known as Dafei 大費, who, according to Sima Qian, assisted Shun in taming the birds and beasts. See Shi ji 5.173. Shun gave him the surname Ying. See also Shi ji 6.276; and Chavannes, Mh 2: 2–3, 218. Ban Gu obviously is punning on Bo Yi's name by referring to him as "regulator of the hundreds" (伯儀 *prak *ngjai). The Guo yu (16.3b), which probably is Ban Gu's immediate source for this line, refers to Bo Yi as one who "is able to arrange properly [yi 議] the hundred types of creatures in order to assist Shun." It should be noted that Bo Yi also has been equated with the Bo Yi 柏 or 伯益 mentioned in the Classic of Documents (Shang shu zhushu 3.24b–25a, 275–76) as Shun's forester (see Han shu 28B.1641). For a discussion of the confusion between these names, see Karlgren, "Legends and Cults," pp. 259–61.

L. 80: The Jiang 姜 clan, the ruling house of the state of Qi, was reputedly founded by Bo Yi 伯儀, who served as master of rites under Shun. See Shi ji 36.1585 and Guo yu 16.3b. He was responsible for regulating the Three Rites, meaning the rites for Heaven, Earth, and Man (i.e., the ancestors). See Shang shu zhushu 3.25b (276). Zhi (*tjəh) 趾, which I have loosely translated "rites," literally means "footsteps." Its extended meaning may be "traces," "legacy," or "foundation." Zhang Yun'ao (Xuanxue jiaoyan, 8.10a–b) suggests it should be construed as zhi (*drjəh) 畤 (altar).

L. 81: Cf. Lun yu 7/14: "Zigong asked, 'What kind of men were Boyi and Shuqi?' Confucius replied, 'They were ancient worthies.' 'Did they complain about anything?' The Master said, 'They sought benevolence and obtained it. What was there for them to complain about?'"

L. 83: The Eastern Neighbor (Dong lin 東鄰) is Zhou Xin 紂辛, the last ruler of the Yin dynasty, which occupied territory east of the Zhou. The "three good men" (san ren 三仁) are Weizi 微子, Jizi 箕子, and Bi Gan 比干. See Lun yu 18/1. Weizi (or, more properly, the viscount of Wei), also known as Qi 啟, was Zhou Xin's elder brother. He left the court after Zhou Xin failed to heed his repeated admonitions about Zhou Xin's neglect of government and profligate ways. Bigan, Zhou Xin's uncle, was put to death for protesting Zhou Xin's cruelty. Jizi (lit., viscount of Ji) also was an uncle of Zhou Xin. He was so horrified by the execution of Bigan that he feigned madness and became Zhou Xin's slave. See Shi ji 3.108; and Chavannes, Mh 1: 206.

*IV*

Chongli's pure radiance dazzled the era of Gaoxin;
The Mi clan grew great and strong on the southern shore.
The Ying clan gained prestige from the regulator of the hundreds;
80    The Jiang clan originated from the minister of the Three Rites.
How true the saying "Benevolence sought is benevolence gained"!
High in the celestial realm the rule is the same.
The cruel Eastern Neighbor slaughtered the good;

L. 84: The *Guo yu* (3.18a-b) records a series of favorable astronomical conjunctions that occurred at the time of King Wu of Zhou's expedition against the Yin. "Formerly, when King Wu attacked the Yin, Jupiter was in Quail Fire [Chun huo 鶉火, in Hydra], the moon was in Heavenly Quadriga [in Scorpio], the moon was at the Ford [Jin 津, the Sky River or Milky Way] of the Split Tree [Ximu 析木, in Scorpio], the *chen* 辰 [the conjunction of the sun and moon] was at the Dipper's Handle, and Mercury was at the Celestial Turtle [Tian yuan 天黿, in Aquarius]. The positions of Mercury together with the sun and *chen* were all in the Northern Quarter. This is where Zhuanxu founded his rule. Diku received the succession from him. Our Ji clan appeared from the Celestial Turtle. Furthermore [see the text in *Han shu* 100A.4219, n. 5], the Split Tree contains the Founding Star [Jian xing 建星, in Sagittarius] and the Herd Boy. It was the spirit relied on by Duke Feng 逢, the descendant of Boling 伯陵, nephew of Da Jiang 大姜, our deceased mother. The location of Jupiter was in our Zhou's astrological division. The location of the moon in the Horses of Dachen 大辰 and the Farmer's Auspice had their coordinates fixed by our grand ancestor Houji. King Wu wished to conform to these five positions [sun, moon, Jupiter, Mercury, and *chen*] and three locations [associated with Duke Feng, the Zhou, and Houji] and use them." For further discussion of this passage, see Hart, "The Discussion of the *Wu-yi* Bells in the *Kuo-yü*," pp. 416-17.

L. 85: The woman of the Rong is Li Ji 驪姬, the daughter of a Rong chieftain, whom Duke Xian 獻 of Jin (reg. 676-651 B.C.) took as his principal wife. Through clever intrigue, Li Ji was able to convince Duke Xian to remove as heir designate Shen Sheng 申生, a son by his first wife, in favor of her own son Xi Qi 奚齊. She then tricked Shen Sheng into presenting his father with poisoned meat he had used in a sacrifice to his mother. Although Shen was not guilty of poisoning the meat, rather than expose his wicked stepmother and thus upset his father, he committed suicide. This was regarded as an act of filial piety. See *Zuo zhuan* Xi 4 (Legge, *The Chinese Classics* 5: 141-42); *Shi ji* 39.1645-46; and Chavannes, *Mh* 4: 264-66.

L. 86: Duke Xian of Jin had two others sons, Chonger 重耳 and Yiwu 夷吾, whom Li Ji had falsely implicated in the "plot" to poison their father. Chonger fled and traveled for nineteen years before returning to Jin to assume the throne. Known also as Duke Wen 文 (reg. 636-628 B.C.), he is one of the hegemons of Zhou. The *Guo yu* (10.11a-12a) records a dialogue between Chonger and an astrologer about his prospects for returning to Jin. The astrologer said that Chonger left Jin under the constellation Chen 辰 (also known as Dahuo 大火, or Antares), which according to Wei Zhao corresponds to the fifth year of Duke Xi of Lu (655 B.C.). Chen is equated with the dragon (see Schlegel, *Uranographie chinoise* 1: 138-39). He would return to Jin under the constellation Shen 申 (seven stars in Orion), which Wei Zhao equates with Duke Xi's twenty-fourth year (636 B.C.). Shen is equated with the tiger (see ibid. 1: 397). For further discussion of the *Guo yu* passage to which Ban Gu alludes, see Chavannes, *Mh* 3: 657-58; 4: 477.

L. 87: Fa 發 is the personal name of King Wu 武 (reg. 1111-1105 B.C.) of Zhou. When he first gathered his troops at Meng Ford 孟津, his lords said, "Zhou can now be attacked." Fa replied, "We do not yet know Heaven's will. We cannot yet do so." Two years later, when the people could no longer bear Zhou Xin's cruelty, Fa led his forces into battle and defeated the Yin. See *Shi ji* 4.120-21; and Chavannes, *Mh* 1: 226-27.

L. 88: During his years as a refugee, Chonger lived for a time in Qi. Duke Huan treated him well and gave him a wife and twenty horse teams. Chonger enjoyed his comfortable life in Qi so much he lost all interest in recovering his throne in Jin. His wife then arranged to get him drunk and have him lured away from Qi. He eventually returned to Jin and took his rightful position as Duke. See *Zuo zhuan*, Xi 23 (Legge, *The Chinese Classics* 5: 187); *Shi ji* 39.1658; Chavannes, *Mh* 4: 287-88.

King Wu made his position conform to the three and five.
85   A woman from the Rong viciously destroyed a filial son;
A hegemon left and returned under the Dragon and Tiger.
After sending back his army, Fa fulfilled Heaven's decree;
After becoming drunk on a journey, Chonger met his destiny.

LL. 89–90: The Zhen 震 (Arousing) trigram represents the dragon. At the end of the Xia dynasty two dragons appeared in court claiming they were the two rulers of Bao 褒. Their spittle was collected and stored in a box. The box was transmitted to the Yin and Zhou without being opened. At the end of the reign of King Li 厲, someone opened it, and the spittle poured over the courtyard. It transformed into a black turtle, which entered the palace ladies' chamber and made a palace maid pregnant. The resulting child was abandoned, but later ended up in Bao. She was called Bao Si 褒姒 and became the favorite of King You 幽 (reg. 779–771 B.C.), the last of the Western Zhou rulers. His infatuation with her is often cited in Chinese accounts as the major cause of the fall of the Western Zhou. See *Guo yu* 16.5b–6a; *Shi ji* 4.147; Chavannes, *Mh* 1: 281–84; and *Han shu* 27C–1.1465.

LL. 91–92: The Xun 巽 (Gentle) trigram represents the chicken. In the reign of Emperor Xuan of the Former Han, a hen in the barns of the Everlasting Palace had changed into a rooster. Although its feathers had changed, it did not crow or lead the flock, and it had no spurs. In the reign of Emperor Yuan, someone presented a cock that had grown horns. Liu Xiang interpreted the strange phenomena as omens of the increasing influence of a female favorite at court, namely Empress Wang. See *Han shu* 27B1.1370–71. Through Wang Mang the Wang family usurped the throne. The five rulers are the emperors from Xuan to the last Former Han emperor, Ping, from whom Wang Mang seized the throne.

L. 95: The word *xu* 胥 can be construed in two different ways. Ying Shao (*Wen xuan* 14.16a and *Han shu* 100A.4220) glosses it as *xu* 須, "must." He paraphrases the lines as follows: "The sage must rely on divination, and then he may consult with the spirits." *Xu* also can mean "mutually," "together." Thus, Lu Xiang (*Liuchen zhu Wen xuan* 14.12a) paraphrases the line to read: "Things that are mutually dependent use the spirits for consultation." Neither of these readings is satisfactory. Lü Xiang's interpretation does not seem grammatically acceptable (*reng* 仍 certainly is a main verb). Ying Shao's "rely on divination" does not easily derive from the text, which literally says "rely on things." I follow him, however, for lack of a better solution.

L. 96: The term *zhou* 宙, which commonly occurs in the expression *yuzhou* 宇宙, means "time." Cf. *Huainanzi* 11.9b: "Going back to antiquity and coming to the present is called *zhou* [time]."

L. 97: Gui 媯 was the ruling clan of the state of Chen 陳. The Jiang 姜 clan ruled the state of Qi. Jingzhong Wan 敬仲完 (b. 705 B.C.), also known as Wan of Chen, was the son of Duke Li 厲 of Chen (reg. 706–700 B.C.). When he was a young child, his father consulted a Zhou astrologer about Wan's future. After divining with the *Classic of Changes*, the astrologer predicted that the lad would become a powerful ruler in a state ruled by the Jiang clan. In 672 B.C. Wan fled to Qi in fear of a threat against his life. His descendants became the Tian 田 family, which eventually seized power from the Jiang clan in Qi. See *Zuo zhuan*, Zhuang 22 (Legge, *The Chinese Classics* 5: 103); *Shi ji* 36.1576–78; and Chavannes, *Mh* 4: 172–74.

L. 98: Dan 旦 is the Duke of Zhou, who served as regent for his nephew King Cheng 成 (reg. 1104–1068 B.C.). When King Cheng moved the famous nine tripods to Jiaru 郟鄏, he had a divination performed. The oracle revealed that the dynasty would last thirty reigns, or seven hundred years. See *Zuo zhuan*, Xuan 3 (Legge, *The Chinese Classics* 5: 293); *Shi ji* 40.1700–1; and Chavannes, *Mh* 4: 352–53. None of these sources specifically mentions Dan's role in performing the divination. For the expression "notched tortoise shell," see *Mao shi* 237/3.

L. 99: Xuan is King Xuan 宣 of Zhou (reg. 827–782 B.C.), who is credited with achieving the restoration of the Zhou dynasty. *Mao shi* 190/4 alludes to a herdsman's dream of "locusts, fish, tortoise-and-snake banners, and falcon banners." A diviner interpreted the

Scales of the "Arousing" let its spittle flow in the courtyard of Xia;
90  After three dynasties it destroyed the clan of Ji.
Feathers of the "Gentle" transformed in Emperor Xuan's palace;
Five reigns later, the result was calamity.


## V

The Way is long and far, human life is short;
The course of things is distant and dark—one cannot fully
           comprehend it.
95  Thus, one must rely on divination and consult with the gods;
Then he may explore time and communicate with the hidden.
That Gui would live with the Jiang was divined in infancy;
Dan calculated the years from a notched tortoise shell.
Xuan's restoration and Cao's defeat were predicted in dreams;

dream as a sign of bountiful harvest and a long-lasting reign. According to the "Lesser Mao Preface," this poem is addressed to King Xuan (see *Mao shi zhushu* 11/2.11b, 938). Ban Gu probably understood the dream omens of the *Mao shi* song as auspicious signs of the Zhou restoration.

Boyang 伯陽 of Cao 曹 (reg. 501–489 B.C.) was the last ruler of the state of Cao. A man of Cao dreamed that a crowd of gentlemen was standing at the altar of soil, planning to overthrow the state. One of the gentlemen advised them to wait for someone named Gongsun Qiang 公孫彊. The next day, the person who had the dream searched throughout the city for a man by this name. Qiang was nowhere to be found, and so the man told his son, "If you hear that Gongsun Qiang has control of the government, you must leave the state." Later, Boyang became ruler of Cao. He spent much of his time hunting with a companion named Gongsun Qiang. Qiang advised Boyang on political matters and encouraged him to compete for the Hegemony. Cao became embroiled in a war against Song, and as a result Cao was defeated and destroyed. See *Zuo zhuan*, Ai 7 (Legge, *The Chinese Classics* 5: 814); *Shi ji* 35.1573; and Chavannes, *Mh* 4: 167–68.

L. 100: The *Zuo zhuan* (Zhao 25; Legge, *The Chinese Classics* 5: 709) alludes to an oracular "children's ditty" that predicted the demise of Duke Zhao 昭 (reg. 540–507 B.C.) and his replacement by Duke Ding 定 (reg. 508–494 B.C.). Wei refers to Duke Ling 靈 (reg. 534–493 B.C.) of Wei 衛. According to the *Zhuangzi* (8.29b), when Duke Ling's grave was being dug at Shaqiu 沙丘, the diggers discovered a stone coffin inscribed· "You cannot rely on your descendants—Duke Mu will seize your plot." Ling was the duke's posthumous name.

L. 101: Shuxiang 叔向 of the Yangshe 羊舌 clan went against his mother's wishes and married a girl from the Wuchen 巫臣 clan. They had a child named Bo Shi 伯石. Shuxiang's mother went to see him, but upon hearing his cry, she refused to enter the room. She said, "This is the cry of a wolf. The offspring of a wolf is of a wild disposition. None other than he will destroy the Yangshe clan." See *Zuo zhuan*, Zhao 28 (Legge, *The Chinese Classics* 5: 726–27).

L. 102: Zhou Yafu 周亞夫, marquis of Tiao 條, consulted with the renowned physiognomist Xu Fu 許負. Xu examined his features and found "vertical lines entering his mouth," a sign that he would eventually die of starvation. Later, he was arrested for participating in a rebellion. He refused to eat and died within a few days. See *Shi ji* 57.2074, 2079; Watson, *Records of the Grand Historian of China* 1: 433–34, 439.

L. 103: Cf. *Laozi* 25: "There is a thing chaotically formed, born before Heaven and Earth. . . . I do not know its name, and I thus call it the Way." Cao Daogu (*Wen xuan* 14.17a) explains: "When a man is born, his will is within him, his voice manifests itself without, his bones and body have form, events and changes have fate conjunctions. All of these things are interdependent and create a single form. This is the way of nature."

L. 104: Cao Dagu (*Wen xuan* 14.17a) explains: "As for the methods of the Way, in evaluating success or failure, ascertaining poverty and low status, or judging wealth and honor, each is based on a single standard. Thus, whether one listens to sounds, looks at the shape of bones, divines colors and innate properties, observes deportment, ascertains intent, examines conduct, consults oracles, or bases himself on ancestors, all of these methods are like water that comes from a common source and flows into separate streams."

LL. 105–6: Cao Daogu (ibid.) comments that fate is predetermined by the gods, and therefore can be revealed beforehand in the form of omens. At the same time, depending upon how one acts, one's fate can be exacerbated or ameliorated. "Mind" here has connotations of will or volition, which is controlled by fate.

LL. 109–10: The Earl of Qin asked Shi Yang 士鞅 which of the Jin grandee clans would be destroyed first. He replied that the Luan 欒 would be the first to go. Their father Shu 書 was a good man, but his son Yan 黶 was excessively cruel. When he died, his son

100 Lu and Wei had their names and titles revealed in inscriptions and
ditties.
A mother heard bawling and accused Shi;
Xu examined the lines of face and informed Tiao.
The Way, chaotically formed, is natural and spontaneous;
Only its methods flow in separate streams from a common source.
105 The gods determine fate before mind,
But fate also fluctuates in accord with human action.
Revolving, flowing, moving—it cannot be overcome;
Thus, with every encounter there is either gain or loss.
The Three Luan ultimately sprang from a single body;
110 Although times changed, Heaven was unerring in dispensing fate.

Ying 盈 would be unable to atone for his father's misdeeds, and his clan would be doomed. See *Zuo zhuan*, Xiang 14 (Legge, *The Chinese Classics* 5: 465). Shi Yang's prediction proved to be accurate, for in 543 B.C. the entire Luan clan was wiped out. See *Zuo zhuan*, Xiang 23 (Legge, *The Chinese Classics* 5: 501). The *Han shu* reads Ying 盈 (the name of the last head of the Luan family) for *yi* 易, "change," of the *Wen xuan*. The *Han shu* text would read: "Although transferred to Ying, their fate was inevitable." Cao Dagu (*Wen xuan* 14.17b) comments that Heaven is unerring in decreeing blessings on good persons and disaster on evil persons.

LL. 111-12: Cao Dagu (ibid.) remarks that retribution is variously and unevenly dispensed. Thus, men are confused and do not trust the Way of Heaven.

LL. 113-14: Both Zhuang Zhou (author of *Zhuangzi*) and Jia Yi (see "Rhapsody on the Houlet," this volume) claimed that death and life were equal in the sense that they both were part of the process of constant transformation. Life was thus not worth clinging to, and death need not be lamented. Cao Dagu (*Wen xuan* 14.17b) comments that although Zhuang Zhou and Jia Yi were men of wisdom and talent, they did not follow the norms of the sages. Thus, they confused good and evil, and engaged in reckless and fanciful talk.

L. 116: A ruler of a state sent an envoy to invite Zhuangzi to join his government. Zhuangzi replied, "Have you seen a sacrificial ox? They garb him in patterned embroidery, feed him hay and soy beans. But when he is led out and enters the Great Temple, although he might wish to be a solitary calf, would it be possible?" Zhuangzi refuses to accept office because he does not wish to suffer the fate of the sacrifical ox. See *Zhuangzi* 10.12a-b. When an owl perched on Jia Yi's mat, he took this as a sign that he was about to die. See "Rhapsody on the Houlet," this volume. Ban Gu cites these stories as examples of even Zhuang Zhou and Jia Yi expressing fear of death despite their claims to be indifferent to it.

L. 117: Cao Dagu (*Wen xuan* 14.18a) says the supreme doctrines are the classics.

LL. 119-20: Cf. *Lun yu* 4/5: "The Master said, 'Wealth and honor, these are what men desire. If they can be obtained only by violating the Way, they should not be owned. Poverty and low position, these are what men detest. If they can be avoided only by violating the Way, they should not be avoided."

L. 122: Cf. *Mao shi* 260/6: "People have a saying, 'Virtue is as light as a hair.'"

L. 123: On the three good men, see L. 83n above.

L. 124: Cf. *Lun yu* 18/8: "The recluses are Boyi, Shuqi, Yuzhong, Yiyi, Zhuzhang, and Shaolian. The Master said, 'Not lessening their resolve or disgracing themselves, such were Boyi and Shuqi. One may say that Liuxia Hui and Shaolian lessened their resolve and disgraced themselves, but their words matched ethical principles and their actions matched the thoughts of other men.'" Boyi and his brother Shuqi refused to serve the Zhou and starved to death. Although he was dismissed three times from his post, Liuxia Hui refused to leave the land of his parents to seek another position. See *Lun yu* 18/2.

L. 125: Duangan Mu 段干木 was a recluse who adamantly refused to serve in office. Marquis Wen 文 (424-387 B.C.) of Wei 魏, after trying unsuccessfully to induce him to take a post, continued to treat him with deference. When Qin was about to attack Wei, someone told the Qin ruler that Wen was respectful to worthy men, and the people praised his benevolence. Since the ruler and his subjects were so concordant and united, it would not be wise to plot against him. Qin then withdrew its troops. See *Shi ji* 44.1839; Chavannes, *Mh* 4: 141-43; and *Lüshi chunqiu* 21.4b-5a.

L. 126: Shen Baoxu 申包胥, a Chu grandee (Jing 荆 is the archaic name for Chu), traveled on foot from Chu to Qin seeking Qin's assistance in repelling an invasion by Wu. "He climbed steep mountains, entered deep ravines, swam rivers and streams. He braved fords and passes, trekked through jungles, trod over sand and stones. From foot to knee, he had thick blisters and heavy callouses." Upon reaching Qin, he wailed in the court for seven

The Way of Heaven is abstruse, uneven, complex;
Thus, the multitudes are confounded and confused.
Zhou and Jia, with wild and reckless fancy,
Equated life and death, fortune and misfortune.
115 They put forth erroneous words to distort the truth:
One took fright at a sacrificial ox, the other was superstitious of
       an owl.

## VI

What we honor most are the supreme doctrines of the sages;
One must accord with Heaven's will and determine what is right.
There are things we desire but should not own;
120 There are also things we detest but should not avoid.
If one's grasp is firm and never wavers,
Virtue becomes light and there are no burdens.
The three good men were different but shared a single ideal;
Yi and Hui were opposites but enjoyed equal fame.
125 Mu rested at ease to defend the Wei;
Shen used blistered feet to save Chu.

days without eating. Finally, Qin agreed to send an army, and Chu was able to drive off the Wu invaders. See *Huainanzi* 19.10b.

L. 127: Ji Xin 紀信 was one of Liu Bang's trusted generals. When Xiang Yu surrounded Liu Bang at Xingyang 滎陽, Ji offered to disguise himself as Liu Bang and surrender to Xiang Yu. While the Chu forces dashed forth to capture the false Han leader, Liu Bang escaped. When Xiang Yu discovered the deception, he burned Ji Xin alive. See *Shi ji* 7.326; Watson, *Records of the Grand Historian of China* 1: 64.

L. 128: During the Qin the Four Hoaryheads (Si hao 四皓) became hermits in the mountains of Shangluo 商雒 and remained there "nurturing their resolve" until the empire was peaceful again. Emperor Gaozu 高祖 (reg. 202–195 B.C.) wished to invite them to his court, but they refused to come. Empress Lu 呂 (reg. 187–180 B.C.) then sent the heir designate with presents and a special carriage to bring them to the capital. This time they consented to come, and Gaozu treated them with great deference. See *Shi ji* 55.2047; Watson, *Records of the Grand Historian of China* 1: 148–49; and *Han shu* 72.3056. The names of the Four Hoaryheads are pseudonyms: Lord of the Garden (Yuan gong 園公), original name Yu Xuanming 庾宣明; Yellow Lord of Xia (Xia Huang gong 夏黃公), original name Cui Guang 崔廣; Master of Lu Hamlet (Luli xiansheng 角里先生), original name Zhou Shu 周術; and Ji of Qi Hamlet (Qili Ji 綺里季). See *Shi ji* 55.2045, n. 1. For a full treatment of the lore concerning the Four Hoaryheads, see Berkowitz, "Patterns of Reclusion in Early and Early Medieval China," pp. 139–63.

L. 129: Cf. *Lun yu* 19/12: One "compares them [i.e., the disciples] to plants and trees. They are divided into classes."

L. 130: The idea is that if one has good character ("is able to bear fruit"), he will have a good reputation ("flourish").

L. 131: Cf. ibid. 15/10: "The gentleman detests the prospect that after his death his name would not be praised"; and *Zuo zhuan*, Xiang 24: "The thing of highest importance is to establish virtue. Next is to establish merit. After that is to establish good speech. If even after a long time they are not in disuse, one may say 'they are imperishable.'"

L. 132: Cf. *Mao shi* 195/4: "They do not model themselves on the ancient people."

L. 134: Ban Gu alludes to two sources here. First, is the *Classic of Documents* (*Shang shu zhushu* 13.21a, 423): "Heaven helps those with sincere words" (for a variant interpretation, see Karlgren, "Glosses on the Book of Documents," no. 1609, 271–72). Second, is the *Classic of Changes*, "Great Commentary" (*Zhou yi zhushu* 7.30b, 169): "The one whom Heaven assists is the compliant. The one whom men assist is the faithful." *Han shu* reads *shun* 順 for *xun* 訓 of *Wen xuan*. Cao Dagu's commentary also reads *xun*. I have followed this reading.

L. 135: Cf. *Mao shi* 198/4: "Orderly is the Great Way, / The sages have planned it."

L. 136: Cf. *Lun yu* 4/25: "The virtuous is never alone. He always has neighbors."

L. 137: Yu 虞 is the sage ruler Shun. The expression *yi feng* 儀鳳 (decorous phoenix?) alludes to the *Classic of Documents* (*Shang shu zhushu* 5.14b, 302): "The 'Shao' music of the panpipes is played in nine movements. The phoenixes come and arrive." For different explanations of *yi*, see Karlgren, "Glosses on the Book of Documents," no. 1346, pp. 142–43.

L. 138: Cf. *Lun yu* 7/13: "When the Master was in Qi, he heard the 'Shao.' For three months he did not know the taste of meat. He said, 'I did not think that music could be so sublime!'"

L. 139: The writing is the *Chunqiu*, or *Annals*, of the state of Lu, which is attributed to Confucius. Han Confucians often referred to Confucius as *su wang* 素王 (uncrowned king). The final entry in the *Chunqiu* reads: "In the fourteenth year, in spring, on a hunt to the west, we captured a unicorn." Although there are various interpretations of the significance of the unicorn's appearance, Ban Gu must have believed the unicorn arrived as a tribute to Confucius's fidelity.

Ji Xin was roasted alive guarding his lord;
The Hoaryheads could not be deterred from nurturing their resolve.
Plants and trees are divided into many classes;
130 As long as they bear fruit they will flourish.
One strives that after death his name shall not perish;
This was the standard of the ancients.
Behold the vast unfolding of Heaven's net!
In truth it aids the sincere, offering them instruction.
135 When one seeks the Great Way of former sages,
He will neighbor the virtuous and assist the faithful.
Yu's "Shao" music was so beautiful it attracted a phoenix;
A thousand years later Confucius forgot the taste of meat.
The uncrowned king's writing was so faithful it brought forth a
      unicorn;

L. 140: In the Han period Confucius was honored in various ways. The Han founding emperor, Gaozu, visited Lu and made a special sacrifice, presumably at the Confucian temple. See *Shi ji* 47.1946 In A.D. 1 one of Confucius's descendants, Kong Jun 孔均, was enfeoffed as Marquis in Recompense for Perfection 褒成侯, and Confucius was given the posthumous name Duke Xuanni 宣尼 in Recompense for Perfection. See *Han shu* 12.351; and Dubs, *HFHD* 2. 69.

L. 143: Yang Youji 養由基 was a famous archer from Chu. The king of Chu ordered him to shoot a gibbon. Before he could release his bow, the gibbon, which was alarmed by Yang's intense concentration, began to howl. This and the following line are examples of the great effect of vital essence (*jing* 精) and spirit (*shen* 神). See *Huainanzi* 16.10b.

L. 144: Li Guang 李廣, one of Emperor Wu's generals, once went out hunting. He saw a rock in the grass that he thought was a tiger. He hit the rock with such force his arrow penetrated it to the end of the shaft. See *Shi ji* 109.2871; and Watson, *Records of the Grand Historian of China* 2: 141.

L. 147: The minor skills include shooting such game as gibbons and tigers.

L. 149: Taihao 太昊 is another name for Fuxi.

L. 150: The dragons are the sages.

L. 151. Cf. *Lun yu* 4/8: "At dawn hear the Way, and at dusk die content." The expression *zhen guan* 貞觀 (correct view) comes from the "Great Commentary" of the *Classic of Changes* (*Zhou yi zhushu* 8.3a, 178): "The Way of Heaven and Earth is to perceive things correctly."

L. 153: Pengzu 彭祖 and Laozi were reputed to have lived a long time.

L. 155: This is a direct quotation from the "Commentary on the Decision" of hexagram 3 in the *Classic of Changes* (*Zhou yi zhushu* 1.28b, 33).

L. 156: Cf. *Classic of Changes*, "Commentary on the Decision," hexagram 24 (*Zhou yi zhushu* 3.19b, 77): "Does not Return [the name of hexagram 24] reveal the mind of Heaven and Earth"? See also *Lun yu* 15/28: "It is man who makes the Way great and not the Way that makes Man great."

L. 163: Cf. *Mengzi* 6A/10: "Life is something that I desire. Rightness is also something that I desire. If I cannot obtain them both, I shall reject life and choose rightness."

LL. 169–70: Cf. *Classic of Changes*, "Great Commentary" *Zhou yi zhushu* 8.13a, 183. "The Master said, 'To know the infinitesimal, is that not godlike?'"

140 In a different era the Han honored his descendant.
　　Vital essence communicates with the spirits and affects other things;
　　Spirit activates *pneuma* and penetrates the unseen world.
　　Yang Youji cast a glance and a gibbon howled;
　　Li Guang shot at a tiger but split a rock instead.
145 Without vital essence or power how could they have an effect?
　　If they lacked substance would who believe them?
　　If even such minor skills must be effected this way,
　　How much more so when immersing oneself in the Way.
　　Up to Taihao and down to Confucius,
150 Many dragons have woven their woofs and wefts.
　　If at dawn my view is correct, I die at dusk content;
　　This is like forgetting self and casting off the body.
　　If I could follow Pengzu or Laozi,
　　I would speak with future sages and tell them my feelings.
　　The Finale says:
155 When Heaven created things out of dim darkness,
　　It determined their nature and fate.
　　Returning to original nature, broadening the Way—
　　Only the sage and worthy can do so.
　　A vast primal force propels things;
160 It flows and never stops.
　　Preserving self, bequeathing a good name,
　　These are examples for men to follow.
　　Choosing what is right and rejecting life
　　Is to follow the workings of the Way.
165 To be afflicted with grief and die young,
　　Nothing is more disgraceful than this.
　　Keep yourself unsullied and pure—
　　Why change colors?
　　I hope to reach the infinitesimal,
170 And enter the realm of the gods.

LL. 1–2: The profound teachings are literally "dark instructions" (*xuan xun* 玄訓) that Zhang Heng sees residing above. Since *xuan* is synonymous with Heaven, presumably the source of these teachings is Heaven. Cf. *Lun yu* 9/10: "Yan Yuan said, 'I look up to them [Confucius's teachings], and they are ever more lofty.'"

L. 3: Cf. *Lun yu* 4/1: "A neighborhood's benevolence is what constitutes goodness."

L. 7: Cf. "Li sao," LL. 289–90 (*Chuci buzhu* 1.29b): "As long as my inner soul is fond of goodness, / Why do I need a matchmaker?"

L. 11: The *Wen xuan* reads *tuantuan* 慱慱; the *Hou Han shu* reads *tuantuan* 團團. Both are probably variants of *tuantuan* 慱慱 (sad). See Zhu Jian, *Wen xuan jishi* 14.3b. The expression occurs in *Mao shi* 147/1: "My weary heart is twisted with grief." The banner flapping in the wind is a figure for mental torment and anguish. Cf. *Zhanguo ce* 14.6b: "Lying down, I am not at ease, and eating, I do not enjoy the taste. My heart flutters like a streamer, and I cannot decide anything."

L. 12: Cf. *Mao shi* 147/3: "My heart full of sorrow / Feels as if tightly bound."

L. 13: The girdle is am emblem of virtue. Cf. *Baihu tongyi* 4.4b. "The reason one must wear girdle pendants is to display one's virtue and show one's abilities."

L. 14: Both the night-glower and carnelian branch represent firmness and purity. Cf. "Li sao," L. 218 (*Chuci buzhu* 1.24a): "I break a carnelian branch and add it to my girdle."

# 15

## ASPIRATIONS AND FEELINGS, PART II

# Rhapsody on Contemplating the Mystery

## ZHANG PINGZI

### I

I admire the profound teachings of the former sages;
However lofty they may be, never shall I go against them.
Other than a neighborhood of benevolence, where can one live?
Other than the path of propriety, what can one follow?
5    Holding them deep in my heart, long do I ponder them;
Through passing days and months my devotion does not flag.
Deep in my soul I remain true and good,
And yearn for the upright integrity of the ancients.
Standing straight and erect, I comply with the norms,
10    And never stray from the marking-line.
My heart, twisted with grief, is like a fluttering streamer;
Yet my devotion and resolve remain firm as if tightly bound.
I display my virtue and conduct by making girdle pendants;
On them I wear night-glowers and a carnelian branch.

ACCORDING TO THE *Hou Han shu* (59.1914), Zhang Heng (*zi* Pingzi) wrote this rhapsody while he was serving as palace attendant during the reign of Emperor Shun 順 (reg. 126–144). "The emperor took him behind the palace curtains, where Zhang gave criticism and advice. The emperor once asked Heng who were the most hateful men in the empire. Fearing that he would malign them, the eunuchs all glared at him. Heng gave an evasive response and left. Still fearing that Heng would make trouble for them, the eunuchs all slandered him. Heng constantly pondered the question of how he should act. He believed that good and bad fortune were intertwined, and their dark subtleties were hard to understand. He then wrote 'Contemplating the Mystery' to express his thoughts and feelings." In this rhapsody Zhang Heng poses for himself the question of whether in the face of a corrupt

LL. 15–16: The thoroughwort and gracilary are conventional figures for good virtues. Cf. "Li sao," L. 210 (ibid. 1.23a): "Knotting thoroughworts, I wait in indecision"; and "Li sao," L. 11 (ibid. 1.4a): "I dressed in gracilary and shady angelica."

L. 18: Cf. "Li sao," L. 328 (ibid. 1.32b): "The fragrance, sweet and strong, does not fade."

L. 25: The Two Eights are the eight sons of Gaoxin and the eight sons of Zhuanxu. They were all employed by Shun. See *Zuo zhuan*, Wen 18 (Legge, *The Chinese Classics* 5: 280, 282).

L. 26: Fu Yue 傅説 worked as a builder at the cliffs of Fu. King Wuding of the Yin dynasty saw him in a dream. He then summoned him to his court and appointed him a minister. See Jia Yi, "Rhapsody on the Houlet," this volume, LL. 41–42n.

L. 31: The simurgh and phoenix represent men of virtue.

15  I tie on the autumn blossoms of the thoroughwort,
Fasten to it the fragrant gracilary.
In their multifold beauty the fragrance is strong;
Truly long-lasting, it will not fade.

My raiment is truly fair and without peer,
20  But it is not prized in this present age.
I scatter my blossoms but no one sees them;
I waft my sweet scent but no one smells it.
Quiet and content, I abide in this lowly place;
But dare I shirk hard work for idleness and sloth?
25  I felicitate the Two Eights for meeting Shun,
Rejoice that Fu Yue lived in the time of Yin.

I revere the mores handed down by former worthies,
Sorrow that I am born too late to meet them.
Why do I walk alone in solitude?
30  Why do I stand apart, cut off from the crowd?
I am moved by the simurgh and phoenix, who nest alone,
And grieve that the good man rarely accords with the world.

## II

But why grieve that the good man does not accord with the world?
For the thing to fear is falseness concealing the truth.

---

world of slander and hostility he should escape to a realm far from his home, or whether he should remain in the world, and in spite of adversity persist in the cultivation of his character. To resolve the question he undertakes a long imaginary journey, in which he visits the gods of each of the four directions. On his journey he consults diviners, who offer him advice on how he should proceed. Each place he visits offers him no comfort from his despair, and he concludes that the unseen world not only provides no solace, but in fact cannot be known or trusted. At the end of the piece Zhang rejects the idea of the imaginary journey, and resolves to return to his home, where he continues to study ancient classics, write poetry, and lead the life of a country scholar. For a fuller discussion of the piece see Knechtges, "A Journey to Morality."

The text of this piece also is found in *Hou Han shu* 59.1914–39. For a modern annotated text see Zhang Zhenze, *Zhang Heng shiwen ji jiaozhu*, pp. 195–241. There are translations by von Zach, *Die Chinesische Anthologie* 1: 217–28; and Obi and Hanabusa, *Monzen* 2: 242–71. For *baihua* translations see Chen Hongtian et al., *Zhaoming wen xuan yizhu* 2: 786–824; Li Jingying, *Zhaoming Wen xuan xinjie* 2: 146–73; and Chi et al., *Lidai fu cidian*, pp. 201–11.

Li Shan often cites an anonymous work designated as the Old Commentary. The date and authorship of this commentary are not known.

LL. 35–36: When King Wu of Zhou was gravely ill, Zhou Dan 周旦, duke of Zhou, made a prayer sacrifice to the gods offering to die in King Wu's place. After obtaining confirmation of his request through divination, he placed the prayer in a metal-bound coffer. King Wu recovered and lived for another five years. After King Wu's death, his younger brothers Guan Shu 管叔 and Cai Shu 蔡叔 slandered Zhou Dan to King Cheng, Wu's successor, accusing him of disloyalty. Zhou Dan left the court. Shortly thereafter the metal-bound coffer was opened, and King Cheng discovered that Zhou Dan was a paragon of loyalty to the Zhou house. This story is the subject of the "Jin teng" 金縢 ("Metal-bound Coffer") chapter of the *Shang shu*; see *Shang shu zhushu* 13.6a–14a (415–19).

LL. 37–38: Line 38 literally reads: "I fear they will set up laws in order to endanger my person." These lines are based on *Mao shi* 254/6: "The people have much perfidy; / Do not set up your own laws." This line probably refers to the eunuchs who had slandered Zhang Heng.

LL. 39–40: Cf. Yan Ji, "Lamenting Time's Fate," LL. 145–46, *Chuci buzhu* 14.8a: "Alone and distraught, I am vexed and tormented; / How can I expel my anger and unfold my feelings?"

L. 45: The striped tiger represents poverty and low position; challenging the elephant stands for spending one's full effort. *Shizi*, B.3a, seems to be the source of this and the following line: "Zhonghuang Bo 中黃伯 [who lived during the time of the Yellow Lord] said, 'With my left hand I grasp the ape of Taihang; with my right I attack the striped tiger. It is only the elephant against which I have not tested myself. I was deluded by this. A strong man would wish to be an ox and would like to test himself in a contest against an elephant. Now you gentlemen consider this the way to propriety. Why should I test myself against such things? Poverty and privation are my ape of Taihang; estrangement from the court and low position are my striped tiger of propriety. I daily encounter them, and they are a sufficient test for me.' "

L. 46: Zhang Heng here is saying that he will brave any danger to preserve propriety. Cf. *Shizi*, B.3b: "The state of Ju had a boulder called Jiaoyuan 焦原. Eight feet wide and fifty paces long, it overlooked a chasm of a hundred fathoms. No one in the state of Ju dared to approach it. There was a man who, on account of his bravery, was invited to visit Ju. Only he could walk backward over the boulder with both heels together. In this way he won over the state of Ju. Propriety is as high as Jiaoyuan [following the *Hou Han shu* 59.1917, n. 5 reading]. Therefore, a worthy man in his propriety must walk with both heels together. In this way he can win over the world."

L. 47: Cf. *Zuo zhuan*, Wen 18 (Legge, *The Chinese Classics* 5: 282): "Jiwen sent the grand scribe Ke to reply as follows: 'The late grandee Zeng Wenzhang taught Hangfu [Jiwen] the rites by which to serve his ruler. He received them and applied them everywhere.' "

L. 48: The You Mao text of *Wen xuan* reads 惡 for 要 of the *Hou Han shu* and the *Liuchen zhu Wen xuan*. The *Wen xuan* reading is difficult to construe. Hu Shaoying (*Wen xuan jianzheng* 17.9b) suggests that 惡 is an error based on graphic similarity to 要.

LL. 49–50: Cf. "Li sao," LL. 89–90 (*Chuci buzhu* 1.12a): "Truly the world is cunning and crafty; / Ignoring square and compass, they change the measures."

LL. 51–52: The southernwort (*xiao* 蕭) and mugwort (*ai* 艾) are foul-smelling plants that represent men of base virtue. The fragrant sweet basil and angelica stand for worthy men.

LL. 53–54: The famous beauty Xi Shi 西施 and the fabulous steed Yaoniao 腰褭 represent men of talent.

L. 57: Cf. "Distant Roaming," L. 9 (*Chuci buzhu* 5.1b–2a): "I ponder the infinitude of Heaven and Earth."

L. 58: Cf. *Zhou yi*, "Wen yan" commentary (*Zhou yi zhushu* 1.14b): "Ascent and descent follow no constant rule."

35    Zhou Dan was slandered by his younger brothers;
Only after the metal-bound coffer was opened was he again trusted.
Upon viewing the perfidies of the multitudes,
I am afraid they shall use the law to do me harm.

Vexed and tormented, I am perplexed and confused;
40    Alas, to whom can I express my plaint?
Gravely worried, I deeply ponder my lot;
My thoughts, tangled and confused, are disordered.
I vow to give my all in preserving propriety;
Although poor and destitute, I shall not change my course.
45    I shall seize the striped tiger and challenge the elephant;
Approaching Jiaoyuan, I shall stop with my heels at the chasm's
          edge.
I hope to uphold these principles and apply them everywhere,
Pursuing them relentlessly until I die.

The world shifts and moves with changing events,
50    Destroying the round of the compass, the straightness of the square.
It values southernwort and mugwort and stores them in layered
          boxes,
While they call sweet basil and angelica unfragrant.
They expel Xishi and deprive her of favor;
They harness Yaoniao to draw their carts.
55    Men of depraved conduct attain their ambitions,
While he who sets norms and standards encounters disaster.
I ponder the infinitude of Heaven and Earth;
How inconstant the fate that one meets!

L. 62: Zhang Heng here uses a common *Chuci* formula. Cf. "Li sao," L. 62 (*Chuci buzhu* 1.9b): "This is not what my heart considers important"; "Grieving I Make My Plaint," L. 30 (ibid. 4.3b): "This is not what my heart aims for"; "Nine Changes," VII, 8 (ibid. 8.10a): "This is not what my heart enjoys."

LL. 63–64: Cf. *Mao shi* 130/2: "The lord has arrived, / Wearing patterned robe and embroidered gown."

LL. 63–68: The sartorial images here all represent Zhang Heng's virtues of goodness and integrity. In L. 67, the *Wen xuan* reads *diaolu* 琱璖 for *diaozhuo* 雕琢 of the *Hou Han shu*. Hu Shaoying (*Wen xuan jianzheng* 16.10b) argues that 璖 should be read *zhuan* 瑑, which is graphically similar to *zhuo* 琢.

L. 69: Zhang Heng's desire presumably is to live long enough to implement the teachings of the sages for the benefit of the world.

L. 70: The Spirit of Brightness (Yao ling 耀靈) is the sun. Cf. "Distant Roaming," L. 42 (*Chuci buzhu* 5.3b): "Resplendent, the Spirit of Brightness traveled west."

L. 71: Cf. "Mountain Spirit," L. 16 (ibid. 2.21a): "Since the year is late, who will adorn me with flowers?"

L. 72: The call of the cuckoo at the autumnal equinox was thought to sound the end of summer, and thus was a sign from nature that plants and flowers were about to wither and die. Zhang Heng probably alludes here to "Li sao," LL. 299–30 (ibid. 1.30b–31a), in which Qu Yuan says: "I fear the untimely call of the cuckoo, / Which causes the many flowers to lose their fragrance." For Qu Yuan and Zhang Heng, the loss of fragrance represents failure to influence the world with their virtue.

LL. 73–74: The thrice-blooming herb (*san xiu* 三秀) is the mushroom (*zhi* 芝), which reputedly bloomed three times in a year. Zhang Heng here is alluding to "Mountain Spirit," L. 17 (ibid 2.2a), which refers to the thrice-blooming herb used by a shaman to "adorn" himself. Zhang Heng uses the plant to represent virtue that is attacked by the biting frost of slander. The figure of dew changing to frost has an antecedent in *Mao shi* 129/1.

L. 75: Cf. "Nine Changes," L. 17 (*Chuci buzhu* 8.3a): "The seasons inexorably advance: they have already passed midpoint"; and "Distant Roaming," L. 41 (ibid. 5.3a): "I fear the alternating sequence of Heaven's seasons."

L. 77: The *Hou Han shu* and the *Wuchen* version of the *Wen xuan* read *du* 妒 (jealous) for *gou* 姤 (evil) of the You Mao text.

L. 78: Han Zhong 韓終 (or 眾) was an alchemist of Qi. He gathered herbs for a king who refused to eat them. Han Zhong then ate them himself and became an immortal. See *Lexian zhuan* as cited in *Chuci buzhu* 5.2b–3a. Cf. "Li sao," L. 94 (*Chuci buzhu* 1.12b): "I would rather quickly die and flow off into oblivion."

L. 81: Cf. "Li sao," L. 278 (ibid. 1.28b): "I wished to follow Ling Fen's auspicious oracle, / But my heart was undecided, uncertain."

L. 82: Mount Qi 岐 (northeast of modern Qishan 岐山, Shaanxi) was the home of King Wen of Zhou. See *Mengzi* 1B/5.

L 83: Lord Wen is King Wen of Zhou, the reputed compiler of the *Zhou yi*, or *Classic of Changes*.

L. 84: Zhang Heng alludes to hexagram 33 ䷠, titled Dun 遯, "Fleeing" or "Retiring." The line-text for the top line reads: 飛遯, 无不利 "Flying into retirement. Nothing unfavorable." The reading for the *Zhou yi* followed by Zhang Heng differs from that of the Wang Bi text (*Zhou yi zhushu* 4.8b, 97), which has *fei* 肥 (fat) for *fei* 飛 (fly). Zhang Heng seems to have followed a Han reading. See Hui Dong, *Zhou yi shu*, p. 161

L. 85: The lower trigram of the Dun hexagram is Gen ☶ 艮, which, according to the "Explanations of the Trigrams" chapter of the *Zhou yi*, is a symbol for mountain. See *Zhou yi*

Not compromising one's standards and yet seeking acceptance in the
      world,
60   Is like trying to cross a river without a craft.
To court favor by resorting to cunning smiles
Is something my heart cannot bear.
I don the patterned robe of gentility and reverence,
Dress in the embroidered gown of ritual and propriety,
65   Weave uprightness and clarity for my belt,
Combine skill and learning as my girdle pendants.
Resplendent are their colored patterns and carved designs;
The sounds of my pendant jades carry long and far.
Long do I linger to give free rein to my desires;
70   But suddenly the Spirit of Brightness hides in the west.
I rely on an understanding friend to adorn me with flowers;
But the cuckoo has called, and flowers have lost their fragrance.
I had hoped for three blooms in one year,
But I was beset by white dew turning to frost.
75   The seasons inexorably advance, alternating in sequence;
In whom can I find a proper companion?
Alas, it's hard for evil and goodness to coexist;
I would like to follow Han Zhong and flow off into oblivion.
I fear that even with time I could not emulate him;
80   Yet by remaining in the world I shall be obscured and unnoticed.

## III

My heart still is undecided, uncertain,
And thus to Mount Qi I go and unfold my feelings.
Lord Wen lays out the milfoil stalks for me;
" 'Tis favorable to fly and flee to preserve your good name.
85   Cross the mountains and travel far and wide;

*zhushu* 9.10a, 198. Thus, the oracle predicts travel to the mountains. This refers to Zhang's travel to the remote mountains of the west below.

L. 86: The lower nuclear trigram (lines 2–4) of the Dun hexagram is Xun ☴, which represents the wind; thus, the reference to flying off on the wind.

L. 87: If the top line of the Dun hexagram is changed to a broken line, one obtains hexagram 31 ䷞, titled Xian 咸, "Influence" or "Wooing." Xian consists of two trigrams, Dui ☱, "Youngest Daughter," and Gen ☶, "Mountain" (Zhang Heng's "lofty peak"). Dui, combined with the lower nuclear trigram (lines 2–4) Xun ☴, "Eldest Daughter," give the "two maidens" of Zhang Heng's text. This oracle predicts Zhang Heng's encounter with two beautiful goddesses in the western mountains (see LL. 265–66 below). The word *gan* 感 (aroused) is used here because it is the meaning assigned to the hexagram Xian in "Commentary on the Decision." See *Zhou yi zhushu* 4.1b.

L. 88: The meaning of this line is not entirely clear. Ice is derived from Qian 乾 ☰, the upper nuclear trigram (lines 3–5) of the Xian hexagram. According to "Explanation of the Trigrams," one of the attributes of the Dui ☱ trigram is "breaking and splitting." The idea that Zhang Heng probably wishes to convey is that even though it is favorable for him to undertake a long journey to meet the two maidens, the road he travels will be difficult. Li Xian (*Hou Han shu* 59.1932, n. 1) says this line predicts Zhang Heng's decision to leave Fu Fei and the Jade Maiden of Taihua in L. 290 below. Hu Shaoying (*Wen xuan jianzheng* 17.11a) proposes that *ying* 瀯 should be understood in the sense of *huo* 惑 (confused). Following his interpretation, the line would be rendered: "Perhaps ice breaks, but one is not confused." I find this contorted explanation does not contribute much to understanding this enigmatic line.

LL. 89–90: When the Dun hexagram changes to Xian, the upper trigram Qian, or Heaven, becomes Dui, which represents the lake (*ze* 澤). Thus, although Heaven is high and hard to reach, as represented by the transformation of Dun into Xian, the situation is changeable, and thus the journey can still be undertaken ("the road is smooth").

L. 91: Cf. *Zhou yi*, hexagram 1, "Commentary on the Images" (*Zhou yi zhushu* 1.8a, 23): "Heaven's movement is strong. The gentleman strengthens himself and never rests."

L. 92: The Qian trigram represents jade. According to the Old Commentary (*Wen xuan* 15.4b–5a), the jade stairs are the stairs of the imperial palace. This means that even though Zhang Heng "wishes to leave, he still longs for the jade steps and does not wish to go. That is to say he still desires to offer his loyalty and wisdom to the emperor."

L. 93: "Short" should designate milfoil stalks, while "long" refers to the tortoise shell. See *Zuo zhuan*, Xi 4 (Legge, *The Chinese Classics* 5: 141). However, since Zhang Heng resorts to tortoise shell divination in the line that follows, possibly he intends long and short to refer to the varying length of the milfoil stalks.

L. 94: The eastern tortoise is one of six types of tortoise the *Zhou li* mentions as being used for divination. See *Zhou li zhushu* 24.19a (1736). In Chinese correlative thought, east represents green. Thus, the eastern tortoise presumably was green.

L. 95: The great bird is the crane, a symbol of retirement and reclusion. Cf. *Mao shi* 184/1: "The crane calls in the ninth marsh."

L. 97: Wang Niansun shows that *bie* 瞥 should be understood as *bie* 撇 (to strike; to brush against). See *Dushu zazhi*, "Zhiyu," B.33a–b.

L. 99: The eagle and osprey represent vicious slanderers.

L. 100: The "I" refers to the crane, which in turn represents Zhang Heng.

L. 101: The dark bird is the crane.

L. 102: The Mother is the Tao. Cf. *Laozi* 52: "The world has an origin. It may be called the Mother of the world. He who has understood the Mother understands her sons.

Wing on the swift wind to spread your fame.
Two Maidens are aroused on a lofty peak;
Perhaps ice breaks and is not repaired.
The canopy of Heaven is high, yet becomes a lake;
90   Who says the road is not smooth?
Strive unceasingly to strengthen yourself;
Tread the towering steepness of the jade stairs."
Fearing the "long and short" of the milfoil diviner,
I drill the eastern tortoise to view my fortune.
95   I meet the great bird of the ninth marsh;
He complains that his basic wishes are unfulfilled.
He roams beyond the dusty world and touches the heavens;
Clinging to the gloomy darkness, he sadly cries.
The eagle and osprey pursue their greedy desires,
100  While I cultivate purity to enhance my fine name.
"Thou hast affinity with the dark bird;
Return to the Mother and thou shalt find peace."

## IV

Since the oracle is auspicious and predicts no harm,
I choose a propitious time and make ready to depart.

He who has understood the sons and keeps to the Mother will never be imperiled his entire life."

LL. 105–6: Cf. "Distant Roaming," LL. 73–74 (*Chuci buzhu* 5.5a–b): "At dawn I wash my hair in Dawn Valley; / At dusk I dry myself at Nine Yang."

L. 107: Cf. "Distant Roaming," L. 75 (ibid. 5.5b): "I sip the flowing liquid of gushing springs."

L. 109: The Old Commentary (*Wen xuan* 15.5b) explains *xuan* 翾 as "to fly." Wang Niansun points out that this meaning does not fit with "fish leaping." He convincingly shows that *xuan* means "swift." See *Dushu zazhi*, "Zhiyu," B.34b–35a.

L. 111: Shaohao 少皞, also known as Jintianshi 金天氏 (see L. 147 below), reputedly lived in Qiongsang 窮桑 or Kongsang 空桑, which Zhang Heng refers to as Qiongye 窮野 (Remote Wilderness). Commentators locate Qiongsang in the eastern state of Lu. See *Zuo zhuan zhushu* 53.9b (4611), Du Yu's commentary (Zhao 29); and *Huainanzi* 8.6a, Gao You's commentary. For more detailed accounts of Qiongsang, see *Zuo zhuan*, Zhao 17 and 29 (Legge, *The Chinese Classics* 5: 667–68, 731); Karlgren, "Legends and Cults," p. 208; and Chan Ping-leung, "Zhongguo gudai shenhua xinshi liangze," pp. 206–10. Traditionally, Shaohao is identified as sovereign of the west, but here Zhang Heng clearly associates him with the east.

L. 112: The three hills are the three mountain islands of the immortals in the Eastern Sea: Penglai, Fangzhang, and Yingzhou. Goumang 句芒 is god of the east.

L. 113: The True are the immortals.

L. 116: Zhang Heng alludes to a legendary giant turtle that carried Penglai Island on its back. See "Celestial Questions," L. 83 (*Chuci buzhu* 3.13b).

LL. 119–20: The returning cloud means "evening cloud." On Fusang, see Xie Zhuang, "Rhapsody on the Moon," this volume, LL. 30–31n.

L. 122: For the term *hangxue* 沆瀣 (midnight vapors), see *Chuci buzhu* 5.4a.

LL. 123–24: The tree-grain (*mu he* 木禾), an auspicious tree that grew in the wastes of the Kunlun Mountains, is described as five hundred feet tall and five spans in circumference. See Yuan Ke, *Shanhai jing jiaozhu* 6.294.

L. 125: On Dawn Valley, see Xie Zhuang, "Rhapsody on the Moon," this volume, LL. 30–31.

L. 126: Lord Yu 伯禹 refers to Yu's title as earl of Chong. See *Shang shu zhushu* 3.21a (284). Yu once convened a meeting of his vassal lords in the Mao 茅 Mountains, which he renamed Guiji 會稽. (Ji is an abbreviated form for Guiji). See *Wu Yue chunqiu* 6.3b.

LL. 127–28: The *Wen xuan* reads *jia* 嘉 (to praise) for the *Hou Han shu*'s *ji* 集 (to assemble). The spirits refer to the rulers of the mountains and rivers whom Yu assembled in the Guiji Mountains. In L. 127, Zhang Heng borrows from a *Zuo zhuan* passage (Ai 7; Legge, *The Chinese Classics* 5: 814) that says "Yu assembled the lords on Mount Tu 塗 [a peak of the Guiji Mountains]. Those bearing jade and silk numbered ten thousand states." According to the *Guo yu* (5.10b–11a), when Yu assembled the spirits at Guiji, Fangfeng 防風 (Wind Blocker?), the ruler of Wangmang 汪芒, arrived late, and Yu had him put to death. See also *Han Feizi* 5.10a; *Shi ji* 47.1912; Chavannes, *Mh* 5: 312–14; and Karlgren, "Legends and Cults," p. 305. Presumably Fangfeng broke his word (lit., "ate his words") by failing to arrived on time as promised.

LL. 129–30: Chonghua 重華 is another name for the legendary sage emperor Shun. According to the *Shanhai jing*, his burial place at Cangwu 蒼梧 in the Jiuyi 九嶷 Mountains was located "within the bounds of Lingling 零陵 and Changsha." See Yuan Ke, *Shanhai jing jiaozhu* 13.459.

LL. 131–32: The two consorts are the wives of Shun, E Huang 娥皇 and Nu Ying 女英. According to some sources, when Shun died they did not go to Cangwu to mourn for him,

114

105 At dawn I wash my hair in a limpid fount,
And dry myself in the morning sun.
I sip the flowing liquid of gushing springs,
Chew the fallen petals of stone mushrooms.
Swift as a soaring bird, a leaping fish,
110 I journey through the eight wastes.
Crossing Shaohao's Remote Wilderness,
I ask Goumang about the three hills.
How pure and untainted the Way of the True!
I shed my filthy bonds and make myself light.
115 I climb Penglai and sally about;
Although a giant turtle thrashes the water, the island does not topple;
I stay at Yingzhou and gather mushrooms,
Hoping with them to prolong my life.
Riding a returning cloud I go off into the distance,
120 And spend the night at Fusang.
I drink the jade elixir from green crags,
Eat midnight vapors for sustenance.
At night I conjure up a dream of the tree-grain,
Growing high on Kunlun's peaks.

## V

125 At daybreak I travel to Dawn Valley,
And accompany Lord Yu to Ji Mountains.
I admire the host of spirits who carried jade,
And detest Fangfeng for breaking his word.
Following an indirect route to Changsha,
130 I visit Chonghua amongst the southern neighbors.
I grieve that his two consorts never joined him there,
But flew off to dwell by the banks of the Xiang.

but remained in the area of the Jiang and Xiang rivers. Some sources claim they became the goddesses of the Xiang River. For a summary of the various accounts, see Zhu Jian, *Wen xuan jishi* 14.9a–10a.

LL. 133–36: Chongli (see Ban Gu, "Rhapsody on Communicating with the Hidden," this volume, LL. 77–78n.) was buried on Mount Heng 衡 (modern Nanyue 南岳, Hunan). Li Xian (*Hou Han shu* 59.1922, n. 3) cites Sheng Hongzhi's *Jingzhou ji*, which says: "South of Mount Heng there is the grave of Chongli, Regulator of the South. During the time of King Ling of Chu, the mountain collapsed, thus destroying his grave."

L. 138: The *Hou Han shu* reads *yuao* 愉敖 for *aoyou* 遊遨 of the *Wen xuan*. According to the *Sihai tu* 四海圖 (Map of the World?) cited by Li Shan (*Wen xuan* 15.7a), Angzhou 卬州, located south of the regions of Jiao 交 and Guang 廣 (modern Guangdong), was a place of extreme heat.

L. 139: Kunwu 昆吾 is a volcano in the extreme south. The *Shenyi jing* 神異經 (Canon of Divine Marvels), cited in *Hou Han shu* 59.1922, n. 5, reports that it was forty *li* high and four to five *li* wide. According to the *Huainanzi* (3.10a), when the sun reaches Kunwu, it is high noon.

L. 145: Cf. "Nine Changes," I, L. 9 (*Chuci buzhu* 8.2b): "Desolate, he wanders with nary a friend."

L. 147: The Old Commentary (*Wen xuan* 15.7b) identifies Jintian 金天 as Shaohao. In some sources, Shaohao is associated with the element metal, and thus he was identified as the sovereign of the west. However, since Zhang Heng mentions visiting Shaohao during his travels to the east (see L. 111 above), this line would seem to refer to another deity. Hu Shaoying (*Wen xuan jianzheng* 17.14b) identifies Jintian as Rushou 蓐收. The *Zuo zhuan* (Zhao 29; Legge, *The Chinese Classics* 5: 731) says he was Master of the Metal Phase. Rushou also is associated with the west in "Distant Roaming," L. 114 (*Chuci buzhu* 5.7b): "I meet Rushou in the western heaven." If Jintian refers to Shaohao, the only way to construe the line is to understand *gu* 顧 in the strict sense of "to look back at." Although he is in the south, by going west he removes himself even farther from the eastern home of Shaohao. Thus, he heaves a sigh. I have deliberately left the line ambiguous.

L. 149: Zhurong is the sovereign of the south. See Ban Gu, "Rhapsody on Communicating with the Hidden," this volume, LL. 77–78n.

L. 150: The Vermilion Bird (Zhu niao 朱鳥) is the guardian of the southern sky. It also is an astral configuration that designates the seven lunar mansions that occupy the Southern Palace of the heavens. See *Shi ji* 27.1299.

L. 151: The Jian mu 建木, which I have tentatively rendered "Standing Tree," is a mythical tree located in the southern mountains of Duguang 都廣 (also called Guangdu 廣都). The *Shanhai jing* describes it as shaped like an ox, with leaves like gauze, and fruit resembling a pomelo. See Yuan Ke, *Shanhai jing jiaozhu* 10.279. The *Huainanzi* (4.3a–3b) says that it was the tree on which the heavenly lords ascended from and descended to earth. The exact location of Duguang or Guangdu is not known. According to Guo Pu (see ibid. 11.291), it was the site of Houji's grave. Some authorities claim it is another name for Chengdu, Sichuan. See ibid.18.445, n. 1.

L. 152: The Ruo Tree lay west of the Standing Tree. See Xie Zhuang, "Rhapsody on the Moon," this volume, LL. 30–31n.

L. 153: Xuanyuan 軒轅 is the state of the Yellow Lord. See Yuan Ke, *Shanhai jing jiaozhu* 2.51, Guo Pu's commentary.

L. 154: The dragon fish is described as resembling a carp. It lived in the highlands north of Sishe 四蛇, near Xuanyuan. Wangshi 汪氏 probably is a variant for the area of the remote west called Womin 沃民 or Woye 沃野 (Fertile Wilds). See *Huainanzi* 4.4a; Yuan Ke, *Shanhai jing jiaozhu* 7.222–23; and Hu Shaoying, *Wen xuan jianzheng* 17.15a–b.

Wandering my gaze over Mount Heng's crags,
I sight Chongli's ruined grave.
135 I sorrow that the Fire Regulator has no place to return;
His solitary soul has been entrusted to the mountain slopes.
With grief welling deep within me, I yearn for the distance;
I cross Angzhou and wander happily.
I ascend Kunwu when the sun reaches noon,
140 And rest in a place seared by blazing fire.
It throws up sparks and flames that redden the sky;
Water froths and foams, spurts and spouts.
A warm wind, blowing hard, increases the heat;
Distraught and sad, I cannot rest at ease.
145 Wandering alone, with nary a friend,
How can I remain here?

## VI

Looking toward Jintian, I heave a sigh;
I shall go west to seek enjoyment.
I order Zhurong to go before me and raise the signal flag;
150 Following behind is the Vermilion Bird, who carries the banner.
I halt at the Standing Tree in Guangdu.
Pause to pluck Ruo's blossoms.
I traverse Xuanyuan in the Western Sea,
Stride across Wangshi and its mighty dragon fish.

L. 155: The people of the land of Xuanyuan reputedly had a longevity of eight hundred years. See Yuan Ke, *Shanhai jing jiaozhu* 7.221 and the corrected reading as cited in *Hou Han shu* 59.1923, n. 4.

L. 157: The nine lands refer to the nine regions.

L. 158: On Rushou, see L. 147n above.

L. 161: White Portal (Bai men 白門) is the farthest reaches of the southwest, where the metal pneuma is generated. See *Huainanzi* 4.4b.

L. 163: Weak River (Ruo shui 弱水) flowed at the base of the Kunlun Mountains. Its name reputedly came from its inability to float even something as light as a goose feather. See Yuan Ke, *Shanhai jing jiaozhu* 11.407.

L. 164: Huayin 華陰 literally is the north ridge of Mount Hua. It also was the name of a prefecture (modern Huayin, Shaanxi) near the Luo River.

L. 165: Pingyi 馮夷 here probably is Lord of the He, the supreme deity of the Yellow River. According to Gao You (*Huainanzi* 11.10a), Pingyi was a native of Dishou 隄首 hamlet of Tongxiang 潼鄉 in Huayin.

L. 167 Lord Xuan is the Yellow Lord. Li Xian (*Hou Han shu* 59.1925, n. 6) says this line refers to the story of the Yellow Lord casting a bronze tripod at Hu 湖 (the Tang prefecture of Hucheng 湖城, southwest of modern Ruicheng 芮城, Shanxi), near the Yellow River and Mount Hua. He then rose up to heaven as an immortal, and thus "never returned." According to the *Shi ji* (28.1394), the Yellow Lord cast the tripod at the base of Mount Jing 荊山, just north of Huayin.

L. 169: It is not clear exactly what Helin 河林 refers to. There is a Helin that the *Shanhai jing* locates in the Aoan 敖岸 Mountains. However, even the learned Guo Pu does not seem to know much about it. See Yuan Ke, *Shanhai jing jiaozhu* 5.124. Helin could also simply mean "Yellow River groves." This seems to fit the context of the next line, which alludes to a *Classic of Songs* piece about an islet in the Yellow River.

L. 170: "The Osprey" is the title of *Mao shi* 1. The opening lines read: "*Gwa, gwa* calls the osprey, / On an islet in the River." Wang Niansun (*Dushu zazhi*, "Zhiyu," B.35a-b) shows that "The Osprey" was commonly interpreted in the Han as an admonitory piece directed against the licentiousness of court ladies. See *Han shu* 60 2669, 60.2683.

L. 173: "The distant" may refer to the Way of Heaven, and the near, the Way of Man. Cf *Zuo zhuan*, Zhao 18 (Legge, *The Chinese Classics* 5: 671): "The Way of Heaven is far, but the Way of Man is near."

LL. 177-78: Niu Ai 牛哀 was ill for seven days and turned into a tiger. When his elder brother entered his room to look in on him, Niu Ai pounced on him and killed him. See *Huainanzi* 2.2b.

LL. 179-80: Bieling 鼈令, a man of Jing 荊, died, and his corpse disappeared. During this time Wangdi 望帝 ruled the town of Pi 郫 at the foot of the Min Mountains in Shu. Bieling's corpse floated down the river to Pi, where it was found by Wangdi. Wangdi had the corpse revived, and he appointed Bieling his minister. Bieling was able to tame a great flood that soon inflicted the Pi area. Later, Wangdi had sexual relations with Bieling's wife. Ashamed of his conduct, Wangdi abdicated his throne to Bieling. Bieling's imperial title, Kaiming 開明, was assumed by five generations of his descendants. See *Shu wang benji* 蜀王本紀 (Basic Annals of the Kings of Shu), "Quan Han wen," in Yan Kejun, *Quan shanggu Sandai Qin Han Sanguo Liuchao wen* 53.5a.

L. 182. The Master of Fate (Siming 司命) was the deity who controlled life and death. In the "Nine Songs" of the *Chuci* there are two songs dedicated to him. See David Hawkes, *The Songs of the South*, pp. 109-12.

LL. 183-84: Lady Dou 竇姬 refers to Empress Dou of Emperor Wen of the Former Han. Lady Dou's home was in Qinghe 清河 (east of modern Qinghe, Shanxi). When she

155 I have heard of the thousand-year-olds of this state;
But how can this give me any pleasure?


## VII

Pondering the different customs of the nine lands,
I go forth in pursuit of Rushou.
Suddenly my spirit transforms, and I shed my old body;
160 Pure essence now is my friend and companion.
Marching through White Portal, I gallop eastward,
Where I trek the midst of the wilds.
I ford the burbling waters of Weak River,
Halt at an islet in the rapids of Huayin.
165 I shout to Pingyi to clear the ford;
Rowing a dragon boat, he ferries me across.
But Lord Xuan has not yet returned;
Sadly I wander about, pacing to and fro.
As I rest in the thick grass of Helin,
170 I praise "The Osprey," which was a warning to women.


## VIII

The Yellow Lord's spirit arrives, and I ask him my fate:
"In seeking the Heavenly Way, where do I go?"
He says, "Trust the near, doubt the distant;
The Six Classics failed to write about this.
175 The path of the spirits is dark and hard to explore;
Who can understand and follow it?
When ill, Niu Ai transformed into a tiger;
Even his own brother he was bound to eat.
Bieling died, and his corpse disappeared,
180 Yet later he assumed the Shu succession, and for many generations
                his clan ruled.
The process of life and death is complex and uneven;
Even the Master of Fate does not comprehend it.
Lady Dou wailed as she traveled the road to Dai;
Later, she was blessed as empress and her family flourished.

was selected to be included in a group of women who were to be presented to the Han kings, she expected to be sent to Zhao, which was near her home. The eunuch in charge mistakenly included her in the group to be sent to Dai 代. When the time came for her to make her journey, Lady Dou burst into tears and refused to go. She departed only after much persuasion. In Dai, the king bestowed on her great favor, and when he eventually became emperor, Lady Dou was named empress. Her son was Emperor Jing, and members of her family held high positions at court. See *Shi ji* 49.1972–73; Watson, *Records of the Grand Historian of China* 1: 383–84; and *Han shu* 97A.3942–43.

LL. 185–86: Lady Wang is Empress Wang, the daughter of Wang Mang. Wang Mang arranged for her to marry the boy emperor Ping 平 (reg. A.D. 1–6), and she was named empress. After Emperor Ping's death, Wang Mang took the throne for himself. Claiming illness, Empress Wang refused to attend court. When Wang Mang was assassinated, her palace caught fire and she committed suicide by throwing herself in the flames. See *Han shu* 97B.4009–11.

LL. 187–88: The gray-browed commandant refers to Yan Si 顏駟. According to the *Han Wu gushi* 漢武故事 (Precedents of Emperor Wu of the Han), cited by Li Shan (*Wen xuan* 15.9a), he held the low position of gentleman through reigns of Emperor Wen, Emperor Jing, and into the reign of Emperor Wu. One day Emperor Wu's carriage passed the office of the gentlemen, and he saw the aged Yan Si, with his huge eyebrows and white hair. Emperor Wu asked him how long he had served as gentleman Yan Si replied, "I became gentleman in the reign of Emperor Wen. Emperor Wen loved *wen* 文 (nonmartial virtues), but I was fond of *wu* 武 (martial values). Emperor Jing loved beauty, but my face is ugly. When Your Majesty ascended the throne, you loved youth, but I was already old. Thus, for three reigns I have not been successful in office. Thus, I have become old in the office of gentleman." Emperor Wu was moved by Yan Si's plight and appointed him commandant of Guiji.

LL. 189–90: Dong Xian 董賢 (fl. 5–1 B.C.) was a favorite of Emperor Ai 哀 of the Former Han (reg. 6–1 B.C.). The handsome young man served as the emperor's catamite and eventually was named grand minister of war. Emperor Ai had a large tomb built for him. After Emperor Ai's death, Dong Xian committed suicide. His body was buried in the imperial prison. See *Han shu* 93.3733–40.

LL. 193–94: Mu 穆 is the posthumous name of Shusun Bao 叔孫豹, a grandee of Lu. Niu is Shu Niu 豎牛 (Servant Niu), Shusun Bao's son. Shusun Bao was guilty of an offense in Lu and fled to Qi. At Gengzong 庚宗 he met a woman and slept with her. She gave birth to a son. While in Qi, he dreamed that the sky was pressing down upon him, and he could not hold it up. Looking around, he saw a man, black and hunchbacked, with deep-set eyes and a pig's snout. He called out to him, "Niu [Ox], help me!" He was then able to hold up the sky. Later Shusun Bao returned to Lu. The woman of Gengzong visited him and gave him a pheasant that she claimed was raised by her son. When he summoned the son, Shusun Bao discovered that he resembled the man about whom he had dreamed. He named the boy Niu and appointed him a servant in his household. Later, when Shusun Bao became ill, Niu plotted to seize control of the Shusun clan. He shut his father in a chamber, refused him all visitors, and gradually starved him to death See *Zuo zhuan*, Zhao 4; and Legge, *The Chinese Classics* 5: 598–99. The *Wen xuan* reads *jie* 屆 (to reach) for *fu* 負 (to support) of the *Hou Han shu*.

LL 195–96: Bo refers to Bo Chu 伯楚, the style name of Bodi 勃鞮, a eunuch in the state of Jin. Duke Xian of Jin sent Bodi to attack Chonger, the future Duke Wen, at Pucheng 蒲城. As Chonger was escaping, Bodi cut off his sleeve. Later, after Chonger assumed the throne in Jin, Bodi warned him that the ministers Lü Sheng 呂甥 and Ji Rui

185 Lady Wang flourished in the Han court,
    But in the end, harboring grief, she died heirless.
    The gray-browed commandant fell into obscurity as gentleman,
    But after three reigns he met Emperor Wu.
    At twenty, Dong Xian wore ministerial robes;
190 They built him a royal tomb, but he never occupied it.
    Fortune and misfortune are intertwined;
    They are constantly reversing and shifting with no fixed rule.
    Mu, who dreamed the sky was pressing down on him, was pleased
             with Niu;
    But this man wreaked havoc on the Shusun clan and imprisoned his
             master.
195 Duke Wen resented Bo for cutting off his sleeve,
    But this same eunuch informed of a plot and made his lord secure.

冀芮 were conspiring to assassinate him. With the aid of Qin, Chonger was able to put down their coup. See *Guo yu* 10.12a–13a.

L. 198: The *Hou Han shu* reads *ai* 愛 (favor) for *hun* 昏 (muddled) of the *Wen xuan*.

LL. 199–200: Ying 嬴 is the surname of the First Qin Emperor. He received a warning in a prognostication text that read, "The one who destroys Qin will be Hu." Thinking that the threat came from the Hu tribes of the north, the emperor had the general Meng Tian 蒙恬 attack the Hu and seize the territory of Henan. After the death of the First Qin Emperor, Li Si 李斯 and Zhao Gao 趙高 conspired to place Hu Hai 胡亥, the emperor's second son, on the throne. Hu Hai eventually caused the downfall of the Qin empire. See *Shi ji* 6.252, 6.264.

LL. 201–2: The Old Commentary (*Wen xuan* 15.10a) and Li Xian (*Hou Han shu* 59.1927, n. 22) record the following story credited to the *Sou shen ji* (for a similar version see Wang Shaoying, *Sou shen ji* 10.123). A poor man named Zhou Chou 周韄 worked very hard in his fields. The Lord of Heaven took pity on him, and asked the Master of Fate, "Can he be made wealthy?" The Master of Fate replied, "He is fated to be poor, but he may borrow the assets of the unborn child named Cart [Chezi 車子]." After receiving the money, they made an agreement to return it when the child Cart was born. Zhou Chou gradually became so wealthy his assets were worth a million in cash. When the time came to repay the loan, Zhou and his wife loaded their wealth in a wagon and fled. On the road they met a husband and wife who spent the night under a cart. During the night the woman gave birth to a son, whom she named Cart. Zhou Chou then had no choice but to turn over his fortune to this boy.

LL. 203–4: Shen is Zi Shen 梓慎, a Lu grandee who once interpreted a solar eclipse as an omen of a future flood. Another official predicted there would be a drought. Zi Shen was wrong, and in the autumn there was a drought. See *Zuo zhuan*, Zhao 24; Legge, *The Chinese Classics* 5: 702. Zao is Bei Zao 裨竈, who twice predicted fire in Zheng. Both times the minister Zichan 子產 rejected his advice. After the second prediction, Zichan said, "The Way of Heaven is far, but the Way of Man is near. We cannot grasp the former. How can we understand it? How could Zao understand the Way of Heaven?" See *Zuo zhuan*, Zhao 17–18, Legge, *The Chinese Classics* 5: 668, 671.

LL. 205–6: Zhang Heng alludes here to the story of a demon of Liqiu 黎丘 in the state of Liang 梁 who was fond of assuming the form of a living person. One day an old man went to the market and got drunk. All the way home the demon, having taken the form of the man's son, scolded him. When the man recovered from his drunken stupor, he reprimanded the real son for his behavior. When the son denied the accusation, the old men realized he had been deceived by a demon. He then vowed if he were accosted by the demon again, he would kill him. The next day the old man got drunk again in the market. This time the real son, fearing that his father would not return, went out to look for him. Seeing what he thought was the demon, the father pulled out his sword and killed his own son. See *Lüshi chunqiu* 27.5b.

L. 210: Cf. *Mao shi* 206/1,2,3: "Do not brood on all of your cares."

L. 212: See Ban Gu, "Rhapsody on Communicating with the Hidden," this volume, L. 134 and n.

LL. 213–14: After five years of drought in his kingdom, Tang 湯, founder of the Shang dynasty, went to the grove of Sang 桑 and prayed to have the gods grant his people rain. He shaved off his hair, filed down his nails, and offered himself as a sacrificial victim. Rain then poured in torrents. See *Lüshi chunqiu* 9.3b–4a.

LL. 215–16: During the reign of Duke Jing 景 (reg. 515–451 B.C.) of Song, Yinghuo 熒火 (Mars) lodged in the Heart mansion (three stars in Scorpio). Frightened, the duke summoned the astrologer Ziwei 子韋 to interpret the portent. Ziwei replied, "Yinghuo is the

If discerning men do not understand how to distinguish good from
       evil,
How can the muddled and confused make proper judgments?
Ying received a warning to beware of Hu;
200  Although he prepared for an external attack, the real threat came
       from within.
Someone loaded his wealth in a wagon in order to elude a child
       named Cart;
But on the road a pregnant woman gave birth to a boy by this
       name.
Shen and Zao became prominent through their ability to explain
       Heaven,
But in predicting fire and flood they made false pronouncements.
205  The old man of Liang was vexed by the demon of Liqiu;
Encountering his son, he stabbed him with a sword.
If what one sees with his own eyes cannot be understood,
How can the hidden and dark be trusted?
Do not become entangled or led by personal concerns;
210  Brooding on your cares only makes you ill.
Heaven's purview is truly discerning;
Thus, it aids the sincere and helps the benevolent.
Tang purified his body to pray and sacrifice;
He received great blessings and thereby saved his people.
215  Duke Jing felt three concerns in managing his state;
Thus, Mars lodged in another stellar station.

punishment of Heaven. The Heart mansion is the astral field of Song. Calamities will befall you. Nevertheless, you can transfer them to the chancellor." The duke replied, "The chancellor is the one with whom I govern the state. If I transfer my death to him, that will be inauspicious." Ziwei then advised him to transfer the calamities to the people. The duke responded, "If the people die, whose ruler shall I be? I would rather die alone." Finally, Ziwei suggested he transfer the calamities to the harvest. The duke answered, "If the harvest is injured, the people will be hungry. If the people are hungry, they will die. If I act as a ruler and kill the people in order to keep myself alive, who will regard me as their ruler? Thus, my life certainly will come to an end." Ziwei then congratulated the duke on his wise response and informed him that the Yinghuo star would move three stations that night as a sign that he would prolong his twenty-one years. He explained: "Because you have thrice spoken such good responses. Heaven will thrice reward you. Tonight Yinghuo will move three stations. Each station comprises seven stars. One move of each star equals seven years. Three times seven is twenty-one. Thus, I say Your Majesty will prolong your life twenty-one years." See *Lüshi chunqiu* 6.8a–b.

LL. 217–18: Wei Ke 魏顆 was the son of Wei Chou 魏犨 of Jin also known as Wuzi 武子. Wei Chou was ill, and he ordered Wei Ke in the event of his death to make sure his favorite concubine remarried. Later, when he was more gravely ill, Wei Chou changed his mind, and ordered that the concubine be buried with him. When Wei Chou died, Wei Ke found her a husband, saying, "When my father was so very ill, his senses were confused. I will follow the charge he gave when he was in his right mind." At a later time, Wei Ke led an army to meet an invasion by Qin. The fierce warrior Du Hui 杜回 was fighting for Qin. Du tripped on a grass rope in a field and was captured. At night Wei Ke dreamed that the old man who had made the rope said to him, "I am the father of the woman whom you provided with a husband. Because you followed the charge your father gave you when he was in his right mind, I have thus recompensed you." See *Zuo zhuan*, Xuan 15; Legge, *The Chinese Classics* 5: 326, 328.

LL. 219–20: Gaoyao 咎繇 was a minister of punishments under Shun. The line "Gaoyao goes forth to sow his virtue" is taken from "Counsels of the Great Yu" in the *Classic of Documents* see *Shang shu zhushu* 4.6a, 284. Ying 英 and Liu 六 are the two states in which Gaoyao's descendants were enfeoffed. See *Shi ji* 2.83, 36.1585, 91.2607.

LL. 221–22: This refers to the mulberry epiphyte (*Loranthus yadoriki* called *sangshang jisheng* 桑上寄生 that attaches itself to a mulberry and continues to flourish even after the top of the tree withers. This analogy illustrates that the descendants of Gaoyao continued to flourish after the other states were destroyed. See Li Xian in *Hou Han shu* 59.1928, n. 31 and Li Shan in *Wen xuan* 15.11b.

L. 223: Cf *Mao shi* 256/6: "There is no word that goes unanswered; / There is no meritorious deed that goes unrequited."

L. 224: Cf. *Zhou yi*, hexagram 11, 9/3 *Zhou yi zhushu* 2.22a, 54: "There is no plain that is not followed by a slope, and there is no departure that is not followed by a return."

L. 227 Cf. Yang Xiong's "Sweet Springs Palace Rhapsody," L. 62: "Raising and lifting his head to look on high." See Knechtges, *Wen xuan* 2: 25.

L. 229. Cf. Sima Xiangru, "Rhapsody on the Great Man" *Han shu* 57B.2592: "I grieve at the pressing narrowness of the profane world."

L. 231: Accumulated Ice Ji bing 積冰 is a name for the extreme reaches of the north. See *Huainanzi* 4 4a. The binome *weiwei* 磑磑 probably is equivalent to *aiai* 皚皚 (white and glistening. See *Hou Han shu* 59.1929, n.3

L. 235: The Dark Warrior Xuan wu 玄武 is the spirit of the north. He is usually depicted as part tortoise, part snake. See *Hou Han shu* 22.774, n. 1.

Wei Ke loyally followed his father's clearminded charge;
Thus, the ghost repelled Hui, thereby defeating Qin.
Gaoyao went forth to sow his virtue;
220 The virtue he planted flourished in Ying and Liu.
An epiphyte attaches its roots to the top of the mulberry;
Although the host plant withers, it continues to grow.
There is no word that goes unanswered;
How can one depart without returning?
225 Why not journey in order to display your good name?
Who says time can be stayed?"

## IX

I raise my head and gaze into the distance;
My soul is unsettled, perplexed, without a companion.
Pressed by the narrow confinement of the central realm,
230 I shall northward go, wandering far and wide.
I walk the glistening whiteness of Accumulated Ice;
Clear springs, frozen solid, no longer flow.
Freezing winds, biting cold, incessantly blowing,
Strike lofty peaks with howling fury.
235 The Dark Warrior shrinks into his shell;

L. 236: The Leaping Serpent (Teng she 騰蛇 or 螣蛇) is a type of dragon that reputedly was able to cause clouds and mist to rise. See *Erya yishu* C4.10a.

L. 239: Greater Yin (Tai yin 太陰) here designates the extreme north, where the concentration of the yin force is greatest.

LL. 241–42: On Gaoyang and Zhuanxu, see Bun Gu, "Rhapsody on Communicating with the Hidden," this volume, L. 1n. The word "dark" (you 幽) probably alludes to the Dark Capital (You du 幽都), which was the portal of the north, where darkness gathered. See *Huainanzi* 4.5b.

L. 243: The *Wen xuan* reads *lu* 路 (road) for *luo* 絡 (weft) of the *Hou Han shu*.

L. 245: Cf. "Distant Roaming," L. 156 (*Chuci buzhu* 5.10b): "Far away we go to the world's end at the Gate of Coldness." The Gate of Coldness (Han Men 寒門) is a mountain in the extreme north. See *Huainanzi* 4.4b.

L. 246: Buzhou 不周 is a mountain of the extreme northwest, where the Dark Capital was located. See *Huainanzi* 4.4b.

L. 249: Zhang Heng may be referring to the subterranean passage at Buzhou that led to the underworld.

L. 252: The subterranean goat (*fenyang* 墳羊) is a creature that reputedly lived deep underground. See *Guo yu* 5.7a.

L. 255: The *Hou Han shu* reads 右密 for 石密 of the *Wen xuan*. I am not sure what 石密 might mean. 右密 means "Mount Mi of the west." Mount Mi probably is the same as Mount Mi 峚, which the *Shanhai jing* locates 420 *li* northwest of Buzhou Mountain. See Yuan Ke, *Shanhai jing jiaozhu* 2.41; Zhu Jian, *Wen xuan jishi* 14.11a; and Hu Shaoying, *Wen xuan jianzheng* 17.19a.

LL. 257–58: The Candescent Dragon (see Xie Huilian, "Rhapsody on Snow," this volume, LL. 75–76n) dwelled on Mount Zhong 鐘山, which the *Shanhai jing* locates 420 *li* northwest of Mount Mi. See Yuan Ke, *Shanhai jing jiaozhu* 2.42.

LL. 259–60: Carnelian Ravine (Yao xi 瑤谿) was located east of Mount Zhong. Above it was the scarlet precipice called Carnelian Cliff (Yao ya 瑤崖). Zujiang 祖江 seems to be another name for a man named Baojiang 葆江. According to the *Shanhai jing*, the son of Mount Zhong was a spirit named Gu 鼓 (also written Fu 敷), who had a human face and dragon body. He and another spirit killed Baojiang on the southern slope of Kunlun. The Lord of Heaven then executed them at Carnelian Ravine. See Yuan Ke, *Shanhai jing jiaozhu* 4.42.

L. 261: "Silver terrace" (*yin tai* 銀臺) is a common name for the residence of a god or immortal. See *Shi ji* 28.1378; and *Hou Han shu* 59.1931, n. 4. The Queen Mother is Xi Wangmu, who resided on Mount Yu 玉山, which the *Shanhai jing* locates 350 *li* west of Kunlun. See Yuan Ke, *Shanhai jing jiaozhu* 2.50.

L. 262: The *Bencao jing* 本草經 (Canon of Herbs), cited in *Hou Han shu* 59.1931, n. 5, says jade mushroom (*yu zhi* 玉芝) is another name for white mushroom (*bai zhi* 白芝), which is one of the six principal types of mushrooms. See *Bencao gangmu* 28.1709.

L. 263: The Queen Mother of the West is often described as "wearing a headdress" (*dai sheng* 戴勝); see Yuan Ke, *Shanhai jing jiaozhu* 2.52, 16.407. In one place this headdress is called *sheng zhang* 勝杖 (ibid. 12.306), the precise meaning of which is unclear. The *sheng* is commonly depicted in Han art. It usually consists of "a pair of jade discs that are linked by a straight rod" (Loewe, *Ways to Paradise*, p. 105).

L. 265: The Jade Maiden (Yu nu 玉女) of Taihua 太華 was a goddess of Mount Hua (located south of Huayin). She was a Taoist deity, probably identical to the Hairy Maiden (Mao nü 毛女) mentioned in the *Liexian zhuan* B.7a. According to tradition, she once was a palace lady of the First Qin Emperor. After the fall of Qin, she fled to the mountains, where she prolonged her life eating pine needles. See Pokora, *Hsin-lun*, pp. 247–48, n. 19.

The Leaping Serpent twists and coils itself.
Scales quivering, fish freeze into the ice;
Alighting on trees, birds slip from branches.
Sitting in a sealed chamber in the land of Greater Yin,
240 I sigh and sob and am increasingly sad.
I resent that Gaoyang divined this dwelling;
I am indignant at Zhuanxu for residing in this dark place.
With labored effort I weave my way over the four marches;
Neither this way nor that offers any relief.
245 Gazing toward the Gate of Coldness at the world's end,
I slacken the reins and head for Buzhou.
A swift whirlwind rapidly pushes me along;
Light and fast I gallop, unimpeded.
I dash through a yawning, gaping cavern,
250 Drift over a deep, plunging pool,
Cross the quiet stillness of layered shadows,
Pity the subterranean goat hidden so deep in the ground.

## X

I chase the wispy ephemera beneath the earth,
Overleap the formless and float above.
255 When I emerge at the dark plain of Mi in the west,
I do not know which path to follow.
I hasten the Candescent Dragon to carry the torch;
We cross Mount Zhong and rest there.
I look at the scarlet banks of Carnelian Ravine,
260 And condole with Zujiang, who was murdered here.

## XI

I am invited to the silver terrace of the Queen Mother;
She offers jade mushrooms to allay my hunger.
Wearing a headdress, smiling her pleasure,
She teases me for arriving late.
265 She sends a carriage for the Jade Maiden of Taihua,

L. 266: Consort Fu (Fufei 宓妃) is the goddess of the Luo River. She is the subject of Cao Zhi's "Rhapsody on the Luo River Goddess" (this volume).

L. 273: The *Hou Han shu* reads *yu* 璵 (fine jade) for *chen* 琛 (jewel).

L. 274: The "black and yellow" can refer to the color of the pendants (Old Commentary in *Wen xuan* 15.14a) or to silks (Li Xian in *Hou Han shu* 59.1931, n. 11). Cf. *Shang shu zhushu* 11.23b: "Its men and women basketed their black and yellow silks."

LL. 281–82: The calling crane alludes to the *Classic of Changes*, hexagram 6, 9/2 (*Zhou yi zhushu* 6.16a): "A crane calls in the shade. Its chicks answer it." The cranes and the ospreys (see *Mao shi* 1) represent conjugal harmony.

L. 283: Cf. *Mao shi* 23/1: "There is a girl harboring spring thoughts." Spring thoughts are feelings of love.

L. 286: Cf. *Mao shi* 132/1,2,3: "Why is it, why is it, / You ignore me so completely?"

L. 290: Cf. *Mao shi* 57/4: "The He's waters swell and surge." The He (Yellow River) was thought to have its source in the Kunlun Mountains. See *Shi ji* 123.3179; and *Huainanzi* 4.3a.

LL. 291–92: Cf. "Li sao," LL. 351–52 (*Chuci buzhu* 1.35a): "I signal the water-dragons to bridge the ford; / Summon the Sovereign of the West to take me across."

LL. 293–94: Mount Langfeng 閬風 was the highest peak of the Kunlun Mountains. The Storied Wall, over 11,000 *li* high, lay below the Kunlun wastes. To the west grew a tree of immortality. See *Huainanzi* 4.2b.

L. 295: Cf. "Li sao," L. 336 (*Chuci buzhu* 1.33a): "I grind jasper powder for my provisions."

L. 296: The White Water (Bai shui 白水) was one of five colored streams that had their source in the Kunlun Mountains. According to a "River Chart" (He tu 河圖) cited by Li Xian (*Hou Han shu* 59.1932, n. 4), the White Water flowed southeast into the Middle Kingdom, where it became the Yellow River.

L. 297: Shaman Xian (Wu Xian 巫咸) was one of ten shamans who lived on Mount Ling 靈山 in the Great Barrens. See Yuan Ke, *Shanhai jing jiaozhu* 16.396. An expert diviner, he performed a divination for Qu Yuan. See "Li sao," L. 279 (*Chuci buzhu* 1.28b). Zhang Heng has him interpret the dream of the tree-grain mentioned in L. 123 above.

Summons Consort Fu from the Luo River banks.
Both are winsome and fair, entrancing and alluring;
Add to that lovely eyes and moth eyebrows.
They bend their dainty waists so fine and slender,
270 Fluttering jacket ribbons of assorted hues and kinds.
They part their vermilion lips in a coy smile;
Their faces, glistening and gleaming, cast a brilliant luster.
They present me jade pendants and a studded belt,
Express their affection with black and yellow silks.
275 Although their features are fair, and their gifts beautiful,
My heart, pure and detached, finds them unpraiseworthy.
The two maidens are saddened at not being accepted;
Together they intone a poem, singing in clear voice.
Their song goes:
"Heaven and Earth combine their generative forces;
280 The hundred plants are laden with blossoms.
Calling cranes intertwine their necks;
Ospreys cry in harmonious accord.
Young maidens harbor spring thoughts;
Their spirits and souls are restless, perturbed.
285 Why does one so pure and wise,
Ignore us so completely?"

## XII

I would answer their poem, but I have no time;
Thereupon, I prepare my carriage and abruptly depart.
Gazing upon the majestic heights of Kunlun,
290 I look down upon the swollen waters of the winding He.
Subduing the sacred turtle, I bid him bear the river isle;
I cross a soaring bridge formed by krakens and dragons,
Climb Langfeng's Storied Wall,
Build a bed from the tree of immortality.
295 I grind carnelian petals for my provisions,
Dip from the White Water for my drink.
I order Shaman Xian to interpret my dream;
It truly was a good sign auspiciously divined.
"Let your good virtue flourish in proper centrality;
300 Embrace your fine grain and let it spread.

LL. 301–2: The ears of grain hanging down signify longing for home. Cf. *Huainanzi* 10.4b: "Confucius observed the three changes of grain. Sighing deeply, he said, 'The fox dies facing its burrow. Am I the head of the grain [that looks to the root]?'" Gao You explains: "When the ears of the grain hang down toward the root, this means that the gentleman does not forget his roots."

L. 304: I follow Wang Niansun, who argues that *gu* 姑 should be understood in the sense of "to rest." See *Dushu zazhi*, "Zhiyu," B.36a–b (1058).

L. 305: The officers are the gods of clouds and thunder mentioned below.

LL. 307–8: Fenglong 豐隆 is variously identified as god of clouds or god of thunder. See Zhang Yun'ao, *Xuanxue jiaoyan* 8.14a. Here he must be the god of thunder. Lightning was thought to issue from cracks in an area of the sky 2,400 *li* from earth. See *Han shu* 57B.2599, n. 5; and Zhu Jian, *Wen xuan jishi*, 11.3b. Cf. "Li sao," L. 221 (*Chuci buzhu* 1.24a): "I command Fenglong to ride off on a cloud."

L. 310: Cf. "Greater Master of Fate," L. 4 (*Chuci buzhu* 2.12a): "I cause driving rain to sprinkle the dust."

L. 311: On *yi* 輢 in the sense of "to ready a chariot," see Hu Shaoying, *Wen xuan jianzheng*, 17.21b. The flowery canopy probably is decorated with plumes.

L. 313: Cf. "Li sao," L. 281 (*Chuci buzhu* 1.29a): "The hundred spirits densely descend in full array."

L. 321: Cf. "Nine Regrets," "Thoughts on Loyalty Bent," LL. 11–12 (*Chuci buzhu* 15.9a): "I join the Five Constellations to make a banner, / Wave misty vapors for my banner."

L. 323: Hu Shaoying (*Wen xuan jianzheng* 17.21b–22a) proposes that *ling zhi* 軨帜 should be understood as *ling xuan* 軨軒 (grilled dashboard). For a detailed explanation of the term, see Knechtges, *Wen xuan* 2: 24, n. 68n.

L. 325: The supernal city is the capital of the Lord of Heaven. Cf. "Li sao," L. 365 (*Chuci buzhu* 1.36b): "As I ascend the dazzling splendor of August Heaven, / I suddenly look down on my old home."

LL. 327–28: Cf. *Li ji zhushu* 3.8b (2702): "At the front is the Vermilion Bird, taking up the rear, the Dark Warrior; on the left is the Green Dragon, on the right, the White Tiger." The white eminence is the White Tiger, the guardian deity of the west.

L. 329: Changli 長離 is a mythical bird that may be another name for the Vermilion Bird. See *Han shu* 57B.2595.

L. 330: The You Mao *Wen xuan* reads 後委衡 (rearward entrust control to) for 委水衡 (appoints as director of waters) in the *Hou Han shu* and *Wuchen* edition. Xuanming 玄冥, god of the north, was also known as Director of Waters. See *Kongzi jiayu* 6.2a. Thus, the *Hou Han shu* and *Wuchen* reading is correct. See Hu Shaoying, *Wen xuan jianzheng* 17.22a.

L. 331: Winnow Earl (Ji Bo 箕伯) refers to the Wind Master, who corresponded to the Winnow Star. This star was in charge of summoning wind and air. See Wu Shuping, *Fengsu tongyi jiaoshi* 8.303.

L. 333: Cf. "Li sao," L. 360 (*Chuci buzhu* 1.36a): "We carry cloud banners fluttering and flapping."

Since its ears hang down and look toward the roots,
You must direct your thoughts toward your old home.
Be content with harmony and tranquility, flow with the times;
Rest in the place where perfect goodness abides."

## XIII

305 I command the various officers to assemble early;
All dutifully come and greet me.
Fenglong unleashes his thunderbolts;
The fiery fissures brilliantly light up the sky.
The Cloud Master darkly masses clouds together;
310 Driving rain, in torrents, sprinkles the road.
Readying my jade-inlaid chariot, I raise the flowery canopy;
Tame a winged dragon to draw my carriage.
The hundred spirits in great numbers follow in full array;
The grouped horsemen in orderly files scatter like stars.

## XIV

315 Shaking my sleeves, I mount the chariot;
I wield a long sword, thrusting it upward and downward.
My cap, tall and high, reflects in the canopy;
My girdle, luxuriant and full, brightly glistens.
My coachman sternly adjusts the whip,
320 And my eight-horse team, prancing proudly, gallops off.
Vapor banners swell up and whirl in the sky;
Rainbow streamers flutter and flap in the wind.
Stroking the grilled dash, I look back;
My heart is burning hot like boiling water.
325 Since I admire the dazzling splendor of the supernal city,
Why am I so beguiled by home I cannot forget it?
On the left, a green patterned dragon raises a mushroom canopy;
On the right, the white eminence handles the bell.
In front, I send Changli to spread his wings;
330 To the rear, I entrust the Directorship of Waters to Xuanming.
I appoint Winnow Lord to embrace the wind;
He purges filth and dust and makes things clean.
Trailing behind me are cloud banners flapping and fluttering;

L. 334: Cf. "Li sao," L. 344 (*Chuci buzhu* 1.34a): "Jade carriage bells resound, jingling and tinkling."

L. 337: Cf. "Nine Regrets," "Raising Barriers," L. 8 (*Chuci buzhu* 15.10a): "Soaring smoothly amidst spirit hosts, upward I ascend."

L. 338: Cf. "Li sao," L. 203 (*Chuci buzhu* 1.29a): "August Heaven, blazing bright, casts off a numinous glow."

L. 339: Cf. "Li sao," L. 207 (*Chuci buzhu* 1.23a): "I bid the Celestial Porter to open the gate."

L. 341: The "All-embracing Music" ("Guang yue" 廣樂) is the music of Heaven. See *Shi ji* 43.1787, 105.2786–87.

L. 342: Cf. *Zuo zhuan*, Yin 1 (Legge, *The Chinese Classics* 5: 6): "Duke Zhuang of Zheng entered the great underground passageway and recited, 'Within the great passageway, / How harmonious the joy!' Lady Jiang came out and recited, 'Outside the great passageway, / How concordant the joy!'"

L. 343: What I have translated "musical pitches and sounds" is literally "pitchpipes and string tuner." The string tuner (*jun* 鈞) was used to tune musical pitchpipes. See *Guo yu* 3.15b–16a. Zhang Heng here expresses the ancient Chinese idea that music reflected the order and disorder of society. Cf. Huan Tan's "Qin dao" 琴道 ("Way of the Zither"): "The seven strings of the zither are sufficient to bring one into communion with the ten thousand things, and to permit one to investigate order and disorder." See "Quan Hou Han wen," in Yan Kejun, *Quan shanggu Sandai Qin Han Sanguo Liuchao wen* 15.9a; and Pokora, *Hsin-lun*, p. 182.

L. 347: The White Maiden (Su nü 素女) is a legendary musician who played a fifty-string zither for Fuxi. The song she played was so sad, Fuxi tried to make her stop. When she refused, he broke the zither in two, leaving an instrument of twenty-five strings. See *Shi ji* 12.472, 28.1396; and Watson, *Records of the Grand Historian of China* 1: 55.

L. 348: Tairong 太容 was music master to the Yellow Lord. The phrase "Think on this" (see *Shang shu zhushu* 4.4b, 283) is a warning against unrestrained pleasure.

L. 350: Cf. *Mao shi* 165/3: "When we have leisure / We shall drink this unstrained wine."

LL. 351–52: The Purple Palace (Zi gong 紫宮) was the residence of the Lord of Heaven. It also was the name of a constellation (corresponding to fifteen stars mostly in Draco) encircling the celestial pole. Taiwei 太微, the court of the Lord of Heaven, contained the thrones of the Five Celestial Lords. On these two constellations, see Schlegel, *Uranographie chinoise* 1: 508–10; and Ho, *The Astronomical Chapters of the Chin shu*, pp. 67–76.

L. 353: Cf. *Han shu* 26.1279: "The four stars within the Han River [Milky Way] are called Celestial Quadriga. The star to the side of it is called Wang Liang. Wang Liang spurs on the horses." Wang Liang 王良 (or 王梁), the charioteer of the Lord of Heaven, also is an asterism that corresponds to five stars in Cassiopeia. See Schlegel, *Uranographie chinoise* 1: 329; and Ho, *The Astronomical Chapters of the Chin shu*, p. 96. On the Celestial Quadriga, see Yan Yanzhi, "Rhapsody on the Russet and White Horse," this volume, LL. 21–22n.

L. 354: The Lofty Gallery (Gao ge 高閣), more commonly known as Raised Gallery (Ge dao 閣道), is an asterism located northeast of Wang Liang. It corresponds to six stars in Cassiopeia. See Ho, *The Astronomical Chapters of the Chin shu*, p. 89.

L. 355: The Net Cart (Wang ju 罔車) is another name for the Bi 畢 (Net) constellation (the Hyades). See Schlegel, *Uranographie chinoise* 1: 365–71.

L. 356: Blue Grove (Qing lin 青林) is another name for the Celestial Park (Tian yuan 天苑), a circular constellation of stars in Eridanus. See Schlegel, *Uranographie chinoise* 1: 364.

Jade carriage bells resound, jingling and tinkling.
335 Crossing the clear empyrean, I ascend the distant heights;
Drifting the misty murk, I journey upward.
Soaring smoothly amidst spirit hosts, I slowly advance;
The light, flashing and flaring, casts off a numinous glow.
I call to the Celestial Porter to open the door,
340 So that I may visit the Sovereign of Heaven in the Jasper Palace.
I listen to the nine movements of the "All-embracing Music";
It pours forth joyfully, harmonious and concordant.
Observing that order and disorder are expressed in musical pitches
        and sounds,
I reflect on how things begin, ponder how they end.
345 But the craving for delight and ease is never sated,
And I fear that once joy departs sadness will return.
The White Maiden strums a zither, and the melody lingers on;
Tairong sighs and says, "Think on this!"
Having restrained my passion, I calm my mind;
350 When I have leisure I shall soar away.

## XV

I leave the solemn majesty of the Purple Palace,
And arrive at the towering heights of Taiwei.
I command Wang Liang to spur on the Quadriga;
We cross the Lofty Gallery towering on high.
355 I deploy the Net Cart, its mesh broadly spread,
And hunt the vast expanse of Blue Grove.

L. 357: The Bow (Hu 弧) is an asterism of nine stars in Canis Major and Argonavis. Shaped like a bow with arrow affixed, it is aimed at the Celestial Wolf (Tian lang 天狼) to its north. See Schlegel, *Uranographie chinoise* 1: 434.

L. 358: Bozhong 嶓冢 is a mountain south of modern Tianshui, Gansu. According to a "River Chart" apocryphon cited by Li Xian (*Hou Han shu* 59.1936, n. 27), the spiritual essence of Bozhong rose to become the Wolf Star.

L. 359: The Ramparts (here Bilei 壁壘, also Leibi 壘壁), is a twelve-star constellation located west of the Quill Grove Army (Yu lin 羽林, forty-five stars in Aquarius and Piscis Austrini). It corresponds to four stars each in Aquarius, Capricorn and Pisces. The Northern Settlement (Bei luo 北落) is a single star southeast of the Quill Grove Army. It corresponds to Fomalhaut (α Piscis Austrini). See Schlegel, *Uranographie chinoise* 1: 293–94; and Ho, *The Astronomical Chapters of the Chin shu*, p. 108.

L. 360: The River Drum (He gu 河鼓) was so named because it was located in the Sky River (Milky Way). It corresponds to α, β, γ Aquilae. See Schlegel, *Uranographie chinoise* 1: 184–87; and Ho, *The Astronomical Chapters of the Chin shu*, p. 86.

L. 361: The Celestial Torrent (Tian huang 天潢) is another name for the Celestial Ford (Tian jin 天津), the stellar crossing of the Sky River. It corresponds to nine stars in Cygnus. See Schlegel, *Uranographie chinoise* 1: 207–10.

L. 362: Han in the Clouds (Yun Han 雲漢) is another name for the Sky River. See Edward Schafer, "The Sky River."

L. 363: The Twinkler or Twinkling Indicator (Zhaoyao 招搖) is a bright star that was sometimes imagined as a ninth star of the Northern Dipper. It corresponds to γ Boötes. See Ho, *The Astronomical Chapters of the Chin shu*, p. 81. The Conductors (Sheti 攝提) were two groups of three stars each, one on the left, and one on the right, located in Boötes Pointed toward the handle of the Northern Dipper, they were used to indicate time and the seasons. See Schlegel, *Uranographie chinoise* 1: 499–502.

L. 364: The Two Norms (Er ji 二紀) are the sun and moon. The Five Wefts (Wu wei 五緯) were the five known planets: Mercury, Venus, Mars, Jupiter, and Saturn.

L. 367: Cf. "Distant Roaming," L. 142 (*Chuci buzhu* 5.9b): "Flowing in an amorphic blur, alone I drift."

L. 372: The Upturned Phosphors (Dao jing 倒景) are luminous bodies in the highest part of the sky (4,000 *li* above the earth), past the sun and moon. Because sunlight and moonlight shone upward to it, it was called the region of the Upturned Phosphors. See *Han shu* 25C.1261, n. 3 and 57B.2599.

L. 375: Kaiyang 開陽 is the sixth star of the Northern Dipper. See Schlegel, *Uranographie chinoise* 1 503; and Ho, *The Astronomical Chapters of the Chin shu*, p. 74.

Drawing the fearsome Bow, bending it full,
I shoot the giant Wolf of Bozhong.
I inspect the Ramparts at Northern Settlement,
360 Beat the rumbling River Drum.
── Riding the surging swell of Celestial Torrent,
I float the fluvial flow of Han in the Clouds.
Leaning on the Twinkler and Conductors, I whirl and turn,
And perceive the continuous coursing of Two Norms and Five
Wefts.
365 Proudly prancing, supple and lissome, upward they leap, turning and
twisting;
Diversely disposed, in teeming throngs, suddenly they disperse.
Whizzing and whooshing along, flowing in an amorphic blur,
They scatter and spread, far away, passing one another.
I ride into the droning din of frightening thunder,
370 Play with the fiery flash of frenzied lightning,
Overtake the primal vapors of the boundless murk,
Pass the Upturned Phosphors, soaring on high.
All is broad, vast, stretching to infinity;
Now I can explore the realm beyond the heavens.
375 Reclining on Kaiyang, I gaze downward,
And behold my old home dimly revealed.
I am sad that living apart troubles the heart;
My feelings turn sad, and I think of returning home.
My soul is full of longing, and I look back again and again;
380 My horse leans against the chariot shaft, reluctant to go on.
Although through wandering I find enjoyment,
How can I bear the sorrowful yearning?

## XVI

Leaving the Gate of Heaven, I descend the celestial road,
Riding the whirling wind, galloping over the empty void.
385 Clouds, thickly gathered, curl round my wheels;
Wind, blowing from afar, shakes my falcon banners.
Out of this unremitting maelstrom, begloomed in darkness,
Suddenly, in a flash, I return to my old abode.

L. 391: Cf. "Li sao," L. 112 (*Chuci buzhu* 1.13b): "I refashion my former attire." Zhang Heng's attire is his moral integrity and virtue.

L. 392: Cf. "Li sao," L. 118 (*Chuci buzhu* 1.14a): "I lengthen the spangled beauty of my girdle pendants."

LL. 401–2: The *Qin cao* 琴操 (Zither Tunes) of Cai Yong 蔡邕 (133–92), cited by Li Shan (*Wen xuan* 15.19a), mentions the song "Returning to the Plow," which reputedly was composed by Zengzi after he had awakened one morning longing for his aged parents, from whom he had been separated for over ten years:

That which passes and does not return are the years;
Those who cannot be served again are parents.
Alas! Let me return to the plow!
Where can I plow? The foot of Mount Li.

According to legend, Mount Li 歷 was where Shun had once tilled the soil.

L. 405: Cf. *Zhou yi*, hexagram 1, 9/3 (*Zhou yi zhushu* 1.3b, 21): "At night [the gentleman] trembles, as if in danger."

L. 411: Cf. *Laozi* 47: "One can know the world without leaving his house."

L. 413: Cf. ibid. 7: "Heaven is eternal, Earth is everlasting."

L. 414: The water of the Yellow River was thought to run clear only during times of peace and order.

L. 419: Cf. *Lun yu* 19/25: "Heaven cannot be scaled."

## XVII

I now curb my idle indulgences of the past,
390 Rein in my desire to roam afar in wild abandon.
I refashion the flowing fullness of my former attire,
Lengthen the streaming splendor of my girdle pendants.
Their elegant pattern dazzles with vivid brilliance;
In resplendent beauty, they flutter in the wind.
395 I drive the precious equipage of the Six Classics,
Roam the plain and forest of the Way and Virtue,
Tie scriptures and texts into a net,
Chase Ruism and Mohism as my game.
I play with the alternations of yin and yang,
400 Intone sweet songs the "Odes" and "Hymns."
I praise Zengzi's song "Returning to the Plow,"
Admire the soaring steepness of Li Hill.
Day and night I never waver from my devotion to virtue;
From beginning to end I steadfastly carry out my tasks.
405 Trembling at night as if in danger, I examine my faults,
Fearful that my character still is unperfected.
As long as my heart remains straight and true,
Though no one knows me, I am not ashamed.
Silent, nonacting, my mind fully focused,
410 I now wander freely with goodness and propriety.
One can know the world without leaving his house;
Why must one exert himself on a distant journey?

## XVIII

The Epilogue says:
Heaven is eternal, Earth is everlasting, time cannot be delayed;
To wait for the Yellow River to clear only brings one grief.
415 I wished to travel afar and enjoy myself,
Ascending and descending by no fixed rule to explore the six
      directions.
Rising above, springing into the sky, I cut myself off from the world;
Light and airy, my soul soared, and I gave free rein to my desires.
But Heaven cannot be scaled, and immortals are few.

L. 420: "Cypress Boat" is the title of *Mao shi* 26. In stanza 4 the poet says: "My anxious heart is troubled and sad, / I am hated by the mass of petty men." The concluding stanza contains the following line: "I quietly brood on it, / But I cannot flap my wings and fly away." The "Mao Preface" says that this poem is about a good man who does not meet a wise ruler to employ him. Zheng Xuan explains that the boat, which should be used to transport things, is idle, drifting about aimlessly in the water. This stands for the good man who is not used and must consort with petty men. See *Mao shi zhushu* 2/1.5a–b (624).

L. 421: Song and Qiao are Chi Song 赤松 and Wang Qiao 王喬, two famous immortals.

L. 423: The profound counsels are the teachings of the sages mentioned in L. 1. The *Hou Han shu* reads *mou* 謀 for *Wen xuan's ji* 諆. Both words have roughly the same meaning of "plan," "counsel."

L. 1: The capital refers to Luoyang, where Zhang Heng served for most of his official career.

L. 3: This line is based on a proverb cited in several Han texts. Cf. *Huainanzi* 17.12a: "Standing by the riverbank and craving the fish is not as good as returning home and weaving a net." See also *Han shu* 56.2506 and 87A.3535. According to Lü Yanji (*Liuchen zhu Wen xuan* 15.25b), Zhang Heng uses this proverb to state that he vainly craved honor and wealth, and because of his lack of success, it was better to return home to cultivate his virtue.

L. 4: Cf. *Zuo zhuan*, Xiang 8: "Wait for the Yellow River to clear; can a man live long enough?" The Yellow River reputedly ran clear once every thousand years, only when the empire was well governed and well ordered. Zhang Heng is saying that he does not live in such a time. Cf. Zhang Heng, "Rhapsody on Contemplating the Mystery," this volume, L. 414.

L. 5: Cai Ze 蔡澤 was a traveling persuader from Yan. After wandering from state to state without obtaining employment, he met the physiognomist Tang Ju 唐舉, who predicted that Cai Ze would live another forty-three years. Cai Ze then persisted with his quest to find a state that would employ him. He eventually became prime minister in Qin. See *Shi ji* 79.2418.

420 Like the "Cypress Boat" poet, troubled and sad, I regretted I could
      not fly away;
Song and Qiao on their lofty perches—who can approach them?
To concentrate vitality in distant roaming causes the heart to be
      drawn away;
I thus change my course and come back to follow the profound
      counsels;
I obtained what I sought—why brood on it further?

# Rhapsody on Returning to the Fields

## ZHANG PINGZI

### I

In the capital I have spent an eternity,
With nary a wise plan to aid the world.
In vain have I stood on the riverbank admiring the fish,
And futilely waited for the Yellow River to run clear.
5    I feel the same frustrations as Cai Ze,

AFTER A LONG career at court, in 138 Zhang Heng retired to his home in Xi'e 西鄂
(north of modern Nanyang, Henan), where he wrote this short lyrical rhapsody praising the
delights of living in the countryside. He begins by explaining his reasons for retiring. First,
he modestly claims that he had served a long time in office without having any of his
plans accepted by the emperor. Second, although some men in the past have been able to
resolve their doubts, Zhang Heng finds the way of Heaven difficult to fathom, and thus he
concludes that he would be better off withdrawing from the world. The remainder of the
rhapsody recounts the pleasures he derives from living in the countryside. It is a pleasant,
warm day in the second month of spring, and the poet cheers his spirits by viewing the
burgeoning plants and listening to singing birds. During the day he hunts and fishes, and at
night he retires to his study, where he plays a zither, studies the classics, and writes poetry.
    For annotated texts see Zhang Zhenze, *Zhang Heng shuwen ji jiaozhu*, pp. 242–46; *Liang
Han wenxue shi cankao ziliao*, pp. 82–84; Li Hui and Yu Fei, *Lidai fu yishi*, pp. 63–69; Pei
Jinnan et al., *Han Wei Liuchao fu xuanzhu*, pp. 58–61; and Huang Ruiyun, *Lidai shuqing xiaofu
xuan*, pp. 33–36. For translations, see Hightower, "The Fu of T'ao Ch'ien," pp. 214–16;
A.R. Davis, in Kotewall and Smith, *The Penguin Book of Chinese Verse*, pp. xlix–l; and Obi and
Hanabusa, *Monzen* 2: 272–74. There are *baihua* translations by Chen Hongtian et al.,
*Zhaoming Wen xuan yizhu*, 2: 825–28; Li Jingying, *Zhaoming Wen xuan xinye* 2: 174–76; and
Kong Jingqing and Han Quanxin, *Liang Han zhujia sanwen xuan*, pp. 269–74.

139

L. 7: Cf. Sima Qian, "Rhapsody on the Frustrated Scholar" *(Yiwen leiju* 30.541): "The Way of Heaven is obscure."

L. 8: The Fisherman is the hermit who lectured Qu Yuan on the folly of contending with the world. See *Shi ji* 84.2486; and *Chuci buzhu* 7.1a–3a.

L. 19: This line is drawn verbatim from *Mao shi* 186/1.

L. 20: Cf. "Outpouring of Sad Thoughts," L. 68 *(Chuci buzhu* 4.18a): "Wildly gazing about, I travel south and thereby cheer my heart."

LL. 21–22: Cf. *Huainanzi* 3.2a: "The tiger roars and the valley wind comes blowing in, the dragon rises and propitious clouds gather." Zhang compares himself to the tiger and dragon, both of which are in harmony with nature.

L. 28: The *sha* 鯋 probably is the *chui sha* 吹沙, a small river fish known as the goby. See Read, *Chinese Materia Medica*, pp. 46–47. Zhu Jian *(Wen xuan jishi* 14.14b) tentatively identifies the *liu* 鰡 with the *lou* 鰦, another name for the *jian* 鰜 *(Psettodes erumei)*. Because of the uncertain identification, I have simply translated the name as "minnow."

LL. 29–30: The Spirit of Brightness is the sun. See Zhang Heng, "Rhapsody on Contemplating the Mystery," this volume L. 70n. Wangshu 望舒 is the charioteer of the moon.

L. 33: Cf. *Laozi* 11: "Galloping and hunting cause one's mind to become mad."

Who found a Tang Ju to resolve his doubts.
But the Way of Heaven is obscure and difficult to know,
And thus I join the Fisherman and share my joys with him.
Rising above the dust and dirt, I shall travel afar,
10   And bid a final farewell to worldly affairs.

## II

Then
In the finest month of mid-spring,
When the weather is fair and the air clear,
On highland and lowland vegetation luxuriantly grows,
And all plants profusely bloom.
15   The osprey thrums his wings,
The oriole sadly calls.
Neck to neck, they soar and swoop,
Crying *gwa gwa, yee yee*.
Among them I freely wander,
20   And thereby cheer my spirits,

## III

And now, I am a dragon singing in the great marsh,
A tiger howling in the mountains and hills.
Above, I let fly my slender arrow-cord,
Below, I angle in a long-flowing stream.
25   Struck by the arrow, a bird falls;
Craving the bait, a fish swallows the hook.
I fell a stray bird from among the clouds;
Dangle from my line gobies and minnows from the depths.

## IV

And then, the Spirit of Brightness suddenly shifts its rays,
30   And is soon followed by Wangshu.
I am so enthralled by the perfect pleasure of rambling and roaming,
Even as the sun sets, I am oblivious of fatigue.
Moved by the warning left by Laozi,
I shall turn my carriage back to my thatched hut.

141

L. 36: Zhou is the Duke of Zhou; Kong is Confucius.

35   I strum the sublime airs of the five-stringed zither,
     Recite the writings of Zhou and Kong.
     I take up brush and ink to write,
     To set forth the patterns of the Three Emperors.
     If I let my mind roam free beyond the material world,
40   Why need I worry about honor and disgrace?

# 16

## ASPIRATIONS AND FEELINGS, PART III

# Rhapsody on Living in Idleness

## PAN ANREN

In reading the "Biography of Ji An," whenever I came to the passage that refers to Sima An's four times rising to the rank of the nine ministers, I noticed that the good historian labeled him as a "shrewd official."[1] At this point I would never fail to lay down my book and heave a deep sigh, saying, "Ah, if there truly is a method behind shrewdness, then there must be one behind ineptitude as well." In reflecting on this, I have always thought that when a gentleman is born into the world, unless he is a supreme sage who leaves no traces behind or is a man of minute subtlety and profound understanding,[2] he must attain achievements and perform deeds that will be of use to his times. Thus, by relying on loyalty and observing fidelity he promotes virtue, and by cultivating his words and establishing his sincerity he preserves his achievement.[3]

IN THIS RHAPSODY Pan Yue recounts his disillusionment with official service and expresses delight at retirement to his country estate. He begins with a long prose introduction that contains a detailed account of the various offices he held before he took up a brief retirement between 295 and 297. The rhapsody is one of the main sources from which we can now reconstruct important events in Pan Yue's life. In the rhymed portion of the piece he first provides a description of the capital, Luoyang, including its ritual buildings, military headquarters, and educational institutions. He then follows with a delightful account of his villa in the Luoyang suburbs, with its orchards and vegetable garden. In an unusual touch for a rhapsody, Pan Yue mentions the outings taken by his mother to ease her ailments and promote the circulation of the medicine she takes. He also refers to family gatherings on the third day of the third month in which they go down to the river, float winecups in the water, and sing and dance.

For another text of this piece see *Jin shu* 55.1504-6. There are previous translations by von Zach, *Deutsche Wacht* (November 1928), rpt. in *Die Chinesische Anthologie* 1 299-33; Watson, *Chinese Rhyme-Prose*, pp. 64-71; Obi and Hanabusa, *Monzen* 2: 275-87; and Kōzen Hiroshi, *Han Gaku Riku Ki*, pp. 79-110. For *baihua* translations, see Chen Hongtian et al., *Zhaoming Wen xuan yizhu*, 2: 829-43; Li Jingying, *Zhaoming Wen xuan xinjie*, 2: 177-87, and Chi et al., *Lidai fu cidian*, pp. 302-4.

145

When I was young, I enjoyed undeserved acclaim in my village, and I disgraced the charges of the minister of works and grand commandant.[4] The master whom I served was none other than the grand minister, Duke Wu of Lu.[5] He recommended me as a flourishing talent and appointed me gentleman. When I entered service under the Ancestor of Generations, Emperor Wu, I became prefect of Heyang and Huai, gentleman of the secretariat, and adjudicator under the commandant of justice.[6] While the current Son of Heaven was in mourning,[7] I was appointed master of records to the grand tutor.[8] When the bureau chief was executed,[9] I had my name removed from the official roster and became a commoner. Soon thereafter I was restored to office and appointed prefect of Chang'an.[10] I then was transferred to the position of erudite,[11] but before I could be summoned to the court to accept the appointment, my mother became ill, and I immediately resigned from office.

From the time I took the youth cap until the age when I commenced "to understand fate,"[12] I changed positions eight times. I once advanced in rank,[13] and twice resigned.[14] I once had my name removed from the official roster,[15] and I once was unable to accept a position.[16] Three times was I transferred.[17] Although my successes and failures have something to do with fate, I rather believe what happened to me is the result of my ineptitude.

A perspicacious man, He Changyu,[18] once evaluated me by saying: "You are certainly 'inept in using your many talents.'"[19] When he refers to my "many" talents, how dare I consider myself worthy? But what he says about my ineptitude is true and amply demonstrated by the evidence.[20] At the present time, when "good and able men are in office," and "all officials properly attend to their duties,"[21] this inept person should give up the idea of gaining favor and honor. Furthermore, my esteemed mother still resides with me, and she suffers from maladies of infirmity and old age. How could I ignore my duty to remain by her side and care for her with cheerful expression merely for the sake of pursuing a petty bushel-and-peck office?

Thereupon, having seen the measure of knowing enough and knowing where to stop,[22] I hope that my desires may become like drifting clouds.[23] I have built a house and planted trees where I may roam and ramble in self-contentment. My ponds are sufficient for fishing, and the income from grain-husking can take the place of tilling the land. I water my garden, sell vegetables in order to supply food for my morning and evening meals. I raise sheep and sell dairy products in order to anticipate

L. 1: The You Mao *Wen xuan* reads *chang* 場 (garden) for *chang* 長 of the *Jin shu* and the *Liuchen zhu Wen xuan*. "Canons and scriptures" is my free rendering of *fen su* 墳素, which refers to texts attributed to Chinese antiquity. The Pseudo–Kong Anguo preface to the *Shang shu* (see *Wen xuan* 45.22a–b) gives this expression in the form of *san fen ba suo* 三墳八索 (lit., "three mounds and eight knots"). The Pseudo–Kong Anguo identifies the former as the writings of Fuxi, Shennong, and Huangdi, and the latter as the explanations of the eight trigrams. *Su* 素 is interchangeable with *suo* 索, and in this sense is interpreted as the writings of the "uncrowned king" (*su wang* 素王), Confucius. For a detailed explanation, see Zhu Jian, *Wen xuan jishi* 14.15a.

L. 3: Cf. *Mao shi* 198/5: "Clever words are like a reed organ; / They are thick skinned indeed!"

LL. 4–6: Cf. *Lun yu* 5/20: "The Master said, 'When the Way prevailed in the state, Ning Wuzi acted wise. When the Way did not prevail in the state, he feigned stupidity'"; and ibid. 15/6: "A gentleman indeed is Qu Boyu! When the Way prevails in the state, he serves. When the Way does not prevail in the state, he rolls up his principles and tucks them in his breast." Ning Wuzi 寧武子 was a grandee of the state of Wei in the seventh century B.C. Qu Boyu 蘧伯玉 was a grandee in Wei during the late sixth and early fifth centuries B.C.

LL. 7–8: Cf. *Guanzi* 20.13a: "The shrewd person has a surplus [of guile] and the inept does not have enough."

L. 12: The *Mengzi* stipulates a five-rank hierarchy, of which "lesser gentleman" (*xia shi* 下士) was the lowest. See *Mengzi* 5B/2.

L. 13: Pan Yue makes an interesting play on the term *pei jing* 陪京, which originally meant "auxiliary capital." In Zhou times, Luoyang was referred to as the "auxiliary capital." Here, Pan Yue uses *pei* in the sense of *bei* 背 (to be located at one's back). Thus, from Pan Yue's perspective the Jin capital Luoyang lay to the back of his residence. The Yi River entered the Luo River southeast of the city.

L. 14: Luoyang's markets were located in the suburbs. There were three main markets: the Metal Market (Jin shi 金市), the largest, situated southwest of the city; the Horse Market (Ma shi 馬市), to the east; and the Luoyang Prefecture Market, south of the city. See Lu Ji's *Luoyang ji* 洛陽記 (Notes on Luoyang) cited by Li Shan (*Wen xuan* 16.4a–b). Li Shan says Pan Yue's residence was near the Luoyang Prefectural Market.

L. 15: The Floating Bridge (Fu qiao 浮橋) was formed by boats linked together across the Luo River. Hu Shaoying (*Wen xuan jianzheng* 18.2b–3a) argues that *you* (\**?jioh*) 勠 is similar in meaning and pronunciation to *jiu* (\**kjioh*) 糾. The binome *youjiu* 勠糾 occurs in Wang Yanshou's "Rhapsody on the Hall of Numinous Brilliance" (*Wen xuan* 11.17b; Knechtges, *Wen xuan* 2: 271, L. 95) in the sense of "conjoined and connected" In Pan Yue's line *you* could describe the line of boats that formed the bridge

L. 16: The Divine Terrace (Ling tai 靈臺), located three *li* south of the city, was used as an astronomical observatory. See Lu Ji, *Luoyang ji*, cited by Li Shan (*Wen xuan* 16.4b)

L. 17: "Heaven's patterns" (*tian wen* 天文) is the Chinese word for the stars and planets.

L. 19: The forbidden encampments are those of the regiment of the five colonels, presumably located west of Pan Yue's residence. Lu Ji's *Luoyang ji* (cited by Li Shan, *Wen xuan* 16.4b) says the headquarters of the colonels of the five encampments was located within the city wall.

L. 21: The Xizi 谿子 was a crossbow made of the silkworm thorn that grew in the land of the southern tribe called Xizi. See *Shi ji* 69.2251, n. 7. The Jushu 巨黍 probably is an alternate name for the bow called Julai 距來 in some texts (see *Shi ji* 69.2251; *Zhanguo ce* 26.1b). Wang Niansun (*Dushu zazhi* 3.4.13a–b) has shown that the correct name for this bow is Jushu.

the expenses of the summer and winter offerings. Oh, to be filial above all else and to be amicable with one's brothers is the way the inept person engages in government.[24] Thus, I have now written this "Rhapsody on Living in Idleness" in order to sing of my situation and express my feelings. The piece goes:

## I

I have roamed the long orchards of the canons and scriptures,
Strolled the lofty courses of the ancient sages,
And thick skinned though I may be,
Within I blush before Ning and Qu.
5    When the Way prevails I do not serve;
When the Way does not prevail, I do not feign stupidity.
How insufficient my shrewdness and guile!
What a surplus of ineptitude and misfortune!

## II

Thus, I have retired to live in idleness
10   On the banks of Luo River.
My status now equals that of a recluse,
And my name is now linked with the lesser gentlemen.
With my back to the capital, gazing toward the Yi,
I face the suburbs and have the markets behind me.
15   The Floating Bridge, long-extended, directly crosses the river;
The Divine Terrace, grand and imposing, stands on high.
Here one peers into the hidden secrets of Heaven's patterns,
And explores the beginning and end of human affairs.

To the west there are the great war chariots and forbidden
        encampments,
20   With their black curtains and green banners;
The Xizi and Jushu crossbows,

L. 22: The *Jin shu* reads 歸 for 機 of the *Wen xuan*. The graph *quan* 桊 probably is a loan for *quan* 弮 (crossbow). See Zhu Jian, *Wen xuan jishi* 14.15b.

L. 24: The special "snipe-fly" arrow is probably referred to here. See *Guangya shuzheng* 8A.26a.

L. 25: Cf. *Mao shi* 177/4: "War carts ten in number / Lead off the march."

L. 27: According to Lu Ji's *Luoyang ji* (cited by Li Shan, *Wen xuan* 16.5a), the Circular Moat was located one *li* east of the Divine Terrace.

L. 30: The "sea" here is the Circular Moat pond, which was thought of as a replica of the four seas.

L. 32: The later ancestor Wen is Sima Zhao 司馬昭 (211–265), also known as Prince Wen 文王. The father of Sima Yan, he was given the posthumous title of Emperor Wen.

L. 33: Cf. *Mao shi* 304/3: "His sage reverence [of the ancestors] day by day advances."

L. 34: The Circular Moat hall was used for rites performed to honor aged men called Quintuply Experienced and Thrice Venerable.

L. 39: Harmonious Heaven (Jun Tian 鈞天) was the central part of the Nine Heavens. See *Lushi chunqiu* 13.1a. See Zhang Heng, "Rhapsody on Contemplating the Mystery," this volume, L. 341n. on the "All-embracing" Music.

L. 47: The two academies are the State Academy (Guo xue 國學), five *li* northeast of the Circular Moat, and the Grand Academy (Tai xue 太學), 200 paces east of the State Academy. See Guo Yuansheng 郭緣生 (n.d.), *Shu zheng ji* 述征記 (Notes on Journeys), cited by Li Shan (*Wen xuan* 16.6a).

LL. 49–50: The State Academy (on the right, or west) was a school for sons of noble families. The Grand Academy (on the left, or east) was an academy of learning to which men of talent, regardless of status, were admitted.

LL. 53–54: Pan Yue alludes here to *Lun yu* 11/14, in which Confucius is quoted as evaluating Zilu's progress in learning: "You [Zilu] have ascended the hall, but have yet to enter the inner chamber." The expressions "ascend the hall" and "enter the inner chamber" thus signify stages in the progress of a student's study.

Differently made but triggered alike;
Ballista stones that startle like thunder,
Speeding arrows that soar like snipe-flies:
25 All these lead off the march,
And lend luster to our sovereign's might.

To the east there are the Luminous Hall and the Circular Moat
Solemn and majestic, spacious and still,
Their surrounding groves a coiling reflection,
30 The circular sea a swirling pool.
Here the emperor carries out filial remembrance to venerate his
        father,
Honors the late ancestor Wen as counterpart to Heaven,
Worships the ways of "sage reverence" to illustrate compliance with
        Heaven,
And nurtures elders to show respect for old age.

## III

35 And then, with winter behind us, we enter into spring;
When yin recedes and yang expands:
The Son of Heaven attends to the rite of burnt offerings,
And through suburban sacrifice to ancestors he promotes propriety.
He orders the performance of the All-embracing Music of
        Harmonious Heaven;
40 And has deployed a thousand chariots, ten thousand riders.
Their uniforms, solemn and stately, are solid black;
Pipes, tooting and tweeting, play in unison.
How bright and brilliant,
Grand and glorious!
45 This is the most magnificent spectacle of ritual observance,
The most resplendent display of imperial rites.

The two academies stand side by side,
Their twin roofs seem as one.
The one on the right invites scions of the state;
50 The one on the left admits men of virtue and talent.
Students in great numbers,
Scholars of dignified demeanor:
Some "ascend the hall,"

L. 55: Cf. *Lun yu* 19/22: "What need was there for a constant master?"

LL. 59–60: Cf. ibid. 12/19: "The virtue of the gentleman is like the wind; the virtue of the lesser man is like the grass. When the wind blows over the grass it is bound to bend."

L. 61: Cf. ibid. 4/1: "A neighborhood's benevolence is what constitutes goodness. In selecting a residence, if one does not dwell in a place of benevolence, how can he attain wisdom?" Cf. Ban Gu, "Rhapsody on Communicating with the Hidden," this volume, LL. 9–10n and Zhang Heng, "Rhapsody on Contemplating the Mystery," this volume, L. 3n.

L. 62: Mencius and his mother first lived near a graveyard, but when she saw her son imitating the grave diggers, she decided to move near the market. There Mencius played at being a pedlar hawking his goods. Finally, they moved near a school, where he imitated the sacrificial and ceremonial observances of the scholars. See *Lienu zhuan* 1.10a–b.

L. 71: The *Guang zhi* 廣志 (Gazetteer of the Guang region), cited by Li Shan (*Wen xuan* 16.6b), says that the summer pears of Sir Zhang 張公, who resided in the Beimang Hills north of Luoyang, were especially sweet. The Great Valley probably is that mentioned in Zhang Heng's "Eastern Metropolis Rhapsody", Knechtges, *Wen xuan* 1: 250, L. 116. See Zhu Jian, *Wen xuan jishi* 14.16b.

L. 72: The *wubei* 烏椑 is *Diospyros Embryopteris*, or varnish persimmon. See Read, *Chinese Medicinal Plants*, p. 48, no. 187. The identity of the Marquis of Liang is not known.

L. 73: According to the *Guang zhi* (cited by Li Shan, *Wen xuan* 16.), during the time of King Wen of Zhou there were extremely beautiful soft-branch jujubes. King Wen planted them in his park.

L. 74: Zhu Zhong 朱仲 was an immortal who stole the plums of Fangling 房陵 Prefecture (north of modern Fang 房 *xian*, Hubei). For a clarification of this line, see Zhu Jian, *Wen xuan jishi* 14.17a.

L. 76: The word *tao* 桃 can apply to many varieties of trees. Pan Yue specifies here two kinds, *yingtao* 櫻桃 (cherry), and *hutao* 胡桃 (walnut). Pan Yue does not mention the third type. It could be peach or *houtao* 侯桃, a type of magnolia.

Others "enter the inner chambers."
55   Yet, in teaching there is no constant master;
     Wherever the Way resides one can be found.
     Thus, prominent officials discard their seal cords,
     Renowned princes tuck away their insignia.
     Instruction is like the action of the wind:
60   People respond as the grass bends.
     This is why it is good to dwell in a humane locality,
     And why Mencius's mother moved three times.


## IV

     And now I have established my abode,
     Built a house, and dug a pond.
65   Tall poplars reflect in the pools,
     Fragrant spiny lime bushes are planted as a hedge.
     Playful fish splash and leap,
     Lotus blossoms unfold and spread.
     Bamboo trees are lush and luxuriant,
70   There are wondrous fruits of assorted kinds:
     The pears of Sir Zhang's Great Valley,
     The varnish persimmons of the Marquis of Liang,
     The soft-branch jujubes of King Wen of Zhou,
     The plums of Zhu Zhong of Fangling,
75   All have been planted here.

     The three *tao* mark the difference between cherry and walnut;
     The two sour apples glisten with hues of crimson and white.
     Such rarities of pomegranate and grape,
     Drooping heavily, spread out at their side.
80   Black plum, apricot, dwarf cherry,
     Are dressed in profuse blooms and pretty patterns.
     Flowers and fruit glisten so brightly
     Words cannot completely describe them.

     Of vegetables there are onions, leeks, garlic, taro,
85   Green bamboo shoots, purple ginger,
     Sweet flavors of water dropwort and shepherd's purse,
     Pungent aroma of smartweed and cutchery,
     Mioga ginger clinging to the shade,

153

L. 96: The grand lady is Pan Yue's mother.

L. 115: Cf. *Lun yu* 4/21: "One must know the age of his parents. On the one hand, it is something to rejoice in, and on the other hand it is something to fear."

LL. 122–23: When Chonger was in Qi, Duke Huan offered him his daughter in marriage and twenty teams of horses. Chonger was so enthralled with his life, he said, "Since human life is so contentful and happy, who could wish for anything else?" See *Guo yu* 10.2a.

Bean leaves in season facing the sun,
90   Green mallows laden with dew,
White scallions covered with frost.
And then, in chill autumn, when heat retreats,
And in mellow spring, when cold departs,
When gentle showers have newly lifted,
95   In the six directions all is clear and bright.


## V

Then, the grand lady climbs into a plain cart,
Or mounts a light chariot,
To ride into the distance to view the royal domain,
Or nearby to tour the house and garden.
100  The movement serves to harmonize her body,
And the exertion helps to circulate the medicine.
She now partakes of more than her usual fare,
And her old ailments are cured.

We unroll long mats,
105  Line up the grandchildren.
Where willows cast their shade,
We halt our carriages.
On the hills we pluck purple fruits;
In the water we catch ruddy carp.
110  Sometimes we feast in the groves;
Other times we perform purgations on the riverbank.
My brothers and I, hair flecked with white,
Our children still young in years,
Pledging mother long life with offered cups,
115  All are both fearful and glad.

As the toasting goblets are raised,
Mother's face takes on a cheerful expression.
Floating our cups, we heartily drink;
Strings and reeds are ranged in rows.
120  Stamping feet, we rise to dance,
Raise our voices in loud singing.
Since human life is so pleasant and happy,
Who could wish for anything else?

L. 124: Cf. *Lun yu* 15/20: "What the gentleman seeks is in himself;" and ibid. 4/6: "When one sees a worthy man, he thinks of equaling him. When one sees an unworthy man, he turns inward and examines himself."

LL. 126–27: Cf. ibid. 16/1: "Qiu, a saying of Zhou Ren goes, 'He who can exert himself may join the ranks.'"

L. 130: The "many wonders" refers to the Tao. See *Laozi* 1.

## VI

In retirement I seek within to examine myself;
125 Truly my usefulness is slight and my talents poor.
I hold to Zhou Ren's fine words—
But dare I exert myself and join the ranks?
Barely have I protected my humble self;
How could I emulate the sage and wise?
130 I look up to the "many wonders" and cut off profane thoughts,
Living carefree, nurturing my ineptness to the end of my days.

SORROWFUL LAMENTS

# Rhapsody on the Tall Gate Palace

## SIMA ZHANGQING

The Filial Emperor Wu's Empress Chen had enjoyed imperial favor for a period of time.[1] She was extremely jealous, and he had her sequestered in the Tall Gate Palace.[2] Dejected and sad, she heard that Sima Xiangru was the most skillful writer in the empire. She offered one hundred catties of gold for Xiangru and Wenjun to obtain wine,[3] and she entrusted Xiangru with composing a piece that would relieve her sorrow.

THE THEME OF this rhapsody attributed to Sima Xiangru (zi Zhangqing) is the abandoned palace lady. According to the preface that is attached to it, the abandoned lady is Empress Chen 陳, who was the principal wife of Emperor Wu of the Former Han. Around 130 B.C. Emperor Wu became attracted to a beautiful singer named Wei Zifu 衛子夫. Empress Chen was exceedingly jealous and began to plot against her. After Emperor Wu was informed of her behavior, he had her dismissed and sent to live in the Tall Gate Palace. The preface says that Empress Chen commissioned Sima Xiangru to write a poem about her plight. His rhapsody reputedly was so moving, Emperor Wu allowed Empress Chen to return to her former position of favor. Scholars now agree that the preface, which contains several obvious anachronisms, could not be by Sima Xiangru. In addition, some have argued that the rhapsody section itself is not by Sima Xiangru. For a discussion of the arguments see Knechtges, "Ssu-ma Hsiang-ju's 'Tall Gate Palace Rhapsody.'"

Previous translations include von Zach, *Deutsche Wacht* (November 1928), rpt. in *Die Chinesische Anthologie* 1: 233–36; Hsu, *Anthologie de la littérature chinoise*, pp. 104–5 (abridged); Itō Masafumi and Ikkai Tomoyoshi, *Kan Gi Rikuchō Tō Sō sambun sen*, pp. 20–22; and Obi and Hanabusa, *Monzen* 2: 288–94. There are *baihua* translations in Chen Hongtian et al., *Zhaoming Wen xuan yizhu* 2: 844–52; Li Jingying, *Zhaoming Wen xuan xinjie* 2: 188–93; and Chi et al., *Lidai fu cidian*, pp. 67–69. The translation here is a revised version of Knechtges, "Ssu-ma Hsiang-ju's 'Tall Gate Palace Rhapsody,'" 54–58. For modern annotated texts, see Qu Tuiyuan, *Han Wei Liuchao fu xuan*, pp. 26–31; *Gujin wenxuan* 4: 1657–60; Li Hui and Yu Fei, *Lidai fu yishi*, pp. 52–62; Li Zhenxiang and Li Fangchen, *Lidai cifu xuan*, pp. 134–40; Bi et al., *Zhongguo lidai fuxuan*, pp. 286–96; and Jin Guoyong, *Sima Xiangru ji jiaozhu*, pp. 111–24. Studies include Xu Shiying, "'Changmen fu' zhenwei bian" and "Sima Xiangru yu 'Changmen fu'"; Chien Tsung-wu, "'Changmen fu' bianzheng," rpt. in *Han fu shi lun*, pp. 53–61; and Zhao Jian, "Changmen gong he 'Changmen fu.'"

L. 1: This opening is a convention in *fu* on beautiful women. See Hightower, "The Fu of T'ao Ch'ien," p. 170, n. 6 for a list of similar examples.

L. 2: Or "Pacing aimlessly to amuse herself," as suggested by Hu Shaoying, *Wen xuan jianzheng* 18.6a–b.

LL. 3–4: Cf. "Distant Wandering," LL. 17–18 (*Chuci buzhu* 5.2a): "My soul suddenly flew away, never to return; / My body, wasted and withered, abides alone."

L. 14: The detached palace is the Tall Gate Palace.

L. 19: This terrace presumably was located in the Tall Gate Palace compound and has nothing to do with the archival office of the same name. See *Han shu* 19A.725.

Xiangru wrote a composition designed to open up their emperor's mind, and Empress Chen again obtained favor.[4]

### I

Ah, this lovely lady,
How she paces, aimlessly, deep in thought!
Her ethereal soul has flown away never to return,
And her body, wasted and withered, abides alone.
5   Her lord promised, "I must depart at dawn, but I shall return at
            dusk;"
But in his feasting and drinking he has forgotten her.
Now displeased with her, his affections shift, and he no longer
            remembers an old favorite;
He now consorts with one who suits him better.

### II

Although my mind is dull and stupid,
10  My love shall ever remain faithful and true.
I wish the favor of an audience to present myself,
And thereby receive my lord's precious command.
I received an empty promise that I thought sincere:
I awaited him in the detached palace south of the wall.
15  I arranged humble fare, which I prepared myself,
But my lord never favored me with his presence.

### III

Disheartened in my lonely seclusion, I am absorbed in thought;
Across the sky, furious and fast, a strong wind blows.
I climb Magnolia Terrace and look into the distance;
20  My spirit, troubled and confused, spills out of my body.
Drifting clouds, thickly gathered, cover the entire sky;
The heavens turn black, and the day darkens.
The sound of thunder, rumbling and roaring,
Reminds me of the sounds of my lord's chariot.
25  A whirlwind blasts round my chamber,
Lifting the curtains, which shake and shudder.

L. 32: The simurgh goes one direction, the phoenix, another, thus symbolizing the empress's separation from the emperor.

L. 45: The "floating uprights" (*you shu* 遊樹) refer to "slanting struts" (*xie zhu* 斜柱) or "king-posts" *zhuru zhu* 侏儒柱. See Ye Dasong, *Zhongguo jianzhu shi*, p. 419.

L. 47: On the term *bolu* 欂櫨 in the sense of "bracket," see Glahn, "Some Chou and Han Architectural Terms," p. 106.

L. 48: Li Shan (*Wen xuan* 16.10a) paraphrases this line to read: "[The brackets] are gathered in assorted sizes to support the empty rafters." Wang Niansun, however, argues that *kangliang* *khang-liang* 榱梁 is a rhyming binome that means "hollow inside." See *Dushu zazhi*, "Zhi yu," B.38a–b (1059).

L. 50: Piled Boulders (Ji shi 積石) was a mountain range southwest of the Han prefecture of Heguan 河關 (west of Daohe 導河 xian, Gansu). It is a source of the Yellow River. See *Han shu* 28A.1532, 26B.1611.

Cinnamon trees, branches twined and tangled,
Send forth a fragrance pungent and strong.
Peacocks come to roost as if paying courtesy calls;
30  Black gibbons shriek and howl.
Kingfishers flock together with folded wings;
Simurgh and phoenix soar off, one north and one south.

## IV

My heart is choked with sorrow that I cannot release;
Foul humors, swelling strong, attack me within;
35  I descend Magnolia Terrace and gaze around me;
Pacing slowly, deep in the palace I walk.
The main hall solitarily reaches into the sky,
Amidst a mass of towers rising and arching upward.
I linger for a while in the eastern chamber,
40  Gazing at the decor and its unending beauty.
I push the jade-inlaid door, shake the golden knocker,
Which peals and chimes like clangorous bells.

## V

Carved magnolia serves for the beams,
Engraved ginko wood for the rafters.
45  Floating uprights, in plenteous profusion, ranged in rows,
Thickly clustered, are joined and braced together.
They are affixed with brackets made of rare timbers;
Gathered in assorted sizes, they are hollow inside.
At times they vaguely resemble natural objects,
50  Just like the lofty heights of Piled Boulders.
The multicolored hues glitter and shine back and forth,
Bright and blazing, shooting beams of light.
Mosaic tiles of assorted stones, compactly laid,
Resemble the intricate patterns of turtle shells.
55  The windows are hung with curtains of gauze and silk,
Tied with sashes made of Chu cord.

L. 58: Winding Terrace (Qu tai 曲臺) was a hall in the Everlasting Hall Palace complex. See *Han shu* 75.3175.

L. 65: The type of zither mentioned here is the *ya qin* 雅琴 (lit., "zither of restraint and decorum"). Li Shan (*Wen xuan* 16.10b) cites Liu Xin's *Qi lüe* 七略 (Seven Summaries) catalogue, which explains the meaning of *ya qin*: "Qin is a way of saying 'to restrain' [*jin* 禁], and *ya* is a way of saying 'proper' [*zheng* 正]. The gentleman observes propriety in order to restrain himself."

L. 67: *Zhi* 徵 is the fourth note of the pentatonic scale. "Flowing *zhi*" seems to be a high-pitched mode associated with melancholy tunes. Cf. "Rhapsody on the Flute," attributed to Song Yu: "They intone the shrill *shang*, / Follow the 'Flowing *zhi*'" (*Guwen yuan* 1.5b).

L. 69: "Proper tune" (*zhong cao* 中操) probably means a moderate tune. There also may be pun on *cao* in the sense of "control."

L. 78: The expression *tui si* 穨思 is ambiguous. I follow Wang Niansun (*Dushu zazhi*, "Zhi yu," B.38b), who argues that it should be understood as *tuixi* 穨息 (to sigh).

L. 88: Net (Bi 畢), or Hyades, and Mane (Mao 昴), or Pleiades, in the astronomy chapter of the *Huainanzi* (3.3a), are identified as the asterisms of the west. According to Li Shan (*Wen xuan* 16.11a), their appearance in the east indicates it is the fifth or sixth moon.

## VI

Languidly I stroke the door lintel,
Gaze toward Winding Terrace, spacious and wide.
A white crane calls plaintively—
60 A solitary bird roosts on a withered willow.
Day turns to dusk, and I am bereft of hope;
Sad and alone, I take refuge in an empty hall.
The moon suspended above shines down on me;
I pass the cool night in my cavernous room.
65 I take up my zither and change the mode,
Play a tune of unbearable sadness.
Then turning back, I strum the "Flowing *zhi*,"
Its notes first faint, then high and shrill.
I run through the melodies to find a proper tune,
70 And my feelings become ever more fervid and intense.
Those about me sadly weep,
And tears flow in streams down their faces.
Heaving long sighs, with repeated sobs,
I slip on my sandals, get up, and pace the room.
75 I pull up my long sleeves to cover myself,
And recount my past misdeeds.
Lacking the face to show myself,
I heave a sigh and go to bed.
I use sweet pollia for my pillow;
80 Fragrant iris, thoroughwort, and angelica form my mat.
Suddenly I fall asleep and begin to dream;
It seems as if my soul is by my lord's side.
Waking with a start, I see nothing;
My soul is terror-stricken, as if it had lost something.
85 The crowing of the cocks saddens me;
I get up and look at the moon's gleaming light.
I view the stars arrayed in the sky;
Net and Mane appear in the east.
I gaze toward the fading moonlight in the courtyard:
90 It is as if frost were falling in late autumn.
The night drags on and on—I feel a year has passed;
My grief becomes heavier—I cannot endure it further.
Trembling, I stand and await the dawn—

First dim and remote it becomes bright again.
95  A woman such as I can only secretly sorrow for herself;
Yet I dare not forget him, even till the end of my days.


# Rhapsody on Recalling Old Friends

## XIANG ZIQI

I lived very close to the residences of Xi Kang and Lü An. Both were men of unbridled talent. However, Xi Kang had lofty ideals yet was oblivious of human affairs, and although Lü An was bighearted, he was given to wild abandon. Later, because of a certain affair, both ran afoul of the law. Xi Kang was broadly versed in the arts, and was especially skilled at playing string and wind instruments. When he was about to be executed, he looked back at his shadow, called for his zither, and began to play.[1] When I was on my way to the west,[2] I passed by their old homes.[3] At this time the sun had reached the Gulf of Yu,[4] and the cold was icy and bitter. One of the neighbors was playing a flute, the sound of which was loud and shrill, and this made me remember the pleasures of the outings and banquets I used to have with Xi and Lü. Moved by the sounds of the flute, I began to sigh. Thus, I have composed this rhapsody.

IN THIS RHAPSODY Xiang Xiu (zi Ziqi) laments the deaths of his good friends Xi Kang and Lü An. In 262 Lü An's brother, Lu Xun 呂巽, committed adultery with An's wife. Lu Xun in turn accused Lu An of beating his mother. Xi Kang came to Lu An's defense, with the result that Sima Zhao had Xi Kang and Lu An arrested. After a brief investigation, both were executed. Xiang Xiu's preface to this rhapsody contains a brief account of Xi Kang's execution. In the body of the piece he recounts his visit to the area of Shanyang where Xi Kang once lived. For another text see *Jin shu* 49.1374–75.

This rhapsody has been translated by von Zach, *Deutsche Wacht* (January 1929), rpt. in *Die Chinesische Anthologie* 1: 236–37; Watson, *Chinese Rhyme-Prose*, pp. 61–63; and Obi and Hanabusa, *Monzen* 2: 295–98. For *baihua* translations, see Chen Hongtian, et al., *Zhaoming Wen xuan yizhu* 2: 853–57; Li Jingying, *Zhaoming Wen xuan xinyi* 2: 194–96; and Chi et al., *Lidai fu cidian*, pp. 278–79. There are numerous modern annotated texts, including *Wei Jin Nanbeichao wenxueshi cankao ziliao* 1: 234–37; Huang Ruiyun, *Lidai shuqing xiao fu xuan*, pp. 65–68; Liu Zhenxiang and Li Fangchen, *Lidai cifu xuan*, pp. 196–99; Lin Junrong, *Wei Jin Nanbeichao wenxue zuopin xuan*, pp. 133–36; Li Hui and Yu Fei, *Lidai fu yishi*, pp. 103–9; Wang Chenguang, *Wei Jin Nanbeichao cifu xuancui*, pp. 21–28; and Wei Fengjuan, *Wei Jin Nanbeichao zhujia sanwen xuan*, pp. 149–53. For a study, see Kai Katsuji, "Xiang Xiu 'Si jiu fu' shi shi."

L. 9: "Millet Song" ("Shu li" 黍離) is the title of *Mao shi* 65. It traditionally was interpreted as a lament for the old capital of Zhou, which had fallen into ruins. See *Mao shi zhushu* 4.1.3b (697).

L. 10: "Song of the Wheat in Bloom" ("Mai xiu" 麥秀) reputedly was written as a lament for the ruins of the fallen capital of Yin. See *Shi ji* 38.1620; and Chavannes, *Mh* 4: 230.

LL. 15–16: Li Si was prime minister in the state of Qin. Under the Second Qin Emperor he was condemned to be executed in the marketplace of Xianyang. As he left the prison, he took the hand of his middle son and said, "I wish I could once more go with you leading my yellow dog outside the east gate of Shangcai chasing wily hares, but is this now possible?" See *Shi ji* 87.2562; and Zhang Heng, "Rhapsody on Contemplating the Mystery," this volume, LL. 199–200n.

# I

Obeying official command, I travel to the distant capital;
Then, turning about, northward I go,
Cross the Yellow River by boat,
And pass Xi Kang's old home in Shanyang.
5   I gaze at the broad plain, bleak and lonely,
And rest my team by a corner of the city wall.
I tread the path my two friends once walked,
Pass their empty houses in a secluded lane.
I sigh over the "Millet Song," which laments the house of Zhou;
10   Grieve at "Wheat in Bloom," which sorrows over the ruins of Yin.
Pondering the past evokes thoughts of my friends;
My heart feels hesitant as I pause and pace.
Roof and ridgepole are still intact, undamaged,
But body and spirit—where have they gone?
15   Of old, when Li Si was condemned to death,
He sighed for his yellow dog with countless moans.
I grieve that Master Xi has eternally parted,
Looking back at his shadow and playing his zither.
Understanding that he was dependent on the turn of fortune,
20   He entrusted his remaining fate to the final moment.
As I listen to the moving sounds of the singing flute,
The sublime notes break off and then continue again.
I halt my chariot before I travel farther,
And take up a brush to express my heart.

L. 1: The word "vapors" does not occur in this line, which literally reads "Heaven and Earth turn and flow." Li Shan (*Wen xuan* 16.14b) says the implied subject is *qi* 氣 (pneuma, vapors). He then cites a passage from the "Yue ling" 月令 (Monthly Ordinances) chapter of the *Li ji* to illustrate his interpretation: "In early spring the vapors of Heaven descend while the vapors of Earth rise." In early winter the process is reversed. See *Li ji zhushu* 14.21b (2934) and 17.11b (2988).

# Rhapsody on Lamenting the Departed

## LU SHIHENG

Of the lifelong friends and relatives about whom I used to hear my elders recount stories, some have faded and died, and only a handful are still living. I have just turned forty, and of my dearest kin, many have passed away and only a few are still alive. And of my closest companions and most intimate friends, not even half are around any longer. Some with whom I traveled on the same road or feasted within the same hall within the past decade are dead and gone. If one pines away and grieves on this account, the extent of his grief can be known.[1] Thus, I have written a rhapsody that goes:

### I

Oh, how the vapors of heaven and earth swirl and flow,
Thickly they ascend and descend, one upon another.
Across the sky the sun drives like a racing courser;
Out of the void each season sets in with startling swiftness.
5   I sigh at the brief span of human life—
Who indeed can attain long life?

LU JI (*zi* Shiheng) wrote this rhapsody at age forty, just after witnessing the death of many friends and associates in the political turmoil of the Western Jin. In the year 300 his patron Zhang Hua was executed, and many members of the Jia Mi clique at the court also lost their lives. Although Lu Ji does not mention any person in particular, it is clear that his "Lament for the Departed" has these men in mind. Probably for political reasons, he writes in more general terms, and refers in the body of the piece to the inexorability of death, which is simply part of the natural process of change and transformation. Lu Ji does personalize his lament by focusing on his own mortality, and his awareness that he, too, will soon pass away. He ends his rhapsody by saying that he will no longer worry about the prospect of death, but will enjoy himself until his fated time comes.

Previous translations include von Zach, *Deutsche Wacht* (January 1929), rpt. in *Die Chinesische Anthologie*, 1: 237–39; Obi and Hanabusa, *Monzen* 2: 299–305; Itō Masafumi and Ikkai Tomoyoshi, *Kan Gi Rikuchō Tō Sō sanbun sen*, pp. 157–59; Kōzen Hiroshi, *Han Gaku Riku Ki*, pp. 173–90; and Lai, "River and Ocean," pp. 278–87. For *baihua* translations, see Chen Hongtian, et al., *Zhaoming Wen xuan yizhu* 2: 858–84; Li Jingying, *Zhaoming Wen xuan xinjie* 2: 197–202; and Chi et al., *Lidai fu cidian*, pp. 370–71.

L. 7: "Lady of the Xiang," L. 39 (*Chuci buzhu* 2.11b): "Time cannot be obtained a second time."

LL. 9–10: The carnelian stamens and morning mists were ingested to prolong life. Cf. "Distant Roaming," L. 56 (*Chuci buzhu* 5.4a): "I rinse my mouth in solar vapor, dine on morning mists."

L. 11: On Dawn Valley, see Xie Zhuang, "Rhapsody on the Moon," this volume, LL. 30–31.

L. 20: The morning dew that disappears once the sun comes out is a figure for the brevity of human life.

L. 23: The "sunrise only" (*riji* 日及), more commonly known as *mujin* 木槿, is *Hibiscus syriacus*, or shrubby althea. Its blossoms opened at sunrise and closed at night.

L. 29: The "ancestral roots" (*ling gen* 靈根) refer to Lu Ji's grandfather Lu Xun 陸遜 (183–245) and his father, Lu Kang 陸抗 (226–274). Cf. Zhang Heng, "Southern Capital Rhapsody" (*Wen xuan* 4.9b), L. 249: "He solidified the ancestral roots in the Xia period."

L. 30: The expression "all those near me" (*ju er* 具爾) refers to Lu Ji's brothers. Cf. *Mao shi* 246/1: "Dear are my elder and younger brothers, / None is far away, all are near." Lu Ji's elder brothers Lu Yan 陸晏 and Lu Jing 陸景 were killed in a battle just before their state of Wu was defeated by Jin in 280.

L. 31: Cf. *Shang shu*, "Grand Proclamation," *Shangshu zhushu* 13.23a: "If a father builds a house, when he has fixed the plan, his son is unwilling to lay the foundation, let alone build the structure." Here "foundation and structure" refer to the achievements of Lu Ji's ancestors.

L. 32: Here Lu Ji probably refers to the fall of the kingdom of Wu.

LL. 35–36: Cf. *Mao shi* 192/4: "The people are now in danger; / They see Heaven as dark and uncaring." The You Mao *Wen xuan* reads *jin* 今 (now) for *ming* 命 (fate) of the *Liuchen* text.

Time suddenly passes, never to be repeated;
Old age, advancing toward dusk, soon arrives.
I regret that carnelian stamens have no effect;
10   Resent that morning mists cannot be ladled.
Standing on tiptoe, I gaze toward Dawn Valley,
And grieve that sunlight remains long concealed.

## II

Alas, a stream is created by gathering water,
And its waters, frothing and foaming, daily pass away.
15   A generation is formed by gathering people,
But people steadily advance toward their evening years.
In what generation are new people not born?
In what generation do old people not die?
Each spring the plain always blooms with flowers,
20   But there is no morning on which dew remains on the grass.
Ever since antiquity this has always been true—
All things of nature are as of old.
Just like "sunrise only" on its branch—
Of its constant fading it is unaware.

25   Although unaware of its fading, this is lamentable still;
My heart is sad for it, and I sorrow for myself.
Truly since the natural process is like this,
How can I obtain a long and enduring life?
I grieve for the "ancestral roots" that fell so early,
30   Regret that of "all those near me" most are gone,
Lament that foundation and structure have collapsed and crumbled,
Sorrow that wall and tower have turned to weed-covered ruins.
My dearest kin have departed this world;
How could my closest companions be forgotten?
35   Alas, my life is now in peril!
I gaze upon Heaven—how dark and gloomy it is!

Pained in heart, sad and sorrowful, many are my cares;
Afflicted with grief, face haggard, few are my joys.
My deep-held feelings come forth, forming threads of sorrow;
40   My pent-up thoughts are stirred, giving rise to a myriad cares.

LL. 49–50: Cf. *Huainanzi* 2.14a: "On Wu Mountain, when a fire is set downwind, the ointment tree and purple mushrooms perish along with artemisia." The idea is that all plants, regardless of their goodness and nobility, equally burn up in the fire.

LL. 51–52: Li Shan (*Wen xuan* 16.15b) explains that human life does not differ in its briefness, just as the water of wave and swell are the same.

I regret the lack of joy in this age;
Singing of the past, I set down these words.
At home, my friends and kin filled halls, overflowed chambers;
Traveling forth, their teams and chariots raced hub to hub.
45    But in the end, how many years did they have?
Which of them has gone forth unscathed by death?
Some, now darkly distant, have already perished;
Only a few, now lonely and forlorn, remain.
Indeed, when the pine flourishes, the cypress rejoices;
50    But, alas, when the mushroom burns, the basil sighs.
Truly life and fate are unvarying,
For how can a single wave have different swells?
Having seen the chariots ahead overturn,
I know this road is hard indeed!
55    I gaze on my four limbs and feel profound grief,
For I fear this form, too, will likewise perish.
I am pained that I lack the means to cheer my heart,
Regret the many faces that appear before my eyes.


## III

Truly many faces appear before my eyes;
60    Where can my spirit go to obtain repose?
I seek memories of the living from echoes and images,
But looking upon their former things makes me long for them even
                more.
Walking in a wintry grove, I feel downcast and dejected;
I would enjoy spring's luxuriant growth, yet am filled with brooding.
65    Encountering the myriad things of nature gives rise to sorrow,
And I sigh that the seasons are unchanging, yet time is never the
                same.

With each passing year my cares become ever greater;
As my life's path reaches its twilight, I am tormented by my
                thoughts.
Kinsmen have steadily fallen away and become daily fewer;
70    Friends have gradually perished and hardly any remain.
I look for old companions among the living,
And find only ten out of a thousand, one out of a hundred.

L. 81: The Grand Twilight (Da mu 大暮) is death. Lu Ji wrote a *fu* on death entitled "Rhapsody on the Grand Twilight." For a text, see "Quan Jin wen" in Yan Kejun, *Quan shanggu Sandai Qin Han Sanguo Liuchao wen*, 96.8b–9a.

LL. 89–90: Cf. *Zhou yi zhushu*, "Grand Commentary," 8.3b–4a (178): "The greatest virtue of Heaven and Earth is called life, and the greatest treasure of the sages is called position." Lu Ji here declares his intention to give up his official career.

Joy passes from my heart as if forgotten;
Sorrow, springing from my feelings, comes to lodge within me.
75 I entrust my humble affection to the younger generation,
For I am growing old and am now a mere sojourner in life.

## IV

Then, slowing my pace, I calm my heart,
And ponder the workings of nature.
My spirit drifts forth, my soul sinks down,
80 And suddenly they are beyond this world.
I am now aware that all alike must go to sleep in the Grand
                    Twilight;
Thus, why boast of late passing or complain of early death?
I now look toward the coming of that fateful day;
Why let my fears trouble my heart?
85 If one is moved by autumn flowers on withered trees,
Or grieves at fallen dew on thick grass,
And is beset with deep worries that he cannot cast off,
How can this be called knowing the Way?
I shall nurture the greatest virtue of Heaven and Earth,
90 And cast off the greatest treasure of the sages.
At life's end I shall remove my heart's burdens,
And roam free and easy enjoying my old age.

L. 1: Kaiyang 開陽 was one of the southeast gates of Luoyang. It looked directly onto the Luo River.

L. 8: Cf. "Nine Movements," VIII, L. 7 (*Chuci buzhu* 8.10b–11a): "The sun, dim and dark, is about to set."

# Rhapsody on Recalling Old Friends and Kin

## PAN ANREN

When I was twelve, I had the opportunity to meet my father's friend, the venerable Yang, Marquis Dai of Dongwu.[1] At our first encounter he already knew my reputation.[2] Later, he offered his daughter to me in marriage.[3] His sons Daoyuan and Gongsi also prized the many generations of esteem between our families.[4] Unfortunately, their fated spans were brief, and father and sons passed away. I first had a personal hardship,[5] and then sought employment outside my home area.[6] It has now been nine years since I have visited the mountains of Songqiu.[7] Now as I pass through this place, heaving a sigh, I recall old friends and kin, and compose the following rhapsody:

### I

With the opening of Kaiyang Gate I set out at dawn,
And directly proceed to cross the clear River Luo.
The morning wind is biting cold;
Evening snow, whitely glistening, covers the road;
5    In the ice-clogged ruts chariot tracks have vanished;
The wheel skids, soaked with water, freeze solid.
The road is hard, and travel is difficult;
The sun, dim and dark, is about to set.
Looking up, I gaze upon returning clouds;

IN THIS RHAPSODY Pan Yue recounts his visit to the grave sites of his father-in-law Yang Zhao 楊肇 (ob. 275) and Yang Zhao's two sons, Yang Tan 楊譚 (ob. 278) and Yang Shao 楊邵 (n.d.). This visit probably took place in 284. See Lu Kanru, *Zhonggu wenxue xinian* 2: 710. Their graves were located in the Mount Song 嵩 area about fifty miles south of Luoyang.

Previous translations include von Zach, *Deutsche Wacht* (January 1929), rpt. in *Die Chinesische Anthologie* 2: 239–41; and Obi and Hanabusa, *Monzen* 2: 306–9. For *baihua* translations, see Chen Hongtian et al., *Zhaoming Wen xuan yizhu* 2: 865–69; Li Jingying, *Zhaoming Wen xuan xinjie* 2: 203–5.

179

LL. 11-12: According to the *Xi zheng ji* 西征記 (Notes on a Western Journey) by Dai Yanzhi 戴延之 (n.d.), cited by Li Shan (*Wen xuan* 16.18a), Mount Songgao 嵩高 is the Middle Marchmount. Its eastern peak was called Taishi 太室, and its eastern peak, Shaoshi 少室. The general name for the mountains is Song. The *Xiao shuo* 小説 (Collection of Tales), probably by Yin Yun 殷芸 (471-529), cited by Li Shan (*Wen xuan* 16.18a; see also Lu Xun, ed., *Gu xiaoshuo gouchen* 1: 120) contains an anecdote that reports a conversation between Fu Liang 傅亮 (374-426) and an unnamed questioner. The questioner asked, "When Pan Yue composed his 'Rhapsody on Recalling Old Friends and Kin,' he wrote: 'Before me I sight Taishi, / To the side I glimpse Songqiu.' Songqiu and Taishi are a single mountain. Why does he mention sighting one to the front and glimpsing another to the side?" Fu Liang replied, "There is a Songqiu Mountain that is seventy [this probably should read seventeen, DRK] *li* from Taishi. This is simply a mistake by the copyist." Zhu Jian (*Wen xuan jishi* 14.20b) claims that Taishi is another name for Songgao, and that the name Songqiu does not appear elsewhere as a name for Songgao. He suggests that it is used only for purposes of rhyme.

L. 18: The phrase that I translate "profound reflection" is literally "I think" (*yu si* 予思), which Pan Yue borrows from the "Yi and Ji" chapter of the *Classic of Documents* (*Shangshu zhushu* 5.1a, 296): "I think only of working hard day by day."

LL. 19-20: Lord Dai is Yang Zhao. Yuan and Si refer to Yang Tan and Yang Shao respectively.

L. 26: "Pure dust" is a figure of speech for "favor."

L. 30: The two sons are Yang Tan and Yang Shao.

L. 32: Pan Yue draws on *Lun yu* 4/25: "Virtue does not stand alone, but must have neighbors." *De* 德, which in the *Lun yu* passage means "virtue," is used in Pan Yue's line in the sense of "kindness" or "favor."

L. 41: This line is identical to line 6 of "Distant Roaming" (*Chuci buzhu* 5.1b).

10  Looking down, I see flowing springs reflecting like mirrors.
Before me I sight Taishi,
To the side I glimpse Songqiu.
The body of the Lord of Dongwu was entrusted here;
They opened up a plot and built a grave.
15  Tall and stately stand twin grave markers;
Neatly arrayed, a row of catalpas.

## II

Gazing upon these catalpas
Moves me to profound reflection.
Having offered my respects to Lord Dai,
20  I also mourn Yuan and lament Si.
Their graves rest one upon another, mound touching mound;
Cypresses, lush and luxuriant, in thick clusters are planted.
Why did they pass away so swiftly one after another?
For even the perennial grass on the grave did not change.

## III

25  From the time I first met him in my youth,
I was fortunate to be sprinkled with Lord Dai's pure dust.
He dubbed me a scholar of state,
And granted me his daughter in marriage.
Beginning with my grandfather, our families' bonds were strong,
30  And the amity of generations has continued down to the two sons.
I had hoped to grow old with them hand in hand,
And as their good neighbor, to repay their father's kindness.
This is the first time I have come here in nine years,
Only to find the house empty, silent, and the people gone.
35  Thick weeds overspread the hall steps;
The old garden has been turned into a woodpile.
I walk courtyard and corridor, pacing and pausing;
Tears, flowing in streams, soak my kerchief.
At night, tossing and turning, I cannot sleep,
40  And heaving many a deep sigh, I await the dawn.
All alone, despondent and depressed, with whom can I speak?
For now, I shall pour out my cares in this poem.

L. 1: Cf. *Mao shi* 286/1: "Pity me the little child! / Our house has met an unlucky fate!" Cf. Ding Yi's "Rhapsody on a Widow" (*Yiwen leiju* 34.601): "How unlucky was my fate, / To meet such difficulty and travail on the road of life!"

L. 3: The term *pian gu* 偏孤 "partially orphaned" refers to the death of a child's father while the mother is still alive.

LL. 5–6: "Cold Springs," *Mao shi* 32/3, expresses the torment of a mother who has lost her husband. "Tall Lousewort," *Mao shi* 202, about a child who has lost both father and mother.

# Rhapsody on a Widow

## PAN ANREN

Ren Zixian of Le'an was a man whose magnanimity embraced the entire world.[1] From youth we enjoyed a friendship that was unmatched even by affection between brothers. Unfortunately, he died at the age of twenty. What grief can compare with the passing of a good friend? Furthermore, his wife was my wife's younger sister.[2] She lost both of her parents when she was young,[3] and now after her marriage, her "heaven" has also died.[4] Ren's orphan daughter was very small and still a "babe in arms."[5] This is the greatest calamity of human life, and the suffering that brings the greatest grief. In years past, when Ruan Yu died, Emperor Wen of Wei mourned for him, and commanded Ruan's friends to compose rhapsodies for his widow.[6] I now have written an imitation of their pieces in order to express the feelings of the lonely widow. The piece goes:

## I

Alas, I was born to an unlucky fate!
I lament that Heaven, deeming me insincere, cast calamity down
      upon me.
In my early years I was alone and forsaken, a "partial orphan";
The grief, sad and painful, broke my heart.
5   Reading "Cold Springs," I still felt the lingering sighs;
Singing "Tall Lousewort," I could still hear its lasting strains.
My heart was always sad with constant longing;

PAN YUE wrote this rhapsody on behalf of his wife's younger sister, who was married to Ren Hu 任護, a boyhood friend of Pan Yue's. Ren died in 276 or 277. See Chiu-mi Lai, "River and Ocean," p. 67; and Lu Kanru, *Zhongguo wenxue xinian* 2: 668–69. The writing of a rhapsody to console a wife on the death of her husband was a well-established custom by Pan Yue's period. Among the earliest examples are the *fu* written by Cao Pi, Wang Can, and probably other poets for the widow of Ruan Yu 阮瑀, who died in 212. See Cao Pi's "Rhapsody on a Widow" in "Quan Sanguo wen," in Yan Kejun, *Quan shanggu Sandai Qin Han Sanguo Liuchao wen* 4.4a–b; Wang Can's "Rhapsody on a Widow" in "Quan Hou Han wen," ibid., 90.3a–b; and the "Rhapsody on a Widow" variously attributed to the wife of Ding Yi 丁廙 (see *Yiwen leiju* 34.601 and "Quan Hou Han wen," in Yan Kejun, *Quan shanggu*

LL. 9–10: Cf. Ding Yi's "Rhapsody on a Widow" (*Yiwen leiju* 34.601). "All girls go forth to be married; / This indeed is a constant norm of the ages."

L. 11: Li Shan (*Wen xuan* 16.20a) says "auspicious clouds" stand for the lady's parents.

LL. 13–14· Cf. *Mao shi* 4/1: "In the south there is a tree with drooping branches; / The creeper vine twines round it." The creeper vine attaching itself to the tall tree is a figure for a lady's transference of loyalty and respect to her new husband's household. Cf. Ding Yi's "Rhapsody on the Widow" (*Yiwen leiju* 34.601): "I was like the hanging lichen that clings to the pine."

LL. 15–16: Cf. Cao Zhi, "Rhapsody on a Parrot," in Zhao Youwen, *Cao Zhi ji jiaozhu* 1.57: "I regret that though my virtue is slight, favors are generously bestowed; / I fear that the beneficence of the past will cease in mid-course"; and Ding Yi's "Rhapsody on a Widow" (cited by Li Shan, *Wen xuan* 16.20a; *Yiwen leiju* 34.601): "I was fearful of receiving generous favor despite my meager virtue; / I felt as if treading on thin ice, standing on the edge of an abyss."

L. 17· Cf. Cai Yong, "Epitaph for the Wife of Minister over the Masses Yuan, née Ma" ("Quan Hou Han wen," in Yan Kejun, *Quan Shanggu Sandai Qin Han Sanguo Liuchao wen* 77.5b): "The injunctions on proper conduct, / Are like a river's flow."

L. 18 Cf. Favorite Beauty Ban, "Rhapsody of Self-commiseration," *Han shu* 97B.3985: "I spread out paintings of women to serve as guiding mirrors. / Consulting the lady scribe, I asked about the *Songs*." According to the *Zhou li*, the female scribe (*nu shi* 女史) was an official position charged with managing the ritual duties of the empress. See *Zhou li zhushu* 8.3a (1485). Although there was no such formal post in the Jin bureaucracy, Pan Yue probably was using it to designate the equivalent of a female tutor. Zhang Hua's "Admonition on the Female Scribe" in chapter 56 of the *Wen xuan* is a Western Jin piece on the subject of the female scribe tradition.

L. 20 Cf. Favorite Beauty Ban, "Rhapsody of Self-commiseration," *Han shu* 97B.3986. "I dutifully sprinkle and sweep amidst the curtains; / Ever shall I do so, until my death "

LL. 21–22. These lines allude to *Mao shi* 62/4, which is supposedly in the voice of a woman who longs for her departed husband: "With longing I pine for my lord; / It makes my heart painful."

LL. 25–26: Cf. Ding Yi's "Rhapsody on a Widow" (*Yiwen leiju* 34.601; compare the reading in Li Shan's commentary, *Wen xuan* 16 20b)· "Just as his bright blossoms had begun to flourish, / The one on whom I relied suddenly perished."

LL. 27–28: Cf Ding Yi's "Rhapsody on a Widow" (Li Shan's commentary, *Wen xuan* 16.20a; *Yiwen leiju* 34.601) "I quietly close the door, refuse to sweep the path: / Solitary, alone, I dwell in seclusion"; and Wang Can's "Rhapsody on a Widow" (*Yiwen leiju* 34.601): "I close the door, refuse to sweep the path, / And dwell in seclusion in a high hall."

LL. 29–30: Cf Ding Yi's "Rhapsody on a Widow" (*Yiwen leiju* 34.601)· "I brush the vermilion gatetower with white chalk, / Replace black drapes with a white shroud." It was customary during the mourning period to sleep on a cushion of grass and pillow made from a clump of dirt. See *Li ji zhushu* 57.10a (3601).

The longer I brooded, the deeper my cares.
All girls go forth to be married,
10  And I was betrothed to a noble clan.
Having basked in the lustrous protection of auspicious clouds,
I then received the beneficent favor of my lord.
I recalled the creeper vine growing so tenderly
That attaches its slender stalks to a tree with drooping branches.
15  I was fearful that though my virtue is slight, favors would be
            generously bestowed;
And I felt as if treading on thin ice, standing over a ravine.
I complied with the clear injunctions on proper conduct,
Modeled myself on the precepts and warnings of the lady scribe.
I carried out the winter and autumn sacrifices to show my docility
            and obedience,
20  And performed sprinkling and sweeping unceasingly throughout the
            year.

## II

Just like the *Songs* poet who sighed for her departed husband,
In vain was my longing, which only pained my heart.
How unlucky was my fate!
I met calamity from Heaven, which has been unforgiving.
25  Just as his bright blossoms had begun to flourish,
My good husband suddenly abandoned this world forever.
I quietly closed the door to dwell in seclusion;
Solitary, alone, I have no one on whom to rely.
I replace brocade cushions with a grass mat,
30  Replace silk drapes with a white shroud.
I order my wet nurse to accompany me to the place of mourning;

---

*Sandai Qin Han Sanguo Liuchao wen* 96.10a–11a), the wife of Ding Yi 丁儀 (*Wen xuan* 16.19a–22b, Li Shan's commentary), or, more probably, Ding Yi 丁廙. See Lu Kanru, *Zhonggu wenxue xinian* 2: 388. Pan Yue seems to draw heavily upon the latter piece, the parallels with which are cited in Li Shan's commentary. I shall refer to the piece below as Ding Yi's "Rhapsody on a Widow."

For previous translations, see von Zach, *Deutsche Wacht* (October 1928), rpt. in *Die Chinesische Anthologie* 1: 241–44; and Obi and Hanabusa, *Monzen* 2: 310–29. There are *baihua* translations in Chen Hongtian et al, *Zhaoming Wen xuan yizhu* 2: 870–82; and Li Jingying, *Zhaoming Wen xuan xinjie* 2: 206–13. For a modern annotated text see Liu Zhenxiang and Li Fangchen, *Lidai cifu xuan*, pp. 200–209.

LL. 35–36: Cf. Ding Yi, "Rhapsody on a Widow" (*Yiwen leiju* 34.601): "I am laden with bitter grief; to whom can I tell it? / I hug my young child to console myself"; and Wang Can, "Rhapsody on a Widow" (*Yiwen leiju* 34.601): "Carrying my child, I go out the door, / And walk with him to the eastern chamber."

LL. 37–38: Cf. "Li sao," L. 209 (*Chuci buzhu* 1.23a): "The day is growing dark and drawing toward dusk"; and "Nine Laments," "Going Far Away," L. 57 (ibid. 16.14a): "The sun, fading in the distance, declines in the west." Cf. also Ding Yi's "Rhapsody on a Widow" (*Yiwen leiju* 34.601): "The day is growing dark and is now lightless in the east; / The sun, fading into twilight, sets in the west."

LL. 39–40: Cf. Ding Yi, "Rhapsody on a Widow" (*Yiwen leiju* 34.601): "Chickens fold their wings and climb onto their roosts; / Sparrows scatter and head for their flock."

L. 45: The Spirit of Brightness is the sun. See Zhang Heng, "Rhapsody on Contemplating the Mystery," this volume, L. 20n.

L. 49: The spirit hall (*shen yu* 神宇) probably was the room in which the deceased person was put to rest. Cf. Ding Yi, "Rhapsody on a Widow" (*Yiwen leiju* 34.601): "I gaze on the empty void of the spirit hall."

L. 50: The word I have translated here as "cerements" is literally "spirit garment" (*ling yi* 靈衣). Cf. "Nine Songs," "Greater Lord of Lives," L. 13 (*Chuci buzhu* 2.13a): "My spirit garment billows in the wind."

LL. 57–58: Cf. Ding Yi, "Rhapsody on a Widow" (Li Shan, *Wen xuan* 16.21b; *Yiwen leiju* 34.601): "I am saddened that life and death are different paths"; "I shall have the coffin removed and begin the funeral procession."

LL. 59–60: Cf. Ding Yi, "Rhapsody on a Widow" (*Yiwen leiju* 34.601): "They yoke the dragon-painted hearse by the side of the gate"; and (Li Shan, *Wen xuan* 16.22a): "The funeral banner flaps and flutters in the wind."

Upon seeing his handkerchief and fan, I pour forth sorrow.
With choked sobs, I let forth a loud cry,
And tears, streaming down my face, soak my gown.

35  All of the pent-up grief in my heart, to whom can I tell it?
I carry my orphan child to the side of the bier.
The day is growing dark and drawing toward dusk;
The sun, fading into twilight, is setting in the west.
Sparrows, flying in flocks, head for their nest in the pillars;
40  Chickens climb onto their roosts and fold their wings.
I return to the empty chamber and commiserate with myself;
Stroking quilt and bed-curtain, I heave a deep sigh.
My thoughts are tangled and twisted in dark confusion;
My heart is broken and filled with bitter sorrow.

## III

45  The Spirit of Brightness, resplendently shining, swiftly proceeds on its
        course;
The four seasons are in constant rotation, changing and moving;
The congealing dew from the sky comes down as frost;
Falling leaves from the trees drop from the branches.
I look up at the empty stillness of the spirit hall,
50  Gaze on the cerements billowing in the wind.
I withdraw to a corner of the hall and inwardly grieve;
Advance to the edge of the bier and make a solitary bow.
Listening intently, I think I hear his voice of old,
And my eyes can dimly descry his former visage.
55  Although everything is so dark and hazy, nothing can be seen,
I can still vaguely sense his presence.
Saddened that life and death are different states,
I shall have the coffin removed and placed in the grave.
The dragon-painted hearse is solemnly yoked by starlight;
60  Fluttering in the wind, the funeral banner leads the way.
Following the track, the wheels slowly advance;
The horse, sadly neighing, pauses and looks back.
The soul, deeply buried, has gone far away never to return,
And I am bound up in deep cares with no one to whom I may
        confide them.

LL. 67–68: Mid-autumn is the eighth month. The widow's mourning continues into winter. Pan Yue draws on the *Classic of Changes* (hexagram 2, 6/1; *Zhou yi zhushu* 1.23a, 31): "Treading the frost. Solid ice will soon appear." Cf. Ding Yi, "Rhapsody on a Widow" (Li Shan, *Wen xuan* 16.22a): "From the time I began to be laden with grief and sorrow, / I have been through the four seasons of the entire year."

LL. 69–70: Cf. *Mao shi* 167: "Snow falls thick and heavy"; Ding Yi, "Rhapsody on a Widow" (Li Shan, *Wen xuan* 16.22a): "The wind, shrieking and howling, blows daily stronger; / Snow, in wild flurries, thickly falls."

LL. 71–72: Cf. Ding Yi, "Rhapsody on a Widow" (*Yiwen leiju* 34.601): "Frost, biting cold, falls at night; / Water, slowly crystalizing, freezes at dawn."

L. 74: Cf. "Nine Pieces," "The Outpouring of Sad Thoughts," L. 57 (*Chuci buzhu* 4.17b): "The road to Ying is distant and far, / But nine times each night my soul journeys there."

L. 78: Cf. "Lament for Time's Fate," L. 7 (*Chuci buzhu* 14.1b)· "All night, my eyes are wide open, and I cannot sleep."

L. 80: Cf. Ding Yi, "Rhapsody on a Widow" (ibid. 34.601): "The cold, freezing to the bone, is increasingly cutting."

LL. 81–82: Cf. Ding Yi, "Rhapsody on a Widow" (Li Shan, *Wen xuan* 16.22b): "Anger wells up, tangling and twisting within; / Stroking the white silk pillow, I sigh and sob."

LL. 83–84: Cf. "Nine Changes," III, 23 and VIII, 5 (*Chuci buzhu* 8.5b, 8.11a): "The year hastens by and soon will end"; and Ding Yi, "Rhapsody on a Widow" (Li Shan, *Wen xuan* 16.22b): "His soul daily recedes farther in the distance; / The year's work is suddenly done."

LL. 85–86: Cf. Ding Yi, "Rhapsody on a Widow" (Li Shan, *Wen xuan* 16.22b): "Glancing at the pale cast of my visage, / I face my companions and wipe away the tears."

LL. 87–88: The Three Good Men (San liang 三良) are three members of the Ziyu 子輿 clan who followed Duke Mu of Qin into death after he passed away in 620 B.C. *Mao shi* 131 is a lament for them. For a good study of this tradition, see Robert Joe Cutter, "On Reading Cao Zhi's 'Three Good Men.'"

LL. 89–90: Cf. Wang Can, "Rhapsody on a Widow" (Li Shan, *Wen xuan* 16.23a): "I wish to raise a knife and kill myself, / But glancing at my orphan child, I hold myself back."

L. 94: This line is drawn verbatim from "Nine Changes," II, 16 (*Chuci buzhu* 8.4a).

L. 98: Cf. Ding Yi, "Rhapsody on a Widow" (Li Shan, *Wen xuan* 16.23a): "A bird soaring into the void, flying back and forth."

65   Although I see his body and shadow on the table and mat,
     His spirit has already sped away to the grave.


## IV

     Since mid-autumn I have been in deep sorrow;
     Now I must tread on frost and ice.
     Snow, flurrying thick and heavy, suddenly begins to fall;
70   Wind, blowing hard and swift, rises at dawn.
     Runoff from gutters, dripping steadily, pours down at night;
     Water, slowly freezing, forms thin ice.
     My mind, muddled and confused, is transported away;
     Nine times each night my soul flies off.
75   I hoped that as time gradually passed my grief would abate,
     But my feelings become more and more laden with sorrow.
     I wished to meet his spirit in a dream,
     But my eyes are open wide, and I cannot sleep.
     The night, stretching on and on, is interminably long;
80   The cold, bitter and biting, chills me to the bone.
     Anger wells up within me, filling my breast;
     Tears stream down my face, flowing over my pillow.
     The soul of the deceased has departed forever;
     The year hastens on and soon will end.
85   My face has become wasted and haggard;
     My companions, sorrowing, take pity on me.
     Moved by the Three Good Men martyred in Qin,
     I shall gladly give my life in suicide.
     But I hug my young child to my breast,
90   And hesitate, unable to bring myself to it.
     I point to the sun and swear a silent oath;
     Although my body is alive my will has died.

     The finale says:
     I look up at august Heaven and heave a sigh;
     My self-pity, when will it end?
95   Perceiving that my humble person is so helpless and alone,
     And that my young child does not yet understand,
     I seem as if crossing a river without a bridge,
     Or soaring into the void without wings.

L. 100: The ground below the springs is the netherworld or land of the dead.

LL. 105–6: Cf. Ding Yi, "Rhapsody on a Widow" (Li Shan, *Wen xuan* 16.23b): "This humble concubine, solitary and alone, / Gazes at her shadow as her only companion."

L. 111: Cf. "Li sao," L. 18 (*Chuci buzhu* 1.5b): "Spring and autumn follow in continuous succession."

L. 114: Starry Han is the Sky River or Milky Way.

L. 126: Cf. Favorite Beauty Ban, "Rhapsody of Self-commiseration" (*Han shu* 97B.3987): "And twin streams of tears pour down my face."

LL. 127–28: Gong Jiang 恭姜 was the wife of Gong Bo 恭伯, heir-designate in the state of Wei. After he died young, his parents tried to force her to remarry. She refused and composed the "Cypress Boat" song (*Mao shi* 26) to express her resolve not to give in to their pressure. See *Mao shi zhushu* 3.1.1a (659).

LL. 129–30: Cf. Favorite Beauty Ban, "Rhapsody on Self-commiseration" (*Han shu* 97B.3986): "I hope they return my bones to the foot of a hill, / Where they may rest in the lingering shade of pine and cypress."

L. 131: Cf. *Mao shi* 73/3: "While alive you shall have a separate chamber, / But when dead we shall share the same grave."

L. 132: Cf. *Mao shi* 45/1: "He swore until death he would have no other."

I gaze up at the portrait of my late husband,
100   Look down upon the ground below the springs,
    Where in the gloomy darkness he is hidden in sombrous shade,
    But he is there in my heart, and I envision him with my eyes.
    I pay my respects to the still solemnity of the vacant bier,
    And make my plaint to the empty vastness of the deserted hall.
105 I stand apart and alone, gazing at my shadow,
    Speaking only to myself, and listening to echoes.
    Gazing at my shadow, I feel pain in my heart;
    Listening to echoes only adds to my grief.
    His soul has departed, and draws ever farther away;
110 He has gone into the remote distance and left me forever.
    The four seasons course onward in rapid succession;
    The year is coming to its twilight, and the sun sets in the west.
    Frost covers the courtyard, wind enters my chamber,
    Midnight has come, and Starry Han has begun to turn its course.
115 I dream that my husband has journeyed to me here,
    As if the gates of Heaven had opened wide.
    Then, I awaken with a start and, hearing nothing,
    I am crestfallen, confused and confounded, sad at heart.

    I am sad at heart, but what is to be done?
120 I then climb to the top of the mound.
    The door to the tomb is solemn and still;
    The high barrow is tall and towering.
    A solitary bird sadly chirps;
    On a tall pine, lushly growing, the branches shudder.
125 Pent-up grief gathers within me,
    And tears pour down my face in heavy streams.
    Emulating the lady Gong Jiang, I shall make a clear oath,
    And sing in clear voice the "Cypress Boat" song.
    When I die they shall return my bones to the foot of a hill,
130 But while alive I shall rely on his lingering glory.
    I vow to share the same grave with my lord,
    And I swear until death I shall have no other.

LL. 10–13: This section refers to the First Qin Emperor (reg. 246–209 B.C.), who led the western state of Qin to victory over the rival states of the east and south. Under his regime the writing system was unified and the system of measures including those for the wheel gauges was made uniform. See Bodde, *China's First Unifier*, pp. 146–61.

LL. 14–15: Cf. Jia Yi's "Finding Fault with Qin" (*Wen xuan* 51.4a): "The Qin tamped Mount Hua into the ramparts and used the Yellow River for a moat." Mount Hua, one of the five sacred mountains of China, is located south of Huayin in modern Shaanxi. Purple Gulf Zi yuan 紫淵 may refer to the same river mentioned in Sima Xiangru's "Rhapsody on the Imperial Park" see Knechtges, *Wen xuan* 2, L. 31). Its exact location is a matter of debate among Chinese scholars.

L. 18: This line is based on a passage in the *Zhushu jinian* (B.6a) in which the deed of ordering turtles and alligators to form a bridge is credited to King Mu of Zhou.

L. 19: This line refers to the numerous tours of inspection undertaken by the First Qin Emperor. However, the language is reminiscent of the *Liezi* 3.4b, which recounts the story of King Mu of Zhou, who journeyed westward "to observe where the sun sets." "Right" in ancient Chinese orientation is "west."

# Rhapsody on Resentment

## JIANG WENTONG

As I look across the level plain, I see creeper plants twining around bones, and giant "arm-spanning" trees where the souls of the dead gather.[1] When human life reaches this point, why bother to discourse on the Way of Heaven? Thus, I have become basically a man of resentment, whose apprehension never ceases. All I can think of are the ancients who died laden with resentment.

*I*

Such as

10  The Qin emperor, leaning on his sword,
While the vassal lords galloped west to submit:
He pared down their land and pacified the empire,
Unified the script, standardized wheel gauges.
Mount Hua served as his ramparts,
15  Purple Gulf was his moat.
His breast was filled with ambitious plans,
And he never used his martial might to the full.
He built a bridge of turtles and alligators,
And toured the area right of the sea to escort the sun westward.

THE THEME of this rhapsody by Jiang Yan (*zi* Wentong) is *hen* 恨, which carries the double meaning of "resentment" and "frustration." Jiang Yan describes six different types of people, all of whom died full of "resentment and frustration": an emperor (the First Qin Emperor), who was able to enjoy his reign as ruler of the united empire only a brief time; a Warring States king (King Qian of Zhao), who ended his life in exile; a loyal Chinese general (Li Ling), who suffered the disgrace of capture by the Xiongnu; an emperor's concubine (Wang Zhaojun), who left China to become the wife of a Xiongnu ruler; a "man of talent" (Feng Yan), who was dismissed from office and spent the remainder of his life in retirement; and a man of lofty ideals (Xi Kang), who was thrown into prison and executed. Jiang Yan concludes by describing the feelings of resentment felt by exiles and even the rich and powerful.

It is not clear whether this piece reflects any personal feelings of the author. It could be simply a virtuoso exercise on a traditional theme. However, Cao Daoheng 曹道衡 and Shen Yucheng 沈玉成 argue that Jiang Yan must have composed this piece as the result of his

193

LL. 20–21: The First Qin Emperor died while conducting an inspection tour of south and east China (see *Shi ji* 6.260–64; and Chavannes, *Mh* 2: 184–92). The expression "the imperial carriage is late to depart" is a euphemism for the death of an emperor. Ying Shao (cited in *Shi ji* 79.2415 and *Han shu* 26.1302) explains that the emperor ordinarily arose early to conduct court business. Thus, upon his death, the ministers declared, "The imperial carriage is harnessed late."

LL. 22–23: King Qian 遷, also known as Youmu 幽繆, of Zhao (reg. 235–228 B.C.), was defeated by Qin and taken captive (see *Shi ji* 43.1832). He was then exiled to Fangling 房陵 (modern Fang *xian*, Hubei). Longing for his home in Zhao, he composed a nostalgic piece, "Song of the Rivers and Hills." Everyone who heard it was moved to tears. See *Huainanzi* 20.16b–17a.

L. 30: The expression "a thousand autumns, ten thousand years later" is a euphemism for the death of a ruler. Cf. *Zhanguo ce* 14.3b: "[The king of Chu said,] 'A thousand autumns and ten thousand years from now with whom will I be able to enjoy this?' "

L. 32: Li Ling 李陵 was a general during the reign of Emperor Wu of the Former Han. In 99 B.C. he led an army of five thousand men on an expedition against the Xiongnu. His army was surrounded by a larger Xiongnu force, and Li Ling had no choice but to surrender. Emperor Wu was furious upon learning of this humiliating defeat, and he eventually had Li Ling's entire family put to death. Li Ling remained with the Xiongnu for some twenty years, until his death in 74 B.C. See *Han shu* 54.2450–59; and Watson, *Courtier and Commoner*, pp. 24–33.

L. 34: There probably were no pillars in the Central Asian yurts in which Li Ling lived. The striking of the pillar is a gesture symbolic of Li's deep frustration.

L. 35: Li Ling had no one but his shadow and soul to whom to express his sorrow and shame. The line seems derived from a passage in the *Yanzi chunqiu* (7.13b): "When standing alone a gentleman feels no shame before his shadow, and when sleeping alone he feels no shame before his soul."

LL. 36–37: Shangjun 上郡 (in the area of modern Yan'an and Yulin, Shaanxi) and Yanmen 雁門 (northwest of modern Dai 代 *xian*, Shanxi) were two important Han commanderies located on the northern frontier. They represent here the "China" for which Li Ling still maintained his loyalty.

L. 38: The letter written on silk alludes to a story about Li Ling's friend Su Wu 蘇武, who also was captured by the Xiongnu. A Han envoy came to the Xiongnu territory to inquire about Su Wu, whom the Xiongnu had falsely reported dead. One of Su Wu's attendants instructed the envoy to inform the Xiongnu that Emperor Wu, while hunting in the imperial park, had shot a goose and found on its leg a letter stating where Su Wu could be found. See *Han shu* 54.2466; and Watson, *Courtier and Commoner*, p. 40.

LL. 40–41: These lines allude to the parting of Li Ling and Su Wu. The poem "To Su Wu" (*Wen xuan* 29.8b), attributed to Li Ling, contains the lines "Clutching hands / we linger on the moor." In Su Wu's biography in the *Han shu* (54.2464), Li Ling addresses Su: "Human life is like the morning dew. Why have you suffered so long like this?"

20   But one day his soul left him,
     And the imperial carriage was late to depart.


## II

Such as
The king of Zhao, who was taken prisoner,
And exiled to Fangling:
As dusk fell his heart was stirred,
25   And at daybreak his spirits were aroused.
     He parted from his gorgeous concubines and lovely ladies,
     And lost his gilt chariots and jade carriages.
     As he set out wine and was about to drink,
     Sorrow came to fill his breast.
30   A thousand autumns, ten thousand years later—
     Such resentment is hard to bear.


## III

Such as
Li Ling, who surrendered in the north,
His name disgraced, his person wronged:
Drawing his sword, he struck a pillar;
35   Grieving to his shadow, he felt shame in the depth of his soul.
     His affection still was with Shangjun,
     And his heart held fast to Yanmen.
     He shredded silk to attach a letter,
     Vowing to repay Han's favor.
40   But morning dew is here in an instant;
     Clutching hands, what is there to say?

---

own personal frustration, perhaps after he was dismissed from his position and sent into exile to Wuxing 吳興 (modern Pucheng 浦城, Fujian). See Cao Daoheng and Shen Yucheng, *Nanbeichao wenxue shi* 南北朝文學史, pp. 118–19.

For previous translations, see Obi and Hanabusa, *Monzen* 2. 320–25; and John Marney, *Chiang Yen*, pp. 133–35. For *baihua* translations, see Chen Hongtian et al., *Zhaoming Wen xuan yizhu* 2: 883–89; and Li Jingying, *Zhaoming Wen xuan xinjie* 2: 214–18. This piece also is included in Jiang Yan's collected works. See *Jiang Wentong ji* 1.10a–b; and Hu Zhiji 胡之驥, *Jiang Wentong ji huizhu* 1.7–10. There are several annotated texts: Zhang Renqing 張仁青, *Lidai pianwen xuan* 1: 109–16; Huang Ruiyun, *Lidai shuqing xiaofu xuan*, pp. 135–41; and Fu Lipu, *Fu xuan zhu*, pp. 260–63.

L. 43: The Radiant Consort (Ming fei 明妃), also known as Zhaojun 昭君, is the celebrated Lady Wang (Wang Qiang 王嬙), a concubine of Emperor Yuan of the Former Han. In 33 B.C. she was selected to become the wife of the Xiongnu ruler. See *Han shu* 9.297; and Dubs, *HFHD* 2: 335. There are many legends and stories surrounding her name. See Zhang Shoulin, "Wang Zhaojun gushi yanbian zhi diandian didi"; Nienhauser, "Once Again, the Authorship of the *Hsi-ching tsa-chi*," pp. 227–29; and Eoyang, "The Wang Chaochün Legend."

L. 44: Purple Terrace (Zi tai 紫臺) stands for Purple Palace, a common designation for the residence of the emperor.

LL. 48–49: Long 隴 is a mountain range that stretches from modern Long *xian* in Shaanxi to Qingshui 清水, Gansu. Dai 代 (also written 岱) was a Han commandery on the northwestern frontier (northwest of modern Yu 蔚 *xian*, Hebei). The clouds and vapors of this area "were all black" (see *Han shu* 26.1297).

L. 52: Jingtong 敬通 is the style name of Feng Yan 馮衍 (ca. 15 B.C.–A.D. 59), a prominent scholar and writer of the early Eastern Han period. He was a member of the Gengshi Emperor's staff until he offered to defect to Emperor Guangwu, who refused to employ him. He eventually was appointed to several posts, but was forced to leave office in a crackdown on close associations of the consort clan. He then "returned westward to his home commandery and barred his gate" (*Hou Han shu* 27A.978).

L. 56: *Ruren* 孺人 is technically a term for a grandee's wife. See *Li ji zhushu* 5.11b (2740).

L. 57: The You Mao edition of the *Wen xuan* reads 顧弄 (turning around, he caressed) for 右顧 (looking right) of the *Liuchen zhu Wen xuan.*

L. 60: This line alludes to Feng Yan's "Letter to Yin Jiu" (cited in *Hou Han shu* 28A.978): "My long-cherished aspirations have not been rewarded, and I enter the realm of darkness harboring resentment."

L. 62: The Palace Grandee is Xi Kang (see biographical sketches, this volume), who held the sinecure title of Palace Grandee without Specified Appointment.

L. 63: This line may refer to Xi Kang's poem "Anger in Prison," which he composed while in prison. See *Wen xuan*, chap. 23; and Holzman, "La Poésie de Ji Kang," pp 354–56.

LL. 64–65. Cf. Xi Kang's "Letter Severing Friendship with Shan Tao" (*Wen xuan* 43.7a): "A cup of unstrained wine, a song to strum on my zither, and my aspirations and desires are fulfilled."

L. 68: "Cerulean clouds" is a conventional figure for "lofty aspirations."

L. 69: Cf. Emperor Wu of Han's "Rhapsody on Lady Li" (*Han shu* 97A.3953): "She left cart and horse at barrow's ridge, / To tarry in the eternal night of the unshining sun."

## *IV*

Such as
The Radiant Consort, who, upon her departure,
Gazed heavenward and heaved a deep sigh:
The Purple Terrace gradually faded into the distance,
45   And the passes and mountains stretched on without end.
Whirlwinds rose all around,
And the bright sun sank in the west.
Over Long Mountain geese seldom flew;
Over Dai the clouds are gloomy and dull.
50   She watched for her lord, but when could they meet?
Finally she perished in an alien land.

## *V*

Such as
Jingtong, who, rebuffed by the emperor,
Quit office and returned to his country hamlet:
Barring the gate, he left his path unswept;
55   Sealing his entrance, he refused to serve.
To the left he had his wife for company;
Turning around, he caressed his young children.
No longer constrained by lords and chancellors,
He abandoned himself in literature and history.
60   He died still harboring unfulfilled aspirations,
And his eternal longing never ceased.

## *VI*

Then there was
The Palace Grandee, thrown into prison,
His anger and resentment furiously seething.
Unstrained wine he poured in the evening;
65   A plain zither he tuned in the morning.
The autumn sun was cheerless,
And drifting clouds had lost luster.
Still pent up inside was a singular desire to soar the cerulean clouds,
But he entered the eternal night of the unshining sun.

LL. 70–71: These lines allude to *Mengzi* 7A/18: "The estranged minister and the son of a concubine maintain their minds in a state of apprehension and take precautions against trouble. Li Shan (*Wen xuan* 16.26b) notes that these lines are an example of "reciprocal phrasing": "the 'mind' ought to be 'apprehensive' and 'tears' ought 'to fall.' "

L. 72: After being captured by the Xiongnu, Su Wu was "transported to an uninhabited area of the Northern Sea [Lake Baikal?], and was forced to herd rams" (*Han shu* 54.2463).

L. 73: This could refer to Lou Jing 婁敬, who originally was from Qi. He was sent to guard the northwestern frontier at Longxi. See *Shi ji* 99.2715.

L. 82: This is a metaphorical expression meaning death. Cf. Wang Chong, *Lun heng* 20.12b: "A death is like the quenching of a fire. The fire is quenched, and its blazing brilliance no longer shines."

L. 87: "Silks and chiffons" is metonymy for the rich and powerful.

L. 89: Cf. *Lun yu* 12/7: "Since antiquity death has been the lot of all men."

## VII

Sometimes there are:
70 An estranged minister weeping in apprehension,
A concubine's son with crestfallen heart,
A banished stranger on the northern sea,
An exile guarding the frontier north of Long.
These men have only to hear the mournful wind swiftly rising,
75 And bloody tears soak their lapels.
They too, filled with bitterness, stifling sighs,
Fall into extinction, plunge into oblivion.

## VIII

Once where
Horsemen rode track upon track,
Chariots followed rut upon rut,
80 With yellow dust covering the ground,
Song and flute sounding in all directions:
None failed to have their smoke and fires unextinguished,
Or have their bones unburied in the nether springs.

## IX

Alas! All is over!
85 Spring grass withers, autumn winds begin to blast;
The autumn winds cease, spring grass grows.
When the "silks and chiffons" expire, ponds and lodges are no more;
When the strains of zithers no longer sound, grave mounds are
            leveled.
Since antiquity death has been the lot of all men;
90 And all have had to swallow their resentment and mute their shouts
            of protest.

LL. 3–4: Qin (northwest) and Wu (southeast) lay at opposite ends of the empire. Yan (in modern Hebei) was in the northeast, far from Song (modern Shangqiu 商丘, Henan) to the south.

LL. 5–6: Cf. "Summoning the Soul," L. 45 (*Chuci buzhu* 9.15a): "My gaze stretches a thousand leagues, saddening my heart"; and Bao Zhao, "Eastern Gate" (*Wen xuan* 28.20a): "The wind from the plain blows the autumn trees, / The traveler's heart is broken."

L. 11: Cf. "Crossing the River," L. 21 (*Chuci buzhu* 4.9a): "My boat glides slowly, making no progress; / Stayed by the eddying waters, it stalls."

# Rhapsody on Separation

## JIANG WENTONG

### I

Of the things that bring gloom and dissolve the soul,
Nothing can match separation!
It is felt most acutely between those distant lands of Qin and Wu,
Or Yan and Song, a thousand leagues apart,
5    When spring moss begins to grow,
Or autumn winds suddenly arise.

Thus, a traveler's heart is broken,
A hundred cares afflict him.
The wind sighs and sobs with an unfamiliar sound,
10   Clouds, stretching endlessly, take on an unusual cast.
His boat stalls at the riverbank,
His chariot pauses by the hill's edge.
The oars dip slowly—how can he advance?
Horses neigh in the cold, their sounds unceasing.

"RHAPSODY ON SEPARATION" by Jiang Yan is the companion piece to "Rhapsody on Resentment" above. It recounts the parting and separation encountered in seven situations: banquets of the wealthy and powerful, departures of knights-errant, campaigns of soldiers, the embarking of a man on an important mission, separation of husband and wife, abandonment of the world by a Taoist alchemist, and parting of young girls from their lovers.

For previous translations, see Margouliès, *Le "Fou" dans le Wen-siuan*, pp. 75–81, and *Anthologie*, pp. 307–9; Watson, *Chinese Rhyme-Prose*, pp. 96–101; Frankel, *The Flowering Plum and the Palace Lady*, pp. 73–78; and Obi and Hanabusa, *Monzen* 2: 327–36. There are *baihua* translations in Chen Hongtian et al., *Zhaoming Wen xuan yizhu* 2: 890–99; Li Jingying, *Zhaoming Wen xuan xinyi* 2: 219–26; and Wei Fengjuan, *Wei Jin Nanbeichao zhujia sanwen xuan*, pp. 295–307. The piece also is found in Jiang Yan's collected works. See *Jiang Wentong ji* 1.8a–9b; and Hu Zhiji, *Jiang Wentong ji huizhu* 1.35–42. There are numerous modern annotated texts. The most useful are Wang Li, *Gudai Hanyu* 3: 1214–23; *Wei Jin Nanbeichao wenxueshi cankao ziliao*, pp. 630–39; Zhang Renqing, *Lidai pianwen xuan* 1: 95–108; Qu Tuiyuan, *Han Wei Liuchao fuxuan*, pp. 190–200; Hu Chusheng, "*Wen xuan* 'Bie fu' Li zhu buzheng"; Li Hui and Yu Fei, *Lidai fu yishi*, pp. 129–43; Liu Zhenxiang and Li Fangchen, *Lidai cifu xuan*, pp. 292–300; Pei Jinnan, *Han Wei Liuchao fu xuanzhu*, pp. 158–67; and Qu Shouyuan, *Zhaoming Wen xuan zashu ji xuanjiang*, pp. 65–80.

# JIANG WENTONG

L. 31: Cf. Pan Yue, "Western Journey Rhapsody," L. 379. Shu Guang 疏廣 and his nephew Shu Shou 疏受 (both fl. ca. 70 B.C.) were tutors to the heir-designate of the Former Han, the future Emperor Xuan. When they retired, the emperor presented them with twenty catties of gold, and the heir-designate gave them fifty catties of gold. High officials provided a parting banquet outside the Eastern Capital gate. See *Han shu* 71.2040; and Watson, *Courtier and Commoner*, p. 164.

L. 32: Golden Valley (Jin gu 金谷) was the villa of Shi Chong 石崇 (249–300), one of the wealthiest men of the Western Jin period. His villa was the site of numerous gatherings of prominent people, who feasted on rare delicacies, listened to many kinds of musical performance, strolled in the lavish gardens, and composed poetry. See *Jin shu* 33.1006–7; and Hellmut Wilhelm, "Shih Ch'ung and His Chin-ku-yüan."

L. 33: *Yu* 羽 is the highest note of the pentatonic scale.

L. 34: Yan and Zhao are particularly famous for beautiful women. Cf. "Nineteen Old Poems" (*Wen xuan* 29.6a): "In Yan and Zhao are many fine ladies, / Beauties with faces like jade."

LL. 37–38: Cf. *Han shu waizhuan* 6.7a: "When Huba strummed his lute, fish hiding in the depths came up to listen; when Boya strummed his zither, his six horses looked up from their grazing."

L. 40: The You Mao edition of the *Wen xuan* reads *gan* 感 (to feel) for *xian* 咸 (all) of the *Liuchen zhu Wen xuan*.

L. 42: James J. Y. Liu has pointed out that *shaonian* 少年 (lit., "youth"), when applied to knights-errant, has the sense of "hooligan" or "unruly youth"; see *The Chinese Knight Errant*, p. 209. Cf. *Han shu* 92.3701: "[Guo Xie] offered his life to help friends avenge wrongs.... Young hooligans, admiring his actions, often would avenge wrongs for him without informing him." See also Ch'ü, *Han Social Structure*, p. 420.

L. 43: The state of Han 韓 alludes to a story of the dog butcher Nie Zheng 聶政, who was hired to assassinate Xialei 俠累, the prime minister of Han. He boldly entered the palace and stabbed Xialei to death. See *Shi ji* 86.2522–24; Watson, *Records of the Historian*, pp. 50–54; *Zhanguo ce* 27.6a–7b; and Crump, *Chan-Kuo Ts'e*, pp. 455–58. The Zhao privy refers to a story about Yu Rang 豫讓, who was hired to plaster a privy in the palace of the ruler of Zhao, who had killed Yu's former master. Hoping to avenge his master's death, he waited for an opportunity to stab the Zhao ruler. Just as the ruler was about to enter the privy, he noticed Yu Rang and had him seized. See *Shi ji* 86.2519; Watson, *Records of the Historian*, pp. 48–49; *Zhanguo ce* 18.4b–6a; and Crump, *Chan-Kuo Ts'e*, pp. 285–87.

L. 44: The palace of Wu refers to Zhuan Zhu 專諸, who assassinated King Liao 僚 of Wu (reg. 526–515 B.C.) with a dagger concealed in a fish. See *Shi ji* 86.2516–18; Watson, *Records of the Historian*, pp. 46–48; and *Wu Yue chunqiu* 3.5a–6b. The marketplace of Yan was where Jing Ke 荊軻 (ob. 227 B.C.) met with his friend Gao Jianli 高漸離 to drink wine. Jing Ke later became famous for his failed assassination of the First Qin Emperor. See *Shi ji* 86.2528.

15    He covers his golden goblet—to whom can he offer it?
He lays aside the jade-pegged zither, and tears wet his carriage-rail.

The one left behind lies abed, sad at heart;
She is bewildered, as if having lost something.
The sun sets behind the wall, plunging its brilliance downward;
20    The moon rises above the veranda, sending forth its flying beams.
She sees red thoroughwort soaked with dew,
Gazes at green catalpas struck by frost.
She walks about the towering hall, leaving the doors unclosed;
Strokes the brocade curtains, which feel empty and cold.
25    She knows that the distant one still pauses and paces in his dreams,
And imagines that the departed one's soul has flown away.


## II

Thus, although separation is a single emotion,
Its manifestations are of a myriad kinds.
Such as dragon steeds with silver saddles,
30    Vermilion coaches with ornate axles,
Tent banquets at the Eastern Capital gate,
Sending off guests at Golden Valley:
Zithers playing the *yu* mode, pipes and drums arrayed,
From Yan and Zhao, beauties singing their sad songs,
35    Adorned with pearls and jade, so gorgeous in late autumn,
Garbed in chiffons and silks, so lovely in early spring.
The music startles draft horses to look up from their grazing,
Stirs red-scaled fish to rise from their pools.
When it is time to let go hands, they become choked with tears;
40    Lonely and forlorn, they all feel their spirits wracked with grief.


## III

Then there is a swordsman ashamed of unearned favor,
A young knight bent on vengeance:
In the state of Han, a privy in Zhao,
At the palace of Wu, the marketplace of Yan.
45    Severing family affection, withholding his love,
He departs his homeland, leaves his village.

L. 48: The eyes are blood-stained because of prolonged shedding of tears.

L. 49: Cf. *Shi ji* 86.2534: "Jing Ke then went to his chariot and left, never once looking back."

L. 52: That is, they did not seek to earn a reputation as martyrs. Their sole intention was to be of service to their benefactors.

L. 53: According to the story of Yan Danzi 燕丹子 (cited by Li Shan, *Wen xuan* 16.28b), when Jing Ke and his companion Wu Yang 武陽 entered the presence of the First Qin Emperor, bells and drums began to sound, the emperor's courtiers began to shout, and Wu Yang became so frightened his face "seemed a deathly ashen color."

L. 54: The "flesh and blood" alludes to Nie Zheng's (see L. 43n above) elder sister, who died of grief while mourning over her brother's corpse, which had been left in the market-place for someone to identify. See *Shi ji* 86.2525; Watson, *Records of the Historian*, p. 54; *Zhanguo ce* 27.7a–b; and Crump, *Chan-Kuo Ts'e*, p. 458. For the expression *xin si* 心死 (lit., "heart dies"), see *Zhuangzi* 7.16b: "Confucius said . . . 'There is no greater sorrow than the death of the heart.'" The expression thus has the sense of extreme grief and sorrow.

LL. 57–58: The Liao 遼 River flows through modern Liaoning province of northeast China. Mount Yan 雁, also known as Yanman 雁門, is located northwest of modern Dai *xian*, Shanxi. These were areas where military expeditions against foreign invaders and marauders were conducted.

L. 65: According to Lu Yanji (*Liuchen zhu Wen xuan* 16.38b), peaches and plums stand for husband and wife. I prefer to take them simply as another indication of spring in full bloom.

LL. 67–68: Cf. *Shuo yuan* 11.9b: "Yongmen Zhou used his skill as a zither player to gain an audience with Lord Mengchang. Lord Mengchang said, 'When you play the zither, can you make me sad?' Yongmen replied, 'How can I make you sad? Those whom I can make sad include those who were first honored and then reduced to humble circumstances, who were first wealthy and then poor. . . . Nothing is comparable to loving and adoring someone, yet separating for no rancorous cause and going away to a faraway land, with no chance of seeing each other again." See also Pokora, *Hsin-lun*, p. 186.

L. 70: The North Bridge cannot be identified. Jiang Yan draws here from Wang Bao's "Nine Regrets," "Raising Barriers," L. 20 (*Chuci buzhu* 15.10b): "Leaving North Bridge, I bid a final farewell."

L. 73: Cf. *Zuo zhuan*, Xiang 26 (Legge, *The Chinese Classics* 5: 526): "Wu Ju fled to Zheng and was about to flee to Jin. Shengzi was on his way to Jin and met him on the outskirts of Zheng. They spread out vitex branches, ate together, and discussed returning to their home-land."

L. 74: Cf. "Parting Poem" attributed to Su Wu (*Wen xuan* 29.10a):

I have a goblet of wine;
I wish to send it to one far away.
I wish you would draw from it,
And recount our life-long affection.

Shedding tears, he bids loved ones a last farewell;
He wipes his blood-stained eyes, exchanging glances for a final time.
Then, spurring on his traveling mount, he does not look back,
50   But fixes his gaze on the dust of the road that rises unceasingly
              before him.
He shall repay favor received with a single sword,
And does not seek to purchase fame in the nether springs.
The sounds of bells and chimes give him fright, and his expression
              pales;
His flesh and blood feel such sorrow their hearts are numb with
              grief.

## IV

55   And then, border commanderies are not yet pacified,
And a man, bearing plumed arrows, marches with the army.
The Liao River stretches on without end,
Mount Yan soars into the clouds.
For the lady in her bedchamber, the breeze is warm,
60   And on the field paths, the grass is fragrant.
The sun rises, its beams brilliantly shining in the sky;
Dew falls, casting scintillating patterns over the ground.
In the reflected light, the glittering glare of vermilion dust,
Enveloping the air, the ethers of spring, thick and heavy.
65   Breaking sprigs of peach and plum, they cannot bear to part;
She sends off her beloved son, tears soaking her gauze skirt.

## V

Then if a man suddenly departs for a foreign land,
How can he meet his loved ones again?
He looks at the tall trees in his home village,
70   Leaving North Bridge, he bids a final farewell.
His companions' souls tremble;
Friends and relatives shed copious tears.
All they can do is spread out vitex branches and exchange sorrowful
              poems,
Or with a goblet of wine recount their sorrows.
75   Just in the season when autumn geese take to flight,

205

L. 79: The Zi 淄 River flows near modern Laiwu 萊蕪 *xian*, Shandong.

L. 84: What I have translated here as "gem plant" is my invention for *yao cao* 瑤草, which grew on 姑媱 Peak. According to legend, the Lord of Heaven's daughter died there and was transformed into the gem plant. See Yuan Ke, *Shanhai jing jiaozhu* 5.142. As Jiang Yan uses it here, this plant stands for the young wife left at home.

LL. 91–92: These lines allude to the famous palindrome made by the lady Su Hui 蘇蕙 (style name Ruolan 若蘭). According to the "Preface to the Palindrome of Woven Brocade," cited by Li Shan (*Wen xuan* 16.30a), Su Hui's husband Dou Tao 竇滔 (fl. ca. 350) was transferred to the northwestern frontier, where he took another wife. Su Hui wove a long palindrome of 841 characters, which she sent to her husband to express her indignation. See also *Jin shu* 96.2523.

L. 93: According to the *Liexian zhuan* (A.16b), a man named Xiu Yang 修羊 (also read Xiu Qian 修芊), who lived in a stone chamber of Mount Huayin, attained immortality by eating a concoction made from a piece he broke off from stone couch and Solomon's seal.

L. 94: Or, following *Liuchen zhu Wen xuan*, "Who ingests elixirs and becomes an immortal."

LL. 101–2: Cf. Bao Zhao, "Ascending the Heavens" (*Wen xuan* 28.24a): "In a brief journey I cross a myriad miles; / A momentary parting amounts to a thousand years."

Right at the time when white dew falls:
They complain and complain again of the twisting turns of the
    distant hills,
Where he must travel on and on along the banks of an endless
    stream.

## VI

Again, suppose the husband dwells on the right bank of the Zi,
80   And his wife lives north of the Yellow River:
They used to share the morning sunshine glistening on their
    carnelian pendants,
And together enjoyed the evening fragrance of a bronze incense
    burner.
Now the husband, wearing his official seals, has gone a thousand
    leagues away;
What a pity the gem plant wastes its sweet aroma!
85   She is loath to play the zither in her chamber,
And she keeps the yellow silk curtains in her high terrace darkly
    drawn.
The spring palace is enveloped in green moss,
Autumn curtains are filled with the light of the moon.
Summer mats are cool, daylight never ends;
90   Winter lamps freeze—how long the nights.
Weaving a song on brocade, she weeps her eyes dry;
Composing a palindrome, alone to her shadow she grieves.

## VII

Supposing a great master of Huayin:
Ingesting elixirs, he returns to the mountains.
95   The techniques are subtle, but he studies them still.
His mastery of the Way is profound, yet the true mystery he has yet
    to learn.
He tends to the refining of cinnabar, oblivious of the world;
Smelting it in a bronze cauldron, his will is unyielding and firm.
Riding a crane, he ascends to the Sky River;
100  Drawn by a simurgh, he soars through the heavens.
A brief journey is a myriad miles;

LL. 103–4: These lines may allude to the story of the immortal Wang Ziqiao 王子喬, who, before bidding a final farewell to the world, summoned his family to the crest of Goushi 緱氏 Mountain Riding a white crane, Wang flew near the peak, where the people of the area saw him disappear into the distance. See *Liexian zhuan* A.12a–b.

L. 105: The "poem on the peony" alludes to *Mao shi* 95, which depicts a tryst between lovers. The second stanza mentions that the man presents the girl with a peony. The introductory phrase that I have rendered "in the world below" may simply mean "there also are."

L. 106: The "song of the lovely lady" was composed by Li Yannian 李延年 (fl. 120 B.C.) to praise the beauty of his sister to Emperor Wu of the Former Han. After hearing the song, Emperor Wu selected the girl as a concubine. See *Han shu* 97A.3951.

LL. 107–8: Sangzhong 桑中 Amongst the Mulberries and Shanggong 上宮 (Upper Chamber are rendezvous spots for young lovers. They are mentioned in *Mao shi* 48 and were part of the Zhou state of Wei 衛 (northern Henan and southern Hebei). The beauty of Chen alludes to *Mao shi* 28 Chen 陳 was a Zhou state near Wei in what is now southeastern Henan and northern Anhui. According to the interpretation that was probably prevalent in Jiang Yan's time, the song tells of Zhuang Jiang 莊姜, wife of Duke Zhuang of Wei reg. 757–735 B.C., who is sending off her friend the lady Dai Gui 戴媯 back to her home state of Chen. See *Mao shi zhushu* 2.1.11b (627).

LL. 111–12: The "southern bank," a poetic term designating a place at which one sends off a friend, originally comes from "River Earl" (LL. 15–16 in the *Chuci* (see *Chuci buzhu* 2.19a: "My master crosses his arms and journeys eastward, / He sends off the Fair One at the southern bank."

L. 116: "Light and darkness" (*guang yin* 光陰) means "time."

L. 125: Yuan refers to Wang Bao, whose style name was Ziyuan 子淵. Yun is Yang Xiong, whose style name was Ziyun 子雲. Both are famous *fu* writers of the Former Han.

L. 126: Yan is Yan An 嚴安, and Le is Xu Le 徐樂, both of whom were among the prominent writers and experts on political rhetoric during the reign of Emperor Wu of the Former Han. See *Han shu* 64A.2775, 64A.2804–6, 64B.2809–14.

L. 127: The Bronze Chamber is the Bronze Horse Gate (Jin ma men 金馬門), a large portal in the Everlasting Palace of Former Han Chang'an. Here scholar-officials waited to be summoned by the emperor. See Knechtges, *Wen xuan* 1: 92, n. 6.

L. 128: The Magnolia Terrace (Lan tai 蘭臺) housed the official archives in which compilers and scholars worked. See *Han shu* 19A.725.

L. 129: This line alludes to Sima Xiangru's "Rhapsody on the Great Man," which, when presented to Emperor Wu, gave him "an air of buoyancy, as if he had soared to the clouds." See *Shi ji* 117.3063.

L. 130: "Dragon-carving" (*diao long* 雕龍), which in Jiang Yan's time meant "literary ornament," alludes to the Zhou philosopher Zou Shi 騶奭 (4th cent. B.C.), whose writings were praised as "dragon-carving." See *Shi ji* 74.2348.

A short separation is a thousand years.
But the world takes separation seriously;
In bidding farewell, even he feels reluctant to leave.

## VIII

105  In the world below there is the poem on the peony,
And a song of a lovely lady,
The girl from Wei in Sangzhong,
A beauty from Chen in Shanggong:
On spring grasses, the color of green jade,
110  By a spring stream, its ripples clear,
She sends off her lord at the southern bank.
How painful, but what can be done?
Then, when autumn dewdrops fall like pearls,
The autumn moon is like a disc of jade:
115  Bright moon, white dew—
Light and darkness come and go.
When she parts from her loved one,
Her thoughts of longing linger on.

## IX

Thus, although the ways of separation are not fixed,
120  And the reasons for separation have a thousand names,
Separation always leads to regret;
And when regret comes, it overflows one's breast,
Thus causing a man's mind to despair, his spirit to tremble,
His heart to shatter, and his bones to shake.
125  Even if there were men with the writing skills of Yuan and Yun,
The literary talent of Yan and Le,
Or all the masters of the Bronze Chamber.
And there were the countless talents of Magnolia Terrace,
Whose rhapsodies are acclaimed for their "cloud-soaring spirit,"
130  And whose eloquence is famed for its "dragon-carving":
Yet who could portray the manner of temporary parting,
Or describe the feelings of a final farewell?

209

## 17

LITERATURE

# Rhapsody on Literature

## LU SHIHENG

Whenever I read what men of talent have written, I presume to think that I have understood how they have used their minds.[1] When a writer sets forth words and disposes his phrases, there are many variations indeed, but nevertheless one can still say whether they are beautiful or ugly, good or bad. Every time I write, I am especially aware of this situation. I am constantly concerned that my ideas may be out of balance with the objects, and that the writing may not match my ideas.[2] This is not because of the difficulty of knowing, but the difficulty of doing.[3] Thus, I have written "Rhapsody on Literature" to tell of the splendid elegance

THIS RHAPSODY by Lu Ji is one of the most important early Chinese writings on literature. Although it is not a systematic treatise, it contains a broad and comprehensive treatment of the process of literary creation. Lu Ji first examines the sources of literary creation, which he attributes to the writer's emotional response to the cosmos, nature, and the passing of the seasons, as well as his experience with other literary works. To Lu Ji, writing is a contemplative, spiritual act in which the writer, much like a Taoist mystic, suspends his sight and hearing to embark on a spirit journey for his literary inspiration. Thus, he is able "to view past and present in a single instant, / And touch the entire world in the blink of an eye." Lu Ji also says much about the relationship between thought and language, and the difficult effort the writer makes in his attempt to express his feelings and thought. One of the most important sections of this rhapsody discusses the major genres and the norms that Lu Ji associates with them. His statements on the rhapsody and lyric poem (shi) have been especially influential. Lu Ji also establishes aesthetic criteria for judging good writing, notably harmony (he 和), resonance (ying 應), dignity (ya 雅), beauty (yan 豔), and strong feeling (bei 悲).

Scholars do not agree on when Lu Ji may have written "Rhapsody on Literature." The Tang poet Du Fu claimed in his "Zui ge xing" 醉歌行 ("Sung While Drunk") that Lu Ji composed "Rhapsody on Literature" at the age of twenty (see Du Gongbu shiji 1.6a), but it is more likely that it is a much more mature composition that dates from around the year 300, three years before Lu Ji's death. For detailed discussion, see Lu Qinli, " 'Wen fu' zhuanchu niandai kao," pp. 421–34; Chen Shih-hsiang, Essay on Literature, pp. xxxiii–xxxv; Chen

L. 1: Li Shan (*Wen xuan* 17.2a) relates the expression *xuan lan* 玄覽, which I have rendered "darkly observes," to *Laozi* 10: "Can you cleanse and purify your dark insight (*xuan lan*) and keep it without blemish?" The Heshang Gong 河上公 commentary, which Li Shan also cites, explains that "the mind dwells in a place of darkness, and there observes and knows the myriad things." The translation of *xuan* as "darkness" is somewhat misleading, for the term actually refers to a kind of mystical journey into the mind that results in absolute clarity of vision. In fact, one of the common interpretations of *xuan lan* is "mysterious mirror" (cf. Lau, *Lao Tzu*, p. 66). The process is similar to that described in *Huainanzi* 21.13b: "A man who has attained perfectly clear vision grasps the mysterious mirror in his heart, and reflects things clearly." Lu Yanji (in *Liuchen zhu Wen xuan* 17.2a) glosses *xuan lan* as "viewing from afar." This interpretation is followed by Qian Zhongshu (*Guan zhui bian* 3: 1181) and several other modern commentators. As Owen points out (*Readings*, p. 88), this reading does not fit this context, which emphasizes literary imagination as a kind of spiritual journey.

L. 2: On the word *fen* 墳 as "classical text" see Pan Yue, "Rhapsody on Living in Idleness," this volume, L. 1n.

L. 3: The expression *tan shi* 歎逝, which I have rendered here as "lament their passing," also is the title of Lu Ji's "Rhapsody on Lamenting the Departed." In this context *shi* 逝 refers not to death but rather the passage of time.

L. 4: For *si fen* 思紛, which I have rendered "ponders their complexity," another possible interpretation is "his cares burgeon."

LL. 7–8: Frost is an image of purity and moral integrity; clouds here represent lofty detachment from the world.

L. 12: My "perfect balance" translates *binbin* 彬彬, which means the perfect blending between *wen* 文 (form; ornament; refinement) and *zhi* 質 (content; substance). The locus classicus for the expression is *Lun yu* 6/16.

L. 13: *Tou pian* 投篇, which I have rendered "puts aside his books," may also be understood as "setting out his paper" (lit., "bamboo strips"). See C. H. Wang, "Lu Ji Wen fu jiaoshi," p. 9 (167).

of former writers, and then to discuss the causes for the success and failure in writing. I hope that perhaps some day one can say that I have thoroughly exhausted the subtleties of this subject.[4] When one comes to the point of hewing an axe-handle with axe in hand, the model is not far away.[5] But still, how the changes follow the movements of the hand is truly difficult to convey in words.[6] All that I am able to say I have set forth here.

# I

The writer stands at the center of things, darkly observes,
Nurturing his feelings and his mind in canons and scriptures.
Following the changing seasons, he laments their passing;
Gazing upon the myriad things, he ponders their complexity.
5   He grieves at falling leaves in stark autumn,
Rejoices at tender branches in fragrant spring.
His heart, shaking and shivering, embraces the frost;
His mind, distant and detached, looks down on the clouds.
He sings of the great achievements attained by generations of virtue,
10  And declaims on the pure fragrance of his forebears.
He roams the groves and storehouses of literature,
And admires the perfect balance of elegant artistry.
Then, moved, he puts aside his books and picks up his brush,

---

Shih-hsiang and Ikkai Tomoyoshi, "Riku Ki no shōgai to 'Bun fu' seikakuna nendai"; and Zhou Xunchu, " 'Wen fu' xiezuo niandai xintan."

Previous translations include Margouliès, Le "Fou" dans le Wen-siuan, pp. 82–97, and Anthologie, pp. 419–25; Chen Shih-hsiang, "Literature as Light Against Darkness"; Fang, "Rhymeprose on Literature"; E. R. Hughes, The Art of Letters; Wong, Early Chinese Literary Criticism, pp. 39–60; Hamill, The Art of Writing; Owen, Readings in Chinese Literary Thought, pp. 73–181; and Obi and Hanabusa, Monzen 2: 337–57. There are numerous baihua translations, including Chen Hongtian et al., Zhaoming Wenxuan yizhu 2: 900–22; Li Jingying, Zhaoming Wenxuan xinjie, 2: 227–42; Zhang Huaijin, Wen fu yizhu; Zhao Zecheng et al., Zhongguo gudai wenlun yijiang, pp. 22–52; and Guo Zhengyuan, Wen Jin Nanbeichao wenxue lunwen mingpian yizhu, pp. 29–80. There are many commentaries in Chinese. The most useful and authoritative are Wei Jin Nanbeichao wenxueshi cankao ziliao 1: 252–75; Guo Shaoyu, Zhongguo lidai wenlun xuan 1: 136–54; Qian Zhongshu, Guan zhui bian 3: 1176–1207; Xu Fuguan, "Lu Ji 'Wen fu' shushi chugao"; Zhang Shaokang, Wen fu jishi; and C. H Wang, "Lu Ji Wen fu jiaoshi." For a comprehensive listing of studies of "Rhapsody on Literature," see Hong Shunlong, Zhongwai Liuchao wenxue yanjiu wenxian mulu, pp. 97–101. There are a number of variant readings, most of them minor. I do not note them all in my notes. For a critical text, see Jin Taosheng, Lu Ji ji.

L. 21: What I have translated as "multitude of words" is *qun yan* 群言, which refers to the vast variety of things that have been written. C. H. Wang suggests that the expression implies the inclusion of the classics and the works of the hundred schools of thought; see ibid., p. 19 (177). Cf. Yang Xiong, *Fa yan* 13.4a: "Someone asked: 'What has the highest standing among the multitude of words, and what is foremost among the varieties of human conduct?' Yang Xiong replied, 'Virtuous words have highest standing among the multitude of words, and virtuous conduct is foremost among the varieties of human conduct.' "

L. 22. The Six Classics (*Liu yi* 六藝) are the categories of the Confucian canon: *Changes, Documents, Songs, Rites, Music,* and *Annals.* Li Shan (*Wen xuan* 17.2b) certainly is wrong in identifying them as the six arts (ritual, music, archery, chariot driving, calligraphy, and mathematics). See Hu Shaoying, *Wen xuan jianzheng* 18.15b–16a.

L. 23: *Tian yuan* 天淵, which I have rendered "pool of Heaven," may be another name for the constellation Tian huang 天潢 mentioned in Zhang Heng, "Rhapsody on Contemplating the Mystery," this volume, L. 361. Li Shan (*Wen xuan* 17.2b) seems to understand it in the sense of "Heaven and the Abyss," as in Yang Xiong's "Denigrating Qin and Praising Xin" (*Wen xuan* 48.9b).

L. 29: The locus classicus for the expression *que wen* 闕文, which I have rendered here "phrases that were lacking," is the passage of *Lun yu* 15/25, in which Confucius complains about the failure of the scribes of his time to follow the ancient practice of leaving a blank in a text at points of uncertainty about the correct reading or meaning: "Even in my time a scribe would omit something in the text." Lu Ji uses *que wen* in a very different sense, for phrases that have not been used before.

L. 30: The word I have translated as "euphonius words" is *yun* 韻, which many commentators and translators understand as "rhyme." However, the word can have a more general sense of "euphonious" or "mellifluous" sounds.

L. 37: The You Mao edition of the *Wen xuan* reads *shu* 暑 (heat) for *jing* or *ying* 景 (light; shadow) of the *Liuchen zhu Wen xuan.* I have incorporated the senses of both "light" and "shadow" in my translation of *jing.* It is not clear to what "light and shadow" actually refer. I suspect *jing* simply evokes visual aspects of the world, as opposed to its auditory aspects in the following line. Whatever their reference, the writer's task is to seek them out (lit., "tap on them") and bring them into expression.

L. 43: Lu Ji draws on a phrase in hexagram 49 (9/5) in the *Classic of Changes (Zhou yi zhushu* 5.19b–20a, 124): "The great man changes like a tiger." The "Commentary on the Images" to this line says: "The great man changes like a tiger. This means his markings are bright and distinct." Commentators have variously explained the sense of this line. The basic idea is that the tiger represents the dominant pattern (or meaning?), which, when properly manifested, brings the rest of the piece into order and compliance with it.

214

In order to express himself in writing.

## II

15   In the beginning he withdraws sight, suspends hearing,
Deeply contemplates, seeks broadly,
Letting his spirit race to the eight limits,
Letting his mind roam ten thousand spans.
Then, at the end, his feelings, first glimmering, become ever brighter;
20   Things, clear and resplendent, reveal one another.
He distills tiny drops from a multitude of words,
Sips the sweet moisture of the Six Classics.
He flows calmly along, drifting on the pool of Heaven;
Soaking himself, he bathes in the springs below.
25   Then, submerged phrases struggle forth,
Like a swimming fish, hook in mouth, surfacing from the deepest
          pool;
And floating elegance flutters down,
Like a soaring bird, struck by a stringed-arrow, falling from the lofty
          clouds.
He gathers in phrases that were lacking for a hundred generations;
30   Picks euphonious words that have been neglected for a thousand
          years,
Casts aside the morning blossom that has already bloomed,
Brings to flower the evening bud that has yet to open.
He views past and present in a single instant,
And touches the entire world in the blink of an eye.

## III

35   Then, he selects ideas, arranged in proper places;
Examines words, set out in proper order.
Everything that contains light and shadow he touches;
All that embodies sound and tone he plays forth.
Sometimes he grasps a branch and shakes the leaves;
40   Or follows the ripples to seek the source.
Sometimes beginning with the hidden, he reaches the manifest;
Or seeking the simple, he finds the difficult.
Sometimes the tiger changes its stripes and beasts submit;

L. 44: On *lan* 瀾 in the sense of "scatter" see Hu Shaoying, *Wen xuan jianzheng* 18.16b. The image of the dragon, which also is common in the *Classic of Changes* tradition, is comparable to that of the tiger in the preceding line and represents the controlling force of a work.

L. 48: This line uses phrasing that comes from a passage in the "Explaining the Trigrams" commentary to the *Classic of Changes* (*Zhou yi zhushu* 9.9a, 196): "What is meant by spirit is that which subtly works through all things" 神也者, 妙萬物而為言者也. The precise meaning of *miao* 妙, which should be a transitive verb, is unclear. However, Wang Bi in his commentary to this *Classic of Changes* passage explains that *shen* 神 (spirit) is not a material substance and thus can be spoken of as subtly working through all things. See Lynn, *The Classic of Changes*, p. 122. I suspect that in Lu Ji's line the idea behind *miao zhong lu* 妙眾慮 is similar to the preceding line: the writer must somehow rarefy his thoughts beyond those of the mundane realm. Thus, my translation: "He rarefies all of this cares."

L. 49: It is not clear whether "form" (*xing* 形) here refers to literary form, physical form, or some abstract notion of the form (or forms) of the myriad things. For a good summary of the possible interpretations, see Owen, *Readings*, pp. 111–12.

L. 68: Or, alternatively, "The more thought is pursued, the more profound it becomes."

L. 73: It is not clear whether Lu Ji uses *ti* 體 here in the sense of "literary forms," or the more abstract sense of the forms of everything in existence. Guo Zhengyuan (*Wei Jin Nanbeichao wenxue lunwen mingpian yizhu*, p. 39) persuasively argues that in this line, which emphasizes the vast variety of things in general, the best interpretation of *ti* is "objective reality."

Or the dragon appears and birds scatter.
45    Sometimes he finds the way smooth and steady, easily executed;
Other times it is rough and rugged, difficult to manage.
He completely purifies his mind and focuses his thoughts;
Or rarefies all of his cares before putting them into words.
He encases Heaven and Earth within the realm of form,
50    And crushes the myriad things against the tip of his brush.
At first words hesitate on his dry lips;
Finally they smoothly flow onto his moist brush.
The ordering principle, supporting substance, steadies the trunk;
Outward pattern, like hanging branches, produces rich fruit.
55    Truly feeling and expression are never in conflict;
Thus, each change brings a new mood to his face.
When his thoughts turn to joy, he is bound to smile;
But when he speaks of grief, he has already sighed.
Sometimes he grasps his writing tablet and composes effortlessly;
60    Or he holds his writing brush in his mouth, his mind far away.

## *IV*

In this endeavor one can find joy;
Long has it been revered by sages and worthies.
The writer examines the void and demands being;
He taps on silence, seeking sound.
65    He contains a boundless expanse in a foot of silk;
He pours forth a swelling torrent from a tiny heart.
As words expand, the broader their scope;
As thought is restrained, the more profound it becomes.
The writing spreads forth the rich fragrance of sweet blossoms,
70    Bursts forth in the lush luxuriance of green twigs.
Brightly it shines, flying like the breeze, rising like a whirlwind;
It thickly gathers, like clouds rising from the grove of letters.

## *V*

There are a myriad different kinds of forms,
And things of nature lack a fixed measure.
75    Chaotic and confused, swift and illusory,
Their shapes are hard to describe.

LL. 77–78: The expression *si qi* 司契, "holding the creditor's tally" (the left half of a tally given to the creditor) alludes to *Laozi* 79: "The man of virtue holds the creditor's tally." By extension, the term means "exercising control and judgment in writing." Li Shan (*Wen xuan* 17.4a) understands these lines as referring to the process of putting words together in a work, which "is like showing a talent, displaying a skill," and selecting ideas. These all have the role of the creditor's tally, "which acts as the craftsman." Other commentators (see, inter alia, Guo Zhengyuan, *Wei Jin Nanbeichao wenxue lunwen mingpian yizhu*, p. 39) argue that Lu Ji is talking here about the writer's talent and skill: his phrasing shows the efficacy of his skill, and the way he expresses his ideas demonstrates his craftsmanship.

LL. 79–80: Cf. *Mao shi* 35/4:

Coming to where the water was deep,
I crossed it by raft or boat.
Coming to where it was shallow,
I waded and swam.
What was there, what not?
I strove to get it.

Lu Ji borrows phrases from this poem, but uses them in a different sense. For example, he uses *you wu* 有無 from the line 何有何無 ("What was there, what not?") in the sense of "being and nonbeing."

L. 85: This line seems to refer back to L. 82.

L. 86: A "penetrating discourse" (*lun da* 論達) is one that conveys its message and argument directly and to the point. Cf. *Lun yu* 15/40: "Language should convey meaning [*da*] and that is all." The exact sense of *kuang* 曠 (expansive; open) is difficult to convey here. Stephen Owen (*Readings*, p. 129), who summarizes some of the interpretations, suggests the possibility that *kuang* refers to the meaning that lingers after the discourse has expressed its meaning. Thus, he translates this line: "Discourse attains its ends only in broadening." In my translation, I have placed the emphasis not on the meaning that is left over, which I find difficult to extract from the usual meanings of *kuang*, but on the "vast clarity" that results from the meaning of the discourse being conveyed.

L. 89: Lu Ji here points to the primary quality that an epitaph should ideally possess, that of presenting a factual account of the deceased person's virtues. In this genre, literary ornament is also important, but subordinate to substance.

L. 91: Li Shan (*Wen xuan* 17.4b) explains that the "matters" (*shi* 事) treated in the inscription are broad, but the writing is concise. The conciseness of the inscription was determined by the medium on which it was written: a small object such as a vessel, fan, sword, or mirror.

L. 92: The admonition (*zhen* 箴) is a short monitory piece written in a terse, often archaic style. Most consist of a series of moral aphorisms that enumerate warnings about proper conduct, especially for various categories of officeholders. The quality of *duncuo* 頓挫 that Lu Ji attributes to this genre is difficult to construe. The most common usage describes the modulations of sound or the variations (pauses and turns) in movement. Li Shan (*Wen xuan* 17.4b) links *duncuo* with the critical and satirical function of admonition, but he does not actually explain what it means. Zhang Xian (in *Liuchen zhu Wen xuan* 17.6a) explains that the function of the admonition is to criticize past failings, and thus it "restrains the minds of men of the past" (sic). Based on these imprecise explanations, I have translated *duncuo* here as "restrains."

L. 98: There may be a reference here to *Lun yu* 2/2: "The *Songs* are three hundred, and one phrase from them covers them all: 'No wayward thoughts.' "

Through phrasing a writer shows his talent, displays his skill,
But through ideas he holds the creditor's tally and acts as craftsman.
He strives between being and nonbeing,
80 And whether confronted with deep or shallow, he does not yield.
Although he may depart from the square, withdraw from the round,
He hopes fully to realize the shape, fully depict the form.
Thus, one who would dazzle the eyes prizes the extravagant;
He who would satisfy the heart values the appropriate.
85 One whose words are exhaustive encounters no obstacle;
And he whose discourse is penetrating achieves a vast clarity.

## VI

Lyric poetry springs from feelings and is exquisitely ornate;
The rhapsody gives form to an object, and is limpid and clear.
The epitaph displays outer form to support substance;
90 The dirge wrenches the heart and is mournful and sad.
The inscription is broad yet concise, gentle and smooth;
The admonition restrains, and is crisp and bold.
The eulogy is dignified and relaxed, lush and luxuriant;
The treatise is subtle and exact, pellucid and coherent.
95 The memorial is calm and clear, refined and elegant;
The discourse dazzles and glitters, but is deceptive and deceitful.
Although there are distinctions among these forms,
They all repress the wayward, control wild abandon.

L. 99: This is another restatement of the *Lun yu* 15/40 passage in which Confucius is quoted as saying, "Language should convey [*da*] meaning and that is all."

LL. 101–2: These lines are a restatement of LL. 73–74 above. Another possible rendering is that of Achilles Fang ("Rhymeprose," p. 536): "As an object, literature puts on numerous shapes; as a form, it undergoes diverse changes."

L. 103: Some commentators understand *hui yi* 會意 as "understanding the meaning." See *Wei Jin Nanbeichao wenxueshi cankao ziliao* 1: 262. Note that *huiyi* also is the name for one of the six types of script in which two simple graphs are combined to form what is often mistranslated into English as an "ideogram."

L. 105: This line is sometimes understood as being the first statement on the rules that govern the distribution of tones in a poetic line. However, Lu Ji's line seems to refer more to the euphonic features of writing in general, and need not be understood as saying anything about tones.

L. 107: "Departing and dwelling" (*shi zhi* 逝止) refer to the changes of language and/or sounds of a literary work.

L. 113: Black (*xuan* 玄) and yellow (*huang* 黃) are the fundamental cosmic colors of Heaven and Earth. According to Li Shan (*Wen xuan* 17.5a), the analogy here is to embroidery in which the colors are out of sequence.

L. 121: "Relative merits" is *dian zui* 殿最 (lit., "the bottom and the top"), an expression used to rank court officials in the Han. See *Han shu* 8.253.

LITERATURE

Words must convey meaning, and principle must be properly set forth;
100  Thus, there is no need for prolix verbiage.

## VII

It is the nature of things to take on many postures,
And forms are frequently changing.
In putting together the ideas, craft is foremost;
In arranging words, beauty is paramount.
105  When it comes to the sounds, they should alternate,
Just as the five colors enhance one another.
Although they depart or remain by no fixed rule,
And truly follow a tortuous path hard to make smooth,
If one can understand the variations and know the proper order,
110  It would be like opening a channel to receive the spring.
But if one loses the moment and misses the opportunity,
He will always place the end following the head.
If one disorders the proper sequence of black and yellow,
Things look muddied and mired, lacking in clarity.

## VIII

115  Sometimes, looking back in the text, one impinges upon an earlier
         section,
Or looking forward, one encroaches upon a later passage.
Sometimes the phrasing is impeded, yet the reasoning smoothly
         follows;
Or the wording is smooth, yet the meaning is hindered.
Taken separately, they both appear beautiful,
120  But placed together, they do each other harm.
Consider relative merits by minute measures;
Determine selection by the breadth of a hair.
If one cuts according to a strict standard,
One must follow the marking line for a proper fit.

## IX

125  Sometimes the style is luxuriant and the reasoning is rich,
But the main idea is not clearly indicated.

221

L. 141: The loom is a metaphor for literary creativity. The act of writing is often compared to weaving cloth on a loom. Li Shan (*Wen xuan* 17.6a) says that "even though [the writing] came from my own feelings, I am afraid that someone else has preceded me." Thus, even though what one has written is original, if it resembles something that has been written before, it cannot be allowed.

LL. 153–54: Cf. *Xunzi* 1.4a: "When jade is in a mountain, the grass and trees are sleek and moist; when a pool produces pearls, the bank does not dry up." The idea seems to be that an isolated rarity can impart beauty and luster to its surroundings.

LL. 155–56: These lines pose several problems of interpretation. First, *zhen* 榛 and *hu* 楛 are two trees (filbert and thorn) mentioned together in *Mao shi* 239 as flourishing luxuriantly. However, Li Shan (*Wen xuan* 17.6b) construes them as images for "ordinary sounds," that is, an undistinguished passage of writing. Zhu Jian (*Wen xuan jishi* 14.23b) argues that *zhenhu* is a descriptive word that indicates rank, undesirable growth. Second, the combination *ji cui* 集翠 can be understood either as "roosting kingfisher" or "gathered verdure" (of the vegetation). Whatever the interpretation of individual words in these lines, the general sense is clear: even the ordinary and commonplace has a function within a literary work.

LL. 157–58: "Lower Hamlet" and "White Snow" are songs mentioned in "Responding to a Question by the King of Chu," attributed to Song Yu (see *Wen xuan* 45.2a). The first, the full title of which was "Xiali Baren" 下里巴人 ("The Man of Ba from the Lower Hamlet"), was a popular song performed in an easy low mode to which a thousand people reputedly could join in. "White Snow" is short for "Yangchun baixue" 陽春白雪. This was a more difficult song in a higher mode, and less than several dozen people could sing along. The two songs thus represent "vulgar" and "noble" music respectively.

Reaching the end, there cannot be two meanings;
What is fully expressed cannot be added to.
Set down an incisive phrase in a strategic place,
130 And it will serve as the whip for the entire piece.
Even though the multitude of other words is well ordered,
This is needed to produce maximum effect.
Truly achievements will be many and encumbrances few;
Thus, choose what is sufficient and leave it unchanged.


## X

135 At times literary thoughts blend as in a fabric,
Limpid and lovely, resplendent and bright,
Glistening like intricately colored embroidery,
Plaintive like an ensemble of strings.
It if must be that what one writes is not unusual,
140 Then it imperceptibly accords with some earlier work.
Even though the loom is my heart,
I am afraid that someone has preceded me.
If I damage integrity and violate propriety,
Although I am fond of it, I must give it up.


## XI

145 Sometimes a blossom bursts forth, or a grain stalk stands tall,
Each apart from the crowd, cut off from the main thought,
Like a shape unpursued by a shadow,
An echo unconnected to a sound.
Alone, solitary, it conspicuously stands,
150 Not woven in with common sounds.
The heart then feels desolate, without a mate,
Yet the idea, wandering and wavering, is not abandoned.
When a stone contains jade, the mountain glows;
When waters bear pearls, the stream is alluring.
155 Rank growth need not be cut down;
For it may receive luster from a roosting kingfisher.
Join "Lower Hamlet" to "White Snow,"
And the greatness of the work will be enhanced.

LL. 159–60: According to Li Shan (*Wen xuan* 17.6b), *duan yun* 短韻 means a short piece in which "matters" (*shi* 事) are few. What Lu Ji seems to criticize here is a piece short on "resonance" (*ying* 應), that is, the elements in a composition fail sufficiently to interact and correspond with one another. Siu-kit Wong captures this meaning aptly by translating *duan yun* "unsustained song"; see *Early Chinese Literary Criticism*, p. 46. On this section and its connection with resonance, see DeWoskin, "Early Chinese Music and the Origins of Aesthetic Terminology," pp. 199–200.

L. 160: I suspect the "bleak expanse" (*qiong ji* 窮迹) refers not to tracks that run out, as Stephen Owen suggests (*Readings*, p. 157), but to the lack of content that gives the line a sense of desolation, dullness, and solitariness (*gu xing* 孤興).

L. 165: "Feeble tones" (*cui yin* 瘁音) refers to writing that lacks strength and "bone" (*gu* 骨). See Chen Hongtian et al., *Zhaoming Wen xuan yizhu* 2: 913, n. 157.

L. 169: In ancient musical performance at state ceremonies, there was a division between music played in the upper hall and the lower hall. The lower-hall music (*xia guan* 下管) was played by wind instruments. See *Zhou li zhushu* 23.14b–15a (1718–19).

L. 181: On "Keeping off the Dew," see Xie Zhuang, "Rhapsody on the Moon," this volume, L. 72n. Sangjian 桑間 (Among the Mulberries), on the Pu 濮 River (modern Henan), was a place traditionally associated with the so-called music of a fallen state. See *Li ji zhushu* 37.7a (3311). King Zhou, the last ruler of the Yin dynasty, ordered his music master to compose licentious music. Later, when the Yin dynasty was defeated by the Zhou, the music master drowned himself in the Pu River. Several centuries later the music master Juan 涓 passed through this area and heard the sound of a zither playing. He transcribed the tune and played it for Duke Ping 平 (reg. 557–532 B.C.) of Jin in the presence of the music master Kuang 曠. Before he could finish, Kuang stopped him, declaring, "This is the music of a fallen state." See *Shi ji* 24.1235; and Chavannes, *Mh* 3: 288–89.

## XII

Sometimes a poet entrusts his words to a foreshortened verse;
160 Facing a bleak expanse, they rise alone.
One looks down on empty stillness and sees no friend;
Looks up at vast space and finds no connection.
It is like a side string, strung alone;
It contains a clear song, but lacks resonance.

## XIII

165 Or he entrusts his phrases to feeble tones;
The words are merely decorous but are not resplendent.
He mixes the beautiful and ugly in the same form,
Encumbering the good substance and creating defects.
It is like the isolated prestissimo of a lower-hall pipe;
170 Although there is resonance, there is no harmony.

## XIV

Or he abandons meaning and preserves the strange,
Vainly seeking the empty, pursuing the obscure.
Words will lack feeling, be devoid of love;
Phrases will drift about, without attachment.
175 This is like thin strings rapidly strummed;
Although music is harmonious, it is not moving.

## XV

Sometimes, galloping forth in wild abandon, he blends the sounds,
Seeking only the loud and enticing.
This only pleases the eyes, suits vulgar taste;
180 The pitch may indeed be high, but the quality of the song is low.
One is reminded of "Keeping off the Dew" and "Among the
            Mulberries":
Although the music is moving, it is not dignified.

225

LL. 185–86: These lines allude to a passage in the "Record of Music" chapter of the *Record of Rites* (*Li ji zhushu* 37.8a–b, 3311), which says that the ceremonial music and food of ancient rites were deliberately not the most appealing. The zither used plain vermilion silk for the strings and had broadly spaced holes, which produced a dull sound. Nevertheless, as "one person sang, three sighed in response." The ceremonial foods consisted of plain water and fresh meats. The grand broth was not seasoned, and thus "taste was ignored."

L. 194: "Light" (*qing* 輕) implies lack of seriousness.

L. 201: See Lu Ji's preface to this rhapsody, n. 6.

L. 210: This line alludes to *Mao shi* 196/3: "There are beans in the middle of the plain; / The common people pick them." The idea is that a rare and precious stone, and by extension superb writing, is as common as beans in the field.

L. 211: Cf. *Laozi* 5: "Is not the space between Heaven and Earth like a bellows? It is empty without giving out; the more it moves, the more it emits."

## XVI

Sometimes the writing is bland and empty, gentle and restrained,
With all complexity excised, superfluity removed.
185 It lacks even the "ignored taste" of the grand broth,
And is the same as the pure simplicity of vermilion strings.
Although one sings and three sigh in response,
It may be dignified, but lacks beauty.

## XVII

As for the way the work is tailored, either full or thin,
190 And the way the form moves, ascending and descending:
Following what is appropriate, it adapts to changes,
And their convolutions have many subtle aspects.
Sometimes the language is clumsy, yet the figures are well crafted,
Sometimes the sense is plain, yet the phrasing is light.
195 Sometimes adhering to the old produces something new;
Sometimes following the turbid brings greater clarity.
Sometimes a brief inspection results in greater perception;
Sometimes thorough study must be done to grasp the subtle essence.
It is like a dancer flinging her sleeves in time with the beat,
200 Or a singer letting forth his voice in response to the strings.
This is what Wheelwright Bian could not express in words,
And even the most florid discourse could not capture its essence.

## XVIII

I surveyed the rules of phrasing and the laws of writing,
And they truly are things that I most admire in my heart.
205 I am intimately familiar with the common errors of this age,
And know what is good in the writing of past worthies.
Although something may come deep from within an ingenious mind,
It may be ridiculed in the eyes of the dim-sighted.
Carnelian flourishes and jade ornament
210 Are like beans on the middle of the plain;
Like the inexhaustible bellows,
Growing together with Heaven and Earth.
Although they thickly flourish in this age,

L. 214: Cf. *Mao shi* 226/1: "All morning I gather arthraxon, / It does not even fill my two hands."

L. 215: The water pitcher is a conventional figure for limited knowledge. Cf. *Zuo zhuan*, Zhao 7: "Although a man has the knowledge of a pitcher carrier, he guards his vessel closely and will not lend it."

L. 217: The You Mao text of the *Wen xuan* reads *duan yuan* 短垣 (short wall) for *duan yun* 短韻 (foreshortened verse) of the *Liuchen zhu Wen xuan*. I follow Zhu Jian (*Wen xuan jishi* 14.24a), who argues that *duan yuan* is the proper reading on the grounds that it fits better with the verb *chen zhuo* 踸踔 (to limp; to stumble).

L. 221: The earthenware pot was used to produce musical accompaniment. Dust presumably would diminish the quality of its humble sound.

L. 223: "Stirring and responding" (*gan ying* 感應 in the *Sbck* edition of the *Liuchen zhu Wen xuan*, *ying gan* in other texts) refers to the moment of literary creation or inspiration.

LL. 226–27: Cf. *Zhuangzi* 7.21a, in which Sunshu Ao explains how he viewed the attaining and loss of position: "I believed that its coming could not be rejected, and its departure could not be stopped." Lu Ji of course borrows the phrasing to refer to literary inspiration.

L. 237: Li Shan (*Wen xuan* 17.9a) cites the "Chang yan" 昌言 ("Sincere Words") of Zhongchang Tong 仲長統 (180–220), which identifies the six emotions as pleasure, anger, sorrow, joy, fondness, and hatred.

L. 244: The You Mao edition of the *Wen xuan* reads *yaya* 乙乙 for *yaya* 軋軋 of the *Liuchen zhu Wen xuan*.

L. 245: The regret presumably is for the mistakes one has made in writing.

L. 247: "This thing" refers to writing.

L. 249: Or, as Stephen Owen (*Readings*, p. 178) translates: "At times I consider the emptiness in my heart and turn against myself."

They do not fill my two hands.
215 Distressed that my water pitcher is always empty,
I deplore that "good words" are so hard to compose.
Thus, I stumble over even a low wall,
And sing forth banal sounds to complete my song.
A lingering regret always concludes my piece;
220 How can I feel fully satisfied?
I am afraid of becoming a dust-covered earthenware pot,
To be laughed at by the tinkling jade.

## XIX

As for the moment of stirring and response,
And the principle that governs obstruction and flowing freely:
225 What comes cannot be stopped,
What departs cannot be stayed.
When hiding, it vanishes like a shadow;
When active, it rises like an echo.
When the motive force of Heaven becomes swift and smooth,
230 There is no confusion that cannot be put into order.
A wind of thought bursts from the breast,
A fountain of words flows between lips and teeth.
Such splendid luxuriance and plenteous profusion
Can only be traced with brush and paper.
235 Writing, glittering and glistening, fills the eyes;
Sounds, rich and flowing, overflow the ears.
Then, when the six emotions stagnate and stall,
When the mind departs while the spirit remains:
One becomes numb as a withered tree,
240 Empty as a dried-up stream.
Then, gripping the soul, one explores the inner depths,
Gathering the inner essence, he seeks within himself.
The ordering principle, darkly shrouded, lies more deeply concealed;
Thought, repressed and held back, is hard to draw out.
245 Thus, at times one becomes emotionally spent and feels much regret;
At other times one composes at will, and faults are few.
Although this thing is within me,
Even my concerted powers cannot bring it out.
Thus, I always stroke my empty breast and sigh to myself;

229

L. 257: Cf. *Lun yu* 19/22: "The way of Kings Wen and Wu has not yet fallen to the ground."

L. 258: What I have translated as "moral influence" is *feng sheng* 風聲 (lit., "influence and reputation"). Cf. *Shang shu zhushu* 19.8a (521): "Show forth the good, bring ill on the evil, and establish for them moral influence and reputation."

L. 263: Metal and stone here refer to the materials on which inscriptions were commonly written.

250 For I do not understand the cause behind obstruction and flowing
        freely.

## XX

As for the function of literature,
It is indeed that on which a multitude of principles rest.
Over an expanse of a myriad leagues nothing blocks it;
It is a ford that links millions of years.
255 Looking forward, it offers models for future generations;
Looking back, it views patterns left by the ancients.
It rescues the way of Wen and Wu, which was about to fall;
And spreads their moral influence so that it does not perish.
No path is too far for it to embrace,
260 No principle is too subtle for it to encompass.
It equals clouds and rain in its rich moisture,
Resembles ghosts and spirits in its transformations.
It covers metal and stone and makes virtue known;
Flowing through pipes and strings, it is daily renewed.

L. 2: The mountain barrens of Jiangnan probably is Cimu Mountain 慈母山, also written 慈姆, located north of modern Maanshan 馬鞍山 City, Anhui. See Tan Qixiang, *Zhongguo lishi ditu ji* 4: 27–28, 13–10. Li Shan (*Wen xuan* 17.10b) cites a gazetteer of this area, the *Danyang ji* 丹陽記 (Notes on Danyang), which specifically identifies Cimu Mountain as the place Wang Bao describes in his rhapsody.

# Rhapsody on the Panpipes

## WANG ZIYUAN

### I

Trace the original site where panpipe bamboos grow:
And it is on a hilly waste south of the Yangtse.
Their hollow culms are straight and smooth, and sparsely noded;
Their tips, leafy and lush, luxuriantly spread.

5    Just behold the sides of the hills to which they cling!
Ruggedly rising, precipitously plunging,
They stand sheer and steep, continuously sloping:
Truly one may grieve at their instability!
But in full view one sees a vast expanse,
10   Stretching on and on, broad and boundless.
And one further rejoices at its open tranquility.
The trees entrust their bodies to Sovereign Earth,
For a myriad years they have remained unchanged.
They breathe in the rich luster of perfect essence,

---

THIS RHAPSODY by Wang Bao (*zi* Ziyuan) is also known by the title "Eulogy to the Panpipes" ("Dongxiao song" 洞簫頌); see *Han shu* 64B.2629. *Dongxiao* literally means "open pipe." It was given this name because the bottom holes of the pipes were left unsealed. See Ru Chun, *Han shu yinyi*, cited by Li Shan (*Wen xuan* 17.10b). According to Li Shan, in Han times the instrument had either twenty-three or sixteen pipes. For an excellent study of the Chinese panpipes, see Zhuang Benli, *Zhongguo gudai zhi paixiao*.

    The only other previous foreign language translation of this piece is by Obi and Hanabusa, *Monzen* 2: 358–67. There are *baihua* translations in Chen Hongtian, et al., *Zhaoming Wenxuan yizhu* 2: 923–33; Li Jingying, *Zhaoming Wenxuan xinjie* 2: 242–51; and Chi et al., *Lidai fu cidian*, pp. 95–98. A good annotated text is in Bi et al., *Zhongguo lidai fu xuan*, pp. 328–40.

L. 23: The jade fluid probably refers to spring waters.

L. 28: The cicada is known for living only on dew.

L. 38: Cf. *Lun yu* 20/2: "The gentleman is generous with making great expense."

L. 40: Ban is the famous carpenter Gongshu Ban 公輸般. See Knechtges, *Wen xuan* 1: 192, L. 186n, on Zhang Heng's "Western Metropolis Rhapsody." Jiang is Jiang Shi 匠石 (Craftsman Shi). His skills are celebrated in *Zhuangzi* (2.12a, 8.16b).

L. 41: Kui 夔 was Shun's minister in charge of music. See *Shang shu zhushu* 3.26a (276). Li Shan (*Wen xuan* 17.11b) cannot identify Fei 妃. The *Liuchen zhu Wen xuan* reads Xiang 襄, which probably refers to Shi Xiang 師襄. He was music master in the state of Wei 衛 during the Chunqiu period. Confucius reputedly studied the zither under him. See *Shi ji* 47.1925. I have followed the *Liuchen* reading here.

L. 45: The "lips" are the mouth holes.

15 Take in the moist firmness of verdurous hues.
Stirred by the changes of yin and yang,
They attach their lives to August Heaven.
Soaring breezes, soughing and sighing, blow through their branches;
Eddying rivers and coursing streams water their mountain.
20 Raising white ripples, spraying beads of water,
Roaring and raging, they pour into a deep chasm.
Morning dew, fresh and cool, falls by their sides;
Jade fluid, rich and moist, soaks their roots.
A solitary hen, a lone crane,
25 Joyfully frolic below them.
Spring birds, playing in flocks,
Soar at their tops.
Autumn cicadas, eating nothing,
Cling to their bark, chirring endlessly.
30 Black apes, howling sadly,
Seek and search within them.
They dwell in dark concealment, deeply secluded,
Thickly clustered, joined one to another.
Just carefully examine their pure form:
35 They seem fit for silence and not making sound.
Yet they were fortunate to be named "panpipe" material,
And receive the generous favor of a sage lord.
This can be called "being generous without great expense";
And also conforms to the natural essence of things.

## II

40 And then, Ban and Jiang display their craft,
Kui and Xiang determine the scale.
It is banded with ivory,
Which melds the joints and seams.
It is carved into intricate patterns;
45 Red-lacquered "lips" are diversely disposed.
Closely joined, linked and laced together,
The pipes are arrayed like fish scales, long and short.
They are compactly combined in orderly rows,
So the various fingerings can easily be applied.

L. 63: Hu Shaoying equates *uushu* (\*mjət-zjwət) 勿術 with *huyu* (\*hwət-zjwət) 汩潏, a rhyming binome used to describe the jetting and bubbling of water from a spring. In Wang Bao's line, Li Shan (*Wen xuan* 17.12b) explains it as "unimpeded." Thus, I have rendered it "smoothly flowing."

50 And then, they bid one whose sight has been blurred and dimmed,
From birth unable to perceive the forms and contours of Heaven and
       Earth,
Unable to distinguish hues and shapes of white and black,
Pent up with rage, bitter with sorrow,
Aggrieved that his eyes have lost acuity,
55 And lacking a means to release his cares,
To vent all his frustration in music.

Thus, he purses his lips in tune with *gong* and *shang*,
His harmonies, rich and strong, fill the air.
His body sways and swings in time with his blowing;
60 Glowering, he puffs up his cheeks, his rage unspent.
His breath, blasting through the pipes, suddenly bursts out,
To go forth, scattering and spreading, slowly dispersing,
Then dashing off, free and easy, smoothly flowing,
Racing off in a profusion of sound, eerie and strange.
65 Sometimes the notes blend together, burbling softly;
Or they may make a cracking sound like a snapping branch.
Sometimes they flood and flow without cease,
Brimming full as they contend to spill forth.
Then the sound is chilly and cold, tranquil and serene,
70 And abruptly dies out, as if completely stopped.
But suddenly, fast and furious, a spate of sound
Pours forth again from the pipes.

## III

Then, if one quietly listens to the rhythm,
Carefully hearkens to the tune, he will hear:
75 Manifold sounds of tweeting and tooting singing out,
Beginning slowly, gradually resounding in unison.
Like an unremitting breeze blowing without cease,
Gracefully, gently, swinging and swaying.
Then, floating away they continue on, thin and faint,
80 Until they abruptly stop to form another tune.
There they wait, blocking the road,
Until they play forth in harmony with a song.

Thus, now listen to the greater tones:

L. 104: Zhu Jian (*Wen xuan jishi* 15.3b) shows that *fenqi* 奮棄 should be read *fenqi* 糞棄, which means "cast aside"; hence, my "swept away."

L. 115: Zhong Qi is Zhong Ziqi 鍾子期, a famous music connoisseur of the Chunqiu period. Bo Ya 伯牙 was a great zither player who often performed for Zhong Ziqi. As he strummed the strings, his mind was on Mount Tai, and Zhong Ziqi exclaimed, "How skillful indeed! The music is tall and stately as Mount Tai!" Sometime later, his mind was focused on flowing water. Zhong Qizi then said, "How skillful indeed. The music is full and flowing like a coursing stream!" When Zhong Ziqi died, Bo Ya smashed his zither and refused to play again. See *Lüshi chunqiu* 14.4a. Kuang 曠 was a music expert in the state of Jin during the Chunqiu period. See Lu Ji, "Rhapsody on Literature," this volume, L. 181n.

L. 116: Qi Liang 杞梁 was a man of Qi. After he died in battle, his wife, who was childless and without kin, wailed over his corpse, which lay beneath a wall. After ten days, the intensity of her crying and lamentation caused the wall to collapse. See *Lienü zhuan* 4.5a.

They course and flow like a river in flood,
85  Engorging and disgorging everything in their embrace,
Just like a kind father nurturing his sons.
The more subtle sounds
Are calm and quiet, subdued and still,
Docile and compliant, humble and meek,
90  Like a filial son serving his father.
The morals and lessons contained in its measures and rhythms,
Correspond indeed to principles of propriety and good conduct.
They surge with fury, are roused to passion—
Oh, how like the brave warrior!
95  But in their dignified gentility, and gentle amiability
They also resemble the gentleman.

Thus, their martial sounds
Are like booming blasts of thunder,
Speeding swiftly, rumbling and roaring.
100  Their benevolent sounds
Are like the mild warmth of a southern breeze,
Generously dispensing kindness.
Sometimes they coalesce, gather en masse;
Sometimes they are scattered and swept away.
105  Sometimes the sounds are grave and despairing, sad and sorrowful;
Sometimes they are quiet and tranquil, calm and composed.
At times they are fine and delicate like tiny drops,
Or flow strong and easily like a river bursting its banks.
When mournful and plaintive, one's heart is beset with care;
110  Yet the sweet and mellifluous tones are something to savor.


## IV

Thus, when the greedy and grasping listen to this music, their
            character becomes pure;
The fierce and malicious hear it, and do not grumble or complain.
The firm and resolute, the vicious and cruel return to benevolence
            and kindness;
The idle and indolent refrain from misdeeds.
115  Zhong Qi, Ya, and Kuang become disconcerted and dismayed,
Qi Liang's wife could not match its spirited feeling,

239

L. 117: Shi Xiang was a music master of the state of Wei. See L. 41n above. Yan Chun 嚴春 probably refers to Zhuang Chun 莊春, who is mentioned in the *Qi lüe* (cited by Li Shan, *Wen xuan* 17.14a) catalog as an expert on the zither. He also is mentioned in "Rhapsody on the Flute," attributed to Song Yu. See *Guwen yuan* 1.5b.

L. 118: Li Shan (*Wen xuan* 17.14a) explains *qinyin* 浸淫 as "like *jianran* 漸冉 [gradually]," which Li claims has the meaning here of "closely approach." He thus takes it as descriptive of Shuzi, whom he identifies as Yan Shuzi 顏叔子. The Mao commentary to the *Classic of Songs* (see *Mao shi zhushu* 12.3.20b, 978) says he lived alone next to a widow. One night a windstorm destroyed her home, and she fled to Shuzi's house. Shuzi took her in, but kept his house illuminated by holding a candle all night to avoid suspicions of impropriety. Li Shan probably construed *qinyin* as somehow descriptive of Yan Shuzi's conduct, but I am not sure exactly what it would mean in this context, or what the story of Yan Shuzi and the widow has to do with Wang Bao's line. Based on parallelism with the preceding line, Qin Yin could be a name, as Zhang Xian (in *Liuchen zhu Wen xuan* 17.20b) construes it. However, if it is a name, this person is not otherwise known. My translation is a tentative one that follows Li Shan, and I have rendered *qinyin* as "approachable" (Shuzi).

L. 119: Zhu is Dan Zhu 丹朱, the doltish son of Yao; Jun is Shang Jun 商均, the unworthy son of Shun. The expressions *yin* 嚚 (stupid) and *wan* 頑 (stubborn) are actually applied to Shun's father and mother respectively in the "Canon of Yao" (see *Shang shu zhushu* 2.24b).

L. 120: Jie is the evil last ruler of the Xia dynasty. Zhi is the notorious Robber Zhi. Yu 驚 probably refers to the warrior Xia Yu 夏育. See Knechtges, *Wen xuan* 1: 220, L. 564n. Li Shan (*Wen xuan* 17.14a) says Bo is Shen Bo 申博, about whom nothing is known. He cites "Encomium to Xia Yu," which mentions the ferocity of Xia Yu and the bravery of Shen Bo.

L. 121: Li Shan (17.14a) explains *cenci* 參差 (lit., "the long and short") as another name for the panpipes. Thus, following him, the line would read: "Playing the panpipes, one enters into the realm of morality." However, it is not the performer who enters into morality, but rather the listener. Recently, Sun Changxu has adduced good arguments to show that *cenci* did not originally mean panpipes, and that in Wang Bao's line the word describes the manifold variety of the pipe music (e.g., high and low, strong and weak, long and short). He also argues that *chui* 吹 means "pipe music." See " 'Chui cenci' fei 'chui dongxiao' shuo." I have followed Sun's interpretation.

LL. 129–30: These lines are extremely difficult and unclear. Hu Shaoying (*Wen xuan jianzheng* 17.14a) argues that *bosuo* (\*bak-sak) 薄索 represents *pocu* (\*prak-tshjuk) 迫促 (hurried; urgent). However, I am not sure how this meaning fits this context. Thus, I have followed Li Shan (*Wen xuan* 17.4b), who glosses it as "urgently search." The meaning of *wangxiang* 罔象 (formless) also is difficult to construe. Zhang Xian (in *Liuchen zhu Wen xuan* 17.21a) says it refers to "lingering sound," presumably meaning that which lingers after the music stops.

LL. 133–35: Wang Niansun (*Dushu zazhi*, "Zhiyu," B.39b) proposes that the reading 聞其悲聲 of the You Mao text should be emended to 其為悲聲, which is the *Wuchen* text reading. Wang takes the line as applying to the panpipe player, who is the subject of the following two lines. However, the entire emphasis of the piece is the effect the music has on those who hear it, and thus I have retained the You Mao reading.

L. 137: Wang Niansun (*Dushu zazhi*, "Zhiyu,"B.39b) shows that *yan* 衍 of the You Mao text is an error for *kan* 衎 (happy). See also Hu Shaoying, *Wen xuan jianzheng* 19.7a.

L. 139: Zhu Jian (*Wen xuan jishi* 15.4a) shows that *chihuo* 蚚蠖 is a variant for *chihuo* 尺蠖 (measuring worm).

L. 140: Wang Bao here describes the effect the music has even on lowly insects.

L. 141: Zhu Jian (*Wen xuan jishi* 15.4a–b) shows that *yanyan* 蝘蜓 should be emended to *yanting* 蝘蜓 (gecko).

Shi Xiang and Yan Chun would not dare to display their skill,
Even the approachable Yan Shuzi would keep his distance from his
        kind,
The stupid and stubborn Zhu and Jun would be startled and have
        their intelligence restored,
120 Jie, Zhi, Yu, and Bo would become weak and fatigued.
The music of the pipes, so varied and diverse, enters the realm of
        morality,
And thus always can be enjoyed and honored.


## V

At times the panpipe plays a rapid tune:
The sounds wander and waver,
125 Sometimes pausing, unmoving,
Sometimes moving without pause.
Quiet and soft they scatter,
Without partner, bereft of mate.
Then urgently searching, repeating and repeating,
130 They find each other in the realm beyond form.
Thus, those who truly understand music both rejoice and sorrow
        over it;
Those who do not understand music find it wondrous and grand.
Those who hear its sad sounds
Do not fail to heave sad sighs,
135 And wipe away copious tears.
And with the playing of a joyful melody,
None fails to feel cheerful and glad,
Calm and relaxed.
Thus, the cricket and measuring worm
140 Slow their crawl, gasping and panting.
The molecricket, ant, and gecko

L. 158: Li Shan (*Wen xuan* 17.15a) glosses *jiaosou xiaoshao* 攪搜澤捎 as the sound of water. Hu Shaoying (*Wen xuan jianzheng* 19.8b) shows that the phrase has the sense of "shaking."

L. 159: Hu Shaoying (*Wen xuan jianzheng* 19.8b) proposes that *xiaoyao* 逍遙 should be understood as *xiaotiao* 踃跳 (leaping and jumping).

L. 169: Cf. *Lun yu* 3/20: "'The Osprey' is joyous without being licentious, it is sorrowful without being injurious."

L. 170: *Tiaochang* 條暢, here rendered "ordered and smooth," is the word used in L. 3 above to describe the bamboo canes. Here it describes the music.

L. 171: *Jiecao* 節操, which I have rendered "strict rhythm," also means "integrity and principle." This is another example of Wang Bao's imbuing panpipe music with moral qualities.

Creeping along, languid and listless,
Move to and fro, back and forth,
Goggling like fish, gaping like fowl.
145  Lowering their mouths, they whirl and twirl,
Staring intently, forgetting to eat.
How much more would this affect humankind, which is stirred by
              the harmony of yin and yang,
And transformed by moral custom!


## VI

The finale says:
Its manner of sounds is like a nimble acrobat,
150  Leaping and vaulting, springing and bounding,
Fleet and quick, agile and graceful.
It also is like dashing waves,
Foaming and frothing, rushing and raging,
Racing through a tortuous channel.
155  The music blares and blasts,
Rises and falls, stops and starts,
In a jarring and jostling of sounds.
Quaking and quivering, jolting and shaking,
Roaming at will, surging and swelling,
160  As if something had toppled and collapsed.
Relaxed and easy the rhythm flows,
Lingering briefly, hesitating and pausing —
One becomes almost spellbound.
Then, fading and falling, the sounds depart:
165  Bidding a final farewell, they vanish in the distance,
Drifting about, never to return.
The music is bestowed the transforming influence of the sages,
Calm and composed it accords with the Way,
And is joyous without being licentious.
170  Ordered and smooth, clear and penetrating,
It follows a strict rhythm.
When the song ends and the music stops,
There still is a lingering melody.
The remnant sounds of the piper's breath
175  Continuing on, reverberating in the pipes,

Generate a light breeze.
The music goes on in an unceasing stream,
Changing and transforming without end.

# Rhapsody on Dance

## FU WUZHONG

### I

After King Xiang had toured the Yunmeng park,[1] he had Song Yu rhapsodize on the events of Gaotang.[2] He had prepared a banquet and was about to begin feasting and drinking, when he said to Song Yu, "I would like to entertain all of my courtiers. What can I use to amuse them?"

Song Yu replied, "I have heard that song is used to intone words,[3] and dance is used to give full expression to meaning. Thus, discoursing on a song cannot compare with hearing its sounds, and hearing its sounds

---

IN THIS RHAPSODY Fu Yi (*zi* Wuzhong) describes a favorite form of entertainment in the Han, a type of dance known as the "Qi pan" 七盤 ("Seven Plate-Drums"). Seven flat drums shaped like plates (*pan gu* 盤鼓) were placed on the ground. The performers beat out the rhythm on the drums as they danced around them. There is a Han mural painting from Yi'nan 沂南, Shandong, that clearly portrays this dance. See Wang Zhongshu, "Yi'nan shike huaxiang zhong de Qi pan wu." For another Han rhapsody on this dance see Zhang Heng's "Rhapsody on Dance" in Zhang Zhenze, *Zhang Heng shiwen ji jiaozhu*, pp. 257–62. There also is a study of the "Qi pan" dance by Konishi Noburo, "Shichiban mai ni kansuru shosetsu ni tsuite." Fu Yi does not set his *fu* in the Han, but uses the poet Song Yu, who was reputedly an expert on music, to describe the dance for the king of Chu Song Yu begins with a brief discourse on music, and surprisingly defends the music of Zheng and Wei as appropriate as a means of providing entertainment. Fu Yi first describes the dancers, their costumes, and adornments, then follows with a curious song about leaving worldly cares and travails behind. The description of the dance is typical of the rhapsodies on music, and focuses on the varied movements of the dancers as well as the "spirit" or unseen aspects of the dance ("Their spirit is like floating clouds, / Their mood is like autumn frost"). The rhapsody concludes with a charming account of the guests leaving the gathering.

Previous translations include von Zach, *Deutsche Wacht* (September 1928), rpt. in *Die Chinesische Anthologie* 1: 245–49; and Obi and Hanabusa, *Monzen* 2: 368–78. There are *baihua* translations in Chen Hongtian, et al., *Zhaoming Wen xuan yizhu* 2· 934–46; Li Jingying, *Zhaoming Wen xuan xinjie* 2: 252–61; and Chi et al., *Lidai fu cidian*, pp. 191–94.

cannot compare with observing its outer manifestation.[4] The dances of 'Turbulent Chu,' 'Binding Wind,' and 'Sunny Bank'[5] are the grandest spectacles of the female talents,[6] and are the greatest wonders of the empire. I wonder, could these be presented?"

The king said, "How about the music of Zheng?"

Song Yu said, "The lesser and greater are put to different uses. The Zheng and the "Elegantiae" are appropriate for different occasions. Laxness and tautness were measures applied by the sage and wise.[7] Thus, the *Book of Music* records the gestures of the "Axe-and-Shield,"[8] the "Elegantiae" praises the dancing of "graceful stepping,"[9] the *Rites* sets forth rules for the three toasts,[10] and the "Eulogia" has a song about returning drunk.[11] "All-encompassing Pond" and "Six Blossoms" are for display in the ancestral temple and harmonizing spirits and man.[12] The music of Zheng and Wei is for the purpose of entertaining a group of guests and providing pleasure and joy. Pleasant dissipation on idle days may not be for the purpose of instructing the people, but what harm does it do?"

The king said, "Please try to rhapsodize on this for me."

Song Yu said, "Very well."

## II

On this quiet night so bright and clear,
The moon shines down, spreading its light.
Long rows of vermilion torches, blazing forth,
Light up ornate rooms, illumine secluded chambers.
5   Embroidered curtains, tied with sashes, are drawn open;
Door knockers flare with glaring glitter.
Cushions and mats are spread, seats arranged;
Bronze wine jars are filled, jade goblets are put in place.
Beakers and cups, brimming full, are passed around;
10   Once drunk, everyone feels happiness and joy.
Solemn faces turn pleasant and cheerful;
Deep-held feelings come forth, outwardly expressed.
The man of letters cannot withhold his artistry;
The intrepid warrior cannot hide his bravery.
15   Lazily, idly, they begin to dance,
Joyfully frolicking hand in hand.
Deep indeed is their wild abandon,
How different from their normal reserve!

L. 20: Cf. "Summoning the Soul," L. 74 (*Chuci buzhu* 9.7a): "Double lines of eight attend you through the night"; L. 113 (ibid. 9.11b): "Double lines of eight, in perfect accord, begin a dance of Zheng."

L. 40: Li Shan (*Wen xuan* 17.17b) interprets *moshi* 末事 (petty affairs) as referring to the music of Zheng and Wei, which "bends and twists" to suit the ruler's whims. I am not sure how he arrived it this interpretation, for in the lines above Fu Yi actually seems to praise the music of Zheng and Wei. However, I am not certain what *weiqu* 觟曲 (bends and twists) refers to. Thus, I have left my translation deliberately vague.

L. 43: Cf. Wang Bao, "Rhapsody on the Panpipes," this volume, L. 169n.

L. 44: "Cricket" is the title of *Mao shi* 114. According to the Mao Preface (*Mao shi zhushu* 6.1.3a), this song criticizes Duke Xi 僖 of Jin for his excessive frugality and urges him to enjoy himself according to the Rites. In contrast to the preceding line, which praised "The Osprey" for not being licentious, this line condemns the narrow viewpoint of refraining from all pleasures.

L. 45: Dance was attributed with the power to remove blockage in the pneumas and to enhance their circulation. See *Lüshi chunqiu* 5.8a. Here, the pneumas are called Grand Reality (*Tai zhen* 泰真).

L. 46: Cf. *Zhuangzi* 7.17b: Confucius said to Lao Dan, who had just come out of his bath: "Is this a delusion? Or is it really so? A moment ago, sir, your body was as stiff as a withered tree, as though you had left everything behind, parted from humankind, and were standing in solitude."

LL. 47–48: "Ardent *Zhi*" ("Ji zhi" 激徵) and "Clear *Jiao*" ("Qing jiao" 清角) are musical modes. In the *Hanfeizi* (3.3b–4a), the music master Kuang describes "Clear *Jiao*" as the ultimate musical mode.

L. 50: I am unsure of the exact meaning of *jun qu* 均曲, which I have tentatively rendered "melodic tune." *Jun* is a device used to tune zither strings. Perhaps *jun qu* means a well-modulated tune.

## III

    And then, maidens from Zheng present themselves;
20  Stepping slowly in double lines of eight, they attend their lord.
    Their lovely garments are the ultimate in beauty;
    Pleasant and cheerful, perfect is their demeanor.
    Their features, so comely and fair, are bewitching;
    Their rosy faces, radiant, resplendently glow.
25  Their eyebrows, drawn delicate and fine, form repeated curves;
    Their eyes, rolling and glancing, are like flowing waves.
    Pearls and kingfisher plumes glisten and glitter;
    Colored jackets with flying sashes are adorned with dainty gauze.

    Looking back at the shadows cast by their forms,
30  They straighten and adjust their clothes.
    With every puff of a gentle breeze,
    They send forth the sweet scent of pollia.
    Parting their vermilion lips,
    Furrowing their clear brows,
35  They open their throats and sing aloud,
    All in accord with musical rules.

## IV

    The song goes:
    "I dispel my thoughts, broaden my vision,
    Release the bonds that confine my soul,
    Loosen the tightly stretched strings,
40  And spurn the bends and twists of petty affairs,
    Expanding my scope even broader and wider,
    Removing myself from trifling troubles.
    I praise the absence of licentious conduct in 'The Osprey,'
    And sorrow at the narrow vision of 'The Cricket.'
45  Opening the blockage in Grand Reality,
    Rising on high, I leave everything behind and transcend the world.'

    Then, striking up "Ardent *Zhi*,"
    And sounding forth "Clear *Jiao*,"
    Accompanied by a dance rhythm,
50  They perform a melodic tune.

LL. 80–81: Cf. Wang Bao, "Rhapsody on the Panpipes," this volume, L. 115n

Form and gestures are graceful and smooth,
Spirit and mood are in perfect harmony.
All is done with effortless ease,
And nothing perturbs their minds.


## V

And then, the dancers step to the beat of outspread drums,
55   Their mood relaxed and carefree.
They let their minds wander in the boundless,
Yearning for the distant, contemplating the far away.
When they first begin:
They seem to be looking up, yet looking down,
60   They seem to be arriving, yet departing.
They are calm and composed, yet sad and sorrowful.
They simply cannot be described.

Advancing slightly:
They seem to be flying, yet walking,
65   They seem to be standing, yet falling.
Still or moving, they follow the beat;
Their gestures and glances accord with the tune.
Gossamer gowns blow in the breeze,
Long sleeves tangle and twine together.
70   On and on, unceasing, they flit about,
Whirling and twirling together with the music.
They flutter about like hovering swallows,
And soar into the air like startled swans.
Comely and graceful, dignified and fair,
75   They are nimble and quick, light of form.
Their demeanor is fine beyond compare,
And their hearts are true and pure.
They cultivate virtuous conduct to make known their good intent,
And they let their hearts race alone into the distant darkness.
80   When their thoughts are on mountains, the dancing seems "tall and
        stately";
When their hearts are with water, it seems "full and flowing."
Their movements shift and change with their mood,
And no gesture is done without purpose:

L. 99: Li Shan (*Wen xuan* 17.19a) construes *ni* 儗 as "analogy" or "comparison," and interprets the line to say that the gestures and movements of the dancers contain symbolic significance. However, he does not explain how *ni* fits in with *qie* 切 (close), which immediately precedes it. Thus, I have taken *qieni* together to mean "pressed closely together."

They interpret the song and express its meaning,
85  First with heavy sighs, then with spirited excitement.
Their spirit is like floating clouds,
Their mood is like autumn frost.
Those who view it gasp in wonder,
For such performers are beyond compare.

## VI

90  And then, the full ensemble comes forth,
One after another, each dancer waiting her turn.
They vie in displaying talent, in showing skill,
And their beautiful faces are all adorned.
Splendid poses are continuously born,
95  Magnificent postures wondrously appear.
Gazing at the plate-drum, they roll their limpid eyes;
Intoning seductive sounds, they flash their glistening teeth.
They even their ranks, order their rows,
To and fro, pressed closely together.
100  Vaguely they resemble moving spirits,
Soaring in circles, then coming to rest.
The drum does not miss a beat,
And the dancers' feet never seem to touch the ground.
As if on wing they abruptly depart,
105  And suddenly the dancing stops.

## VII

Then, as they turn about and reenter the stage,
Urged on by a quickened tempo, they dance:
Now leaping into the air, then dropping to their knees,
Now walking on their toes, then on their heels.
110  Suddenly twisting their bodies, far off they go,
Bending so supplely they seem about to snap.
Thin gossamer flies like moths,
Fluttering about as if severed from their gowns.
They leap forward like flocking birds,
115  Then disperse, their pace relaxed and slow.
Dainty and delicate, they turn and twirl,

253

Rolling like clouds, swift as the wind.
Their bodies are like cavorting dragons,
Their sleeves are like white rainbows.
120 Slow and solemn, they bow,
And the dance number comes to an end.
Then, pausing briefly, smiling faintly,
They withdraw and return to their places.
The spectators all shout "bravo,"
125 And nary a one is not delighted.

## VIII

Then, they revel and feast late into the night,
When the host orders the guests to be sent off.
They quickly dash to their chariots,
Their coachmen steadying the reins.
130 Chariots and horse-riders, crowded together,
Closely clustered, press and push.
Fine chargers, with unsurpassed speed,
Swiftly galloping, pass one another,
Prancing like dragons, heads held high,
135 Straining at their bits, foam spuming from their mouths.
The horses, each with different skill,
Try to overtake each other.
One, outracing the dust in the dash for the road,
Swift as the shock of thunder, the flash of lighting,
140 His hooves pounding the ground, far from the group,
Suddenly leaps ahead, alone and unrivaled.
One, stomping in place, filled with fury,
Hesitates, unwilling to set off.
He is the last to depart, but the first to arrive,
145 And becomes the object of the others' pursuit.
And one, his manner dignified and sedate,
Steps in stately solemnity, in refined harmony,
Moving slow or fast at the driver's will,
His speed completely under control.
150 The sound of the chariots is like thunder,
As they gallop by one after another.
Flurrying past in a steady stream, they return home,

Like a bank of clouds suddenly lifting, leaving the city empty and
        still.
The heavenly king feasts
155 And is joyful, but not to excess.
Cheering his spirit, and ignoring old age,
Are methods of prolonging his years.
Relaxed and at ease,
He shall spend his days.

# 18

MUSIC, PART II

# Rhapsody on the Long Flute

## MA JICHANG

I am widely read in the ancient canons and odes,[1] and am thoroughly conversant with numerical arts.[2] Also, by nature I am fond of music, and I am able to strum the zither and play the flute. Since I began working in the Bureau of Merit,[3] I have had no pressing matters, and have been idling away my time alone in Pingyang Settlement in Mei Prefecture.[4] There was a guest staying in the hostel who played on the flute the songs for instrumental accompaniment "Qi chu" and "Jing lie."[5] I have been away from the capital for over a year and, upon hearing this music, I suddenly felt both sad and happy over it. I recalled that there were odes by Wang Ziyuan,[6] Mei Sheng,[7] Liu Bokang,[8] Fu Wuzhong,[9]

IN THIS RHAPSODY Ma Rong (*zi* Jichang) describes the blowing instrument known as the *chang di* 長笛 (long flute). The *Shuowen* (see *Shuowen jiezi gulin* 5A.1980b–82a) and the *Fengsu tongyi* (see Wu Shuping, *Fengsu tongyi jiaoshi* 6.243) say the flute had seven holes. Ma Rong wrote this rhapsody around 126 when he was stationed in the Youfufeng area (see n. 3 to this rhapsody).

Ma Rong's rhapsody follows the model of Wang Bao's "Rhapsody on the Panpipes." He begins with a long description of the Zhongnan Mountains, on which the bamboo used to make flutes grows. He describes the rugged slopes and the raging rivers that flow past the bamboo groves. This perilous terrain has a terrifying effect on animals and even the bamboo, which moan sadly in the wind. Intrepid climbers are then sent to the mountains to cut bamboo, with which craftsmen make a flute. The flute is used in a performance for young nobles, and Ma Rong describes the manifold aspects of the flute music, comparing its sounds to everything from a pounded forge to the whistling wind and flowing water. This music has a transforming effect on listeners, who learn from the music the proper norms of behavior. The music stirs animals and evil men, as well as hermits, officials, and even fish. Upon hearing it, famous singers and musicians are forced to cease their performance, and the audience is struck dumb in awe of its marvelous sound. Ma Rong ends with a section comparing the flute with other instruments, to which it is vastly superior. Instead of a finale, he inserts a song attributed to the musician Qiu Zhong of the Former Han period, who tells of the origins of the flute in the land of the Qiang 羌 (proto-Tibetans), and how it was

259

L. 1: The *zhonglong* 鐘籠 is a type of bamboo used for making wind instruments such as the flute. See Hagerty, "Tai K'ai-chih's *Chu-p'u*," pp. 386–87.

L. 2: Zhongnan 終南 Mountain, located south of modern Xi'an, is a peak in the Qinling range.

L. 5: Li Shan (*Wen xuan* 18.2a) explains *jian* 箭 (arrow bamboo) and *gao* 槀 as two types of bamboo. However, elsewhere in his commentary he cites Zheng Xuan's *Zhou li* commentary, which explains *gao* as the stalk of the arrow bamboo. (This actually is from Zheng Zhong's commentary; see *Zhou li zhushu* 28.10b [1795].)

L. 6: The combination *lingfeng* 聆風 is ambiguous. Liu Liang (in *Liuchen zhu Wen xuan* 18.2a) explains it as "hearing the wind." However, based on parallelism with the preceding line, it could be a type of bamboo. Thus, Li Shan (18.2a; for the corrected reading, see Hu Kejia's *Kaoyi* in *Wen xuan* 2.33a) cites Zheng Xuan's gloss on the bamboo called *junlu* 箘簬 (see *Shangshu zhushu* 6.16a), which he equates with *lingfeng* 笭風. *Junlu* seems to be another name for *shetong* 射筒 (blowpipe bamboo); see *Shuowen jiezi gulin* 5A.1908a–b, Duan Yucai's commentary. I follow this interpretation without any great confidence that it is correct. For a detailed discussion of this passage, see Zhu Jian, *Wen xuan jishi* 15.7a.

L. 18: Li Shan's (*Wen xuan* 18.2a) explanation of this line (嵍窞巖覆) is confusing. He equates kan 嵍 with *kan* 坎 (chasm). He then cites *Shuowen* (*Shuowen jiezi gulin* 7B.3287–88), which explains dan 窞 as "a small chasm within a chasm." He then glosses 巖覆 as "the appearance of not being level." However, he goes on to cite *Guangya* (*Guangya shuzheng* 7A.5a), which explains fu 覆 as "cavern." Thus, one is not sure how Li Shan understood the line. Noting Li Shan's confusion, Hu Shaoying (*Wen xuan jianzheng* 19.16a) proposes that the line simply means "small chasms within chasms, caverns within crags." I follow his explanation for lack of anything better.

L. 21: Li Shan (*Wen xuan* 18.2b) explains *xiao* 篠 as equivalent to *xiao* 篠 (dwarf bamboo). However, Hu Shaoying (*Wen xuan jianzheng* 19.16a–b) rightly argues that *linxiao* 林篠 should be a descriptive binome parallel with *senshan* 森槮 in the following line. I follow him in rendering *linxiao* as "leafy and lush." "Spreading vinebush" is my invention for *manjing* 蔓荆 (*Vitex trifolia*), a large shrub with vinelike branches. See Smith, p. 457.

L. 22: Two types of oak are mentioned in this line, the *zuo* 柞 (*Quercus dentata*, Chinese oak) and *bu* 樸 (*Quercus acutissima*, bigleaf oak). See Lu Wenyu, *Shi caomu jinshi*, p. 12, no. 17, and p. 67, no. 76.

and others on the panpipes, zither, and mouth organ. Only the flute had none. Thus, in order to fill in the gap, I have composed "Rhapsody on the Long Flute," which reads as follows:

## I

The rare *zhonglong* bamboo
Grows on the shady slopes of Zhongnan.
It rests on a solitary mount, nine tiers high,
And overlooks a stony ravine, a myriad yards deep.
5   Solitary stands of arrow bamboo rise straight and tall,
Alone, blowpipe bamboo rests on the most precipitous heights.
Autumn downpours cleanse their base,
Winter snows pile up on their branches.
Standing with roots clinging to the summit, they are perilously
        poised;
10  When struck by a whirling gale, they seem about to fall.

To the front and sides are layered crests piled with boulders,
Clustered together, evenly placed.
They rise sheer and steep, tall and towering;
They slope and slant, abrupt and sharp.
15  Gaping wide, hollow and open,
Are coombs and corries, one joined to another.
There are gullies and ravines, deep and smooth,
Chasms inside chasms, caverns in crags.
Twining and twisting, winding and weaving,
20  Ridges join, summits intersect.
Leafy and lush grows spreading vinebush;
Luxuriant and thick rise tall oaks.

---

altered by the *Classic of Changes* expert Jing Fang 京房. This poem is a tour de force of rhapsodic description, replete with numerous binomial descriptives and rare words that defy translation. My renderings of many of these expressions are only vague approximations.

    The only previous translation into a foreign language of this piece is Obi and Hanabusa, *Monzen* 2: 379–96. There are *baihua* translations in Chen Hongtian, et al., *Zhaoming Wen xuan yizhu*, 2: 947–69; Li Jingying, *Zhaoming Wenxuan xinjie* 2: 262–78; and Chi et al., *Lidai fu cidian*, pp. 216–21.

L. 24: Hu Shaoying (*Wen xuan jianzheng* 19.17a) suggests that *zhang* 障 means "to stop up," "to dam." Clearly what Ma Rong describes here are the pools overflowing with water. Thus, I have rendered *zhang kui* 障潰 somewhat freely as "swell and burst."

L. 26: Li Shan (*Wen xuan* 18.2b) explains that *dui tou* 碓投 means the waters beat into the caves like a pestle pounding grain. Hu Shaoying (*Wen xuan jianzheng* 19.17a–b) argues that *dui* 碓 is a variant for *dui* 堆 (mound). Here it possibly means *sha dui* 沙堆 (sandbar).

L. 57: Sounding Bell (Hao zhong 號鐘) was a zither played by the famous musician Bo Ya. See *Chuci buzhu* 16.22b.

## *II*

And then mountain streams arrive in torrents,
Ponds and pools swell and burst their banks.
25 The waters roil and rage in copious flow,
Tossing aside sandbars, pouring into caves.
Turbulent rapids whirl and swirl,
Gurging and gushing, swelling and surging.
Ripples and waves, patterned like fish scales,
30 Rising and falling, colliding and clashing,
Spurting foam, spewing froth,
Race away, battering and beating the rocks.

That which rocks the mountain,
And jolts the roots of the trees,
35 Comes five or six times a year.

Thus, there are no paths in the open spaces,
And human tracks rarely reach here.
Gibbons and monkeys scream at dawn,
Flying squirrels chatter in the night,
40 A wintry bear opens his jowls,
A great stag looks back at his mane.
Golden pheasants flock in the morning,
Wild pheasants cry at daybreak.
Seeking their mates, cooing to their chicks,
45 Sadly they shriek, long they call.
Walking slowly over familiar paths,
They loudly chatter and chitter.
Whether passing left and right of the grove,
Or chirring to its front and rear,
50 Day or night they do not rest.

This indeed is a place oppressed by daunting danger and precipitous
       terrain,
Where a multitude of sorrows and manifold grief gathers.

Thus, in response to a cool breeze,
Their tender branches shudder and shake,
55 Resounding loud and soft,
Like a tautly strung zither, the stops tightly wound,
Or Sounding Bell playing a high-pitched tune.

L. 60: Peng is Peng Xian 彭咸, a Shang official who drowned himself after his ruler failed to heed his advice. See *Chuci buzhu* 1.11a, 1.37a. Xu refers to Wu Zixu 伍子胥 (ob. 485 B.C.), an official who loyally served King Fucha of Wu. Angered by Wu Zixu's admonition not to make peace with Yue, Fucha ordered him to commit suicide. Wu's body was wrapped in a leather sack and thrown into the Yangtze River. See *Shi ji* 66.2180. Boqi 伯奇 is a famous filial son. According to the *Qin cao* (cited by Li Shan, *Wen xuan* 18.3b), he was the son of Jifu 吉甫, the minister to King Xuan of Zhou. After Boqi's mother died, Jifu took another wife, who gave birth to a son named Bobang 伯邦. The new wife accused Boqi of licentious intentions toward her. When Jifu expressed his doubt about her charges, she proposed to put Boqi to a test by having Jifu observe his son's behavior from a nearby tower. The wife placed a poisonous wasp inside her collar, and the kindly and filial Boqi immediately came to her rescue and pulled it out. Thinking his son had made improper advances, Jifu had Boqi expelled to the countryside. One day King Xuan was out on an excursion accompanied by Jifu. The king heard Boqi playing a moving song, which he immediately recognized as a tune by a banished son. Jifu then recalled his son and had the scheming wife put to death.

L. 61: Sorrowful Jiang (Ai Jiang 哀姜) was the senior wife of Duke Wen 文 of Lu. After Duke Wen died in 609 B.C., Lady Jiang's two sons were murdered by the minister Xiangzhong 襄仲, who conspired to install the son of Duke Wen's secondary wife, Jingying 敬嬴, on the throne. Lady Jiang was then obliged to return to her home state of Qi. As she passed the marketplace she began to weep, crying out, "Oh, Heaven! Xiangzhong has acted contrary to the proper Way. He has murdered the legitimate heir and installed a concubine's son on the throne!" Those in the market all wept, and the people of Lu called her Sorrowful Jiang. See *Zuo zhuan*, Wen 18 (Legge, *The Chinese Classics* 5: 282); *Shi ji* 33.1536; and Chavannes, *Mh* 4: 116–17. Filial Ji (Xiao Ji 孝己) was the son of King Wuding of Yin. His mother died when he was young, and he was mistreated by his father's second wife, who was able to persuade Wuding to expel him. Ji, who was renowned for his filial piety, died in exile. See *Diwang shiji* 帝王世紀 (Annals of Emperors and Kings), cited by Li Shan (*Wen xuan* 18.3b).

L. 64: Cf. Liu Xiang, "Nine Longings," "Impatience with the World," L. 40 (*Chuci buzhu* 17.7a): "My moans and sighs resound like thunder."

L. 70: Ban of Lu is the famous craftsman Gongshu Ban. See Wang Bao, "Rhapsody on the Panpipes," this volume, L. 40n. Di of Song is the philosopher and expert on technology Mo Di (Mozi).

LL. 81–82: On Kui and Xiang, see Wang Bao, "Rhapsody on the Panpipes," this volume, L. 41n. Ziye refers to Music Master Kuang. There were six yang pitches, which were called *lü* 律, and six yin pitches, which were called *lü* 呂.

L. 84: The "yellow bell" is one of the twelve pitchpipes.

L. 85: Based on their position in this line, *jin* 斤 and *xie* 械 should be verbs. Following the *Shuowen* (see *Shuowen jiezi gulin* 14A.6371a–72a, 6A.3634b–35a), Li Shan glosses *jin* 斤 as "to cut wood," and *xie* 械 as "to put in order" (to plane?). Thus, I have translated them as "pare and plane."

L. 88: Chen Hongtian et al., *Zhaoming Wen xuan yizhu* (2: 956, n. 86) suggests that "sizing the outside" means placing the holes at specified intervals.

LL. 89–90: Li Shan (*Wen xuan* 18.5a) explains that because of its capacity "to cleanse filth" (\**diek* 笛, "flute," is homphonous with \**diek* 滌, "to cleanse"), the flute can be used to observe worthy men.

## III

And then, an exiled official, a banished son,
An abandoned wife, a departed friend,
60   Peng, Xu, and Boqi,
Sorrowful Jiang and Filial Ji,
All gather downwind,
Concentrating their energy, listening intently.
Moaning and sighing with thunderous noise,
65   They pound their chests, beat their breasts.
They weep copious tears of blood,
That flow in torrents down their faces.
From night till dawn they cannot sleep,
And are unable to restrain their emotions.

## IV

70   And then they send Ban of Lu and Di of Song
To build scaling ladders,
Erect floating columns:
They climb over slender roots,
Walk on tender vines,
75   Their chests rubbing against the cliff,
Their bellies glued to the slope.
When they reach the top,
Crawling and creeping, they begin to cut,
Lopping and pruning both root and branch.
80   Following proper pattern and measure,
Kui and Xiang arrange the yang pitches,
Ziye tunes the yin pitches.
The twelve pitches are then all prepared,
With the yellow bell as the guide.

85   They straighten and bend, pare and plane,
Cut and trim, measure and match.
They drill and polish, shavings flying and falling from their tools;
Having sized the outside, they paint the inside red.
They determine its name and call it "flute,"
90   And use it to observe the character of good men.
It is set out by the eastern stairway,

265

L. 92: The eight musical sounds are the various timbres of musical instruments made of eight different materials: metal, stone, silk, bamboo, gourd, earth, leather, and wood. See *Zhou li zhushu* 23.10b (1716).

L. 93: *Shi ju* 食舉 (lit., "to perform while eating") also is a type of banquet music used in the Han period. See Guo Maoqian, *Yuefu shiji* 13.181. "Concord" ("Yong" 雍) is the title of *Mao shi* 282. The singing of this piece for the clearing of the vessels is mentioned in *Lun yu* 3/2 and *Zhou li zhushu* 23.4b (1713), Zheng Xuan's commentary.

L. 95: The Yellow Gate (Huang men 黃門) designated the private living quarters of the Han emperor. According to Huan Tan, musicians and singers were stationed there, presumably to provide entertainment for the emperor. See Pokora, *Hsin-lun*, p. 118.

LL. 96–97: Zhongqiu 重丘 is a prefecture in Pingyuan 平原 Commandery. It was located east of modern Ling 陵 *xian*, Shandong. See Tan Qixiang, *Zhongguo lishi ditu ji* 2: 19–20, 1–4. Song, Guan, Guo, and Zhang presumably are famous musicians.

L. 114: Li Shan (*Wen xuan* 18.5b) refers to *Heguanzi* B.18a, in which the expression *hua yu* 華羽 is also used: "In the south, the myriad things all have resplendent outer adornment [*hua yu*]. Thus, it is tuned to the *yu* 羽 note." There is an obvious pun on *yu* 羽 (outer adornment) and *yu* (the fifth of the five notes). Ma Rong seems to associate it with emotional intensity.

L. 123: This line seems to refer to the sudden retardation after the tempo had increased to breakneck speed.

And played together with the eight musical sounds.
They begin the meal with music, conclude it with "Concord,"
To enhance the appetite of worthy gentlemen.

95 And then, retiring to the Yellow Gate to put the music in order are:
Song and Guan from Zhongqiu,
Famous masters Guo and Zhang,
Accomplished musicians and artistes,
Practice their art, master its sounds.

## V

100 And then, young lords seeking leisure and play,
Princes bent on pleasure and amusement,
Who rejoice in the harmony of the five notes,
And delight in the sonority of the eight sounds,
Then gather together in the courtyard,
105 And raptly listen to a mixed medley of songs and tunes.

Oh, how rich the music!
The sounds profusely spread, fresh and bright —
How truly delightful!
They scatter like waves broad and wide —
110 Oh, marvelous indeed!
They thrust and parry, back and forth —
Oh how worthy of wonderment!

The tooting and tweeting
Is like the resplendent *yu* note,
115 Fervent and troublous, then increasingly strong.
Then throbbing with pent-up fury, seething anger,
Loud and clear, they suddenly bolt forth, turbulent and unrestrained.
The breath-force, vigorous and strong, broadly spreads,
Then abruptly halts and stands fierce and menacing,
120 Reverberating thunderously, like the banging and clanging of a
              pounded forge,
Or whining and whistling like a chilling breeze.
Finally, all of the sounds gather and merge, outrunning the tempo,
Dashing into convergence, only to stumble and fall.

L. 142: I follow Wang Niansun (*Dushu zazhi*, "Zhiyu," B.42b–43a), who construes *zhuang* 裝 in the sense of *zhuang* 壯 (strong).

L. 153: Cf. *Shang shu zhushu* 3.26a (Legge, *The Chinese Classics* 3: 48): "When the eight musical sounds can be harmoniously blended, and do not interfere with each other, the spirits and men are in harmony."

L. 156: Ma Rong borrows the phrase *wu jiang* 五降 (receding five times) from a passage in the *Zuo zhuan*, Zhao 1 (Legge, *The Chinese Classics* 5: 580), in which a physician named He explains the way in which music should be properly played: "The music of the former kings was a means of providing restraint for a multiplicity of affairs. Thus, there were five rhythms. From beginning to end, whether fast or slow, the tempos followed one upon another, and receded only upon reaching the point of central harmony. After receding five times, further playing was not allowed." The idea of this difficult passage seems to be that each of the five rhythms has a point of central harmony. When this point is reached, the music then recedes (*jiang* 降, lit., "falls"), only to be revived again with the next rhythm. After all five rhythms are dispensed with in this fashion, the playing ceases.

## VI

And then, the sounds that one hears take on various forms:
125  Their manner is like flowing water,
And they further resemble soaring geese.
Like water in flood, broad and boundless,
They flow mighty and vast, powerful and strong,
Drawing into the distance, as far as the eye can see,
130  Reeling and rebounding, wavering and wandering about.
Then a host of sounds, repressed and restrained,
Suddenly burst forth, spewing and spurting,
Loud and blaring, clear and sharp,
Spreading broad and boundless.
135  The selection of notes accords with proper timing,
And the selection of tempo follows a fixed rule.
The crescendos and decrescendos follow proper sequence;
Whether thick or thin, it must match the tune.
Delicate and subtle as a light breeze,
140  It is now here, then gone.
The trailing notes slow as if about to cease,
Then stop in mid-course only to become stronger.
Suddenly they fade and die out,
Then powerfully resurge.

145  At times, his thoughts fully focused, firmly fixed,
The flutist plays with unrivaled beauty, unmatched skill,
Far surpassing zither and mouth organ,
Silencing drum and bell.
Sometimes the notes are held fast as if bound with a rope,
150  Sounding easy and relaxed, slack and slow.
Pipes and reeds all play forth;
Metal and stone all loudly chime:
The sounds, which do not interfere with one another,
Are thereby dispersed to the eight winds.
155  Once the pitches are harmoniously tuned,
And the mournful sounds five times recede,
The tune ceases, the piece ends,
Yet lingering strains rise again.
Intricate cadences sound forth again and again,
160  Overlapping and repeating, close as comb teeth.

L. 179: Li Shan (*Wen xuan* 18. 7b) vaguely explains *minhu yiyin* 箆笏抑隱 as descriptive of the fingers moving over the holes. However, Zhu Jian (*Wen xuan jianzheng* 15.8b–9a) argues that *minhu* is equivalent to *miehu* 蔑忽, which describes the faintness of the sounds. He goes on to explain *yiyin* 抑隱 as describing low and deep tones. Although I am not certain that Zhu's explanation is correct, I follow him for lack of a better alternative.

L. 185: This line seems to refer to a change in the musical mode. Li Shan (in *Wen xuan* 18.7b) says that *fan shang* 反商 is "like *bian shang*" 變商 (altered *shang*), a musical term mentioned in the *Huainanzi* (4.8a): "The altered *gong* produces *zhi*, the altered *zhi* produces *shang*, the altered *shang* produces *yu*, the altered *yu* produces *jiao*, and the altered *jiao* produces *gong*." The altered *shang* must be an "adjusted pitch" comparable to the more commonly mentioned *bian gong* 變宮 and *bian zhi* 變徵, which were added to the pentatonic scale to create additional modes. *Xia zhi* 下徵 (lower *zhi*) is a type of flute mode in which *linzhong* 林鐘 acts as *gong* 宮 (doh). It is described in the monograph on music and calendar of the *Song shu* (11.216). The grammar of this line is not clear, for *fan* 反 and *xia* 下 could be verbs, as in Obi Kōichi and Hanabusa Hideki's parsing of the text (*Monzen* 2: 388). However, I am not sure what *fan* and *xia* would mean as verbs in this context, and thus I follow Li Shan in taking them as names of musical modes.

Then, pressed and pushed together, compactly clustered,
The notes swarm like bees, converge like ants.
A multitude of sounds gather about,
To send off the finale.

## VII

165 Then, after a brief rest, a momentary pause,
Diverse tunes are randomly played.
Changing the mode startles the ears,
Sways and tugs the heart.
Lightly soaring, easily drifting,
170 Calm and composed, slow and leisurely,
Sad and sorrowful, plangent and plaintive,
The sounds are played low and relaxed.
Then, rapid and quick, seeking and searching,
Now near, now far,
175 As if looking down from a height, they let themselves go,
Seeming about to fall, yet pulling themselves up again,
Then weaving and winding together, tangled and twisted,
They mingle and merge, coiling and curling about.
Faint and soft, deep and low,
180 The melody goes through various changes.
Grinding together, fast and furious,
The five notes alternate in turn.
Pushing and pressing, fingers pass over the holes,
All in proper order, moving from one to the next:
185 "Altered *Shang*" and "Lowered *Zhi*,"
Each mode is excellent in its own way.

## VIII

Thus, those who hear the tunes and refrains,
May observe proper norms in the rhythm,
And discern changes from the phrasing,
190 And thereby know that the rites and regulations cannot be
                    transgressed;
And those who hear the miscellaneous airs,
May ponder the ancients of the distant past,

271

L. 199: Lao and Zhuang refer to Laozi and Zhuangzi.

LL. 200–201: Cf. *Shang shu zhushu* 4.19a (291), "Counsels of Gaoyao": Gaoyao enumerates the nine virtues, among which he mentions "To be docile, yet bold, be direct yet gentle." Kong and Meng are Confucius and Mencius.

L. 203: Bian Sui 卞隨 and Wu Guang 瞀光 were recluses during the time of Jie, the last ruler of the Xia dynasty. After Tang, the founder of the Shang, had overthrown Jie, he offered Bian Sui the throne. Bian Sui indignantly refused and threw himself into the Chou River and drowned. Tang then offered the throne to Wu Guang, who likewise declined and drowned himself in the Lu River. See *Zhuangzi* 9.16a.

L. 205: Zhu refers to Zhuan Zhu. See Jiang Yan, "Rhapsody on Separation," this volume, L. 44n. Ben refers to Meng Ben 孟賁, a famous warrior of the Chunqiu period who was so brave he did not fear snakes and dragons or tigers and wolves. See *Shi ji* 101.2739, n. 2.

L. 207: Guan and Shang are Guan Zhong 管仲 (ca. 720–645 B.C.) and Shang Yang 商鞅 (390–338 B.C.), legalist thinkers famous for their decisiveness and concern with rules and regulations. Guan Zhong was adviser to Duke Huan of Qi and is attributed with the book of political and economic philosophy *Guanzi* 管子. For a partial translation, see Rickett, *Guanzi*. His biography is found in *Shi ji* 62.2131–34. Shang Yang was prime minister in the state of Qin. He is well known for introducing a series of political and economic reforms. He is attributed with the *Shang jun shu* 商君書 (Book of Lord Shang). For a study and translation see Duyvendak, *The Book of Lord Shang*.

L. 208: I follow the *Wuchen* reading of *li* 理 for *fen* 紛. This undoubtedly is the original Li Shan reading. See Hu Kejia's, *Kaoyi*, *Wen xuan* 3.36b.

L. 209: Shen and Han are the famous statesmen Shen Buhai 申不害 (400–337 B.C.) and Han Fei 韓非 (280–233 B.C.). Shen Buhai was a minister in the state of Han who introduced a series of administrative reforms. For a study of his thought, see Creel, *Shen Pu-hai*. Han Fei was the leading proponent of legalist ideas, which may be found in the *Han Feizi* 韓非子. For a translation, see Liao, *The Complete Works of Han Fei Tzu*.

L. 211: Fan and Cai are Fan Ju 范睢 (fl. 266–256 B.C.) and Cai Ze 蔡澤 (n.d.), who were famous traveling persuaders of the Warring States period. They have biographies in *Shi ji* 79.2401–25.

L. 213: Xi and Long are Deng Xi 鄧哲 (ca. 554–501 B.C.) and Gongsun Long 公孫龍 (n.d.). Deng Xi was a political adviser in the state of Zheng, and was famous for writing a legal code. He also was known for his complicated argumentation. See *Lushi chunqiu* 18.8a. Gongsun Long was a famous logician to whom many complicated logical arguments are attributed.

L. 214: "Shao xiao" 韶簫 was a dance attributed to the sage emperor Shun. See *Zuo zhuan*, Xiang 29; *Zuo zhuan zhushu* 39.18b (4358), Du Yu's commentary. "Southern Flute" ("Nan yue" 南籥) is a dance song attributed to King Wen of Zhou. See *Zuo zhuan*, Xiang 29; ibid. 39.39.16b (4357), Du Yu's commentary.

L. 215: On "White Snow," see Xie Huilian, "Rhapsody on Snow," this volume, L. 29n. "Limpid Waters" ("Lu shui" 渌水) is a song about which nothing is known. See *Huainanzi* 2.12b, where it is mentioned together with "Sunny Bank" as a dance song. It also is mentioned in *Baopuzi* 49.2b.

L. 216: "Dew Prolonged" ("Yan lu" 延露) was a popular song. See *Huainanzi* 18.17b. On "Man of Ba," see Lu Ji, "Rhapsody on Literature," this volume, L. 73n.

L. 221: "Bear-hanging" (*xiong jing* 熊經) and "bird-stretching" (*niao shen* 鳥申) are Taoist calisthenics. See *Zhuangzi* 6.1a.

Inferring their thoughts from the mournful strains,
And thereby know that one beset with constant worry cannot live an
        idle life.

195 Thus, here we discuss and recount its greater meaning,
And draw analogies to the things it resembles:
The sounds roam at will, in wild abandon,
Relaxed and carefree, expansive and detached:

Just like the manner of Lao and Zhuang.
200 They are gentle yet direct, docile yet bold:
Just like Kong and Meng.
They are fervent and forthright, pure and principled:
Just like the integrity of Sui and Guang.
They are cranky and cross, contentious and quarrelsome:
205 Just like the spirit of Zhu and Ben.
The rhythm is clipped, the phrasing concise,
Just like the rules of Guan and Shang.
Order is determined, complications are unraveled,
Just like the discerning judgments of Shen and Han.
210 Their elaborate intricacies go on and on,
Just like the persuasions of Fan and Cai.
They are precise and controlled,
Just like the clever arguments of Xi and Long.

At the beginning they derive their model from "Shao xiao" and
        "Southern Flute,"
215 In the middle take their measures from "White Snow" and "Limpid
        Waters,"
And at the end draw their pattern from "Dew Prolonged" and "Man
        of Ba."

## IX

Thus, noble and mean, pretty and plain,
Wise and foolish, brave and timid,
Fish and turtles, birds and beasts,
220 All who hear it prick up their ears, skittish as deer.
Hanging like bears, stretching like birds,
Gawking like owls, looking backwards like wolves,
Hooting and howling, jumping and leaping.

273

L. 228: Qu Ping 屈平 is another name for Qu Yuan. Cf. *Mao shi* 113/2: "We go to that happy state." The idea is that Qu Yuan would no longer be unhappy in the state of Chu, and thus would not find it necessary to commit suicide.

L. 229: Jietui is Jie Zhitui 介之推, an official who served Chonger 重耳, Duke Wen of Jin. Jie faithfully assisted Chonger during his long exile. When Chonger assumed the throne in Jin, he failed to reward Jie Zhitui, and Jie left the court to become a recluse on Mount Mianshang 綿上. See *Zuo zhuan*, Xi 24 (Legge, *The Chinese Classics* 5: 191); *Shi ji* 39.1662; and Chavannes, *Mh* 4: 296.

L. 230: Tantai is Tantai Mieming 澹臺滅明, who was a disciple of Confucius. His son drowned in a river, and his followers wished to retrieve the body and bury it, but Tantai refused, saying, "When alive, he was my son. Now that he is dead, he is my ghost." Li Shan (*Wen xuan* 18.9b) attributes this story to the *Bowu zhi*, but I cannot find it in the received version of this work.

L. 231: Gao Yu 皋魚 possibly is Gao Chai 高柴, one of Confucius's disciples. Confucius once encountered him weeping bitterly by the roadside. He wept until he died. See *Han shi waizhuan* 9.1b.

L. 232: Changwan is Nangong Changwan 南宮長萬, a grandee of Song in the Chunqiu period. One day he accompanied Duke Min (691–682 B.C.) on a hunt. After the duke insulted him, Changwan became angry and killed the duke with a chess board. See *Zuo zhuan*, Zhuang 12 (Legge, *The Chinese Classics* 5: 89); *Shi ji* 38.1624; and Chavannes, *Mh* 4: 235–36.

L. 233: Qumi is Gao Qumi 高渠彌, a grandee of Zheng during the Chunqiu period. When Duke Zhao (reg. 696–695 B.C.) was heir designate, he detested Qumi. His father, Duke Zhuang, appointed Qumi as a dignitary despite his son's objections. When Duke Zhao took the throne, Qumi feared that he would be put to death. He took advantage of a hunt to kill the duke with an arrow. See *Zuo zhuan*, Huan 17 (Legge, *The Chinese Classics* 5: 69); *Shi ji* 42.1763; and Chavannes, *Mh* 4: 459.

L. 234: Kuai Kui 蒯聵 was the son of Duke Ling of Wei. He plotted to assassinate the duke's wife, Nanzi 南子. When Duke Ling discovered the plot, Kuai Kui fled the state. After Duke Ling died in 493 B.C. Kuai Kui's son, known posthumously as Duke Chu 出公 (reg. 492–481 B.C.), was installed on the throne. With the aid of Jin, Kuai Kui was able to occupy the city of Qi 戚 in Wei. In 492 B.C. a Wei army supported by troops from Qi lay siege to Qi. See *Zuo zhuan*, Ding 14, Ai 2–3 (Legge, *The Chinese Classics* 5: 788, 799, 802).

L. 235: Buzhan is Chen Buzhan 陳不占, a native of Qi. After Cui Zhu 崔杼 assassinated Duke Zhuang of Qi in 548 B.C., Chen Buzhan rushed to defend the ducal house. However, as soon as he heard the war drums outside the gate of the duke's residence, he died of fright. Li Shan (*Wen xuan* 18.9b–10a) refers to the *Han shi waizhuan* for this story, but it is not contained in the received version of this work.

LL. 240–41: The motif of fish and horses reacting to the sounds of music is a common one. Cf. *Xunzi* 1.4a: "Of old, when Huba played the zither, swimming fish came up to listen; when Bo Ya played the zither, his six horses looked up from their grazing." On the dancing cranes, see Bao Zhao's "Rhapsody on Dancing Cranes," this volume.

L. 242: Mian Ju 綿駒 was a famous musician of Qi. According to *Mengzi* (6B/6), when he lived in Gaotang 高唐 (northeast of modern Gaotang *xian*, Shandong), the people in western Qi all imitated his form of singing.

L. 244: Huba is the zither player mentioned in LL. 240–41 above.

L. 245: Qingxiang 磬襄 (lit., "Xiang who plays the stone chimes") is a musician mentioned in *Lun yu* 18/9.

L. 255: Ma Rong here borrows a phrase from the "Yi and Ji" chapter of the *Classic of*

Each attains his proper measure.
225 Every person satisfies his desires,
And all return to central harmony,
And thereby improve customs and mores.
Qu Ping would go to a happy state,
Jietui would return to Jin and receive reward,
230 Tantai would carry his son's corpse back home,
Gao Yu would restrain his weeping.

Changwan would cease his traitorous schemes,
Qumi would no longer engage in evil acts,
Kuai Kui would be able to force the enemy to retreat,
235 And Buzhan would become a man of integrity and fortitude.
Kings and lords would protect their positions,
Recluses would be content in their forest retreats,
Officials would rejoice in their work,
And for generations the common people would preserve their houses.
240 Sturgeon poke out their heads by the riverbank to listen,
Horses look up from their grazing and black cranes begin to dance.


## X

At this time, Mian Ju would lose his voice,
Bo Ya would break his zither strings,
Huba would readjust his stops,
245 And Qingxiang would take down his hanging stone chimes.
People gawk and gaze with wonder,
Praising and lauding it again and again.
Losing composure, they fall from their mats,
Clapping and applauding as loud as thunder.
250 They squint, then stare wide-eyed,
Snivel and tears flowing copiously.

Thus, flute music can commune with the spirits, stir natural beings,
Express spirit, reveal thoughts,
Convey heartfelt feelings, manifest true intent,
255 Lead the people to rise and perform their work.

*Documents*: Gaoyao said, "Lead the people to rise and perform their work"; *Shang shu zhushu* 5.17a (304); Legge, *The Chinese Classics* 3: 89.

LL. 258–59: Baoxi 庖羲, better known as Fuxi 伏羲, was a culture hero of remote antiquity. Zhu Jian (*Wen xuan jishi* 15.9a) points out that the more common tradition attributes him with inventing the lute (*se* 瑟); Shennong is usually credited with creating the *qin*.

L. 260: Nuwa 女娲 (also read Nugua) is a complex figure about whom there is a great amount of lore. Karlgren summarizes most of the accounts in "Legends and Cults," pp. 229–32. The *Record of Rites* mentions Nüwa's invention of the mouth organ; see *Li ji zhushu* 31.16b (3228).

L. 261: Little is known about Baoxin 暴辛. The *Fengsu tongyi* cites the *Shi ben* 世本 (Origins of the Ruling Houses), which refers to him as Duke Xin of Bao. See Wu Shuping, *Fengsu tongyi jiaoshi* 6.226. Li Shan (*Wen xuan* 18.10b) cites Song Jun 宋均, who identifies Baoxin as a noble of the period of King Ping 平 of Zhou (reg. 770–720 B.C.).

LL. 262–63: Chui 倕 was a musician during the time of Yao. Shu 叔 was a musician from the time of Shun. Ma Rong's lines are taken verbatim from *Li ji zhushu* 31.16b (3228).

LL. 276–77: Ma Rong alludes here to the "Grand Commentary" of the *Classic of Changes* (*Zhou yi zhushu* 7.3a–4a): "Since it is easy, it is easy to know; since it is simple, it is simple to follow. Being easy to follow, there can be close association with it; being easy to follow, work can be successfully completed. If there is close association, one can long endure; if work is successfully completed, one may become great. Being able to endure is the virtue of the sage; becoming great is the undertaking of the worthy man."

L. 279: The Two Emperors are Fuxi and Shennong. The sage and wise refer to Nuwa, Baoxin, Chui, and Shu.

L. 284: Qiu Zhong 丘仲 was a musician of the Emperor Wu period of the Han. Nothing else is known about him.

It washes away foul filth,
Purges dirty grime.

## XI

Of old, when Baoxi invented the zither,
Shennong created the lute,
260  Nüwa constructed the mouth organ,
Baoxin made the ocarina,
Chui harmonized the bells,
And Shu put the stone chimes in order:

Sometimes they smelted metal, polished stone,
265  Painting and planing, paring and filing,
Molding and kneading, carving and chiseling,
Cutting and engraving, boring and drilling.
They applied consummate artistry, the greatest skill,
Working for days and months,
270  And finally completed their instruments.
But their sounds were only of a certain kind.
Only the flute makes use of its natural qualities,
And does not change its basic character.
Bamboo is simply cut down and blown,
275  And its sounds are as splendid as this.
Presumably this accords with the principle of simplicity and ease,
And makes playing it an endeavor of a worthy man.
The six instruments mentioned above
At least were elaborated and augmented by the Two Emperors, the
              sage and wise.
280  But what about the flute that was first created in the Great Han?
Scholars, who do not know that it can enhance the splendor and
              glory of our age,
Have ignored it and do not give it praise.
How sad indeed!

## XII

There was a menial official named Qiu Zhong who has explained
how the flute came into being, but he did not understand how great or
wonderful its music is. The words of his song go:

L. 292: Jing Junming 京君明 is Jing Fang 京房 (ca. 76–37 B.C.). There are records of two men named Jing Fang in the Former Han. The Jing Fang whose style name was Junming was the younger of the two. On him, see Hulsewé, "The Two Early Han *I Ching* Specialists Called Jing Fang 京房."

"In recent times the double flute originated in the land of the Qiang;
A Qiang man was cutting some bamboo, and before he had finished,
He heard a dragon calling in the water, but could not see it.
290  He then cut off a piece of bamboo, and blew on it to resemble the
        dragon's call;
He carved it into the shape of a tube so that it was easy to hold.

"Master of the *Changes* Jing Junming well understood musical pitches,
And he added one hole to the original four.
The hole added by Junming was on the back;
In this way the *shang* tone and five notes were complete."

# Rhapsody on the Zither

## XI SHUYE

When I was young I was fond of music, and as I grew older, I was
able to study it. I believe that all things flourish and decay, but music
never changes, and although one may eat his fill of rich flavors, he never
tires of music. It can guide and nourish spirit and breath, relax and
harmonize the emotions and feelings. For dwelling alone in dire straits
without feeling sad, nothing is better than music. For this reason, if
repeated performance on an instrument is insufficient, then one may hum
or sing in order to release his feelings. If humming and singing are not

THIS RHAPSODY by Xi Kang (zı Shuye) is on the noblest of all Chinese musical instruments, the *qin* 琴 (zither). The *qin* was the instrument of the cultivated gentleman. In Xi
Kang's time it probably had seven strings. The body was made of paulownia wood. On the
side farthest from the player are thirteen *hui* 徽 (studs) which mark where the strings should
be pressed down. For a detailed treatment of the history of the zither in Chinese civilization,
see van Gulik, *The Lore of the Chinese Lute*.
  Xi Kang himself was an accomplished *qin* player, and in his preface he is critical of
earlier works on musical instruments because their authors did not have adequate knowledge
of music. His rhapsody, however, clearly is indebted to such earlier pieces as Wang Bao's
"Rhapsody on the Panpipes" and Ma Rong's "Rhapsody on the Long Flute." In conventional fashion, he first describes the area in which the paulownia trees grow, with a long
rhapsodic passage on the mountains and rivers. Xi Kang portrays the area as one inhabited

sufficient, then one may confer his words to writing in order to express his thoughts.[1] Thus, talented men throughout the ages have written rhapsodies and odes for the instruments of the eight musical sounds,[2] and the various types of song and dance. In the form and style of their works they all imitate one another. When they acclaim the material from which an instrument is made, they place paramount importance on its perilous and precarious location. When they describe its sounds, they place emphasis on sadness and sorrow. When they praise its influence and effect, they place highest value on the shedding of tears. These works are beautiful to be sure, but they do not fully convey the inherent principle of the instrument. If one were to deduce the reason for this, it would seem that it is basically because they do not understand music. And if one examines the fundamental ideas of their pieces, one finds that they do not comprehend the feelings involved in rites and music.[3] Of all of the various musical instruments, the virtue of the zither is the highest. Thus, I have put my feelings in writing, and I have composed a rhapsody on this subject. The piece reads:

## I

The place where the paulownia grows
Rests on a high ridge of a lofty mountain.
Pushing its roots through the layered earth, tall it rises;
Reaching to the Northern Dipper, it soars on high.
5    Enveloped in the pure harmony of Heaven and Earth,
It inhales the auspicious radiance of sun and moon.
Lush and thick, it stands in unique luxuriance,

---

by hermits and immortals, who go there not only to escape the entanglements of the profane world, but to cut wood from which to make a *qin*. He then follows with passages on the making of the zither, its tuning, and the zither music itself, with special mention of various tunes. He ends his rhapsody with a description of the effects the zither music has on those who hear it. In the finale, Xi Kang hails the *qin* as the musical instrument for the perfected man.

There is another carefully edited text with extensive annotation in Dai Mingyang *Xi Kang ji jiaozhu* 2: 82–111. Previous translations include von Zach, *Deutsche Wacht* 10 (1932), rpt. in *Die Chinesische Anthologie* 1: 250–58; van Gulik, *Hsi K'ang and His Poetical Essay on the Lute;* Goormaghtigh, *L'Art du Qin*, pp. 25–41; and Obi and Hanabusa, *Monzen* 2: 397–418. There are *baihua* translations in Chen Hongtian, et al., *Zhaoming Wen xuan yizhu*, 2: 970–94; Li Jingying, *Zhaoming Wenxuan xinjie*, 2: 279–95; and Chi et al., *Lidai fu cidian*, pp. 281–88. For a brief analysis of the piece see Li Ruiqing, "Xi Kang 'Qin fu' xiaolun."

L. 9: The Gulf of Yu is where the sun sets.

L. 10: I have literally translated *jiu yang* 九陽 as "nine suns." Xi Kang imitates a line in "Distant Wandering" (L. 74, *Chuci buzhu* 5.5b): "At dusk I dry my body in the nine suns." This probably refers to the Fusang tree of the east, which, according to ancient Chinese legend, contained nine suns. Cf. Zhang Heng, "Rhapsody on Contemplating the Mystery," this volume, LL. 105–6n.

L. 16: The You Mao text of the *Wen xuan* reads *hu* 互. Other editions of the Li Shan text, plus the *Liuchen zhu Wen xuan*, read *xuan* 玄 (dark), which I have followed here. Hu Kejia (see *Wen xuan* 3.38b) suggests that the You Mao text is in error.

L. 34: The central realm refers to the central plain area.

Letting its blossoms fly into the great azure.
At dusk it receives the rosy rays from the Gulf of Yu;
10    At dawn it dries its trunk in the nine suns.
For a thousand years it waits to have its worth recognized,
Quiet it stands, spiritlike, eternally healthy and strong.

## II

As for the shape and contours of the mountains and rivers around it:
Twisting and twining, dark and deep,
15    Tall and towering, perilously poised,
Dark peaks, sharp cliffs,
Spire upwards rugged and steep.
Vermilion banks precipitously plunge,
Green walls soar a myriad fathoms high.

20    And then, layered crests rising one upon another,
Soar so high they seem enveloped in clouds.
From afar, they arch over all in supreme grandeur,
Standing tall and imposing in solitary splendor.
They exhale numinous vapors to scatter the clouds,
25    From their divine founts they spurt flowing water.
And then, tumbling waves dash forth,
Wildly coursing in contentious flow,
Smashing into cliffs, battering crooks and crannies,
Seething with anger, roaring with rage.
30    Soaring and leaping, clashing and colliding
Rushing and racing, swelling and surging
Sinuously snaking, as if coiled together,
With wild abandon they pour into great rivers,
And cross the central realm.
35    Now placidly swirling, slowly coursing,
The waters quietly flow into the distance,
Calmly spreading and sprawling,
Encircling and embracing mountains and hills.

Carefully observe what grows in this region,
40    What treasures it produces in its most secret domains:
Rubies, rare and wondrous,
Carnelian and jade, rich and glittering,

283

L. 47: Master Juan 涓子 was a recluse famous for his zither playing. He is attributed with a treatise on the zither entitled *Qin xin* 琴心 (Heart of the Zither). See *Liexian zhuan*, A.5a.

L. 59: Rong Qi is Rongqi Qi 榮啟期, a recluse known for his playing of the zither. According to the *Huainanzi* (9.4a), after Confucius heard him pluck one string, he was so moved by the harmony, he was joyful for three days. Qi Ji is Qili Ji, one of the Four Hoaryheads. See Ban Gu, "Rhapsody on Communicating with the Hidden," this volume, L. 128n.

L. 72: Mount Ji 箕 (located southeast of modern Dengfeng 登封 *xian*, Henan) was the retreat of the recluse Xu You 許由. Yao wanted to abdicate to Xu You, but he refused each time. Finally Xu You fled to Mount Ji, where he died. See Huangfu Mi, *Gaoshi zhuan* A.2b–3a.

L. 76: Xuanyuan is Huangdi (the Yellow Lord), who in some accounts is attributed with inventing the zither.

L. 77: The Aged Boy (Lao Tong 老童) was the son of Zhuanxu. He resided on Mount Gui. His voice was like that of bells and stone chimes. See Yuan Ke, *Shanhai jing jiaozhu* 2.55, 11.395.

Gathered in clusters, collected in piles,
Are scattered about the sides of the tree.

45 Then, spring boneset spreads to the east,
Crab apple trees grow on the west.
Master Juan resides on the southern slope,
Elixir of jade bubbles in the front.
Dark clouds cover its top,
50 Soaring simurghs perch on the crest,
Pure dew soaks its bark,
A gentle breeze blows through it.
Its branches thrust upward in silent solemnity,
Its lush leaves unfold in quiet repose.

55 The reason that people linger about it is truly because of its natural
divine beauty, which is enough to inspire admiration and interest.

## III

Then, gentlemen who have fled from the world,
Men like Rong Qi and Qi Ji:
60 Together climb soaring bridges,
Cross dark ravines,
Grasp jasper branches,
Climb steep slopes,
In order to play beneath it.

65 Long they gaze all about them —
Their vista is as broad as that of birds soaring the skies.
Sidewards they glimpse Kunlun,
See below them the shores of the sea.
They point out Cangwu far in the distance,
70 Look down on winding rivers, turning and twisting.
Aware of the many burdens of the profane world,
They see above them the lingering brilliance of Mount Ji.
They admire the broad expanse of this peak,
And their hearts are so stirred they forget to return.

75 Their feelings released, they gaze into the distance,
And receive the melody left by Xuanyuan.
They revere the Aged Boy in his Mount Gui nook,

L. 78: On Tairong, see Zhang Heng, "Rhapsody on Contemplating the Mystery," this volume, L. 348n.

L. 85: Master Li is Li Lou 離婁, who was known for his acute vision. See *Mengzi* 4A/1.

L. 86: On Craftsman Shi, see Wang Bao, this volume, "Rhapspody on the Panpipes," L. 40n.

L. 87: On Kui and Xiang, see ibid., 41n.

L. 88: On Chui, see Ma Rong, "Rhapsody on the Long Flute," this volume, LL. 260–61n. On Ban, see Wang Bao, this volume, "Rhapsody on the Panpipes," L. 40n.

L. 95: Yuan Ke 園客 was a native of Jiyin 濟陰 who obtained a secret method for growing silkworms that produced cocoons as large as jars. See *Liexian zhuan* B.3b–4a.

L. 96: Mount Zhong 鍾山 is another name for the Kunlun. See *Huainanzi* 2.4b.

LL. 99–100: On Bo Ya and Zhong Qi see Wang Bao, "Rhapsody on the Panpipes," this volume, L. 115n.

L. 104: Ling Lun 伶倫 or 泠綸 was a musician whom Huangdi sent into Xie Valley 嶰谷 north of the Kunlun Mountains to cut bamboo that was used to make the twelve pitchpipes. See *Han shu* 21A.959

L. 105: Tian Lian 田連, also known as Cheng Lian 成連, was a famous zither player. See *Han Feizi* 14.1a. According to the *Qin cao* (cited by Li Shan, *Wen xuan* 18.15b), he was a teacher of Bo Ya. Hu Shaoying (*Wen xuan jianzheng* 20.2a) shows that *zhang* 張 is equivalent to *chang* 暢, a generic name for "zither tune." Cf. *Fengsu tongyi jiaoshi* 6.235.

Admire the lofty singing of Tairong.
Beholding this paulownia gives rise to thoughts,
80 And they wish to avail themselves of it to convey their feelings.
They then lop off a young bough,
Measure a piece that can be put to use.
Using it to release their cares, these Perfected Men
Make it into an Elegant Zither.

## IV

85 Then, they have Master Li inspect the marking line,
Craftsman Shi wield the axe,
Kui and Xiang present the rules of construction,
Ban and Chui display their divine craft.
They chisel out the center, join the seams, fitting them tightly
        together,
90 Achieving a perfect balance between gaps and joints.
They paint and carve it,
Adorn it with designs and patterns.

They inlay it with rhinoceros horn and ivory,
Apply a layer of blue and green.
95 The strings are made of Yuan Ke's silk,
For the studs they use Mount Zhong jade.

It has figures of dragons and phoenixes,
The forms of ancient worthies.
Bo Ya moves his fingers across the strings,
100 And Zhong Qi listens to the sounds.
Its ornate surface glitters and glistens,
Casting off color and light.
Oh how beautiful it is!

Ling Lun arranges the pitches,
105 Tian Lian plays the tune.
As performed by a worthy gentleman,
New melodies are clear and loud.
How grand indeed they are!

ʟʟ. 110–11: The *jiao, yu, gong,* and *zhi* designate the third, fifth, first, and fourth strings respectively. I assume that Xi Kang means that *gong* and *zhi* are used as a reference for tuning the strings.

ʟ. 117: The proper music is *zheng sheng* 正聲, which is the name given to the orthodox music. Also known as *ya yue* 雅樂 (elegant music), it is the morally uplifting form of music that is the antithesis of the music of Zheng and Wei.

ʟ. 119: On "White Snow," see Xie Huilian, "Rhapsody on Snow," this volume, ʟ. 29n.

ʟ. 120: On "Clear *Jiao*," see Fu Yi, "Rhapsody on Dance," this volume, ʟʟ. 47–48n.

ʟ. 124: Li Shan (*Wen xuan* 18.16a) explains *jiji* 岌岌 as "descriptive of being high." However, Hu Shaoying (*Wen xuan jianzheng* 20.2a–b) convincingly shows that it means "swift."

ʟʟ. 127–30: See Wang Bao, "Rhapsody on the Panpipes," this volume, ʟ. 115n.

ʟ. 137: The phrase *jing ming* 兢名 (striving for fame) seems out of place here, but I have translated it literally for lack of anything better to suggest.

ʟ. 142: Grand Simplicity (Tai su 泰素) is ambiguous here. I suspect that Xi Kang uses it in the sense of the original state of things, that is, the condition when sound and forms are undifferentiated.

## V

When the strings are first tuned,
110 The *jiao* and *yu* resound together,
The *gong* and *zhi* confirm one another.
Notes separately go forth, then blend together,
From high to low continuously resonating.
First weak and feeble, then strong and robust,
115 Lovely melodies begin to sound.
They are smooth and harmonious indeed, all worthy of providing
       joy.

And now can the proper music be played,
And sublime melodies be performed.
They play forth "White Snow,"
120 Sound forth "Clear *Jiao*."
A flurry of sounds, steadily streaming, smoothly flowing,
Profusely pours forth, rich and mellow.
Tones, bright and vigorous, rise on high,
Racing swiftly one after another.
125 Full and strong, leaping into one another, they race forth,
Then blend together, vibrant and rich, delicate and fine.

Their manner is like lofty mountains,
And also resembles rolling waves:
Now full and flowing,
130 Then tall and stately.
Rumbling and grumbling, troubled and tormented,
The sounds twist and twine, whirl and twirl.
Then with wild abandon, they disperse and drift,
Rolling and swelling, unfolding and spreading.

135 With solemn expression, the musician follows the rhythm,
Adapting to changing harmonies, conforming to proper measure.
Striving for fame, he masters his art:
All in accord with the rules, slow and sure.
In stately solemnity, in refined harmony,
140 The notes grandly spread into the distance,
Then, clear and graceful, they send off the finale,
As their lingering echoes drift into Grand Simplicity.

L. 149: The phrase *qin leng* 琴冷 (the zither instrument is cold) is ambiguous. Another possible interpretation is that "cold" describes the sounds made by the zither. See *Zhaoming Wenxuan yizhu* 2: 982, n. 149.

L. 153: On "Limpid Waters," see Ma Rong, "Rhapsody on the Long Flute," this volume, L. 215n.

L. 154: "Clear *Zhi*" ("Qing *zhi*" 清徵) is an especially moving musical mode. See *Hanfeizi* 3.3a.

LL. 155–56: "Tang Yao" 唐堯 probably refers to the zither song "Yao chang" 堯暢, which is mentioned in the "Qin dao" 琴道 ("Way of the Zither") of Huan Tan 桓譚, a fragmentary treatise on the zither. That work mentions "Weizi cao" 微子操 (The Song of the Viscount of Wei), which the viscount reputedly composed on a zither to lament the imminent fall of the Yin dynasty. These fragments are cited by Li Shan (*Wen xuan* 18.16b). See also Pokora, *Hsin-lun*, pp. 181, 183–84.

L. 162: On Yingzhou, see Zhang Heng, "Rhapsody on Contemplating the Mystery," this volume, L. 112n.

L. 163: Liezi was a well-known philosopher. However, here Xi Kang probably refers to him as the figure in the *Zhuangzi* (1.4b) who was able to ride off on the wind for five days.

## VI

Then, on high verandas, soaring towers,
In tall mansions, secluded chambers,
145  On winter nights, cold and still,
The bright moon shining down its light,
New clothes rustling and swishing,
Colored tie-strings wafting a sweet scent:

Then, the instrument is cold, but its strings are tuned;
150  The heart is relaxed, but the hands are nimble.
One touches and plucks the strings at will,
And all is played only as intended.

One first launches into "Limpid Waters,"
Midway plays "Clear *Zhi*,"
155  Gracefully plays "Tang Yao,"
Ends by intoning "Viscount of Wei."
These melodies are magnanimous and wise, broad and rich,
Relaxed and at ease, hesitant and slow.
To the strumming of strings songs are gently sung,
160  New melodies begin one after another.

The song goes:
"Soaring on the whirling wind, I come to rest in Yingzhou;
I invite Liezi as my boon companion.
I dine on midnight vapors, weave morning mists into a belt;
165  Gliding and soaring afar, near Heaven I roam.
Viewing all things as the same, I am free from worldly cares;
I yield to fate, go or stay at will."

The sounds resonate clearly, in accord with the cadence;
How harmoniously blended are song and zither tune!

## VII

170  And then, as the song comes to a close,
And the various sounds are about to cease,
Chords are changed, modes are altered,
And a wonderful melody sounds forth.

The players raise their heads and reveal a mild expression,

L. 190: The exactly meaning of *jian sheng* 間聲 is unclear. Van Gulik (*Hsi K'ang*, p. 102, n. 52) explains *jian* as "chords," meaning sounds that are produced by simultaneously pulling several strings. Dai Mingyang (*Xi Kang ji jiaozhu* 2.98) equates 間 with *jian* 姦 (licentious). The "licentious sounds" are those that are opposed to the orthodox sounds mentioned above. Dai's explanation is not convincing, for the expression 姦聲 is well established, and if this were Xi Kang's intended meaning, he likely would not have substituted 間聲 for it. Another meaning of 間 is "miscellaneous" or "mixed," as in the expression *za se* 雜色, "mixed colors," i.e., those which diverge from the five standard colors (*zheng se* 正色). Perhaps the "mixed sounds" are the harmonies that depart from the *zheng sheng* 正聲.

LL. 196–97: Xi Kang borrows here from Ji Zha's praise of the "Eulogia" section of the *Classic of Songs*. See *Zuo zhuan*, Xiang 29 (Legge, *The Chinese Classics* 5: 550).

L. 200: I follow Hu Shaoying (*Wen xuan jianzheng* 20.3b), who explains *jie ji* 劫掎 as "coerced."

175 Lift their sleeves and display gleaming wrists.
Their slender fingers swiftly fly over the strings,
And a profusion of tones flows forth.
At times the sounds are hesitant, as if looking back with longing:
Held in and held back, restrained and repressed,
180 Lingering and loitering, reticent and reserved,
All is calm and composed, well-practiced.
Then swiftly they race off,
Like a startling breeze agitating the clouds:
Thin and faint, they fly into the air,
185 Scattering and spreading in all directions,
Full and strong, broadly dispersed,
Resplendently beautiful, vibrant and bright.
Grand strains issue forth,
Richly colored, brilliantly toned.
190 Sometimes mixed harmonies are intermingled,
As if two separate melodies are counterpoised.
Two beautiful strains advance together,
Like two horses galloping in double-harness.
At first they seem about to part,
195 Then, blend together at the end.
At times they bend, but are not obsequious,
Are straightforward, but not overbearing.
Sometimes they cross into one another, but are never disorderly,
Sometimes they separate, but never break apart.
200 Sometimes they seem compelled and constrained, beset with
                    frustration;
Sometimes they are plaintive and sad, timid and tentative.
Suddenly they whirl away, as if lightly traveling on the wind,
Then linger for a moment before spreading out in all directions.

Sometimes they follow each other in hasty pursuit,
205 Resounding and re-echoing, as if pushed and pressed together.
This way and that, in an unending stream,
They race and run, pushing each other along,
And the audience repeatedly claps and sighs its praise;
There is not even a moment to draw a breath.
210 This melody is so ornate and rich, so wondrous and grand,
One cannot comprehend it completely.

L. 213: Broad (*hong* 洪) and delicate (*xian* 纖) are loud and soft notes respectively.

L. 223: Li Shan (*Wen xuan* 18.18b) explains *qianshan* 慊縿 and *lisa* 離縭 as "descriptive of down and feathers." Dai Mingyang (*Xi Kang ji jiaozhu* 2.100) shows that *qianshan* is descriptive of things hanging down, and that *lisa* is related to a whole series of descriptive binomes with the general meaning of "continuous," "unbroken," "streaming." My rendering attempts to incorporate the meanings assigned these words by Dai.

L. 226: I have given only a paraphrase translation of the four verbs in this line, each of which is thought to represent a different manner of pulling the strings of the zither. In spite of attempts by later scholars to explain these terms, their meaning long has been lost.

L. 229: I follow Hu Shaoying (*Wen xuan jianzheng* 20.3b–4a), who construes *hua* 爐 as *hua* 劃 (distinct).

## VIII

Then, if one plays slowly and refined,
The broad and delicate tones are in their proper place.
The sounds are clear and harmonious, graceful and smooth,
215 Now high, now low, in manifold forms,
Gentle and soft, joyful and gay,
Mild and compliant, swaying to and fro.
Sometimes through a difficult passage the notes follow the beat,
Then, awaiting an opening, they go to a more perilous height:
220 Screeching like a stray jungle fowl crying by a limpid pond,
Winging like a wandering swan soaring over steep cliffs.
The tones, diversely hued, brightly colored,
Hang thickly like drooping fringe.
The echoing sounds carried by a gentle breeze,
225 Dainty and delicate, linger in the air.
Sometimes the strumming and thrumming
Is like the sound of the plashing and splashing of waves.
The strings are lightly touched, barely plucked,
Yet the sounds are clearly and distinctly perceived.
230 They are fast but never hurried,
Slow but never sluggish.
Fluttering about, distant and far,
Faint tones swiftly depart.

Heard from afar,
235 They are like the harmonious singing of simurgh and phoenix
                playing amidst the clouds;
Examined more closely,
They are like a cluster of spreading blossoms glistening in a spring
                breeze.
The music is rich and of manifold elegance,
Is excellent from beginning to end.
240 Oh, what charming grace and grand beauty!
How inexhaustible its changing forms!

## IX

In the first of the three spring months,
Clad in pretty clothes fit for the season,

LL. 254–55: According to Huan Tan's *Qin dao* (cited by Li Shan in *Wen xuan* 18.19a), after Shun (Chonghua) became Son of Heaven, he longed so much for his parents, he did not feel that his position was worth keeping. He then took up a zither and composed a song. See also Pokora, *Hsin-lun*, p. 183.

LL. 260–63: "Southern Jing" 南荊 presumably is a song of the state of Chu. Nothing is known about "Western Qin" 西秦. According to Li Shan (*Wen xuan* 18.19a), "Lingyang" 陵陽 is mentioned in the version of Song Yu's "Response to the King of Chu" found in Song Yu's collected works (it is not mentioned in the version found in *Wen xuan* 45.2a). On "Man of Ba," see Lu Ji, "Rhapsody on Literature," this volume, L. 73n.

L. 264: The terms *bian* 變 and *yong* 用 are unclear. Chen Hongtian et al. (*Zhaoming Wenxuan yizhu* 2: 986, n. 247) construe them as referring to elegant and vulgar songs respectively. This interpretation does have some support, for *bian sheng* 變聲 (mutated sounds) is a word for the music that is the antithesis of *ya yue* 雅樂. *Yong* literally means "useful," and perhaps refers here to the didactic function of the *ya yue*. Although this interpretation is somewhat speculative, I follow it for lack of anything better to suggest.

LL. 269–70: "Guangling" 廣陵, which is better known as "Guangling san" 廣陵散 ("Guangling Melody"), is one of the most famous zither tunes. Xi Kang reputedly played it just before his execution. See Yang Yong, *Shishuo xinyu jiaozhu* 6.265 (6/2); and Mather, *Shih-Shuo Hsin-yu* p. 180. In the later musical tradition "Stopping the Breath" ("Zhi xi" 止息) was the name of the finale of "Guangling san." However, nothing is known about it as an independent tune. See van Gulik, *Hsi K'ang*, pp. 47–48. "Dongwu" 東武 and "Mount Tai" 泰山 are *yuefu* titles. See Guo Maoqian, *Yuefu shiji* 41.605–9. Li Shan (*Wen xuan* 18.19b) cites a commentary to Zuo Si's "Three Capitals Rhapsody" that identifies "Dongwu" and "Mount Tai" as old songs of Qi.

LL. 271–72: "Flying Dragon" ("Fei long" 飛龍) could refer to the Han ritual song in which the phrase "flying dragon" occurs. See *Han shu* 22.1048. "Deer Calls" ("Lu ming" 鹿鳴) is the title of *Mao shi* 161. According to Cai Yong's *Qin cao* (as cited by Li Shan, *Wen xuan* 18.19b), it was also the name of a zither song. Li Shan (*Wen xuan* 18.19b) identifies "Jungle Fowl" ("Kun ji" 鵾雞) as a *xianghe* song. Nothing else is known about it or "Roaming Strings" ("You xuan" 遊弦). They are mentioned in Guo Maoqian, *Yuefu shiji* 41.599, but are not explained further.

Hand in hand with good friends,
245 We go for a stroll to amuse ourselves.
We enter a garden of fragrant herbs,
Climb a lofty knoll.
With a tall grove at our backs,
Covered by a flowery sunshade,
250 We go down to a limpid stream,
And compose new songs.
We admire the relaxed ease of fish and dragon,
Enjoy the fecund splendor of the many plants.
We then play the zither song handed down from Chonghua;
255 Heaving sighs, we long for the distant, ponder the far away.

### X

Then, at an informal banquet in an ornate hall,
With intimate friends and close companions:
Savory viands are served to all,
Fine wine is clear and mellow.
260 We then present "Southern Jing,"
Sound forth "Western Qin,"
Continue with "Lingyang,"
Play "Man of Ba."
Vulgar and elegant sounds, mingling and rising together,
265 Stir the listeners' ears and startle their souls.
Judging the zither's incomparable merits and comparing its tunes,
How could it be matched by mouth organ and flute?

### XI

If one orders the tunes in their proper places,
There are "Guangling" and "Stopping the Breath,"
270 "Dongwu" and "Mount Tai,"
"Flying Dragon" and "Deer Calls,"
"Jungle Fowl" and "Roaming Strings."
They are alternately sung and played,
Their sounds seem as if spontaneously born.
275 Smooth and clear, gracile and graceful,
They dispel anxiety, wash away cares.

297

L. 278: Master Cai is Cai Yong. Li Shan (*Wen xuan* 18.19b) identifies his five songs as "Roaming in Spring" ("You chun" 遊春), "Limpid Waters," "Sitting in Sadness" ("Zuo chou" 坐愁), "Autumn Thoughts" ("Qiu si" 秋思), and "Dwelling in Seclusion" ("You ju" 幽居).

L. 279: Wang Zhao is Wang Zhaojun, on whom see Jiang Yan, "Rhapsody on Resentment," this volume, L. 42n. There are numerous songs about her. See Guo Maoqian, *Yuefu shiji* 29.424–435. The Consort of Chu 楚妃 is Fan ji 樊姬, who was the wife of King Zhuang 莊 of Chu (reg. 613–591 B.C.). Citing her own example of yielding to younger and more beautiful concubines, she convinced the king to dismiss the minister Yu Qiuzi 虞邱子, who had served in office for more than ten years without recommending able men or dismissing the incompetent. The king then appointed the able Sunshu Ao 孫叔敖 to take his place. See *Lienü zhuan* 2.8a–9a. There is a series of songs about Fan ji in *Yuefu shiji*, Guo Maoqian, 29.435–37.

L. 280: "Crane Separated a Thousand Leagues" ("Qian li bie he" 千里別鶴) is a zither song attributed to Muzi 牧子 of Shangling 商陵. He was married for five years, and his wife had not given birth to a son. Thus, his parents wanted him to take another wife. Upon hearing this, his wife got up in the middle of the night, leaned on the door, and listened to the bugling of cranes. Muzi was so moved, he composed the zither song that became known as "Crane Separated a Thousand Leagues." See Cai Yong's *Qin cao* (cited in *Wen xuan* 18.19b) and *Gujin zhu* B.1a.

L. 281: Li Shan (*Wen xuan* 18.19b) explains *yiqie* 一切 as *quan shi* 權時 (temporary; provisional), which does not make much sense in this line. I construe *yiqie* in the sense of "general" or "ordinary"; cf. *Shi ji* 79.2425: "Fan Ju and Cai Ze were what the world regards as ordinary sophists."

Next come popular ballads,
Master Cai's five tunes,
Songs of Wang Zhao and the Consort of Chu,
280 "Crane Separated a Thousand Leagues,"
As well as ordinary tunes
That can be used to fill in the gaps,
And these, too, may be appreciated.

However, only he who is detached and carefree
285 Can share in the enjoyment of the zither music.
Only he whose thoughts are profound and tranquil
Can comfortably dwell with it.
Only he who is unrestrained and untrammeled
Can devote himself to it without begrudging the effort.
290 And only he who is of the most refined attainment
Can understand its inherent principle.

## XII

Now let us discuss its form and structure,
And examine the manner of its tones:
The instrument has a mellow quality and thus its sounds are
       resonant;
295 Its strings are strung tight and thus the tones are clear.
The spacing between the strings is far, and thus low notes can be
       played;
The strings are long, and thus the studs can be used to sound the
       notes.
Its nature is pure and tranquil, upright and true,
And it embraces the harmonious peace of perfect virtue.
300 Truly it can be used to stir the heart,
And release deep emotions.

Thus, if the downhearted and dejected hear it,
They will not fail to shudder and shake from sorrow and sadness;
Anguish and care will pain their hearts.
305 The grief they feel will be so bitter and strong,
They will be unable to restrain their feelings.
If the content and happy hear it,
They will be joyful and glad.

L. 317: Boyi 伯夷 and his younger brother Shuqi 叔齊 were sons of the Lord of Guzhu 孤竹 (southern Lulong 盧龍 *xian*, Hebei). Their father wanted to name Shuqi his heir, but Shuqi yielded to Boyi. However, after Boyi refused the position, both brothers went into hiding. When King Wu conquered the Yin, they refused to "eat the grain of Zhou." They retired to Mount Shouyang 首陽, where they subsisted on ferns and eventually died of starvation. See *Shi ji* 61.2123.

L. 318: Confucius's disciple Yan Hui was especially known for his devotion to *ren* 仁 (benevolence); see also Ban Gu, "Rhapsody on Communicating with the Hidden," this volume, L. 64n.

L. 319: Bi Gan 比干 served at the court of Zhou, the last ruler of the Yin dynasty. He dared to admonish the king for his cruelty, and was put to death by having his heart torn out. See *Lun yu* 18/1; *Shi ji* 3.108; and Chavannes, *Mh* 1: 206.

L. 320: Wei Sheng 尾生, also known as Wei Shenggao 尾生高, was a native of Lu. He had an engagement to meet a woman under a bridge. Even though she did not arrive, he refused to leave. When the water rose, he drowned hugging a pillar of the bridge. See *Zhuangzi* 9.21a; *Shi ji* 69.2265; and *Huainanzi* 13.11b.

L. 321: Hui Shi 惠施 was a famous logician of the Warring States period. In the *Zhuangzi*, he and Zhuang Zhou are often portrayed engaging in debate.

L. 322. Lord Wanshi 萬石 is Shi Fen 石奮 (ob. 124 B.C.). He and his sons served with distinction in the early Western Han. Shi Fen was well known for his circumspect conduct. See *Shi ji* 103.2763–66; and Watson, *Records of the Grand Historian of China* 1: 543–46.

LL. 332–33: Metal and stone refer to bells and stone chimes respectively. The gourd refers to the mouth organ, and bamboo the flute.

L. 334: Wang Bao 王豹 was a famous singer of antiquity. According to *Mengzi* (6B/6), when he lived on the Qi 淇 River, people on the west bank of the Yellow River learned to sing in his manner.

L. 335: Di Ya 狄牙, also known as Yi Ya 易牙, was famous for his sensitive taste. He reputedly could even distinguish between the waters of different rivers. See *Huainanzi* 12.1b.

L. 336: Tianwu 天吳 was a river spirit about whom nothing much is known. See Yuan Ke, *Shanhai jing jiaozhu* 9.256.

L. 337: Wang Qiao 王喬, also known as Wang Jin 王晉, was the heir designate to King Ling of Zhou (reg. 571–545 B.C.). He played the mouth organ and could imitate the call of the phoenix. He learned the technique of attaining immortality from a Taoist, and flew off into the sky. See *Liexian zhuan* A.1, A.23–24.

Clapping and dancing, they will leap about,
310  Lingering on in wild abandon,
Laughing heartily all day long.

If the placid and serene hear it,
They will be contented and pleased.
Solemn and sedate, natural and unaffected,
315  Unperturbed and empty of care, rejoicing in antiquity,
They abandon worldly affairs and are oblivious of self.
Thus, from the zither Boyi obtained his incorruptibility,
From it Yan Hui obtained his benevolence,
From it Bi Gan obtained his loyalty,
320  From it Wei Sheng obtained his fidelity,
From it Hui Shi obtained his gift for argument,
And from it Wanshi obtained his circumspection.

A list of other worthies can be extended from these examples.
The effects the music achieves are manifold—
325  They attain the same ends, albeit by different paths:
Sometimes it is elaborate, sometimes plain.
It embraces central harmony and thereby controls all things,
And one can use it every day and never be led astray.
Its influence on humankind, its effects on things
330  Are great indeed!

## XIII

At the time it is played:
Metal and stone silence their sounds,
Gourd and bamboo hold back their air,
Wang Bao stops singing,
335  Di Ya loses his sense of taste,
Tianwu leaps from his deep pool,
Wang Qiao unfolds the clouds and descends to earth,
The phoenix dances on the courtyard steps,
River nymphs come floating in and gather here.
340  Since zither music influences Heaven and Earth and thereby brings
            about harmony,
How much more does it affect common creatures that creep on the
            ground?

301

ll. 1–2: Pan Yue refers here to the area of Hedong 河東, located in modern central Shanxi, where the Fen 汾 River flows south into the Yellow River. Quwo 曲沃 was the ancient name for the prefecture of Wenxi 聞喜 (northeast of modern Wenxi, Shanxi). See Tan Qixiang, *Zhongguo lishi ditu ji* 2: 15–16, 3–7; and *Han shu* 28B.1550.

ll. 3–4: Zou 鄒 and Lu 魯 were ancient states in the area of modern Shandong. Wenyang 汶陽 was a prefecture of the Lu kingdom in Han times. See *Han shu* 28B.1637. It was located northeast of modern Ningyang 寧陽, Shandong; see Tan Qixiang, *Zhongguo lishi ditu ji* 2: 19–20, 3–5. The bamboo mentioned here is *xiao* 篠, which was particularly valued for making the reeds of the mouth organ. See Hagerty, "Tai K'ai-chih's *Chu-p'u*," pp. 417–18.

To praise the great splendor of this instrument
I intone this poem to console myself.
Never shall I tire of its use,
345 For in truth it has been treasured, both in the past and present.

## XIV

The finale says:
Quiet and gentle is the zither's virtue—
It cannot be fathomed.
Its purity of essence, detachment of purpose
350 Are truly hard to attain.
Instruments of good quality and fine players
Can be found in this age.
Its rich and harmonious sound
Surpasses all other arts.

355 But those who understand its music are few,
And who can truly treasure it?
For fully comprehending the elegant zither,
There is only the Perfected Man.

# Rhapsody on the Mouth Organ

## PAN ANREN

### I

Among the treasures of the land between the Fen and Yellow rivers,
There is the gourd of Quwo.
The rarities of Zou and Lu
Include the unique bamboo of Wenyang.

IN THIS RHAPSODY Pan Yue describes the *sheng* 笙 (mouth organ). In ancient times, its body was made from a gourd, and thus it usually is classifed as a "gourd" instrument. The ancient *sheng* had various numbers of tubes. Most (but not all) tubes had bamoo reeds called *huang* 簧. Pan Yue's rhapsody departs from the conventional rhapsodies on musical

303

L. 5: This line refers to the gourd, which was used to make the wind-box of the mouth organ.

L. 21: This line refers to the reeds, which are inside the pipes.

LL. 25–26: The mouth organ was thought to resemble the shape of a *fenghuang* (phoenix). Thus, another name for the instrument is *feng guan* 鳳管 (phoenix pipes). Presumably the pipes represent the wings of the phoenix.

L. 30: The bright pearl probably refers to the mouthpiece.

L. 32: This line refers to the two longest tubes of the *sheng*. If they are "open within," these perhaps are tubes that are without reeds.

5 As for the lush and spreading beauty of their trailing stalks,
 The richness of the divine moisture that soaks them,
 The level and rugged contours of the nooks and bends that surround
   them,
 The delightful play of the birds that soar and land in them:
 These are things that have been thoroughly described by numerous
   writers,
10 And I thus allow myself to omit them from my piece.

 Simply behold how the instrument is made:
 After carefully examining the size,
 And measuring the length,
 They cut off a fresh culm,
15 And fashion it into cured reeds.
 They set the *gong* note in place, demarcate the *yu*,
 Arrange the *zhi*, order the *shang*.
 Expel air through the tube and all is silent;
 But cover a finger hole, and sounds come forth.
20 The pipes are arrayed on the outside, gathered together;
 The sound is clear within, subtle and refined.
 Each tube holds a single pitch, and thereby controls the resonance of
   the sounds;
 And a large-headed gourd serves as the wind-box.
 With yellow bell as the base note, euphonious melodies are played;
25 From the demeanor of the phoenix it takes its shape.
 It emulates the phoenix by thrusting out its wings,
 And imitates the voice of the simurgh with its piercing sound.

 Like a bird standing on tiptoe,
 It cranes its neck as if ready to fly.
30 The bright pearl is in its beak,
 Seemingly about to be swallowed, about to be dropped.
 The long tubes are open within,
 The remaining pipes bend outward,

---

instruments and eliminates the elborate description of the environment in which the materials used to make the instrument grow. Instead, he launches immediately into a description of the instrument and the music that it plays.

 There is a translation into modern Japanese by Obi and Hanabusa in *Monzen* 2: 419–29. There are *baihua* translations in Chen Hongtian et al., *Zhaoming Wen xuan yizhu* 2: 995–1009; and Li Jingying, *Zhaoming Wenxuan xinyu* 2: 296–302.

Closely clustered, diversely disposed,
35  Aligned like fish scales, short and long.


## II

And then, one who once lived in luxury and now is in straitened
     circumstances,
Who formerly basked in glory but is now haggard and worn,
Who feels frustrated by his present lowly condition,
Who constantly yearns for honors of the past:
40  While all those in the hall merrily drink,
He sits alone facing the wall, wiping his tears.
He picks up the mouth organ and is about to play,
But first he clears his throat to control his breath.
At first, he plays calm and composed, relaxed and at ease,
45  Then, midway he seems troubled and tormented, pent-up with grief.
At the end, the sounds are high and stately, straightforward and
     direct,
And also welling and swelling like seething waters.
Distraught and dispirited, sad and sorrowful,
They seem about to cease, then pour forth again.
50  They briefly halt, then swiftly dash off,
As if racing in wild abandon, then breaking off midway.
They are mournful and plaintive,
Yet vibrant and bright.
Full and overflowing, they pour forth,
55  Whizzing and whirring along, fast and furious.
Sometimes they meander about, level and low;
Sometimes they leap up, vigorous and quick.
Sometimes, once gone, they do not return;
Sometimes, having departed, they enter again.
60  Pausing, delaying, then dispersing,
They slowly spread, one following upon another.
The dancers stop their stepping in mid-course,
And the one who taps the rhythm stick cannot keep up with the
     beat.
Happy sounds come forth, and the entire hall rejoices;
65  Sad sounds are played, and the whole company weeps.

L. 72: "Lady Zhang" 張女 is a old tune about which nothing is known.

L. 73: On "Guangling," see Xi Kang, "Rhapsody on the Zither," this volume, LL. 269–70.

L. 74: There is a *yuefu* tune titled "Yuan tao xing" 園桃行 ("Song of Peaches in the Garden"), to which Pan Yue probably alludes here. "Yuan tao xing" is a variant title for "Huanghuang Jing Luo xing" 煌煌京洛行 ("Song of the Resplendent Capital Luo"); see Lu Qinli, *Xian Qin Han Wei Jin Nanbeichao shi* 1: 391–92.

L. 75: Li Shan (*Wen xuan* 18.24a) cites lines from a *yuefu* piece entitled "Duoyin ge" 咄喑歌 ("Song of Sighs") that praises the lushness of the date tree.

L. 78: Cf. *Mao shi* 174/3: "The paulownia and idesia, / Their fruits thickly hang."

LL. 83–84: On "Flying Dragon" and "Jungle Fowl," see Xi Kang, "Rhapsody on the Zither," this volume, LL. 271–72n.

LL. 85–86: These songs probably refer to *yuefu* tune titles. Li Shan (18.24a) mentions an old *yuefu* entitled "Feilai shuang bai he" 飛來雙白鶴 ("A Pair of White Cranes Flying In").

L. 87: Ziqiao is Wang Ziqiao, on whom, see Xi Kang, "Rhapsody on the Zither," this volume, L. 337n.

L. 88: On Mingjun, see Jiang Yan, "Rhapsody on Separation," this volume, L. 42n; and Xi Kang, "Rhapsody on the Zither," this volume, L. 279n.

L. 89: Li Shan (*Wen xuan* 18.24a) says this line refers to the "Chu wang yin" 楚王吟 ("Lament of the King of Chu"), an old *yuefu* tune title about which nothing is known. See also Guo Maoqian, *Yuefu shiji* 29.424.

L. 90: See Xi Kang, "Rhapsody on the Zither," this volume, L. 279n.

L. 92: What I have rendered as *yee yee* and *gwa gwa* are *yingying* 嚶嚶 and *guanguan* 關關, sounds made by the oriole and osprey respectively.

Tiny featherlike holes are pressed to rouse the dark reed,
And air reaches the upper pipes, passes to the lower tubes.
In accord with blowing and inhaling, it goes back and forth,
Following the rise and fall, now empty, now full.
70 The blowing is strong and vigorous, and the sound is resonant and
        clear;
Then, looking back hesitantly, he plays leisurely and slowly.
Ceasing the mournful strains of "Lady Zhang,"
He then breaks into the famous melody of "Guangling,"
Praises the tender beauty of the garden peach,
75 Sings of the lush luxuriance of the date tree.

The song goes:
"The date tree, how lush and luxuriant!
Its vermilion fruits thickly hang.
But after it sheds its leaves,
80 It will become a mass of withered branches.
If one cannot make merry while alive,
What good is the empty honorific given after death?"


## III

And then, he plays "Flying Dragon,"
Intones "Jungle Fowl."
85 "A Pair of Swans" soars off,
"White Crane" flies away.
Ziqiao lightly rises,
Mingjun longs to return,
The King of Jing wails his sad lament,
90 The Chu Consort sighs with recurring grief.
The sounds are sad and bitter —
Calling *yee yee, gwa gwa* —
Like a stray swan crying for her young.
Then, muffled and muted, soft and gentle,
95 They harmoniously sound,
Like a flock of baby cranes following their mother.
Pressing his lips to the mouthpiece, he blows a powerful burst of air,
And the sound becomes loud and deep, sustained and long.
The intricate skirling, delicate chirring —

L. 116: Ling 酃, a prefecture near modern Hengyang in south-central Hunan, was famous for its fine ale made from the waters of Lake Ling. See Knechtges, *Wen xuan*, 1: 420, n. 677.

L. 118: The twin phoenixes here presumably refer to the mouth organ. See LL. 25–26n above.

L. 119: Ye of Jin is Music Master Kuang.

L. 127: "Autumn Wind" refers to Cao Pi's "Yan ge xing" 燕歌行 ("Song of Yan"), the first line of which reads: "The autumn wind whines and moans, the weather turns cold." See *Wen xuan* 27.19a.

L. 128: "Heaven's Brilliance" ("Tian guang" 天光) and "Morning Sun" ("Zhao ri" 朝日) are *yuefu* titles. Cao Pi has a piece entitled "Morning Sun"; see *Song shu* 21.613. Li Shan (*Wen xuan* 18.25b) mentions that Fu Xuan 傅玄 (217–278) wrote a piece entitled "Heaven's Brilliance," but nothing by this name survives in his extant works.

LL. 129–30: These lines are taken from *Guo yu* 3.14a.

L. 131: "Zhang" is "Da zhang" 大章, an ancient song in praise of Yao; Xia is "Da Xia" 大夏, which lauded the achievements of Yu.

100 Oh, how clear and distinct!
The notes, shrill and sharp, sad and plaintive,
Oh, how they bend like a stone chime!

## IV

Then, in a sunny season just as the weather is turning warm,
We go down to a stream to send off a parting friend.
105 Merry with drink, we roister and revel;
The music ends as the sun shifts westward.
The few remaining guests begin to leave,
And the host feels a slight fatigue.
They put down the zithers, store the flutes,
110 Clear the ocarinas, remove the pipes.

## V

And then, sitting side by side on the mat,
Holding a companion's hand,
They let their solemn expressions relax,
And release their pent-up feelings.
115 They peel yellow rind and hand out sweet oranges,
They drain green jars from which they pour Ling wine.
The glistening pipes are all neatly ordered,
Twin phoenixes blare forth, resounding in harmony.
If Ye of Jin takes fright and throws down his zither,
120 What about the lute player of Qi and the zither player of Qin?

New sounds, variant tunes,
Wonderful melodies, exuberant and carefree,
Are twined with the strains of singing and drumming,
Gather the tones of bells and pitchpipes in their net.
125 Notes, glittering and glistening brightly, display their allure;
Full, swelling and surging, air comes forth.
"Autumn Wind" is sung on the road to Yan,
"Heaven's Brilliance" is followed by "Morning Sun."
The greater tones do not go beyond *gong*,
130 The finer tones do not go beyond *yu*.
He begins by sounding forth with "Zhang" and "Xia,"

L. 132: "Shao" 韶 is the famous music of Shun. "Wu" is "Da wu" 大武, music in praise of the martial victory of King Wu of Zhou over the Yin.

LL. 135–36: These phrases are drawn from Ji Zha's description of the "Eulogia" music as recorded in *Zuo zhuan*, Xiang 29 (Legge, *The Chinese Classics* 5: 550).

L. 142: See Lu Ji, "Rhapsody on Literature," this volume, L. 181n.

Then leads into "Shao" and "Wu,"
Thereby harmonizing the music of Chen and Song,
Unifying the customs of Qi and Chu.
135  The sounds come near but do not crowd, go afar but do not draw
       apart;
The tones form a pattern, and the rhythm is well ordered.


## VI

The success or failure of government
Is influenced by the quality of popular mores.
Music is the means by which customs turn toward the good,
140  And also is the means by which they are changed to the bad.
Thus, the instruments of string and bamboo never changed,
Yet the degenerate music of Sang-Pu has flourished.
Only the mouth organ
Is able to replicate the purity of all sounds,
145  And only the mouth organ
Is able to encompass the multiplicity of all pure tones.
Wei then is unable to display its depravity,
And there is no place for the licentiousness of Zheng.
If the mouth organ does not produce the most harmonious music in
       the world,
150  And sound forth the most virtuous, inalterable sounds,
What instrument can compare with it?

L. 7: On Mount Ji, see Xi Kang, "Rhapsody on the Zither," this volume, L. 72n

# Rhapsody on Whistling

## *CHENGGONG ZI'AN*

### *I*

A young gentleman, aloof from the crowd,
Eccentric in manner, fond of the strange,
Scornful of the world, oblivious of honor,
Abandons all worldly affairs.
5    He admires the lofty minded, yearns for the ancients,
Thinks of the distant, ponders the far away.
He will ascend Mount Ji to ennoble his character,
Or float the azure sea to let his mind wander free.

And then, he invites good friends,
10    Gathers about him like-minded companions.
He has mastered the supreme subtleties of life and fate,
Discerned the dark secrets of the Way and Virtue.
He grieves that the profane world is unenlightened,
And that he alone, transcending all care, was the first to awaken.
15    Stinted by the narrowness of the mundane road,
He gazes on the concourse of Heaven and treads on high.

THIS RHAPSODY by the Western Jin scholar and poet Chenggong Sui (*zi* Zian) is on the subject of *xiao* 嘯, a word that is usually translated "whistling." Although "whistling" is a close approximation of the manner in which *xiao* was executed, *xiao* actually was a breathing exercise performed by Taoist adepts. In his rhapsody, Chenggong Sui identifies the performer of the *xiao* as a young noble who has abandoned worldly concerns to cultivate his skills in "whistling." Although *xiao* is not a form of song and is not performed with a musical instrument, he describes it in musical terms, and thus this rhapsody properly belongs in the music category of the *Wen xuan*. There are several important studies of *xiao*: Aoki Masaru, "'Shō' no rekishi to jigi no hensen"; Funazu Tomihiko; and Li Fengmao, *Liuchao Sui Tang xiandao lei xiaoshuo yanjiu*, pp. 225–79.

    A text of this piece also is found in *Jin shu* 92.2373–75. Previous translations include von Zach, *Deutsche Wacht* 4 (1932); rpt. in *Die Chinesische Anthologie*, 1: 258–61; Obi and Hanabusa, *Monzen* 2: 430–39; and Douglas White, in Victor Mair, *The Columbia Anthology of Traditional Chinese Literature*, pp. 429–34. There are *baihua* translations in Chen Hongtian et al., *Zhaoming Wen xuan yizhu* 2: 1009–20; Li Jingying, *Zhaoming Wenxuan xinjie* 2: 302–9; and Chi et al., *Lidai fu cidian*, pp. 289–92.

315

L. 19: This refers to the setting sun. Cf. Zhang Heng, "Rhapsody on Returning to the Fields," this volume, LL. 29–30n.

L. 20: Murky Shore is where the Sun sets. See Xie Zhuang, "Rhapsody on the Moon," this volume, LL. 30–31n.

L. 27: "Yellow *gong*" is the yellow bell tone. On "Clear *Jiao*," see Fu Yi, "Rhapsody on Dance," this volume, LL. 47–48n.

L. 28: On "Flowing *Zhi*," see Lu Ji, "Rhapsody on Literature," this volume, L. 67n.

L. 29: Grand Clarity (Tai qing 泰清) is the sky.

L. 37: This phrase comes from the "Grand Commentary" to the *Classic of Changes*. See *Zhou yi zhushu* 8.4b (178).

Removing himself from pomp and vulgarity, he becomes oblivious of
     self,
And with strong feeling makes a long-drawn whistle.

## II

And then, when the Spirit of Brightness inclines its rays,
20    Pouring its light into Murky Shore:
He goes roaming hand in hand with a friend,
His pace leisurely and slow.
He emits marvelous sounds from his vermilion lips,
Stirs mournful tunes from his glistening teeth.
25    The sounds rise and fall, rolling within his throat;
The breath pours forth from his mouth strong and heavy, then
     suddenly rises.
He harmonizes yellow *gong* with "Clear *Jiao*,"
Blends *shang* and *yu* with "Flowing *Zhi*."
The whistle drifts like a wandering cloud in Grand Clarity,
30    Gathers like an unremitting breeze for a myriad leagues.
When the tune is finished, and the sounds cease,
Its lingering echoes may be savored without end.
This truly is a perfect natural sound,
Which not even strings and winds can imitate.

35    Thus, to make this sound one needs no instrument,
To effect it one requires no other thing.
He takes it near at hand from his own body,
And does it by using his mind and controlling his breath.
He simply moves his lips and there is a tune,
40    He opens his mouth and creates a sound.
Moved by whatever he encounters,
He responds in kind, sings forth accordingly.
The sound is loud but never boisterous,
It is faint but never inaudible.
45    In clarity and intensity it matches syrinx and mouth organ,
In richness and smoothness it equals lute and zither.
Its mysterious wonder is sufficient to commune with gods and
     awaken spirits;
Its refined subtlety is sufficient to explore the hidden and fathom the
     deep.

L. 49: On "Turbulent Chu," see Knechtges, *Wen xuan* 2: 106, L. 399n.

L. 50: "Northern Ward" (Bei li 北里) was a generic name for any type of lascivious music. It originally was the name of music composed for Zhou, the last ruler of the Yin dynasty. See *Shi ji* 3.105.

LL. 51–52: Li Shan (*Wen xuan* 18.27b) cites a story from a Taoist Lingbao scripture about the mute daughter of one King Zhui 墜. When she was four, he had her abandoned on the slopes of Southern Fusang 南浮桑. Although without food, she was able to nourish herself on vapors and moonlight. She also learned the techniques for getting rid of calamities. Sometime later she returned to her home state, which was suffering from a severe drought. Raising up her head, she gave out a whistle, and the sky sent down a huge torrent of water one hundred feet deep. "Overpowering yang" (*kang yang* 亢陽), a term in the *Classic of Changes* tradition used to refer to yang at its peak or the top line of a hexagram (see *Zhou yi zhushu* 1.5b, 22), is a conventional term for drought. Cf. *Sanguo zhi* 52.1238: "Thus, drought for several consecutive years is a response to overpowering yang." The expression "double yin" (*chong yin* 重陰) refers to thick clouds and, by extension, heavy rain. Cf. Cao Zhi, "Presented to Wang Can" (*Wen xuan* 24.4a): "Double yin moistens the myriad things."

L. 62: Cf. *Lun yu* 3/20: "'The Osprey' expresses grief without becoming harmful."

L. 69: This probably means that from a slow and relaxed tempo it returns to the original rhythm.

L. 79: The *Liuchen zhu Wen xuan* reads *si* 嘶 (neigh) for *si* 思 (thoughts) of the You Mao and *Jin shu* texts of the *Wen xuan*.

L. 80: The Hu horse (*Hu ma* 胡馬) that leans into the northern wind is a conventional image of longing for home. Cf. "Nineteen Old Poems," no. 1 (*Wen xuan* 29.2a): "The Hu horse leans into the northern wind."

It restrains the mournful abandon of "Turbulent Chu,"
50 Controls the extravagant dissipation of "Northern Ward."
It relieves a great flood with fiery drought,
Turns "overpowering yang" into "double yin."
Its tunes and songs have a myriad variations,
And its modes and modulations have no end:
55 They are harmonious and happy, joyful and gay,
Sad and sorrowful, depressing and dispiriting.
At times the sound is deep and dispersed, as if about to break off,
Then, midway, becomes high and shrill, spirited and strong.
Slow, with graceful restraint, it ambles at ease,
60 Then a flurry of sounds rush off in a rousing crescendo.
It can relieve feelings of brooding and care;
Although the heart is grieved, it is never harmed.
It garners the perfect harmonies of the eight musical sounds,
And truly reaches the height of pleasure without wild abandon.

## III

65 If then, one ascends a high terrace and looks down over the distance,
Opens his painted veranda and lets his gaze wander:
Heaving a sigh, head raised, he looks up and claps his hands,
Loudly giving out a long whistle that resounds clear and strong.
Sometimes it is easy and relaxed, then turns itself back;
70 Sometimes it is halting and hesitant, then races off again.
Sometimes it is tender and supple, soft and yielding;
Sometimes it roars and rushes like pounding waves.
Resounding full and strong, it overflows, then drains off;
Limpid tones drift about clear and smooth.

75 Powerful bursts of breath gush forth,
Mingling and mixing in wild confusion.
Huffing and puffing, it rises like a whirlwind;
Twittering and tweeting, echoes respond.
It renders the longing thoughts of the Hu horse,
80 Which leans into the cold wind on the northern frontier.
It is like a wild goose leading its young,
The flock crying out over the boreal desert.

Thus, in accord with forms, he can create sounds,

L. 92: Li Shan (*Wen xuan* 18.28b) cites the apocryphon *Chunqiu yuanming bao* 春秋元明苞, which says that when a fierce tigers howls (*xiao* 嘯, lit., "whistles"), "a valley wind (eastern wind) arises."

L. 93: The Southern Winnow is the star that controls the wind. See Bao Zhao, "Rhapsody on Dancing Cranes," this volume, L. 28n.

LL. 113–14: Metal refers to the bell, leather to the drum, pottery to the ocarina, and the gourd to the mouth organ.

And following events, he can compose tunes.
85  He responds without limit to things,
As swift as a snapping trigger the echo resounds.
Troubled and tormented, bursting and flowing forth,
It streams on and on like a long bank of clouds.
Now parted, now joined,
90  It seems about to break off, then continues again.

Feilian is roused in his dark cavern,
A fierce tiger responds from within the valley,
The Southern Winnow moves in the vaulted azure,
And a fresh gale shakes through the tall trees.
95  It dispels stagnant air, scattering and carrying it away;
Purges the murky turbidity of dusty haze.
It effects the perfect harmony of yin and yang,
And transforms the vile vulgarity of wanton customs.

### IV

If then, one roams lofty ridges,
100  Crosses great mountains:
He looks down from the side of a cliff,
Gazes on flowing rivers,
Sits on a giant rock,
Rinses his mouth in a clear spring.
105  He makes a mat of the marsh boneset waving in the wind,
Lies in the shade of the bamboo, graceful and tall.
Then, intoning and chanting, he gives forth a whistle,
One tone after another continuously reverberating.
He releases the grief and anger of pent-up thoughts,
110  Rouses the lingering torment of long-harbored care.
His heart is cleansed and free of troubles,
His mind, detached from the profane world, is as if drifting and
            floating.

### V

If then, it obtains a model from metal and leather,
Derives a pattern from pottery and gourd:

LL. 119–22: In these lines, Chenggong Sui draws upon the traditional correspondences between the notes of the pentatonic scale and the four seasons. The *zhi* note corresponds to summer. If played in winter, it could give rise to summer heat. *Yu, shang,* and *jue* are the notes of winter, autumn, and spring respectively. When *yu* is played in summer, winter cold occurs. When *shang* is played in the spring, autumn rains will fall. When *jiao* is played in autumn, a spring breeze blows through the trees. Cf. *Liezi* 5.14b–15a, which tells the following story of a zither player who could change the weather of each season by playing a different note: "In spring he struck the *shang* string and summoned up Nanlü. A cool wind suddenly arrived, and plants and trees produced fruit. In autumn he struck the *jiao* string and stirred Jiazhong. A warm wind slowly whirled, and plants and trees burst into bloom. In summer he struck the *yu* string and summoned up Huangzhong. Frost and snow fell together, and rivers and ponds suddenly froze. In winter he struck the *zhi* string and stirred Ruibin. Sunlight shone brightly, and solid ice instantly melted."

L. 133: For "Shao" and "Xia" see Pan Yue, "Rhapsody on the Mouth Organ," this volume, LL. 131–32n. On "All-encompassing Pond," see Fu Yi, "Rhapsody on Dance," this volume, n. 12.

L. 135: See Ma Rong, "Rhapsody on the Long Flute," this volume, L. 242n.

L. 136: On Wang Bao, see Pan Yue, "Rhapsody on the Mouth Organ," L. 334n.

L. 137: The *Yanzi chunqiu* (1.4b) mentions a Lord Yu 虞公 who performed lascivious music for Duke Jing of Yan. However, Li Shan (*Wen xuan* 18.30a) cites Liu Xiang's *Bie lu*, which says there was a Lord Yu in the early Han period who was a skilled singer.

L. 138: Master Ning is Ning Qi 甯戚, a man of Wei in the Chunqiu period. He unsuccessfully sought a position with Duke Huan of Qi, and then took up a career as a merchant. One night he was singing sadly by his cart when Duke Huan happened to see him. Ning then received an appointment as minister in Qi. See *Lüshi chunqiu* 23.3b.

L. 139: On Zhong Qi, see Wang Bao, "Rhapsody on the Panpipes," this volume, L. 115n.

L. 140: This line alludes to *Lun yu* 7/14, which reports that after Confucius heard the "Shao" music, he was oblivious of the taste of meat for three months.

LL. 141–42: Cf. *Shang shu zhushu* 5.14b–15a: "When all nine parts of the Xiao Shao music were completed, the phoenix came in solemn demeanor. Kui then said, 'Oh, when I strike the stone, when I tap the stone, all the beasts begin to dance.'"

115 A multitude of sounds would be played in unison,
   Like reed pipe, and like bamboo flute.
   Roaring and rumbling, they thunderously resound,
   Blasting and blaring with a deafening din.
   Emit the *zhi* note, and at the peak of winter it becomes hot and
           humid;
120 Release the *yu* note, and severe frost withers things in summer;
   Stir the *shang* note, and autumn rainstorms fall in spring;
   Play the *jiao* note, and an east wind sings through the branches.

   The tones and harmonies are not constant,
   The tunes have no fixed measure.
125 It goes forth, but does not overflow;
   It stops, but is never stagnant.
   From his mouth and lips the whistle comes forth;
   Carried on his fragrant breath, far away it travels.
   The tones, subtle and marvelous, flow off in echoes;
130 The melody, rapid and abrupt, sounds clear and sharp.
   This truly is the most beautiful sound of nature;
   It is distinctive indeed, unmatched in the world!
   It surpasses "Shao," "Xia," and "All-encompassing Pond";
   Why merely point out its differences with the music of Zheng and
           Wei?

## VI

135 At the time it is played, Mian Ju becomes tongue-tied and bereft of
           vitality;
   Wang Bao closes his mouth and turns pale.
   Lord Yu stills his voice and ceases his song;
   Master Ning withdraws his hands and heaves a sigh.
   Zhong Qi throws down his zither and listens instead;
140 Confucius forgets the taste of meat and stops eating.
   All the beasts begin to dance and stamp their feat;
   The phoenix comes in solemn demeanor and flaps its wings.
   From this, one can know the marvelous beauty of the long- drawn
           whistle;
   For this indeed is the highest form of musical sound!

# 19

PASSIONS

# *Rhapsody on the Gaotang Shrine*

## *SONG YU*

### I

Once King Xiang of Chu and Song Yu were strolling about the terrace of Yunmeng,[1] and they sighted the Gaotang shrine. Above it there was only a cloudy vapor:

5    Abruptly it rose straight up,

    Then suddenly changed appearance.

    In the space of a brief moment,

    It made countless changes and transformations.

    The king asked Song Yu, "What manner of vapor is this?"

10   Song Yu replied, "It is what is called Dawn Cloud."

    The king said, "What is meant by Dawn Cloud?"

Song Yu replied, "Once when a former king was visiting Gaotang, he became tired and took a daytime nap. He dreamed that he saw a woman

THIS RHAPSODY and "Rhapsody on the Goddess," which follows it in the *Wen xuan*, are the most famous pieces attributed to Song Yu. Both concern the female deity of Wushan 巫山 (Shaman Mount). Although there are various legends about her, the prevailing image of her in the Chinese literary tradition is that of a sexually captivating goddess who suddenly appears out of the clouds to have a tryst with a Chu king. Song Yu, who is renowned for his expertise on beautiful women, is the appropriate poet to give a detailed account of her. "Rhapsody on the Gaotang Shrine" is basically two pieces in one. The first part, which forms an introduction or preface, is a dialogue between King Qingxiang of Chu and Song Yu, who recounts the various guises in which the goddess appears. The second, and much longer portion, is a description of the marvelous Shaman Mount, as well as the activities that take place on its slopes. It is a mountain inhabited by famous immortals and seekers of longevity, and also a place in which kings may enjoy themselves in excursions and hunting. This section is noted for its long description of the waters that roar beneath the mountain. Although the exact location of this Shaman Mount is not certain, the cataractine character

L. 26: The Sun Terrace (Yang tai 陽臺) perhaps is the same as the Yangyun Terrace 陽雲臺, which Meng Kang (*Han shu* 57A.2544, n. 4) identifies as Gaotang itself. The Yangyun Terrace is associated with Shaman Mount in eastern Sichuan. The *Taiping huanyu ji* by Yue Shi (142.7a), locates it in Wushan Prefecture (modern Wushan, Sichuan). However, it also mentions (132.7a) a Yang tai twenty-five *li* south of Chachuan 汉川 Prefecture (north of modern Hanchuan 漢川, Hubei).

who said to him, 'I am the maiden of Shaman Mount, and I am a guest at Gaotang. Having heard that my lord is visiting this place, I wish to offer him pillow and mat.' The king then favored her with his bed. When she left, she bade farewell saying:

'I live on the sunny side of Shaman Mount,
Among the defiles of a lofty hill.
Mornings I am Dawn Cloud,
Evenings I am Pouring Rain.
25  Dawn after dawn, dusk after dusk,
Below the Sun Terrace.'

"The next morning the king looked there, and it was just as she had said. Thus, he established a temple in her honor, which he named Dawn Cloud."

King Xiang asked, "When Dawn Cloud first appears, how does she look?"

Sung Yu replied:

"When she first appears,
She is lush as a stand of pines.
As she gradually comes nearer,
She is bright and radiant like a fair lady.
35  Raising her sleeve to block the sun, she watches for her lover.
Suddenly, she changes appearance,
Swift as a four-horse team,
With plumed banners raised.
She is cold as the wind,

---

of the waters suggests that this must be the Shaman Mount located near the Yangtze gorges. The rhapsody ends in typical moralistic fashion. The king is allowed to go to the Gaotang shrine only after he has properly fasted and morally purified himself.

A number of scholars have doubted the authenticity of this rhapsody. Among the earlier studies that cast doubt on the attribution to Song Yu is Lu Kanru, *Song Yu* 宋玉, pp. 107–10. Several recent scholars have challenged Lu's conclusions. See Cao Minggang, "Song Yu fu zhenwei bian"; and Chien Tsung-wu, " 'Gaotang fu' zhuancheng shidai zhi shangque".

Previous translations include Arthur Waley, *The Temple and Other Poems*, pp. 65–72; Fusek, "The 'Kao-t'ang Fu'"; and Obi and Hanabusa, *Monzen* 2: 440–52. For *baihua* translations see Chen Hongtian et al., *Zhaoming Wen xuan yizhu* 2: 1021–34; Li Jingying, *Zhaoming Wenxuan xinjie* 2: 310–18; and Chi et al., *Lidai fu cidian*, pp. 14–17. For annotated texts see Xiao Jizong, *Xian Qin wenxue xuanzhu*, pp. 252–58; Fu Lipu, *Fu xuan zhu*, pp. 1–7; and Bi et al., *Zhongguo lidai fu xuan*, pp. 131–49.

L. 64: This line could also be rendered: "The waters rise and surge without a sound."

L. 73: The punctuation here is unclear. Li Shan (*Wen xuan* 19.3a) treats Jieshi 碣石 as a place name, and breaks the line after 石. However, 石 (*djɪak*) does not make a good rhyme with the *yue* 月 (*at-*) group rhymes that precede and follow. Thus, I have broken the line at 碣. See Hu Kejia, *Wen xuan*, 4.1b.

40 Chilly as the rain.
When the wind stops and the rain clears,
The cloud is nowhere to be found."
The king said, "May I now visit there?"
Song Yu replied, "Yes, you may."
45 The king said, "What is this place like?"
Song Yu said: "It is high and prominent;
Looking down from it, one may see far away.
Broad and widely extended,
It is the progenitor of the myriad things.
50 Above, it conjoins with Heaven;
Below it, one can see plunging depths.
Its precious wonders and strange marvels
Cannot be told or discussed."
The king said, "Please try to rhapsodize on it for me."
55 Song Yu said, "Very well."


## II

Verily Gaotang is such a massive form,
There is nothing with which it can compare.
Shaman Mount is majestic without peer;
Paths bend back and forth, following one upon another.
60 Climb its cragged cliffs and gaze downward—
One sees below the massing waters that pour from its great slopes.
When the rain has newly cleared from the sky,
One may view a hundred valleys collected together.
There is no sound but the roar of the surging waters;
65 All joined, calm and full, they flow together.
Swollen, broad and wide, they disperse in the four directions,
Flowing tumid and deep, never ceasing.
A distant wind blows in and waves rise up,
Like solitary balks clinging to a hill.
70 As their force nears shore, the waters collide;
Then pulled together in a narrows, they draw back and meet again.
Gathered together, they rage within, thrusting on high,
Like giant columns sighted while sailing the sea.
Rocks and pebbles, heaped in piles, grind together,
75 Resounding with a roar that rattles the sky.

L. 88: Li Shan does not explain the word *hui* 喙. Hu Shaoying (*Wen xuan jianzheng* 21.2a–b) cites Wang Niansun, who explains *hui* as "shortening of breath." Thus, I have rendered it as "panting."

L. 97: The "dark trees" (*xuan mu* 玄木) probably are the magic trees, the leaves of which when eaten will confer one immortality. See *Lüshi chunqiu* 14.6a. *Xuan* also has cosmological associations. It is the color of the north and winter, and thus a *xuan mu* perhaps is the "boreal tree" or "hibernal tree."

L. 102: Li Shan (*Wen xuan* 18.4a) explains *zhen lin* 榛林 as "chestnut grove." However, both Hu Shaoying (*Wen xuan jianzheng* 21.2b) and Zhu Jian (*Wen xuan jishi* 15.18a–16a) show that *zhen* simply means "dense" or "clustered."

L. 104: The *yi* 椅 is *Idesia polycarpa* Maxim., a tree that blooms in early summer with clusters of small green fragrant flowers. See Lu Wenyu, *Shi caomu jinshi*, pp. 28–29, no. 35.

Giant boulders, drowned and drenched, rise and fall in the plashing
waves;
Foam, spraying and spuming, is thrown aloft.
The waters, tossing and tumbling, twist and twine;
Broad billows, flowing full, shudder and shake.
80   Then, they race off, heaving and leaping, striking one another;
Rising like clouds, they tumble with the sound of pelting rain.
Ferocious beasts take fright, bolt and panic;
Running helter-skelter, they dash off into the distance.
Tiger, leopards, dholes, and gaurs,
85   Bereft of vitality, are afraid to cry out.
Eagles, ospreys, hawks, and kites
Soar away to escape and hide.
Thighs trembling, panting from fear,
They dare not pounce at will.


## III

90   And then, water creatures, fully emerged,
Climb onto the sunny side of the isles.
Turtles, alligators, sturgeons, and paddlefish,
Lie heaped together, one upon another.
Shaking their scales, flapping their fins,
95   They wriggle and writhe, twist and twitch.
On the middle bank one gazes into the distance:
There are dark trees blooming in winter.
Bright and brilliant, gleaming and glistening,
They overwhelm one's power of sight.
100  They sparkle like stars arrayed in the sky;
One cannot fully describe them.

Dense groves grow thick and luxuriant,
Covered and canopied with blossoms and flowers.
Twin idesia heavy with drooping pods,
105  Their twining branches joined one to another,
Shuddering and shaking,
Follow the waves with their dark shadows.
East and west they spread their winglike boughs,
Swinging and swaying in plenteous profusion of

L. 115: The quintuple changes perhaps are the five notes of the pentatonic scale. The changes could be the five changes of rhythm that were prescribed for a musical piece. See Ma Rong, "Rhapsody on the Long Flute," this volume, L. 156n. The quadruple merging perhaps refers to the blending of the music of the four directions. See Li Shan, *Wen xuan* 19.4a.

L. 136: Whetstone Pillar (Di zhu 砥柱), also known as Sanmen shan 三門山, was a mountain near modern Sanmenxia 三門峽, Henan. According to legend, when Yu tamed the flood, he dredged a course through the mountain to let the Yellow River flow through. The river surrounded most of the mountain, leaving a portion resembling a pillar protruding from the water. See *Shui jing zhu* 4.22a.

110  Green leaves, purple fruits,
    Cinnabar stalks, white stems.
    Slender branches sadly moan
    With sounds like syrinx and flute.
    Clear and turbid are blended together,
115  Quintuply changing, quadruply merging.
    The sounds rouse the heart, stir the ears,
    Wrench the bowels, pain the spirit,
    And cause orphaned child and widowed wife
    To tremble with grief, to cry bitterly.
120  High officials discard their posts,
    Worthy scholars abandon their ambitions:
    With no end to their sad thoughts,
    They heave a sigh and let tears fall down their cheeks.


## IV

    Climbing on high and gazing afar
125  Cause one's heart to be pained.
    Winding bluffs, sheer and steep,
    Rise layer upon layer, lofty and tall.
    Giant boulders, poised on high,
    Leaning precariously, topple from the cliffs.
130  Rugged scarps, jaggedly jutting,
    Run hither and thither in mutual pursuit.
    Nooks and crannies crisscrossing the slopes,
    With caverns at their backs, block foot passage.
    The peaks heaped and piled, one upon another,
135  In tiers and layers rise higher and higher,
    In a manner like Whetstone Pillar,
    Lie beneath Shaman Mount.

    Above, one sees the mountain's crest:
    How majestic its verdant luxuriance,
140  Shining, dazzling, bright with rainbows!
    Below one sees a plunging precipice,
    A vast void deep and dark:
    One cannot see its bottom,
    And merely hears the sound of rustling pines.

L. 153: Ben and Yu are the famous warriors Meng Ben and Xia Yu.

L. 179: The *zhengming* 正冥, which I have translated "just-at-dusk," is a bird that cannot be identified.

L. 180: The identity of the *sifu* 思婦 (yearning-wife) bird is not known.

145 By the overhanging bluff where waters race full and strong,
Someone stands nervously hunched like a bear.

For a long time he does not leave,
And he is fully drenched in sweat down to his feet.
He is distant and distracted, befuddled and bemused,
150 Distraught and distressed, lost in thought.
This causes a man's heart to throb;
For no reason he is afraid.
Even men as resolute as Ben and Yu
Could not summon up their courage.
155 Suddenly he meets strange creatures,
But does not know from whence they came.

In teeming throngs they assemble.
As if born of ghosts,
As if issued from spirits.
160 In appearance they are like running beasts,
Or resemble flying birds.
Illusory and strange, wondrous and grand,
They cannot be fully described.

Above, beside the shrine,
165 The ground is smooth and flat.
Spreading out like a winnow's heel,
Fragrant plants rampantly grow.
Autumn thoroughwort, angelica, and basil
Along with lovage all luxuriate.
170 Green sweet flag, blackberry lily,
And cart-halt grow in thick clusters.

Bunched grasses, twined and tangled,
Fine and delicate extend across the slopes.
Fragrance wafts thick and strong;
175 Birds in flocks chirp and chatter.
Male and female, lost from their mates,
Sadly wail, crying for each other.
Ospreys, orioles,
Just-at-dusk, Chu doves,
180 Cuckoos, yearning-wife birds,
Droop-tailed fowl nest on high.

L. 183: I follow Wang Niansun (*Dushu zazhi*, "Zhiyu," B.46a), who emends *dang nian* 當年 to *dangyang* 當羊, which has the sense of *changyang* 尚羊 (relaxed and at ease).

L. 186: The masters of techniques are the *fangshi* 方士, who were experts in divination, prognostication, and prolonging life.

L. 187: Xianmen 羨門, also known as Xianmen Gao 羨門高, was an immortal. Gao Xi 高谿 possibly is a variant for the immortal Gao Shi 高晢. Xianmen and Gao Shi are mentioned together in *Shi ji* 6.251.

L. 188: Li Shan (*Wen xuan* 19.6a) explains Shangcheng 上成 and Yulin 鬱林 as names of *fangshi* and adds that the line could mean that immortals are gathered as thick as a forest. I have followed the latter interpretation.

L. 189: Li Shan (*Wen xuan* 19.6a) says that Gong Le 公樂 and Ju Gu 聚穀 may be names of immortals. However, he goes on to suggest that *gong* 公 is equivalent to *gong* 共 (together). The line thus could mean that immortals gather on the mountain to enjoy a feast. Wang Niansun (*Dushu zazhi* 3/2.26b–27a) equates Ju Gu with Zui Hou 最後, which some commentators understand as the name of a *fangshi*. See *Shi ji* 28.1368. The text seems hopelessly corrupt here, and frankly I am unsure of its exact meaning. My translation is highly tentative.

L. 193: Grand Unity (Taiyi 太一) originally was a Taoist term that was used as another name for the Tao. In the Emperor Wu (reg. 140–87 B.C.) period of the Former Han, Grand Unity became the most important deity of the imperial cult. For this reason, some scholars have argued that this line indicates that "Rhapsody on the Gaotang Shrine" could not have been written by Song Yu. See Fusek, "The 'Kao-t'ang Fu,'" pp. 405–6. Recently Ma Jigao has argued that the deity Grand Unity could have existed as early as the reputed time of Song Yu. See *Fu shi*, pp. 41–42.

L. 206: In the plume hunt (*yu lie* 羽獵), marchers in the entourage wear plumes on their shoulders. See *Han shu* 87A.3541, n. 1 and *Guo yu* 7.6b.

336

Calling *gia gia*,
Relaxed and at ease, they play about,
Alternately singing and chirping in chorus,
185   They follow a set tune in accord with the water's flow.


## V

There are masters of techniques,
Xianmen and Gaoxi,
Gathered on high, thick as groves,
All enjoy a sumptuous feast.
190   They offer single-colored victims,
Pray in the carnelian chamber,
Pour libations to the spirits,
Worship the Grand Unity.
Once the invocation has been prepared,
195   Its words and phrases all complete:

The king then mounts a jade-inlaid chariot:
It is drawn by four green dragons,
With banners and pennons trailing behind,
And streamers harmoniously blended in.
200   A musician plucks the main string and elegant sounds flow forth;
A chilly wind blows in, increasing sadness and grief.
And then, the melodious singing causes men
To feel mournful and grieved,
To bate their breath and sigh repeatedly.

Then, they send forth the hunters;
205   At the base of the mountain they spread out like stars.
They pass the order that the plume hunt is to begin;
Biting on their gags, they make nary a sound.
Bows and crossbows do not shoot,
Nets and meshes are not spread.
210   They wade wide streams,
Gallop through tangled brush.
Birds have no time to fly away,
Beasts have no time to flee.
How swift, how sudden

L. 228: The tryst presumably is with the Wushan goddess.

L. 233: Hu Kejia (see *Wen xuan* 4.3a) notes that the *Wuchen* text does not contain the character *zhi* 滯. He concludes that the original Li Shan text also did not have *zhi*. Thus, this should be understood as a single line instead of two. See also Wang Niansun, *Dushu zazhi*, "Zhi yu," B.46a–b.

215  Their hooves and legs are spotted with blood!
Before the feats of the first catch are proclaimed,
The game carts are already full.

If Your Majesty wishes to visit there,
You must first fast and purify yourself,
220  Select an auspicious time and choose a propitious day.
Ride a simple cart, dress in black,
With cloud standards raised.
Rainbows will form your banners,
Kingfisher plumes will form your canopy.
225  When the wind rises and the rain stops,
You may travel a thousand leagues.
Having thus dispelled your ignorance,
You may then go to your tryst.
With your thoughts on the myriad regions,
230  And anxious about harm to the state,
You become receptive to worthies and sages,
And they will assist you wherever you are deficient.
Your nine apertures will be unclogged, and your vital spirit will be
        unblocked.
You shall extend your years, increase your fated span
235  By a thousand, even ten thousand years!

# Rhapsody on the Goddess

## SONG YU

### I

King Xiang of Chu and Song Yu were strolling along the shore of
Yunmeng, and the king had Yu rhapsodize about the Gaotang shrine.
That night, while Song Yu was asleep,[1] he actually dreamed of having an

THIS RHAPSODY is a companion piece to "Rhapsody on the Gaotang Shrine." In the
"Goddess" Song Yu describes the alluring beauty of the Wushan goddess. The piece
contains many lines on which later poets drew in writing about female beauty.

encounter with a goddess whose appearance was extremely beautiful. Song Yu wondered about this, and the next day he told the king about it. The king said, "What sort of dream did you have?" Song Yu replied, "After the late afternoon watch:

"My spirit felt befuddled and confused,
As if something propitious had occurred.
But I was perplexed and puzzled,
And did not know what it meant.
15   My eyes could only vaguely discern her,
But I can recall my momentary impression.
I saw a woman
Unusual in appearance.
Asleep, I dreamed of her;
20   Awake, I cannot remember her form,
And thus I felt depressed and unhappy,
Sad and frustrated.
And then, stroking my breast, I calmed my spirit, and again
        visualized what I had seen in my dream."
The king said, "What did she look like?"
Song Yu replied:
25   "She is magnificent, she is gorgeous,
Beautiful in all respects!
She is splendid, she is elegant,
Quite difficult to fathom!
Remote antiquity had none like her,
30   And the current world has yet to see her peer.
Her rare features and precious bearing
Cannot be praised enough!
When she first appears, she glitters like the bright sun shining over
        roof beams;
As she gradually draws near, she gleams like the bright moon
        spreading forth its light.

---

Previous translations include Eduard Erkes, "The Song of the Goddess by Sung Yuh"; von Zach, *Deutsche Wacht* (June 1928), rpt. in *Die Chinesische Anthologie* 1: 262–65; Margouliès, *Anthologie*, pp. 321–24; and Obi and Hanabusa, *Monzen* 2: 453–60. For *baihua* translations see Chen Hongtian et al., *Zhaoming Wen xuan yizhu* 2: 1035–43; and Li Jingying, *Zhaoming Wenxuan xinjie*, 2: 319–23. For annotated texts see Xiao Jizong, *Xian Qin wenxue xuanzhu*, pp. 259–61; and Bi et al., *Zhongguo lidai fu xuan*, pp. 149–57.

L. 53: Li Shan (*Wen xuan* 19.7b) explains *tuo* 媠 as "beautiful." However, Hu Shaoying (*Wen xuan jianzheng* 21.7b–8a) argues that *tuo* is equivalent to *tuo* 脫 (to remove). Thus, the line follows from the goddess's change of appearance in L. 51, and perhaps describes her changing dress.

L. 65: Li Shan (*Wen xuan* 19.7b) explains that the goddess has obtained the outer adornment of abundant beauty. Liu Liang (*Liuchen zhu Wen xuan* 19.9b) says that the goddess possesses a beautiful adornment as a generous favor from Heaven and Earth.

35 Within a moment
A beauteous look fully envelops her,
Brilliant as a flower,
Smooth as jade,
A host of colors brilliantly displayed:
40 She cannot be fully described.
Looking at her closely,
Robs one of his power of vision.
She is splendidly adorned with
Gauze and silk, damask and fine remnants, replete with resplendent
designs.
45 The wondrous hues of her magnificent attire illumine the myriad
directions.
She wears an embroidered blouse,
Is garbed in jacket and skirt.
Thick fabric does not make her appear too short,
Thin dress does not make her appear too tall.
50 Walking daintily, she dazzles the hall;
Suddenly, she changes appearance,
Supple as a roaming dragon soaring the clouds.
Removing her garments,
She changes into lighter dress.
55 She bathes in boneset oil,
And exudes the fragrance of sweet pollia.
She is of a pleasant and agreeable nature,
Well suited to attend a king.
Compliant and gentle,
60 She can cheer one's heart."
The king said, "How magnificent indeed she is!
Would you try to rhapsodize about her for me?"
Song Yu said, "Very well."


*II*

How beautiful is this lovely goddess:
65 Endowed with the rich adornment of yin and yang,
She dresses in garments of ornate delight,
Just like a kingfisher flapping its wings.
Her appearance is without peer,

L. 70: Mao Qiang 毛嬙 was a beautiful lady of ancient times. See *Zhuangzi* 1.21a.

L. 85: I emend *wang* 王 to *yu* 玉. See n. 1 to this rhapsody and Hu Shaoying, *Wen xuan jianzheng* 20.8a–b.

Her beauty is beyond description.
70  Mao Qiang would hide her face in her sleeves,
For she would no longer be a standard of beauty;
And Xi Shi would cover her visage,
For in comparison she would have no allure.

Viewed close up, she is ravishing;
75  Seen from afar, she is a stunning vision.
The pattern of her bones is of unusual form,
A physiognomy fitting for the lady of a lord.
As I looked upon her, her beauty filled my eyes;
Who could possibly surpass her?
80  I enjoyed her with secret delight,
And my joy was unbounded.
But since she was so chary of love and favor,
I could not express my full feelings.
No one else could see her;
85  Only I saw her form.

Her form is tall and stately;
How can she be fully described?
Her face is round and full, sedately beautiful—
A jade countenance smooth and moist.
90  Her pupils flash sharp and clear,
And in her bright eyes much beauty can be seen.
Her eyebrows are daintily curved like a moth's antennae;
Her vermilion lips shine bright as cinnabar.
Her pure white figure is full and firm;
95  Her mood is calm and composed, her bearing relaxed.
She maintains a lovely reserve in quiet seclusion,
But also cavorts and frolics in the human world.
It is proper for her to release her feelings in a high hall,
And freely let herself go, graceful and at ease.


## III

100  Rustling her misty gossamer, stepping slowly,
She brushed her jangling jades against the stairs.
Toward my curtain she looked with beckoning gaze,
Her eyes like the surge of rolling waves.

She flounced her long sleeves, straightened her lapels,
105   And stood hesitant, restless and uneasy.
Yet her manner was calm and tranquil, pleasant and mild;
And her mood was quiet and composed, unperturbed.
At times her movements were so easy and subtle,
Her intent could not be fathomed.
110   Her manner seemed intimate, yet aloof;
She appeared to come near, then turn back.
I raised the bed curtains, invited her in,
To express my most earnest feelings.
But she held to her chaste purity,
115   And refused to consort with me.
In a display of fine words, she made her reply,
Exhaling fragrance sweet as boneset.
Our beings went back and forth in spiritual congress,
And our hearts were contented and peaceful, joyful and glad.
120   Although our spirits joined, they were not bound;
And my soul was left lonely and forlorn, without hope.
Although she seemed to say yes, she was unwilling in the end;
Moaning deeply, I cried out, heaving mournful sighs.
Her flushed face showed a trace of anger, yet she remained
                composed,
125   And I did not dare impose myself upon her.


## IV

Then, rustling her girdle ornaments,
Sounding the simurgh bells,
She straightened her clothes,
And resumed a solemn expression.

130   She consulted with her preceptor,
Called to her tutor,
And although our love was not yet consummated,
She was about to bid farewell and depart.
She stepped back and moved away,
135   And she could no longer be approached.

She seemed to have gone, yet was still there;
Midway she appeared to turn toward me,

Her eyes casting furtive glances,
And bestowing their magic luster upon me.
140 The power of her will and bearing was everywhere manifest;
It cannot be completely described.
Although she wished to part, she had not finally severed the ties;
And my heart and spirit overturned with anxiety and fear.
She was too rushed to complete the farewell courtesies,
145 And we had no time to say parting words.
I wished to steal a moment,
But the goddess pleaded haste.
My bowels were wrenched, my spirit wounded,
And I tottered uneasily, with nothing on which to hold.

150 All was cloudy and dark,
And suddenly I did not know where I was.
My feelings hidden in my breast,
To whom could I confide them?
Sad and sorrowful, with tears falling down my face,
155 I sought her till the light of dawn.

# Rhapsody on Master Dengtu the Lecher

## SONG YU

### I

The grandee Master Dengtu was in attendance on the king of Chu, and he spoke disparagingly of Song Yu: "As a person, Song Yu is hand-

THIS RHAPSODY depicts Song Yu in one of his familiar roles, the handsome man who does not succumb to the seduction of a beautiful woman. He also is shown here as a great wit who is able to defeat an opponent with a clever speech. Master Dengtu, who accuses Song Yu of lechery, may be a purely fictional figure.
Previous translations include Waley, 170 Chinese Poems, pp. 43–44, and Translations, pp. 7–8; Margouliès, *Anthologie*, pp. 126–27; and Obi and Hanabusa, *Monzen* 2: 461–66. For

some and refined in appearance, and he has a gift for clever speech, yet by nature he is a lecher. I hope Your Majesty will not allow him access to the rear palace."

When the king questioned Song Yu about Master Dengtu's charges, Song Yu said: "My handsome and refined appearance, I have received from nature, and my gift for clever speech, I have learned from my teacher. As for being a lecher, I deny that I am any such thing."

The king said, "If you are not a lecher, do you have a defense? If you have a defense, that will be the end of the matter. If not, you will be dismissed."

Song Yu said, "Of all the fair women in the world, none can compare with those in Chu. And of the beauties of Chu, none can compare with those of my village. And of the lovely ladies of my village, none can compare with the daughter of my eastern neighbor. The daughter of my eastern neighbor: Add an inch to her height, and she would be too tall; subtract an inch, and she would be too short. Applying powder would make her too white, and applying rouge would make her too red. Her eyebrows are like kingfisher plumes, her skin is like white snow, her waist is like bundled silk, her teeth are like cowry shells. One of her charming smiles would confound Yangcheng and befuddle Xiacai.[1] For three years this girl has been climbing the wall and peeping at me, but I have never given in to her. Master Dengtu is not like this. His wife:

> Has disheveled hair, crooked ears,
> A cleft lip, gaping teeth,
> Walks with a sideward gait, is hunchbacked,
> And also has scabies and piles.

Yet Master Dengtu fell in love with her, and caused her to bear him five children. If Your Majesty would examine this carefully, you would see who really is the lecher."

At this time, a Zhanghua grandee from Qin was standing by the side of the king,[2] and he took the opportunity to step forward and say: "Just now Song Yu has lavishly praised his neighbor's daughter, deeming her a great beauty, but this stupid and lowly courtier believes that in upholding virtue, I cannot compare with those two gentlemen.[3] Moreover, how can

---

baihua translations, see Chen Hongtian et al., *Zhaoming Wen xuan yizhu*, 2: 1044–48; Li Jingying, *Zhaoming Wen xuan xinjie* 2: 324–27; and Chi et al., *Lidai fu cidian*, pp. 10–11. For annotated texts, see Xiao Jizong, *Xian Qin wenxue xuanzhu*, pp. 265–67; and Fu Lipu, *Fu xuan zhu*, pp. 8–10.

a concubine from a humble lane in Southern Chu be worthy of being mentioned to Your Majesty? The ladies this lowly courtier has seen with his own eyes I would not dare mention."

The king said, "Please explain this for me."

The grandee said, "Very well."

## II

"When I was young I went on a distant journey. I viewed the nine regions of the realm, and passed through the cities of the five directions. I left Xianyang to enjoy myself in Handan.[4] I lingered about the Zhen and Wei rivers in Zheng and Wei.[5]

"At this time, at the end of spring,
Just as we greeted the first sun of summer,
Orioles were chirping,
And a group of girls went out to pick mulberry leaves.
The young lasses of this country town
Glow with resplendent color and allure.
Their figures are pretty, their faces ravishing,
And require no makeup or adornment.
As I looked upon the most beautiful one,
I declaimed the following verse:
'I follow the great road, I grasp your sleeve.'[6]

"I gave her a fragrant flower and spoke to her charming words. And then, the young maid

"Seemed to be gazing expectantly, but she would not approach;
Suddenly she seemed about to approach, then disappeared.
Her air seemed cordial, but her person remained distant;
With each movement, up or down, was a different view.
With happy heart, smiling faintly,
Her rolling eyes cast furtive glances at me.
She then declaimed the following song:
'I know that the spring wind stirs fresh flowers into bloom;
Chaste and pure, I await your kind words,
But to receive a gift in this manner, I would prefer not to live.'

She then withdrew and bade me farewell. We used subtle words only to stir each other's feelings, and our spirits joined only in brief union. My

L. 2: Li Shan (*Wen xuan* 19.12a) says Cao Zhi was returning to Juancheng, which was east of Luoyang. However, Cao Zhi probably already had been installed in his new fief of Yongqiu, and thus the eastern fief refers to this place, not Juancheng.

L. 3: Yique 伊闕 was a mountain fifty *li* south of Luoyang. It reputedly was formed at the time Yu dredged the course of the Yi River. He diverted the river between two mountains that faced each other like twin monumental gateways (*que*); hence, the name Yique (Yi River Gateway). See *Shui jing zhu* 15.19b–20a; *Huainanzi* 19.2a, Gao You's commentary; and Zhu Jian, *Wen xuan jishi* 4.3b–4a.

L. 4: Huanyuan 轘轅 was a mountain forty-six *li* southeast of Goushi 緱氏 Prefecture (southeast of modern Yanshi *xian*, Henan). It was called Huanyuan (Switchback) because of its twelve winding slopes. See Li Jifu, *Yuanhe junxian tuzhi* 5.133.

L. 5: Tong Valley 通谷 was also known as Tai Valley 太谷. According to the *Luoyang ji* of Hua Yan 華延 (cited by Li Shan, *Wen xuan* 19.12a), it was located fifty *li* south of Luoyang. See also Li Jifu, *Yuanhe junxian tu zhi* 5.139, which places it ninety *li* south of Tang-time Luoyang.

L. 6: Li Shan (*Wen xuan* 19.12a) cites a work called *Henan jun tu jing* 河南郡圖經 (Texts and Maps of Henan Commandery), which says that Mount Jing 景山 was seven *li* south of Goushi Prefecture. Zhu Jian (*Wen xuan jishi* 15.20a) locates it northwest of Gou Mountain 緱山 in the Goushi Prefecture area.

eyes took pleasure in her pretty face, but in my heart I saw her virtue. In declaiming poems and upholding the rites, we never transgressed the bounds of propriety. Thus, this is worthy of relating to Your Majesty."

Thereupon, the King of Chu proclaimed his praise, and Song Yu was not dismissed.

# *Rhapsody on the Luo River Goddess*

## *CAO ZIJIAN*

In the third year of Huangchu[1] I attended court in the capital. Upon my return I crossed the Luo River. The ancients say that the goddess of this river is called Fufei. Inspired by Song Yu's response to the king of Chu on the matter of the goddess,[2] I have composed this rhapsody. The piece reads:

### *I*

I start out from the capital realm,
To return to my fief in the east.
With Yique at my back,
I traverse Huanyuan,
5     Cross Tong Valley,
Ascend Mount Jing.
The sun has already inclined toward the west,
My chariot is tipping precariously, the horses are tired,
And I then halt my equipage in a pollia marsh,

THE GODDESS who is the subject of this rhapsody by Cao Zhi (*zi* Zijian) is Fufei, who, according to tradition, was the daughter of the ancient culture hero Fuxi. She drowned in the Luo River and was subsequently worshiped as the Luo River goddess. Cao Zhi composed this rhapsody in imitation of "Rhapsody on the Goddess," attributed to Song Yu. His motivation in writing the piece long has been the subject of speculation. There is the tradition, recorded in a "note" (*ji* 記) in the You Mao edition of the *Wen xuan* (it probably was not part of Li Shan's original commentary), that the Luo River goddess actually stands for Empress Zhen 甄, the wife of his elder brother Cao Pi, with whom Cao Zhi reputedly was in love. However, this account clearly does not accord with historical circumstances and

L. 10: This may refer to the place known as Zhitian *zhen* 芝田鎮 forty *li* southwest of Gong 鞏 *xian*, Henan. See *Wei Jin Nanbeichao wenxueshi cankao ziliao* 1: 96, n.4.

L. 11: Li Shan (*Wen xuan* 19.12b) says that Yanglin 陽林 is also written 楊林, and is so named for its many poplar trees.

10 Graze my team in a mushroom field.
   Ambling about the poplar groves,
   I wander my gaze over the Luo River,
   And then my spirit is shaken, my soul startled,
   And suddenly my thoughts scatter.
15 Looking down, I perceive nothing;
   Looking up, I behold an unusual sight.
   I see a beautiful person,
   On the bank below the cliffs.

I then tug at the coachman's arm and say to him, "Do you see that over there? What sort of person is it, one so beautiful as this?"

The coachman replies, "I have heard that the goddess of the He and Luo is called Fufei. What my prince sees, could it possibly be she? What is her appearance like? I would like to hear you tell me."

## *II*

I tell him:

---

should not be given any serious consideration. See Zhang Yun'ao, *Xuanxue jiaoyan* 9.17b; and Cutter, "The Death of Empress Zhen." The piece also is read as a frustration poem in which Cao Zhi uses the beautiful goddess to represent his brother, Emperor Wen, who refused to grant Cao Zhi an important position in the Wei regime. As in Qu Yuan's quest for Fufei in "Li sao," Cao Zhi's encounter with the Luo River goddess is short-lived, and is understood to represent his abortive quest to receive an important position in which to demonstrate his loyalty and talent. This interpretation is more credible than the previous one, but there is no solid evidence that this is a political allegory. For one of the more cogent political interpretations of the piece, see Cao Daoheng, *Han Wei Liuchao cifu*, pp. 109–10. For a summary of the traditional political interpretations see Whitaker, "Tsaur Jyr's Luoshen Fuh." Some recent scholars have hailed this rhapsody for its detailed portrayal of female beauty and frank expression of feelings of love. See Zhang Wenxun, "Kumen de xiangzheng—'Luo shen fu' xinyi." On the influence of this *fu* in Six Dynasties literature, see Hong Shunlong, "Lun 'Luoshen fu' dui Liuchao fu tan de touying."

There are numerous annotated versions of the piece. The more scholarly include *Wei Jin Nanbeichao wenxueshi cankao ziliao* 1: 93–106; Qu Tuiyuan, *Han Wei Liuchao fuxuan*, pp. 63–69; Zhao Youwen, *Cao Zhi ji jiaozhu* 2.282–93; Wang Chenguang, *Wei Jin Nanbeichao cifu xuancui*, pp. 1–20; Wei Fengjuan, *Wei Jin Nanbeichao zhujia sanwen xuan*, pp. 88–99; and Huang Ruiyun, *Lidai shuqing xiaofu xuan*, pp. 54–64. Previous translations include von Zach, *Deutsche Wacht* (August 1928), rpt. in *Die Chinesische Anthologie* 1: 265–68; Whitaker, "Tsaur Jyr's Luoshen Fuh"; Watson, *Chinese Rhyme-Prose*, pp. 55–60; and Obi and Hanabusa, *Monzen* 2: 467–75. For *baihua* translations, see Chen Hongtian et al., *Zhaoming Wen xuan yizhu* 2: 1049–59; Li Jingying, *Zhaoming Wenxuan xinye* 2: 328–34; and Chi et al., *Lidai fu cidian*, pp. 262–65. One important study of the piece is Miao Yue, "Cao Zhi 'Luoshen fu' (*Wen xuan* fu jian 4)."

L. 32: Cf. the "roaming dragon" image in Song Yu, "Rhapsody on the Goddess," this volume, L. 52.

L. 48: "Flower of lead" 鉛華 is a mineral compound, the principal ingredient of which was lead. It was used mainly as makeup on the forehead. See Schafer, "The Early History of Lead Pigments and Cosmetics in China."

L. 60: The paintings presumably are those of immortals and deities, which were common in the Han-Wei period.

In appearance, she lightly flutters like a startled swan,
Curvets like a roaming dragon.
Her luster is more brilliant than autumn chrysanthemum,
Her resplendence is more luxuriant than spring pine.

35  She is dimly descried like the moon obscured by light clouds,
She drifts airily like whirling snow in streaming wind.
Gaze at her from afar,
And she glistens like the sun rising over morning mists,
Examine her close up,
40  And she is dazzling as lotus emerging from limpid ripples.

Between plump and thin, she strikes a mean;
Her height conforms to proper measure.
Her shoulders seem as if sculpted,
Her waist is like bundled silk.
45  On her long throat and slender neck,
White flesh is clearly revealed.
Fragrant oils she does not apply,
Flower of lead she does not use.

Billowy chignons rise high and tall,
50  Long eyebrows are delicately curved,
Scarlet lips shine without,
White teeth gleam within.
Bright eyes do well at casting sidelong glances,
Dimples lie on either cheek.
55  Her wondrous manner is of uncommon beauty;
Her comportment is quiet, her body relaxed.
With tender feeling and graceful bearing,
She enthralls with her lovely words.
Her wondrous attire is unsurpassed in the world;
60  Her figure and form accord with the paintings.
She drapes herself in the shimmering glitter of a gossamer gown,
Wears in her ears ornate gems of carnelian and jade,
Bedecks her hair with head ornaments of gold and halcyon plumes,
Adorns herself with shining pearls that illumine her body.
65  She treads in patterned Distant Roaming slippers,
Trails a light skirt of misty gauze.
Obscured by the fragrant lushness of thoroughwort,
She paces hesitantly in a mountain nook.

L. 73: The divine stream presumably is the Luo River.

L. 87: Li Shan (*Wen xuan* 19.14a) cites the *Han shi neizhuan* 韓詩內傳 (Esoteric Commentary on the Han Version of the *Songs*), which tells the story of a man named Jiaofu 交甫 of Zheng, who met two nymphs on the bank of the Han River. As a parting gift, they gave him their girdle ornaments. After he bade them farewell, the girdle ornaments and the nymphs disappeared.

Then, suddenly she moves light and easy,
70 Rambling and playing about.
On her left rests a colored streamer,
On her right she is shaded by a cassia-staff banner.
Extending her albescent arms toward the margin of the divine
        stream,
She plucks dark mushrooms from the raging rapids.

## III

75 I delight in her chaste beauty,
But my heart, pounding nervously, is not happy.
Having no good go-between to convey my love,
I convey my words to the tiny billows.
Hoping that my sincere feelings first be made known,
80 I untie my jade girdle and offer it as a pledge.
Oh, the fair one, how truly good she is!
She is well versed in the Rites and understands the *Songs*.
Holding high a jasper gem to match my offering,
She points to the hidden depths as a place for our tryst.
85 I hold to my affection that is sincere and true,
Yet I fear this spirit will deceive me.
Recalling the broken promise made to Jiaofu,
I disconsolately pause, doubtful and uncertain.
Then, assuming a mild expression, I calm my feelings,
90 And control myself with the restraints of the Rites.

## IV

And the Luo spirit is moved;
Lingering briefly, she paces to and fro.
Her divine radiance disperses, then joins,
Now dark, now light.
95 Raising her slight form, cranelike she stands,
As if about to soar off, yet not taking flight.
She treads in the strong pungency of pepper-plant paths,
Walks through clumps of pollia, scattering their fragrance.
Disconsolate, she makes a long moan of endless longing;
100 The sound, mournful and shrill, long resounds.

L. 107: The two consorts are E Huang and Nü Ying, the wives of Shun who were worshipped as goddesses of the Xiang River. See Zhang Heng, "Rhapsody on Contemplating the Mystery," this volume, LL. 131–32n.

L. 108: The roaming nymphs are the two goddesses of the Han River who encountered Jiao of Zheng. See L. 87n above.

L. 109: The Gourd Star (Pao gua 匏瓜) consists of five stars in Delphinus. See Schlegel, *Uranographie chinoise* 2: 210–14. Li Shan (*Wen xuan* 19.14b) cites "Rhapsody on Stilling the Desires" by Ruan Yu, which says: "I lament that the Gourd Star has no mate." However, he does not know to what legend this reference to the mateless Gourd Star may refer.

L. 110: The Oxherd (Qian niu 牽牛) and Weaving Maid (Zhi nü 織女) were constellations, equivalent to Altair and Vega, that occupied opposite sides of the Sky River. They were allowed to meet only once a year, on the seventh day of the seventh moon, when a flock of magpies formed a bridge for them to cross the river. See Solger, "Astronomische Anmerkungen zu chinesischen Märchen"; and Fan Ning, "Niu lang Zhi nü gushi de yanbian."

L. 111: The Song edition of the *Cao Zijian ji* 曹子建集 reads *qimi* 綺靡 for *yimi* 猗靡. Zhao Youwen accepts the reading of *qimi*. See *Cao Zhi ji jiaozhu* 2.290, n. 95.

L. 114: Cao Zhi portrays the goddess as human, and thus here he describes her as a divine creature. See ibid. 2.290, n. 97.

L. 127: Pingyi 屏翳 is variously identified as the god of thunder, rain, or wind. However, in Cao Zhi's "Jie jiu wen" 詰咎文 ("Casting Blame"), there is a line that says "Pingyi takes charge of the wind" (see ibid. 3.457). Thus, Cao Zhi may have understood Pingyi to be a wind god.

LL. 128–29: Li Shan (*Wen xuan* 19.15a) says that the River Lord 川后 is Hebo 河伯, god of the Yellow River. However, Ping Yi (see Xie Huilian, "Rhapsody on Snow," this volume, L. 79n) also is identified as He Bo. Thus, it is possible that River Lord is some other river deity.

L. 130: On Nuwa, see Ma Rong, "Rhapsody on the Long Flute," this volume, L. 260n.

And then, a host of spirits, in teeming throngs,
Calling to cohorts, shouting to companions:
Some play in the limpid stream,
Some soar over fairy isles,
105   Some gather shining pearls,
Some collect halcyon plumes.
She accompanies the two consorts from Xiang in the south,
Walks hand in hand with the roaming Han River nymphs.
She sighs that the Gourd Star has no mate,
110   Laments that the Oxherd must dwell alone.
Her light jacket, so delicate and fine, waves in the wind;
Screening her face with a long sleeve, she stands and waits.
Her body, swifter than a soaring duck,
Suddenly drifts away like a god.
115   Crossing the billows, she walks with dainty steps,
Her gauze slippers stirring up dust.
Her movements follow no constant pattern,
As if precariously poised, then standing steady.
Her advances and stops are hard to predict;
120   She seems to depart, then returns again.
Her turning gaze reveals a fiery essence;
Her face is bright and sleek as jade.
The words in her mouth are not yet uttered,
Yet her breath is as sweet as dark boneset.
125   Her lovely countenance so gentle and fair
Makes me forget to eat.

## V

And then, Pingyi withdraws the wind,
The River Lord stills the waves,
Ping Yi beats the drum,
130   Nüwa sings clearly.
They bid the striped fishes to leap forth and warn of her chariot's
                approach,
And sound the jade simurgh-bells to accompany her departure.
With six dragon-chargers sedately prancing head to head,
Her cloud carriage advances slow and easy.
135   Whales rise up alongside the wheel hubs,

L. 155: The "height" possibly is Mount Jing

Water birds soar forth as her guard.

## VI

And then, as she crosses the northern sandbars,
Passes the southern ridge,
She turns her white neck,
140 Looks back with her bright shining eyes.
Moving her vermilion lips, slowly she speaks,
Setting forth the grand principles of amity and love.
She regrets that the ways of humans and spirit are different,
And laments that in her flourishing years she cannot find a fit mate.
145 She raises a gauze sleeve to wipe her eyes,
And tears fall in streams soaking her lapel.
She grieves that this good tryst must cease forever,
And sorrows that, once departed, we shall go to different realms.
"Lacking even the slightest feeling with which to express my love,
150 I present you a shining pearl earring from Yangtze south.
Although I dwell submerged in the Great Yin,
I shall always lodge my heart with you, my prince."
Suddenly I do not know where she has gone,
And I sadly watch as her spirit vanishes, and her brightness becomes
        hidden.

## VII

155 And then, leaving the lowland behind, I scale a height;
My feet go forth, but my spirit remains.
With lingering feeling, I try to conjure up her image;
I look back and my heart is filled with sorrow.
Hoping that her divine form would appear again,
160 I take a light craft and go upstream.
Drifting on the long stream, I forget to return;
My longing, unbroken and unending, increases my yearning.
At night I am restless and cannot sleep,
And I am soaked by heavy frost 'til light of day.
165 I order the driver to prepare the chariot,
For I wish to return to the eastern road.
I grasp harness and bridle and raise my whip,
But disconsolate, I hesitate, and am unable to depart.

# Biographical Sketches

BAN GU 班固 (32–92), *zi* Mengjian 孟堅, native of Anling 安陵 (modern Xian-yang, Shaanxi).

Ban Gu was the son of Ban Biao 班彪 (3–54), and the older brother of Ban Zhao 班昭 (ca. 49–ca. 120), also known as Cao Dagu 曹大家. His twin brother Ban Chao 班超 (32–102) was a famous explorer. Information about Ban Gu's life is found in the "Autobiographical Postface" to the *Han shu* (100) and in Ban Biao's biography in the *Hou Han shu* (40).

From an early age Ban Gu showed unusual literary skill and reputedly was able to recite the *Classic of Songs* and rhapsodies at the age of nine. He was an avid reader and, as he grew older, was thoroughly conversant with the major schools of learning. In A.D. 54, when Ban Gu was twenty-two, his father died. He returned to the family home in Anling, northeast of Chang'an. Greatly saddened by his father's death, Ban Gu spent a period of contemplation and introspection, pondering what direction he should follow in his life. As a way of "setting forth his fate and carrying out his intentions" (see *Han shu* 100A.4213), he wrote the long *fu* "Rhapsody on Communicating with the Hidden," which is contained in the *Wen xuan* (chap. 14).

Ban Gu did not immediately embark on an official career, but remained at home in Anling engaging in scholarship. Before his death, Ban Biao had begun work on a supplement to Sima Qian's *Shi ji*. Ban Gu took up the task of completing his father's work. Around 58 he served on the staff of Liu Cang 劉蒼 (fl. 41–62), king of Dongping.

In A.D. 62 someone informed Emperor Ming 明 (reg. A.D. 58–75) that Ban Gu had privately undertaken to revise the national history. The emperor ordered that Ban Gu be arrested and his family library confiscated. His brother Ban Chao interceded on his behalf, and the emperor consented to have Ban Gu released from confinement. In the same year he was assigned to the Magnolia Terrace as a foreman clerk, in which capacity he worked on compiling the annals of the first Later Han emperor, Guangwu 光武 (reg. A.D. 25–57), along with biographies of important figures of that era. In A.D. 64 Ban Gu was promoted to the post of gentleman and put in charge of editing books in the imperial collection. The emperor was so impressed with the quality of Ban Gu's scholarship that in A.D. 66 he granted him permission to resume compilation of his Former Han history, on which he worked for over twenty-five years, until his death in A.D. 92. The full one-hundred-*juan Han shu* was completed after Ban Gu's death, most likely by his sister Ban Zhao. The "Treatises from the Histories" and "Evaluations from the Histories" sections of the *Wen xuan* (chaps. 49 and 50) contain examples of the critical essays and rhymed appraisals of historical figures that concluded each chapter of Ban Gu's history.

During Emperor Ming's reign, in addition to compiling his history, Ban Gu continued to write *fu*. It was probably during this period that he wrote his longest and most famous *fu*, "Two Capitals Rhapsody" (*Wen xuan*, chap. 1). In 74 Ban wrote an essay titled "Elaboration of the Canon" (*Wen xuan*, chap. 48), which praises the Later Han imperial house as the legitimate successor to the sage ruler Yao.

Although he was much admired as a writer and scholar, Ban Gu held the relatively low position of gentleman, and other than writing pieces at imperial command, he was mainly employed as an editor of texts in the imperial archives. Sensitive to criticism that his learning and literary skills had won him "no merit," Ban wrote "Response to a Guest's Jest" (*Wen xuan*, chap. 45), a justification of his apparent lack of success.

During the reign of Emperor Zhang 章 (reg. 76–88) Ban Gu was promoted (ca. 78) to marshal of the Black Warrior Gate, a position with more prestige and a higher salary (one thousand bushels). In 79 he was given the task of editing the proceedings of an important conference on the classics held in the White Tiger Hall. (The attribution to Ban Gu of the treatise by that name—*Baihu tong* 白虎通—is, however, questioned by some scholars.) As the most accomplished poet at court, Ban Gu enjoyed special favor and often composed eulogies and rhapsodies in celebration of imperial excursions and tours of inspection, in which he was privileged to participate.

After his mother died in 88 Ban Gu resigned his position, but returned to government service the following year as an aide to General Dou Xian 竇憲 (ob. 92) on a military expedition against the Northern Xiongnu. To commemorate Dou Xian's victory, Ban Gu composed "Inscription for the Ceremonial Mounding at Mount Yanran" (*Wen xuan*, chap. 36), which was carved on a stele erected on Mount Yanran 燕然 (in modern Mongolia). Ban Gu also headed the Chinese delegation that accepted the Xiongnu chieftan's surrender.

Although Dou Xian received much honor and acclaim for his successful Xiongnu campaign, Emperor He (reg. 89–105), suspecting him of plotting a coup against the throne, had him arrested and sent to his estate, where he was forced to commit suicide. As a member of Dou Xian's staff, Ban Gu was dismissed from office. The prefect of Luoyang, who had harbored a grudge against Ban Gu, ordered him arrested. Ban Gu died in his sixty-first year in the capital prison.

*References*
Fujiwara Takashi. "Han Ko no fu kan."
Gong Kechang. "Ban Gu fu lun," *Han fu yanjiu*, pp. 208–30.
Jiang Fan. "Ban Gu de wenxue sixiang."
Lo Tchen-ying. *Les Formes et les methodes historiques en Chine.*

Van der Sprenkel, Otto B. *Pan Piao, Pan Ku, and the Han History*.
Zheng Hesheng. *Ban Gu nianpu*.

BAO ZHAO 鮑照 (ca. 414–466), *zi* Mingyuan 明遠. Sources do not agree on his native place. The ancestral home of the Bao clan probably was Shangdang 上黨 (modern Changzi 長子, Shanxi). Later, one branch may have moved to Donghai 東海 of Xuzhou 徐州 (modern Tancheng 郯城, Shandong). Thus, he is variously referred to as a native of Shangdang or Donghai.

Bao Zhao was a skilled writer of poetry, rhapsodies, and parallel prose. What little information there is about his life is found in short notices inserted in the *Song shu* (51.1477–80) and *Nan shi* (13.36) biographies of his patron Liu Yiqing 劉義卿 (403–444). Another valuable source is the preface to Bao's collected works by Yu Yan 虞炎 (fl. 483–493).

We know little about Bao Zhao's early life. Before taking up an official career, he probably worked as a farmer. Bao Zhao spent much of his official career not in the central administration, but on the staffs of Liu-Song princes. From ca. 438 to 444, he served as attendant gentleman to Liu Yiqing, prince of Linchuan 臨川. During Liu Yiqing's tenure as governor of Jiangzhou 江州 (roughly corresponding to modern Jiangxi and Fujian), Bao Zhao trekked the area around Jiujiang and wrote several poems about Mount Lu. In 440 he accompanied Liu Yiqing to Guangling 廣陵 (modern Yangzhou), where Liu assumed the position of governor of Southern Yanzhou 南兗州. After Liu Yiqing died in 444 Bao Zhao resigned his position as attendant gentleman and returned home.

In 445 Bao Zhao was appointed attendant gentleman on the staff of Liu Jun 劉濬, prince of Shixing 始興, who then held the position of governor of Yang-zhou 揚州 (modern Nanjing). In 449 he accompanied the prince to Jingkou 京口 (modern Zhenjiang, Jiangsu), where Bao's family possibly once lived. In January 451 the armies of the Northern Wei invaded the south and reached as far as Guabu 瓜步, on the north bank of the Yangtze across from Jiankang. After the Song army quickly repelled the invaders, Liu Jun led a force to refortify Guabu, and Bao Zhao accompanied him. Bao Zhao probably left Liu Jun's service before Liu and his brother instigated a rebellion against Emperor Wu in 453, for there is evidence that already in 452 he was serving as prefect of Haiyu 海虞 (east of modern Changshou 常熟, Jiangsu).

Around 458, after serving in the capital as erudite in the Imperial Academy and chamberlain in the secretariat, Bao Zhao took up another local government post as prefect of Moling 秣陵, on the southern outskirts of Jiankang. Attributed to this period is "Admiring the Moon in My Office by the West City Gate" (*Wen xuan*, chap. 30), a poem in which Bao reflects on his separation from a loved one as the moon becomes full.

The accounts of Bao's activities between 461 and 464, when he joined the staff of Liu Zixu 劉子頊 (457–466), prince of Linhai 臨海, are confusing. Yu Yan's claim that he served as prefect of Yongjia 永嘉 (modern Wenzhou) is doubtful, for Yongjia was not a prefecture in the Liu-Song period. It is more likely that he served as subprefect of Yongan 永安 (modern Sui 隨 *xian*, Hubei). Claims by some scholars that Bao Zhao visited Guangling after Liu Dan's abortive rebellion in 460 are also difficult to support.

In 462 the five-year-old Liu Zixu held the post of governor of Jingzhou 荊州 (roughly modern Hubei). The actual administration of Jingzhou must have been in the hands of senior officials such as Bao Zhao, who served first as acting adjutant and later as legal adjutant in the forward army. In February 466 Liu Zixun 劉子勛 (457–466), prince of Jin'an 晉安, encouraged by his adviser Deng Wan 鄧琬 (407–466), rebelled and declared himself emperor at Xunyang. Liu Zixu soon joined the insurrection, and thus Bao Zhao had no choice but to serve the rebel regime. By September 466 imperial forces routed the rebel armies, and Liu Zixu was ordered to commit suicide. Soldiers under the command of local Jingzhou commanders entered Jiangling and killed Liu Zixu's staff members, including Bao Zhao.

Bao Zhao's best-known *fu* is "Rhapsody on the Ruined City" (*Wen xuan*, chap. 11), a moving description of the desolate and wasted city of Guangling. Another of Bao's *fu* included in the *Wen xuan* (chap. 14) is "Rhapsody on Dancing Cranes."

As a *shi* poet, Bao Zhao is most distinguished for his *yuefu*. The *Wen xuan* (chap. 28) contains eight of his *yuefu*, including "Departing from the North Gate of Ji" and "Song of Dongwu," both of which are "border poems" about military service beyond the northern frontier. Bao also wrote numerous imitation poems. His three "Imitating Ancient Style" poems and "Imitating the Style of Liu Gonggan" (*Wen xuan*, chap. 31) all express a common Bao Zhao theme, the frustrations of an embittered scholar-official who has failed to achieve high position and meritorious service.

*References*

Cao Daoheng. "Guanyu Bao Zhao de jiashi he jiguan."
——. "Bao Zhao jipian shi wen de xiezuo shijian."
——. "Bao Zhao."
Chen, Robert Shanmu. "A Study of Bao Zhao and His Poetry."
——. "A Biographical Study of Bao Zhao."
Chen Yixin. "Bao Zhao he tade zuopin."
Ding Fulin. "Bao Zhao shi wen xinian kaobian."
——. "Guanyu Bao Zhao de jiguan."
——. "Bao Zhao ren qianjun canjun de shijian."
Frodsham, J. D. "The Nature Poetry of Pao Chao."
Fujii Mamoru. "Hō Shō no fu."
Itō Masafumi. "Hō Shō den ronkō."
Kotzenberg, Heike. *Der Dichter Pao Chao* (+466).
Lin Wen-yüeh. "Bao Zhao yu Xie Lingyun de shanshui shi."
Liu Wenzhong. *Bao Zhao he Yu Xin*.
Lü Zhenghui. "Bao Zhao shi xiaolun."
Miao Yue. "Bao Mingyuan nianpu."
Nakamori Kenji. "Hō Shō no bungaku."
Su, Jui-lung. "Versatility within Tradition: A Study of the Literary Works of Bao Zhao (414?–466)."

Wu Defeng. "Bao Zhao nianpu buzheng."
Wu Piji. *Bao Zhao nianpu* 鮑照年譜.
Zeng Junyi. "Bao Zhao yanjiu."
Zhang Zhiyue. "Bao Zhao ji qi shi xintan."

CAO ZHI 曹植 (192–232), *zi* Zijian 子建, native of Qiao 譙 in the kingdom of Pei 沛 (modern Bo 亳 *xian,* Anhui).

Cao Zhi was the foremost writer of the Jian'an and early Wei periods. The most important sources of information on his life are his biography in the *Sanguo zhi* (19.557–577) and the works cited in the commentary of Pei Songzhi 裴松之 (372–451).

Cao Zhi was the third son of Cao Cao 曹操 (155–220), and the second son of Cao Cao by Lady Bian 卞. He was the younger brother of Cao Pi 曹丕 (187–226), Emperor Wen of the Wei 魏 dynasty. Much of Cao Zhi's early life was spent in the camps of his father's army. From 204 until 220, except for brief periods when he accompanied Cao Cao on military campaigns, he resided in Ye 鄴 (southwest of modern Linzhang 臨漳, Hebei), where he was a leading participant in the literary salon centered around the Cao family.

Cao Zhi began to write *shi* poetry during his early years. In addition to the many occasional poems he composed for the gatherings in Ye, one of which ("Lord's Feast") is included in the *Wen xuan* (chap. 20), he wrote several personal poems. The best of these is "Sending Off Master Ying" (*Wen xuan*, chap. 20). Cao Zhi possibly wrote this poem for Ying Yang 應瑒 (ca. 170–217) as Ying was about to leave for a post in the north. Most of Cao Zhi's presentation poems included in the *Wen xuan* (chap. 24) also must have been written during this time.

From the time he was quite young, Cao Zhi was one of his father's favorites. Cao Cao seriously considered naming him heir, rather than the older son, Cao Pi. Cao Cao's indecision led to rivalry between the two brothers, each of whom had support of different groups at court. Cao Zhi's main supporters were literary men: the brothers Ding Yi 丁儀 (ob. 220) and Ding Yi 丁廙 (ob. 220), and Yang Xiu 楊修 (175–219), who was the nephew of Cao Cao's enemy Yuan Shu 袁術 (ob. 199). Mainly because of his reckless and irresponsible behavior, Cao Zhi eventually fell from his father's favor. In 217 Cao Zhi got drunk and rode his chariot down the imperial speedway and out the Major's Gate. This was a capital offense, for access to the speedway and gate was restricted to the emperor. Angered at his son's impudence, Cao Cao decided in winter of Jian'an 22 (217) to designate Cao Pi heir.

After Cao Pi declared himself emperor in December 220, he immediately introduced measures to curb the power of his brothers, including his chief rival, Cao Zhi. He ordered the execution of the two Ding brothers, and sent all of his own brothers to their estates, allowing them to come to the capital only with special permission. To ensure that they did not plot against him, he established the office of internuncios who supervise the vassal kingdoms. In 221 one of these officials charged Cao Zhi with "being drunk and insolent and trying to intimidate the imperial envoy." Cao Pi then ordered Cao Zhi brought to Luoyang, where officials were asked to deliberate on his punishment. Some recommended that he be reduced to the status of commoner. Others even proposed that he be put to death. However, after the intervention of Empress Dowager Bian, Cao Pi reduced Cao Zhi's rank from marquis of Linzi 臨菑 (northwest of modern Linzi, Shandong) to marquis of Anxiang 安鄉 (southeast of modern Wuji 無極, Hebei). The number of households in his estate was reduced from ten thousand to one thousand. Later in the same year (221), he received the title of marquis of Juancheng 鄄城 (north of modern Juancheng, Shandong). In 222 several officials accused Cao Zhi of an unspecified offense. He then went to the capital to plead his own case. Cao Zhi was allowed to return to his old home in Ye, where he stayed for a short time before returning to Juancheng. In April 222 Cao Zhi had his title elevated to that of prince of Juancheng. However, his status was still lower than that of most of his brothers, whose fiefs were commanderies, for Juancheng was only a prefecture.

In June–July 223 Cao Zhi and his brothers were allowed to come to Luoyang to participate in the seasonal festival. While in the capital he composed his most famous *fu*, "Rhapsody on the Luo River Goddess" (*Wen xuan*, chap. 19). At this time he presented to Cao Pi two tetrasyllabic poems, "Self-chastisement" and "Responding to an Edict" (*Wen xuan*, chap. 20). In the memorial submitted with the poem, Cao Zhi declared his desire to be of service to the state in the campaign against Shu and Wu.

Cao Zhi was never to have the chance to prove himself, for Cao Pi ordered him to return to his estate. As he was about to leave the capital, he presented a six-part poem to his brother Cao Biao 曹彪, who also was visiting the capital. In this poem, entitled "Presented to Biao, Prince of Baima" (*Wen xuan*, chap. 24), Cao Zhi expresses his regret at having to leave the capital and part from his brother Biao. In the second poem of the sequence, he describes the difficulties of travel over muddy roads made almost impassable by steady rain.

In late 223 Cao Pi again transferred Cao Zhi, this time to Yongqiu 雍丘 modern Qi 杞 *xian*, Henan,. In 225, while returning from an expedition against Wu, Cao Pi stopped to visit Cao Zhi in Yongqiu. According to an anecdote in the *Shishuo xinyu*, Cao Pi ordered Cao Zhi to compose a poem while taking seven paces. If he could not complete it, he would receive the maximum penalty. On the spot, Cao Zhi composed the poem now known by the title "Poem of Seven Paces." However, there are doubts about the authenticity of this piece.

In 226 Cao Pi died and was succeeded by his son Cao Rui 曹叡 (Emperor Ming 明帝, reg. 226–239. Although he was treated less harshly by Cao Rui, Cao Zhi continued to be transferred from one fief to another. In 227 he was moved to Junyi 浚儀 near modern Kaifeng,. In 228 he returned to Yongqiu. Disappointed at his failure again to obtain a position of responsibility, Cao Zhi submitted to Cao Rui a memorial requesting an appointment that would allow him to prove his loyalty to the state "Memorial Seeking To Prove Myself," *Wen xuan*, chap. 37).

In March of 228 Cao Rui journeyed to Chang'an to observe military operations against Shu. Soon there was a rumor that Cao Rui had died there, and some officials made preparations to install Cao Zhi on the throne. When Cao

Rui returned to Luoyang in June, there was great consternation in the capital. Although no one was punished, Cao Rui's suspicions toward Cao Zhi must have increased. Thus, in 229 Cao Zhi was transferred again, this time to Dong'e 東阿 (southwest of modern Dong'e, Shandong), where he remained for three years. In 231 he submitted a memorial to Cao Rui requesting that the regulations prohibiting contact among imperial relatives be relaxed ("Memorial Seeking to Convey Familial Affection," *Wen xuan*, chap. 37). Although Cao Zhi received only a laconic reply, later that year Cao Rui invited the princes, including Cao Zhi, to visit the capital. The emperor was especially gracious to Cao Zhi, but was still reluctant to appoint him to a government post.

In 232 Cao Zhi was assigned to Chen 陳 (modern Huaiyang 懷陽, Henan). He died there in 232 at the age of forty-one. He was given the posthumous name Si 思 ("The Thoughtful").

Cao Zhi's *yuefu*, four of which are contained in the *Wen xuan* (chap. 27), are particularly admired. His "Seven Laments" (chap. 23), along with several of his "Miscellaneous Poems" (chap. 29), are moving expressions of frustration using the persona of an abandonded lady. Cao Zhi also was a skilled *fu* writer. In addition to "Rhapsody on the Luo River Goddess," the *Wen xuan* contains "Seven Communications" (chap. 34), in which the protagonist presents a series of seven enticements to a recluse to induce him to leave his wilderness home to take a position at court.

Cao Zhi's prose works are also well represented in the *Wen xuan*. His eloquent memorials are ardent expressions of frustration and deep feeling. Even more personal feelings can be found in his two letters contained in chapter 42. His moving death lament for Wang Can, "Dirge for Wang Zhongxuan," may be found in chapter 56.

*References*
Chen Yibai. *Cao Zijian shi yanjiu.*
Cutter, Robert Joe. "Cao Zhi and His Poetry."
———. "Cao Zhi's (192–232) Symposium Poems."
———. "The Incident at the Gate."
———. "On Reading Cao Zhi's 'Three Good Men.'"
———. "The Death of Empress Zhen."
Deng Yongkang. "Cao Zijian nianpu xinbian."
———. *Wei Cao Jijian xiansheng Zhu nianpu.*
Diény, Jean-Pierre. "Les Septs Tristesses (*Qi Ai*)."
Dunn, Hugh. *Ts'ao Chih.*
Frankel, Hans H. "Fifteen Poems by Ts'ao Chih."
———. "The Problem of Authenticity in the Works of Ts'ao Chih."
Funazu Tomihiko. "Sō Shoku no yūsenshi ron."
Guo Moruo. "Lun Cao Zhi."
Ho, Kenneth P. H. "Xiancun Cao Zhi fu kaolüe."
Holzman, Donald. "Ts'ao Chih and the Immortals."
Honda Wataru. "Sō Shoku to sono jidai."
Ita Masafumi. *Sō Shoku.*

Kent, George W. *Worlds of Dust and Jade.*
Komori Ikuko. "Sō Shoku shi shokan."
———. "Sō Shoku ron."
K'uai Shu-p'ing. "Six Poems of Ts'ao Tzu-chien."
Li Baojun. *Cao shi fuzi he Jian'an wenxue.*
Li Chendong. "Cao Zhi de zuopin fenqi."
Liu Weichong. *Cao Zhi pingzhuan.*
Mok Wing-yin. "Three Poems by Ts'ao Chih."
Park Hyun-kyu. "Cao Zhi yanjiu lunzhu mulu."
Roy, David. "The Theme of the Neglected Wife in the Poetry of Ts'ao Chih."
*San Cao ziliao huibian.*
Ueki Hisayuki. "Sō Shoku den hokō."
Whitaker, K. P. K. "Tsaur Jyr's 'Luohshern fuh.'"
———. "Some Notes on the Background of Tsaur Jyr's Poem on the Three Good
  Courtiers."
———. "Tsaur Jyr and the Introduction of *Fannbay* 梵唄 into China."
Xu Gongchi. "Cao Zhi shige de xiezuo niandai wenti."
———. "Cao Zhi shengping ba kao."
———. "Cao Zhi wei Cao Cao diji zi."
———. "Cao Zhi."
Yu Guanying. "Jian'an shiren daibiao Cao Zhi (192–232)."
Zhang Dejun. "Guanyu Cao Zhi de pingjia wenti."
Zhang Keli. *San Cao nianpu.*
Zhong Youmin. *Cao Zhi xintan.*

CHENGGONG SUI 成公綏 (231–273), *zi* Zian 子安, native of Baima 白馬 in
Dong Commandery (east of modern Hua 滑 *xian*, Henan).

Chenggong Sui was a scholar and poet of the Western Jin. The main source
of information on his life is his biography in the *Jin shu* (92.2371–75).
According to the *Jin shu*, in his youth Chenggong Sui already displayed
unusual learning and intelligence. He was a skilled writer of *fu*, and among his
youthful compositions was a long piece on the cosmos entitled "Rhapsody on
Heaven and Earth" (see *Jin shu* 92.2371–73). He was on good terms with Zhang
Hua (q.v.), with whom he composed poems on imperial command. Around 255
Zhang Hua recommended Chenggong Sui for appointment as erudite. He later
served in the palace library, and ca. 261 he rose to the position of assistant director. Around 263 he was appointed to the secretariat, and at this time probably
composed "Rhapsody on Whistling," which is his only composition contained in
the *Wen xuan* (chap. 18). In 264, while serving as commandant of cavalry, Chenggong Sui was a member of the fourteen-person commission that was charged with
drafting the Jin law code. In 269 he was back in the secretariat as attendant
gentleman. In this year he composed several of the ritual songs used in imperial
ceremonies. The last post he held before his death in 273 was chief compiler.
The *Jin shu* mentions that Chenggong Sui's literary works circulated in a ten-
*juan* collection. The *Sui shu* (35.1061) lists collections in both nine and ten *juan*. All

of these collections long have been lost. He was a prolific *fu* writer, and the texts of his extant *fu*, many of them in fragments, are preserved in "Quan Jin wen" 59 (in Yan Kejun, *Quan shanggu Sandai Qin Han Sanguo Liuchao wen*).

FU YI 傅毅 (ca. 35–ca. 90), *zi* Wuzhong 武仲, native of Maoling 茂陵.

Fu Yi was a contemporary of Ban Gu, and a prominent scholar and poet during the beginning of the Later Han period. The most important source of information on his life is his biography in the *Hou Han shu* (80A.2610–13).

Fu Yi received much of his early education at the imperial university, where he began his studies ca. 52. Around 59 he went to Pingling 平陵 (west of modern Xianyang, Shaanxi) to study the type of commentary known as "chapter and verse" (*zhangju* 章句). At this time he wrote an autobiographical poem in tetrasyllabic verse entitled "Fulfilling My Aims." He also wrote "Seven Incitements," a rhapsody ostensibly intended to admonish men who had chosen to become recluses during the reign of Emperor Ming.

During the reign of Emperor Zhang 章 (reg. 75–88), Fu Yi and Ban Gu were the most prominent writers at the imperial court. Around 77 Fu Yi was appointed foreman clerk of the Magnolia Terrace. Soon thereafter he was promoted to gentleman and participated in the editing of documents with Ban Gu and the learned scholar Jia Kui 賈逵 (20–101). Fu Yi composed a long ten-part "Eulogy for Xianzong" in praise of Emperor Ming. Only fragments of the piece survive.

In 78 Fu Yi was appointed major on the staff of the powerful general Ma Fang 馬防 (ob. 90), who was leading a military expedition against the Western Qiang. When Ma Fang fell from power in 83, Fu Yi was dismissed from office. He apparently had no official position until 88, when General Dou Xian appointed him his private secretary. In the following year Fu Yi held the position of major, also on Dou Xian's staff. Fu Yi died soon thereafter, probably in 90.

Fu Yi's most famous work is "Rhapsody on Dance" (*Wen xuan*, chap. 17).

JIA YI 賈誼 (ca. 200–168 B.C.), native of Luoyang.

Jia Yi was a leading writer and thinker of the early Former Han. The main sources of information on his life are his biographies in the *Shi ji* (84.2491–2503) and the *Han shu* (48.2221–65).

During his youth, Jia Yi was well known in his home commandery of Henan 河南 (modern Luoyang) for his literary skills and his ability to recite the classics. At about the age of eighteen (ca. 183 B.C.), he attracted the notice of the governor of Henan, the Venerable Wu 吳公, who was a prominent legalist and student of the Qin minister Li Si. When Wu became commandant of justice around 179 B.C., he recommended Jia Yi to Emperor Wen (reg. 180–157 B.C.) as a scholar learned in the hundred schools of philosophy. The emperor appointed Jia Yi erudite, a position that in this period probably involved giving instruction in a particular text or school of philosophy. The other erudites, who were much older men, viewed the young Jia Yi with suspicion, particularly after he rose within one year to the post of grand palace grandee, a one-thousand-bushel rank.

Jia Yi submitted proposals for institutional reforms, which Emperor Wen did not dare to implement so early in his reign. Jia Yi also was the intiator of the plan ordering the vassal lords to take up residence in their fiefs. When Emperor Wen considered naming Jia Yi to a ministerial post, the senior officials protested on the grounds that "the man from Luoyang is young and just beginning his studies, yet he concentrates all his desires on arrogating authority to himself, and has brought chaos and confusion to everything" (see *Shi ji* 84.2492 and *Han shu* 48.2222). The men who opposed Jia Yi were part of the so-called Huai-Si 淮泗 faction, a group of old-guard officials that joined the Han founder Liu Bang in his home area and continued to serve in influential positions under Emperor Wen. They not only regarded Jia Yi as an upstart, but undoubtedly considered this reformed-minded genuis a threat to their own positions.

Deciding it was not politic to offend the group that had put him on the throne, Emperor Wen ceased seeking Jia Yi's advice. Finally, probably in 176 B.C., he dismissed Jia from the court and sent him into exile as grand tutor to the king of Changsha 長沙 (roughly corresponding to modern Hunan). Shortly after his arrival in Changsha, Jia Yi composed "Lament for Qu Yuan" (*Wen xuan*, chap. 60). While in Changsha he wrote his most famous poem, "Rhapsody on the Houlet" (*Wen xuan*, chap. 13). According to his *Shi ji* and *Han shu* biographies (see *Shi ji* 84.2496 and *Han shu* 48.2222), Jia Yi wrote this piece after living in Changsha for three years, i.e., 173 B.C.

Around 172 B.C. Emperor Wen summoned Jia Yi back to the capital and appointed him grand tutor to King Huai 懷 of Liang 梁 (reg. 178–169 B.C.). King Huai, Emperor Wen's youngest and favorite son, was a studious lad and fond of books. While serving as his tutor, Jia Yi continued to give advice to the emperor, particularly on how to reduce the power of the vassal kingdoms. King Huai died in 169 B.C. after being thrown from a horse. Jia Yi blamed himself for the accident and reputedly died of grief in 168 B.C.

*References*

Cai Tingji. *Jia Yi yanjiu.*
Emmerich, Reinhard. "Untersuchungen zu Jia Yi (200–168 v.Chr.)."
Gong Kechang. "Saofu zuojia Jia Yi." In *Han fu yanjiu*, pp. 49–60.
Kanaya Osamu. "Ka Gi no fu ni tsuite."

JIANG YAN 江淹 (444–505), *zi* Wentong 文通, native of Kaocheng 考城 Prefecture in Jiyang 濟陽 Commandery (east of modern Lankao 蘭考 Henan).

Jiang Yan was a leading writer of prose and poetry during the Song, Qi, and Liang dynasties. Although his ancestral home was in Kaocheng, his family had lived in the south since the Western Jin. The most important sources of information on his life are his biography in the *Liang shu* (14.247–51) and *Nan shi* (59.2447–51). Jiang Yan also wrote an autobiography, which is contained in his collected works (see *Jiang Wentong ji*).

The Jiang clan of Kaocheng was a distinguished family. However, Jiang Yan's branch did not include any high officials. His grandfather Jiang Dan 江耽 held the position of prefect of Danyang 丹陽 (modern Nanjing), and his father, Jiang Kangzhi 江康之 (ob. 456), served as prefect of Nansha 南沙 (modern Changshu, Jiangsu). His mother, née Liu 劉, was the aunt of Liu Zhao 劉昭 (ob. ca. 510), a prominent writer and scholar of the late Southern Dynasties.

When Jiang Yan was twelve his father died, and the family endured poverty for a number of years. Despite his privation, Jiang Yan acquired a good education, and at an early age earned renown for his learning and skill as a writer.

Jiang Yan began his official career at the age of nineteen (463) as tutor to Emperor Xiaowu's eleventh son, the six-year-old Liu Zizhen 劉子真, prince of Shi'an 始安. Jiang Yan instructed the young prince in the Five Classics, and wrote a number of memorials on the prince's behalf. He also accompanied him to his various posts, including Shitou cheng 石頭城, located about four kilometers west of the capital. It was here that Jiang Yan wrote his first extant poem, "Attending the Prince of Shi'an at Shitou" (see *Jiang Wentong ji* 4.7b).

Jiang Yan was invited to serve on the staff of Liu Ziluan 劉子鸞 (ob. 465), prince of Xin'an 新安, who was nominal inspector of Nan Xuzhou 南徐州 (modern Zhenjiang). Jiang Yan at first declined the appointment (see his "Memorandum to the Prince of Xin'an in Nan Xuzhou" in *Jiang Wentong ji* 3.1a), but eventually accepted the post, and served briefly under Liu Ziluan before returning to the service of Liu Zizhen. In 465 Jiang Yan accompanied Liu Zizhen to his post as inspector of Nan Yanzhou 南兗州 (modern Yangzhou). On 25 October 466 Liu Yu 劉彧 (Emperor Ming 明, reg. 466–472), who wished to eliminate all of the sons of Emperor Xiaowu, had the nine-year-old Liu Zizhen put to death. Jiang Yan was not a prominent member of Liu Zizhen's staff, and thus escaped punishment.

Jiang Yan immediately was able to obtain a position with Liu Jingsu 劉景素 (ob. 476), prince of Jianping 漸平. Liu Jingsu, who was fourteen at the time, was a grandson of Emperor Wen (reg. 424–453). In 466 Liu Jingsu assumed Liu Zizhen's post as inspector in Nan Yanzhou and, probably because Jiang Yan was on Zizhen's staff, he simply continued to serve Liu Jingsu.

Shortly after joining Liu Jingsu's staff the prefect of Guangling 廣陵, Guo Yanwen 郭彥文, was charged with a crime, and in his confession accused Jiang Yan of accepting bribes. Jiang Yan was arrested and sent to prison. From prison, he wrote an eloquent appeal to Liu Jingsu proclaiming his innocence. This piece, entitled "Letter Submitted to the Prince of Jianping" (*Wen xuan*, chap. 39), is a skillful imitation of Zou Yang's "Letter from Prison Submitted to the King of Liang." The prince reputedly was so moved by Jiang Yan's letter he ordered him released and restored to his former position.

In early 466 Jiang Yan was recommended to take the *xiucai* 秀才 (flourishing talent) examination by Liu Zifan 劉子范, prince of Guiyang 桂陽 and inspector of Nan Xuzhou, and Jiang was ranked the highest of all candidates. Presumably as a result of his success on the exam, Jiang Yan was appointed right regular attendant in the administration of the prince of Baling 巴陵, Liu Xiuruo 劉休若, inspector of Yongzhou 雍州 (modern Xiangyang). On the way to Xiangyang, Jiang Yan composed "Gazing toward the Jing Mountains" (*Wen xuan*, chap. 27). (Li Shan says Jiang Yan wrote this poem in 471 when he was accompanying Liu Jingsu to

Jingzhou. However, Cao Daoheng shows that the geographical references in the poem better fit the circumstances of his journey to Xiangyang with Liu Xiuruo. See "Jiang Yan," p. 507, n. 1.) In this poem Jiang Yan expresses sadness as he views the bleak autumn landscape.

Jiang Yan served only briefly with Liu Xiuruo, and then returned to the administration of Liu Jingsu, who was now governor of Danyang 丹陽, which included the capital area. At this time he made the acquaintance of the grandson of Xie Lingyun 謝靈運 (385–433), Xie Chaozong 謝超宗 (ob. 483), with whom he exchanged several poems.

Jiang Yan's best friend was Yuan Bing 袁炳 (*zi* Shuming). In 466 Jiang Yan wrote "Letter in Response to Yuan Shuming," in which he declares his hope to withdraw from official service. Not too long after this letter was written Yuan Bing died, and Jiang Yan lamented his friend's passing in "Biography of My Friend Yuan" (*Jiang Wentong ji* 3.12b) and "Rhapsody Lamenting a Friend" (*Jiang Wentong ji* 1.14b–16b).

Jiang Yan accompanied Liu Jingsu to his various posts, which included grand administrator of Wuxing 吳興 (modern Huzhou 湖州, Zhejiang), inspector of Xiangzhou 湘州 (modern Changsha) in 470, and inspector of Jingzhou 荊州 (modern Jiangling) in 471. While visiting Ji'nan *cheng* 紀南城, the site of the old Chu capital of Ying 郢, Jiang Yan composed a poem entitled "Accompanying the Prince of Jianping on a Journey to Ji'nan cheng" (*Jiang Wentong ji* 4.8a), in which he gazes over the old city of Ying, now in ruins, and concludes that immortality and fame are futile pursuits.

In May 472 Emperor Ming died, and the new emperor, Liu Yu 劉昱 (Emperor Houfei 後廢), who was only ten years old, did not have universal support from some prominent men, who urged Liu Jingsu to depose Liu Yu. Jiang Yan tried to persuade Jingsu to desist from plotting a revolt, but his advice was not heeded.

On 12 September 472 Liu Jingsu assumed the post of inspector of Nan Xuzhou at Jingkou 京口 (modern Zhenjiang), and Jiang Yan continued to serve on his staff as military aide as well as assistant governor of Donghai 東海 commandery, which was located in the same area. Liu Jingsu persisted with his plans for revolt. As a means of indicating his displeasure with the prince's actions, Jiang composed fifteen poems in imitation of Ruan Ji's "Singing My Feelings." Jiang Yan's pieces attack Liu Jingsu only indirectly, through subtle suggestion and allusion.

In 474 the governor of Donghai, Lu Cheng 陸澄, had to return home to attend a funeral. Jiang Yan believed that as assistant governor he was entitled to take charge of the commandery during Lu's absence. However, Lu appointed another man in Jiang's place. After Jiang Yan protested this decision, Liu Jingsu reported him to the bureau of appointments. As a result, Jiang Yan was demoted to the position of prefect of Wuxing 吳興 in Jian'an 建安 Commandery (modern Pucheng 蒲城, Fujian).

While traveling to Wuxing, Jiang Yan wrote poems describing the mountain scenery of Zhejiang and Fujian. He also wrote a number of *fu* during the two years he spent in Wuxing. It was probably here that he wrote his two most famous *fu*, "Rhapsody on Resentment" and "Rhapsody on Separation" (*Wen xuan*, chap. 16).

In August 476 Liu Jingsu staged a revolt to seize the imperial throne for himself. Within a week his army was defeated, and Liu Jingsu was executed. Shortly thereafter, Xiao Daocheng 蕭道成 (ob. 482), who had become regent, and who had instigated the assassination of Emperor Houfei, appointed Jiang Yan adjutant, in which capacity he drafted many of Xiao's proclamations and dispatches. After Xiao Daocheng established himself as first emperor of the Southern Qi in May 479, Jiang Yan was appointed prefect of Dongwu 東武 and was put in charge of drafting edicts. He also was commissioned to compile the Qi history.

Xiao Daocheng died on 11 April 482, and was succeeded by Xiao Ze 蕭賾 (Emperor Wu 武, reg. 483–493). Throughout the Qi dynasty Jiang Yan held high central-government positions. In 485 he was vice-president of the imperial secretariat and director of the national academy.

Very few of Jiang Yan's writings survive from this period down to the time of his death. Among those that he probably wrote during the Qi are his thirty miscellaneous poems imitating of the style of earlier poets (*Wen xuan*, chap. 37).

In 494, after the succession of Xiao Luan 蕭鸞 (Emperor Ming 明, reg. 494–498) to the imperial throne, Jiang Yan was appointed grand administrator of Xuancheng. In 497 he was recalled to the capital and appointed attendant gentleman of the Yellow Gate and colonel of infantry. It was at this time that there was a rumor in the capital that Jiang Yan's talent had been depleted, for he composed virtually no poetry from the time of his elevation to high office.

In 501 Jiang Yan joined Xiao Yan 蕭衍 (464–549) in his revolt against the Qi emperor. After the founding of the Liang in April 502, Jiang Yan was given appointment as cavalier attendant-in-ordinary and general commandant of the left. He also was enfeoffed as earl of Liling 醴陵 and was given the honorific title of grand master of the palace with golden seal and purple ribbon. Jiang Yan died in 505 at the age of sixty-one.

*References*
Cao Daoheng. "Jiang Yan."
Marney, John. *Chiang Yen.*
Takahashi Kazumi. "Kō En no bungaku."
Toyofuku Kenji. "Kō En no fu."
Wu Piji. *Jiang Yan nianpu.*


LU JI 陸機 (261–303), zi Shiheng 士衡, native of Huating 華亭 (modern Songjiang 松江 xian, Shanghai City).

Lu Ji was a distinguished writer of rhapsodies, lyric poetry, and prose in the Western Jin period. The most important source of information on his life is his biography in the *Jin shu* (54.1467–81).

Lu Ji was a member of a prominent family of the Wu kingdom. His grandfather Lu Xun 陸遜 (183–245) was chancellor of Wu, and his father, Lu Kang 陸抗 (226–274), was grand minister of war. Lu Kang died in 274 when Lu Ji was fourteen. He and his brothers then assumed command of their father's army. In 280, when the Jin army invaded Wu and forced the surrender of Sun Hao 孫皓 (242–284), the last Wu emperor, Lu Ji's elder brothers Lu Yan 陸晏 and Lu Jing 陸景 were killed in battle. After Wu was defeated by Jin, Lu Ji and his younger brother Lu Yun 陸雲 (262–303) retired to their estate in Huating. Here Lu Ji devoted himself to study and writing. He composed "Disquisition on the Destruction of a State" (*Wen xuan*, chap. 53), in which he discussed the reasons for the fall of Wu. During the ten years he spent in retirement, Lu Ji began to perfect his craft as a poet. He composed a number of poems in imitation of earlier pieces. His most famous imitation series is "Imitating the Old Poems" (*Wen xuan*, chap. 30), which consists of twelve poems, most of which are inspired by the "Nineteen Old Poems."

In 289 Lu Ji and Lu Yun, together with their good friend Gu Rong 顧榮 (ca. 260–322?), went to Luoyang, presumably at the invitation of one of the former Wu ministers now serving in the Jin administration. Lu Ji wrote two poems recounting his journey north, "On the Way to Luo" and "Written on the Road to Luo" (*Wen xuan*, chap. 26). In Luoyang Lu Ji met Zhang Hua (q.v.), who introduced him and his brother to influential men. In 290 Lu Ji received an appointment to the staff of the grand-tutor Yang Jun 楊駿 (ob. 291). When Empress Jia 賈 (ob. 300) led a coup against Yang Jun in 291, Lu Ji continued in office as attendant to Crown Prince Minhuai 愍懷, Sima Yu 司馬遹 (ob. 300). Lu Ji wrote several occasional poems for gatherings hosted by the prince, including "Poem Composed on Command for the August Heir Designate's Banquet at the You Hall of Mysterious Park" (*Wen xuan*, chap. 20).

In 294 Lu Ji and Lu Yun joined the staff of Sima Yan 司馬晏 (ob. 310), prince of Wu, who led a military expedition to Huainan. In 296 Lu Ji returned to the capital, where he served in the secretariat. Shortly after taking up his post, he was granted leave to visit his home in Huating. Upon his return north he persuaded the brigand Dai Yuan 戴淵 (ca. 260–322) to surrender to the Jin. Lu Ji and Dai then became good friends.

While serving in Luoyang, Lu Ji was a member of the literary salon led by Jia Mi 賈謐 (ob. 300), the nephew of Empress Jia. Among Lu Ji's writings from this period is an eleven-part set of tetrasyllabic poems addressed to Jia Mi (*Wen xuan*, chap. 24).

In 300 Empress Jia instigated the assassination of Crown Prince Minhuai. Sima Lun 司馬倫 (ob. 301) deposed Empress Jia and ordered her and her nephew Jia Mi put to death, along with her associates Zhang Hua and Pan Yue (q.v.). After declaring himself chancellor of state, Sima Lun appointed Lu Ji as his adjutant. Having observed the death of numerous family members and friends during this turbulent period, Lu Ji then composed "Rhapsody on Lamenting the Departed" (*Wen xuan*, chap. 16) to express grief at their passing.

In 301 Sima Lun plotted to seize the throne for himself. After Sima Lun's army was defeated by Sima Jiong 司馬冏 (ob. 302) and Sima Ying 司馬穎 (279–306), Lu Ji was arrested and put on trial. Through the intercession of Sima Ying, Lu Ji was able to have his capital punishment reduced to banishment to the frontier. However, before Lu could depart for his exile, he was released from his punishment by a general amnesty. To express his gratitude to Sima Ying, he composed "Two Poems on the Garden Mallow" (*Wen xuan*, chap. 29). It was probably during this period that Lu Ji wrote his famous "Rhapsody on Literature."

Lu Ji then joined the staff of Sima Ying, who appointed him royal administrator of Pingyuan 平原 (administrative center south of modern Pingyuan, Shandong). The memorial of thanks Lu Ji wrote to Sima Ying for granting him this post is contained in the *Wen xuan* (chap. 37). In 303 Sima Yong 司馬顒 (ob. 306), prince of Hejian 河澗, and Sima Ying joined in an expedition against Sima Yi 司馬乂 (ob. 303), prince of Changsha, who had killed Sima Jiong. Sima Ying appointed Lu Ji commander-in-chief of the vanguard. During the ensuing battle, Lu Ji's army was defeated outside one of the gates of Luoyang. Accused by political enemies of plotting revolt, Lu Ji was put to death along with his two sons and brother Lu Yun.

*References*

Chen Enliang. *Lu Ji wenxue yanjiu.*
Fujii Mamoru. "Sei Shin jidai no gafu shi."
Jiang Liangfu. *Lu Pingyuan nianpu.*
Jiang Zuyi and Han Quanxin. "Lu Ji."
Kang Rongji. *Lu Ji ji qi shi.*
Kōzen Hiroshi. *Han Gaku Riku Ki.*
Lai, Chiu-mi. "River and Ocean."
Liao Weiqing. "Lun Lu Ji de shi."
Lin Wen-yüeh. "Lu Ji de nigu shi."
Lu Qinli. " 'Wenfu' zhuanchu niandai kao."
Takahashi Kazumi. "Riku Ki no denki to sono bungaku."
Wang Yi. "Lu Ji jian lun."

MA RONG 馬融 (79–166), *zi* Jichang 季長, native of Maoling 茂陵 (northeast of modern Xingping 興平, Shaanxi).

Ma Rong was a leading poet and scholar of the Later Han dynasty. He was the grand-nephew of the famous general Ma Yuan 馬援 (14 B.C.–A.D. 40). The most important source of information on his life is his biography in the *Hou Han shu* (60.1953–73).

Ma Rong received his early education from his father, Ma Yan 馬顔 (ob. 98), who was a prominent official during the reign of Emperor He. Later, probably around 101, he studied with the recluse Confucian scholar Zhi Xun 摯恂 (n.d.). Zhi was so fond of Ma, he gave his daughter to him in marriage. Around 106 Ma went to the capital, where he received instruction from Ban Gu's sister, Ban Zhao, in reading the *Han shu*.

In 108 the general-in-chief Deng Zhi 鄧騭 (ob. 121) invited Ma to join his staff, but considering such a post not to his liking, Ma left the capital area and traveled in the area of Gansu and western Shaanxi. Finally, in 110, economic circumstances forced him to accept Deng Zhi's invitation to serve as gentleman collator in the Dongguan library. While working in the capital administration, Ma became concerned about the antimilitary policies advocated by the Deng clan that dominated the court by virtue of the position of Empress Dowager Deng (ob. 121). Ma Rong composed a long rhapsody, "Eulogy on the Guangcheng Park," to protest the failure to pursue a strong military defense policy. As a result of his opposition to the Deng clan, in 120 Ma Rong was forced to "impeach himself" and resign. The empress dowager then ordered that he be banned for life from taking office.

However, after the empress dowager's death in 121, Ma Rong returned to government service. For a decade, from about 123 to 133, he served in the local administration. From 126 to 133, he worked in the bureau of merit in his home commandery of Fufeng 扶風. In 126 he composed "Rhapsody on the Long Flute" (*Wen xuan*, chap. 18).

From 133 to 138 Ma Rong was again in the capital, serving first as gentleman consultant and then as attendant gentleman of the household on the staff of the general-in-chief Liang Shang 梁商 (ob. 141). Between 138 and 144 he was governor of Wudu 武都 (modern Wudu, Gansu). During this time he wrote commentaries to the *Classic of Changes, Classic of Songs, Classic of Documents, Record of Rites* and *Rites of Zhou*.

In 145 Ma Rong returned to the capital, where he became a protégé of Liang Shang's son Liang Ji 梁冀 (ob. 159), who had great influence at court through connections with his sister, the Empress Dowager. Ma Rong may have drafted the impeachment letter that resulted in the execution of the eminent official Li Gu 李固 (ob. 147). Between ca. 148 and 152 Ma served as governor of Nan 南 commandery. By 152 he had incurred the displeasure of Liang Ji, and was charged with corruption and exiled to Shuofang 朔方 (modern Inner Mongolia), where he remained until after the death of Liang Ji in 159.

In 160 Ma Rong received a pardon and was appointed gentleman consultant, a position he held until 164, when he resigned from office on grounds of illness. He returned to his home in Maoling, where he died in 166.

*References*
Künstler, Mieczyslaw Jerzy. *Ma Jong vie et oeuvre.*
Lu Kanru. *Zhonggu wenxue xinian.*

MI HENG 禰衡 (ca. 173–198), *zi* Zhengping 正平, native of Ban 般 Prefecture of Pingyuan 平原 Commandery (modern Linyi 臨邑, Shandong).

Mi Heng was a wit and poet of the late Later Han period. The main source of information on his life is his biography in the *Hou Han shu* (80B.2652–58).

Around 194 Mi Heng fled the turmoil of north China and went south and joined the staff of Liu Biao 劉表 (ob. 208), who was governor general of the Jingzhou 荊州 area (modern Hunan-Hubei). Jingzhou was a major intellectual and literary center in this period, and Liu Biao was able to attract some of the most talented writers of the time to his court. Mi Heng held himself in high regard. He reputedly carried around with him a calling card, but the characters on it wore off before he could give it to someone whom he deemed worthy of visiting.

Around 196 Mi Heng went to Xu 許 (modern Xuchang, Henan), which had recently been built on orders of Cao Cao as a residence for the Han emperor. He was on good terms with the renowned scholar-poet Kong Rong 孔融 (153–208), who wrote a memorial recommending him to Emperor Xian 獻 (reg. 190–220), who was now a puppet of Cao Cao. Kong Rong also frequently spoke of Mi Heng to Cao Cao, who wished to meet him, but Mi Heng had a low opinion of the redoubtable generalissimo, and refused to see him. Cao Cao was outraged, but was reluctant to kill such a talented and famous young man. Hearing that Mi Heng was a skilled drummer, he summoned Mi to perform with other drummers at a gathering of guests. The drummers were ordered to remove their old clothes and change into peaked helmets and unlined yellow-green robes. When it came Heng's turn to perform, without changing his clothes, he began to play a treble drum roll in a sad and plaintive manner. When a footman scolded him for failing to don the required garb, Mi Heng removed all of his clothing and, standing stark naked directly in front of Cao Cao, he slowly picked up the peaked helmet and unlined yellow-green robe and put them on. He then performed another treble drum roll displaying not the slightest embarrassment on his face.

Although Kong Rong arranged another meeting between Cao Cao and Mi Heng, Mi's eccentric and arrogant manner was even more offensive and disrespectful. Unable to tolerate Mi any longer, Cao Cao decided to send him to Liu Biao. In 197 Mi Heng returned to Jingzhou, where he was treated with great deference by the dignitaries and scholars in Liu Biao's entourage. He was considered the arbiter of literary taste. However, he offended Liu Biao with his arrogance and insulting manner. In 198 Liu Biao sent Mi Heng to Huang Zu 黃祖 (ob. 208), governor of Jiangxia 江夏 (modern Wuchang). Mi was on especially good terms with Huang Zu's son, Huang Yi 黃射, governor of Zhangling 章陵 (south of modern Zaoyang 棗陽, Hubei). At a gathering hosted by Huang Yi, Mi Heng composed "Rhapsody on the Parrot" (*Wen xuan*, chap. 13).

Mi Heng insulted Huang Zu at a banquet, and Huang Zu had Mi Heng put to death, probably in 198.

*References*
Graham, William T., Jr. "Mi Heng's 'Rhapsody on a Parrot.'"
Yuan Shishi, ed. *Shandong gudai wenxuejia pingzhuan* 1: 112–24.

PAN YUE 潘岳 (247–300), *zi* Anren 安仁, native of Zhongmou Prefecture 中牟 (modern Zhongmou, Henan, between Kaifeng and Zhengzhou) in Xingyang Commandery. However, his home probably was in Gong 鞏 Prefecture east of Luoyang.

Pan Yue was a leading poet and prose writer of the late third century. The most important source of information on his life is the *Jin shu* (55.1500–7), which seems based in part on Pan Yue's preface to his "Rhapsody on Living in Idleness" (*Wen xuan*, chap. 16). He also is the subject of many ancedotes in the *Shishuo xinyu*.

Pan Yue came from a family of prominent officials. His grandfather Pan Jin 潘瑾 served as governor of Anping 安平 (modern Ji *xian*, Hebei). His father Pan Pi

潘芘 ob. ca. 280 held the post of royal administrator of Langye in modern Shandong while Sima Lun 司馬倫 ob. 301 was prince of Langye reg. 265–ca. 277. The Pan family also was connected by marriage to several important clans. Pan Yue himself was married ca. 274 to the daughter of Yang Zhao 楊肇 ob. 275, who also was from Xingyang.

In 265, the year that Sima Yan took the throne as emperor and Sima Lun was enfeoffed as prince of Langye, Pan Yue's father was appointed royal administrator of Langye. While in Langye, Pan Yue wrote "Rhapsody on Pheasant Shooting" Wen xuan, chap. 9, which describes the pheasant hunting methods of ancient Shandong. Around 266 he assumed his first official post, assistant to the minister of works Xun Yi 荀顗 205–274. While in Luoyang, Pan Yue became good friends with Xiahou Zhan 夏侯湛 243–291. In 268 Pan composed on behalf of Emperor Wu of Jin reg. 265–290 "Rhapsody on the Sacred Field" Wen xuan, chap. 7 in celebration of the revival of the ceremonial plowing of the imperial plot.

For about ten years Pan Yue had little success as an official. His father-in-law, Yang Zhao, died in 275, and Pan wrote the famous "Dirge for Yang Jingzhou" Wen xuan, chap. 56. Around 278 Pan joined the staff of the grand marshall Jia Chong 賈充 217–282. However, he was quite disillusioned with official life. To express his frustration, he composed "Rhapsody on Autumn Inspirations" Wen xuan, chap. 13. Perhaps around this time he also wrote "Rhapsody on a Widow" Wen xuan, chap. 16 to lament the death of Ren Hu 任護, the husband of his wife's sister.

For unknown reasons, around 279 Pan Yue left the capital to serve in the local administration, first in Heyang 河陽 west of modern Meng 孟 xian, Henan, on the north bank of the Yellow River across from Luoyang. In the spring of 282 he left Heyang to assume the post of prefect of Huai 懷 modern Wuzhi 武陟 xian, Henan. Pan Yue's poems "Written in Heyang Prefecture" and "Written in Huai Prefecture" Wen xuan, chap. 26 express his dissatisfaction with official service away from the capital and his home.

Around 285 Pan Yue returned to the capital, where he served first as acting gentleman in the secretariat of revenue and then as adjudicator under the commandant of justice. Immediately upon his return, he visited the graves of Yang Zhao and his brothers-in-law, Yang Tan 楊潭 and Yang Shao 楊韶, near Mount Song, south of Luoyang. Pan Yue's "Rhapsody on Recalling Old Friends and Kin" Wen xuan, chap. 16 is a lamentation over their death.

In 290 Emperor Wu died. The grand tutor Yang Jun 楊駿 ob. 291 served as regent for the young Emperor Hui 惠 reg. 290–306. Yang Jun appointed Pan Yue secretary to the grand tutor. In spring 291 Empress Jia staged a coup to overthrow Yang Jun. On 23 April Sima You 司馬繇 led a troop of four hundred palace guards into Yang's headquarters south of the arsenal. They set fire to the building and stationed crossbowmen on the pavilion to prevent Yang's guards from leaving. Yang Jun fled to the stable, where a soldier killed him. Empress Jia sent out an order to execute Yang's associates, and several thousand men were killed. As a protégé of Yang Jun, Pan Yue had his name removed from the official register. Although all members of Yang's encourage were condemned to

death, Pan Yue escaped by leaving the capital on an emergency. His friend
Gongsun Hong 公孫宏 (ob. 291), who was in charge of the executions, was able
to spare Pan's life by claiming that Pan was only an "acting official" on Yang
Jun's staff.

In 291 Xiahou Zhan died. Pan composed "Dirge for Regular Attendant
Xiahou" (*Wen xuan*, chap. 57) to pay tribute to his good friend.

Pan Yue did not remain off the official roster long. He was appointed prefect
of Chang'an, and left Luoyang on 20 June 292. His journey took him through
many historical sites, which he described in "Rhapsody on the Western Journey"
(*Wen xuan*, chap. 10).

Around 293 Pan returned to the capital, where he became a member of the
entourage of Jia Mi 賈謐 (ob. 300), the empress's nephew. Although he was
summoned to assume the post of erudite, before he could take office he had to
decline the appointment because of his mother's illness. He then lived briefly in
retirement near Luoyang. At this time he wrote "Rhapsody on Living in Idleness"
(*Wen xuan*, chap. 16), in which he contrasts his life as an official with his seemingly
contented existence as a retired gentleman. He also spent part of his leisure time
at the Jingu 金谷 estate of Shi Chong 石崇 (249–300), where many literary figures
gathered to drink and feast, listen to music, and write verse. Pan's "A Poem
Written at a Golden Valley Gathering" (*Wen xuan*, chap. 20) was composed for
one of these occasions. Pan Yue also wrote poems on behalf of his patron Jia Mi.
One of these, addressed to Lu Ji, is contained in the *Wen xuan* (chap. 24).

In late 297 Pan Yue returned to office as gentleman composer and regular
cavalier attendant. In the same year he composed "Dirge for Ma, Overseer of
Qian" (*Wen xuan*, chap. 57), a moving lament for Ma Dun 馬敦, who died in
prison in 297. In autumn 298 Pan Yue's wife died in the Degong Ward 德宮里 of
Luoyang. Pan wrote a prose piece, "Lamenting the Eternally Departed" (*Wen
xuan*, chap. 57), expressing his grief at her passing. In the next year he wrote a
three-part poem, "Lamenting the Deceased," to mourn for his dead wife (*Wen
xuan*, chap. 23). These poems are the earliest known examples in Chinese literature of a poet's lament for his deceased wife.

In autumn 299 Pan Yue returned to official service with the Jia faction.
While serving as gentleman attendant of the Yellow Gate, he composed "Within
the Passes" to commemorate the suppression of an insurrection in the Yongzhou
area (*Wen xuan*, chap. 20). He also wrote "Dirge for Yang Zhongwu" (*Wen xuan*,
chap. 56) to lament the passing of Yang Sui 楊綏 (270–299), his wife's nephew.

In January and February 300 Pan Yue was involved in the plot of Empress
Jia and Jia Mi to depose Crown Prince Minhuai 愍懷, Sima Yu 司馬遹 (ob. 300).
In April Empress Jia sent an assassin to Xuchang to kill the crown prince. In May
Sima Lun and Sima Tong 司馬肜 deposed Empress Jia and had Jia Mi, Zhang
Hua, and Pei Wei 裴頠 (267–300) put to death. Sima Lun then assumed the post
of chancellor and commander of central and internal military affairs. His principal
adviser was president of the secretariat Sun Xiu 孫秀 (ob. 301), who long had
harbored a grudge against Pan and his family. Sun Xiu charged Pan Yue, Shi
Chong, and Ouyang Jian 歐陽建 (Shi Chong's nephew) with plotting to join
Sima Yun 司馬允 (ob. 300), prince of Huainan, and Sima Jiong 司馬冏 (ob. 302),

prince of Qi, against Sima Lun. Sima Lun had them arrested and executed. Also executed were Pan Yue's mother, his brothers, and their sons and daughters.

*References*

Fu Xuancong. "Pan Yue xinian kaozheng."

Kōzen Hiroshi. *Han Gaku Riku Ki.*

Lai, Chiu-mi. "River and Ocean."

Li Changzhi 李長之. "Xi Jin shiren Pan Yue de shengping ji qi chuangzuo."

Matsumoto Yukio. "Han Gaku no denki."

Takahashi Kazumi. "Han Gaku ron."


SIMA XIANGRU 司馬相如 (179–117 B.C.), *zi* Zhangqing 長卿, native of Chengdu 成都 (modern Chengdu, Sichuan), in the commandery of Shu.

Sima Xiangru is the best-known *fu* writer of the Former Han dynasty. The most important sources of information about his life are his biographies in the *Shi ji* (117) and the *Han shu* (57).

Nothing is known about Sima Xiangru's ancestors. He may have been distantly related to the Qin general Sima Cuo 司馬錯, who led an invasion of Shu in the late fourth century B.C. Around 150 B.C., or slightly before, Sima Xiangru traveled to Chang'an, where he was able to purchase an appointment at the imperial court as gentleman. Under Emperor Jing 景 (reg. 156–141 B.C.) he served as military mounted attendent-in-ordinary, a six-hundred-bushel rank. Although the duties of the post were not to his liking, it did give Sima Xiangru an opportunity to participate in the emperor's excursions, and thus he was able to obtain first-hand knowledge of the military reviews, banquets, and sorties in the imperial park that were the principal themes of his *fu*.

One reason for Sima Xiangru's unhappiness with official life in Chang'an might have been that Emperor Jing had an aversion to *fu* poetry. Emperor Jing's principal advisers were legalists, whose distaste for literary embellishment is well known. Thus, Sima Xiangru welcomed the opportunity to become a guest scholar at the court of Liu Wu 劉武 in Liang. At the time of his arrival in Liang around 149 B.C., Liu Wu's entourage already included Zou Yang and Mei Sheng. Sima Xiangru remained in Liang until 144 B.C., when he had to leave after Liu Wu's death. Until that time he presumably was able to enjoy the company of the salon poets and use his leisure time to compose *fu*. His best-known work from this period is "Rhapsody of Sir Vacuous," (*Wen xuan*, chap. 7), a long, effusive description of the Yunmeng hunting preserve in the old kingdom of Chu.

In 144 B.C. after the death of Liu Wu, Sima Xiangru returned to Shu, where by virtue of his poetic talent he became the protégé of a prominent Shu official. In 142 B.C. he scandalized Shu society by eloping with Zhuo Wenjun 卓文君, the daughter of a wealthy iron manufacturer. To support themselves, he and his wife ran a wine shop until Wenjun's father was shamed into recognizing their marriage. Sima Xiangru was living in Chengdu when he received a summons, perhaps in the year 137 B.C., to have an audience with Emperor Wu in the capital. It seems that one day Emperor Wu had chanced upon a copy of Sima

Xiangru's "Rhapsody of Sir Vacuous," which so impressed the young emperor, he exclaimed to his attendant, the keeper of hounds Yang Deyi 楊得意, "Shall We alone not have the privilege of being this man's contemporary?" Yang Deyi, who was a Shu native, informed the emperor that his fellow townsman Sima Xiangru claimed to have written the piece. Emperor Wu immediately issued a summons for Sima Xiangru to appear at court.

In his audience with Emperor Wu, Sima Xiangru belittled the quality of his earlier composition, which after all concerned only the "affairs of the vassal lords." He then offered to compose for the emperor a "*fu* on the excursions and hunts of the Son of Heaven." With brushes and bamboo slips given to him by the master of writing, Sima composed a long rhapsody on the imperial hunting park, the Shanglin yuan 上林苑. Emperor Wu was so pleased with the poem, which is contained in the *Wen xuan* (chap. 8) under the title "Rhapsody on the Imperial Park," he reappointed Sima Xiangru to his former post of gentleman.

Emperor Wu found Sima Xiangru useful for his poetic skill and undoubtedly commissioned him to compose many *fu* for special court occasions. However, none of these pieces survives. In addition to his duties as court poet, Sima served as the emperor's envoy in the southwest, of which his native Shu was a part. Around 131 B.C. he mediated a dispute between the local inhabitants and a Chinese official, who had alienated some of the Shu people with his oppressive policies. Sima wrote an elegant dispatch on behalf of the emperor apologizing for the general's actions ("Proclamation Addressed to Ba and Shu," *Wen xuan*, chap. 44). After returning to the capital, the emperor promoted him to the position of general of the gentlemen of the household, a relatively high two-thousand-bushel post. In this capacity he was put in charge of a road-building project in the southwest. Upon Sima Xiangru's return to Shu with a large entourage, his father-in-law, Zhuo Wangsun 卓王孫, warmly greeted him and bestowed upon his daughter a generous share of his estate, equal to that of a son. In the middle of his mission Sima Xiangru encountered much opposition to his plans to establish regular contacts with the southwestern tribes, particularly from prominent men in Shu. He then wrote a dispatch, "Objecting to the Elders of Shu" (*Wen xuan*, chap. 44), a dialogue between the Shu elders, who plead against opening communication with the tribes, and the imperial envoy, who wins them over with words about imperial beneficence. Reputedly Sima Xiangru's true views are conveyed in the speech of the elders.

Sima Xiangru spent his later years in or near the capital. Shortly after returning from the southwest, he was accused of accepting bribes while serving as emissary in Shu, and he was dismissed from his post of general of the household gentlemen. Although he returned to court within a few years, Sima Xiangru never regained a high-ranking position. He seems to have lost interest in court affairs, and even though he continued to enjoy Emperor Wu's favor, Sima spent his remaining years in semiretirement. His sudden disinterest in politics might have had something to do with his poor health—he suffered from diabetes. In addition, he stuttered, and thus could not participate in court debate. Finally, thanks to his wife's inheritance, he was now independently wealthy, and he no longer needed to rely on a government salary to support his family.

During the period from 130 to 120 B.C., Sima Xiangru's principal activity was that of poet. From time to time he accompanied the emperor on outings and hunts. After one excursion to the Tall Poplars Lodge in the imperial park, where the emperor actually joined in the chase, Sima Xiangru submitted a memorial warning him about the dangers to which he was exposing himself ("Letter of Submission Admonishing on Hunting," *Wen xuan*, chap. 39). On this same tour, the emperor's entourage visited Befitting Spring Palace, which was near the tomb of the Second Qin Emperor. Sima Xiangru took this occasion to compose a short *fu* titled "Lamenting the Second Qin Emperor," which may have been intended as a subtle warning to Emperor Wu to curb his ambitions.

Around 120 B.C. Sima Xiangru received an appointment as prefect of Emperor Wen's funerary park, a six-hundred-bushel rank that may have been a sinecure. About this time he composed "Rhapsody on the Great Man," a long panegyrical description of a godlike immortal, the Great Man, who wanders at will about the heavens with all deities at his command. Around 119 B.C. Sima Xiangru resigned from office on grounds of illness. He retired to the mausoleum town of Maoling, on the Wei River west of the capital, where he died in 117 B.C. Just before his death, he wrote "Essay on the *Feng* and *Shan* Sacrifices" (*Wen xuan*, chap. 48), a memorial addressed to Emperor Wu exhorting him to celebrate his achievements by performing sacrifices on Mount Tai. Also attributed to Sima Xiangru is "Rhapsody on the Tall Gate Palace" (*Wen xuan*, chap. 16), reputedly written to commiserate with Empress Chen, who had fallen out of favor with Emperor Wu.

*References*
Chien Tsung-wu. *Sima Xiangru Yang Xiong ji qi fu zhi yanjiu.*
Gong Kechang. "Han fu dianjizhe Sima Xiangru." In *Han fu yanjiu*, pp. 86–107.
Hervouet, Yves. *Un Poète de cour sous les Han.*
———. *Le Chapitre 117 du Che-ki (Biographie de Sseu-ma Siang-jou).*

SONG YU 宋玉 (fl. 3rd cent. B.C.), reputedly a native of Yan 鄢 (modern Yanling 鄢陵, Henan) in the state of Chu.

Although a large number of *fu* have been attributed to Song Yu, the authenticity of many of these pieces is questionable. What little we know about Song Yu is preserved in anecdotes contained in the *Shi ji, Xin xu,* and *Han shi waizhuan.* The most reliable accounts say that Song Yu served at the court of King Qingxiang 頃襄 of Chu (reg. 298–263 B.C.). Although he was a skilled writer and wit, he never held high position. When he gave advice to the king, he used flattery and indirect suggestion. He also has a reputation as an expert on sex, music, and beautiful women.

"Shi fu lue 詩賦略" ("Summary of Songs and Rhapsodies") in the chapter on literature in the *Han shu* has a listing for Song Yu and credits him with sixteen *fu*. In the *Chuci* (see *Chuci buzhu*), Wang Yi attributes Song Yu with two pieces, "Nine Changes" and "Summoning the Soul," which are contained in the *Wen xuan* (chap. 33). The *Wen xuan* also contains five other pieces under his name:

"Rhapsody on the Wind" (chap. 13), "Rhapsody on the Gaotang Shrine" (chap. 19), "Rhapsody on the Goddess" (chap. 19), "Rhapsody on Master Dengtu the Lecher" (chap. 19), and "Responding to the Question of the King of Chu" (chap. 45). In addition, Tang and Song sources attribute to him seven more *fu*. The authenticity of all of these pieces is suspect.

As late as the early Tang there was a *Song Yu ji* 宋玉集 (Collected Works of Song Yu) in three *juan*. We have no way to determine its contents or date, for the collection was lost sometime in the Song. In the Southern Song, there was a one-*juan Song Yu ji*, which consisted of pieces extracted from the *Wen xuan* and *Guwen yuan*. This collection no longer survives. All later collections are reconstructions.

*References*
Asano Michiari. "Sō Gyoku no sakuhin no shingi ni tsuite."
Cao Minggang. "Song Yu fu zhenwei bian."
Chen Shengyong. "Jianguo yilai Song Yu ji qi zuopin yanjiu zongshu."
Cheng Renqing. "Dui 'Guanyu Song Yu' yiwen de yijian."
Deng Yuanxuan. "Guanyu Song Yu pingjia zhong de yige wenti."
Fujiwara Takashi. "Sōfu to jifu no bukiten."
Guo Moruo. "Guanyu Song Yu."
Hu Nianyi. "Song Yu zuopin de zhenwei wenti."
Inahata Kōichirō. "Sō Gokyu ron."
———. "Sō Gyoku no betsushū."
———. "*Sō Gyoku shū* hosetsu."
Jiang Liangfu. "Song Yu jianshu."
Lu Kanru 陸侃如. "Song Yu pingzhuan."
———. *Song Yu.*
Lu Yongpin. "Song Yu."
Shi Zhimian. "Song Yu wu fu."
Yang Yinzong. "Song Yu fu kao."
Zhu Bilian and Shen Jianying. "Song Yu cifu zhenwei bian."

WANG BAO 王褒 (ob. ca. 61 B.C.), *zi* Ziyuan 子淵, native of Zizhong 資中 (modern Ziyang 資陽, Sichuan). The most important source of information on his life is his biography in the *Han shu* (64B.2821–30).

Wang Bao was a leading poet at the court of Emperor Xuan 宣 of the Former Han (reg. 74 B.C.–48 B.C.). He began his career in Shu under the provincial inspector Wang Xiang 王襄, for whom he composed three panegyrical songs and a rhyme-prose essay explaining the meaning and purpose of the songs. Impressed with his literary talent, Wang Xiang recommended him to Emperor Xuan, who summoned him to court to compose a eulogy entitled "The Sage Ruler Obtains Worthy Officials" (*Wen xuan*, chap. 47). Wang Bao soon become one of the emperor's favorite poets. He and the poet Zhang Ziqiao 張子僑 composed rhapsodies celebrating imperial excursions and hunts. Wang's accomplishments as a poet won him appointment as grandee remonstrant, an eight-hundred-bushel rank.

Wang Bao's duties were not limited to entertaining the emperor. On one occasion he and several other poets were summoned to the palace of Crown Prince Liu Shi 劉奭 the future Emperor Yuan, who was sick in bed suffering from dizziness, loss of memory, and melancholia. From dawn to dusk the poets recited "unusual writings" and poems they had composed themselves. Only when the crown prince recovered did they leave. The crown prince especially enjoyed two of Wang Bao's compositions, "Eulogy on the Sweet Springs Palace" and "Eulogy on the Panpipes," which he ordered the female musicians to chant for him. The latter piece is contained in the *Wen xuan* chap. 17) under the title "Rhapsody on the Panpipes."

When an occult master claimed that a metal horse and jade chicken had been discovered in Wang Bao's native area of Yizhou, Emperor Xuan commanded Wang to go there and present sacrifices to them. He died of illness contracted during the journey.

In addition to the poems mentioned above, Wang Bao is credited with "Nine Longings," which is contained in the *Chuci*. He also is the author of "Slave's Contract," a humorous mock contract reputedly written for a recalcitrant slave.

*Reference*
Cai Xiongxiang. "Wang Bao ji qi zuopin."

XI KANG or Ji Kang 嵇康 (223–262), *zi* Shuye 叔夜, also known as Xi Zhongsan 嵇中散. His ancestral home was Shangyu 上虞 in Guiji 會稽 Commandery (modern Shangyu, Zhejiang, east of Shaoxing). Fleeing from a feud, Xi Kang's ancestors settled in Zhi 銍 Prefecture (west of modern Suzhou 宿州, Anhui) of Qiao 譙 Commandery. According to the *Jin shu* of Wang Yin 王隱, the original family name was Xi 奚. After moving to Zhi, they changed the name to Xi 嵇, which was derived from the final syllable of the name of their native place, Guiji, except that they wrote it with "mountain" in the lower right portion of the character and pronounced Ji as Xi.

Xi Kang was a prominent poet and thinker of the Wei dynasty. He was a member of the group known as the Seven Worthies of the Bamboo Grove. The most important sources of information on his life are his biography in the *Jin shu* 49.1369–1374 and anecdotes preserved in the *Shishuo xinyu* and its commentary.

Xi Kang came from a wealthy family of Confucian scholars. His father, Xi Zhao 嵇昭, held several high positions. He died when Xi Kang was an infant, and Xi Kang was raised by his elder brother, Xi Xi 嵇喜, and his mother, née Sun 孫.

Xi Kang had a strong interest in Taoism, the study of which he began in his youth. He eventually became one of the leading spokesmen of his age in favor of Taoist quietism as well as the more esoteric aspects of Taoism that involved the techniques called *yang sheng* 養生 (nurturing life). Around the year 243 Xi Kang wrote an essay entitled "Disquisition on Nurturing Life" (*Wen xuan*, chap. 53).

Sometime in the 240s Xi Kang married a princess of the Cao clan, Changle Tingzhu 長樂廷主, who is variously identified as a daughter or granddaughter of Cao Lin 曹林, a son of Cao Cao. As a result of his marriage, Xi Kang was appointed palace gentleman. Around 245 he received the honorific title of grandee without specified appointment. He then moved to Shanyang 山陽 (southeast of modern Jiaozuo 焦作 City, Henan), about sixty kilometers northeast of Luoyang. Xi Kang remained there for most of the rest of his life. It was there that he met with many of his friends for "pure conversation." Xi Kang was on especially good terms with the libertine and antiritualist Lü An 呂安 (ob. 262), as well as the eccentrics who belonged to the so-called Bamboo Grove group.

Xi Kang was reluctant to serve in government office, and in this respect he differed from his elder brother, Xi Xi, who accepted positions in the Sima regime. However, Xi Kang apparently considered raising an army in support of the anti-Sima revolt begun in January 255 by Guanqiu Jian 毋秋儉 and Wen Qin 文欽 at Shouchun 壽春 (modern Anhui), but backed out after Shan Tao 山濤 (205–283) advised him not to get involved.

It may have been as a result of his contemplated involvement in this revolt that Xi Kang went into hiding for several years. He may have fled to Hedong 河東 (Shanxi) after Sima Zhao summoned him to take a position. Xi Kang perhaps joined the recluse Sun Deng 孫登, who lived in the mountains of Ji 汲 Prefecture, about forty kilometers east of Shanyang.

Xi Kang's contempt for conventional society and government service is best reflected in a letter he wrote to his friend Shan Tao in 261, when Shan Tao was about to leave the bureau of selection and recommended Xi Kang as his replacement. Xi Kang's "Letter to Shan Tao Breaking off Friendship" (*Wen Xuan*, chap. 43) expresses his indignation at being asked to abandon his principles of non-involvement in political affairs. He also argues that his various eccentricities make him unfit to hold government office.

Xi Kang's contempt for conventions and authority eventually led to his death. In 261 his friend Lü An became embroiled in a dispute with his elder brother, Lü Xun 呂巽 (or Xun 遜). Lü Xun had committed adultry with Lü An's wife. Lü An wanted to make a public accusation against his brother, but Xi Kang persuaded him not to. Meanwhile, Lü Xun, who was a protégé of Sima Zhao, spread a rumor that his younger brother had beaten their mother. He then submitted a memorial urging that he be tried for unfilial conduct. Lü An was exiled to the frontier. Just before departing for his exile, Lü An submitted a plea in which he mentioned Xi Kang's name. As a result, both Lü An and Xi Kang were arrested. Zhong Hui 鍾會 (225–264), an old enemy of Xi Kang's, who then held the post of metropolitan commandant, recommended that Xi Kang and Lü An be put to death for sedition and treason. One charge he made against Xi Kang was that he had wanted to participate in Guanqiu Jian's revolt. Xi Kang was then taken to the Eastern Market of Luoyang and executed, probably in 262.

Among Xi Kang's extant writings there are sixty *shi*. His best poems are those in the four-syllable-line form. He has one particularly well-known eighteen-part piece entitled "Presented to the Flourishing Talent upon Entering the Army," five of which are included in the *Wen xuan* (chap. 24). Another of Xi Kang's important tetrasyllabic poems is "Prison Anguish," a long autobiographical piece he composed while in prison (*Wen xuan*, chap. 23). Xi Kang also was a skilled zither player. His long *fu* "Rhapsody on the Zither" is contained in the *Wen xuan* (chap. 18).

*References*
Henricks, Robert G. "Hsi K'ang (223–262)."
———. *Philosophy and Argumentation in Third-Century China.*
Holzman, Donald. *La Vie et la pensée de Xi Kang (223–262 Ap J.C.).*
———. "La Poésie de Ji Kang."
Kōzen Hiroshi. "Kei Kō shi shōron."
———. "Kei Kō no hishō."
Van Gulik, Robert. "Hsi K'ang's Poetical Essay on the Lute."
———. *Hsi K'ang and His Poetical Essay on the Lute.*
Zhuang Wanshou. *Xi Kang yanjiu ji nianpu.*

**XIANG XIU** 向秀 (230?–285?), *zi* Ziqi 子期, native of Huai 懷 Prefecture in Henei 河內 Commandery (southwest of modern Wuzhi 武陟, Henan).

Xiang Xiu was a leading writer and thinker of the Wei-Jin period. Like Xi Kang, he is included in the group known as the Seven Worthies of the Bamboo Grove. The major source of information on his life is his biography in the *Jin shu* (49.1374–75).

Nothing is known about Xiang Xiu's family background or his early life. During his youth he became acquainted with Shan Tao 山濤 (205–283), whose native place also was Huai Prefecture. Like Shan Tao, he had a strong interest in Laozi and Zhuangzi. Xiang is known for his commentary on the *Zhuangzi*, which has often been confused with the commentary by Guo Xiang 郭象.

Xiang Xiu also was a friend of Xi Kang (q.v.) and Lü An 呂安 (ob. 262). Around 242 Xiang Xiu wrote a refutation of Xi Kang's "Disquisition on Nurturing Life." Around 253 he reputedly joined Xi Kang at his forge, and tended a garden with Lü An.

Around 264 Xiang Xiu was sent to the capital to present the accounts of his home commandery. He visited Xi Kang's home in Shanyang, north of Luoyang, and then composed "Rhapsody on Recalling Old Friends" (*Wen xuan*, chap. 16), in which he laments the passing of Xi Kang and Lü An, who had been executed in 262.

Around 269 Xiang Xiu entered official service as cavalier attendant-in-ordinary, and around 274 was promoted to attendant gentleman of the Yellow Gate. Around 279 he was again in the post of cavalier attendant-in-ordinary. It is not known when Xiang Xiu died; the year 285 is only a guess.

*Reference*
Lu Kanru. *Zhonggu wenxue xinian.*

**XIE HUILIAN** 謝惠連 (407–433), native of Yangjia 陽夏 in Chen 陳 Commandery (modern Taikang 太康, Henan). However, the Xie family had settled in the area of Guiji (modern Shangyu, Zhejiang) after 317.

Xie Huilian was a poet of the Liu-Song period. Information on his life is provided in his biographies in the *Song shu* (53.1524–25) and *Nan shi* (19.537–38).

Xie Huilian was a younger cousin and, since childhood, a good friend of the famous landscape poet Xie Lingyun 謝靈運 (385–433). Xie Huilian's father, Xie Fangming 謝方明 (381–427), served as governor of Guiji from 423–427. In 424 Xie Lingyun returned to his family estate in Shining 始寧 (modern Shangyu 上虞, Zhejiang), and spent much of his time with Huilian. On one occasion, he even scolded Huilian's father for failing to recognize Huilian's literary talent (see *Song shu* 67.1774–75).

Xie Lingyun and Xie Huilian were together again in 428, when Lingyun returned to Shining after serving in the capital. Huilian had to return to his home because of a scandal. It seems that during the mourning period for his father he composed poems to his homosexual lover, one Du Deling 杜德靈, a minor clerk in the Guiji Commandery administration. These poems were circulated, and when the authorities discovered them, they punished Huilian by stripping him of his rank and banning him from holding further office.

Xie Huilian, along with three other friends—He Zhangyu 何長瑜 (ob. 444), Xun Yong 荀雍, and Yang Xuanzhi 羊璿之 (ob. 459)—were known as the four companions of Xie Lingyun. They spent their time attending parties on Xie Lingyun's estate at which they discussed and composed poetry. In 430 Xie Huilian received an imperial pardon and was able to return to official service. He obtained an appointment as judicial aide to Liu Yikang 劉義康 (409–451), prince of Pengcheng 彭城, who was then serving as minister of education. On his journey to take up his post, he stopped at Xiling Lake 西陵 (near modern Xiaoshan 蕭山, Zhejiang), where he was delayed by a windstorm. There he wrote a five-part poem, "At Xiling, Encountering a Storm, Presented to Xie Lingyun" (*Wen xuan*, chap. 25).

In October 430 Liu Yikang wished to refurbish the Eastern Bureau Wall. While the workmen were excavating the moat, they dug up an ancient tomb in which they found two coffins and numerous burial articles. Liu Yikang ordered that the coffins be reburied on the eastern knoll. Xie Huilian composed an offering for the deceased, whose identity was not known. This piece is a famous prose composition, "Offering on an Ancient Tomb" (*Wen xuan*, chap. 60).

Xie Huilian died quite young of unspecified causes in 433. His literary corpus contains about thirty *shi*. Most of these are imitation *yuefu*. He also wrote a few landscape poems in the style of his cousin Xie Lingyun. One of the most moving of these is his "Autumn Inspirations" (*Wen xuan*, chap. 23). Another of Xie Huilian's famous pieces is "Rhapsody on Snow" (*Wen xuan*, chap. 13).

XIE ZHUANG 謝莊 (421–466), *zi* Xiyi 希逸. His ancestral home was Yangjia 陽夏 (modern Taikang, Henan), but he was a member of the renowned Xie clan that had fled north China after the fall of the Western Jin in 317. He thus was related to Xie Huilian (q.v.) and Xie Lingyun. The most important information on his life can be found in his biographies in the *Song shu* (85.2167–77) and *Nan shi* (20.553–57).

Xie Zhuang's father, Xie Mi 謝密 (392–433), also known by his style name, Hongwei 宏微, was a high official. Xie Zhuang was a precocious child and reputedly could compose at the age of seven. Around 449 he joined the staff of Liu Dan 劉誕, prince of Sui, who appointed him director of the bureau of recorders. In 452 Emperor Wen 文 (reg. 424–453) named him palace cadet for the heir-designate. Upon imperial command he composed a *fu* on a beautiful red parrot that was presented to the court; "Rhapsody on the Scarlet Parrot" (*Yiwen leiju* 91.1577) received special praise from Yuan Shu 袁淑 (408–453), a leading scholar and poet of the time.

On 14 March 453 Emperor Wen's eldest son, Liu Shao 劉劭 (ob. 453), known in history as the Arch-fiend 元兇, assassinated his father and declared himself emperor. Emperor Wen's third son, Liu Jun 劉駿 (the future Emperor Xiaowen 孝文, reg. 454–464), led an army against him. He entrusted Xie Zhuang with correcting and polishing the war proclamations issued against Liu Shao. When Liu Jun assumed the throne in May of 453, he appointed Xie palace attendant. In 454 Xie was promoted to left general of the guards and minister of the bureau of personnel. However, because he was suffering from a very painful illness, which he describes in a letter to the prince of Jiangxia 江夏, Liu Yigong 劉義恭 (403–465), he resigned from the bureau of personnel in 456.

Xie Zhuang returned to office in 457 in the position of minister of the section for justice. In 458, as a result of changes in the administrative structure, Xie was appointed head of the bureau of personnel, a position he held jointly with Gu Jizhi 顧覬之. Soon thereafter Xie was promoted to right general of the guards as well as servitor within the palace. Upon imperial command, he composed a rhapsody and song in praise of a dancing horse that had been presented to the court from Henan.

In 461 Xie Zhuang returned to his former position of palace attendant, and was put in command of the general of the forward army. In 462 he again was head of the bureau of personnel and director of the erudites of the academy for the sons of state. In that year he composed "Dirge for Emperor Xiaowu's Honorable Consort Xuan" (*Wen xuan*, chap. 57) and "Lament for Honorable Consort Yin" (*Yiwen leiju* 15) to mourn the passing of Emperor Xiaowu's concubine Yin Shuyi 殷淑儀. The emperor reputedly was moved to tears when he read the lament. So many people in the capital wished to copy it, the price of paper and ink rose (*Nan shi* 11.324).

In 463 the son of Yan Shibo 顏師伯 recommended a commoner for the post of prefect of official carriages. Even after the emperor judged that the man's status was inappropriate for this postion, the officials in charge allowed him to assume the post. When their failure to follow the emperor's edict was discovered, numerous officials were punished. Xie Zhuang, as head of the bureau of personnel, was removed from office (*Song shu* 77.1994–95).

Xie Zhuang then joined the staff of Liu Ziluan 劉子鸞 (ob. 465), prince of Xin'an 新安, as chief clerk, in which post he served until the accession of Liu Ziye 劉子業 (posthumously known as the Former Deposed Emperor, reg. 464–65) as emperor in July 464, when he was reappointed to the central administration as household grandee of the gold and purple. Xie also was commissioned to compose the official lament for the deceased Emperor Xiaowu. However, Liu Ziye long had resented Xie Zhuang, for he was deeply offended by the dirge Xie had written for the Honorable Consort Xuan, which contained a line he considered derogatory to him and his late mother. Although he first proposed having Xie Zhuang put to death, he was persuaded to punish him by assigning him to the office of the Directorate of Imperial Manufactories, where Xie presumably was given the menial task of making utensils and tools.

On 1 January 466 Liu Ziye was assassinated and replaced by the eleventh son of Emperor Wen, Liu Yu 劉彧 (posthumously known as Emperor Ming 明, reg. 466–472). Xie Zhuang was immediately recalled to office and appointed cavalier attendant-in-ordinary, household grandee, and put in charge of the army of the prince of Xunyang 尋陽. He also composed the edict that announced a general amnesty, as well hymns in praise of Emperor Xiaowu. Before he died in 466 at the age of forty-six, Xie Zhuang held the positions of director of the secretariat, regular attendant, and had an official retinue of twenty men.

Xie Zhuang's collection originally was quite large: nineteen *juan* including over four hundred works of verse, *fu*, and prose, most of which have been lost. His best-known work is "Rhapsody on the Moon" (*Wen xuan*, chap. 13).


YAN YANZHI 顏延之 (384–456), *zi* Yannian 延年, native of Linyi 臨沂 in Langye 琅邪 (in the Jin and Song period, Linyi was a so-called emigré prefecture northeast of modern Jiangning 江寧, Jiangsu).

Yan Yanzhi was a prominent writer of prose and poetry in the Liu Song period. The most important sources of information on his life are his biographies in the *Song shu* (73.1891–1904) and *Nan shi* (34.877–881).

Yan Yanzhi came from a family whose ancestors held high positions, but Yan himself lived in poverty as a youth. However, he was a diligent student and a voracious reader. Yan began official service in 415 when he joined the staff of Liu Liu 劉柳, who had just been appointed inspector of Jiangzhou 江州. He accompanied Liu to Xunyang, where he met the poet Tao Qian. Yan and Tao had a lifelong friendship.

In 416 Yan Yanzhi joined the staff of Liu Yifu 劉義符 (406–424), the eldest son of the founder of the Song dynasty, Liu Yu 劉裕 (363–442). In that same year, after Liu Yu defeated the Later Qin and captured Chang'an and Luoyang, Yan Yanzhi was in the group of envoys sent to Luoyang to offer congratulations to Liu Yu, newly named duke of Song. On the way, Yan composed the poem "On a Northern Mission in Luoyang" (*Wen xuan*, chap. 27). This poem impressed Xie Hui 謝晦 (390–426) and Fu Liang 傅亮 (374–426), two of Liu Yu's most important advisers. With the founding of the state of Song in 418, Yan Yanzhi was appointed an erudite and later secretary to Liu Yifu. When Liu Yu officially took the throne as emperor in 420, Yan continued to serve as secretary to Liu Yifu, who was then named heir designate. Although he was a member of Liu Yifu's entourage, Yan, along with Xie Lingyun, was closely associated with Liu Yizhen 劉義真 (407–424), who was competing with Liu Yifu for the succession.

Liu Yu died on 22 June 422, and was succeeded by Liu Yifu (Emperor Shao

少帝, reg. 423-24, who immediately dismissed members of Liu Yizhen's faction from their capital posts. Xie Lingyun was sent to Yongjia 永嘉 (modern Wenzhou, Zhejiang, and Yan Yanzhi was sent to Shi'an 始安 modern Guilin, Guangxi). On the way to Shi'an. Yan passed the Miluo 汨羅 River, where Qu Yuan had committed suicide. On behalf of Zhang Shao 張邵, prefect of Xiangzhou 湘州, he composed "Offering for Qu Yuan" *Wen xuan*, chap. 60 . He also passed through Xunyang. where he visited Tao Qian.

In 426 Liu Yilong 劉義隆 407-453,. posthumously known as Emperor Wen, who had replaced his brother as emperor, recalled members of the Liu Yizhen faction to the capital. Yan and Xie Lingyun both returned to Jiankang to serve in prestigious positions. Yan held the post of attendant gentleman of palace writers. In 427 Tao Qian died. Yan composed "Dirge for Summoned Gentleman Tao" *Wen xuan*, chap. 57 to lament the passing of his good friend. In 433 his other poet friend. Xie Lingyun. was executed.

In the early 430s the most powerful men at court were the palace attendants, who included Yin Jingren 殷景仁 ca. 390-440 , Liu Zhan 劉湛 (392-440), and Liu Yikang 劉義康, prince of Pengcheng 彭城. Yan Yanzhi, who was a heavy drinker and reckless in his behavior, openly expressed contempt for Yin and Liu. Liu Zhan then persuaded Liu Yikang to send Yan Yanzhi into exile as governor of Yongjia. To express his indignation. Yan wrote "Song of the Five Gentlemen" *Wen xuan*. chap. 21 . a set of five poems about five of the Seven Worthies of the Bamboo Grove. Some of the lines of these pieces were intended to be critical of the men in power. Outraged, Liu Zhan and Liu Yikang sought to have Yan Yanzhi banished to an even more remote location. However. Emperor Wen issued an edict to Liu Yikang. ordering him to have Yan removed from office "to ponder his errors in a country village."

Yan Yanzhi spent seven years from 434 to 440 in retirement, depending on his wealthy friend the noble Wang Qiu 王球, for financial support. In 436 Empress Gongsi 恭思 of the Jin died. For her burial. the authorities wanted to appoint officials who had taken office in 405. the year she was named empress. Yan Yanzhi was named palace attendant. When the local official presented him with the letter of appointment. in a drunken rage Yan threw it down and said, "Yan Yanzhi could not serve the living. How can he serve the dead?" On another occasion. Emperor Wen wished to summon Yan to court. He sent out numerous edicts. but Yan did not appear. for he was always sitting drunk in a wineshop, singing funeral songs. Only after he sobered up did he go to court. While out of office. Yan composed the *Ting gao* 庭誥 Instructions from the Courtyard), a book of injunctions for his sons.

In 439 Liu Zhan and members of his faction were executed. Yan Yanzhi was invited to return to office to serve as aide to Liu Jun 劉濬. prince of Shixing 始興. In 441 he composed a *fu*. "Rhapsody on the Russet and White Horse" (*Wen xuan*, chap. 14 . describing a beautiful piebald horse that had originally been presented to Liu Yu. and was very much admired by Emperor Wen.

In 443 Yan Yanzhi was promoted to palace assistant secretary. It is said that he was lax in exercising his duties and made no proposals. However, despite his poor performance in office. in 445 he rose to become libationer for the sons of the state. In this capacity he established Wang Bi's commentary to the *Zhou yi* as the official commentary in place of Zheng Xuan's commentary.

Sometime in the late 440's Yan Yanzhi was charged with refusing to compensate the seller for land he wanted to buy. He was dismissed from office, but later recalled. In 452 he submitted a memorial asking to be allowed to retire. The emperor denied his request. He did retire the next year (453), at the age of seventy.

In March 453 Liu Shao assassinated his father and took the throne. Yan Yanzhi was named imperial household grandee. Yan's eldest son, Yan Jun 顏竣, was on the staff of Liu Jun 劉駿, Emperor Wen's third son, who was leading an army against Liu Shao. Yan Jun drafted the war proclamations. Liu Shao became suspicious of Yan Yanzhi's loyalty and questioned him saying, "Whose writing is this?" Yan Yanzhi said, "It is Yan Jun's writing." "How do you know it is his?" Yan said, "Jun's style is something I definitely can recognize." Liu Shao said, "How can he speak such language as this?" Yan Yanzhi said, "My son does not even pay any attention to me, your old minister. How could he pay any attention to you?" Liu Shao's suspicions were relieved, and Liu Jun decided that Yan Yanzhi was not implicated in his son's treason.

In late May 453 Liu Jun defeated Liu Shao and assumed the throne. He granted Yan Yanzhi the title of imperial household grandee of the gold and purple and put him in charge of the army of the prince of Xiangdong 湘東. Yan's son Yan Jun was ennobled as a marquis, but Yanzhi refused to accept any emolument from the son's estate. Yan Yanzhi died in 456 at the age of seventy- three.

In his time Yan Yanzhi was considered a major writer, both of prose and verse. He and Xie Lingyun were regarded as the leading writers of the south— they were referred to as "Yan and Xie of the area south of the Yangtze." However, Yan was not as gifted a poet as Xie Lingyun. Most of his extant poetry consists of occasional poems written at gatherings. Yan was an accomplished writer of parallel style prose. One of his best-known parallel prose pieces is "Preface for the Poems Composed at the Winding Waterway on the Third Day of the Third Month" (*Wen xuan*, chap. 46), written for the Lustration Festival of 434. This is a long essay written in strict parallel form, and is laden with learned allusions to earlier texts, mostly the classics.

*References*
Chen Meizu. *Nanchao Yan Xie shi yanjiu.*
Kinami Norio. "Gan Enshi no shōgai to shisō."
Li Zhiliang. "Yan Yanzhi xingshi ji *Wen xuan* suoshou shiwen xinian."
Miao Yue. "Yan Yanzhi nianpu."
Oyane Bunjirō. "Gan Enshi no shi."
Takahashi Kazumi. "Gan Enshi no bungaku."
Zhou Jianzhong. "Lun Yan Yanzhi de wenxue chuangzuo."

ZHANG HENG 張衡 (78–139), *zi* Pingzi 平子, native of Xi'e 西鄂 in Nanyang 南陽 Commandery (north of modern Nanyang City, Henan).

Zhang Heng was a leading poet, scholar, and scientist of the Later Han. The most important source of information about his life is his biography in the *Hou Han shu* (58.1897–1940). There also is an epitaph by his close friend Cui Yuan 崔瑗 (78–143), which is contained in the *Guwen yuan* (8.8b–9a).

Zhang Heng came from a distinguished family of scholars and officials. His grandfather Zhang Kan 張堪 was widely admired for his learning and integrity. Around 94, at the age of seventeen, Zhang Heng toured the Chang'an and Luoyang areas, where he began collecting material that he would eventually incorporate into his long rhapsodies on these two Han capitals. His first appointment was in Nanyang, where he served as master of documents under Bao De 鮑德 (ob. 111 or 113), governor of Nanyang from 103 to 111. He composed inscriptions, dirges, and other works on Bao De's behalf.

Around 107 Zhang Heng completed "Western Metropolis Rhapsody" and "Eastern Metropolis Rhapsody" (*Wen xuan*, chaps. 2 and 3). In 111, after Bao De was transferred to the capital, Zhang returned to Xi'e to resume his scholarly studies. At this time he wrote a commentary to Yang Xiong's *Taixuan* 太玄 (Grand Mystery) and did research in mathematics and astronomy. He also composed "Southern Capital Rhapsody" about his home area of Nanyang (*Wen xuan*, chap. 4).

Emperor An 安 (reg. 107–125), having learned of Zhang's expertise in mathematics, summoned Zhang to the capital around 112 and appointed him palace gentleman. Zhang also served twice as prefect grand astrologer in 115–120 and 126–132. In the mid-130s he came into conflict with eunuchs. He composed "Rhapsody on Contemplating the Mystery" (*Wen xuan*, chap. 15) to express his frustration.

In 136 Zhang Heng left his central government post to take up the position of chancellor of Hejian 河間. Hejian (administrative center southeast of modern Xian *xian* 獻, Hebei) was the kingdom of Liu Zheng 劉政 (ob. A.D. 141), who had allowed powerful families special privileges. Zhang Heng was a strict administrator, and after learning the names of those who had violated the law, he had them arrested. For this deed, he earned the respect and admiration of the Hejian people. In this period melancholy and bitterness filled Zhang's writings, the most notable of which is "Four Sorrows" (*Wen xuan*, chap. 29), a lyric poem written as an allegory in which a beautiful woman reputedly represents the ruler, whom the persona seeks to win over with gifts of precious objects, but has his way blocked by high mountains, deep snow, and impassable rivers (petty men).

In 138 Zhang retired from office and composed "Rhapsody on Returning to the Fields" (*Wen xuan*, chap. 15). In 139 he was summoned out of retirement and died that same year after serving briefly as master of writing. Zhang was buried at his home in Xi'e.

*References*
Gong Kechang. "Zhang Heng fu lun." In *Han fu yanjiu*, pp. 231–260.
———. "Zhang Heng."
Liao Guodong. *Zhang Heng shengping ji qi fu zhi yanjiu.*
Sun Wenqing. *Zhang Heng nianpu.*
Yang Qinglong. "Zhang Heng zhuzuo xinian kao shi."

Zhang Caimin. "Zhang Heng 'Yongyuan shiernian wei Nanyang zhubo' xinzheng."
Zhao Jian. "Zhang Heng zhuyao fuzuo xinian."

ZHANG HUA 張華 (232–300, *zi* Maoxian 茂先, native of Fangcheng 方城 in Fanyang 范陽 (south of modern Gu'an 固安, Hebei).

Zhang Hua was a leading scholar, poet, and statesman of the Western Jin. The primary source of information on his life is his biography in the *Jin shu* (36.1068–77). There are also anecdotes about him recorded in the *Shishuo xinyu*.

Born into an official family that had fallen on hard times after the death of his father, Zhang Hua spent his early years as a goatherd. His status was enhanced by marriage to the daughter of Liu Fang 劉放 (ob. 250), a prominent official of the Wei. Upon the recommendation of the Fanyang Commandery governor, ca. 255 he received an appointment as erudite in the ministry of ceremony. Zhang in turn recommended the learned scholar Chenggong Sui (q.v.) for the same post.

Around 258 Lu Qin 廬欽 (ob. 278), a prominent court official from Zhang Hua's home commandery of Fanyang, recommended him to the chancellor Sima Zhao 司馬昭 (211–265), who was de facto ruler of the Wei. Sima Zhao named Zhang Hua assistant governor of Henan, but before he could take up his post, he was transferred to the position of deputy compiler. The next year he became chief clerk, followed in 261 with an appointment as gentleman of palace writers. It was probably at this time that Zhang Hua wrote his most famous poem, "Rhapsody on the Wren" (*Wen xuan*, chap. 13). When the renowned poet Ruan Ji saw the piece, he proclaimed that its author could become a minister of state.

After the establishment of the Western Jin in 265, the Jin emperors held Zhang Hua in high regard for his learning and literary skill. They consulted him on matters of ritual and protocol as well as on political, legal, and military affairs. In 267 he received the noble title of Marquis within the Passes. Zhang Hua was so much in demand, he was recalled to the court before he could complete the mourning period for his deceased mother. In 270 he and Xun Xu 洵勖 (ob. 289) directed the compilation of a catalogue of the imperial library. This catalogue is generally regarded as the first catalogue to organize books by the "four-division" (*si bu* 四部) system.

In 280, as a reward for helping formulate a strategy for the successful campaign that resulted in the defeat of Wu, Zhang Hua was enfeoffed as marquis of Guangwu 廣武. He also devised the ritual program for the *feng* 封 and *shan* 禪 rites, which were to be performed in celebration of the victory over Wu. In 282 he was sent out as military governor of Youzhou 幽州 (modern northern Hebei). Zhang performed his duties so well, he earned the praise of "barbarians" and Chinese alike. As a result, the imperial council recommended that he be appointed prime minister. However, because of opposition from several officials whom Zhang had offended in the past, the emperor appointed him director of the ministry of ceremony instead.

In 287 the ridgepole in the grand hall of the imperial ancestral temple collapsed, and Zhang Hua, who was held responsible for this unlucky omen (the ridgepole was considered a symbol of the stability of the state), was forced to resign from office. Zhang Hua continued to attend court in his capacity as a noble of rank. He also warmly received Lu Ji (q.v.) and his brother Lu Yun when they first arrived from Wu. and he recommended them to prominent men in the capital.

In 290. after the death of Emperor Wu and the accession of Emperor Hui, Zhang Hua was recalled to government service as junior tutor to the heir designate. Sima Yu 司馬遹 (ob. 300). However, because he was disliked by the regent Yang Jun 楊駿 ob. 291 . Zhang's advice was not sought on political matters. After Yang Jun was killed in 291, and Empress Jia seized de facto control of the court, Zhang Hua received high positions, including imperial household grandee of the right. palace attendant, and overseer of masters of writing. Although the empress showed great deference to Zhang and consulted him on important political matters. he was deeply concerned that she had obtained too much power. He then composed "Admonition of the Female Scribe" (Wen xuan, chap. 56), in which he warns female favorites of the dangers that come from assuming prerogatives to which they are not entitled.

In 293 or 294 Zhang Hua received ennoblement as duke of Zhuangwu 壯武 west of modern Jimo 即墨, Shandong). Although he repeatedly declined the rank, he finally accepted it after being ordered to do so by imperial edict. In 294, after reading an essay by the learned scholar Shu Xi 束皙 ca. 264–ca. 303), Zhang Hua had Shu appointed as an administrator. In 296 Zhang attained his highest position, minister of works. In that year he appointed the famous poet Zuo Si libationer.

From 296 on Zhang Hua came into conflict with Sima Lun 司馬倫 (ob. 301), who was openly increasing his own power and influence with the assistance of his aide Sun Xiu 孫秀 (ob. 301). In 299 Zhang opposed their attempt to depose Empress Jia. When he refused to participate in a coup to seat Sima Lun on the throne. Zhang was put to death along with his sons.

*References*
Greatrex. Roger. *The Bowu Zhi.*
Jiang Liangfu. *Zhang Hua nianpu.*
Liao Weiqing. "Zhang Hua yu Xi Jin zhengzhi zhi guanxi."
———. "Zhang Hua nianpu."
Straughair. Anna. *Chang Hua.*

# *Notes*

## INTRODUCTION

1. Selected articles from the conferences have been published. See Zhao Fuhai et al., *Zhaoming Wenxuan yanjiu lunwen ji*; and Zhao Fuhai, *Wen xuan xue lunji*.

2. Wei Shuqin et al., *Zhongwai Zhaoming Wen xuan yanjiu lunzhu suoyin*.

3. See Chen Hongtian et al., *Zhaoming Wenxuan yizhu*.

4. *Wang Can ji*.

5. They all have been published by Jinan chubanshe 暨南出版社 in Tainan.

## "RHAPSODY ON THE WIND"

1. Magnolia Terrace (Lan tai 蘭臺) was the site of a touring palace of the Chu kings. It is traditionally located east of modern Zhongxiang 鍾祥, Hubei. King Xiang is King Qingxiang 頃襄 (reg. 298–263 B.C.). He figures in most of the rhapsodies attributed to Song Yu.

2. Jing Cuo (or Chai) 景差 was a literary figure at the Chu court. He appears in several of the rhapsodies attributed to Song Yu. Little is known about him.

3. Li Shan (*Wen xuan* 13.2a) explains *zhi* 枳 as the name of a tree (probably *Hovenia dulcis* Thunb., or "raisin tree"), and *gou* 句 as descriptive of the bends and twists of the tree. However, Duan Yucai (see *Shuowen jiezi gulin* 9A.2703); Hu Shaoying, *Wen xuan jianzheng* 15.1a–b; and Zhu Jian, *Wen xuan jishi* 13.11a–b show that *zhigou* is a binome meaning "bent and contorted." It also is possible that *zhigou* 枳句 is a variant for *zhiju* 枳椇, a common name for the raisin tree. See Lu Wenyu, *Shi caomu jinshi*, p. 98, no. 108.

4. Li Shan (*Wen xuan* 13.2a) cites a lost passage from the *Zhuangzi*, which expresses the same idea as Song Yu's line: "Holes and crevices attract the wind, seeds of the parasol tree bring [birds] to nest." Zhu Jian (*Wen xuan jishi* 13.2b–3a) shows that *kongxue* 空穴 simply means "places where there are holes and gaps."

## "RHAPSODY ON AUTUMN INSPIRATIONS"

1. Li Shan (*Wen xuan* 13.4a) says this year corresponds to the fourteenth year of Taishi 太始. However, the Taishi period lasted only ten years. As Liang Zhangju

(*Wen xuan pangzheng*, 14.19a) has shown, the fourteenth year of Jin is the fourth year of Xianning 咸寧 (278).

2. The expression I have translated "gray" is *er mao* 二毛, which literally means "two colors of hair." See *Zuo zhuan*, Xi 22 (Legge, *The Chinese Classics* 5: 183): "The gentleman does not wound a second time, and he does not capture persons with grey hair."

3. The *Jin shu* of Zang Rongxu 臧榮緒 (cited by Li Shan, *Wen xuan* 13.4a) says that Pan Yue served as assistant to Jia Chong, who held the position of Grand Commandant.

4. This line is cited in *Shishuo xinyu* to prove that the Tiger-swift Commander of Palace Gentlemen had no headquarters, but instead occupied the bureau of the detached cavalry. See Yang Yong, *Shishuo xinyu jiaozhu* 1.37; and Mather, *Shih-shuo Hsin-yu*, p. 79.

5. The "military cap" worn by regular attendants and palace attendants had gold cicada-shaped ornaments attached to it. The cicada symbolized purity because of its reputation for drinking only dew. The tail of the sable (*diao* 貂), said to represent outward gentleness and inner ferocity, was also used as an ornament. See *Jin shu* 25.768; Harada, *Kan Rikuchō no fukushoku*, pp. 109–13, plates XXVI-2, XXVII-1; Eberhard and Eberhard, *Die Mode der Han-und Chou-zeit*, pp. 59–62; and Zhang Moyuan, *Hanchao fuzhuang tuyang ziliao*, pp. 65–66 and 69.

6. The locus classicus for the phrase *she guan cheng fa* 攝官承乏 (to assume temporary office and take charge where qualified persons are lacking), which I have rendered "temporarily appointed by default," is *Zuo zhuan*, Cheng 2 (Legge, *The Chinese Classics* 5: p. 345): "Han Jue said to the Marquis of Qi, 'I venture to inform you that I am unintelligent. I temporarily assume office to take charge where officials are lacking.' "

7. Cf. *Mao shi* 58/5 and 196/4: "Early to rise and late to bed."

8. Cf. *Mao shi* 162/2: "I have no leisure to kneel or rest."

## "RHAPSODY ON THE HOULET"

1. Jia Yi was dismissed from the court of Emperor Wen 文 (reg. 179–157 B.C.) ca. 176 B.C. after receiving criticism from senior officials at the Han court. He was sent to serve as tutor to Liu Zhu 劉著, king of Changsha 長沙 (reg. 177–157 B.C.). Changsha in this period was a kingdom the territory of which roughly corresponded to modern Hunan. For an excellent study of Changsha during the early Han, see Emmerich, "Chu und Changsha am Ende der Qin-Zeit und zu Beginn der Han-Zeit."

2. The fifth-century gazetteer *Jingzhou ji* 荊州記 (Notes on Jingzhou), cited in *Shi ji* 84.2496, n. 1, mentions that Jia Yi's house was located in the northwest corner of the capital city, Changsha (modern Changsha, Hunan). His house was famous for its small stone bed.

3. The compilers of the *Wen xuan* drew this so-called preface from the *Han shu* 48.2226.

### "RHAPSODY ON THE PARROT"

1. This event probably occurred in 198. See Lu Kanru, *Zhonggu wenxue xinian* 1: 332–33.

2. *Chu shi* 處士 (retired gentleman) designates a man who held no official title. Li Shan (*Wen xuan* 13.20b) cites the *Fengsu tongyi* 風俗通義, which defines *chu shi* as someone who "lives in reclusion and refrains from speech." (This passage is not in the received text of the *Fengsu tongyi*.)

3. The source of this preface is not known. It clearly is not by Mi Heng. Qu Tuiyuan suggests that it was written by a historian or an editor. See *Han Wei Liuchao fuxuan*, p. 53, n. 6.

### "RHAPSODY ON THE WREN"

1. What I have translated "span" is *xun* 尋 (eight Chinese feet). A double-span (*chang* 常) is sixteen feet. *Xunchang* is a small area.

2. The phrase *sheng sheng* 生生 occurs in both the *Laozi* and *Zhou yi*. In the former the phrase means "nurturing life." Cf. *Laozi* 75: "The reason people take death lightly is that they are so intent on nurturing life." In the latter, *sheng sheng* has the sense of "constantly generating life." Cf. *Zhou yi zhushu*, "Grand Commentary," 7.13b: "Constantly generating life is called change." Zhang Hua probably uses the term in the sense of "sustaining life."

3. Zhang Hua borrows the phrase "nothing does it harm" from a passage in the *Lüshi chunqiu* (19.2b) that tells of men who refused offers of the throne by Shun and Tang. "Being men of high integrity and stern deportment, and taking joy in following their own personal will, they were harmed by nothing."

4. Cf. *Lienü zhuan* 3.10a: "One has never seen the osprey living in twos, dwelling in pairs."

5. Cf. Liu Xiang, "Nine Laments," "The Far Off Journey," l. 6 (*Chuci buzhu* 16.27b): "Riding the scarlet clouds, I traverse Grand Purity."

6. Cf. "Distant Wandering," l. 156 (*Chuci buzhu* 5.9b): "We come to the Gate of Coldness in the farthest bounds of the world."

7. Cf. *Shi ji* 109.2878: "There is a proverb that goes: 'The plum and peach do not speak, but a path forms naturally beneath them.' Although these words are simple, they can illustrate a great truth."

### "RHAPSODY ON THE RUSSET AND WHITE HORSE"

1. Cf. *Lun yu* 14/33: "A good steed is praised not for its strength, but for its virtue."

2. In ancient China the horse was often portrayed as possessing the nature of a dragon. The most commonly mentioned dragon-horse is the fabled equine of

the Yellow River on whose back Fuxi perceived markings that inspired him to create the eight trigrams. See n. 4 below.

3. Huang Kan proposes that *bu* 不 is a superfluous word in the line. I have followed his reading. See Huang Kan, *Wen xuan pingdian*, p. 51. Li Shan (*Wen xuan* 14.1b) explains *fu* 駃 (*bjɔk*) as the name of a horse. However, Zhu Jian (*Wen xuan jishi* 13.12b) suggests that it is simply a loan for *fu* 服 (*bjɔk*), "harness."

4. An apocryphon to the *Shang shu*, the *Shang shu zhong hou* 尚書中侯 (The Book of Documents: Exact Observations), cited by Li Shan (*Wen xuan* 14.1b), relates that when Yao was in the seventieth year of his reign, he built altars at the He and Luo rivers. When the sun was about to set, a bright light rose from the He, and a dragon-horse emerged holding a (turtle?) shell in its mouth. The shell was green with red markings. At the altar of the He it spat out a diagram portraying the eight trigrams. This was a sign confirming the great virtue of Emperor Yao.

5. The Exalted Ancestor is Liu Yu.

6. What I have translated as "declared allegiance" literally is "complied with their duties."

7. Cf. *Lun yu* 20/1: "The choice rests with Your Majesty alone."


## "RHAPSODY ON LIVING IN IDLENESS"

1. Ji An 汲黯 was an official during the reigns of Emperors Jing and Wu of the Former Han. Sima An 司馬安 was the son of Ji An's father's elder sister. In their youth they served together as forerunners of the heir designate. Sima Qian (*Shi ji* 120.3111) characterizes him as "shrewd and skilled in acting as an official." Thus, he was appointed to the rank of the nine ministers four times. The good historian must be Sima Qian. Cf. *Han shu* 62.2738: "Men such as Liu Xiang and Yang Xiong, who were broadly learned in a wide variety of books, all praise Sima Qian as a man who has the talents of a good historian."

2. Cf. *Laozi* 27: "He who excels at walking leaves no track or trace"; *Laozi* 15: "In ancient times he who excelled in acting as a gentleman was minutely subtle, and possessed profound understanding."

3. Cf. *Zhou yi zhushu* 1.13a: "The gentleman develops his virtue and tends to his work. Loyalty and fidelity are the means by which he develops virtue. Cultivating his words and establishing his sincerity are the means by which he preserves his achievement."

4. The minister of works and grand commandant is Jia Chong. See Chiu-mi Lai, "River and Ocean," pp. 60–61. Although Pan Yue clearly is referring to Jia Chong, Lai shows that Pan Yue probably served first under Xun Yi 荀顗 (ob. 274), who held the position of minister of works in 266–67 and was Grand Commandant in 268, when Pan Yue first entered official service.

5. Duke Wu of Lu 魯武公 is the noble title bestowed on Jia Chong in 266.

6. Emperor Wu is Sima Yan 司馬炎 (reg. 265–290). Pan Yue was appointed prefect of Heyang 河陽 (west of modern Meng 孟 *xian*, Henan) ca. 279. His

appointment in Huai 懷 (modern Wuzhi 武陟 xian, Henan) took place around 282. See ibid., pp. 67–68. The position with the secretariat probably refers to his temporary posting as acting gentleman in the secretariat of revenue. He was appointed to this position in 285. A year or two later, he was transferred to the position of adjudicator under the commandant of justice. See ibid., p. 73.

7. The "current" emperor is Emperor Hui 惠 (reg. 290–306). He was in mourning for Sima Yan, who died in 290.

8. The grand tutor is Yang Jun 楊駿 (ob. 291), who served as regent for the gravely ill Emperor Wu. He continued as grand tutor under Emperor Hui. See *Jin shu* 40.1177–78.

9. The bureau chief is Yang Jun, who was assassinated on 28 April 291 on orders of Empress Jia. See *Jin shu* 4.90.

10. Pan Yue was appointed prefect of Chang'an in 292.

11. His position was actually that of acting erudite, to which he was named in 293.

12. The taking of the youth cap occurred at the age of twenty. Fifty is the age at which one reputedly "understood Heaven's fate." Cf. *Lun yu* 2/4.

13. Pan Yue rose from prefect of Huai to acting gentleman in the secretariat of revenue.

14. Pan Yue's first resignation from office occurred in the late 280s after he committed an unspecified offense. See *Jin shu* 55.1503. His second resignation occurred in 291, when he was dismissed because of his association with Yang Jun.

15. This refers to the punishment he received after Yang Jun was executed in 291.

16. Because of his mother's illness, Pan Yue did not take up his appointment as erudite.

17. The three transfers were to the positions of adjudicator under the commandant of justice, master of documents for the grand tutor, and erudite.

18. He Changyu 和長輿 is He Qiao 和嶠 (ob. 292), a prominent official during the reign of Sima Yan. For his biography, see *Jin shu* 45.1283–84.

19. This characterization is based on a line in the first chapter of *Zhuangzi* (1.8b) in which Zhuangzi says to Huizi, who found no use for a large gourd: "You are certainly inept in using the large."

20. Cf. *Zuo zhuan*, Zhao 8 (Legge, *The Chinese Classics* 5: 622): "The words of a gentleman are true and corroborated by the evidence."

21. Cf. *Shangshu zhushu* 4.20b (291): "Good and able men are in office, all officials emulate one another, and all officials properly attend to their duties."

22. Cf. *Laozi* 44: "He who is satisfied suffers no disgrace; he who knows when to stop is never imperiled."

23. Cf. *Lun yu* 7/15: "To be rich and honorable by impropriety is to me nothing but a drifting cloud."

24. Cf. *Lun yu* 2/21: "The [*Classic of*] *Documents* says, 'Oh, by being filial above all else and being amicable with one's brothers, one can have an effect on government.' In this way, one also engages in government. Why need one actively engage in government?"

### "RHAPSODY ON THE TALL GATE PALACE"

1. Empress Chen, whose personal name was Ajiao 阿嬌, was the daughter of Emperor Wu's aunt Liu Piao 劉嫖, Princess Zhang 長公主. He took her for his wife when he was still heir designate. When he ascended the imperial throne in 141 B.C., he named her empress. She enjoyed great favor for over ten years, until Emperor Wu began to bestow his attention on the palace singer Wei Zifu. Empress Chen became extremely jealous, and plotted to have Wei Zifu removed from her privileged position. After Emperor Wu discovered that one of Empress Chen's daughters was accused of using black magic against Wei Zifu, he ordered that the empress be sequestered in the Tall Gate Palace, a detached palace twenty kilometers southeast of Chang'an. See *Shi ji* 49.1979; and *Han shu* 97A.3948. Note that the designation "Filial Emperor Wu" is an anachronism, for this is Emperor Wu's posthumous title, and since Sima Xiangru died before Emperor Wu, he could not possibly have known this name.

2. This event occurred in 130 B.C. See *Han shu* 6.164; and Dubs, *HFHD* 2: 41.

3. Zhuo Wenjun 卓文君 was Sima Xiangru's wife. She was the daughter of the wealthy Shu iron manufacturer Zhuo Wangsun 卓王孫, who renounced her when she eloped with Sima Xiangru. They lived in poverty until Wenjun was able to borrow money to open a wine shop in Linqiong 臨邛. Zhuo Wangsun eventually recognized their marriage and presented the couple with a large dowry, whereupon they gave up their wine business. See *Shi ji* 117.3000–1; and *Han shu* 57A.2530–1.

4. This statement does not agree with the historical record, which does not mention that Empress Chen regained the emperor's favor.

### "RHAPSODY ON RECALLING OLD FRIENDS"

1. There are several accounts of Xi Kang's playing the zither before his execution. According to the *Wenshi zhuan* 文士傳 (Biographies of Men of Letters) by Zhang Yin 張隱 (fourth cent.), on the eve of his execution Xi Kang was visited by his brothers and kinsmen. He asked his elder brother, "Did you bring my zither?" When his brother replied that he had done so, Xi Kang picked it up, tuned it, and played "Song of Great Peace." After finishing the song, he sighed and said, "'The Song of Great Peace' dies now with me!" See Li Shan's commentary, *Wen xuan* 16.12a–b; Yang Yong, *Shishuo xinyu jiaojian*, 6.266 (6/2); *Sanguo zhi* 21.606; and Holzman, *La Vie et la pensée de Hi K'ang*, p. 49.

2. Xiang Xiu was on his way to the capital, Luoyang, southwest of Xi Kang's home in Shanyang (see n. 3 below).

3. Xi Kang's home was in the Bailu 白鹿 Mountains. According to Zhu Jian (*Wen xuan jishi* 14.19a–b), this corresponds to the Tianmen 天門 Mountains in the area of modern Hui 輝 *xian* and Jiahuo 嘉獲 *xian*, Henan. See also *Shui jing zhu* 9.3b.

4. The Gulf of Yu 虞淵 is where the sun sets.

## *"RHAPSODY ON LAMENTING THE DEPARTED"*

1. Cf. *Kongzi jiayu*, 1.11b: "Kongzi said to Duke Ai, 'The gentleman enters the ancestral temple . . . and all of the vessels are present, but he does not see the deceased persons. If Your Majesty pines away and grieves on this account, the extent of your grief indeed can be known."

## *"RHAPSODY ON RECALLING OLD FRIENDS AND KIN"*

1. Marquis Dai 戴侯 was the posthumous title given to Yang Zhao. He was given the title of Viscount of Dongwu 東武 in 264 by Sima Zhao.
2. Pan Yue was a child prodigy and probably was well known in his native area of Xingyang 滎陽 (in modern Henan), which was also the home of Yang Zhao.
3. Pan Yue married Yang Zhao's daughter around 274. See Chiu-mi Lai, "River and Ocean," p. 66.
4. Daoyuan 道元 (also written 源) is the style name of Yang Zhao's eldest son, Yang Tan. Gongsi 公嗣 is the style name of the second son, Yang Shao.
5. It is not clear what hardship Pan Yue might be referring to. Chiu-mi Lai (ibid., pp. 71–72) suggests that it might be the death of Pan Yue's father around 275.
6. This could refer to Pan Yue's service in the capital or possibly to his postings in Heyang and Huai. If it is the latter, the line should be translated "outside the capital."
7. Songqiu 嵩丘 is another name for Mount Song. See LL. 11–12n to this rhapsody.

## *"RHAPSODY ON A WIDOW"*

1. Le'an 樂安 was a commandery southwest of the area of modern Zouping 鄒平, Shandong. See Tan Qixiang, *Zhongguo lishi ditu ji* 3: 11–12, 3–9. The *Shan gong biaozhu* 山公表注 (Annotated Tables of Shan Tao?) by Jia Bizhi 賈弼之 (n.d.), cited by Li Shan (*Wen xuan* 16.19a), says that Ren Hu's style name was Zixian 子咸, and that he held the position of chief commandant of imperial equipages.
2. Ren Hu's wife was the second daughter of Yang Zhao. See Jia Bizhi, *Shangong biaozhu* (cited by Li Shan in *Wen xuan* 16.19a).
3. Yang Zhao died in 275. We do not know when his wife died.
4. "Heaven" is a polite term for "husband."
5. The daughter, Zilan 子蘭, must have been about three years old when Ren Hu died. Pan Yue says in his "Lament for Ren Zilan" (cited by Li Shan, *Wen xuan* 16.19a): "Zilan is the daughter of Ren Zixian. Just as she turned three, she died before the mourning period for her father had ended." According to Zhao Qi 趙岐 (ca. 108–201), a child between the ages of two and three was

known as a "babe in arms" (*hai ti* 孩提). See *Mengzi zhushu* 孟子注疏, *Shisan jing zhushu* 13A.9b.

6. Ruan Yu was a prominent literary figure of the Jian'an period. When Ruan died in 212, Cao Pi 曹丕 (Emperor Wen of Wei, 187–226) ordered that poets of the court compose rhapsodies for his widow. See introductory note above.

### "RHAPSODY ON RESENTMENT"

1. The large tree that grew in graveyards was called the "arm-spanning tree" 拱木; see *Zuo zhuan*, Xi 32 (Legge, *The Chinese Classics* 5: 221). The old *yuefu* funeral song "Hao Village" ("Hao li ge" 蒿里歌) describes the gathering of souls in the land of the dead: "In Hao Village, whose lands are these? Here souls gather, wise and fool alike." See *Gu jin zhu* 古今注, *Sbby*, B.2a.

### "RHAPSODY ON LITERATURE"

1. The expression *yong xin* 用心 (lit., "using the heart") is ambiguous here. Owen (*Readings*, p. 78), who follows the usage in *Lun yu* 17/22 ("One who eats to the full all day long and exerts his mind at nothing in particular is a problem indeed!"), understands it in the sense of "strenuous efforts." Another sense of *yong xin* is "workings of the mind" or simply "mental outlook." Cf. *Zhuangzi* 5.15b: "In times past Shun asked Yao, 'How do you use your mind?' Shun replied, 'I am not arrogant toward those who have nowhere to complain, and I do not reject people who are destitute. I suffer for the dead, comfort young children, and grieve for widows. This is how I use my mind." I have deliberately kept my rendering ambiguous.

2. The word *wu* 物, which I have translated here as "objects," is ambiguous. Some Chinese commentators construe wu as "things of the world" or "objective phenomena"; see, inter alia, Guo Zhengyuan, *Wei Jin Nanbeichao wenxue lunwen mingpian yizhu*, p. 30; and Zhang Huaijin, *Wen fu yizhu*, p. 19. Others understand it as the content or "matter" of the literary work; see C. H. Wang, "Lu Ji Wen fu jiaoshi," p. 3 (161).

3. Cf. *Zuo zhuan*, Zhao 10 (Legge, *The Chinese Classics* 5: 630): "This is not a difficulty of knowing, but of putting it into practice." See Qian Zhongshu, *Guan zhui bian* 3: 1178–80.

4. Disturbed by the apparent immodesty of this remark, several scholars have attempted to emend the text, or reinterpret it to make Lu Ji seem less arrogant. These various interpretations have been neatly summarized by Owen (*Readings*, pp. 84–85), who rightly rejects them, partially on the grounds that such boasting was common in the rhapsodies of Lu Ji's time.

5. Lu Ji here draws on *Mao shi* 158/2: "To hew an axe-handle, to hew an axe-handle, / The model is not far away." The model here presumably is the model of the ancient writers.

6. The You Mao edition reads *dai* 逮 (reach) for *zhu* 逐 (pursue) of the *Liuchen*

edition. Li Shan (*Wen xuan* 17.2a) illustrates this line by citing the story of Wheel-wright Bian 扁 in the *Zhuangzi* (5.18b), who described the process of making a wheel as something that can only be done intuitively: "I view it from the perspective of my own work. If I chisel at the wheel too slowly, the chisel slips and does not hold firmly, but if I chisel too fast, the chisel wobbles and does not go in. Not too slow, not two fast—I feel it in my hand and respond from my heart. The mouth cannot express it in words, yet there is a special technique to it somewhere. I cannot teach it to my son, and my son cannot learn it from me." Although again Lu Ji is not completely clear on his meaning, the basic idea is that the process of creativity, whether one is making an axe-handle, a wheel, or a literary work, cannot be fully described in language.

### "RHAPSODY ON DANCE"

1. King Xiang is King Qingxiang 頃襄 of Chu (reg. 298-263 B.C.). Yunmeng 雲夢 was a marshy preserve located in the state of Chu. The kings of Chu used it for hunting and excursions. It extended from modern Yiyang 益陽 in Hunan, north to Jiangling and Anlu 安陸 in Hubei, and east to Wuhan. See Yves Hervouet, *Un Poète de cour sous les Han*, pp. 45-54.

2. Gaotang was a terrace in the Yunmeng park. King Xiang of Chu's encounter with a beautiful goddess reputedly took place there. See "Rhapsody on the Gaotang Shrine," attributed to Song Yu, this volume.

3. This is a classical definition of song that is attributed to Shun in the "Canon of Shun"; see *Shang shu zhushu* 3.26a (276).

4. Its "outer manifestation" (*xing* 形) of course is dance.

5. These are famous dance songs of Chu. On "Turbulent Chu" and "Binding Wind," see Knechtges, *Wen xuan* 2: 106, L. 399n.

6. The female talents (*cairen* 材人) usually refer to members of the imperial harem who were skilled in dance and song.

7. Cf. *Li ji zhushu* 43.8b (3397): "Now taut, now relaxed, this is the way of Kings Wen and Wu."

8. The "Axe-and-Shield" ("Gan qi" 干戚) are martial dances mentioned in the "Yue ji" 樂記 ("Record of Music") of the *Record of Rites* (*Li ji zhushu* 37.17a). The "Yue ji" is a composite text of various early Chinese writings on music. Here, I have called it the *Book of Music*.

9. "Graceful stepping" refers to *Mao shi* 165/3: "Bang, bang, they drum to us; / Stepping gracefully, they dance to us." This is a song in the "Lesser Elegantiae" of the *Classic of Songs*.

10. The *Record of Rites* (see *Li ji zhushu* 29.15b) specifies that at banquets given by a ruler for his officials, toasts should be limited to three.

11. *Mao shi* 298/3, which is in the "Eulogia of Lu" section of the *Classic of Songs*, contains the following lines: "The drums go boom, boom; / They return when drunk."

12. "All-encompassing Pond" ("Xian chi" 咸池) is one of the great pieces of ancient music variously attributed to either Yao or Huangdi. See *Shi ji* 24.1199;

and Chavannes, *Mh* 3:255. "Six Blossoms" ("Liu ying" 六英), also known as "Six Stalks" ("Liu jing" 六莖), is an ancient dance piece attributed to the legendar emperor Diku 帝嚳. See *Han shu* 22.1038.


## *"RHAPSODY ON THE LONG FLUTE"*

1. I assume "canons and odes" (*dian ya* 典雅) refer primarily to the *Classic of Documents* and *Classic of Songs* respectively.

2. Numerical arts (*shushu* 數術) are the various numerological and cosmological theories of *yinyang*, pitchpipes, five elements, etc., that were common in Han times.

3. From 126 to 133 Ma Rong served in the Bureau of Merit in Youfufeng 右扶風 commandery (administrative center: modern Xingping 興平, Shaanxi).

4. Mei 郿 was a prefecture in Youfufeng commandery. It was located east of modern Mei *xian*, Shaanxi. See Tan Qixiang, *Zhongguo lishi ditu ji* 2: 42–43, 4–3.

5. The *xianghe* 相和 (song for musical accompaniment) was a special category of music in Han times. Li Shan (*Wen xuan* 18.1b) cites the *Ge lu* 歌錄 (Song Register), which says that there were eighteen tunes in the *xianghe* category. The first was the "Qi chu" 氣出, the second, "Jing lie" 精列. The monograph on music in the *Song shu* (21.603–4) contains the texts for "Qi chu" and "Jing lie" songs by Cao Cao, which presumably were inspired by Han *xianghe* songs.

6. Wang Ziyuan is Wang Bao, author of "Rhapsody on the Panpipes" (*Wen xuan*, chap. 17).

7. Mei Sheng was a famous poet of the early Former Han. He has no extant piece on a musical instrument. Perhaps Ma Rong is referring to the description of a zither performance in Mei Sheng's "Seven Stimuli" (*Wen xuan* 34.3b–4b).

8. Liu Bokang 劉伯康 is Liu Xuan 劉玄. Li Shan (*Wen xuan* 18.1b) cites the *Wenzhang zhi* 文章志 (Notes on Literature) by Zhi Yu (ob. 312), which identifies Liu Xuan as a man of the Emperor Ming (reg. 58–75) period of the Later Han. He apparently wrote a "Rhapsody on the Mouth Organ," which is not extant.

9. Fu Wuzhong is Fu Yi. His only extant piece on a musical instrument is "Rhapsody on a Zither," fragments of which can be found in *Yiwen leiju* 44.783; and *Chuxue ji* 16.388.


## *"RHAPSODY ON THE ZITHER"*

1. Cf. "Preface to the Mao Version of the *Songs*" (*Wen xuan* 45.21a): "When words are insufficient [to express feeling], one expresses them in sighs. When sighing is insufficient, one sings them forth. When singing is insufficient, one unconsciously dances them with his hands and feet."

2. On the eight musical sounds, see Ma Rong, "Rhapsody on the Long Flute," this volume, L. 92n.

3. Cf. *Li ji zhushu* 37.15b (3315): "He who understands the feelings involved

in rites and music can initiate action, and he who understands the patterns of rites and music can transmit [teaching]."

## "RHAPSODY ON THE GAOTANG SHRINE"

1. Yunmeng is the large preserve and hunting park of the ancient state of Chu.

## "RHAPSODY ON THE GODDESS"

1. The *Wen xuan* text reads *wang* 王 (king) here, but the Song dynasty scholar Shen Gua 沈括 (1031–1095) proposes to emend the text to 玉, on the grounds that it is inappropriate in the following section to have the king's address to Song Yu prefaced by the word *bai* 白. In addition, the logic of the dialogue seems to favor having Song Yu relate his dream and then follow with a description of the goddess for the king, not as in the present version of the *Wen xuan* text. See Shen's detailed discussion in *Xin jiaozheng Mengxi bitan*, pp. 286–87.

## "RHAPSODY ON MASTER DENGTU THE LECHER"

1. According to Li Shan (*Wen xuan* 19.10a), Yangcheng 陽城 (east of modern Luohe 漯河 City, Henan) and Xiacai 下蔡 (north of modern Shou 壽 *xian*, Henan) were cities in which Chu nobility were enfeoffed. Thus, even the sophisticated lords of this area would be overwhelmed by the beauty of the eastern neighbor's daughter.

2. Li Shan (*Wen xuan* 19.10b) explains that Zhanghua 章華 is a place in Chu and that the grandee was a Chu native who was serving as an official in Qin, and had been sent as an envoy from Qin to the Chu court.

3. The meaning and punctuation of these lines is unclear. Li Shan (*Wen xuan* 19.10b) understands 愚亂之邪臣 as a self-deprecatory way for the Zhanghua grandee to refer to himself. Hu Shaoying (*Wen xuan jianzheng* 21.10b–11a) proposes that 愚亂之邪 is a single line and that 臣 should be the initial word in the following line. Hu interprets 邪 as the interrogative/exclamatory particle 耶. However, I am not sure what 愚亂之耶 would mean. Xiao Jizong (*Xian Qin wenxue xuanzhu*, pp. 216–17, n. 15) interprets this phrase as applying to Master Dengtu. Following Xiao, these lines would read: "A stupid licentious courtier [Dengtu] claimed that Song Yu was inferior in upholding virtue." I have followed Li Shan here, but the alternative suggested by Professor Xiao is also possible.

4. Xianyang 咸陽 (northeast of modern Xianyang, Shaanxi) was the capital of Qin. Handan 邯鄲 (modern Handan, Hebei) was the capital of the state of Zhao, and a city renowned for its beautiful women.

5. Zheng and Wei are the states of the Chunqiu period notorious for their

411

so-called licentious customs and music. The Zhen 溱 and Wei 洧 rivers, which flowed through these states, were known as the sites of illicit love trysts. See *Mao shi* 95.

6. This line is derived from *Mao shi* 81, a song in the "Airs of Zheng" section of the *Classic of Songs*.

### "RHAPSODY ON THE LUO RIVER GODDESS"

1. "Third year of Huangchu" should read "fourth year of Huangchu." In Huangchu 3 (222) Cao Zhi was installed as prince of Juancheng 鄄城 (northwest of modern Juancheng, Shandong). According to his biography in the *Sanguo zhi* (19.562), he was transferred to Yongqiu 雍丘 (modern Qi 杞 *xian*, Henan) in Huangchu 4 (223). According to Cao Zhi's preface to his "Poem Presented to Biao, Prince of Baima" (*Wen xuan* 24.5a), in the fifth month of Huangchu 4, he and two of his brothers attended court in the capital. Thus, Li Shan (*Wen xuan* 19.12a) claims that Huangchu 3 is an error. For a detailed discussion see Lu Kanru, *Zhonggu wenxue xinian* 2: 455–57.

2. See "Rhapsody on the Goddess" attributed to Song Yu, this volume.

# Bibliography

## ABBREVIATIONS

| | |
|---|---|
| AM | Asia Major |
| BMFEA | Bulletin of the Musuem of Far Eastern Antiquities |
| BSOAS | Bulletin of the School of Oriental and African Studies |
| CLEAR | Chinese Literature: Essays, Articles, Reviews |
| HFHD | History of the Former Han Dynasty |
| HJAS | Harvard Journal of Asiatic Studies |
| JAOS | Journal of the American Oriental Society |
| Mh | Mémoires historiques |
| MS | Monumenta Serica |
| Sbby | Sibu beiyao |
| Sbck | Sibu congkan |
| TP | T'oung Pao |

Aoki Masaru 青木正兒. "'Shō' no rekishi to jigi no hensen" 嘯の歷史と字義の變遷, *Ritsumeikan bungaku* 150–51 (1957): 179–87.

Asano Michiari 淺野通有. "Sō Gyoku no sakuhin no shingi ni tsuite" 宋玉の作品の真偽について, *Kambun gakkai kaihō* 12 (1961): 3–12.

*Baihu tongyi* 白虎通義. Attributed to Ban Gu 班固 (32–92). In *Han Wei congshu*.

*Bencao gangmu* 本草綱目. Compiled by Li Shizhen 李時珍 (1518–1593). 4 vols. Beijing: Renmin weisheng chubanshe, 1975–1982.

Berkowitz, Alan. "Patterns of Reclusion in Early and Early Medieval China: A Study of the Formulation of the Practice of Reclusion in China and Its Portrayal." Ph.D. diss., University of Washington, 1989.

Bi Wanchen 畢萬忱, He Peixiong 何沛雄, and Luo Kanglie 羅忼烈, ed. and comm. *Zhongguo lidai fu xuan* 中國歷代賦選, *Xian Qin Liang Han juan* 先秦兩漢卷. Nanjing: Jiangsu jiaoyu chubanshe, 1990.

Bielenstein, Hans. *The Bureaucracy of Han Times.* Cambridge: Cambridge University Press, 1980.

Birch, Cyril, and Donald Keene, eds. *Anthology of Chinese Literature: From Early Times to the Fourteenth Century.* New York: Grove Press, 1965.

Birrell, Anne. *Popular Songs and Ballads of Han China.* London: Unwin Hyman, 1988.

Bodde, Derk. *China's First Unifier: A Study of the Ch'in Dynasty as Seen in the Life of Li Ssu.* 1938. Rpt., Hong Kong: Hong Kong University Press, 1975.

413

Boltz, William G. "Evocations of the Moon, Excitations of the Sea," *JAOS* 106.1 (1986): 23–32.

Cai Tingji 蔡廷吉. *Jia Yi yanjiu* 賈誼研究. Taipei: Wen shi zhe chubanshe, 1984.

Cai Xiongxiang 蔡雄祥. "Wang Bao ji qi zuopin" 王褒及其作品, *Xuecui* 19.6 (1977): 14–18.

Cao Daoheng 曹道衡. "Guanyu Bao Zhao de jiashi he jiguan" 關於鮑照的家世和籍貫, *Wen shi* (1979: 7): 191–97. Rpt. in *Zhonggu wenxue shi lunwenji* 中古文學史論文集, pp. 368–77. Beijing: Zhonghua shuju, 1986.

———. "Bao Zhao jipian shi wen de xiezuo shijian" 鮑照幾篇詩文的寫作時間, *Wen shi* 16 (1982): 189–202. Rpt. in *Zhonggu wenxue shi lunwenji*, pp. 378–400.

———. "Jiang Yan" 江淹. In Lü Huijian et al., *Zhongguo lidai zhuming wenxuejia pingzhuan* 中國歷代著明文學家評傳 1: 503–25. Jinan: Shandong jiaoyu chubanshe, 1985.

———. "Bao Zhao" 鮑照. In *Zhongguo lidai zhuming wenxuejia pingzhuan* 1: 459–82.

———. *Han Wei Liuchao cifu* 漢魏六朝辭賦. Shanghai: Shanghai guji chubanshe, 1989.

——— and Shen Yucheng 沈玉成. *Nanbeichao wenxue shi* 南北朝文學史. Beijing: Renmin wenxue chubanshe, 1991.

Cao Minggang 曹明綱. "Song Yu fu zhenwei bian" 宋玉賦真偽辨, *Shanghai shifan xueyuan xuebao* (1984: 2): 53–57.

Chan Ping-leung (Chen Bingliang 陳炳良). "Zhongguo gudai shenhua xinshi liangze" 中國古代神話新釋兩則, *Tsing Hua Journal of Chinese Studies*, n.s. 7 (1969): 206–32.

Chavannes, Edouard, trans. *Les Mémoires historiques de Se-ma Ts'ien*. 6 vols. 1895–1905. Rpt., Taipei: Chengwen, 1969.

Chen Enliang 陳恩良. *Lu Ji wenxue yanjiu* 陸機文學研究. Hong Kong: Guanghua shuju, 1969.

Chen Hongtian 陳宏天, Zhao Fuhai 趙福海, and Chen Fuxing 陳復興, eds. *Zhaoming Wen xuan yizhu* 昭明文選譯注. Vols. 1–2, 1988; vols. 3–4, 1992. Changchun: Jinlin wenshi chubanshe.

Chen Meizu 陳美足. *Nanchao Yan Xie shi yanjiu* 南朝顏謝詩研究. Taipei: Wenjin chubanshe, 1989.

Chen, Robert Shanmu. "A Study of Bao Zhao and His Poetry." Ph.D. diss., University of British Columbia, 1989.

———. "A Biographical Study of Bao Zhao," *Tsing Hua Journal of Chinese Studies* 21.1 (1991): 125–200.

Chen Shengyong 陳勝勇. "Jianguo yilai Song Yu ji qi zuopin yanjiu zongshu" 建國以來宋玉及其作品研究綜述, *Yuwen daobao* (Hangzhou daxue Zhongwen xi) (1985: 6): 9–12.

Chen Shih-hsiang 陳世驤. "Literature as Light Against Darkness," *National Peking University Semicentennial Papers*, no. 11 (Peiping: College of Arts, 1948), pp. 47–70.

———. *Essay on Literature*. Portland, Me.: Anthoensen Press, 1953.

———. Ikkai Tomoyoshi 一海知義, trans., "Riku Ki no shōgai to 'Bun fu' seikakuna nendai" 陸機の生涯と'文賦'の正確な年代, *Chūgoku bungaku hō* 8 (1958): 50–78.

Chen Yibai 陳一百. *Cao Zijian shi yanjiu* 曹子建詩研究. Shanghai: Shangwu yinshuguan, 1928.

Chen Yixin 陳貽焮. "Bao Zhao he tade zuopin" 鮑照和他的作品, *Wenxue yichan* (1957): 182–90.

Cheng Renqing 程仁卿. "Dui 'Guanyu Song Yu' yiwen de yijian" 對'關於宋玉'一文的意見, *Wen shi zhe* (1955: 5): 46–47.

Chi Wenjun 遲文浚, Xu Zhigang 許志剛, and Shen Xulian 沈緒連, eds. *Lidai fu cidian* 歷代賦辭典. Shenyang: Liaoning renmin chubanshe, 1992.

Chien Tsung-wu 簡宗梧. *Sima Xiangru Yang Xiong ji qi fu zhi yanjiu* 司馬相如揚雄及其賦之研究. Taipei: published by the author, n.d.

———. "'Changmen fu' bianzheng"《長門賦》辨證, *Dalu zazhi* 46.2 (1973): 57–60. Rpt. in *Han fu shi lun* 漢賦史論 (Taipei: Dong da tushu gongsi, 1993), pp. 53–61.

———. "'Gaotang fu' zhuancheng shidai zhi shangque"《高唐賦》撰成時代之商榷. In *Han fu shi lun*, pp. 63–97.

Ch'ü T'ung-tsu. *Han Social Structure*. Seattle: University of Washington Press, 1972.

*Chuci buzhu* 楚辭補注. Edited and commented on by Hong Xingzu 洪興祖 (1070–1135). Hong Kong: Zhonghua shuju, 1963.

*Chuxue ji* 初學記. Compiled by Xu Jian 徐堅 (659–729). Beijing: Zhonghua shuju, 1962.

Coblin, W. South. *A Handbook of Eastern Han Sound Glosses*. Hong Kong: Chinese University Press, 1983.

Creel, Herrlee G. *Shen Pu-hai, A Chinese Political Philosopher of the Fourth Century* B.C. Chicago: University of Chicago Press, 1974.

Crump, James I., trans. *Chan-Kuo Ts'e*. Oxford: Oxford University Press, 1970.

Cutter, Robert Joe. "Cao Zhi and His Poetry." Ph.D. diss., University of Washington, 1983.

———. "Cao Zhi's (192–232) Symposium Poems," *CLEAR* 6.1 and 2 (1984): 1–32.

———. "The Incident at the Gate: Cao Zhi, the Succession, and Literary Fame," *TP* 71 (1985): 228–62.

———. "On Reading Cao Zhi's 'Three Good Men': *Yong shi shi* or *Deng lin shi*?" *CLEAR* 11 (December 1989): 1–11.

———. "The Death of Empress Zhen: Fiction and Historiography in Early Medieval China," *JAOS* 112.4 (1992): 567–83.

Dai Mingyang 戴明揚, ed. and comm. *Xi Kang ji jiaozhu* 嵇康集校注. Beijing: Remin wenxue chubanshe, 1962.

Dai Zhen 戴震 (1724–1777). *Fangyan shuzheng* 方言疏證. Shanghai: Shanghai guji chubanshe, 1984.

Deng Yongkang 鄧永康. "Cao Zijian nianpu xinbian" 曹子建年譜新編, *Dalu zazhi* 34.1 (1967): 13–19; 34.2 (1967): 26–32; 34.3 (1967): 30–32.

———. *Wei Cao Zijian xiansheng Zhi nianpu* 魏曹子建先生植年譜. Taipei: Shangwu yinshuguan, 1981.

Deng Yuanxuan 鄧元煊. "Guanyu Song Yu pingjia zhong de yige wenti" 關於宋玉評價中的一個問題, *Sichuan shiyuan xuebao* (1985: 1). Rpt. in *Zhongguo gudai jindai wenxue yanjiu* (1985: 7): 69–76.

415

DeWoskin, Kenneth. "Early Chinese Music and the Origins of Aesthetic Terminology." In *Theories of the Arts in China*, edited by Susan Bush and Christian Murck, pp. 187–214. Princeton: Princeton University Press, 1983.

Diény, Jean-Pierre. "Les Septs Tristesses (*Qi Ai*). A propos des deux versions d'un poème à chanté de Cao Zhi," *TP* 65 (1979): 51–65.

Ding Fulin 丁福林. "Bao Zhao shi wen xinian kaobian" 鮑照詩文系年考辨, *Zhonghua wenshi luncong* 27.3 (1983): 277–87.

———. "Guanyu Bao Zhao de jiguan" 關於鮑照的籍貫, *Wen shi* 20 (1983): 253–58.

———. "Bao Zhao ren qianjun canjun de shijian" 鮑照任前軍參軍的時間, *Wen shi* 22 (1984): 190.

*Du Gongbu shiji* 杜工部詩集. Hong Kong: Zhonghua shuju, 1972.

Dubs, Homer H., trans. *History of the Former Han Dynasty*. 3 vols. Baltimore: Waverly Press, 1938–1955.

Dunn, Hugh. *Ts'ao Chih: The Life of a Princely Chinese Poet*. Taipei: China News, 1970. Rpt. under the title *Cao Zhi: The Life of a Princely Chinese Poet*. Beijing: New World Press, 1983.

Duyvendak, J. J. L., trans. *The Book of Lord Shang*. Chicago: University of Chicago Press, 1928.

Eberhard, Alide, and Wolfram Eberhard. *Die Mode der Han- und Chou-zeit*. Antwerp: DeSikkel, 1946.

Emmerich, Reinhard. "Chu und Changsha am Ende der Qin-Zeit und Beginn der Han-Zeit," *Oriens Extremus* 34 (1991): 85–137.

———. "Untersuchungen zu Jia Yi (200–168 v.Chr.)." Hamburg: Habilitationsschrift, University of Hamburg, 1991.

Eoyang, Eugene. "The Wang Chao-chün Legend: Configurations of the Classic," *CLEAR* 4.1 (January 1982): 3–22.

Erkes, Eduard. "The Feng-Fu (Song of the Wind)," *Asia Major* 3 (1926): 526–33.

———. "The Song of the Goddess by Sung Yüh," *TP* 25 (1927–28): 387–402.

*Erya yishu*. See Hao Yixing.

Fan Ning 范寧. "Niu lang Zhi nü gushi de yanbian" 牛郎織女故事的演變, *Wenxue yichan zengkan* 1 (1955): 42–33.

Fang, Achilles. "Rhymeprose on Literature: The *Wen-fu* of Lu Chi (A.D. 261–303)," *HJAS* 14 (1951): 527–66.

Frankel, Hans H. "Fifteen Poems by Ts'ao Chih: An Attempt at a New Approach," *JAOS* 84 (1964): 1–14.

———. *The Flowering Plum and the Palace Lady*. New Haven: Yale University Press, 1976.

———. "The Problem of Authenticity in the Works of Ts'ao Chih." In *Essays in Commemoration of the Golden Jubilee of the Fung Ping Shan Library (1932–1982)*, pp. 183–201. Hong Kong: Fung Ping Shang Library, 1982.

Frodsham, J. D. "The Nature Poetry of Pao Chao," *Orient/West* 9.5 (1964): 21–30.

Fu Lipu 傅隸樸, ed. and comm. *Fu xuan zhu* 賦選注. Taipei: Zhengzhong shuju, 1977.

Fu Xuancong 傅璇琮. "Pan Yue xinian kaozheng" 潘岳繫年考證, *Wen shi* 14 (1982): 237–57.

Fujii Mamoru 藤井守. "Hō Shō no fu" 鮑照の賦, *Hiroshima Daigaku bungaku hō* 34 (1975): 230–44.

———. "Sei Shin jidai no gafu shi—Riku Ki o chūshin toshite" 西晉時代の樂府詩—陸機お中心として, *Hiroshima Daigaku bungakubu kiyō* 36 (1976): 237–58.

Fujiwara Takashi 藤原尚. "Sōfu to jifu no bunkiten—Sō Gyoku no fu ni tsuite" 騷賦と辭賦の分歧點 —宋玉の賦について. In *Obi hakashi taikyū kinen Chūgoku bungaku ronshū* 小尾博士退休紀念中國文學論集, pp. 113–35. Hiroshima: Daiichi gakushūsha, 1976.

———. "Han Ko no fu kan" 班固の賦觀, *Hiroshima daigaku bungakubu kiyō* (1981: 1): 182–202.

Funazu Tomihiko 船津富彦. "Gi Shin bungaku ni okeru shōgō ni tsuite" 魏晉文學における嘯傲について, *Tōyō bungaku kenkyū* 11 (1963): 34–50.

———. "Sō Shoku no yūsenshi ron" 曹植の遊仙詩論, *Tōyō bungaku kenkyū* 13 (1965): 49–65.

Fusek, Lois. "The 'Kao-t'ang Fu,'" *Monumenta Serica* 30 (1972–73): 392–425.

Ge Hong 葛洪 (ca. 280–ca. 340). *Baopuzi* 抱朴子. *Sbby*.

Giles, Herbert A. "Poe's 'Raven'—in Chinese," *Adversaria Sinica* (1914): 1–10.

Glahn, Else. "Some Chou and Han Architectural Terms," *BMFEA* 50 (1978): 105–25.

Gong Kechang 龔克昌. *Han fu yanjiu* 漢賦研究. Jinan: Shandong wenyi chubanshe, 1990.

———. "Zhang Heng 張衡." In Lü Huijuan et al., *Zhongguo lidai zhuming wenxuejia pingzhuan*, pp. 187–203.

Goormaghtigh, Georges. *L'Art du Qin, Deux textes d'esthétique musicale chinoise*. Brussels: Institut Belge des Hautes Études Chinoises, 1990.

Graham, A. C. *Chuang Tzu: The Inner Chapters*. London: Routledge, Chapman & Hall, 1981.

———. "A neglected pre-Han philosophical text: Ho-kuan-tzu," *BSOAS* 52.3 (1989): 497–509.

Graham, William T., Jr. "Mi Heng's 'Rhapsody on a Parrot,'" *HJAS* 39.1 (1979): 39–54.

Greatrex, Roger. *The Bowu Zhi: An Annotated Translation*. Stockholm: Skrifter utgivna av Föreningen för Orientaliska Studier, no. 20, 1987.

*Guangya shuzheng*. See Wang Niansun.

*Guanzi* 管子. *Sbby*.

*Gujin wenxuan* 古今文選. 4 vols. Taipei: Guoyu ribao, 1962.

*Gujin zhu* 古今注. Compiled by Cui Bao 崔豹 (fl. A.D. 290–306). *Sbby*.

Guo Maoqian 郭茂倩 (12th cent.). *Yuefu shiji* 樂府詩集 Beijing: Zhonghua shuju, 1979.

Guo Moruo 郭沫若. "Lun Cao Zhi" 論曹植. In *Lishi renwu* 歷史人物, pp. 3–29. Shanghai: Haiyan, 1947.

———. "Guanyu Song Yu" 關於宋玉, *Xin jianshe* (1955: 2): 42–46.

Guo Shaoyu 郭紹虞, ed. *Zhongguo lidai wenlun xuan* 中國歷代文論選. 3 vols. 1947. Rpt., Hong Kong: Zhonghua shuju, 1979.

*Guo yu* 國語. In *Sbby*.

Guo Zhengyuan 郭正元, ed. and comm. *Wei Jin Nanbeichao wenxue lunwen mingpian yizhu* 魏晉南北朝文學論文名篇譯注. Wuhan: Hebei renmin chubanshe, 1986.

*Guwen yuan* 古文苑. Probably compiled by Sun Zhu 孫洙 (1032–1080). In *Dainan'ge congshu*.

Hagerty, Michael J. "Tai K'ai-chih's *Chu-p'u*: A Fifth Century Monograph of Bamboos Written in Rhyme with Commentary," *HJAS* 11 (1948): 372–440.

Hamill, Sam. *The Art of Writing*. Minneapolis: Milkweed Editions, 1991.

*Han Feizi* 韓非子. In *Sbby*.

*Han shi waizhuan* 韓詩外傳. In *Xuejin taoyuan*.

*Han shu* 漢書. Compiled by Ban Gu 班固 (32–92). Beijing: Zhonghua shuju, 1962.

*Han Wei congshu* 漢魏叢書. Edited by Cheng Rong 程榮 (Ming). Taipei: Xinxing shuju, 1966.

Hanyu dazidian bianji weiyuanhui 漢語大字典編輯委員會 and Hubei cishu chubanshe 湖北辭書出版社. *Hanyu da zidian* 漢語大字典. 8 vols. Wuhan: Hubei cishu chubanshe and Sichuan cishu chubanshe, 1986–1990.

Hao Yixing 郝懿行 (1757–1825), ed. and comm. *Erya yishu* 爾雅義疏. In *Sbby*.

Harada Yoshito 原田淑人. *Kan Rikuchō no fukushoku* 漢六朝の服飾. 1937. Rev. ed., Tokyo: Tōyō bunko, 1967.

Hart, James. "The Discussion of the *Wu-yi* Bells in the *Kuo-yü*," *MS* 29 (1970–71): 391–418.

Hawkes, David, trans. *The Songs of the South: An Anthology of Ancient Chinese Poems by Qu Yuan and Other Poets*. Harmondsworth: Penguin Books, 1985.

*Heguanzi* 鶡冠子. In *Sbby*.

Henricks, Robert G. "Hsi K'ang (223–262): His Life, Literature, and Thought." Ph.D. diss., University of Wisconsin, 1976.

———. *Philosophy and Argumentation in Third-Century China: The Essays of Hsi K'ang*. Princeton: Princeton University Press, 1983.

Hervouet, Yves. *Un Poète de cour sous les Han: Sseu-ma Siangjou*. Paris: Presses Universitaires de France, 1964.

———. *Le Chapitre 117 du Che-ki (Biographie de Sseu-ma Siang-jou)*. Paris: Presses Universitaries de France, 1972.

Hightower, James Robert. "The Fu of T'ao Ch'ien," *HJAS* 17 (1954): 169–230.

———. "Chia Yi's 'Owl Fu,'" *Asia Major*, n.s., 8 (1959): 125–30.

Ho, Kenneth P. H. 何沛雄. "Xiancun Cao Zhi fu kaolüe" 現存曹植賦考略, *Huaxue yuekan* 149 (1984): 7–22.

Ho Peng-yoke. *The Astronomical Chapters of the Chin shu*. Paris and the Hague: Mouton, 1966.

Holzman, Donald. *La Vie et la pensée de Hi K'ang* (223–262 Ap J. C.). Leiden: E. J. Brill, 1957.

———. "La Poésie de Ji Kang," *Journal asiatique* 268 (1980): 107–77, 323–78.

———. "Ts'ao Chih and the Immortals," *AM*, 3rd series, 1.1 (1988): 15–57.

Honda Wataru 本田濟. "Sō Shoku to sono jidai" 曹植とその時代, *Tōhōgaku* 3 (1952): 53–60.

Hong Shunlong 洪順隆, ed. *Zhongwai Liuchao wenxue yanjiu wenxian mulu* 中外六朝文學研究文獻目錄. Taipei: Hanxue yanjiu zhongxin, 1992.

———. "Lun 'Luoshen fu' dui Liuchao fu tan de touying" 論洛神賦對六朝賦壇的投映, *Xinya xuebao jikan* 13 (1994): 91–114.

*Hou Han shu* 後漢書. Compiled by Fan Ye 范曄 (398–446). Beijing: Zhonghua shuju, 1963.

Hsü, S. N. *Anthologie de la littérature chinoise des origines à nos jours*. Paris: Librarie Delarave, 1933.

Hu Chusheng 胡楚生. "*Wen xuan* 'Bie fu' Li zhu buzheng" 文選別賦李注補正, *Nanyang daxue xuebao* 1 (1967): 69–75.

Hu Nianyi 胡念貽. "Song Yu zuopin de zhenwei wenti" 宋玉作品的真偽問題, *Wenxue yichan zengkan* 1 (1956): 40–55.

Hu Shaoying 胡紹煐, ed. *Wen xuan jianzheng* 文選箋證. Preface dated 1835. Rpt. in *Xuan xue congshu* Taipei: Guangwen shuju, 1966.

Hu Zhiji 胡之驥 (fl. 1598), ed. and comm. *Jiang Wentong ji huizhu* 江文通集彙注. Beijing: Zhonghua shuju, 1984.

*Huainanzi* 淮南子. In *Sbby*.

Huang Kan 黃侃 (1886–1935), comm. Huang Zhuo 黃焯, ed. *Wen xuan pingdian* 文選平點. Shanghai: Shanghai guji chubanshe, 1985.

Huang Ruiyun 黃瑞雲, ed. and comm. *Lidai shuqing xiaofu xuan* 歷代抒情小賦選. Shanghai: Shanghai guji chubanshe, 1986.

Huangfu Mi 皇甫謐 (215–282). *Gaoshi zhuan* 高士傳. In *Sbby*.

Hughes, E. R. *The Art of Letters: Lu Chi's "Wen Fu," A.D. 302*. Princeton: Princeton University Press, 1951.

Hui Dong 惠棟. *Zhou yi shu* 周易述. In *Hu Wei Hui Dong zhi Yixue* 胡渭惠棟之易學. Taipei: Dingwen shuju, 1975.

Hulsewé, A. F. P. *China in Central Asia. The Early Stage: 125 B.C.–A.D. 23*. Sinica Leidensia, vol. 14. Leiden: E. J. Brill, 1979.

———. "The Two Early Han *I Ching* Specialists Called Jing Fang 京房," *TP* 72 (1986): 161–62.

Idema, Wilt L. *Wie zich pas heeft gebaad tikt het stof van zijn kap*. Leiden: Stichting De Lantaarn, 1985.

Inahata Kōichirō 稲田耕一郎. "Sō Gokyu ron—sono bungakuteki hyōka no tei-ritsu o megutte" 宋玉論——その文學的評價の定立おめぐって. In *Chūgoku bungaku ronshū (Mekada Makoto hakushi koki kinen)* 中國文學論集 (目加田誠博士古稀紀念), pp. 67–97. Tokyo: Ryukei, 1974.

———. "Sō Gyoku no betsushū—sono hensan, rufu, sanitsu no aidani" 宋玉の別集——その編纂, 流布, 散佚のあいだに, *Chūgoku koten kenkyū* 20 (1975): 101–21.

———. "*Sō Gyoku shū* hosetsu—*Sō Gyoku shi* kara *Sō Gyoku shū* e" 宋玉集補説——宋玉子から宋玉集へ, *Chūgoku bungaku kenkyū* 7 (1981): 38–56.

Itō Masafumi 伊藤正文 "Hō Shō den ronkō" 鮑照傳論稿, *Kobe daigaku bungakukai kenkyū* 14 (1957): 18–55.

———. *Sō Shoku* 曹植. Tokyo: Iwanami, 1964.

——— and Ikkai Tomoyoshi 一海知義, trans. *Kan Gi Rikuchō Tō Sō sanbun sen* 漢魏六朝唐宋散文選. Tokyo: Heibonsha, 1970.

Itō Tomio 伊藤富雄. "Ka Gi no Fukuchō no fu no tachiba" 賈誼の鵩鳥の賦の立場, *Chūgoku bungakuhō* 13 (1960): 1–24.

Jiang Fan 蔣凡. "Ban Gu de wenxue sixiang" 班固的文學思想, *Fudan xuebao* (1985: 2): 68–76. Rpt. in *Zhongguo gudai jindai wenxue yanjiu* (1985: 9): 67–75.

Jiang Liangfu 姜亮夫. *Lu Pingyuan nianpu* 陸平原年譜. Shanghai: Gudian wenxue chubanshe, 1957.

——. *Zhang Hua nianpu* 張華年譜. Shanghai: Gudian wenxue chubanshe, 1957.

——. "Song Yu jianshu" 宋玉簡述. In Jiang Liangfu, *Chuci xue lunwen ji* 楚辭學論文集, pp. 465–70. Shanghai: Shanghai guji chubanshe, 1984.

*Jiang Wentong ji* 江文通集. In *Sbby*.

Jiang Zuyi 蔣祖怡 and Han Quanxin 韓泉欣. "Lu Ji" 陸機. In Lü Huijian et al., *Zhongguo lidai zhuming wenxuejia pingzhuan* 1: 357–77.

Jin Guoyong 金國永, ed. and comm. *Sima Xiangru ji jiaozhu* 司馬相如集校注. Shanghai: Shanghai guji chubanshe, 1993.

*Jin shu* 晉書. Compiled by Fang Xuanling 房玄齡 (578–648) et al. Beijing: Zhonghua shuju, 1974.

Jin Taosheng 金濤聲, ed. and comm. *Lu Ji ji* 陸機集. Beijing: Zhonghua shuju, 1982.

Johnsgard, Paul A. *Cranes of the World*. Bloomington: Indiana University Press, 1983.

Kai Katsuji 甲斐勝二. "Xiang Xiu 'Si jiu fu' shi shi" 向秀《思舊》賦試釋, *Wen shi zhe* (1990: 5): 53–56.

Kanaya Osamu 金谷治. "Ka Gi no fu ni tsuite" 賈誼の賦について, *Chūgoku bungaku hō* 8 (1958): 1–25.

Kang Rongji 康榮吉. *Lu Ji ji qi shi* 陸機及其詩. Taipei: Jiaxin shuini wenhua jijinhui, 1969.

Karlgren, Bernhard. "Legends and Cults in Ancient China," *BMFEA* (1946): 199–365.

——. "Glosses on the Book of Documents," *BMFEA* 20 (1948): 39–315; 21 (1949): 63–206.

Kent, George W. *Worlds of Dust and Jade: 47 Poems and Ballads of the Third Century Chinese Poet Ts'ao Chih*. New York: Philosophical Library, 1969.

Kinami Norio 木金德雄. "Gan Enshi no shōgai to shisō 顏延之の生涯と思想, *Nihon Chūgoku gakkai hō* 15 (1963): 120–41.

Knechtges, David R. "Ssu-ma Hsiang-ju's 'Tall Gate Palace Rhapsody,'" *HJAS* 41.1 (1981): 47–64.

——. "A Journey to Morality: Chang Heng's *The Rhapsody on Pondering the Mystery*." In *Essays in Commemoration of the Golden Jubilee of the Fung Ping Shan Library*, pp. 162–82. Hong Kong: Fung Ping Shan Library, 1983.

——. trans. Compiled by Xiao Tong (501–531). *Wen xuan, or Selections of Refined Literature*. Vol. 1, *Rhapsodies on Metropolises and Capitals*. Princeton: Princeton University Press, 1982.

——. *Wen xuan, or Selections of Refined Literature*. Vol. 2. *Rhapsodies on Sacrifices, Hunting, Travel, Sightseeing, Palaces and Halls, Rivers and Seas*. Princeton: Princeton University Press, 1987.

Komori Ikuko 小守郁子. "Sō Shoku shi shokan" 曹植詩所感, *Nagoya daigaku bungakubu kenkyū ronshū* 63, *tetsugaku* 21 (March 1974): 91–114.

——. "Sō Shoku ron" 曹植論, *Nagoya daigaku bungakubu kenkyū ronshū* 69, *tetsugaku* 23 (March 1976): 267–302.

Kong Jingqing 孔鏡清 and Han Quanxin 韓泉欣, ed. and comm. *Liang Han zhujia sanwen xuan* 兩漢諸家散文選. Hong Kong: Sanlian shudian, 1994.

*Kongzi jiayu* 孔子家語. In *Sbck*.

Konishi Noburo 小西狩. "Shichiban mai ni kansuru shosetsu ni tsuite" 七盤舞に關する諸説について, *Nihon Chūgoku gakkai hō* 14 (1962): 79–92.

Kotewall, Robert, and Norman L. Smith, eds. *The Penguin Book of Chinese Verse*. Harmondsworth: Penguin Books, 1962.

Kotzenberg, Heike. *Der Dichter Pao Chao (+466): Untersuchungen zu Leben und Werk*. Bonn: Rheinsiche Friedrich-Wilhelms-Universität, 1970.

Kōzen Hiroshi 興膳宏. "Kei Kō shi shōron" 嵇康詩小論, *Chūgoku bungaku hō* 15 (1961): 1–32.

———. "Kei Kō no hishō" 嵇康の飛翔, *Chūgoku bungaku hō* 16 (1962): 1–28.

———. *Han Gaku Riku Ki* 潘岳陸機. Tokyo: Chikuma shobō, 1973.

Kroll, Paul W. "The Dancing Horses of T'ang," *TP* 67 (1981): 240–68.

K'uai Shu-p'ing. "Six Poems of Ts'ao Tzu-chien," *National Peking University Semi-Centennial Papers, College of Arts*, no. 14 (Beijing, 1948): 24–31.

Künstler, Mieczyslaw Jerzy. *Ma Jong vie et oeuvre*. Warsaw: Panstowe Wydawnictwo Naukowe, 1969.

Lai, Chiu-mi. "River and Ocean: The Third-Century Verse of Pan Yue and Lu Ji." Ph.D. diss., University of Washington, 1990.

Lau, D. C., trans. *Lao Tzu Tao Te Ching*. Harmondsworth: Penguin Books, 1963.

Legge, James, trans. *The Chinese Classics*. Vol. 1, *Confucian Analects, The Great Learning and the Doctrine of the Mean*. 1861. Rpt., Taipei: Wenxin shudian, 1963.

———. *The Chinese Classics*. Vol. 5, *The Ch'un Ts'ew with the Tso Chuen*. 1872. Rpt., Taipei: Wenxin shudian, 1963.

———. *The Chinese Classics*. Vol. 3, *The Shoo King*. 1865. Rpt., Taipei: Wenxin shudian, 1963.

Li Baojun 李寶均. *Cao shi fuzi he Jian'an wenxue* 曹氏父子和建安文學. Shanghai: Zhonghua shuju, 1962.

Li Changzhi 李長之. "Xi Jin shiren Pan Yue de shengping ji qi chuangzuo" 西晉詩人潘岳的生平及其創作, *Guowen yuekan* 68 (June 1968): 25–32.

Li Chendong 李辰冬. "Cao Zhi de zuopin fenqi" 曹植的作品分期, *Dalu zazhi* 15.4 (1957): 9–14.

Li Fengmao 李豐楙. *Liuchao Sui Tang xiandao lei xiaoshuo yanjiu* 六朝隋唐仙道類小説研究. Taipei: Xuesheng shuju, 1986.

Li Hui 李暉 and Yu Fei 于非, ed. and comm. *Lidai fu yishi* 歷代賦譯釋. Harbin: Heilongjiang renmin chubanshe, 1984.

*Li ji zhushu* 禮記注疏. In *Shisan jing zhushu*.

Li Jifu 李吉甫 (9th cent.), ed. *Yuanhe junxian tuzhi* 元和郡縣圖志. Beijing: Zhonghua shuju, 1983.

Li Jingying 李景漾, ed. and comm. *Zhaoming Wen xuan xinjie* 昭明文選新解. 5 vols. Tainan: Jinan chubanshe, 1990–92.

Li Ruiqing 李鋭清. "Xi Kang 'Qin fu' xiaolun" 嵇康琴賦小論, *Xinya xuebao jikan* 13 (1994): 65–71.

Li Shan. See *Wen xuan*.

Li Zhiliang 李之亮. "Yan Yanzhi xingshi ji *Wen xuan* suoshou shiwen xinian" 顏延之行實及文選所收詩文系年, *Zhengzhou daxue xuebao* 100 (1994: 1): 58–62.

*Liang Han wenxue shi cankao ziliao* 兩漢文學史參考資料. Beijing: Zhonghua shuju, 1962.

*Liang shu* 梁書. Compiled by Yao Silian 姚思廉 (ob. 637). Beijing: Zhonghua shuju, 1975.

Liang Zhangju 梁章鉅 (1775–1849). *Wen xuan pangzheng* 文選旁證. 1834. Rpt. in *Xuanxue congshu*. Taipei: Guangwen shuju, Taiwan, 1966.

Liao Guodong 廖國棟. *Zhang Heng shengping ji qi fu zhi yanjiu* 張衡生平及其賦之研究. M.A. thesis, National Chengchih University, Taiwan, 1979.

Liao, W. K., trans. *The Complete Works of Han Fei Tzu.* 2 vols. London: Probsthain, 1939–59.

Liao Weiqing 廖蔚卿. "Zhang Hua yu Xi Jin zhengzhi zhi guanxi" 張華與西晉政治之關係, *Wen shi zhe xuebao* 22 (1973): 13–86.

———. "Lun Lu Ji de shi" 論陸機的詩. In *Zhongguo gudian wenxue yanjiu congkan: Shige zhi bu* 中國古典文學研究叢刊: 詩歌之部, edited by Ke Qingming 柯慶明 and Lin Mingde 林明德, pp. 71–105. Taipei: Juliu tushu gongsi, 1977.

———. "Zhang Hua nianpu" 張華年譜, *Wen shi zhe xuebao* 27 (1978): 1–96.

*Lienü zhuan* 列女傳. In *Sbby*.

*Liexian zhuan* 列仙傳. In *Linlang mishi congshu* 琳琅秘室叢書.

*Liezi* 列子. In *Sbby*.

Lin Junrong 林俊榮, ed. and comm. *Wei Jin Nanbeichao wenxue zuopin xuan* 魏晉南北朝文學作品選. Changchun: Jilin renmin chubanshe, 1980.

Lin Wen-yüeh 林文月. "Bao Zhao yu Xie Lingyun de shanshui shi" 鮑照與謝靈運的山水詩. In *Shanshui yu gudian* 山水與古典, pp. 93–123. Taipei: Chun wenxue chubanshe, 1975.

———. "Lu Ji de nigu shi" 陸機的擬古詩. In *Zhonggu wenxue luncong* 中古文學論叢, pp. 123–58. Taipei: De'an chubanshe, 1989.

Liu, James J. Y. *The Chinese Knight Errant.* Chicago: University of Chicago Press, 1967.

Liu Tan 劉坦. "*Lü lan* Tuntan yu 'Fu fu' Chan e *Huainan* bingzi zhi tongkao" 呂覽涒灘與服賦單閼淮南丙子之通考, *Lishi yanjiu* (1965: 4): 77–89.

Liu Weichong 劉維崇. *Cao Zhi pingzhuan* 曹植評傳. Taipei: Liming wenhua shiye gongsi, 1977.

Liu Wenzhong 劉文忠. *Bao Zhao he Yu Xin* 鮑照和庾信. Shanghai: Shanghai guji chubanshe, 1986.

Liu Zhenxiang 劉禎祥 and Li Fangchen 李方晨, ed. and comm. *Lidai cifu xuan* 歷代辭賦選. Changsha: Hunan renmin chubanshe, 1984.

*Liuchen zhu Wen xuan* 六臣注文選. In *Sbck*.

Lo Tchen-ying. *Les Formes et les methodes historiques en Chine: Une famille d'historiens et son oeuvre.* Paris: P. Geuthner, 1931.

Loewe, Michael. *Ways to Paradise: The Chinese Quest for Immortality.* London: George Allen & Unwin, 1979.

Lu Kanru 陸侃如. "Song Yu pingzhuan" 宋玉評傳. In *Zhongguo wenxue yanjiu* 中國文學研究. *Xiaoshuo yuebao* 17, special issue. Shanghai: Shangwu yinshuguan, 1927.

———. *Song Yu* 宋玉. Shanghai: Yadong tushuguan, 1929.

———. *Zhonggu wenxue xinian* 中古文學繫年. 2 vols. Beijing: Renmin wenxue chubanshe, 1985.

Lu Qinli 逯欽立. *Xian Qin Han Wei Jin Nanbeichao shi* 先秦漢魏晉南北朝詩. 3 vols. Beijing: Zhonghua shuju, 1983.

———. "'Wen fu' zhuanchu niandai kao"《文賦》撰出年代考, *Xueyuan* 2.1 (1948): 61–64. Rpt. in *Han Wei Liuchao wenxue lunji* 漢魏六朝文學論集, pp. 421–34. Xi'an: Shaanxi renmin chubanshe, 1984.

Lu Wenyu 陸文郁. *Shi caomu jinshi* 詩草木今釋. Tianjin: Tianjin renmin chubanshe, 1957.

Lu Xun 魯迅, ed. *Gu xiaoshuo gouchen* 古小說鈎沈. Hong Kong: Xinyi chubanshe, 1970.

Lu Yongpin 陸永品. "Song Yu" 宋玉. In Lü Huijian et al., *Zhongguo lidai zhuming wenxuejia pingzhuan* 1: 55–64.

Lucas, Heinz. *Der Tanz der Kraniche und die Hochzeit auf dem Meeresgrund, Ein Beitrag zur vergleichenden Maskenforschung*. N.p.: Verlag Emsdetten, ca. 1971.

Luo Zhufeng 羅竹風, ed. *Hanyu da cidian* 漢語大辭典. 12 vols. Shanghai: Cishu chubanshe, 1986–1993; Hong Kong: Sanlian shudian, 1987–1993.

Lü Huijuan 呂慧鵑, Liu Bo 劉波, and Lu Da 盧達, eds. *Zhongguo lidai zhuming wenxuejia pingzhuan* 中國歷代文學家憑傳. 6 vols. Jinan: Shandong jiaoyu chubanshe, 1983.

Lü Zhenghui 呂正惠. "Bao Zhao shi xiaolun" 鮑照詩小論, *Wenxue pinglun* 6 (1980): 119–34.

*Lüshi chunqiu* 呂氏春秋. In *Sbby*.

Lynn, Richard John, trans. *The Classic of Changes: A New Translation as Interpreted by Wang Bi*. New York: Columbia University Press, 1994.

Ma Jigao 馬積高. *Fu shi* 賦史. Shanghai: Shanghai guji chubanshe, 1987.

Mair, Victor, ed. *The Columbia Anthology of Traditional Chinese Literature*. New York: Columbia University Press, 1994.

*Mao shi zhushu* 毛詩注疏. In *Shisan jing zhushu*.

Margouliès, Georges. *Le "Fou" dans le Wen-siuan*. Paris: Paul Geuthner, 1926.

———. *Anthologie raisonnée de la littérature chinoise*. Paris: Payot, 1948.

Marney, John. *Chiang Yen*. Boston: Twayne, 1981.

Mather, Richard, trans. *Shih-shuo Hsin-yü: A New Account of Tales of the World*. Minneapolis: University of Minnesota Press, 1976.

Matsumoto Yukio 松本幸男. "Han Gaku no denki" 潘岳の傳記, *Ritsumeikan bungaku* 321 (1972): 1–40.

*Mengzi zhushu* 孟子注疏. In *Shisan jing zhushu*.

Miao Yue 繆鉞. "Bao Mingyuan nianpu" 鮑明遠年譜, *Wenxue yuekan* 3.1 (1932): 5–18.

———. "Cao Zhi 'Luoshen fu' (*Wen xuan fu jian* 4)" 曹植洛神賦 (文選賦箋4), *Zhongguo wenhua yanjiu huikan* 7 (1947): 66–72.

———. "Yan Yanzhi nianpu" 顏延之年譜, *Zhongguo wenhua yanjiu huikan* 8 (1948): 31–52.

Mok Wing-yin. "Three Poems by Ts'ao Chih," *Renditions*, no. 2 (Spring 1974): 50–52.

*Mu Tianzi zhuan* 穆天子傳. In *Sbby*.

Nakajima Chiaki 中島千秋. "Chō Ka no 'Shōryō no fu' ni tsuite" 張華の鷦鷯の賦について, *Shinagaku kenkyū* 32 (1966): 28–41.

Nakamori Kenji 中森件二. "Hō Shō no bungaku" 鮑照の文學, *Ritsumeikan bungaku* 364–366 (1975): 119–64.

*Nan shi* 南史. Compiled by Li Yanshou 李延壽. (fl. 629). Beijing: Zhonghua shuju, 1975.

Neugebauer, Klaus. *Hoh-kuan Tsi. Eine Untersuchung der dialogischen Kapitel (mit Übersetzung und Annotationen)*. Frankfurt am Main: Peter Lang, 1986.

Nienhauser, William H., Jr. "Once Again, the Authorship of the *Hsi-ching tsa-chi* (Miscellanies of the Western Capital)," *JAOS* 98.3 (1978): 219–31.

Obi Kōichi 小尾郊一 and Hanabusa Hideki 花房英樹, trans. *Monzen* 文選. 7 vols. *Zenshaku Kanbun taikei* 全釋漢文大系 79. Tokyo: Meiji shoin, 1977.

Ogata Tōru 大形徹. "Kakkanshi no seiritsu" 鶡冠子の成立, *Osaka furitsu daigaku kiyō, Jinbun shakai kagaku* 31 (1983): 11–23.

Owen, Stephen. "Hsieh Hui-lien's 'Snow Fu': A Structural Study," *JAOS* 94.1 (1974): 14–23.

———. *Readings in Chinese Literary Thought*. Cambridge: Harvard University Press, 1992.

Oyane Bunjirō 大矢根文次郎. "Gan Enshi no shi" 顏延之の詩, *Tōyō bunka kyūjo kiyō* 4 (1962): 53–66.

Park Hyun-kyu 朴現圭. "Cao Zhi yanjiu lunzhu mulu" 曹植研究論著目錄, *Shumu jikan* 21.4 (1988): 81–100.

Pei Jinnan 裴晉南 et al., ed. and comm. *Han Wei Liuchao fu xuanzhu* 漢魏六朝賦選注. Shanghai: Shanghai guji chubanshe, 1983.

Pokora, Timoteus, trans. *Hsin-lun (New Treatise) and Other Writings by Huan T'an (43 B.C.–28 A.D.)*. Michigan Papers on Chinese Studies, no. 20. Ann Arbor: Center for Chinese Studies, University of Michigan, 1975.

Qi Zhiping 齊治平, ed. and comm. *Shiyi ji* 拾遺記. Beijing: Zhonghua shuju, 1981.

Qian Daxin 錢大昕 (1728–1804). *Nianer shi kaoyi* 廿二史考異. In *Qianyan tang quanshu* 潛研堂全書.

Qian Zhonglian 錢仲聯, ed. and comm. *Bao Canjun jizhu* 鮑參軍集注. Shanghai: Shanghai guji chubanshe, 1980.

Qian Zhongshu 錢鍾書. *Guan zhui bian* 管錐編. 4 vols. Beijing: Zhonghua shuju, 1979.

Qu Shouyuan 屈守元. *Zhaoming Wen xuan zashu ji xuanjiang* 昭明文選雜述及選講. Tianjin: Tianjin guji chubanshe, 1988.

Qu Tuiyuan 瞿蛻園, ed. and comm. *Han Wei Liuchao fuxuan* 漢魏六朝賦選. Beijing: Zhonghua shuju, 1964.

Read, Bernard E. *Chinese Medicinal Plants from the Pen Ts'ao Kang Mu A.D. 1596*. 1936. Rpt., Taipei: Southern Materials Center, 1977.

———. *Chinese Materia Medica: Fish Drugs*. 1939. Rpt., Taipei: Southern Materials Center, 1977.

Rickett, Allyn W. *Guanzi: Political, Economic, and Philosophical Essays from Early China*. Vol. 1. Princeton: Princeton University Press, 1985.

Roy, David. "The Theme of the Neglected Wife in the Poetry of Ts'ao Chih," *JAS* 19 (1959): 25–31.

*San Cao ziliao huibian* 三曹資料彙編. Beijing: Zhonghua shuju, 1980.

*Sanguo zhi* 三國志. Compiled by Chen Shou 陳壽 (233–297). Beijing: Zhonghua shuju, 1962.

Schafer, Edward H. "The Early History of Lead Pigments and Cosmetics in China," *TP* 44 (1955): 413–38.

———. "Parrots in Medieval China." In *Studia Serica Bernhard Karlgren Dedicata*, edited by Soren Egerod and Else Glahn, pp. 271–82. Copenhagen: Ejnar Munksgaard, 1959.

———. *The Vermilion Bird: T'ang Images of the South*. Berkeley and Los Angeles: University of California Press, 1967.

———. "The Sky River," *JAOS* 94 (1974): 401–7.

———. "The Cranes of Mao Shan." In *Tantric and Taoist Studies*, edited by Michel Strickmann. Vol. 2, pp. 372–93. Brussels: Institut Belge des Hautes Etudes, 1983.

Schauensee, Rodolphe Meyer de. *The Birds of China*. Washington, D.C.: The Smithsonian Institution, 1984.

Schindler, Bruno. "Some Notes on Chia Yi and his 'Owl Song,'" *Asia Major*, n.s. (1959): 161–64.

Schlegel, Gustave. *Uranographie chinoise*. 2 vols. 1875. Rpt., Taipei: Chengwen, 1967.

*Shang shu zhushu* 尚書注疏. In *Shisan jing zhushu*.

Shangwu yinshuguan bianji bu 商務印書館編輯部, ed. *Ci yuan* 辭源. 4 vols. Beijing: Shangwu yinshuguan, 1983.

Shen Gua 沈括 (1031–1095). *Xin jiaozheng Mengxi bitan* 新校正夢溪筆談. Hong Kong: Zhonghua shuju, 1975.

*Shi ji* 史記. Compiled by Sima Qian 司馬遷 (145–ca. 86 B.C.). Beijing: Zhonghua shuju, 1959.

Shi Zhimian 施之勉. "Song Yu wu fu" 宋玉五賦, *Dalu zazhi* 23.2 (1961): 51.

*Shisan jing zhushu* 十三經注疏. Kyoto: Chūbun shuppansha, 1972.

*Shizi* 尸子. In *Sbby*.

*Shui jing zhu* 水經注. Compiled by Li Daoyuan 酈道元 (ob. 526). In *Sbby*.

*Shuo yuan* 說苑. In *Sbby*.

*Shuowen jiezi gulin* 説文解字詁林. Compiled by Ding Fubao 丁福保 (1874–1952). 12 volumes. Taipei: Shangwu yinshuguan, 1959.

Smith, Frederick Porter. *Chinese Materia Medica: Vegetable Kingdom*. Revised by G. A. Stuart. 1911. Rpt., Taipei: Ku T'ing Book House, 1969.

Solger, F. "Astronomische Anmerkungen zu chinesischen Marchen," *Mitteilungen für Natur- und Völkerkunde Ostasiens* 17 (1922): 168–94.

*Song shu* 宋書. Compiled by Shen Yue 沈約 (441–513). Beijing: Zhonghua shuju, 1974.

Spring, Madeline. "The Celebrated Cranes of Po Chü-i," *JAOS* 111.1 (1991): 8–18.

Straughair, Anna. *Chang Hua: A Statesman-Poet of the Western Chin Dynasty*. Australian National University, Faculty of Asian Studies, Occasional Paper 15. Canberra: Australian National University, 1973.

Su, Jui-lung. "Versatility within Tradition: A Study of the Literary Works of Bao Zhao (414?–466)." Ph.D. diss., University of Washington, 1994.

*Sui shu* 隋書. Compiled by Wei Zheng 魏徵 (580–643), Linghu Defen 令狐德棻 (583–661), et al. Beijing: Zhonghua shuju, 1973.

Sun Changxu 孫長敘. " 'Chui cenci' fei 'chui dongxiao' shuo" "吹參差"非"吹簫" 説. In *Chuci yanjiu* 楚辭研究, pp. 260–81. Jinan: Qi Lu shushe, 1988.

Sun Wenqing 孫文青. *Zhang Heng nianpu* 張衡年譜. 1935. Rev. ed., Shanghai: Shangwu yinshuguan, 1956.

Sun Zhizu 孫志祖 (1737–1801). *Wen xuan buzheng* 文選補證. In *Xuanxue congshu* (Taipei: Guangwen shuju, 1966)

Takahashi Kazumi 高橋和己. "Han Gaku ron" 潘岳論, *Chūgoku bungaku hō* 7 (1957): 14–91.

———. "Riku Ki no denki to sono bungaku" 陸機の傳記とその文學, *Chūgoku bungaku hō* 11 (1959): 1–57; 12 (1960): 49–84.

———. "Gan Enshi no bungaku" 顔延之の文學, *Ritsumeikan bungaku* 180 (1960): 108–29.

———. "Kō En no bungaku" 江淹の文學. In *Yoshikawa hakase taikyū kinen Chūgoku bungaku ronshū* 吉川博士退休記念中國文學論集, pp. 253–70. Tokyo: n.p., 1968.

Tan Qixiang 譚其驤, ed. *Zhongguo lishi ditu ji* 中國歷史地圖集. 8 vols. Shanghai: Ditu chubanshe, 1982–87.

Toyofuku Kenji 豐福健二. "Kō En no fu" 江淹の賦, *Chūgoku chūsei bungaku kenkyū* 7 (1968): 55–63.

Ueki Hisayuki 植木久行. "Sō Shoku den hokō—honden no hosoku to shinsetsu no hosei o chūshin toshite" 曹植傳補考—本傳の補足と新説の補正お中心, *Chūgoku koten kenkyū* 21 (1976): 17–31.

Upton, Beth. "The Medieval Animal Book in China and the West: A Comparative Study of Two Thirteenth Century Works," *Phi Theta Papers*, Publication of the Oriental Languages Student Association, University of California, Berkeley, 14 (September 1977): 42–50.

Van der Sprenkel, Otto B. *Pan Piao, Pan Ku, and the Han History*. Australian National University, Centre of Oriental Studies, Occasional Paper no. 3. Canberra: The Australian National University, 1964.

Van Gulik, Robert. *The Lore of the Chinese Lute: An Essay in Ch'in Ideology*. Monumenta Nipponica, no. 3 Tokyo: Sophia University Press, 1940.

——— "Hsi K'ang's Poetical Essay on the Lute," *T'ien-hsia Monthly* 11.4 (1941): 374–84.

———. *Hsi K'ang and His Poetical Essay on the Lute*. 1940. Rpt., Tokyo and Rutland, Vermont: Sophia University and Charles Tuttle Company, 1968.

von Zach, Erwin, trans. *Die Chinesische Anthologie: Übersetzungen aus dem Wen hsüan*. Edited by Ilse Martin Fang. Harvard-Yenching Studies 18. 2 vols. Cambridge: Harvard University Press, 1958.

Waley, Arthur, trans. *170 Chinese Poems*. New York: Alfred A. Knopf, 1919.

———. *The Temple and Other Poems*. New York: Alfred A. Knopf, 1923.

———. *Translations from the Chinese*. New York: Alfred A. Knopf, 1919, 1941.

———. "The Heavenly Horses of Ferghana," *History Today* 5 (1955): 95–103.

Wang, C. H. 王靖獻. "Lu Ji Wen fu jiaoshi" 陸機文賦校釋, *Wen shi zhe xuebao* 32 (1983): 1–98 (159–256). Rpt., Taipei: Hongfan shudian, 1985.

Wang Chenguang 王晨光, ed. and comm. *Wei Jin Nanbeichao cifu xuancui* 魏晉南北朝辭賦選粹. Tianjin: Tianjin jiaoyu chubanshe, 1987.

Wang Chong 王充 (27–ca. 100). *Lun heng* 論衡. In *Sbby*.

Wang Guowei 王國維. *Guantang jilin* 觀堂集林. Hong Kong: Zhonghua shuju, 1973.

Wang Li 王力. *Gudai Hanyu* 古代漢語. 3 vols. Beijing: Zhonghua shuju, 1962–64.

———. *Tongyuan zidian* 同源字典. Beijing: Shangwu yinshuguan, 1982.

Wang Niansun 王念孫 (1744–1832). *Dushu zazhi* 讀書雜志. Taipei: Letian chubanshe, 1974.

———, ed. and comm. *Guangya shuzheng* 廣雅疏證. *Sbby*.

Wang Shaoying 汪紹楹, ed. and comm. *Soushen ji* 搜神記. Beijing: Zhonghua shuju, 1979.

Wang Xianqian 王先謙 (1842–1918), ed. and comm. *Han shu buzhu* 漢書補注. Taipei: Yiwen yinshuguan, 1956.

Wang Yi 王毅. "Lu Ji jian lun" 陸機簡論, *Zhongguo gudian wenxue luncong* 2 (1985): 55–72.

Wang Zhongshu 王仲舒. "Yi'nan shike huaxiang zhong de Qi pan wu" 沂南石刻畫像中的七盤舞, *Kaogu tongxun* (1955: 2): 12–16.

Watson, Burton, trans. *Records of the Grand Historian of China*. 2 vols. New York: Columbia University Press, 1961.

———. *Records of the Historian: Chapters from the Shih chi of Ssu-ma Ch'ien*. New York: Columbia University Press, 1969.

———. *Chinese Rhyme-Prose: Poems in the Fu Form from the Han and Six Dynasties Periods*. New York: Columbia University Press, 1971.

———. *Courtier and Commoner in Ancient China: Selections from the History of the Former Han by Pan Ku*. New York: Columbia University Press, 1974.

Wei Fengjuan 韋鳳娟. *Wei Jin Nanbeichao zhujia sanwen xuan* 魏晉南北朝諸家散文選. Hong Kong: Sanlian shudian, 1991.

*Wei Jin Nanbeichao wenxueshi cankao ziliao* 魏晉南北朝文學史參考資料. 2 vols. Beijing: Zhonghua shuju, 1962.

Wei Shuqin 魏淑琴, Wu Qiong 吳窮, and Jiang Hui 姜惠, eds. *Zhongwai Zhaoming wenxuan yanjiu lunzhu suoyin* 中外昭明文選研究論著索引. Changchun: Jilin wenshi chubanshe, 1988.

*Wen xuan* 文選. Compiled by Xiao Tong 蕭統 (501–531). Commentary by Li Shan 李善 (?–689). Taipei: Zhengzhong shuju, 1971.

*Wenzi* 文子. In *Sbby*.

Whitaker, K. P. K. "Tsaur Jyr's Luohshern Fuh," *AM* 4 (1954): 36–56.

———. "Some Notes on the Background of Tsaur Jyr's Poem on the Three Good Courtiers," *BSOAS* 18 (1956): 91–107.

———. "Tsaur Jyr and the Introduction of *Fannbay* 梵唄 into China," *BSOAS* 20 (1957): 585–97.

Wilhelm, Hellmut. "Shih Ch'ung and His Chin-ku-yüan," *MS* 18 (1959): 315–27.

Wilhelm, Richard. *Die chinesische Literatur*. Wildpark-Potsdam: Akademische Verlagsgesselschaft Athenaion, 1926.

Wong, Siu-kit. *Early Chinese Literary Criticism*. Hong Kong: Joint Publishing Co., 1983.

Wu Dafeng 吳大風. "Bao Zhao nianpu buzheng" 鮑照年譜補証, *Youshi xuezhi* 5.1 (1956): 1–27.

Wu Guang 吳光. *Huang-Lao zhi xue tonglun* 黃老之學通論. Hangzhou: Zhejiang renmin chubanshe, 1985.

Wu Piji 吳丕績. *Jiang Yan nianpu* 江淹年譜. Changsha: Shangwu yinshuguan, 1938.

———. *Bao Zhao nianpu* 鮑照年譜. Changsha: Shangwu yinshuguan, 1940.

Wu Shuping 吳樹平, ed. and comm. *Fengsu tongyi jiaoshi* 風俗通義校釋. Tianjin: Tianjin renmin chubanshe, 1980.

———. *Dongguan Han ji jiaozhu* 東觀漢紀校注. Zhengzhou: Zhongzhou guji chubanshe, 1987.

*Wu Yue chunqiu* 吳越春秋. In *Sbby*.

Xiao Jizong 蕭繼宗, ed. and comm. *Xian Qin wenxue xuanzhu* 先秦文學選注. Taipei: Zhengzhong shuju, 1968.

Xiao Tong. See *Wen xuan*.

*Xijing zaji* 西京雜記. In *Sbck*.

Xu Fuguan 徐復觀. "Lu Ji 'Wen fu' shushi chugao" 陸機文賦疏釋初稿, *Zhongwai wenxue* 97 (1980): 36–41.

Xu Gongchi 徐公持. "Cao Zhi shige de xiezuo niandai wenti" 曹植詩歌的寫作年代問題, *Wen shi* (1979: 6): 147–60.

———. "Cao Zhi shengping ba kao" 曹植生平八考, *Wen shi* (1980: 10): 199–219.

———. "Cao Zhi wei Cao Cao diji zi" 曹植為曹操第幾子, *Wenxue pinglun* (1985: 5): 36–38.

———. "Cao Zhi." In Lü Huijian et al., *Zhongguo lidai zhuming wenxuejia pingzhuan*, pp. 243–83.

Xu Shiying 許士瑛. "'Changmen fu' zhenwei bian" 長門賦真偽辨, *Zhong De xuezhi* 6.1–2 (1944): 146–49.

———. "Sima Xiangru yu 'Changmen fu'" 司馬相如與長門賦, *Xueshu jikan* 6.2 (1957): 39–57.

*Xunzi* 荀子. In *Sbby*.

Yan Kejun 嚴可均 (1762–1843), comp. *Quan shanggu Sandai Qin Han Sanguo Liuchao wen* 全上古三代秦漢三國六朝文. 1815. Rpt., Beijing: Zhonghua shuju, 1959.

Yang Qinglong 楊青龍. "Zhang Heng zhuzuo xinian kao shi" 張衡著作系年考釋, *Shumu jikan* 9.3 (1975): 75–82.

Yang Shuda 楊樹達. *Han shu kuiguan* 漢書窺管. Beijing: Kexue chubanshe, 1955.

Yang Xiong 揚雄 (53 B.C.–A.D. 18). *Fa yan* 法言. In *Sbby*.

Yang Yinzong 楊胤宗. "Song Yu fu kao" 宋玉賦考, *Dalu zazhi* 27.3 (1963): 85–90; 27.4 (1963): 126–32.

Yang Yong 楊勇, ed. and comm. *Shishuo xinyu jiaojian* 世説新語校箋 Hong Kong: Zhonghua shuju, 1973.

*Yanzi chunqiu* 晏子春秋. *Sbby*.

Ye Dasong 葉大松. *Zhongguo jianzhu shi* 中國建築史. Taipei: Xinming chubanshe, 1973.

*Yiwen leiju* 藝文類聚. Compiled by Ouyang Xun 歐陽詢 (557–641). Beijing: Zhonghua shuju, 1965.

Yu Guanying 余冠英. "Jian'an daibiao shiren Cao Zhi (192–232)" 建安代表詩人曹植 (192–232)." In *Han Wei Liuchao shi luncong* 漢魏六朝詩論叢, pp. 91–107. Shanghai: Shanghai gudian wenxue chubanshe, 1956.

Yu Shaochu 俞紹初, ed. *Wang Can ji* 王粲集. Beijing: Zhonghua shuju, 1980.

Yuan Ke 袁珂, ed. and comm. *Shanhai jing jiaozhu* 山海經校注. Shanghai: Shanghai guji chubanshe, 1980.

Yuan Shishi 袁世碩, ed. *Shandong gudai wenxuejia pingzhuan* 山東古代文學家評傳 1: 112–24. Jinan: Shandong renmin chubanshe, 1983.

Yue Shi 樂史 (930–1007), comp. *Taiping huanyu ji* 太平寰宇記. Nanjing: Jinling shuju, 1882.

Zeng Junyi 曾君一. "Bao Zhao yanjiu" 鮑照研究, *Sichuan daxue xuebao* (1957: 4): 1–25. Rpt. in *Wei Jin Liuchao shi yanjiu lunwen ji* 魏晉六朝詩研究論文集, pp. 134–58. Hong Kong: Zhongguo yuwen xueshe, 1969.

Zhang Caimin 張采民. "Zhang Heng 'Yongyuan shiernian wei Nanyang zhubo' xinzheng" 張衡'永元十二年為南陽主簿'新證, *Nanjing shida xuebao* (1985: 3): 40–43. Rpt. in *Zhongguo gudai jindai wenxue yanjiu* (1985: 23): 73–76.

Zhang Dejun 張德鈞. "Guanyu Cao Zhi de pingjia wenti" 關於曹植的評價問題, *Lishi yanjiu* (1957: 2): 49–66.

Zhang Huaijin 張懷瑾. *Wen fu yizhu* 文賦譯注. Beijing: Beijing chubanshe, 1984.

Zhang Keli 張可禮. *San Cao nianpu* 三曹年譜. Jinan: Qi Lu shushe, 1983.

Zhang Moyuan 張末元. *Hanchao fuzhuang tuyang ziliao* 漢朝服裝圖樣資料. Hong Kong: Taiping shuju, 1963.

Zhang Renqing 張仁青, ed. and comm. *Lidai pianwen xuan* 歷代駢文選. 2 vols. Taipei: Taiwan shifan daxue, 1965.

Zhang Shaokang 張少康. *Wen fu jishi* 文賦集釋. Shanghai: Shanghai guji chubanshe, 1984.

Zhang Shoulin 張壽林. "Wang Zhaojun gushi yanbian zhi diandian didi" 王昭君故事演變之點點滴敵, *Wenxue nianbao* 1 (1932): 347–71.

Zhang Wenxun 張文勛. "Kumen de xiangzheng—'Luo shen fu' xinyi" 苦悶的象徵—《洛神賦》新議, *Shehui kexue zhanxian* (1981: 1): 222–27.

Zhang Yun'ao 張雲璈 (1747–1829). *Xuanxue jiaoyan* 選學膠言. 1822. Rpt. in *Xuanxue congshu*. Taipei: Guangwen, 1966.

Zhang Zhenze 張震澤, ed. and comm. *Zhang Heng shiwen ji jiaozhu* 張衡詩文集校注. Shanghai: Shanghai guji chubanshe, 1986.

Zhang Zhiyue 張志岳. "Bao Zhao ji qi shi xintan" 鮑照及其詩新探, *Wenxue pinglun* (1979: 1): 58–65.

*Zhanguo ce* 戰國策. In *Sbby*.

Zhao Fuhai 趙福海, ed. *Wen xuan xue lunji* 文選學論集. Changchun: Shidai wenyi chubanshe, 1992.

———, Chen Hongtian 陳宏天, et al., eds. *Zhaoming Wenxuan yanjiu lunwen ji* 昭明文選研究論文集. Changchun: Jilin wenxue chubanshe, 1988.

Zhao Jian 趙堅. "Zhang Heng zhuyao fuzuo xinian" 張衡主要賦作系年, *Shanghai shifan xueyuan xuebao* (1984: 1): 151–54.

———. "Changmen gong he 'Changmen fu'" 長門宮和《長門賦》, *Shanghai shifan daxue xuebao* (Zhe shi ban) (1985: 3): 139–41.

Zhao Yongfu 趙永復, ed. *Shui jing zhu tongjian jinshi* 水經注通檢今釋. Shanghai: Fudan daxue chubanshe, 1985.

Zhao Youwen 趙幼文, ed. and comm. *Cao Zhi ji jiaozhu* 曹植集校注 Beijing: Renmin wenxue chubanshe, 1984.

Zhao Zecheng 趙則誠, Chen Fuxing 陳復興, and Zhao Fuhai 趙福海, ed. and comm. *Zhongguo gudai wenlun yijiang* 中國古代文論譯講 Changchun: Jilin renmin chubanshe, 1984.

Zheng Hesheng 鄭鶴生. *Ban Gu nianpu* 班固年譜. Shanghai: Shangwu yinshuguan, 1931.

Zhong Youmin 鍾優民. *Cao Zhi xintan* 曹植新探. Hefei: Huangshan shushe, 1984.

Zhou Jianzhong 周建忠. "Lun Yan Yanzhi de wenxue chuangzuo" 論顏延之的文學創作, *Shandong shida xuebao* (1985: 5): 69–75.

*Zhou li zhushu* 周禮注疏. In *Shisan jing zhushu*.

Zhou Xunchu 周勛初. "'Wen fu' xiezuo niandai xintan" 《文賦》寫作年代新探. 1982. Rpt. in *Wen shi tan wei* 文史探微, pp. 48–56. Shanghai: Shanghai guji chubanshe, 1987.

*Zhou yi zhushu* 周易注疏. In *Shisan jing zhushu*.

Zhu Bilian 朱碧蓮 and Shen Jianying 沈劍英. "Song Yu cifu zhenwei bian" 宋玉辭賦真偽辨, *Dousou* 52 (1983): 54–57, 64.

Zhu Jian 朱珔, ed. *Wen xuan jishi* 文選集釋. 1836. Rpt. in *Xuan xue congshu*. Taipei: Guangwen shuju, 1966.

Zhuang Benli 莊本立. *Zhongguo gudai zhi paixiao* 中國古代之排簫. Institute of Ethnology, Academia Sinica, Monograph No. 4. Taipei: Zhongyang yanjiuyuan minzuxue yanjiusuo, 1963.

Zhuang Wanshou 莊萬壽. *Xi Kang yanjiu ji nianpu* 嵇康研究及年譜. Taipei: Xuesheng shuju, 1990.

*Zhuangzi* 莊子. In *Sbby*.

*Zhushu jinian* 竹書紀年. In *Sbby*.

*Zuo zhuan zhushu* 左傳注疏. In *Shisan jing zhushu*.

# Index

ABBREVIATIONS:
AB = alliterative binome; RB = rhyming binome

Aged Boy (Lao Tong), 284, L. 77n, 285
Ai, Emperor of Former Han, 120, LL. 189–90n
Ai Jiang, *see* Sorrowful Jiang
"Airs of Bei," 22, L. 15n
"Airs of Cao," 22, L. 28n, 23
"Airs of Qi," 32, L. 17n
Ajiao (personal name of Empress Chen), 406
Albescent Beauty (Su E), 34, L. 33n, 35
"All-embracing Music," 132, L. 341n, 133, 151
"All-encompassing Pond," 247, 323, 409
"Altered *Shang*," 271
"Among the Mulberries," 225
An, Emperor of Later Han, 398
Angular Array (constellation), 68, L. 34n, 69
Angzhou, 116, L. 138n, 117
Anling, 367
Anping, 383
Anxiang, 372
"Ardent *Zhi*," 248, LL. 47–48n, 249
"Autumn Thoughts" (song), 298, L. 278n
"Axe-and-Shield," 247, 409

Ba (area of southwest), 81, L. 80n
Ba-Yu dance, 80, L. 80n
Bai men, *see* White Portal
*Baihu tongyi*, 104, L. 13n, 368
Bailu Mountains, 406
Baima, 374
Baling, 377
Ban clan, 82, L. 2n
Ban Biao, 83, 367; "Northern Journey Rhapsody," 82, L. 8n
Ban Chao, 367
Ban Gu, 2, 83, 367, 375; "Autobiographical Postface", 82, LL. 3–4n, 83; "Elaboration of the Canon," 368; "Inscription for the Ceremonial Mounding at Mount Yanran," 368; "Response to a Guest Jest," 368; "Rhapsody on Communicating with the Hidden," 2, 367; "Two Capitals Rhapsody," 368
Ban Kuang, 82, LL. 5–6n
Ban Prefecture, 382
Ban Yi, 82, LL. 3–4n
Ban Zhao (Cao Dagu), 367, 369, 381
Bao (ancient state), 94, LL. 89–90n
Bao De, 398
Bao Si, concubine of King You, 94, LL. 89–90n
Bao Zhao, 1, 75, 77, 370; "Admiring the Moon in My Office by the West City Gate," 369; "Ascending the Heaven," 206, LL. 101–2n; "Departing from the North Gate of Ji," 370; "Imitating Ancient Style," 370; "Imitating the Style of Liu Gonggan," 370; "Rhapsody on Dancing Cranes," 1, 370; "Rhapsody on the Ruined City," 370; "Song of Dongwu," 370
Baojiang, 126, LL. 259–60n. *See also* Zujiang
Baoxi (Fuxi), 276, LL. 258–59n, L. 279n, 277
Baoxin (ancient noble), 276, L. 261n, 277
Barrier Gate, 68, L. 47n, 69
Bei lu (Boreal Route), 32, LL. 13–14n
Bei Zao, official in Zheng, 122, LL. 203–4n
Beimang Hills, 152, L. 71n
*Bencao jing*, 126, L. 262n
Bi, *see* Net (constellation)
Bi Gan, 90, L. 83n, 300, L. 319n, 301
Bian, Empress Dowager of Wei, 371, 372
Bian Sui (recluse), 272, L. 203n, 273
Bieling (ancient Shu minister), 118, LL. 179–80n, 119
Bilei, *see* Ramparts (constellation)
"Binding Wind" (song), 409
Black Warrior Gate, 368
Blue Grove (constellation), 132, L. 356n, 133
Bo Chu (eunuch), 120, LL. 195–96n

Bo Juyi, 77
Bo Shi (son of Shuxiang), 96, L. 101n
Bo Ya, 238, L. 115n, 274, LL. 240–41n, 275, 286, L. 105n, 287
Bo Yi (animal tamer), 52, L. 22n, 53, 90, L. 79n, L. 80n
Bobang (son of Jifu), 264, L. 60n
Bodi (eunuch), 120, LL. 195–96n
Bole (horse tamer), 68, LL. 45–46n
Boling (nephew of Da Jiang), 92, L. 84n
Boniu (Ran Geng), 88, L. 64n
Boqi (filial son), 264, L. 60n, 265
Boreal Route, 32, LL. 13–14n, 33
Bow (constellation), 134, L. 357n, 135
Boyang of Cao, 96, L. 99n
Boyi (recluse), 300, L. 317n, 301, 98, L. 124n
*boyu* RB, 10, L. 69n
Bozhong Mountain, 134, L. 358n, 135
Broadview Tower, 70, L. 73n
Bronze Horse Gate (Jin ma men), 208, L. 127n, 209
Bureau of Music, 66, L. 18n
Buzhou (mountain), 126, L. 246n, L. 255n, 127

Cai Yong, 298, L. 278n, L. 280n; "Epitaph for the Wife of Minister over the Masses Yuan, née Ma," 184, L. 17n; *Qin cao* (Zither Tunes), 136, LL. 401–2n, 264, L. 60n, 286, L. 105n
Cai Ze, 138, L. 5n, 139, 272, L. 211n, 273, 298, L. 281n
Caishu, 108, LL. 35–36n
Candescent Dragon (Zhu long), 26, LL. 75–76n, 27, 126, LL. 257–58n, 127
Cangwu, 114, LL. 129–30n, LL. 131–32n, 285
*Canon for Judging Horses*, see *Xiang ma jing*
"Canon of Shun," 409
Cao Biao, 372
Cao Cao, 371, 383, 390, 410
Cao Dagu, 82, LL. 9–10n, 83, 84, L. 16n, L. 20n, L. 22n, L. 32n, LL. 35–36n, 86, L. 44n, 88, LL. 61–62n, 96, L. 103n, L. 104n, LL. 105–6n, 98, LL. 111–12n, LL. 113–14n, L. 117n, 367
Cao Daoheng, 4, 378
Cao Lin, 390
Cao Pi, 30, L. 1n, 183, 310, L. 128n, 355, 371, 372, 408; "Rhapsody on a Widow," 183; "Song of Yan," 13, 310, L. 127n
Cao Rui (Emperor Ming of Wei), 372
Cao Zhi, 30, L. 1n, 31, 33, 70, LL. 87–88n, 354, L. 2n, 355, 371, 373, 412; "Casting Blame," 362, L. 127n; "Dirge for Wang Zhongxuan," 373; "Lord's Feast," 371;

"Memorial Seeking to Convey Familial Affection," 373; "Memorial Seeking to Prove Myself," 372; "Miscellaneous Poems," 373; "Poem of Seven Paces," 372; "Poem Presented to Biao, Prince of Baima," 372, 412; "Presented to Wang Can," 318, LL. 51–52n; "Responding to an Edict," 372; "Rhapsody on the Luo River Goddess," 3, 372, 373; "Rhapsody on a Parrot," 184, LL. 15–16n; "Sending Off Master Ying," 371; "Seven Communications," 373; "Seven Laments," 373; "Song of White Horse", 70, LL. 87–88n
Carnelian Cliff (Yao ya), 126, LL. 259–60n
Carnelian Pond (Yao chi), 76, L. 18n, 77
Carnelian Ravine, 126, LL. 259–60n
Carriage Palace (constellation), 36, LL. 38–39n, 37
Celestial Ford (constellation), 134, L. 361n
Celestial Park (constellation), 132, L. 356n
Celestial Quadriga (constellation), 75, 132, L. 353n, 133
"Celestial Questions," 114, L. 116n
Celestial Torrent (constellation), 134, L. 361n, 135, 214, L. 23n
Celestial Turtle (constellation), 92, L. 84n
Celestial Wolf (constellation), 134, L. 357n, L. 358n, 135
Chamber of Ministers (constellation), 36, LL. 38–39n, 37
*Chan e* (astrological year), 40, LL. 1–3n
Chang (King Wen of Zhou), 22, L. 26n, 23
Chang E, 31, 34, L. 33n
Chang'an, 54, LL. 65–66n, 372, 385, 395, 398, 405
Changle Tingzhu (princess), 390
Changli (mythical bird), 130, L. 329n, 131
Changmen, see Tall Gate Palace
Changsha, 41, 115, L. 129n, 376, 381, 402
Chen, Empress of Former Han, 159, 161, 388, 406
Chen (Wei dynasty fief), 373
Chen (Zhou state), 33, 313
Chen Buzhan, 274, L. 235n, 275
Chen Commandery, 392
Cheng, Duke of Wei, 86, LL. 49–50n
Cheng, Emperor of Former Han, 36, L. 41n
Cheng, King of Zhou, 94, L. 98n
Cheng Lian (zither player), 286, L. 105n
Chengdu, 386
Chenggong Sui, 315, 374, 399; "Rhapsody on Heaven and Earth," 374; "Rhapsody on Whistling," 3, 374
Chi Song (immortal), 138, L. 421n
Chiwen, see Dapple Red
Chong'er, 92, L. 86n, L. 88n, 93, 120,

LL. 195–96n, 154, LL. 122–23n, 274, L. 229n

Chonghua (Shun), 114, LL. 129–30n, 115, 297

Chongli (director of fire), 90, LL. 77–78n, 91, 116, LL. 133–36n, 117

Chou River, 272, L. 203n

Chu (ancient state), 82, L. 1n, 313, 386

Chu, Duke of Wei, 274, L. 234n

"Chu wang yin" (Lament of the King of Chu), 308, L. 89n

*Chuci*, 388, 390

Chui (musician), 276, LL. 262–63n, L. 279n, 277, 287

Chun tai, *see* Spring Terrace

*Chunqiu*, 100, L. 139n

*Chunqiu qiantan ba*, 22, L. 31n

*Chunqiu yuanming bao*, 320, L. 92n

Cimu Mountain, 232, L. 2n

Circular Moat, 150, L. 27n, L. 30n, L. 34n, 151

*Classic of Changes*, 86, L. 45n, 94, L. 97n, 100, L. 134n, 261, 382

*Classic of Documents*, 382

*Classic of Songs*, 382

"Clear *Jiao*," 248, LL. 47–48n, 249, 289, L. 120, 317

"Clear *Zhi*," 290, L. 154n, 291

Cloud Master, 131

Cloud-Han (= Milky Way), 16, L. 51n, 17

"Concord" (song), 266, L. 93n, 267

Conductors (constellation), 134, L. 363n, 135

Confucius, 72, LL. 129–39n, 88, L. 64n, L. 70n, 89, 101, 103, 142, L. 36n, 150, LL. 53–54n, 248, L. 46n, 272, LL. 200–201n, 323

Consort Fu (Fufei), 128, L. 266n, 129

"Crane Separated a Thousand Leagues" (song), 298, L. 280n, 299

"Crossing the River," 200, L. 11n

Cui Bao, *Gu jin zhu*, 408

Cui Guang (Yellow Lord of Xia), 100, L. 128n

Cui Yuan, 398

Cui Zhu, 274, L. 235n

Da Jiang, 92, L. 84n

"Da wu" (song), 312, L. 132n

"Da Xia" (song), 310, L. 131n

"Da zhang" (song), 310, L. 131n

Dafei (Bo Yi), 90, L. 79n

Dahuo (star), 92, L. 86n

Dai (place), 54, L. 67n, 55, 62, L. 51n, 63, 120, LL. 183–84n, 196, LL. 48–49n, 197

Dai Gui (lady of Chen), 208, LL. 107–8n

Dai Yanzhi, *Xi zheng ji* (Notes on a Western

Journey), 180, LL. 11–12n

Dai Yuan, 380

Dan (Duke of Zhou), 94, L. 98n, 95

Dan Zhu, 240, L. 119n, 241

Danyang, 377, 378

*Danyang ji* (Notes on Danyang), 232, L. 2n

Dao jing, *see* Upturned Phosphors

Dapple Red, 66, LL. 11–12n, 67

Dark Capital (You du), 126, LL. 241–42n

Dark Warrior, 124, L. 235n, 125, 130, LL. 327–28n

Dawn Valley, 34, LL. 30–31n, 115, 173

Degong Ward, 385

Deng, Empress Dowager of Later Han, 382

Deng Grove, 57

Deng Wan, 370

Deng Xi, 272, L. 213n, 273

Deng Zhi, 381

Denglin (Deng Grove), 56, L. 88n

"Dew Prolonged" (song), 272, L. 216n, 273

Di of Song, 265

Di tai, *see* Lord of Heaven's Platform

Di Ya (Yi Ya), 300, L. 335n, 301

Di zhu, *see* Whetstone Pillar

Diku, 90, LL. 77–78n, 92, L. 84n

*Dili shu* (Book of Geography), 70, L. 73n

Ding, Duke of Lu, 96, L. 100n

Ding Yi, 183, 185, 371; "Rhapsody on a Widow," 184, LL. 9–10n, LL. 13–14n, LL. 15–16n, LL. 25–26n, 186, LL. 35–36n, LL. 39–40n, L. 49n, LL. 57–58n, LL. 59–60n, 188, LL. 67–68n, LL. 71–72n, L. 80n, LL. 81–82n, LL. 83–84n, LL. 85–86n, 190, LL. 105–6n

"Distant Roaming," 18, L. 67n, 108, L. 57n, 110, L. 70n, L. 75n, 114, LL. 105–6n, L. 107n, 116, L. 147n, 126, L. 245n, 134, L. 367n, 160, LL. 3–4, 172, LL. 9–10n, 180, L. 41n, 282, L. 10n, 403

Ditai (spirit), 72, LL. 105–6n, 73

Divine Terrace, 148, L. 16n, 149

*Diwang shiji*, 264, L. 61n

Dixuan (Yellow Lord), 66, LL. 9–10n, 67

Dong lin, *see* Eastern Neighbor

Dong Xian, 120, LL. 189–90n, 121

Dong yuan, *see* Eastern Park

Dong'e, 373

Dongguan library, 381

Donghai Commandery, 378

Dongting, 37

Dongwu (place), 379

"Dongwu" (song) 296, LL. 269–70n, 297

Dou, Lady, 118, LL. 183–84n, 119

Dou Tao, 206, LL. 91–92n

Dou Xian, 368, 375

Du Deling, 393

Du Fu, "Sung While Drunk," 211
Du Hui, 124, LL. 217–18n
Duangan Mu, 98, L. 125n
Duguang (place), 116, L. 151n
Dui trigram, 112, L. 87n
Duke of Zhou, 94, L. 98n, 142, L. 36n
Dun hexagram, 112, L. 86n, LL. 89–90n
"Duoyin ge" (Song of Sighs), 308, L. 75n
"Dwelling in Seclusion" (song), 298, L. 278n

E Huang, 362, L. 107n
Earl of Qin, 96, LL. 109–10n
Eastern Neighbor, 90, L. 83n, 91
Eastern Park, 20, L. 6n
Eight Lords of Huainan, 74, L. 1n
eight musical sounds, 281, 319
"Elegantiae," 247
"Encomium to Xia Yu," 240, L. 120n
"Eulogia," 247
Everlasting Palace, 164, L. 58n, 208, L. 127n

Fa (King Wu of Zhou), 92, L. 87n, 93
Fan ji (wife of King Zhuang of Chu), 298, L. 279n
Fan Ju, 298, L. 281n
Fang (Chamber constellation), 66, LL. 21–22n
"Fang lu," see "Keeping off the Dew"
Fangcheng, 399
Fangfeng (Wind Blocker?), 114, LL. 127–28n, 115
Fangling, 152, L. 74n, 153, 195
fangshi, 336, L. 186n
Fangzhang (island), 114, L. 112n
Fanyang, 399
fanyuan RB, 10, L. 69n
Farmer's Auspice (star), 92, L. 84n
Favorite Beauty Ban, "Rhapsody of Self-commiseration," 184, L. 18n, L. 20n, 190, L. 126n, LL. 129–30n
fei (lunar term), 34, L. 35n
Fei tan, see Frothing Pool
Feihuang, see Flying Yellow
Feilian, 321
Fen River, 302, LL. 1–2n, 303
Feng, Duke of Zhou, 92, L. 84n
feng and shan rites, 399
feng guan (phoenix pipes), 304, LL. 25–26n
Feng Yan, 193, 196, L. 52n; "Letter to Yin Jiu," 196, L. 60n
Fenglong (god of clouds), 130, LL. 307–8n, 131
Fengsu tongyi, 276, L. 261n, 286, L. 105n, 403
fenyang (subterranean goat), 126, L. 252n
Filial Ji (Xiao Ji), 264, L. 61n, 265
Fire Star, 16, L. 43n

First Qin Emperor, 44, LL. 39–40n, 122, LL. 199–200n, 126, L. 265n, 192, LL. 10–13n, L. 19n, 193, 194, 204, L. 53n
Five Commands, 68, L. 57n, 69
Five Lords, 82, L. 1n
five rhythms, 268, L. 156n
Five Wefts, 134, L. 364n, 135
Floating Bridge (Fu qiao), 148, L. 15n, 149
"Flowing zhi," 164, L. 67n, 165, 317
"Flying Dragon" (song), 296, LL. 271–72n, 297, 309
Flying Yellow (horse), 66, LL. 9–10n, 67
Founding Star, 92, L. 84n
Four Hoaryheads, 100, L. 128n, 101, 284, L. 59n
Frothing Pool, 24, L. 40n
Fu Fei, 3, 112, L. 88n, 355, 357
Fu Liang, 180, LL. 11–12n, 395
Fu qiao, see Floating Bridge
Fu Xuan, 310, L. 128n
Fu Yi, 245, 375, 410; "Eulogy for Xianzong," 375; "Fulfilling My Aims," 375; "Rhapsody on Dance," 3, 375; "Seven Incitements," 375
Fu Yue, 44, LL. 41–42n, 45, 106, L. 25n, 107
Fucha, King of Wu, 44, LL. 35–38n, 45, 264, L. 60n
Fuqiu Bo, 74, L. 1n
Fuqiu Gong, 74, L. 1n
Fusang, 34, LL. 30–31n, 35, 115, 282
Fuxi, 102, L. 149n, 132, L. 347n, 148, L. 1n, 276, LL. 258–59n, L. 279n, 404

Gan Bao, 36, L. 40n
Gao Chai (Confucius' disciple), 274, L. 231n
Gao ge, see Lofty Gallery
Gao Jianli, 202, L. 44n
Gao Qumi (Chu grandee), 274, L. 233n, 275
Gao Shi (immortal), 336, L. 187n
Gao Xi (immortal), 336, L. 187n, 337
Gao Yu, 274, L. 231n, 275
Gaotang (place in Shandong), 274, L. 242n
Gaotang (shrine in Chu), 245, 339, 409
Gaoxin, 90, LL. 77–78n, 91, 106, L. 25n
Gaoyang (= Zhuanxu), 82, L. 1n, 127
Gaoyao, 124, LL. 219–20n, 272, LL. 200–201n
Gaozu, Emperor of Former Han, 100, L. 128n, 102, L. 140n
Gate of Coldness (Han men), 68, L. 47n, 126, L. 245n, 127
Ge lu (Song Register), 410
Gen (trigram), 112, L. 87n
Gengshi Emperor, 196, L. 52n
Gengzong (place), 120, LL. 193–94n

Golden Valley, 202, L. 32n, 203
Gong Bo of Wei, 190, LL. 127–28n
Gong Jiang (wife of Gong Bo), 190, LL. 127–28n, 191
Gong Le (immortal), 336, L. 189n
Gong Prefecture, 383
Gongshu Ban, 234, L. 40n, 235, 264, L. 70n, 265, 287
Gongsi, Empress of Liu-Song, 396
Gongsun Hong, 385
Gongsun Long, 272, L. 213n, 273
Gongsun Qiang (adviser to Boyang of Cao), 96, L. 99n
*Gongyang zhuan*, 86, LL. 49–50n
Goujian, 44, LL. 35–38n
Goumang, 114, L. 112n, 115
Gourd Star, 362, L. 109n, 363
Goushi Mountain, 208, LL. 103–4n
Goushi Prefecture, 354, L. 4n, L. 6n
Graham, William, 54, LL. 65–66n
Grand Academy, 150, L. 47n, LL. 49–50n
Grand Clarity, 316, L. 29n, 317
Grand Simplicity, 288, L. 142n, 289
Grand Stairway (constellation), 66, L. 5n, 67
Grand Unity, 336, L. 193n, 337
Great Valley, 152, L. 71n, 153
"Greater Master of Fate," 130, L. 310n
Greater Yin, 126, L. 239n, 127
Green Dragon, 130, LL. 327–28n
Green Kraken, 72, LL. 101–4n, 73
"Grieving I Make My Plaint," 110, L. 62n
Gu Jizhi, 394
Gu Rong, 380
Guabu, 369
*guan* (bulrush), 16, L. 26–29n
Guan shu, 108, LL. 35–36n
Guan Zhong, 86, LL. 51–52n, 87, 272, L. 207n
*Guang zhi*, 152, L. 71n, L. 73n
Guangling, 369, 370, 377
"Guangling" (tune), 296, LL. 269–70n, 297, 309
"Guangling san" (zither tune), 296, LL. 269–70n
Guangwang, *see* Broadview Tower
Guangwu, Emperor of Later Han, 72, L. 116n, 73, 196, L. 52n, 367
Guangwu (place), 399
*Guangya*, 260, L. 18n
Guanqiu Jian, 391
*Guanzi*, 46, L. 79n, 148, LL. 7–8n, 272, L. 207n
Gui (ruling clan of Chen), 94, L. 97n, 95
Gui, Mount, 284, L. 77n, 285
Guiji, 114, L. 126n, LL. 127–28n, 390, 392, 393

Guiyang, 377
Gulf of Yu, 167, 282, L. 9n, 283, 406
Guo Pu, "Encomium for the Horse," 66, LL. 21–22n
Guo Xiang, 392
Guo xue, *see* State Academy
Guo Yanwen, 377
*Guo yu*, 62, LL. 55–56n, 90, LL. 77–78n, 92, L. 84n, L. 86n, 94, LL. 89–90n, 114, LL. 127–28n, 154, LL. 122–23n, 156, L. 124n, LL. 126–27n
Guo Yuansheng, 150, L. 47n
*Guwen yuan*, 389, 398
*Guwen Zhou shu*, 72, L. 120n
Guzhu, 300, L. 317n

Hairy Maiden, 126, L. 265n
Haiyu Prefecture, 369
Han Fei, 272, L. 209n, 273
*Han Feizi*, 248, LL. 47–48n, 272, L. 209n, 286, L. 105n
Han in the Clouds, 134, L. 362n
Han Jue, 402
Han men, *see* Gate of Coldness
Han River, 132, L. 353n, 360, L. 87n, 363
*Han shi neizhuan*, 360, L. 87n
*Han shi waizhuan*, 202, LL. 37–38n, 274, L. 231n, L. 235n, 388
*Han shu*, 132, L. 353n, 194, LL. 40–41n, 302, LL. 3–4n, 358, 375, 376, 381, 386, 389, 410
*Han Wu gushi*, 120, LL. 187–88n
Han Zhong, 110, L. 78n, 111
Handan, 80, LL. 83–84n, 81, 353, 411
Handan Chun, 70, L. 87–88n
*hangxie* (midnight vapors), 114, L. 122n
"Hao Village" (song), 408
Hao zhong, *see* Sounding Bell
Hare Garden, 20, L. 6n, 21
Harmonious Heaven, 150, L. 39n, 151
He, Emperor of Later Han, 368, 381
*he* (crane), 77
He Changyu, 147, 405
He gu, *see* River Drum (constellation)
He Qiao, 405
He Zhangyu, 393
Heart (mansion), 16, L. 43n
"Heaven's Brilliance" (song), 310, L. 128n, 311
Heavenly Horses, 70, LL. 89–90n
Heavenly Quadriga (constellation), 66, LL. 21–22n, 74, L. 137n, 92, L. 84n
Hebo (god of Yellow River), 26, L. 79n, 362, LL. 128–29n
Hedong, 302, LL. 1–2n, 391
*Heguanzi*, 42, LL. 23–24n, 43, 44, L. 30n,

LL. 31–32n, LL. 35–38n, LL. 43–44n,
LL. 47–48n, LL. 49–50n, LL. 55–56n,
L. 57n, 46, LL. 63–64n, LL. 75–76n,
LL. 77n, L. 79n, LL. 85–86n, L. 87n, 48,
L. 102n, 266, L. 114n
Hejian, 381, 398
Helin, 118, L. 169n, 119
Helü, King of Wu, 80, L. 86n
Henan, 375, 399
*Henan jun tu jing* (Texts and Maps of Henan
Commandery), 354, L. 6n
Henei Commandery, 392
Heng, Mount, 116, LL. 133–36, 117
Heng E, 34, L. 33n
Herd Boy (constellation), 92, L. 84n
Heshang Gong, 212, L. 1n
Heyang, 384, 404, 407
"Hidden Boneset" (song), 22, L. 29n, 23
Hongmen, 80, L. 81n
Honorable Consort Xuan, 395
Horse Market (Ma shi), 148, L. 14n
Horses of Dachen, 92, L. 84n
*Hou Han shu*, 375, 381, 398
Houfei, Emperor of Liu-Song, 379
Houji, 92, L. 84n, 116, L. 151n
Hu (Han prefecture), 118, L. 167n
Hu (land of Xiongnu), 56, L. 84n, 57
Hu Hai, 122, LL. 199–200n
Hu Kejia, 3
Hua, Mount, 118, L. 164n, L. 167n, 126,
L. 265n, 192, LL. 14–15n, 193
Huai, King of Liang, 376
Huai Prefecture, 384, 392, 405, 407
Huai-Si faction, 376
Huainan, 385
*Huainanzi*, 56, L. 84n, 60, L. 32n, 116,
L. 139n, 130, LL. 301–2n, 138, L. 3n, 140,
LL. 21–22n, 164, L. 88n, 174, LL. 49–50n,
194, LL. 22–23n, 270, L. 185n, 272,
L. 215n, L. 216n, 284, L. 59n, 300,
L. 320n, L. 335n, 354, L. 3n
Huan, Duke of Qi, 86, LL. 51–52n, 92,
L. 88n, 154, LL. 122–23n, 272, L. 207n,
322, L. 138n
Huan Tan, 266, L. 95n, 290, LL. 155–56n;
*Qin dao* (Way of the Zither), 132, L. 343n,
296, LL. 254–55n
Huang men, *see* Yellow Gate
Huang Yi, 49, 383
Huang zhu, *see* Yellow Bamboo
Huang Zu, 49, 54, LL. 65–66n, 383
Huangdi (Yellow Lord), 84, L. 29n, 148,
L. 1n, 284, L. 76n, 286, L. 104n, 409
*Huangdi changliu meng*, 84, L. 29n
Huangfu Mi, 284, L. 72n
Huangtai (hills), 22, L. 27n

Huangzhu (Yellow Bamboo), 22, L. 27n
Huanyuan, 354, L. 4n, 355
Huating, 78, L. 41n, 379, 380
Huayin, 118, L. 164n, 119, 207
Huba (musician), 202, LL. 37–38n, 274,
LL. 240–41n, L. 244n, 275
Hui, Emperor of Western Jin, 384, 400, 405
Hui Shi, 18, LL. 60–63n, 300, L. 321n, 301
*huixue* AB, 8, L. 29n

Jade Maiden, 112, L. 88n, 126, L. 265n,
127, L. 265
jade mushroom (*yu zhi*), 126, L. 262n
Jasper Palace, 133
Ji, Mount, 284, L. 72n, 285, 315
Ji (star), *see* Winnow Star
Ji An, 404
Ji Bo, *see* Winnow Earl
Ji clan, 92, L. 84n, 95
Ji of Qi Hamlet, 100, L. 128n
Ji Prefecture, 391
Ji Rui, 120, LL. 195–96n
Ji shi, *see* Piled Boulders
Ji Xin, 100, L. 127n, 101
Ji Zha, 292, LL. 196–97n, 312, LL. 135–36n
Ji'nan cheng, 378
Jia, Empress of Western Jin, 380, 384, 400
Jia Bizhi, 407
Jia Chong, 13, 384, 402, 404
Jia Kui, 375
Jia Mi, 171, 380, 385
Jia Yi, 1, 41, 98, 99, L. 116n, 375, 402;
"Finding Fault with Qin," 192, LL. 14–
15n; "Lament for Qu Yuan," 376;
"Rhapsody on the Houlet," 1, 98, LL. 13–
14n, 376; *Xin shu*, 388
Jian mu, *see* Standing Tree
Jian xing, *see* Founding Star
Jian'an, 371, 378
Jiang clan, 94, L. 97n, 95
Jiang Dan, 376
Jiang Kangzhi, 377
Jiang Shi (craftsman), 234, L. 40n, 235
Jiang Yan, 193, 201, 376, 377; "Accom-
panying the Prince of Jianping on a
Journey to Ji'nan cheng," 378;
"Attending the Prince of Shi'an at
Shitou," 377; "Biography of My Friend
Yuan," 378; "Gazing toward the Jing
Mountains," 377; "Letter in Response to
Yuan Shuming," 378; "Letter Submitted
to the Prince of Jianping," 377; "Memo-
randum to the Prince of Xin'an in Nan
Xuzhou," 377; "Rhapsody Lamenting a
Friend," 378; "Rhapsody on Resentment,"
2, 379; "Rhapsody on Separation," 2,

379; thirty miscellaneous poems, 379
Jiangxia, 383, 394
Jiangzhou, 369, 395
Jiankang, 369, 396
Jianping, 377
Jiantu, 86, LL. 49–50n
Jiao of Zheng, 362, L. 108n
Jiao quan, *see* Scorching Springs
Jiao xi, *see* Scorching Creek
Jiaofu, 360, L. 87n
*jiaoliao* (wren), 57
*jiaoming* (tiny creature), 62, L. 67n, 63
Jiaoyuan (giant boulder), 108, L. 46n, 109
Jiaru, 94, L. 98n
Jie (last ruler of Xia), 240, L. 120n, 241, 272, L. 203n
Jie Zhitui, 274, L. 229n, 275
Jie'ni, 88, LL. 65–66n, LL. 67–68n
Jieshi (place), 328, L. 73n
Jifu (minister to King Xuan of Zhou), 264, L. 60n
Jilian (Chu ancestor), 90, LL. 77–78n
Jin (Ford constellation), 92, L. 84n
Jin ma men, *see* Bronze Horse Gate
*Jin shu* (Zang Rongxu), 59, 60, L. 27n
Jing (ancient state), 68, LL. 49–50n, 69
Jing, Duke of Qi, 14, L. 17n
Jing, Duke of Song, 122, LL. 215–16n, 123
Jing, Duke of Yan, 322, L. 137n
Jing, Emperor of Former Han, 86, L. 57n, 120, LL. 183–84n, LL. 187–88n, 386, 402, 404
Jing, King of, 309, L. 89
Jing, Mount, 118, L. 167n, 354, L. 6n, 355, 364, L. 155n
Jing Cuo, 7, 401
Jing Fang, 278, L. 292n
Jing Ke, 202, L. 44n, 204, L. 53n
"Jing lie" (song), 259, 410
Jingkou, 369, 378
Jingying, 264, L. 61n
Jingzhong Wan, 94, L. 97n
Jingzhou, 370, 378, 382, 383
*Jingzhou ji,* 116, LL. 133–36n, 402
Jintian (Shaohao), 114, L. 111n, 116, L. 147n, 117
Jiujiang, 369
Jiuyi Mountains, 114, LL. 129–30n
Jiyang, 376
Jiyin (place), 286, L. 95n
Jizi (official under Zhou Xin), 90, L. 83n
Ju Gu (immortal), 336, L. 189n
Juan (music master), 224, L. 181n
Juancheng, 354, L. 2n, 372, 412
Jujun (style name of Wang Mang), 82, L. 7n
Julai (crossbow), 148, L. 21n

*jun* (zither-tuning device), 248, L. 50n
Jun Tian, *see* Harmonious Heaven
"Jungle Fowl" (song), 296, LL. 271–72n, 297, 309
Junyi, 372
Jushu (crossbow), 148, L. 21n, 149

Kaiyang (star in Northern Dipper), 134, L. 375n, 135
Kaiyang Gate, 179
Kaocheng, 376
"Keeping off the Dew" (song), 38, L. 72n, 39, 225
Kerchief dance, 80, L. 81n
Kong Jun, 102, L. 140n
Kong Rong, 383
Kongsang, 114, L. 111n
*Kongzi jiayu,* 407
Kuafu, 56, L. 88n
Kuai Kui, 274, L. 234n, 275
Kuang (music master), 224, L. 181n, 238, L. 181n, 239, L. 115, 248, LL. 47–48n, 264, LL. 81–82n, 310, L. 119n
Kui (music master), 234, L. 41n, 235, 265, 287, 322, LL. 141–42n
Kun, Mount, 27
Kun lang, 76, L. 6n
Kunlun Mountains, 53, 57, 72, LL. 105–6n, 73, 76, L. 17n, L. 18n, 114, LL. 123–24n, 115, 118, L. 163n, 126, LL. 259–60n, 128, L. 290n, LL. 293–94n, 129, 285, 286, L. 104n
Kunwu, 116, L. 139n, 117, L. 333n, 132, L. 334n, L. 338n, L. 339n

"Lady of the Xiang," 172, L. 7n
"Lady Zhang" (song), 308, L. 72n, 309
Lan tai, *see* Magnolia Terrace
Langfeng, Mount, 76, L. 6n, 128, LL. 293–94n, 129
Lao Dan, 248, L. 46n
Laozi, 102, L. 153n, 103
*Laozi,* 18, L. 52n, L. 55n, L. 59n, 41, 44, L. 46n, 96, L. 103n, 112, L. 102n, 136, L. 411n, L. 413n, 156, L. 130n, 212, L. 1n, 218, LL. 77–78n, 226, L. 211n, 272, L. 199n, 403, 404, 405
Lapping Waters, Platform of, 34, L. 32n
Le'an, 407
Leaping Serpent, 126, L. 236n, 127
Leibi, *see* Ramparts (constellation)
Li, King of Zhou, 94, LL. 89–90n
Li, Lady, 86, L. 57n, 87
Li, Mount, 136, LL. 401–2n
Li Gu, 382
Li Guang, 102, L. 144n, 103

Li Guangli, 66, L. 18n
Li Hill, 137
Li Ji, daughter of Rong chieftain, 92, L. 85n
*Li ji*, 88, L. 70n, 170, L. 1n, 184, LL. 29–30n, 224, L. 181n, 226, LL. 185–86n, 276, L. 260n, LL. 262–63n, 409, 410
Li Jifu, 354, L. 4n, L. 5n
Li Jingyin, 4
Li Liang, 193
Li Ling, 194, L. 32n, LL. 40–41n, 195; "To Su Wu," 194, LL. 40–41n
Li Lou, 286, L. 85n
Li River, 272, L. 203n
"Li sao," 14, L. 1n, 104, L. 7n, L. 14n, 106, LL. 15–16n, L. 18n, 108, LL. 49–50n, 110, L. 62n, L. 72n, L. 78n, 128, LL. 291–92n, L. 295n, L. 297n, 130, LL. 307–8n, L. 313n, L. 325n, 136, L. 391n, L. 392n, 186, LL. 37–38n, 190, L. 111n
Li Shan, 3, 401
Li Si, 44, LL. 39–40n, 45, 122, LL. 199–200n, 168, LL. 15–16n, 169, 375
Li Yannian, 208, L. 106n
Liang (Former Han kingdom), 20, L. 5n, 21
Liang Ji, 382
Liang Shang, 382
*Liang shu*, 376
Liao, King of Wu, 202, L. 44n
Liao River, 204, LL. 57–58, 205
*Lienü zhuan*, 152, L. 62n, 238, L. 116n, 298, L. 279n, 403
*Liexian zhuan*, 110, L. 78n, 126, L. 265n, 206, L. 93n, 284, L. 47n, 286, L. 95n
*Liezi*, 68, LL. 45–46n, 192, L. 19n, 290, L. 163n, 291, 322, LL. 119–22n
Liling (place), 379
"Limpid Waters" (tune), 272, L. 215n, 273, 291, 298, L. 278n
Linchuan, 369
Ling, Duke of Wei, 96, L. 100n, 274, L. 234n
Ling, King of Chu, 116, LL. 133–36n
Ling, King of Zhou, 300, L. 337n
Ling, Mount, 128, L. 297n
Ling Lun, 286, L. 104n, 287
Ling Prefecture, 310, L. 116n
Ling tai, *see* Divine Terrace
Ling wine, 311
"Lingyang" (tune), 296, LL. 260–63n, 297
Linhai, 369
Linqiong, 406
Linyi, 395
Linzi (place), 372
Liqiu, demon of, 122, LL. 205–6n, 123
Liu (ancient state), 124, LL. 219–20n, 125
Liu An, 74, L. 1n

Liu Bang, 80, L. 81n, 86, L. 55n, L. 56n, 87, 100, L. 127n, 376
Liu Biao, 382, 383
Liu Bokang, 259, 410
Liu Cang, 367
Liu Dan, 370, 394
Liu Fang, 399
Liu Jingsu, 377, 378, 379
Liu Jun (Emperor Xiaowen of Liu-Song), 394, 397
Liu Jun (prince of Shixing), 369, 396
Liu Liu, Liu-Song prince, 395
Liu Pi (King of Wu), 20, LL. 9–11n
Liu Piao (Princess Zhang of Former Han), 406
Liu Rong, 86, L. 57n
Liu Shao, 394, 397
Liu Shi (Emperor Yuan of Former Han), 390
Liu Wu (King of Liang), 20, L. 5n, 386
Liu Xiang, 94, LL. 91–92n, 403, 404; *Bie lu*, 322, L. 137n; "Nine Longings," 264, L. 64n
Liu Xin, *Qi lüe*, 164, L. 65n
Liu Xiuruo, 377, 378
Liu Xuan, 410
Liu Yifu, 395
Liu Yigong, 394
Liu Yikang, 393, 396
Liu Yilong, 396
Liu Yiqing, 77, 369
Liu Yizhen, 395, 396
Liu Yu (Emperor Houfei of Liu-Song), 378
Liu Yu (Emperor Ming of Liu-Song), 377
Liu Yu (Emperor Wu of Liu-Song), 65, 395, 404
Liu Zhan, 396
Liu Zhao, 377
Liu Zhen, 30, L. 1n, 31
Liu Zheng, 398
Liu Zhu, 402
Liu Zifan, 377
Liu Ziluan, 377, 394
Liu Zixu, 369, 370
Liu Zixun, 370
Liu Ziye, 394, 395
Liu Zizhen, 377
Liuxia Hui, 98, L. 124n, LL. 27–28n, LL. 29–30n
Lofty Gallery (constellation), 132, L. 354n, 133
Long Mountains, 50, L. 1n, 196, LL. 48–49, 197, L. 48, 199
Longdi, 52, L. 21n, 53, 62, L. 52n, 63
Lord Ding, 86, L. 56n, 87
Lord Ku, *see* Diku

Lord of Heaven's Platform (constellation), 34, L. 32n, 35
Lord of the Garden, 100, L. 128n
Lord of the He, 118, L. 165n
Lord Wanshi (Shi Fen), 300, L. 322n, 301
Lord Yu (musician), 322, L. 137n, 323
Lou Jing, 198, L. 73n
Loufan, 82, LL. 3–4n
"Lower Hamlet" (song), 222, LL. 157–58n
"Lowered Zhi," 271
Lu (ancient state), 97, 302, LL. 3–4n, 303
Lu Cheng (compiler of Dili shu), 70, L. 73n
Lu Cheng (governor of Donghai), 378
Lu Ji, 38, L. 72n, 78, L. 41n, 171, 211, 379, 385, 400; "Disquisition on the Destruction of a State," 380; "Imitating the Old Poems," 380; Luoyang ji (Notes on Luoyang), 148, L. 14n, L. 16n, L. 19n, 150, L. 27n; "On the Way to Luo," 380; "Poem Composed on Command for the August Heir Designate's Banquet at the You Hall of Mysterious Park," 380; "Rhapsody on the Grand Twilight," 176, L. 81n; "Rhapsody on Lamenting the Departed," 2, 212, L. 3n, 380; "Rhapsody on Literature," 3, 381; "Two Poems on the Garden Mallow," 381; "Written on the Road to Luo," 380
Lu Jing, 172, L. 30n, 380
Lu Kang, 172, L. 29n, 379
Lu Qin, 399
Lu Xun, 167, 172, L. 29n, 379
Lu Yan, 172, L. 30n, 380
Lu Yun, 380, 381, 400
Lu Zhong, 90, LL. 77–78n
Lü, Empress of Former Han, 100, L. 128n
Lü An, 2, 167, 391, 392
Lu she, see Green Kraken
Lü Sheng, 120, LL. 195–96n
Lü Xun, 391
Luan (clan), 96, LL. 109–10n
Luli xiansheng (Master of Lu Hamlet), 100, L. 128n
Luminous Hall, 151
Lun heng, 198, L. 82n
Lun yu, 14, L. 16n, 82, LL. 9–10n, 88, LL. 65–66n, L. 71n, L. 72n, 90, L. 81n, 98, LL. 119–20n, 100, L. 129n, L. 131n, L. 136n, L. 138n, 102, L. 151n, L. 156n, 104, LL. 1–2n, 136, L. 419n, 148, LL. 4–6n, 150, LL. 53–54n, 152, L. 55n, LL. 59–60n, L. 61n, 154, L. 115n, 180, L. 32n, 198, L. 89n, 212, L. 12n, 214, L. 29n, 218, L. 86n, L. 98n, 220, L. 99n, 230, L. 257n, 234, L. 38n, 242, L. 169n, 266, L. 93n, 274, L. 245n, 300, L. 319n,

318, L. 62n, 322, L. 140n, 403, 404, 405, 408
Luo River, 148, L. 15n, 149, 179, 355, 357
Luoguo (Country of the Naked), 24, L. 43n
Luoyang, 138, L. 1n, 145, 148, L. 13n, L. 14n, 354, L. 3n, 371, 372, 376, 380, 384, 385, 391, 395, 398, 406
Luoyang ji (by Hua Yan), 354, L. 5n
Luoyang Prefecture Market, 148, L. 14n
Lüshi chunqiu, 122, LL. 205–6n, 124, LL. 215–16n, 238, L. 115n, 248, L. 45n, 272, L. 213n, 330, L. 97n, 403

Ma Dun, 385
Ma Fang, 375
Ma Rong, 381, 382; "Eulogy on the Guangcheng Park," 382, "Rhapsody on the Long Flute," 3, 279, 382
Ma Yan, 381
Ma Yuan, 381
Magnolia Terrace, 7, 161, L. 19, 163, 208, L. 128n, 209, 367, 375, 401
Major's gate, 371
Man, 55, L. 61
"Man of Ba" (song), 273, L. 216, 297
Man of the Ji, 22, L. 27n, 23
Mane (constellation), 164, L. 88n, 165
Mao constellation, see Mane (constellation)
Mao Mountains, 114, L. 126n
Mao nü, see Hairy Maiden
"Mao Preface," 138, L. 420n
Mao Qiang, 344, L. 70n, 345
Mao shi: #1, 16, L. 45n,118, L. 170n; #4, 184, LL. 13–14n; #23, 128, L. 283n; #26, 16, L. 44n, 190, LL. 127–28n; #28, 208, LL. 107–8n; #32, 182, LL. 5–6n; #35, 218, LL. 79–80n; #41, 22, L. 15n; #45, 190, L. 132n; #48, 208, LL. 107–8n; #57, 128, L. 29n; #58, 402; #62, 184, LL. 21–22n; #65, 168, L. 9n; #73, 190, L. 131n; #81, 412; #95, 208, L. 105n, 412; #99, 32, L. 8n; #114, 248, L. 44n; #130, 110, LL. 63–64n; #131, 188, LL. 87–88n; #132, 128, L. 286n; #138, 52, L. 46n; #141, 42, L. 7n; #147, 104, L. 11n, L. 12n; #150, 22, L. 28n; #158, 408; #162, 402; #165, 132n, L. 350n, 409; #174, 308, L. 78n; #177, 150, L. 25n; #184, 38, L. 68n; #186, 140, L. 19n; #188, 167, LL. 69–70n; #190, 94, L. 99n; #192, 172, LL. 35–36n; #195, 100, L. 132n; #196, 226, L. 210n; #197, 16, L. 32n; #198, 100, L. 135n, 148, L. 3n; #202, 182, LL. 5–6n; #203, 14, L. 18n; #206, 122, L. 210n; #210, 22, L. 16n, L. 30n; #226, 228, L. 214n; #239, 222,

LL. 155–56n; #246, 172, L. 30n; #256, 84, L. 20n, LL. 33–34n, LL. 35–36n, 124, L. 223n; #260, 98, L. 122n; #282, 266, L. 93n; #298, 409; #304, 150, L. 33n
Maoling, 381, 382, 388
Marquis of Liang, 152, L. 72n, 153
Master Dengtu, 349, 351
Master Juan, 284, L. 47n, 285
Master Ling, 323
Master of Fate, 22, LL. 201–2n, 118, L. 182n, 119
Master of Lu Hamlet, 100, L. 128n
Mei Gu, *see* Western Gloom
Mei Prefecture, 410
Mei Sheng, 20, LL. 9–11n, 21, 28, LL. 124–27n, 29, 386; "Seven Stimuli," 410
Mencius, 152, L. 62n, 272, LL. 200–201n
Meng Ben, 272, L. 205n, 273, 334, L. 153n, 335
Meng Ford, 92, L. 87n
Meng Tian, 122, LL. 199–200n
Mengchang, Lord, 204, LL. 67–68n
*Mengzi*, 22, 28, LL. 124–27n, 84, L. 12n, 102, L. 163n, 124, L. 223n, 148, LL. 12n, 198, LL. 70–71n, 274, L. 242n, 286, L. 85n, 300, L. 334n
Metal Market (of Luoyang), 148, L. 14n
Metal-bound Coffer, 108, LL. 35–36n
Mi, Mount, 126, L. 255n, 127
Mi clan, 90, LL. 77–78n, 91
Mi Heng, 1, 49, 51, 382, 383; "Rhapsody on the Parrot," 1, 383
Mian Ju (musician), 274, L. 242n, 275, 323
"Millet Song," 168, L. 9n, 169
Miluo River, 396
Min, Duke of Song, 274, L. 232n
Min Mountains, 52, L. 41n, 53
Ming, Emperor of Later Han, 367, 410
Ming, Emperor of Liu Song, 395
Ming fei, *see* Radiant Consort
Mingjun (Wang Zhaojun), 309
Minhuai, Crown Prince, 380, 385
Mo Di, 264, L. 70n
Moling, 369
"Morning Sun" (song), 310, L. 128n, 311
"Mount Tai" (song), 296, LL. 269–70n, 297
"Mountain Spirit," 110, L. 71n, LL. 73–74n
Mu, Duke of Qin, 68, LL. 45–46n, 188, LL. 87–88n
Mu, Duke of Zhou, 22, L. 27n, 24, L. 63n
Mu, King of Zhou, 72, LL. 105–6n, L. 115n, L. 120n, 73, 76, L. 18n, 192, L. 18n, L. 19n
Mu Kehong, 4
*Mu Tianzi zhuan*, 22, L. 27n
*mujin* (shrubby althea), 172, L. 23n

Murky Shore, 316, L. 20n, 317
Muzi of Shangling, 298, L. 280n

Nan commandery, 382
*Nan shi*, 376, 393, 395
Nan Xuzhou, 377, 378
Nan Yanzhou, 377
Nangong Changwan, 274, L. 232n, 275
Nansha Prefecture, 377
Nanyang, 397, 398
Nanzi, 274, L. 234n
Net (constellation), 36, L. 37n, 132, L. 355n, 164, L. 88n, 165
Net Cart (constellation), 132, L. 355n, 133
Nie Zheng, 202, L. 43n, 204, L. 54n
"Nine Changes," 13, 14, LL. 10–13n, 16, L. 33n, L. 34n, L. 46n, 110, L. 62n, L. 75n, 116, L. 145n, 188, LL. 83–84n, 388
"Nine Laments," 186, LL. 37–38n, 403
"Nine Longings," 390
"Nine Movements," 178, L. 8n
"Nine Pieces," 188, L. 74n
"Nine Songs," 36, LL. 44–45, 118, L. 182n, 186, L. 50n
"Nineteen Old Poems," 54, L. 67n, 202, L. 34n, 318, L. 80n, 380
Ning Qi, 322, L. 138n
Ning Wuzi, 148, LL. 4–6n
Niu, Mount, 14, L. 17n
Niu Ai, 118, LL. 177–78n, 119
Northern Settlement (constellation), 134, L. 359n, 135
"Northern Ward" (song), 318, L. 50n, 319
Northern Xiongnu, 368
Nü Ying, 114, LL. 131–32n, 362, L. 107n
Nüwa, 276, L. 260n, L. 279n, 277, 363

Old Man of the North, 86, L. 60n, 87
"Outpouring of Sad Thoughts," 140, L. 20n
Ouyang Jian, 385
"Overpowering yang" (*kang yang*), 318, LL. 51–52n
Oxherd (constellation), 362, L. 110n

"Pair of White Cranes Flying In" (song), 308, L. 85–86n, 309
Pan Jin, 383
Pan Pi, 383
Pan Yue, 1, 13, 145, 179, 180, LL. 11–12n, 303, 380, 383, 402; "Dirge for Ma, Overseer of Qian," 385; "Dirge for Regular Attendant Xiahou," 385; "Dirge for Yang Jingzhou," 384; "Dirge for Yang Zhongwu," 385; "Lament for Ren Zilan," 407; "Lamenting the Deceased," 385;

"Lamenting the Eternally Departed," 385; "Poem Written at a Golden Valley Gathering," 385; "Rhapsody on Autumn Inspirations," 1, 384; "Rhapsody on Living in Idleness," 2, 383, 385; "Rhapsody on the Mouth Organ," 3, 410; "Rhapsody on Pheasant Shooting," 384; "Rhapsody on Recalling Old Friends and Kin," 2, 384, 392; "Rhapsody on the Sacred Field," 384; "Rhapsody on the Western Journey," 202, L. 31n, 385; "Rhapsody on a Widow," 2, 384; "Within the Passes," 385; "Written in Heyang Prefecture," 384; "Written in Huai Prefecture," 384

Pao gua, see Gourd Star
Pei (place), 371
Pei Songzhi, 371
Pei Wei, 385
Peng Xian, 264, L. 60n, 265
Pengcheng, 393, 396
Penghu, 74, L. 5n
Penglai, 74, L. 5n, 114, L. 116n, 115
Pengzu, 102, L. 153n, 103
Penumbra, 88, LL. 75–76n, 89
Pi (place), 118, LL. 179–80n
Picheng, 120, LL. 195–96n
Piled Boulders, 162, L. 50n, 163
pili RB, 8, L. 33n
Ping, Duke of Jin, 224, L. 181n
Ping, Emperor of Former Han, 120, LL. 185–86n
Ping, King of Zhou, 276, L. 261n
Pingling, 375
Pingyi (god of Yellow River), 26, L. 79n, 27, 118, L. 165n, 119, 362, L. 127n, 363
Pingyuan, 381, 382
po (lunar term), 34, L. 35n
Pot of Peng, 74, L. 5n, 75
"Preface to the Mao Version of the Songs," 410
Pu River, 224, L. 181n
pure conversation, 391
Purple Gulf, 192, LL. 14–15n, 193
Purple Palace, 32, LL. 351–52n, 133
Purple Swallow (horse), 72, LL. 101–4n, 73
Purple Terrace, 196, L. 44n, 197

Qi (older brother of Zhou Xin), 90, L. 83n
Qi (ancient state), 313
Qi, Mount, 110, L. 82n, 111
"Qi chu" (song), 259, 410
Qi Ji, 285
Qi Liang, 238, L. 116n, 239
Qi lüe, 240, L. 117n
Qi Mountain, 22, L. 26n
"Qi pan" (Seven Plate-Drums), 245

Qian, King of Zhao, 193, 194, LL. 22–23n
Qian Dian, 62, L. 51n
Qian trigram, 112, L. 88n, LL. 89–90n, L. 92n
Qiang (proto-Tibetans), 259, 279
Qiao Commandery, 371, 390
Qili Ji (Ji of Qi Hamlet), 100, L. 128n, 284, L. 59n
Qin (ancient state), 125
qin (zither), 279
qin heng (fragrant plant), 8, L. 46n
Qin xin, 284, L. 47n
Qinglin, see Blue Grove (constellation)
Qingxiang, King of Chu, 388, 401, 409
Qingxiang (musician), 274, L. 245n, 275
Qiongsang, 114, L. 111n
Qiongye, 114, L. 111n
Qiu Zhong (Han musician), 259, 276, L. 284n, 277
Qu Boyu, 148, LL. 4–6n
Qu Ping, 274, L. 228n, 275. See also Qu Yuan
Qu tai, see Winding Terrace
Qu Yuan, 128, L. 297n, 140, L. 8n, 274, L. 228n, 357, 396
quadruple merging, 332, L. 115n
Quail Fire (star), 92, L. 84n
Queen Mother of the West, 72, LL. 105–6n, 73, L. 105, 76, L. 18n, 126, L. 263n
Quill Grove Army (constellation), 134, L. 359n
quintuple changes, 332, L. 115n
Quwo Prefecture, 302, LL. 1–2n, 303

Radiant Consort (Wang Zhaojun), 196, L. 43n, 197
Raised Gallery (constellation), 132, L. 354n
Ramparts (constellation), 134, L. 359n, 135
Ran Geng, 88, L. 64n
Ran You, 88, LL. 75–76n, 89
Rear Palace (imperial harem), 68, L. 34n
Record of Rites, 382, 409
Ren Hu, 2, 183, 384, 407
"Returning to the Plow" (song) 136, LL. 401–2n, 137
Rites of Zhou, 382
River Drum (constellation), 134, L. 360n, 135
River Earl, 208, LL. 111–12n, 361, LL. 128–29n
"Roaming in Spring" (song), 298, L. 278n
"Roaming Strings" (song), 296, LL. 271–72n, 297
Robber Zhi, 240, L. 120n, 241
Rongqi Qi, 284, L. 59n, 285

Ruan Ji, 18, LL. 68–69n, 399; "Singing My Feelings," 378
Ruan Yu, 183, 408; "Rhapsody on Stilling the Desire," 362, L. 109n
*ruo* (common cattail), 16, L. 26–29n
Ruo Tree, 34, LL. 30–31n, 35, 116, L. 152n, 117
Ruoxia (wine), 26, L. 91n
Rushou, 54, LL. 69–70n, 55, 116, L. 147n, 119

Sai men, *see* Barrier Gate
san ren, *see* Three Good Men
San Tai, *see* Three Platforms (constellation)
Sang (grove), 122, LL. 213–14n
Sang-Pu, 313
Sangjian, 224, L. 181n
*Sanguo zhi*, 371
Sangzhong, 208, LL. 107–8n, 209
Sanmen Mount, 332, L. 136n, 333
Scalding Vale, 22, L. 37n, 23
Scarlet Watchtower, 68, L. 48n, 69
Scorching Creek, 22, L. 36n, 23
Scorching Springs, 22, L. 36n
Second Qin Emperor, 44, LL. 39–40n, 168, LL. 15–16n, 388
Seven Rong, 68, LL. 29–30n, 69
Seven Worthies of the Bamboo Grove, 390, 392
Shaman Xian (Wu Xian), 128, L. 297n, 129
Shan Bao, 88, LL. 61–62n, 89
*Shan gong biaozhu*, 407
Shan Tao, 391, 392
Shang Jun (doltish son of Shun), 240, L. 119n, 241
*Shang jun shu*, 272, L. 207n
*Shang shu*, 32, LL. 26–27n, 36, L. 37n, 100, L. 134n, L. 137n, 108, LL. 35–36n, 124, LL. 219–20n, 128, L. 274n, 132, L. 348n, 172, L. 31n, 180, L. 18n, 230, L. 258n, 234, L. 41n, 240, L. 119n, 268, L. 153n, 272, LL. 200–201n, 276, L. 255n, 322, LL. 141–42n, 405, 409
*Shang shu zhong hou*, 404
Shang Yang, 272, L. 207n
Shangcheng, 336, L. 188n
Shangdang, 369
Shanggong (Upper Chamber), 208, LL. 107–8n, 209
Shangjun (place), 194, LL. 36–37n, 195
Shanglin yuan, 387
Shangyu, 390
*Shanhai jing*, 56, L. 88n, 114, LL. 129–30n, 116, L. 151n, 126, LL. 259–60n, 284, L. 77n, 300, L. 336n
Shanyang, 169, 392

Shao, Emperor of Liu-Song, 395
"Shao" music, 101, 312, L. 132n, 313, 323
"Shao xiao," 272, L. 214n, 273
Shaohao, 54, LL. 69–70n, 55, 114, L. 111n, 115, L. 147n
Shaolian (recluse), 98, L. 124n
Shaoshi (peak), 180, LL. 11–12n
Shaqiu (grave site), 96, L. 100n
Shen Baoxu, 98, L. 126n
Shen Bo (warrior), 240, L. 120n
Shen Buhai, 272, L. 209n, 273
Shen Gua, 411
Shen Sheng (heir designate in Jin), 92, L. 85n
Shen Yucheng, 4
*sheng* (mouth organ), 303
Sheng Hongzhi, 116, LL. 133–36n
Sheng Ji (concubine of King Mu of Zhou), 24, L. 63n
Shennong, 148, L. 1n, 276, LL. 258–59n, L. 279n, 277
*Shenyi jing*, 116, L. 139n
Sheti, *see* Conductors (constellation)
*Shi ben*, 276, L. 261n
Shi Chong, 202, L. 32n, 385
Shi Fen, 300, L. 322n
"Shi fu lüe," 388
*Shi ji*, 96, L. 102n, L. 125n, 100, L. 127n, 204, L. 49n, 300, L. 317n, 367, 375, 376, 386, 388, 403
Shi Xiang, *see* Xiang (music master)
Shi Yang, 96, LL. 109–10n
Shi'an, 377, 396
Shining, 393
*Shishuo xinyu*, 296, LL. 269–70n, 372, 383, 390, 399, 402
Shitou cheng, 377
Shixing, 396
*Shiyi ji*, 74, L. 5n, 76, L. 17n
*Shizi*, 108, L. 46n
Shouchun, 391
Shu (musician), 276, LL. 262–63n, 277
Shu (commandery), 386, 387, 389
Shu (kingdom), 372
Shu Guang (tutor to Emperor Xuan), 202, L. 31n
Shu Niu (Servant Niu), 120, LL. 193–94n
Shu Shou (tutor to Emperor Xuan), 202, L. 31n
*Shu wang benji*, 118, LL. 179–80n
Shu Xi, 400
*Shu zheng ji*, 150, L. 47n
*Shui jing zhu*, 354, L. 3n
Shun, 52, L. 22n, 100, L. 137n, 106, L. 25n, 114, LL. 129–30n, LL. 131–32n, 124, LL. 219–20n, 136, LL. 401–2n, 240,

L. 119n, 272, L. 214n, 276, LL. 262–63n, 296, LL. 254–55n, 312, L. 132n, 362, L. 107n, 403, 408
Shun, Emperor of Later Han, 105
Shuofang, 382
*Shuowen*, 260, L. 18n, 264, L. 85n
Shuqi (recluse), 98, L. 124n, 300, L. 317n
Shusun Bao, 120, LL. 193–94n, 121
Shuwu, Viscount of of Wei, 86, LL. 49–50n, 87
Shuxiang of Yangshe clan, 96, L. 101n
Si hao, *see* Four Hoaryheads
Silver terrace, 126, L. 261n
Sima An, 145, 404
Sima Cuo, 386
Sima Jiong, 380, 385
Sima Lun, 380, 384, 385, 400
Sima Qian, 404; "Rhapsody on the Frustrated Scholar," 140, L. 7n
Sima regime of Western Jin, 391
Sima Tong, 385
Sima Xiangru, 20, LL. 9–11n, 21, 23, 159, 386, 388, 406; "Essay on the *feng* and *shan* Sacrifices," 388; "Lamenting the Second Qin Emperor," 388; "Letter of Submission Admonishing on Hunting," 388; "Objecting to the Elders of Shu," 387; "Proclamation Addressed to Ba and Shu," 387; "Rhapsody on the Great Man," 208, L. 129n, 388; "Rhapsody on the Imperial Park," 192, LL. 14–15n; 387; "Rhapsody of Sir Vacuous," 386, 387; "Rhapsody on the Tall Gate Palace," 2, 388
Sima Yan, 380, 384, 404, 405
Sima Yi, 381
Sima Ying, 380, 381
Sima You, 384
Sima Yu, 380, 385, 400
Sima Yun, 385
Sima Zhao, 150, L. 32n, 399, 407
Sir Zhang, 152, L. 71n, 153
"Sitting in Sadness" (song), 298, L. 278n
Six arts, 214, L. 22n
"Six Blossoms" (tune), 247, 410
Six Classics, 214, L. 22n, 215
Six Dependencies, 68, LL. 29–30n, 69
"Six Stalks" (tune), 410
Sky River (Milky Way), 32, LL. 13–14n, 36, L. 51, 79, 92, L. 84n, 134, L. 360n, L. 361n, L. 362n, 190, L. 114n, 207, 362, L. 110n
Slender Black (horse), 72, LL. 101–4n, 73
Snow Palace, 22, L. 24n
Solar Realm, 77
Song (ancient state), 313, 395

Song, Mount, 179, 384, 407
Song Jun, 276, L. 261n
"Song of Great Peace," 406
"Song of the Heavenly Horses," 74, LL. 139–40n
"Song of the Wheat in Bloom," 168, L. 10n, 169
*Song shu*, 270, L. 185n, 393, 395, 410
Song Yu, 13, 15, 22, L. 29n, 38, L. 72n, 245, 325, 339, 349, 351, 388, 401; "Responding to the Question of the King of Chu," 222, LL. 157–58n, 296, LL. 260–63n, 389; "Rhapsody on the Flute," 164, L. 67n, 240, L. 117n; "Rhapsody on the Gaotang Shrine," 3, 389; "Rhapsody on the Goddess," 3, 389; "Rhapsody on Master Dengtu the Lecher," 3, 389; "Rhapsody on Persuasion," 22, L. 29n; "Rhapsody on the Wind," 1, 389
*Song Yu ji*, 389
Songgao, Mount, 74, L. 1n, 180, LL. 11–12n
Songqiu, 407
Sorrowful Jiang, 264, L. 61n, 265
*Sou shen ji*, 36, L. 40n, 122, LL. 201–2n
Sounding Bell, 262, L. 57n, 263
"Southern Flute" (tune), 272, L. 214n, 273
Southern Fusang, 318, LL. 51–52n
"Southern Jing" (tune), 296, LL. 260–63n, 297
Southern Qi, 379
Southern Winnow (constellation), 320, L. 93n, 321
Southern Yanzhou, 369
Spirit of Brightness, 110, L. 70n, 111, 140, LL. 29–30n, 141, 186, L. 45n, 187, 317
Splendid Blue, 72, LL. 101–4n, 73
Split Tree (star), 92, L. 84n
Spring Terrace, 18, L. 52n
Standing Tree, 116, L. 151n, 117
State Academy, 150, L. 47n, LL. 49–50n
"Stopping the Breath" (tune), 296, LL. 269–70n, 297
Su Hui, 206, LL. 91–92n
Su Wu, 194, L. 38n, LL. 40–41n, 198, L. 72n; "Parting Poem," 204, L. 74n
*Sui shu*, 374
"Summoning the Soul," 200, LL. 5–6n, 248, L. 20n, 388
Sun Ce, 36, L. 40n
Sun Deng, 391
Sun Hao, 380
Sun Jian, 36, L. 40n
Sun Quan, 36, L. 40n
Sun Terrace, 326, L. 26n
Sun Xiu, 385, 400
"Sunny Bank" (song), 38, L. 73n, 39, 247

Sunshu Ao, 228, LL. 226–27n, 298, L. 279n
*suonu* (lunar term), 34, L. 34n
Supreme Man, 18, L. 56n, 19

Tai, Mount, 8, L. 24n, 238. L. 115n
Tai jie, *see* Grand Stairway (constellation)
Tai qing, *see* Grand Clarity
Tai shi, *see* Chamber of Ministers
Tai Valley, 354, L. 5n
Tai xue, *see* Grand Academy
Tai yin, *see* Greater Yin
Taihang. 108, LL. 45n
Taihao, 102, L. 149n, 103
Taihua, 126, L. 265n, 127
*Taiping huangyu ji*, 326, L. 26n
Tairong, 132, L. 348n, 133, 286, L. 78n, 287
Taishi (peak), 180. LL. 11–12n, 181
Taiyi, *see* Grand Unity
Taiwei, 34, L. 33n, 132, LL. 351–52n, 133
Tall Gate Palace, 159, 160, L. 14n, 406
Tall Poplars Lodge, 388
Tang (founder of Shang), 122, LL. 213–14n
Tang (Yao), 66, LL. 11–12n, 67
Tang gu. *see* Scalding Vale
Tang Ju, 138, L. 5n, 141
"Tang Yao" (song) 290, LL. 155–56n, 291
Tantai Mieming, 274, L. 230n
Tao Qian, 395, 396
*teng she, see* Leaping Serpent
Three Emperors, 143
Three Good Men, 90, L. 83n, 188, LL. 87–88n, 189
Three Platforms (constellation), 36, LL. 38–39n, 66, L. 5n
thrice-blooming herb, 110, LL. 73–74n
Tian family, 94, L. 97n
Tian huang, *see* Celestial Torrent
Tian jin, *see* Celestial Ford (constellation)
Tian lang, *see* Celestial Wolf (constellation)
Tian Lian, 286, L. 105n, 287, L. 105
Tian si, *see* Celestial Quadriga (constellation); Heavenly Quadriga (constellation)
Tian yuan, *see* Celestial Turtle (constellation)
Tianwu (river spirit), 300, L. 336n, 301
Tiao, Marquis of, 96, L. 102n, 97
*tiao* (lunar term), 34, L. 34n
Tiaozhi, 62, LL. 57–58n, 63
Tong Valley, 354, L. 5n, 355
*Tongsu wen* (Common Graphs), 70, L. 63n
Tu, Mount, 114, LL. 127–28n
Tu yuan, *see* Hare Garden
"Turbulent Chu" (song), 247, 319, 409
Twinkling Indicator (star), 134, L. 363n, 135
Two Eights, 106, L. 25, 107
Two Norms, 134, L. 364n, 135

Uncrowned king, 100, L. 139n
Upturned Phosphors (Dao jing), 134, L. 372n, 135

Venerable Wu, 375
Vermillion Bird, 116, L. 150n, 130, LL. 327–28n
"Viscount of Wei" (song), 290, LL. 155–56, 291

Wang, Empress of Former Han, 86, L. 58n, 87, 120, LL. 185–86n
Wang Bao, 208, L. 125n, 233; "Nine Regrets," 130. L. 321n, 132, L. 337n, 204, L. 70n; "Rhapsody on the Panpipes," 3, 279
Wang Bi, 397
Wang Can, 4. 32, L. 20n, L. 22n, 183; "Rhapsody on a Widow," 183, 184, LL. 27–28n, 186, LL. 35–36n
Wang Jin (Wang Qiao), 300, L. 337n
Wang Liang. 132, L. 353n, L. 354n, 133
Wang Mang, 36. L. 41n, L. 7n, L. 8n, 94, LL. 91–92n, 120, LL. 185–86n
Wang Niansun, 54, LL. 83n
Wang Qiang (Wang Zhaojun), 196, L. 43n
Wang Qiao (Wang Jin), 300, L. 337n, 301
Wang Qiu, 396
Wang Xiang, 389
Wang Yin, 390
Wang Zhaojun, 193, 196, L. 43n, 298, L. 279n, 300
Wang Zhengjun, 36, L. 41n
Wang Zijin (immortal), 74, L. 1n
Wang Ziqiao, 208, LL. 103–4n, 308, L. 87n
Wangdi (legendary Shu ruler), 118, LL. 179–80n
Wangmang (legendary state), 114, LL. 127–28n
Wangshi (legendary place), 116, L. 154n, 117
Wangshu (charioteer of the moon), 140, LL. 29–30n, 141
Wangzi Wuqi, 72, L. 119n
Wastes of Kun, 76, L. 6n, 77
Weak River, 118, L. 163n, 119
Weaving Maid (constellation), 362, L. 110n
Wei, King of Chu, 18, LL. 64–65n
Wei (ancient state), 313, 323, 353
Wei Ao, 82, L. 8n
Wei Chou, 124, LL. 217–18n
Wei Ke, 124, LL. 217–18n, 125
Wei River, 353, 412
Wei Sheng, 300, L. 320n, 301
Wei Shenggao, 300, L. 320n
*Wei zhu*, 66, L. 14n
Wei Zifu, 159, 406

Wen, Duke of Lu, 264, L. 61n
Wen, Duke of Jin, 92, L. 86n, 121
Wen, Emperor of Former Han, 72, L. 116n,
  73, 118, LL. 183–84n, 196, L. 43n, 375,
  376, 402
Wen, Emperor of Wei, 183
Wen, Emperor of Western Jin, 150, L. 32n
Wen, Emperor of Liu Song, 65, 66, L. 1n,
  394, 395, 396
Wen, King of Zhou, 22, L. 26n, 110, L. 82n,
  L. 83n, 111, 152, L. 73n, 153, 231, 272,
  L. 214n
Wen, Marquis of Wei, 98, L. 125n
Wen Qin, 391
*Wenshi zhuan*, 406
Wenyang Prefecture, 302, LL. 3–4n, 303
*Wenzi*, 52, L. 26n, 60, L. 31n
Western Gloom, 34, LL. 30–31n, 35
Western Jin, 399
Western Qiang, 375
"Western Qin" (song), 296, LL. 260–63n, 297
Wheelwright Bian, 227, 409
Whetstone Pillar, 332, L. 136n, 333
Whisk Dance, 80, L. 81n, 81
"White Crane" (song), 309
White Maiden, 132, L. 347n, 133
white mushroom, 126, L. 262n
White Portal, 118, L. 161n, 119
"White Snow" (song), 22, L. 29n, 222,
  LL. 157–58n, 223, 273, 289
White Tiger, 130, LL. 327–28n
White Tiger Hall, 368
White Water, 128, L. 296n, 129
Wind Master, 130, L. 331n
Winding Terrace, 164, L. 58n, 165
Winnow Earl, 130, L. 331n, 131
Winnow Star, 36, L. 37n, 78, L. 28n, 79,
  130, L. 331n
Wowa River, 66, L. 18n
Woye (Fertile Wilds), 116, L. 154n
Wu, Duke of Lu, 147
Wu, Emperor of Former Han, 66, L. 13n,
  72, L. 115n, 73, 102, L. 144n, 120,
  LL. 187–88n, 121, 159, 194, L. 32n, 208,
  L. 106n, 386, 387, 388, 404, 406;
  "Rhapsody on Lady Li," 196, L. 69n
Wu, Emperor of Liu-Song, 369
Wu, Emperor of Western Jin, 147, 400, 404
Wu, King of Zhou, 92, L. 84n, L. 87n, 93,
  108, LL. 35–36n, 231, 312, L. 132n
Wu (Former Han kingdom), 20, LL. 9–11n
"Wu" (dance tune), 313
Wu Guang, 272, L. 203n, 273
Wu Hui, 90, LL. 77–78n
Wu Ju, 204, L. 73n
*Wu lu*, 26, L. 91n

Wu Polu, 36, L. 40n
Wu wei, *see* Five Wefts
Wu Yang, 204, L. 53n
Wu Zixu, 264, L. 60n, 265
Wuchen clan, 96, L. 101n
Wucheng, 26, L. 91n
Wuding, King of Yin, 45, 106, L. 25n, 264,
  L. 61n
Wudu Commandery, 382
Wushan (Shaman Mount), 325
Wuxing, 26, L. 91n, 27, 378

Xi, Duke of Jin, 248, L. 44n
Xi (family name of Xi Kang), 390
Xi Kang, 2, 167, 169, L. 4, 193, 196, L. 62n,
  279, 390, 391, 392; "Disquisition on
  Nurturing Life," 390, 392; "Letter to
  Shan Tao Breaking off Friendship," 391;
  "Presented to the Flourishing Talent
  upon Entering the Army," 391; "Prison
  Anguish," 196, L. 63n, 392; "Rhapsody
  on a Zither," 3, 392, 410
Xi Qi, 92, L. 85n
Xi Shi, 108, LL. 53–54n, 109, 345
Xi Xi, 390, 391
Xi'e, 139, 397, 398
"Xia" (song), 311, 323
Xia dynasty, 94, LL. 89–90n, 95
Xia Huang gong (Yellow Lord of Xia), 100,
  L. 128n
Xia Yu, 240, L. 120n, 334, L. 153n, 335
Xiacai, 351, 411
Xiahou Zhan, 384, 385
Xialei (prime minister of Han), 202, L. 43n
"Xiali Baren" (The Man of Ba from the
  Lower Hamlet), 222, LL. 157–58n, 223
Xian, Duke of Jin, 92, L. 85n, L. 86n, 120,
  LL. 195–96n
Xian, Emperor of Later Han, 383
Xian hexagram, 112, L. 87n, LL. 89–90n
Xian li, *see* Slender Black
Xiang, King of Chu, 7, 245, 325, 339
Xiang (music master), 234, L. 41n, 235, 240,
  L. 117n, 241, 265, 287
Xiang River, 115, 116, LL. 131–32n, 362
*Xiang he jing*, 74, L. 1n, L. 2n, 76, L. 10n,
  L. 11n
*Xiang ma jing* (Canon for Judging Horses),
  68, L. 39n, L. 41n, L. 42n
Xiang Xiu, 167, 392, 406; "Rhapsody on
  Recalling Old Friends," 2, 292
Xiang Yu, 80, L. 81n, 86, L. 55n, 100,
  L. 127n
Xiang Zhuang, 80, L. 81n
Xiangchuan, 26, L. 91n
Xiangdong, 397

*xianghe* song, 296, LL. 271–72n, 410
Xiangyang, 377, 378
Xiangzhong, 264, L. 61n
Xiangzhou, 378, 396
Xianmen Gao, 336, L. 187n, 337
Xianyang, 353, 411
Xiao, King of Liang, 20, L. 5n, L. 6n
*xiao* (bamboo), 302, LL. 3–4n
Xiao Daocheng, 379
Xiao Luan (Emperor Ming of Qi), 379
Xiao Shao, 322, LL. 141–42n
*Xiao shuo*, 180, LL. 11–12n
Xiao Yan (Emperor Wu of Liang), 379
Xiao Ze (Emperor Wu of Qi), 379
Xiaowen, Emperor of Liu-Song, 394
Xiaowu, Emperor of Liu Song, 377, 395
Xie Chaozong, 378
Xie Fangming, 393
Xie Hui, 395
Xie Huilian, 1, 392, 393; "At Xiling,
    Encountering a Storm, Presented to Xie
    Lingyun," 393; "Autumn Inspirations,"
    393; "Offering on an Ancient Tomb,"
    393; "Rhapsody on Snow," 1, 393
Xie Lingyun, 378, 393, 395, 397; "Rhap-
    sody on Dwelling in the Mountains," 38,
    L. 72n
Xie Mi, 394
Xie Valley, 286, L. 104n
Xie Zhuang, 1, 393, 394; "Dirge for
    Emperor Xiaowu's Honorable Consort
    Xuan," 394; "Lament for Honorable
    Consort Yin," 394; "Rhapsody on the
    Moon," 1, 395; "Rhapsody on the Scarlet
    Parrot," 394
*Xijing zaji*, 42, L. 12n
Xiling Lake, 393
Ximu, *see* Split Tree
Xin'an, 377, 394
Xingyang Commandery, 383, 384, 407
Xiongnu. 56, L. 84n, 193, 194, L. 32, L. 38n,
    196, L. 43n, 198, L. 72n
Xiu qi, *see* Splendid Blue
Xiu Yang (immortal), 206, L. 93n
*xucai*, 377
Xizi (crossbow), 148. L. 21n, 149
Xu, Empress of Former Han, 86, L. 58n
Xu (Cao Cao's residence), 383
Xu Fu (physiognomist), 96, L. 102n, 97
Xu Le (early Han writer), 208, L. 126n
Xu Yimin. 4
Xu You. 284. L. 72n
Xuan. Emperor of Former Han, 86, L. 58n,
    94. LL. 91–92n, 95, 202, L. 31n, 389
Xuan, Empress of Former Han, 94,
    LL. 91–92n

Xuan, King of Qi, 22, L. 24n
Xuan, King of Zhou, 94, 95, L. 99n, 264,
    L. 60n
Xuan, Mount, 72, LL. 105–6n, 73
Xuan Gong, *see* Carriage Palace (constella-
    tion)
Xuanming, 130, L. 330n, 131
Xuanni, Duke, 102, L. 140n
Xuan wu, *see* Dark Warrior
Xuanyuan (land of long-lived people), 118,
    L. 155n
Xuanyuan (Yellow Lord), 116, L. 153n, 117,
    118, L. 167n. 119, 284, L. 76n, 285
Xuchang, 385
Xue gong, *see* Snow Palace
Xun trigram, 94, LL. 91–92n
Xun Xu, 399
Xun Yi, 384, 404
Xun Yong, 393
Xunyang, 370, 395, 396
*Xunzi*, 222, LL. 153–54n, 274, LL. 240–41n

Yan (ancient state), 68, LL. 49–50n, 69, 81
Yan (place), 388
Yan, Mount, 204, LL. 57–58n, 205
Yan An (early Han writer), 208, L. 126n
Yan Chun, 240, L. 117n, 241
Yan Danzi, 204, L. 53n
Yan Hui, 88, L. 64n, LL. 75–76n, 89, 301
Yan Ji (= Zhuang Ji), 108, LL. 39–40n
Yan Jun, 397
Yan Shibo, 394
Yan Shuzi, 240, L. 118n
Yan Si, 120, LL. 187–88n
Yan Yanzhi, 1, 65, 395, 396; "Dirge for
    Summoned Gentleman Tao," 396;
    "Offering for Qu Yuan," 396; "On a
    Northern Mission in Luoyang," 395;
    "Preface for the Poems Composed at the
    Winding Waterway on the Third Day of
    the Third Month," 397; "Rhapsody on
    the Russet and White Horse," 1, 396;
    "Song of the Five Gentlemen," 396; *Ting
    gao*, 396
Yan Yuan, 104, LL. 1–2n, L. 3n
Yang Deyi, 387
Yang gu, *see* Dawn Valley
Yang Jun, 380, 384, 385, 405
Yang Shao, 179, 180, LL. 19–20n, L. 30n,
    384, 407
Yang Sui, 385
Yang tai, *see* Sun Terrace
Yang Tan, 179, 180, L. 30n, 384, 407
Yang Xiong, 36, L. 41n, 208, L. 125n, 404;
    "Denigrating Qin and Praising Xin,"
    214, L. 23n; *Fa yan*, 214, L. 21n; "Sweet

Springs Palace Rhapsody," 124, L. 227n; *Taixuan,* 398
Yang Xiu, 371
Yang Xuanzhi, 393
Yang Youji, 102, L. 143n, 103
Yang Zhao, 179, 384, 407
"Yang'e" (song), 38, L. 72n, 80, LL. 83–84n, 81
Yangcheng, 351, 411
"Yangchun baixue" (song), 222, LL. 157–58n
Yangjia, 392, 393
Yanglin, 356, L. 11n
Yangyun Terrace, 326, L. 26n
Yangzhou, 369
Yanmen, 194, LL. 36–37n, 195, 204, LL. 57–58n
Yanran, Mount, 368
Yanyai, 275, L. 230
*Yanzi chunqiu,* 14, L. 17n, 194, L. 35n, 322, L. 137n
Yao, 66, LL. 11–12n, 276, LL. 262–63n, 310, L. 131n, 404, 408, 409
"Yao chang" (tune), 290, LL. 155–56n
Yao chi, *see* Carnelian Pond
Yao ling, *see* Spirit of Brightness
Yao xi, *see* Carnelian Ravine
Yao ya, *see* Carnelian Cliff
Yaoniao (horse), 108, LL. 53–54n, 109
Ye (Cao Cao's capital), 371, 372
Ye of Jin, 310, L. 119n, 311
Yellow Bamboo, 22, L. 27n
Yellow Gate, 74, L. 143n, 75, 266, L. 95n, 267, 379, 392
"Yellow *gong,*" 316, L. 27n, 317
Yellow Lord, 66, LL. 9–10n, 116, L. 153n, 118, L. 167n, 119, 132, L. 348n
Yellow Lord of Xia, 100, L. 128n
Yellow River, 162, L. 50n, 303, 403
Yellow Springs, 19
Yi, Duke of Wei, 80, L. 85n
Yi (stealer of herb of immortality), 34, L. 33n
*Yi jing* (Canon of Arts and Skills), 70, LL. 87–88n
Yi River, 148, L. 13n, 149, 354, L. 3n
Yi Ya, 300, L. 335n
Yin Jingren, 396
Yin Shuyi, 394
*yin tai, see* Silver terrace
Yin Yun, 180, LL. 11–12n
Ying (ancient state), 124, LL. 219–20n, 125
Ying (Chu capital), 378
Ying (surname of First Qin Emperor), 90, L. 79n, 122, LL. 199–200n, 123
Ying Yang, 30, L. n, 31, 371
Yinghuo, 122, LL. 215–16n
Yingzhou, 114, L. 112n, 115, 291

Yique, 354, L. 3n, 355
Yiwu, 92, L. 86n
Yiyi (recluse), 98, L. 124n
Yizhou, 390
Yong Chi, 86, L. 55n, 87
Yongan, 369
Yongjia, 369, 396,
Yongqiu, 372, 412
Yongzhou, 377, 385
You, King of Zhou, 94, LL. 89–90n
You (ancient territory), 68, LL. 49–50n, 69
You du, *see* Dark Capital
Youmu, King of Zhao, 194, LL. 22–23n
Youzhou, 399
Yu (Great Yu of Xia), 114, L. 126n, 115, 310, L. 131n, 332, L. 136n
Yu (Shun), 100, L. 137n
Yu, Mount, 126, L. 261n
Yu lin, *see* Quill Grove Army (constellation)
Yu nu, *see* Jade Maiden
Yu Qiuzi, 298, L. 279n
Yu Rang, 202, L. 43n
Yu Shaochu, 4
Yu Shu, 60, L. 29n
Yu Xuanming (Lord of the Garden), 100, L. 128n
Yu Yan, 369
Yuan, Emperor of Former Han, 36, L. 41n
Yuan Bing, 378
Yuan gong, 100, L. 128n
Yuan Ke, 286, L. 95n, 287
Yuan Shu, 371, 394
"Yuan tao xing" (Song of Peaches in the Garden), 308, L. 74n
*Yuanhe junxian tuzhi,* 354, L. 4n, L. 5n
*yuanyu* (frigate bird), 62, LL. 55–56n
Yue (ancient state), 45, 54, L. 67n, 55, 56, L. 84n, 57, 68, LL. 49–50n, 69
"Yue ji," 409
"Yue ling," 170, L. 1n
*yuefu,* 370, 373
Yuezhi, 70, LL. 87–88n
Yulin, 336, L. 188n
Yun Han, *see* Cloud-Han; Han in the Clouds
Yunmeng Park, 245, 386, 409, 411
Yuzhong, 98, L. 124n

Zang Rongxu, 402
*ze ma* (horse from the marshes), 66, L. 14n
Zeng Wenzhang, 108, L. 47n
Zengzi, 137
Zhang, Emperor of Later Han, 368, 375
Zhang, Princess of Former Han, 406
"Zhang" (song), 311
Zhang Boxi, 58, LL. 7–8n

Zhang Heng, 105, 139, 397, 398; "Eastern Metropolis Rhapsody," 398; "Four Sorrows," 398; *Ling xian*, 34, L. 32n; "Rhapsody on Contemplating the Mystery," 1, 2, 398; "Rhapsody on Dance," 245; "Rhapsody on Returning to the Fields," 2, 398; "Southern Capital Rhapsody," 172, L. 29n, 398; "Western Metropolis Rhapsody," 398

Zhang Hua, 1, 57, 171, 374, 380, 385, 399, 400; "Admonition of the Female Scribe," 184, L. 18n, 400; *Bowu zhi*, 274, L. 230n; "Rhapsody on the Wren," 1, 399

Zhang Kan, 398

Zhang Mountain, 52, L. 41n, 53

Zhang Quan, "Viewing the Celestial Phenomena," 34, L. 32n, L. 33n

Zhang Shao, 396

Zhang Yi, 88, LL. 61–62n, 89

Zhang Yin, 406

Zhang Ziqiao, 389

*Zhangguo ce*, 104, L. 11n, 194, L. 119n

Zhanghua (place in Chu), 351, 411

Zhangling, 383

Zhao, Duke of Lu, 96, L. 100n

Zhao, Duke of Zheng, 274, L. 233n

Zhao Gao, 122, LL. 199–200n

Zhao Jianzi, 72, L. 119n

Zhao Qi, 407

Zhaojun, 196, L. 43n

Zhaoyao, *see* Twinkling Indicator

Zhen, Empress of Wei, 355

Zhen River, 353, 412

Zhen trigram, 94, LL. 89–90n

Zheng (ancient state), 249, 313, 323, 353

Zheng and Wei, 411

Zheng music, 247

Zheng Xuan, 138, L. 420n, 397

*zhengrong* RB, 78, L. 23n

Zhi Prefecture, 390

Zhi Xun, 381

Zhi Yu, *Wenzhang zhi* (Notes on Literature), 410

Zhong, Mount, 126, LL. 257–58n, 127, 286, L. 96n, 287

Zhong Hui, 391

Zhong Qi, 238, L. 115n, 239, 287, 323

Zhongchang Tong, "Sincere Words," 228, L. 237n

Zhonghuang Bo, 108, L. 45n

Zhongmou Prefecture, 383

Zhongnan Mountain, 259, 260, L. 2n, 261

Zhongqiu Prefecture, 266, LL. 96–97n, 267

Zhou, King of Yin, 224, L. 181n, 318, L. 50n

Zhou Chou, 122, LL. 201–2n

Zhou Dan, 108, LL. 35–36n, 109

*Zhou li*, 112, L. 94n, 184, L. 18n, 224, L. 169n, 260, L. 5n, 266, L. 93n

Zhou Ren, 156, LL. 126–27n, 157

Zhou Shu (Master of Lu Hamlet), 100, L. 128n

Zhou Xin, 92, L. 87n

Zhou Yafu, 96, L. 102n

*Zhou yi*, 14, L. 3n, 18, L. 58n, 22, L. 32n, 54, LL. 55–56n, 100, L. 134n, 102, L. 151n, L. 155n, L. 156n, LL. 169–70n, 108, L. 58n, 110, L. 83n, L. 84n, L. 85n, 112, L. 91n, 124, L. 224n, 128, LL. 281–82n, 136, L. 405n, 176, LL. 89–90n, 188, LL. 67–68n, 214, L. 43n, 216, L. 48n, 276, LL. 276–77n, 316, L. 37n, 318, LL. 51–52n, 403, 404

Zhu long, see Candescent Dragon

Zhu Zhong, 152, L. 74n, 153

Zhuan Zhu, 202, L. 44n, 272, L. 205n, 273

Zhuang, Duke of Qi, 274, L. 235n

Zhuang, Duke of Wei, 208, LL. 107–8n

Zhuang, Duke of Zheng, 274, L. 233n

Zhuang, King of Chu, 298, L. 279n

Zhuang Ji, "Lamenting Time's Fate," 108, LL. 39–40n, 188, L. 78n

Zhuang Jiang, 208, LL. 107–8n

Zhuang Zhou, 98, LL. 113–14n, 99, 273, 300, L. 321n

Zhuangwu, 400

*Zhuangzi*, 8, L. 20n, 18, L. 56n, L. 57n, LL. 60–63n, LL. 64–65n, L. 73n, 41, 46, LL. 59–60n, LL. 63–64n, LL. 65–67n, L. 72n, L. 74n, LL. 75–76, L. 77n, L. 92n, 48, LL. 99–100n, L. 102n, L. 105n, 58, L. 17n, 88, LL. 61–62n, 96, L. 100n, 98, L. 116n, 226–27n, 234, L. 40n, 248, L. 46n, 272, L. 199n, L. 203n, 290, L. 163n, 300, L. 320n, L. 321n, 392, 401, 405, 408, 409

Zhuanxu, 82, L. 1n, L. 84n, 106, L. 25n, 127

Zhui, King, 318, LL. 51–52n

Zhuo Wangsun, 387, 406

Zhuo Wenjun, 386, 406

Zhurong, 90, LL. 77–78n, 116, L. 149n, 117

*Zhushu jinian*, 192, L. 18n

Zhuzhang (recluse), 98, L. 124n

Zi gong, *see* Purple Palace

Zi River, 206, L. 79n, 209

Zi Shen (Lu Grandee), 122, LL. 203–4n

Zi tai, *see* Purple Terrace

Zi yan, *see* Purple Swallow

Zi yuan, *see* Purple Gulf

Zichan, 122, LL. 203–4n

Zilu, 88, LL. 65–66n, L. 70n, LL. 75–76n, 89, L. 65, 150, LL. 53–54n

Ziwen (founder of Ban clan), 82, L. 2n
Ziye, 264, LL. 81–82n, 265
Ziyu, 188, LL. 87–88n
Zizhong, 389
Zou (ancient state), 302, LL. 3–4n, 303
Zou Shi, 208, L. 130n
Zou Yang, 20, LL. 9–11n, 21, 27, 386; "Letter from Prison Submitted to the King of Liang," 377
Zujiang, 126, LL. 259–60n, 127
Zuo Si, 13, 400
*Zuo zhuan*, 58, LL. 7–8n, 60, L. 29n, 68, LL. 51–54n, 86, LL. 49–50n, LL. 51–52n, 92, L. 85n, L. 88n, 94, L. 97n, L. 98n, 96, L. 99n, L. 100n, L. 101n, 98, LL. 109–10n, 100, L. 131n, 108, L. 47n, 112, L. 93n, 114, L. 111n, LL. 127–28n, 118, L. 173n, 122, LL. 203–4n, 124, LL. 217–18n, 132, L. 342n, 138, L. 4n, 204, L. 73n, 228, L. 215n, 264, L. 61n, 268, L. 156n, 272, L. 214n, 274, L. 229n, L. 232n, L. 233n, L. 234n, 292, LL. 196–97n, 312, LL. 135–36n, 402, 405, 408

David R. Knechtges is Professor of Chinese literature at the University of Washington. He is the editor and translator of *Wen xuan*, Volumes One and Two, and the author of *The Han Rhapsody: A Study of the "Fu" of Yang Hsiung (53 B.C.–A.D. 18)*.

GPSR Authorized Representative: Easy Access System Europe - Mustamäe tee
50, 10621 Tallinn, Estonia, gpsr.requests@easproject.com